PLAYING WITH IDEAS

Modern and Contemporary Philosophies of Education

JAIME G. A. GRINBERG
TYSON E. LEWIS
Montclair State University

MEGAN LAVERTY
Columbia University

KENDALL/HUNT PUBLISHING COMPANY
4050 Westmark Drive   Dubuque, Iowa 52002

CONTENTS

Introduction   vi

Chapters:

1. Jean-Jacques Rousseau   1
   PREFACE
   BOOKS I, II, AND V

2. Ralph Waldo Emerson   27
   THE AMERICAN SCHOLAR

3. Leo Tolstoy   49
   ARE THE PEASANT CHILDREN TO LEARN
      TO WRITE FROM US?

4. Alfred North Whitehead   55
   THE RHYTHMIC CLAIMS OF FREEDOM AND DISCIPLINE

5. Friedrich Nietzsche   71
   SCHOPENHAUER AS EDUCATOR

6. John Dewey   85
   THE SCHOOL AND SOCIAL PROGRESS
   THE CHILD AND THE CURRICULUM
   THE NEED OF A THEORY OF EXPERIENCE

7. W. E. B. Du Bois   135
   THE IMMORTAL CHILD

8. Antonio Gramsci   153
   THE INTELLECTUALS
   ON EDUCATION

9. Martin Heidegger   183
   HEIDEGGER ON THE ART OF TEACHING

10. George Counts   209
    DARE THE SCHOOL BUILD A NEW SOCIAL ORDER?

11. Theodor Adorno   219
    EDUCATION AFTER AUSCHWITZ
12. Erich Fromm   233
    TO HAVE OR TO BE?
13. Michel Foucault   249
    DOCILE BODIES
14. Paulo Freire   285
    UNDER THE SHADE OF A MANGO TREE
    THERE IS NO TEACHING WITHOUT LEARNING
    TEACHING IS A HUMAN ACT
    THE ADULT LITERARY PROCESS AS CULTURAL ACTION
      FOR FREEDOM
15. Jacques Ranciere   341
    FIVE LESSONS IN INTELLECTUAL EMANCIPATION
16. Richard Rorty   351
    PHILOSOPHY WITHOUT MIRRORS
17. Maxine Greene   385
    TEACHER AS STRANGER
18. Nel Noddings   427
    CARING
    CARING FOR IDEAS
19. Ann Margaret Sharp   469
    THE COMMUNITY OF INQUIRY: EDUCATION FOR
      DEMOCRACY
20. Cleo Cherryholmes   485
    POSTSTRUCTURALISM, PRAGMATISM,
      AND CURRICULUM
21. Nicholas Burbules   509
    THE LIMITS OF DIALOGUE AS A CRITICAL PEDAGOGY
22. bell hooks   527
    EMBRACING CHANGE
    PAOLO FREIRE
23. David Kennedy   547
    THE ROOTS OF CHILD STUDY: PHILOSOPHY, HISTORY
      AND RELIGION
24. Sandra Harding   565
    HOW CAN WOMEN'S STANDPOINT ADVANCE THE
      GROWTH OF SCIENTIFIC KNOWLEDGE?

25. Douglas Kellner   581
    MULTIPLE LITERACIES IN EDUCATION:
      AN INTRODUCTION
26. Philip Wexler   593
    THE MYSTICAL SOCIETY
    HOLY SPARKS

POSTSCRIPT by Jaime Grinberg   609

INTRODUCTION

The title of this volume is an invitation to play with ideas. But how do we play with ideas? Of course, as young children, we can remember playing with toys, but as young adults, there are few models of play. People of all ages seem to play with games, yet these games differ qualitatively from the more fantasy-oriented games of childhood which lack strict rules, objectives, and termination points.

Thus, it might seem rather odd that a volume on contemporary and modern philosophical perspectives would have us turn toward childhood play as a method for thinking. Isn't the seriousness of philosophy the exact opposite of childhood play? To answer this question, let's return once again to thinking about childhood and play. In a state of play, we are fully absorbed into the moment and give each action our full attention and concentration. We are also open to the possibilities of experimenting when we play. Because play is play and not homework, we are not afraid of consequences and instead prefer to enjoy the activity itself. We are not motivated by grades, GPAs, the worries of our parents, or the demands of the teacher. We are instead fully self-motivated and our attention is self-directed toward the playful activity at hand. Because of the joy we experience in the activity of play, we do not worry about consequences and instead focus almost exclusively on the process of play as an end in itself. In other words, to play is to be intrinsically motivated rather than extrinsically motivated, yet this indifference to consequences of play does not mean that play is frivolous. Rather, when the young child plays, she is very serious, indeed. Her efforts are concentrated, careful, and extremely sensitive to the situation of play. Play is therefore far from a mindless, irrational, and senseless activity.

Bearing these characteristics in mind, let's return once again to philosophy. If we often caricature play as nothing more than the whimsical, irrational, and directionless musings of young children, then we often think of philosophy as the reverse. Here philosophy is a "serious" adult activity that is difficult, strenuous, and only possible for highly trained, highly "intelligent" specialists in the field. If thinking about play makes us nostalgic and brings a smile to our faces, then, for most, thinking about the prospects of doing philosophy makes us nervous and brings a sigh of resignation if not frustration, yet is it not possible that below this opposition lies a deeper relationship between play and philosophy? It is our contention that philosophy is a unique space where we can precisely learn (or perhaps relearn) how to play . . . play with ideas. This playfulness is not dissimilar from childhood play. Both are open to the possibilities of playful experimentation. In terms of philosophy this means the examination of some of our most basic assumptions about the world. Being open in relation to thought is to reject all dogmatic positions in favor of a curiosity toward new possibilities and alternative ways of thinking and knowing about the world. To do philosophy is to concern oneself with the process of questioning rather than with firm conclusions. Both are thus very serious yet also about joy, discovery, and most importantly invention. To play with ideas is to rekindle this relationship between "adult" thinking and a "childish" wonder that sees the world and the ideas contained within with curiosity, puzzlement, and a refreshing openness.

So how do we play with ideas? Simply put, we begin to ask questions. These questions are the most general questions concerning everyday assumptions and practices of education. Such questions are highly speculative and as such cannot be answered easily through scientific research. For instance, philosophy asks of education

1. What is a child? If we are going to be teaching children, then we must examine our implicit or explicit assumptions concerning what constitutes childhood. Is a child a rational being, is a child inherently good, or is a child a "blank slate" brought into the world as a pure potential for newness? How we answer such questions will affect teaching practices. Furthermore, if we are to understand what constitutes childhood, then perhaps we must also call into question what exactly an adult is. How do we know an adult from a child? Is an adult simply a more mature child, or is an adult a totally different life stage divorced from the world of childhood? And finally, how are children and adults supposed to relate to one another? What are the proper ethical, pedagogical, and political relations between the two?

2. What is knowledge? Such a question seems so simple, so "naïve," and so "commonsense" that it normally would not appear to be worthwhile to ask, yet if we are teachers, we are surly teaching something, and more often than not, this something is knowledge. But how do we know what we are teaching is knowledge? What are the properties of knowledge (its characteristics), what is the value of knowledge, and how is it acquired? If national standards for K–12 concern what knowledge should be taught, philosophy of education asks what knowledge is in the first place.

3. What is the relationship between education and society? Is education supposed to help students become a part of society, or is it supposed to challenge society and stand against it? Is education political, should it be political, and can the politics of education critically evaluate dominant social politics? What are the places of education in society (is it restricted to schools or does it take place in multiple situations)?

4. What is the goal of education? What is the good education should strive to attain? What is the purpose of education? Another way of asking this question is what qualifies as an educated person? Such questions again will deeply impact the methods of education and as such need to be carefully yet playfully examined.

When we play with ideas, we begin with these "naïve" yet highly provocative questions that are often taken for granted. As such, the practice of playing with ideas contrasts sharply with other classes you might take outside of the educational foundation department. For instance, in curriculum and instruction classes students are exposed to a wide variety of skills that will assist in classroom management. Students learn the tools, techniques, and proficiencies necessary for class instruction (how to write a rubric for evaluation, how to organize a curriculum, how to discipline unruly students, etc.). These are practical classes with direct application to real-world educational experiences. There is, in other words, an immediate payoff for the teacher by learning "best practices." In such classes, the common question asked concerns particular students and their learning: "What should I do in the classroom?"

Apprenticeship classes offer "hands-on" experiences in the field. In the apprenticeship classes, students get to implement what they have learned in C & I while shadowing a professional in the field. Emphasis here is on navigating both the classroom and the bureaucracy of schooling. The common question here concerns administration policy: "What are proper procedures and policies I should follow?"

These are familiar classes to many students and are deemed useful, yet by focusing only on the latest educational innovations (what works for teachers) or on existing practices (what are the standards of professional conduct according to national standards, state standards, and the norms of the school), teacher education programs often neglect to cultivate the skills needed to play with ideas. By playing with ideas, future teachers are given an opportunity to analyze assumptions, speculate as to alternatives, and cultivate a comprehensive sense of the relationships between all aspects of schooling. In other words, educational philosophy offers a space of questioning and imagination where students are asked to suspend what they think they have come to know and think critically, imaginatively, and playfully about the status quo. Such questioning might not have the direct impact on everyday teaching practices seen in C & I courses; nevertheless, playing with ideas teaches future educators to be mindful of the meaning of their experiences. Being open and philosophically mindful allows us to bridge the artificial gap that often comes to separate the pragmatism and realism of adults from the openness, wonder, and curiosity of the children we teach, thus creating new spaces for educational experimentation.

With that said, we invite all of you to come and play with us for a semester!

1

Jean-Jacques Rousseau

Jean-Jacques Rousseau (1712–1778) is one of the most colorful figures in the history of philosophy of education. Born in Geneva, his early life was characterized by upheaval, uncertainty, and constant change. He was largely self-taught. He discovered philosophy when he entered and won an essay contest in 1749. His books include *Julie or the New Eloise* (1761), *The Social Contract* (1762), *Emile or on Education* (1762), and his highly amusing autobiography, *Confessions* (1781).

Emile is not an essay, a treatise, or a handbook on education; it is a utopian work that describes Rousseau's dream of an ideal education. You will most likely have strong reactions to it, as Rousseau intended. He wants the reader to learn just how much his or her thinking is biased by contemporary norms. The text's pedagogy reflects Rousseau's fundamental belief that, if an experience—including the act of reading—is to be genuinely educational, then it must engage both an individual's intellect *and* sentiments. Rousseau is well known for his eschewal of social convention and reason in favor of nature and emotion. He believed that children were closer to nature and that educators should study them in order to understand humanity better. For this reason he is often described as the father of Romanticism and child-centered education.

Rousseau's basic premise is that human beings are born free but become enslaved by public opinion. This results in moral turpitude because public opinion endorses a morality of false propriety. For Rousseau, the challenge that faces education is to create first an

1

individual who desires to live truthfully and, second, a society that supports the flourishing of such individuals. Rousseau thought that humans would live together virtuously if they could only be taught to seek the truth. He aspired to unify humanity through nature. Nature represents the appropriate equilibrium between an individual's desires and faculties: the individual desires to perform only those activities for which he or she has a capacity. In this context, Rousseau distinguishes between *amour de soi*, defined as a healthy love of self, and *amour de propre*, defined as an unhealthy love of self which is mediated by a reliance on the opinions of others. Rousseau argues that our desire for one another compels us to make comparisons that fuel our sense of hurt, anger, resentment, disappointment, envy, and jealousy. We only need to think about, beauty culture, materialism, and academic competitiveness in this regard.

Emile is divided into five books, which depict the imaginary life of its two central characters, Emile and Sophie. Addressed to "thinking mothers," Book 1 advises the reader on infancy, nursing, and swaddling. By Book 2, Emile is under the supervision of a tutor who is the "character" representing Rousseau. Isolated from society, Emile is thoroughly engaged in experiential learning—occupying himself with playing, running, navigation, competition, problem-solving, and planting—and discovering how to differentiate between necessary and unnecessary suffering. In Book 3, Emile learns a trade in order to contribute to society and to be financially self-sufficient. In Book 4, he reaches puberty. The awakening of Emile's sexual passions makes it difficult for him to be true to himself, and Rousseau recommends hunting and travel as tactical diversions. Book 5 describes Emile's courtship with, and eventual marriage to, Sophie.

Book 4 introduces the character of the Savoyard Vicar. The Vicar is usually interpreted as a cipher for Rousseau's own views. The Vicar argues that it is unnecessary and offensive to mandate people's thinking on civil and religious issues because people's ability to make judgments is essentially trustworthy, particularly if educated according to Rousseau's utopian vision, for if an individual's ability to make correct judgments in relationship first to nature and then to things is trustworthy, then so, too, is his or her ability to make correct political and moral judgments.

Rousseau is one of education's most paradoxical thinkers. Like the ancient philosophers, he has a deep interest in virtue, yet his celebration of the individual is distinctly modernist. He is a philosopher of the Enlightenment and one of its severest critics. He is one of the earliest philosophers to address femininity and women's education, yet in this area his work has only essentialized female difference. In sum, Rousseau can be described equally as a romantic, progressivist, pragmatist, or behaviorist. Drawing on Plato's myth of the cave, Rousseau referred to himself as the individual who, having seen the sun, returns to the cave to educate his fellow cave-dwellers, only to be vilified for his insights and to die in relative obscurity.

REFERENCES

Kukla, Rebecca. "Making and Masking Human Nature: Rousseau's Aesthetics of Education." *Journal of the British Society for Phenomenology* 29, no. 3 (1998): 228–249.

Lovlie, Lars. "Rousseau's Insight." *Studies in Philosophy and Education* 21 (2002): 335–41.

Rorty, Amelie-Okensberg. "Rousseau's Therapeutic Experiments." *Philosophy,* 91 (1991): 413–34.

Scholz, Sally. *On Rousseau.* Belmont, CA: Wadsworth, 2001.

PREFACE

This collection of reflections and observations, disordered and almost incoherent, was begun to gratify a good mother who knows how to think. I had at first planned only a monograph of a few pages. My subject drew me on in spite of myself, and this monograph imperceptibly became a sort of opus, too big, doubtless, for what it contains, but too small for the matter it treats. For a long time I hesitated to publish it; and often, in working at it, it has made me aware that it is not sufficient to have written a few pamphlets to know how to compose a book. After vain efforts to do better, I believe I ought to present it as it is, judging that it is important to turn public attention in this direction; and that although my ideas may be bad, if I cause others to give birth to good ones, I shall not entirely have wasted my time. A man, who from his retirement casts his pages out among the public, without boosters, without a party that defends them, without even knowing what is thought or said about them, need not fear that, if he is mistaken, his errors will be accepted without examination.

I will say little of the importance of a good education; nor will I stop to prove that the current one is bad. Countless others have done so before me, and I do not like to fill a book with things everybody knows. I will only note that for the longest time there has been nothing but a cry against the established practice without anyone taking it upon himself to propose a better one. The literature and the learning of our age tend much more to destruction than to edification. A magisterial tone fits censure; but another kind of tone—one less agreeable to philosophic haughtiness—must be adopted in order to make proposals. In spite of so many writings having as their end, it is said, only what is useful for the public, the first of all useful things, the art of forming men, is still forgotten. After Locke's book my subject was still entirely fresh, and I am very much afraid that the same will be the case after mine.

Childhood is unknown. Starting from the false idea one has of it, the farther one goes, the more one loses one's way. The wisest men concentrate on what it is important for men to know without considering what children are in a condition to learn. They are always seeking the man in the child without thinking of what he is before being a man. This is the study to which I have most applied myself, so that even

From "Preface," "Books I, II and V" in *Emile or On Education* by Allan Bloom, 1979. Reprinted by permission of Basic Books, a member of Perseus Books Group.

though my entire method were chimerical and false, my observations could still be of profit. My vision of what must be done may have been very poor, but I believe I have seen clearly the subject on which one must work. Begin, then, by studying your pupils better. For most assuredly you do not know them at all. Now if you read this book with this in view, I believe it will not be without utility for you.

As to what will be called the systematic part, which is here nothing but the march of nature, it is the point that will most put the reader off, and doubtless it is here that I will be attacked. And perhaps it will not be wrong to do so. It will be believed that what is being read is less an educational treatise than a visionary's dreams about education. What is to be done about it? It is on the basis not of others' ideas that I write but on that of my own. I do not see as do other men. I have long been reproached for that. But is it up to me to provide myself with other eyes or to affect other ideas? No. It is up to me not to go overboard, not to believe that I alone am wiser than everybody. It is up to me not to change sentiments but to distrust mine. That is all I can do; and that is what I do. If I sometimes adopt an assertive tone, it is not for the sake of making an impression on the reader but for the sake of speaking to him as I think. Why should I propose as doubtful what, so far as I am concerned, I do not doubt at all? I say exactly what goes on in my mind.

In expounding freely my sentiment, I so little expect that it be taken as authoritative that I always join to it my reasons, so that they may be weighed and I be judged. But although I do not wish to be obstinate in defending my ideas, I nonetheless believe that it is my obligation to propose them; for the maxims concerning which I am of an opinion different from that of others are not matters of indifference. They are among those whose truth or falsehood is important to know and which make the happiness or the unhappiness of mankind.

"Propose what can be done," they never stop repeating to me. It is as if I were told, "Propose doing what is done," or at least, "Propose some good which can be allied with the existing evil." Such a project, in certain matters, is much more chimerical than mine. For in this alliance the good is spoiled, and the evil is not cured. I would prefer to follow the established practice in everything than to follow a good one halfway. There would be less contradiction in man. He cannot pursue two opposite goals at the same time. Fathers and mothers, what can be done is what you want to do. Ought I to be responsible for your will?

In every sort of project there are two things to consider: first, the absolute goodness of the project; in the second place, the facility of execution.

In the first respect it suffices that the project be acceptable and practicable in itself, that what is good in it be in the nature of the thing; here, for example, that the proposed education be suitable for man and well adapted to the human heart.

The second consideration depends on relations given in certain situations—relations accidental to the thing, which consequently are not necessary and admit of infinite variety. Thus, one education may be practicable in Switzerland and not in France; one may be for the bourgeois, and another for the noble. The greater or lesser facility of execution depends on countless circumstances that are impossible to determine otherwise than in a particular application of the method to this or that country, to this or that station. Now all these particular applications, not being essential to my subject, do not enter into my plan. Other men will be able to concern themselves with them, if they wish, each for the country or estate he may have in view. It is enough for me that wherever men are born, what I propose can be done with them; and that, having done with them what I propose, what is best both for themselves and for others will have been done. If I do not fulfill this engagement, I am doubtless wrong. But if I do fulfill it, it would also be wrong to exact more from me. For that is all I promise.

BOOKS I AND II

Everything is good as it leaves the hands of the Author of things; everything degenerates in the hands of man. He forces one soil to nourish the products of another, one tree to bear the fruit of another. He mixes and confuses the climates, the elements, the seasons. He mutilates his dog, his horse, his slave. He turns everything upside down; he disfigures everything; he loves deformity, monsters. He wants nothing as nature made it, not even man; for him, man must be trained like a school horse; man must be fashioned in keeping with his fancy like a tree in his garden.

Were he not to do this, however, everything would go even worse, and our species does not admit of being formed halfway. In the present state of things a man abandoned to himself in the midst of other men from birth would be the most disfigured of all. Prejudices, authority, necessity, example, all the social institutions in which we find ourselves submerged would stifle nature in him and put nothing in its place. Nature there would be like a shrub that chance had caused to be born in the middle of a path and that the passers-by soon cause to perish by bumping into it from all sides and bending it in every direction.

It is to you that I address myself, tender and foresighted mother,* who are capable of keeping the nascent shrub away from the highway and securing it from the impact of human opinions! Cultivate and water the young plant before it dies. Its fruits will one day be your delights. Form an enclosure around your child's soul at an early date. Someone else can draw its circumference, but you alone must build the fence.

Plants are shaped by cultivation, and men by education. If man were born big and strong, his size and strength would be useless to him until he had learned to make use of them. They would be detrimental to him in that they would keep others from thinking of aiding him.** And, abandoned to himself, he would die of want before knowing his needs. And childhood is taken to be a pitiable state! It is not seen that the human race would have perished if man had not begun as a child.

We are born weak, we need strength; we are born totally unprovided, we need aid; we are born stupid, we need judgment. Everything we do not have at our birth and which we need when we are grown is given us by education.

---

*The first education is the most important, and this first education belongs incontestably to women; if the Author of nature had wanted it to belong to men, He would have given them milk with which to nurse the children. Always speak, then, preferably to women in your treatises on education; for, beyond the fact that they are in a position to watch over it more closely than are men and always have greater influence on it, they also have much more interest in its success, since most widows find themselves almost at the mercy of their children; then their children make mothers keenly aware, for good or ill, of the effect of the way they raised their children. The laws—always so occupied with property and so little with persons, because their object is peace not virtue—do not give enough authority to mothers. However, their status is more certain than that of fathers; their duties are more painful; their cares are more important for the good order of the family; generally they are more attached to the children. There are occasions on which a son who lacks respect for his father can in some way be excused. But if on any occasion whatsoever a child were unnatural enough to lack respect for his mother—for her who carried him in her womb, who nursed him with her milk, who for years forgot herself in favor of caring for him alone—one should hasten to strangle this wretch as a monster unworthy of seeing the light of day. Mothers, it is said, spoil their children. In that they are doubtless wrong—but less wrong than you perhaps who deprave them. The mother wants her child to be happy, happy now. In that she is right. When she is mistaken about the means, she must be enlightened. Fathers' ambition, avarice, tyranny, and false foresight, their negligence, their harsh insensitivity are a hundred times more disastrous for children than is the blind tenderness of mothers. Moreover, the sense I give to the name *mother* must be explained; and that is what will be done hereafter.

**Similar to them on the outside and deprived of speech as well as of the ideas it expresses, he would not be in a condition to make them understand the need he had of their help, and nothing in him would manifest this need to them.

This education comes to us from nature or from men or from things. The internal development of our faculties and our organs is the education of nature. The use that we are taught to make of this development is the education of men. And what we acquire from our own experience about the objects which affect us is the education of things.

Each of us is thus formed by three kinds of masters. The disciple in whom their various lessons are at odds with one another is badly raised and will never be in agreement with himself. He alone in whom they all coincide at the same points and tend to the same ends reaches his goal and lives consistently. He alone is well raised.

Now, of these three different educations, the one coming from nature is in no way in our control; that coming from things is in our control only in certain respects; that coming from men is the only one of which we are truly the masters. Even of it we are the masters only by hypothesis. For who can hope entirely to direct the speeches and the deeds of all those surrounding a child?

Therefore, when education becomes an art, it is almost impossible for it to succeed, since the conjunction of the elements necessary to its success is in no one's control. All that one can do by dint of care is to come more or less close to the goal, but to reach it requires luck.

What is that goal? It is the very same as that of nature. This has just been proved. Since the conjunction of the three educations is necessary to their perfection, the two others must be directed toward the one over which we have no power. But perhaps this word *nature* has too vague a sense. An attempt must be made here to settle on its meaning.

Nature, we are told, is only habit. What does that mean? Are there not habits contracted only by force which never do stifle nature? Such, for example, is the habit of the plants whose vertical direction is interfered with. The plant, set free, keeps the inclination it was forced to take. But the sap has not as a result changed its original direction; and if the plant continues to grow, its new growth resumes the vertical direction. The case is the same for men's inclinations. So long as one remains in the same condition, the inclinations which result from habit and are the least natural to us can be kept; but as soon as the situation changes, habit ceases and the natural returns. Education is certainly only habit. Now are there not people who forget and lose their education? Others who keep it? Where does this difference come from? If the name *nature* were limited to habits conformable to nature, we would spare ourselves this garble.

We are born with the use of our senses, and from our birth we are affected in various ways by the objects surrounding us. As soon as we have, so to speak, consciousness of our sensations, we are disposed to seek or avoid the objects which produce them, at first according to whether they are pleasant or unpleasant to us, then according to the conformity or lack of it that we find between us and these objects, and finally according to the judgments we make about them on the basis of the idea of happiness or of perfection given us by reason. These dispositions are extended and strengthened as we become more capable of using our senses and more enlightened; but constrained by our habits, they are more or less corrupted by our opinions. Before this corruption they are what I call in us *nature.*

In the natural order, since men are all equal, their common calling is man's estate and whoever is well raised for that calling cannot fail to fulfill those callings related to it. Let my student be destined for the sword, the church, the bar. I do not care. Prior to the calling of his parents is nature's call to human life. Living is the job I want to teach him. On leaving my hands, he will, I admit, be neither magistrate nor soldier nor priest. He will, in the first place, be a man. All that a man should be, he will in case of need know how to be as well as anyone; and fortune may try as it may to make him change place, he will always be in his own place. *Occupavi te fortuna atque cepi omnesque aditus tuos interclusi, ut ad me aspirare non posses.* *

Our true study is that of the human condition. He among us who best knows how to bear the goods and the ills of this life is to my taste the best raised: from which it follows that the true education consists less in precept than in practice. We begin to instruct ourselves when we begin to live. Our education begins with us. Our first preceptor is our nurse. Thus this word *education* had another meaning for the ancients which we no longer give to it. *Educit obstetrix,* says Varro, *educat nutrix, instituit pedagogus, docet magister.* †

Thus education, instruction, and teaching are three things as different in their object as are the governess, the preceptor, and the master. But these distinctions are ill drawn; and, to be well led, the child should follow only a single guide.

We must, then, generalize our views and consider in our pupil abstract man, man exposed to all the accidents of human life. If men

---

**Tuscul.* V.[10]
†Non. Marcell.[11]

were born attached to a country's soil, if the same season lasted the whole year, if each man were fixed in his fortune in such a way as never to be able to change it—the established practice would be good in certain respects. The child raised for his station, never leaving it, could not be exposed to the disadvantages of another. But given the mobility of human things, given the unsettled and restless spirit of this age which upsets everything in each generation, can one conceive of a method more senseless than raising a child as though he never had to leave his room, as though he were going to be constantly surrounded by his servants? If the unfortunate makes a single step on the earth, if he goes down a single degree, he is lost. This is not teaching him to bear suffering; it is training him to feel it.

One thinks only of preserving one's child. That is not enough. One ought to teach him to preserve himself as a man, to bear the blows of fate, to brave opulence and poverty, to live, if he has to, in freezing Iceland or on Malta's burning rocks. You may very well take precautions against his dying. He will nevertheless have to die. And though his death were not the product of your efforts, still these efforts would be ill conceived. It is less a question of keeping him from dying than of making him live. To live is not to breathe; it is to act; it is to make use of our organs, our senses, our faculties, of all the parts of ourselves which give us the sentiment of our existence. The man who has lived the most is not he who has counted the most years but he who has most felt life. Men have been buried at one hundred who died at their birth. They would have gained from dying young; at least they would have lived up to that time.

The fate of man is to suffer at all times. The very care of his preservation is connected with pain. Lucky to know only physical ills in his childhood—ills far less cruel, far less painful than are the other kinds of ills and which far more rarely make us renounce life than do the others! One does not kill oneself for the pains of gout. There are hardly any but those of the soul which produce despair. We pity the lot of childhood, and it is our own that should be pitied. Our greatest ills come to us from ourselves.

A child cries at birth; the first part of his childhood is spent crying. At one time we bustle about, we caress him in order to pacify him; at another, we threaten him, we strike him in order to make him keep quiet. Either we do what pleases him, or we exact from him what pleases us. Either we submit to his whims, or we submit him to ours.

No middle ground; he must give orders or receive them. Thus his first ideas are those of domination and servitude. Before knowing how to speak, he commands; before being able to act, he obeys. And sometimes he is chastised before he is able to know his offenses or, rather, to commit any. It is thus that we fill up his young heart at the outset with the passions which later we impute to nature and that, after having taken efforts to make him wicked, we complain about finding him so.

Far from being attentive to protecting Emile from injury, I would be most distressed if he were never hurt and grew up without knowing pain. To suffer is the first thing he ought to learn and the thing he will most need to know. It seems that children are little and weak only in order that they may get these important lessons without danger. If the child falls down, he will not break his leg; if he hits himself with a stick, he will not break his arm; if he grabs a knife, he will hardly tighten his grip and will not cut himself very deeply. I do not know of a child at liberty who was ever seen to kill, cripple, or do himself any considerable harm, unless he was carelessly exposed on high places or alone near fire, or dangerous instruments were left in his reach. What is to be said about these arsenals of machines set up around a child to arm him at all points against pain, so that when he is grown, he is at its mercy without courage and without experience, believes he is dead at the first prick, and faints on seeing the first drop of his blood?

Our didactic and pedantic craze is always to teach children what they would learn much better by themselves and to forget what we alone could teach them. Is there anything more foolish than the effort made to teach them to walk, as if anyone were ever seen who, due to his nurse's negligence, did not when grown know how to walk? How many people, on the contrary, does one see walk badly for their whole lives because they were badly taught how to walk?

Emile will not have padded bonnets, strollers, buggies, or leading strings; or, at least, as soon as he begins to know how to put one foot before the other, he will be supported only in paved places, and we shall hastily pass them by.* Instead of letting him stagnate in the stale air of a room, let him be taken daily to the middle of a field. There let him run and frisk about; let him fall a hundred times a day. So much the better.

---

*There is nothing more ridiculous and more lacking in assurance than the step of people who were led too much by leading strings when they were little. This is another of those observations that are trivial by dint of being accurate and that are accurate in more than one sense.

That way he will learn how to get up sooner. The well-being of freedom makes up for many wounds. My pupil will often have bruises. But, in compensation, he will always be gay. If your pupils have fewer bruises, they are always hindered, always enchained, always sad. I doubt whether the advantage is theirs.

Another progress makes complaint less necessary to children; this is the progress of their strength. Able to do more by themselves, they need to have recourse to others less frequently. With their strength develops the knowledge which puts them in a condition to direct it. It is at this second stage that, strictly speaking, the life of the individual begins. It is then that he gains consciousness of himself. Memory extends the sentiment of identity to all the moments of his existence; he becomes truly one, the same, and consequently already capable of happiness or unhappiness. It is important, therefore, to begin to consider him here as a moral being.

Although the furthest limit of human life can be pretty nearly determined, as well as one's probabilities at each age of approaching that limit, nothing is more uncertain than the duration of each man's life in particular. Very few attain this furthest limit. Life's greatest risks are in its beginnings; the less one has lived, the less one ought to hope to live. Of the children born, half, at the most, reach adolescence; and it is probable that your pupil will not reach the age of manhood.

What, then, must be thought of that barbarous education which sacrifices the present to an uncertain future, which burdens a child with chains of every sort and begins by making him miserable in order to prepare him from afar for I know not what pretended happiness which it is to be believed he will never enjoy? Even if I were to suppose this education reasonable in its object, how can one without indignation see poor unfortunates submitted to an unbearable yoke and condemned to continual labor like galley slaves, without any assurance that so many efforts will ever be useful to them? The age of gaiety passes amidst tears, punishments, threats, and slavery. The unlucky fellow is tormented for his own good; and the death that is being summoned is unseen, the death which is going to seize him in the midst of this gloomy setup. Who knows how many children perish victims of a father's or a master's extravagant wisdom? Happy to escape his cruelty, the only advantage they get from the ills he has made them suffer is to die without regretting life, of which they knew only the torments.

Men, be humane. This is your first duty. Be humane with every station, every age, everything which is not alien to man. What wisdom is there for you save humanity? Love childhood; promote its games, its pleasures, its amiable instinct. Who among you has not sometimes regretted that age when a laugh is always on the lips and the soul is always at peace? Why do you want to deprive these little innocents of the enjoyment of a time so short which escapes them and of a good so precious which they do not know how to abuse? Why do you want to fill with bitterness and pains these first years which go by so rapidly and can return no more for them than they can for you? Fathers, do you know the moment when death awaits your children? Do not prepare regrets for yourself in depriving them of the few instants nature gives them. As soon as they can sense the pleasure of being, arrange it so that they can enjoy it, arrange it so that at whatever hour God summons them they do not die without having tasted life.

How many voices are going to be raised against me! I hear from afar the clamors of that false of wisdom which incessantly projects us outside of ourselves, which always counts the present for nothing, and which, pursuing without respite a future that retreats in proportion as we advance, by dint of transporting us where we are not, transports us where we shall never be.

This is, you answer me, the time of correct man's bad inclinations; it is during the age of childhood, when we are least sensitive to pains, that they must be multiplied so as to spare them in the age of reason. But who tells you that this whole arrangement is at your disposition, and that all this fair instruction with which you overwhelm the child's feeble mind will not one day be more pernicious to him than useful? Who assures you that you are sparing him something by the sorrows you lavish on him? Why do you give him more ills than his condition entails without being sure that these present ills are for the relief of the future? And how will you prove to me that these bad inclinations, of which you claim you are curing him, do not come to him from your ill-considered care far more than from nature? Unhappy foresight which makes a being unhappy now in the hope, well or ill founded, of making him happy one day! In case these vulgar reasoners confuse license with liberty and the child one makes happy with the child one spoils, let us teach them to distinguish the two.

In order not to pursue chimeras let us not forget what is appropriate to our situation. Humanity has its place in the order of things; childhood has its in the order of human life. The man must be considered in the man, and the child in the child. To assign each his place and settle him in it, to order the human passions according to man's constitution is all that we can do for his well-being. The rest depends on alien causes which are in no way in our power.

We do not know what absolute happiness or unhappiness is. Everything is mixed in this life; in it one tastes no pure sentiment; in it one does not stay two moments in the same state. The affections of our souls, as well as the states of our bodies, are in a continual flux. The good and the bad are common to us all, but in different measures. The happiest is he who suffers the least pain; the unhappiest is he who feels the least pleasure. Always more suffering than enjoyment; this relation between the two is common to all men. Man's felicity on earth is, hence, only a negative condition; the smallest number of ills he can suffer ought to constitute its measure.

Every feeling of pain is inseparable from the desire to be delivered from it; every idea of pleasure is inseparable from the desire to enjoy it; every desire supposes privation, and all sensed privations are painful. Our unhappiness consists, therefore, in the disproportion between our desires and our faculties. A being endowed with senses whose faculties equaled his desires would be an absolutely happy being.

In what, then, consists human wisdom or the road of true happiness? It is not precisely in diminishing our desires, for if they were beneath our power, a part of our faculties would remain idle, and we would not enjoy our whole being. Neither is it in extending our faculties, for if, proportionate to them, our desires were more extended, we would as a result only become unhappier. But it is in diminishing the excess of the desires over the faculties and putting power and will in perfect equality. It is only then that, with all the powers in action, the soul will nevertheless remain peaceful and that man will be well ordered.

It is thus that nature, which does everything for the best, constituted him in the beginning. It gives him with immediacy only the desires necessary to his preservation and the faculties sufficient to satisfy them. It put all the others, as it were, in reserve in the depth of his soul, to be developed there when needed. Only in this original state are power and desire in equilibrium and man is not unhappy. As soon as his potential faculties are put in action, imagination, the most active of all, is awakened and outstrips them. It is imagination which extends for us the measure of the possible, whether for good or bad, and which consequently excites and nourishes the desires by the hope of satisfying them. But the object which at first appeared to be at hand flees more quickly than it can be pursued. When one believes that one has reached it, it transforms and reveals itself in the distance ahead of us. No longer seeing the country we have already crossed, we count it for nothing; what remains to cross ceaselessly grows and extends. Thus one exhausts oneself without getting to the end, and the more one gains on enjoyment, the further happiness gets from us.

On the contrary, the closer to his natural condition man has stayed, the smaller is the difference between his faculties and his desires, and consequently the less removed he is from being happy. He is never less unhappy than when he appears entirely destitute, for unhappiness consists not in the privation of things but in the need that is felt for them.

The real world has its limits; the imaginary world in infinite. Unable to enlarge the one, let us restrict the other, for it is from the difference between the two alone that are born all the pains which make us truly unhappy. Take away strength, health, and good witness of oneself, all the goods of this life are in opinion; take away the pains of the body and the remorse of conscience, all our ills are imaginary. This principle is common, it will be said. I agree. But its practical application is not common, and we are dealing solely with practice here.

The only one who does his own will is he who, in order to do it, has no need to put another's arms at the end of his own; from which it follows that the first of all goods is not authority but freedom. The truly free man wants only what he can do and does what he pleases. That is my fundamental maxim. It need only be applied to childhood for all the rules of education to flow from it.

Society has made man weaker not only in taking from him the right he had over his own strength but, above all, in making his strength insufficient for him. That is why his desires are multiplied along with his weakness, and that is what constitutes the weakness of childhood compared to manhood. If the man is a strong being and the child is a weak being, this is not because the former has more strength absolutely than the latter, but it is because the former can naturally be sufficient unto himself and the latter cannot. The man should, hence, have more will and the child more whim, a word by which I mean all desires which are not true needs and which can only be satisfied with another's help.

I have given the reason for this state of weakness. Nature provides for it by the attachment of fathers and mothers; but this attachment can have its excess, its defect, its abuses. Parents who live in the civil state transport their child into it before the proper age. In giving him more needs than he has, they do not relieve his weakness; they increase it. They increase it still more by exacting from him what nature did not exact. They do so by subjecting to their will the bit of strength which he has for serving his own, by changing into slavery on one side or the other the reciprocal dependence in which his weakness keeps him and their attachment keeps them.

The wise man knows how to stay in his place; but the child, who does not know his place, would not be able to keep to it. Among us he is given a thousand exits by which to leave it. It is for those who govern him to keep him in his place, and this is not an easy task. He ought to be neither beast nor man, but child. It is necessary that he feel his weakness and not that he suffer from it. It is necessary that he be dependent and not that he obey. It is necessary that he ask and not that he command. He is only subject to others by virtue of his needs, and because they see better than he does what is useful to him, what can contribute to, or be harmful to, his preservation. No one, not even the father, has a right to command the child what is not for his good.

Before prejudices and human institutions have corrupted our natural inclinations, the happiness of children, like that of men, consists in the use of their freedom. But in the case of children this freedom is limited by their weakness. Whoever does what he wants is happy if he is self-sufficient; this is the case of the man living in the state of nature. Whoever does what he wants is not happy if his needs surpass his strength; this is the case of the child in the same state. Children, even in the state of nature, enjoy only an imperfect freedom, similar to that enjoyed by men in the civil state. No longer able to do without others, each of us becomes in this respect weak and miserable again. We were made to be men; laws and society have plunged us once more into childhood. The rich, the nobles, the kings are all children who, seeing that men are eager to relieve their misery, derive a puerile vanity from that very fact and are very proud of care that one would not give to them if they were grown men.

These considerations are important and serve to resolve all the contradictions of the social system. There are two sorts of dependence: dependence on things, which is from nature; dependence on men, which is from society. Dependence on things, since it has no morality, is in no way detrimental to freedom and engenders no vices. Dependence on men, since it is without order,* engenders all the vices, and by it, master and slave are mutually corrupted. If there is any means of remedying this ill in society, it is to substitute law for man and to arm the general wills with a real strength superior to the action of every particular will. If the laws of nations could, like those of nature, have an inflexibility that no human force could ever conquer, dependence on men would then become dependence on things again; in the republic all of the advantages of the natural state would be united with those of the civil state, and freedom which keeps man exempt from vices would be joined to morality which raises him to virtue.

Dare I expose the greatest, the most important, the most useful rule of all education? It is not to gain time but to lose it. Common readers, pardon me my paradoxes. When one reflects, they are necessary and, whatever you may say, I prefer to be a paradoxical man than a prejudiced one. The most dangerous period of human life is that from birth to the age of twelve. This is the time when errors and vices germinate without one's yet having any instrument for destroying them; and by the time the instrument comes, the roots are so deep that it is too late to rip them out. If children jumped all at once from the breast to the age of reason, the education they are given might be suitable for them. But, according to the natural progress, they need an entirely contrary one. They ought to do nothing with their soul until all of its faculties have developed, because while the soul is yet blind, it cannot perceive the torch you are presenting to it or follow the path reason maps out across the vast plain of ideas, a path which is so faint even to the best of eyes.

Thus, the first education ought to be purely negative. It consists not at all in teaching virtue or truth but in securing the heart from vice and

---

*In my *Principles of Political Right*[9] it is demonstrated that no particular will can be ordered in the social system.

the mind from error. If you could do nothing and let nothing be done, if you could bring your pupil healthy and robust to the age of twelve without his knowing how to distinguish his right hand from his left, at your first lessons the eyes of his understanding would open up to reason. Without prejudice, without habit, he would have nothing in him which could hinder the effect of your care. Soon he would become in your hands the wisest of men; and in beginning by doing nothing, you would have worked an educational marvel.

Take the opposite of the practiced path, and you will almost always do well. Since what is wanted is not to make a child out of a child but a doctor out of a child, fathers and masters can never soon enough scold, correct, reprimand, flatter, threaten, promise, instruct, talk reason. Do better: be reasonable, and do not reason with your pupil, especially to get his approbation for what displeases him. Bringing reason to bear on unpleasant things only makes reason tedious for him and discredits it early in a mind not yet in a condition to understand it. Exercise his body, his organs, his senses, his strength, but keep his soul idle for as long as possible. Be afraid of all sentiments anterior to the judgment which evaluates them. Restrain, arrest alien impressions; and in order to prevent the birth of evil, do not hurry to do good, for good is only truly such when reason enlightens it. Regard all delays as advantages; to advance toward the end without losing anything is to gain a lot. Let childhood ripen in children. And what if some lesson finally becomes necessary to them? Keep yourself from giving it today if you can without danger put it off until tomorrow.

Another consideration confirms the utility of this method. One must know well the particular genius of the child in order to know what moral diet suits him. Each mind has its own form, according to which it needs to be governed; the success of one's care depends on governing it by this form and not by another. Prudent man, spy out nature for a long time; observe your pupil well before saying the first word to him. To start with, let the germ of his character reveal itself freely; constrain it in no way whatsoever in order better to see the whole of it. Do you think this time of freedom is lost for him? Not at all. This is the best way to use it, for you are learning now not to lose a single moment in a more valuable time; while if you begin to act before knowing what must be done, you will act haphazardly. Subject to error, you will have to retrace your steps; you will be farther removed from the goal than if you had been in less of a rush to reach it. Do not therefore act like the miser who loses a great deal for wanting not to lose anything. In the earliest age sacrifice time that you will regain with interest at a more advanced age. The wise doctor does not at first sight giddily give prescriptions but in the first place studies the constitution of his patient before prescribing anything to him. He may begin to treat the patient late but he cures him, whereas the doctor who is in too much of a rush kills him.

Remember that before daring to undertake the formation of a man, one must have made oneself a man. One must find within oneself the example the pupil ought to take for his own. While the child is still without knowledge, there is time to prepare everything that comes near him in order that only objects suitable for him to see meet his first glances. Make yourself respectable to everyone. Begin by making yourself loved so that each will seek to please you. You will not be the child's master if you are not the master of all that surrounds him; and this authority will never be sufficient if it is not founded on the esteem for virtue. It is not a question of emptying one's purse and spending money by the handful. I have never seen that money has made anyone loved. One ought not to be miserly and hard nor merely pity the poverty that one can relieve. But you can open your coffers all you want; if you do not also open your heart, others' hearts will always remain closed to you. It is your time, your care, your affection, it is you yourself that must be given. For no matter what you do, people never feel that your money is you. There are tokens of interest and benevolence which produce a greater effect and are really more useful than any gifts. How many unfortunate people, how many sick people need consolation more than alms! How many oppressed people need protection more than money! Reconcile people who have quarreled; forestall litigations; bring children to their duty, fathers to indulgence; encourage happy marriages; prevent harassment; use, lavish the influence of your pupil's parents in favor of the weak man to whom justice is denied and who is crushed by the powerful man. Loudly proclaim yourself the protector of the unfortunate. Be just, humane, and beneficent. Give not only alms; give charity. Works of mercy relieve more ills than does money. Love others, and they will love you. Serve them, and they will serve you. Be their brother, and they will be your children.

BOOK V

Now we have come to the last act in the drama of youth, but we are not yet at the dénouement. It is not good for man to be alone. Emile is a man. We have promised him a companion. She has to be given to him. That companion is Sophie. In what place is her abode? Where shall we find her? To find her, it is necessary to know her. Let us first learn what she is; then we shall better judge what places she inhabits. And even when we have found her, everything will still not have been done. "Since our young gentleman," says Locke, "is ready to marry, it is time to leave him to his beloved." And with that he finishes his work. But as I do not have the honor of raising a gentleman, I shall take care not to imitate Locke on this point.

Sophie OR THE WOMAN

Sophie ought to be a woman as Emile is a man—that is to say, she ought to have everything which suits the constitution of her species and her sex in order to fill her place in the physical and moral order. Let us begin, then, by examining the similarities and the differences of her sex and ours.

In everything not connected with sex, woman is man. She has the same organs, the same needs, the same faculties. The machine is constructed in the same way; its parts are the same; the one functions as does the other; the form is similar; and in whatever respect one considers them, the difference between them is only one of more or less.

In everything connected with sex, woman and man are in every respect related and in every respect different. The difficulty of comparing them comes from the difficulty of determining what in their constitutions is due to sex and what is not. On the basis of comparative anatomy and even just by inspection, one finds general differences between them that do not appear connected with sex. They are, nevertheless, connected with sex, but by relations which we are not in a position to perceive. We do not know the extent of these relations. The only thing we know with certainty is that everything man and woman have in common belongs to the species, and that everything which distinguishes them belongs to the sex. From this double perspective, we find them related in so many ways and opposed in so many other ways that it is perhaps one of the marvels of nature to have been able to construct two such similar beings who are constituted so differently.

These relations and these differences must have a moral influence. This conclusion is evident to the senses; it is in agreement with our experience; and it shows how vain are the disputes as to whether one of the two sexes is superior or whether they are equal—as though each, in fulfilling nature's ends according to its own particular purpose, were thereby less perfect than if it resembled the other more! In what they have in common, they are equal. Where they differ, they are not comparable. A perfect woman and a perfect man ought not to resemble each other in mind any more than in looks, and perfection is not susceptible of more or less.

In the union of the sexes each contributes equally to the common aim, but not in the same way. From this diversity arises the first assignable difference in the moral relations of the two sexes. One ought to be active and strong, the other passive and weak. One must necessarily will and be able; it suffices that the other put up little resistance.

Once this principle is established, it follows that woman is made specially to please man. If man ought to please her in turn, it is due to a less direct necessity. His merit is in his power; he pleases by the sole fact of his strength. This is not the law of love, I agree. But it is that of nature, prior to love itself.

If woman is made to please and to be subjugated, she ought to make herself agreeable to man instead of arousing him. Her own violence is in her charms. It is by these that she ought to constrain him to find his strength and make use of it. The surest art for animating that strength is to make it necessary by resistance. Then *amour-propre* unites with desire, and the one triumphs in the victory that the other has made him win. From this there arises attack and defense, the audacity of one sex and the timidity of the other, and finally the modesty and the shame with which nature armed the weak in order to enslave the strong.

Who could think that nature has indiscriminately prescribed the same advances to both men and women, and that the first to form desires should also be the first to show them? What a strange depravity of judgment! Since the undertaking has such different consequences for the two sexes, is it natural that they should have the same audacity in abandoning themselves to it? With so great an inequality in what each risks in the union, how can one fail to see that if reserve did not impose on one sex the moderation which nature imposes on the other, the result would soon be the ruin of both, and mankind would perish by the means established for preserving it? If there were some unfortunate region on earth where philosophy had introduced this practice—especially in hot countries, where more women are born than men—men would be tyrannized by women. For, given the ease with which women arouse men's senses and reawaken in the depths of their hearts the remains of ardors which are almost extinguished, men would finally be their victims and would see themselves dragged to death without ever being able to defend themselves.

If females among the animals do not have the same shame, what follows from that? Do they have, as women do, the unlimited desires to which this shame serves as a brake? For them, desires comes only with need. When the need is satisfied, the desire ceases. They no longer feign to repulse the male* but really do so. They do exactly the opposite of Augustus' daughter; they accept no more passengers when the ship has its cargo. Even when they are free, their times of good will are short and quickly pass. Instinct impels them, and instinct stops them. What will be the substitute for this negative instinct when you have deprived women of modesty? To wait until they no longer care for men is equivalent to waiting until they are no longer good for anything.

The Supreme Being wanted to do honor to the human species in everything. While giving man inclinations without limit, He gives him at the same time the law which regulates them, in order that he may be free and in command of himself. While abandoning man to immoderate passions, He joins reason to these passions in order to govern them. While abandoning woman to unlimited desires, He joins modesty to these desires in order to constrain them. In addition, He adds yet another real recompense for the good use of one's faculties—the taste we acquire for decent things when we make them the rule of our actions. All this, it seems to me, is worth more than the instinct of beasts.

Whether the human female shares man's desires or not and wants to satisfy them or not, she repulses him and always defends herself—but not always with the same force or, consequently, with the same success. For the attacker to be victorious, the one who is attacked must permit or arrange it; for does she not have adroit means to force the aggressor to use force? The freest and sweetest of all acts does not admit of real violence. Nature and reason oppose it: nature, in that it has provided the weaker with as much strength as is

---

*I have already noticed that affected and provocative refusals are common to almost all females, even among animals, even when they are most disposed to give themselves. One has to have never observed their wiles not to agree with this.

needed to resist when it pleases her; reason, in that real rape is not only the most brutal of all acts but the one most contrary to its end—either because the man thus declares war on his companion and authorizes her to defend her person and her liberty even at the expense of the agressor's life, or because the woman alone is the judge of the condition she is in, and a child would have no father if every man could usurp the father's rights.

Here, then, is a third conclusion drawn from the constitution of the sexes—that the stronger appears to be master but actually depends on the weaker. This is due not to a frivolous practice of gallantry or to the proud generosity of a protector, but to an invariable law of nature which gives woman more facility to excite the desires than man to satisfy them. This causes the latter, whether he likes it or not, to depend on the former's wish and constrains him to seek to please her in turn, so that she will consent to let him be the stronger. Then what is sweetest for man in his victory is the doubt whether it is weakness which yields to strength or the will which surrenders. And the woman's usual ruse is always to leave this doubt between her and him. In this the spirit of women corresponds perfectly to their constitution. Far from blushing at their weakness, they make it their glory. Their tender muscles are without resistance. They pretend to be unable to lift the lightest burdens. They would be ashamed to be strong. Why is that? It is not only to appear delicate; it is due to a shrewder precaution. They prepare in advance excuses and the right to be weak in case of need.

The progress of the enlightenment acquired as a result of our vices has greatly changed the old opinions on this point among us. Rapes are hardly ever spoken of anymore, since they are so little necessary and men no longer believe in them.* By contrast, they are very common in early Greek and Jewish antiquity, because those old opinions belong to the simplicity of nature, and only the experience of libertinism has been able to uproot them. If fewer acts of rape are cited in our day, this is surely not because men are more temperate but because they are less credulous, and such a complaint, which previously would have persuaded simple peoples, in our days would succeed only in attracting the laughter of mockers. It is more advantageous to keep quiet. In Deuteronomy there is a law by which a girl

---

*There can be such a disproportion of age and strength that real rape takes place; but treating here the relation between the sexes according to the order of nature, I take them both as they ordinarily are in that relation.

who had been abused was punished along with her seducer if the offense had been committed in the city. But if it had been committed in the country or in an isolated place, the man alone was punished: "For," the law says, "the girl cried out and was not heard." This benign interpretation taught the girls not to let themselves be surprised in well-frequented places.

The effect of these differences of opinion about morals is evident. Modern gallantry is their work. Finding that their pleasures depended more on the will of the fair sex than they had believed, men have captivated that will by attentions for which the fair sex has amply compensated them.

Observe how the physical leads us unawares to the moral, and how the sweetest laws of love are born little by little from the coarse union of the sexes. Women possess their empire not because men wanted it that way, but because nature wants it that way. It belonged to women before they appeared to have it. The same Hercules who believed he raped the fifty daughters of Thespitius was nevertheless constrained to weave while he was with Omphale; and the strong Samson was not so strong as Delilah. This empire belongs to women and cannot be taken from them, even when they abuse it. If they could ever lose it, they would have done so long ago.

There is no parity between the two sexes in regard to the consequences of sex. The male is male only at certain moments. The female is female her whole life or at least during her whole youth. Everything constantly recalls her sex to her; and, to fulfill its functions well, she needs a constitution which corresponds to it. She needs care during her pregnancy; she needs rest at the time of childbirth; she needs a soft and sedentary life to suckle her children; she needs patience and gentleness, a zeal and an affection that nothing can rebuff in order to raise her children. She serves as the link between them and their father; she alone makes him love them and gives him the confidence to call them his own. How much tenderness and care is required to maintain the union of the whole family! And, finally, all this must come not from virtues but from tastes, or else the human species would soon be extinguished.

The strictness of the relative duties of the two sexes is not and cannot be the same. When woman complains on this score about unjust man-made inequality, she is wrong. This inequality is not a human institution—or, at least, it is the work not of prejudice but of reason. It is up to the sex that nature has charged with the bearing of children to be responsible for them to the other sex. Doubtless it is not permitted to anyone to violate his faith, and every unfaithful husband who deprives his wife of the only reward of the austere duties of her sex is an unjust and barbarous man. But the unfaithful woman does more; she dissolves the family and breaks all the bonds of nature. In giving the man children which are not his, she betrays both. She joins perfidy to infidelity. I have difficulty seeing what disorders and what crimes do not flow from this one. If there is a frightful condition in the world, it is that of an unhappy father who, lacking confidence in his wife, does not dare to yield to the sweetest sentiments of his heart, who wonders, in embracing his child, whether he is embracing another's, the token of his dishonor, the plunderer of his own children's property. What does the family become in such a situation if not a society of secret enemies whom a guilty woman arms against one another in forcing them to feign mutual love?

It is important, then, not only that a woman be faithful, but that she be judged to be faithful by her husband, by those near her, by everyone. It is important that she be modest, attentive, reserved, and that she give evidence of her virtue to the eyes of others as well as to her own conscience. If it is important that a father love his children, it is important that he esteem their mother. These are the reasons which put even appearances among the duties of women, and make honor and reputation no less indispensable to them than chastity. There follows from these principles, along with the moral difference of the sexes, a new motive of duty and propriety which prescribes especially to women the most scrupulous attention to their conduct, their manners, and their bearing. To maintain vaguely that the two sexes are equal and that their duties are the same, is to lose oneself in vain declaiming; it is to say nothing so long as one does not respond to these considerations.

2

RALPH WALDO EMERSON

Born in Boston, Massachusetts, in 1803, Emerson began his career as a Unitarian minister steeped in the liberal theology of William Ellery Channing that upheld the primacy of Reason, the rejection of Christian orthodoxy as dogma, and the promotion of a spirit of optimism founded in the potential of every person to obtain a likeness to God. However, Emerson quickly quit his ministerial duties for the then burgeoning lyceum circuit, becoming a profound and prolific journalist, essayist, poet, and public lecturer who fashioned an intellectual vision that integrated aspects of Unitarianism, German Transcendental philosophy, Platonic and Neo-Platonic ideas, British Romanticism, the meditations of Montaigne, Asian philosophy, Swedenborgian mysticism, and the latest scientific insights of his day. While Emerson's mind engaged with a wide variety of matters, including the proper role of education, the relationship of culture to nature, and metaphysical issues of process and power, his work is best characterized as a form of polemical protest against what he perceived to be the uninspired state of (particularly American) society, politics, and culture during the mid-19th century.

By contrast, Emerson lobbied for and attempted to model a form of life that could transcend the minutiae of status quo expectations and traditions in favor of deeply independent and creative expressions of intuited universal truths that he felt became apparent when one looked upon nature's workings as a pedagogical source of mystery and ecstasy or

Author: Richard Kahn

upon cultural productions from a world-historical perspective that disclosed the hidden *telos* of day-to-day happenings. This countercultural philosophy, first announced in his book *Nature* (1836), is normally considered to have fomented the American Transcendentalist movement as a whole and the lives of figures such as Henry David Thoreau and Walt Whitman, as well as Transcendentalist utopian communities, such as Brook Farm and Fruitlands. But Emerson's influence also extended far beyond the Transcendentalist movement, and his writings were a key source for the philosophy later developed by Friedrich Nietzsche, on the one hand, and for the articulation of American pragmatism as developed by key thinkers such as William James and John Dewey on the other. Indeed, the role of Emerson's thought in the work of John Dewey remains to be more greatly explored and should be enough to mandate Emerson's future relevance for students of education generally.

A key insight for Emerson was that what is more typically perceived as external nature has its internal correspondent in personal feelings. According to Emerson, then, the challenge for people was to achieve enough freedom from authoritarian conventions that they could become literate in these internal/external correspondences, thereby allowing them a truer understanding of how the unfolding of the history of the world and their own personal biographies were ultimately one. This process which incarnates in both individual moods and social events was called "the Oversoul" by Emerson. Just as there are differing levels of print or media literacy, though, so, too, did Emerson believe that ever-deepening levels of literacy into the Oversoul could be achieved. At the very heights of such literacy stood, what Emerson referred to as "the Poet," a constructivist vocation in which personal sensibilities had become so refined that the correspondence between internal feelings and external experiences could be powerfully represented and intuitively named as spoken ideas. These poetic ideas, which accorded closely with the ontological state of the world as such, would then also transform the world through the powerful vision and will of their creators, germinating as seeds of action throughout society and provoking new forms of cultural production that aimed at emancipation, creativity, and the realization of individual power. Emerson's philosophy of education sought to defend and nurture the poetic possibilities of students, to challenge them to recognize the role they play in shaping their own lifeworlds, and to turn them away from a reliance upon penchants for rote reading and scholastic bookishness toward discovering for themselves how to become the great, self-reliant authors of lives that could be lived as literature for future others.

However, just as nature itself reveals a form of periodicity between life and death, so, too, did Emerson's own philosophy undergo noticeable changes during the second half of his life. Though critics disagree as to when exactly this shift took place, with some pointing to the essay "Experience" (1844) and others placing it much later in a book such as *The Conduct of Life* (1860), readers of Emerson's later work will doubtless find a tempering of his youthful enthusiasm, a questioning of whether individual will-to-power is, in fact, enough to ultimately live well, an increasing commitment to engage the political evils of his day (e.g., slavery), and a growing recognition of the fact that epochs are historically conditioned such that even the greatest of poets will experience a plethora of limitations and disappointments. In other words, while the later Emerson remained pedagogically committed to the visionary power of dreaming, he became ever-more accepting and saddened that it was in the nature of things that many dreams were essentially unrealizable within the mortality of a single lifetime. He thus thought that the challenge was to dream beyond one's own timeframe, to cast one's vision outward with such force and integrity that the ideas and truths contained within might remain fertile and provocative for many ages of students to come.

Writing a generation after the American Revolution, in what ways is Emerson offering a form of postcolonial pedagogy in his writing? Likewise, in offering a vision of a strong and active American spirit, in what ways is Emerson problematically invoking a future of American imperialism in his educational philosophy? What does it mean to have direct experiences of nature and are schools today hindrances to or promoters of this sort of learning? What could a contemporary form of Emersonian pedagogy look like at the elementary level? For a secondary school? In adult education circles?

REFERENCES

Bickman, Martin. "From Emerson to Dewey: The Fate of Freedom in American Education." *American Literary History* 6, no. 3 (1994): 385–408.

Bickman, Martin. *Minding American Education: Reclaiming the Tradition of Active Learning.* New York: Teachers College Press, 2003.

Conant, James. "Emerson as Educator." *ESQ: A Journal of the American Renaissance* 43 (1997): 181–206.

Garrison, Jim. "Emerson's 'The American Scholar' and the Current Status of Philosophy of Education." *Taboo* 4 (2000): 101–7.

Helm, Bert. "Emerson Agonistes: Education as Struggle and Process." *Educational Theory* 42 (1992): 165–80.

THE AMERICAN SCHOLAR

Mr. President and Gentlemen,

I greet you on the re-commencement of our literary year. Our anniversary is one of hope, and, perhaps, not enough of labor. We do not meet for games of strength or skill, for the recitation of histories, tragedies, and odes, like the ancient Greeks; for parliaments of love and poesy, like the Troubadours; nor for the advancement of science, like our contemporaries in the British and European capitals. Thus far, our holiday has been simply a friendly sign of the survival of the love of letters amongst a people too busy to give to letters any more. As such, it is precious as the sign of an indestructible instinct. Perhaps the time is already come, when it ought to be, and will be, something else; when the sluggard intellect of this continent will look from under its iron lids, and fill the postponed expectation of the world with something better than the exertions of mechanical skill. Our day of dependence, our long apprenticeship to the learning of other lands, draws to a close.

The millions, that around us are rushing into life, cannot always be fed on the sere remains of foreign harvests. Events, actions arise, that must be sung, that will sing themselves. Who can doubt, that poetry will revive and lead in a new age, as the star in the constellation Harp, which now flames in our zenith, astronomers announce, shall one day be the pole-star for a thousand years?

In this hope, I accept the topic which not only usage, but the nature of our association, seem to prescribe to this day,—the AMERICAN SCHOLAR. Year by year, we come up hither to read one more chapter of his biography. Let us inquire what light new days and events have thrown on his character, and his hopes. It is one of those fables, which, out of an unknown antiquity, convey an unlooked-for wisdom, that the gods, in the beginning, divided Man into men, that he might be more helpful to himself; just as the hand was divided into fingers, the better to answer its end.

The old fable covers a doctrine ever new and sublime; that there is One Man,—present to all particular men only partially, or through one

The American Scholar. *An Oration Before the Phi Beta Kappa Society, at Cambridge, August 31, 1837* by Ralph Waldo Emerson.

The complete works of Ralph Waldo Emerson: Nature addresses and lectures [Vol. 1] Emerson, Ralph Waldo, 1803–1882, Emerson, Edward Waldo, 1844–1930. Boston; New York: Houghton, Mifflin, [1903–1904].

faculty; and that you must take the whole society to find the whole man. Man is not a farmer, or a professor, or an engineer, but he is all. Man is priest, and scholar, and statesman, and producer, and soldier. In the *divided* or social state, these functions are parceled out to individuals, each of whom aims to do his stint of the joint work, whilst each other performs his. The fable implies, that the individual, to possess himself, must sometimes return from his own labor to embrace all the other laborers. But unfortunately, this original unit, this fountain of power, has been so distributed to multitudes, has been so minutely subdivided and peddled out, that it is spilled into drops, and cannot be gathered. The state of society is one in which the members have suffered amputation from the trunk, and strut about so many walking monsters,—a good finger, a neck, a stomach, an elbow, but never a man.

Man is thus metamorphosed into a thing, into many things. The planter, who is Man sent out into the field to gather food, is seldom cheered by any idea of the true dignity of his ministry. He sees his bushel and his cart, and nothing beyond, and sinks into the farmer, instead of Man on the farm. The tradesman scarcely ever gives an ideal worth to his work, but is ridden by the routine of his craft, and the soul is subject to dollars. The priest becomes a form; the attorney, a statute-book; the mechanic, a machine; the sailor, a rope of a ship.

In this distribution of functions, the scholar is the delegated intellect. In the right state, he is, *Man Thinking.* In the degenerate state, when the victim of society, he tends to become a mere thinker, or, still worse, the parrot of other men's thinking.

In this view of him, as Man Thinking, the theory of his office is contained. Him nature solicits with all her placid, all her monitory pictures; him the past instructs; him the future invites.

Is not, indeed, every man a student, and do not all things exist for the student's behoof? And, finally, is not the true scholar the only true master? But the old oracle said, 'All things have two handles: beware of the wrong one.' In life, too often, the scholar errs with mankind and forfeits his privilege. Let us see him in his school, and consider him in reference to the main influences he receives.

I. The first in time and the first in importance of the influences upon the mind is that of nature. Every day, the sun and; after sunset, night and her stars. Ever the winds blow; ever the grass grows. Every day, men and women, conversing, beholding and beholden. The scholar is he of all men whom this spectacle most engages. He must settle its value in his mind. What is nature to him? There is never a beginning, there is never an end, to the inexplicable continuity of this web of God, but always circular power returning into itself. Therein it resembles his own spirit, whose beginning, whose ending, he never can find,—so entire, so boundless. Far, too, as her splendors shine, system on system shooting like rays, upward, downward, without centre, without circumference,—in the mass and in the particle, nature hastens to render account of herself to the mind. Classification begins. To the young mind, every thing is individual, stands by itself. By and by, it finds how to join two things, and see in them one nature; then three, then three thousand; and so, tyrannized over by its own unifying instinct, it goes on tying things together, diminishing anomalies, discovering roots running under ground, whereby contrary and remote things cohere, and flower out from one stem. It presently learns, that, since the dawn of history, there has been a constant accumulation and classifying of facts. But what is classification but the perceiving that these objects are not chaotic, and are not foreign, but have a law which is also a law of the human mind? The astronomer discovers that geometry, a pure abstraction of the human mind, is the measure of planetary motion. The chemist finds proportions and intelligible method throughout matter; and science is nothing but the finding of analogy, identity, in the most remote parts. The ambitious soul sits down before each refractory fact; one after another, reduces all strange constitutions, all new powers, to their class and their law, and goes on for ever to animate the last fibre of organization, the outskirts of nature, by insight.

Thus to him, to this school-boy under the bending dome of day, is suggested, that he and it proceed from one root; one is leaf and one is flower; relation, sympathy, stirring in every vein. And what is that Root? Is not that the soul of his soul?—A thought too bold,—a dream too wild. Yet when this spiritual light shall have revealed the law of more earthly natures,—when he has learned to worship the soul, and to see that the natural philosophy that now is, is only the first gropings of its gigantic hand, he shall look forward to an ever expanding knowledge as to a becoming creator. He shall see, that nature is the opposite of the soul, answering to it part for part. One is seal, and one is print. Its beauty is the beauty of his own mind. Its laws are the laws of his own mind. Nature then becomes to him the measure of his attainments. So much of nature as he is ignorant of, so much of his own mind does he not yet possess. And, in fine, the ancient precept, "Know thyself," and the modern precept, "Study nature," become at last one maxim.

II. The next great influence into the spirit of the scholar, is, the mind of the Past,—in whatever form, whether of literature, of art, of institutions, that mind is inscribed. Books are the best type of the influence of the past, and perhaps we shall get at the truth,—learn the amount of this influence more conveniently,—by considering their value alone.

The theory of books is noble. The scholar of the first age received into him the world around; brooded thereon; gave it the new arrangement of his own mind, and uttered it again. It came into him, life; it went out from him, truth. It came to him, short-lived actions; it went out from him, immortal thoughts. It came to him, business; it went from him, poetry. It was dead fact; now, it is quick thought. It can stand, and it can go. It now endures, it now flies, it now inspires. Precisely in proportion to the depth of mind from which it issued, so high does it soar, so long does it sing.

Or, I might say, it depends on how far the process had gone, of transmuting life into truth. In proportion to the completeness of the distillation, so will the purity and imperishableness of the product be. But none is quite perfect. As no air-pump can by any means make a perfect vacuum, so neither can any artist entirely exclude the conventional, the local, the perishable from his book, or write a book of pure thought, that shall be as efficient, in all respects, to a remote posterity, as to contemporaries, or rather to the second age. Each age, it is found, must write its own books; or rather, each generation for the next succeeding. The books of an older period will not fit this.

Yet hence arises a grave mischief. The sacredness which attaches to the act of creation,—the act of thought,—is transferred to the record. The poet chanting, was felt to be a divine man: henceforth the chant is divine also. The writer was a just and wise spirit: henceforward it is settled, the book is perfect; as love of the hero corrupts into worship of his statue. Instantly, the book becomes noxious: the guide is a tyrant. The sluggish and perverted mind of the multitude, slow to open to the incursions of Reason, having once so opened, having once received this book, stands upon it, and makes an outcry, if it is disparaged. Colleges are built on it. Books are written on it by thinkers, not by Man

Thinking; by men of talent, that is, who start wrong, who set out from accepted dogmas, not from their own sight of principles. Meek young men grow up in libraries, believing it their duty to accept the views, which Cicero, which Locke, which Bacon, have given, forgetful that Cicero, Locke, and Bacon were only young men in libraries, when they wrote these books.

Hence, instead of Man Thinking, we have the bookworm. Hence, the book-learned class, who value books, as such; not as related to nature and the human constitution, but as making a sort of Third Estate with the world and the soul. Hence, the restorers of readings, the emendators, the bibliomaniacs of all degrees.

Books are the best of things, well used; abused, among the worst. What is the right use? What is the one end, which all means go to effect? They are for nothing but to inspire. I had better never see a book, than to be warped by its attraction clean out of my own orbit, and made a satellite instead of a system. The one thing in the world, of value, is the active soul. This every man is entitled to; this every man contains within him, although, in almost all men, obstructed, and as yet unborn. The soul active sees absolute truth; and utters truth, or creates. In this action, it is genius; not the privilege of here and there a favorite, but the sound estate of every man. In its essence, it is progressive. The book, the college, the school of art, the institution of any kind, stop with some past utterance of genius. This is good, say they,—let us hold by this. They pin me down. They look backward and not forward. But genius looks forward: the eyes of man are set in his forehead, not in his hind-head: man hopes: genius creates. Whatever talents may be, if the man create not, the pure efflux of the Deity is not his;—cinders and smoke there may be, but not yet flame. There are creative manners, there are creative actions, and creative words; manners, actions, words, that is, indicative of no custom or authority, but springing spontaneous from the mind's own sense of good and fair.

On the other part, instead of being its own seer, let it receive from another mind its truth, though it were in torrents of light, without periods of solitude, inquest, and self-recovery, and a fatal disservice is done. Genius is always sufficiently the enemy of genius by over influence. The literature of every nation bear me witness. The English dramatic poets have Shaksparized now for two hundred years.

Undoubtedly there is a right way of reading, so it be sternly subordinated. Man Thinking must not be subdued by his instruments. Books are for the scholar's idle times. When he can read God directly, the hour is too precious to be wasted in other men's transcripts of their readings. But when the intervals of darkness come, as come they must,—when the sun is hid, and the stars withdraw their shining,—we repair to the lamps which were kindled by their ray, to guide our steps to the East again, where the dawn is. We hear, that we may speak. The Arabian proverb says, "A fig tree, looking on a fig tree, becometh fruitful."

It is remarkable, the character of the pleasure we derive from the best books. They impress us with the conviction, that one nature wrote and the same reads. We read the verses of one of the great English poets, of Chaucer, of Marvell, of Dryden, with the most modern joy,— with a pleasure, I mean, which is in great part caused by the abstraction of all *time* from their verses. There is some awe mixed with the joy of our surprise, when this poet, who lived in some past world, two or three hundred years ago, says that which lies close to my own soul, that which I also had wellnigh thought and said. But for the evidence thence afforded to the philosophical doctrine of the identity of all minds, we should suppose some preestablished harmony, some foresight of souls that were to be, and some preparation of stores for their future wants, like the fact observed in insects, who lay up food before death for the young grub they shall never see.

I would not be hurried by any love of system, by any exaggeration of instincts, to underrate the Book. We all know, that, as the human body can be nourished on any food, though it were boiled grass and the broth of shoes, so the human mind can be fed by any knowledge. And great and heroic men have existed, who had almost no other information than by the printed page. I only would say, that it needs a strong head to bear that diet. One must be an inventor to read well. As the proverb says, "He that would bring home the wealth of the Indies, must carry out the wealth of the Indies." There is then creative reading as well as creative writing. When the mind is braced by labor and invention, the page of whatever book we read becomes luminous with manifold allusion. Every sentence is doubly significant, and the sense of our author is as broad as the world. We then see, what is always true, that, as the seer's hour of vision is short and rare among heavy days and months, so is its record, perchance, the least part of his volume. The discerning will read, in his Plato or Shakespeare, only that least part,—only the authentic utterances of the oracle;— all the rest he rejects, were it never so many times Plato's and Shakespeare's.

Of course, there is a portion of reading quite indispensable to a wise man. History and exact science he must learn by laborious reading. Colleges, in like manner, have their indispensable office,—to teach elements. But they can only highly serve us, when they aim not to drill, but to create; when they gather from far every ray of various genius to their hospitable halls, and, by the concentrated fires, set the hearts of their youth on flame. Thought and knowledge are natures in which apparatus and pretension avail nothing. Gowns, and pecuniary foundations, though of towns of gold, can never countervail the least sentence or syllable of wit. Forget this, and our American colleges will recede in their public importance, whilst they grow richer every year.

III. There goes in the world a notion, that the scholar should be a recluse, a valetudinarian,—as unfit for any handiwork or public labor, as a penknife for an axe. The so-called 'practical men' sneer at speculative men, as if, because they speculate or *see,* they could do nothing. I have heard it said that the clergy,—who are always, more universally than any other class, the scholars of their day,—are addressed as women; that the rough, spontaneous conversation of men they do not hear, but only a mincing and diluted speech. They are often virtually disfranchised; and, indeed, there are advocates for their celibacy. As far as this is true of the studious classes, it is not just and wise. Action is with the scholar subordinate, but it is essential. Without it, he is not yet man. Without it, thought can never ripen into truth. Whilst the world hangs before the eye as a cloud of beauty, we cannot even see its beauty. Inaction is cowardice, but there can be no scholar without the heroic mind. The preamble of thought, the transition through which it passes from the unconscious to the conscious, is action. Only so much do I know, as I have lived. Instantly we know whose words are loaded with life, and whose not.

The world,—this shadow of the soul, *or other me,* lies wide around. Its attractions are the keys which unlock my thoughts and make me acquainted with myself. I run eagerly into this resounding tumult. I grasp the hands of those next me, and take my place in the ring to suffer and to work, taught by an instinct, that so shall the dumb abyss be vocal with speech. I pierce its order; I dissipate its fear; I dispose of it within the circuit of my expanding life. So much only of life as I know by experience, so much of the wilderness have I vanquished and planted, or so far have I extended my being, my dominion. I do not see how any man can afford, for the sake of his nerves and his nap, to spare any action in which he can partake. It is pearls and rubies to his discourse. Drudgery, calamity, exasperation, want, are instructors in eloquence and wisdom. The true scholar grudges every opportunity of action past by, as a loss of power.

It is the raw material out of which the intellect moulds her splendid products. A strange process too, this, by which experience is converted into thought, as a mulberry leaf is converted into satin. The manufacture goes forward at all hours.

The actions and events of our childhood and youth, are now matters of calmest observation. They lie like fair pictures in the air. Not so with our recent actions,—with the business which we now have in hand. On this we are quite unable to speculate. Our affections as yet circulate through it. We no more feel or know it, than we feel the feet, or the hand, or the brain of our body. The new deed is yet a part of life,—remains for a time immersed in our unconscious life. In some contemplative hour, it detaches itself from the life like a ripe fruit, to become a thought of the mind. Instantly, it is raised, transfigured; the corruptible has put on incorruption. Henceforth it is an object of beauty, however base its origin and neighborhood. Observe, too, the impossibility of antedating this act. In its grub state, it cannot fly, it cannot shine, it is a dull grub. But suddenly, without observation, the selfsame thing unfurls beautiful wings, and is an angel of wisdom.

So is there no fact, no event, in our private history, which shall not, sooner or later, lose its adhesive, inert form, and astonish us by soaring from our body into the empyrean. Cradle and infancy, school and playground, the fear of boys, and dogs, and ferules, the love of little maids and berries, and many another fact that once filled the whole sky, are gone already; friend and relative profession and party, town and country, nation and world, must also soar and sing.

Of course, he who has put forth his total strength in fit actions, has the richest return of wisdom. I will not shut myself out of this globe of action, and transplant an oak into a flower-pot, there to hunger and pine; nor trust the revenue of some single faculty, and exhaust one vein of thought, much like those Savoyards, who, getting their livelihood by carving shepherds, shepherdesses, and smoking Dutchmen, for all Europe, went out one day to the mountain to find stock, and discovered that they had whittled up the last of their pine-trees. Authors we have, in numbers, who have written out their vein, and who, moved by a commendable prudence, sail for Greece or Palestine, follow the trapper into the prairie, or ramble round Algiers, to replenish their merchantable stock. If it were only for a vocabulary, the scholar would be covetous of action. Life is our dictionary. Years are well spent in country labors; in town,—in the insight into trades and manufactures; in frank intercourse with many men and women; in science; in art; to the one end of mastering in all their facts a language by which to illustrate and embody our perceptions. I learn immediately from any speaker how much he has already lived, through the poverty or the splendor of his speech. Life lies behind us as the quarry from whence we get tiles and copestones for the masonry of to-day. This is the way to learn grammar. Colleges and books only copy the language which the field and the work-yard made.

But the final value of action, like that of books, and better than books, is, that it is a resource. That great principle of Undulation in nature, that shows itself in the inspiring and expiring of the breath; in desire and satiety; in the ebb and flow of the sea; in day and night; in heat and cold; and as yet more deeply ingrained in every atom and every fluid, is known to us under the name of Polarity,—these "fits of easy transmission and reflection," as Newton called them, are the law of nature because they are the law of spirit.

The mind now thinks; now acts; and each fit reproduces the other. When the artist has exhausted his materials, when the fancy no longer paints, when thoughts are no longer apprehended, and books are a weariness,—he has always the resource *to live*. Character is higher than intellect. Thinking is the function. Living is the functionary. The stream retreats to its source. A great soul will be strong to live, as well as strong to think. Does he lack organ or medium to impart his truths? He can still fall back on this elemental force of living them. This is a total act. Thinking is a partial act. Let the grandeur of justice shine in his affairs. Let the beauty of affection cheer his lowly roof. Those 'far from fame,' who dwell and act with him, will feel the force of his constitution in the doings and passages of the day better than it can be measured by any public and designed display. Time shall teach him, that the scholar loses no hour which the man lives. Herein he unfolds the sacred germ of his instinct, screened from influence. What is lost in seemliness is gained in strength. Not out of those, on whom systems of education have exhausted their culture, comes the helpful giant to destroy the old or to build the new, but out of unhandselled savage nature, out of terrible Druids and Berserkirs, come at last Alfred and Shakespeare.

I hear therefore with joy whatever is beginning to be said of the dignity and necessity of labor to every citizen. There is virtue yet in the hoe and the spade, for learned as well as for unlearned hands. And labor is everywhere welcome; always we are invited to work; only be this limitation observed, that a man shall not for the sake of wider activity sacrifice any opinion to the popular judgments and modes of action.

I have now spoken of the education of the scholar by nature, by books, and by action. It remains to say somewhat of his duties. They are such as become Man Thinking. They may all be comprised in self-trust. The office of the scholar is to cheer, to raise, and to guide men by showing them facts amidst appearances. He plies the slow, unhonored, and unpaid task of observation. Flamsteed and Herschel, in their glazed observatories, may catalogue the stars with the praise of all men, and, the results being splendid and useful, honor is sure. But he, in his private observatory, cataloguing obscure and nebulous stars of the human mind, which as yet no man has thought of as such,—watching days and months, sometimes, for a few facts; correcting still his old records;—must relinquish display and immediate fame. In the long period of his preparation, he must betray often an ignorance and shiftlessness in popular arts, incurring the disdain of the able who shoulder him aside. Long he must stammer in his speech; often forego the living for the dead. Worse yet, he must accept,—how often! poverty and solitude. For the ease and pleasure of treading the old road, accepting the fashions, the education, the religion of society, he takes the cross of making his own, and, of course, the self-accusation, the faint heart, the frequent uncertainty and loss of time, which are the nettles and tangling vines in the way of the self-relying and self-directed; and the state of virtual hostility in which he seems to stand to society, and especially to educated society. For all this loss and scorn, what offset? He is to find consolation in exercising the highest functions of human nature. He is one, who raises himself from private considerations, and breathes and lives on public and illustrious thoughts. He is the world's eye.

He is the world's heart. He is to resist the vulgar prosperity that retrogrades ever to barbarism, by preserving and communicating heroic sentiments, noble biographies, melodious verse, and the conclusions of history. Whatsoever oracles the human heart, in all emergencies, in all solemn hours, has uttered as its commentary on the world of actions,—these he shall receive and impart. And whatsoever new verdict Reason from her inviolable seat pronounces on the passing men and events of to-day,—this he shall hear and promulgate.

These being his functions, it becomes him to feel all confidence in himself, and to defer never to the popular cry. He and he only knows the world. The world of any moment is the merest appearance. Some great decorum, some fetish of a government, some ephemeral trade, or war, or man, is cried up by half mankind and cried down by the other half, as if all depended on this particular up or down. The odds are that the whole question is not worth the poorest thought which the scholar has lost in listening to the controversy. Let him not quit his belief that a popgun is a popgun, though the ancient and honorable of the earth affirm it to be the crack of doom. In silence, in steadiness, in severe abstraction, let him hold by himself; add observation to observation, patient of neglect, patient of reproach; and bide his own time,—happy enough, if he can satisfy himself alone, that this day he has seen something truly. Success treads on every right step. For the instinct is sure, that prompts him to tell his brother what he thinks. He then learns, that in going down into the secrets of his own mind, he has descended into the secrets of all minds. He learns that he who has mastered any law in his private thoughts, is master to that extent of all men whose language he speaks, and of all into whose language his own can be translated. The poet, in utter solitude remembering his spontaneous thoughts and recording them, is found to have recorded that, which men in crowded cities find true for them also. The orator distrusts at first the fitness of his frank confessions,—his want of knowledge of the persons he addresses,—until he finds that he is the complement of his hearers;—that they drink his words because he fulfill for them their own nature; the deeper he dives into his privatest, secretest presentiment, to his wonder he finds, this is the most acceptable, most public, and universally true. The people delight in it; the better part of every man feels, This is my music; this is myself.

In self-trust, all the virtues are comprehended. Free should the scholar be,—free and brave. Free even to the definition of freedom, "without any hindrance that does not arise out of his own constitution." Brave; for fear is a thing, which a scholar by his very function puts behind him. Fear always springs from ignorance. It is a shame to him if his tranquility, amid dangerous times, arise from the presumption, that, like children and women, his is a protected class; or if he seek a temporary peace by the diversion of his thoughts from politics or vexed questions, hiding his head like an ostrich in the flowering bushes, peeping into microscopes, and turning rhymes, as a boy whistles to keep his courage up. So is the danger a danger still; so is the fear worse. Manlike let him turn and face it. Let him look into its eye and search its nature, inspect its origin,—see the whelping of this lion,—which lies no great way back; he will then find in himself a perfect comprehension of its nature and extent; he will have made his hands meet on the other side, and can henceforth defy it, and pass on superior. The world is his, who can see through its pretension. What deafness, what stone-blind custom, what overgrown error you behold, is there only by sufferance,—by your sufferance. See it to be a lie, and you have already dealt it its mortal blow.

Yes, we are the cowed,—we the trustless. It is a mischievous notion that we are come late into nature; that the world was finished a long time ago. As the world was plastic and fluid in the hands of God, so it is ever to so much of his attributes as we bring to it. To ignorance and sin, it is flint. They adapt themselves to it as they may; but in proportion as a man has any thing in him divine, the firmament flows before him and takes his signet and form. Not he is great who can alter matter, but he who can alter my state of mind. They are the kings of the world who give the color of their present thought to all nature and all art, and persuade men by the cheerful serenity of their carrying the matter, that this thing which they do, is the apple which the ages have desired to pluck, now at last ripe, and inviting nations to the harvest. The great man makes the great thing. Wherever Macdonald sits, there is the head of the table. Linnaeus makes botany the most alluring of studies, and wins it from the farmer and the herb-woman; Davy, chemistry; and Cuvier, fossils. The day is always his, who works in it with serenity and great aims. The unstable estimates of men crowd to him whose mind is filled with a truth, as the heaped waves of the Atlantic follow the moon.

For this self-trust, the reason is deeper than can be fathomed,—darker than can be enlightened. I might not carry with me the feeling of my audience in stating my own belief. But I have already shown the ground of my hope, in adverting to the doctrine that man is one. I believe man has been wronged; he has wronged himself. He has almost lost the light, that can lead him back to his prerogatives. Men are become of no account. Men in history, men in the world of to-day are bugs, are spawn, and are called 'the mass' and 'the herd.' In a century, in a millennium, one or two men; that is to say,—one or two approximations to the right state of every man. All the rest behold in the hero or the poet their own green and crude being,—ripened; yes, and are content to be less, so *that* may attain to its full stature. What a testimony,—full of grandeur, full of pity, is borne to the demands of his own nature, by the poor clansman, the poor partisan, who rejoices in the glory of his chief. The poor and the low find some amends to their immense moral capacity, for their acquiescence in a political and social inferiority. They are content to be brushed like flies from the path of a great person, so that justice shall be done by him to that common nature which it is the dearest desire of all to see enlarged and glorified. They sun themselves in the great man's light, and feel it to be their own element. They cast the dignity of man from their downtrod selves upon the shoulders of a hero, and will perish to add one drop of blood to make that great heart beat, those giant sinews combat and conquer. He lives for us, and we live in him.

Men such as they are, very naturally seek money or power; and power because it is as good as money,—the "spoils," so called, "of office." And why not? for they aspire to the highest, and this, in their sleep-walking, they dream is highest. Wake them, and they shall quit the false good, and leap to the true, and leave governments to clerks and desks. This revolution is to be wrought by the gradual domestication of the idea of Culture. The main enterprise of the world for splendor, for extent, is the upbuilding of a man. Here are the materials strown along the ground. The private life of one man shall be a more illustrious monarchy,—more formidable to its enemy, more sweet and serene in its influence to its friend, than any kingdom in history. For a man, rightly viewed, comprehendeth the particular natures of all men.

Each philosopher, each bard, each actor, has only done for me, as by a delegate, what one day I can do for myself. The books which once we valued more than the apple of the eye, we have quite exhausted. What is that but saying, that we have come up with the point of view which the universal mind took through the eyes of one scribe; we have been that man, and have passed on. First, one; then, another; we drain all cisterns, and, waxing greater by all these supplies, we crave a better and more abundant food. The man has never lived that can feed us ever. The human mind cannot be enshrined in a person, who shall set a barrier on any one side to this unbounded, unboundable empire.

It is one central fire, which, flaming now out of the lips of Etna, lightens the capes of Sicily; and, now out of the throat of Vesuvius, illuminates the towers and vineyards of Naples. It is one light which beams out of a thousand stars. It is one soul which animates all men.

But I have dwelt perhaps tediously upon this abstraction of the Scholar. I ought not to delay longer to add what I have to say, of nearer reference to the time and to this country.

Historically, there is thought to be a difference in the ideas which predominate over successive epochs, and there are data for marking the genius of the Classic, of the Romantic, and now of the Reflective or Philosophical age. With the views I have intimated of the oneness or the identity of the mind through all individuals, I do not much dwell on these differences. In fact, I believe each individual passes through all three. The boy is a Greek; the youth, romantic; the adult, reflective. I deny not, however, that a revolution in the leading idea may be distinctly enough traced.

Our age is bewailed as the age of Introversion. Must that needs be evil? We, it seems, are critical; we are embarrassed with second thoughts; we cannot enjoy any thing for hankering to know whereof the pleasure consists; we are lined with eyes; we see with our feet; the time is infected with Hamlet's unhappiness, "Sicklied o'er with the pale cast of thought. Is it so bad then? Sight is the last thing to be pitied. Would we be blind? Do we fear lest we should outsee nature and God, and drink truth dry? I look upon the discontent of the literary class, as a mere announcement of the fact, that they find themselves not in the state of mind of their fathers, and regret the coming state as untried; as a boy dreads the water before he has learned that he can swim. If there is any period one would desire to be born in,—is it not the age of

Revolution; when the old and the new stand side by side, and admit of being compared; when the energies of all men are searched by fear and by hope; when the historic glories of the old, can be compensated by the rich possibilities of the new era? This time, like all times, is a very good one, if we but know what to do with it.

I read with joy some of the auspicious signs of the coming days, as they glimmer already through poetry and art, through philosophy and science, through church and state.

One of these signs is the fact, that the same movement which effected the elevation of what was called the lowest class in the state, assumed in literature a very marked and as benign an aspect. Instead of the sublime and beautiful; the near, the low, the common, was explored and poetized. That, which had been negligently trodden under foot by those who were harnessing and provisioning themselves for long journeys into far countries, is suddenly found to be richer than all foreign parts. The literature of the poor, the feelings of the child, the philosophy of the street, the meaning of household life, are the topics of the time. It is a great stride. It is a sign,—is it not? of new vigor, when the extremities are made active, when currents of warm life run into the hands and the feet.

I ask not for the great, the remote, the romantic; what is doing in Italy or Arabia; what is Greek art, or Provencal minstrelsy; I embrace the common, I explore and sit at the feet of the familiar, the low. Give me insight into to-day, and you may have the antique and future worlds. What would we really know the meaning of? The meal in the firkin; the milk in the pan; the ballad in the street; the news of the boat; the glance of the eye; the form and the gait of the body;—show me the ultimate reason of these matters; show me the sublime presence of the highest spiritual cause lurking, as always it does lurk, in these suburbs and extremities of nature; let me see every trifle bristling with the polarity that ranges it instantly on an eternal law; and the shop, the plough, and the ledger, referred to the like cause by which light undulates and poets sing;—and the world lies no longer a dull miscellany and lumber-room, but has form and order; there is no trifle; there is no puzzle; but one design unites and animates the farthest pinnacle and the lowest trench. This idea has inspired the genius of Goldsmith, Burns, Cowper, and, in a newer time, of Goethe, Wordsworth, and Carlyle. This idea they have differently followed and with various success.

In contrast with their writing, the style of Pope, of Johnson, of Gibbon, looks cold and pedantic. This writing is blood-warm. Man is surprised to find that things near are not less beautiful and wondrous than things remote. The near explains the far. The drop is a small ocean. A man is related to all nature. This perception of the worth of the vulgar is fruitful in discoveries. Goethe, in this very thing the most modern of the moderns, has shown us, as none ever did, the genius of the ancients. There is one man of genius, who has done much for this philosophy of life, whose literary value has never yet been rightly estimated;—I mean Emanuel Swedenborg. The most imaginative of men, yet writing with the precision of a mathematician, he endeavored to engraft a purely philosophical Ethics on the popular Christianity of his time. Such an attempt, of course, must have difficulty, which no genius could surmount. But he saw and showed the connection between nature and the affections of the soul. He pierced the emblematic or spiritual character of the visible, audible, tangible world. Especially did his shade-loving muse hover over and interpret the lower parts of nature; he showed the mysterious bond that allies moral evil to the foul material forms, and has given in epical parables a theory of insanity, of beasts, of unclean and fearful things.

Another sign of our times, also marked by an analogous political movement, is, the new importance given to the single person. Every thing that tends to insulate the individual,—to surround him with barriers of natural respect, so that each man shall feel the world is his, and man shall treat with man as a sovereign state with a sovereign state;—tends to true union as well as greatness. "I learned," said the melancholy Pestalozzi, "that no man in God's wide earth is either willing or able to help any other man."

Help must come from the bosom alone. The scholar is that man who must take up into himself all the ability of the time, all the contributions of the past, all the hopes of the future. He must be an university of knowledges. If there be one lesson more than another, which should pierce his ear, it is, The world is nothing, the man is all; in yourself is the law of all nature, and you know not yet how a globule of sap ascends; in yourself slumbers the whole of Reason; it is for you to know all, it is for you to dare all.

Mr. President and Gentlemen, this confidence in the unsearched might of man belongs, by all motives, by all prophecy, by all preparation, to the

American Scholar. We have listened too long to the courtly muses of Europe. The spirit of the American freeman is already suspected to be timid, imitative, tame. Public and private avarice make the air we breathe thick and fat. The scholar is decent, indolent, complaisant. See already the tragic consequence. The mind of this country, taught to aim at low objects, eats upon itself. There is no work for any but the decorous and the complaisant. Young men of the fairest promise, who begin life upon our shores, inflated by the mountain winds, shined upon by all the stars of God, find the earth below not in unison with these,—but are hindered from action by the disgust which the principles on which business is managed inspire, and turn drudges, or die of disgust,—some of them suicides. What is the remedy? They did not yet see, and thousands of young men as hopeful now crowding to the barriers for the career do not yet see, that, if the single man plant himself indomitably on his instincts, and there abide, the huge world will come round to him. Patience,—patience;—with the shades of all the good and great for company; and for solace, the perspective of your own infinite life; and for work, the study and the communication of principles, the making those instincts prevalent, the conversion of the world. Is it not the chief disgrace in the world, not to be an unit;—not to be reckoned one character;—not to yield that peculiar fruit which each man was created to bear, but to be reckoned in the gross, in the hundred, or the thousand, of the party, the section, to which we belong; and our opinion predicted geographically, as the north, or the south? Not so, brothers and friends,—please God, ours shall not be so. We will walk on our own feet; we will work with our own hands; we will speak our own minds. The study of letters shall be no longer a name for pity, for doubt, and for sensual indulgence. The dread of man and the love of man shall be a wall of defence and a wreath of joy around all. A nation of men will for the first time exist, because each believes himself inspired by the Divine Soul which also inspires all men.

3

LEO TOLSTOY

A highly recognized and accomplished writer and novelist, Leo Tolstoy wanted to rethink and explore the role of education in Russian society. For that purpose, in 1859 he created an experimental school for peasant children at Yasnaya. In 1862 he collected many of his essays and reflections about the experience. Influenced by the ideas of the French philosopher Rousseau, combined with his mistrust for the power of the state and his deep hope on human capacity and freedom, his school attempted to implement these ideas in the organization and curriculum. In line with many classics, he considered that his chief concerns for freedom and equality could be addressed with the right pedagogical experience.

He was born in Russia in 1928 to an aristocratic, influential, and affluent family. The experimental school he established was in the same area where he was born and where his family had a large estate, Yasnaya Polyana. He studied languages and law in the university, but he was not fond of the traditional ways of teaching, as well as of how authority was practiced in education. For a few years he also served in the military. His fame mostly came from his novels, which include two masterpieces— *War and Peace*, first published in 1869, and *Anna Karenina*, published in 1978. He passed away in 1910.

His writing extended to philosophical, political, and educational essays. Although considered an anarchist by many as he embraced some of the libertarian principles involved in this ideology, he rejected vehemently any form of violence, since he also was a pacifist and a Christian, as discussed in his essay "On Anarchy," published in 1900. These principles of freedom and individual potential for greatness manifest in his educational ideals. His experimentation and reflections are in sharp contrast to the dominant practices and philosophies of education at the time in Europe. For instance, the school was free, but not compulsory, and in spite of having a morning and afternoon schedule, students often stayed longer and sometimes came in late.

One important reason for his choosing to open the school was his interest in reaching out to the large number of illiterate Russian peasants and spreading literature among the people of Russia, not only the educated few. As a writer he pondered for whom he was writing if the masses could not read. But he also understood that the development of Russia as a modern and industrialized nation-state would not occur if the peasants, who constituted large numbers of the population, did not receive a formal public education and teachers were not trained.

The selection for this chapter is a provocative essay in which Tolstoy suggests that while teachers were teaching the peasant children, the children also were teaching the teachers. This essay offers a glimpse at his reflections and ideas as result of his practical experience teaching.

REFERENCE

Archambault, R. D., ed. *Tolstoy on Education.* Chicago: University of Chicago Press, 1967.

TOLSTOY ON EDUCATION

Are the Peasant Children to Learn to Write from Us?

The feelings of truth, beauty, and goodness are independent of the degree of development. Beauty, truth, and goodness are conceptions which express only the harmony of relations in the sense of truth, beauty, and goodness. Lie is only a non-correspondence of relations in the sense of truth; there is no absolute truth. I am not lying when I say that the tables whirl about under the touch of my fingers, if I believe it to be so, even though it is an untruth; but I am lying when I say that I have no money when, according to my ideas, I have money. No immense nose is monstrous, but it is monstrous on a small face. Monstrosity is only a disharmony in relation to beauty. To give away my dinner to a mendicant, or to eat it up myself has nothing of badness in it; but to give it away, or eat it up myself, while my mother is starving is a disharmony of relations in the sense of goodness.

In bringing up, educating, developing, or in any way you please influencing the child, we ought to have and unconsciously do have one aim in view,—to attain the greatest harmony possible in the sense of truth, beauty, and goodness. If time did not run, if the child did not live with every side of himself, we should be able quietly to attain this harmony by supplementing there where there seems to be a lack, and by reducing where there seems to be a superfluity. But the child lives; every side of his existence strives after development, trying to outstrip every other side, and, for the most part, we mistake the progress of these sides of his being for the aim, and cooperate in this development only, instead of aiding the harmony of the development. In this lies the eternal mistake of all pedagogical theories.

We see our ideal before us, whereas it is behind us. The necessary development of man is far from being a means of attaining that ideal of harmony which we bear within us; it is, on the contrary, a hindrance, put in our way by the Creator, in the attainment of the highest ideal of harmony. In this necessary law of forward motion lies the meaning of that fruit of that tree of the knowledge of good and evil, which our first ancestor tasted.

"Becoming Educated: A Journey of Alienation or Integration?" by Jane Roland Martin, *Journal of Education*, Volume 167, #3, 1985. Reprinted with permission of Blackwell Publishers.

A healthy child is born into the world, completely satisfying all the demands of unconditional harmony in relation to truth, beauty, and goodness, which we bear within us; he is near to inanimate beings,—to the plant, to the animal, to Nature, which always represents to us that truth, beauty, and goodness, which we are seeking and wishing for. In all the ages and with all men, the child has been represented as a model of innocence, sinlessness, goodness, truth, and beauty. "Man is born perfect" is a great word enunciated by Rousseau, and this word will remain firm and true, like a rock. At birth man represents the prototype of harmony, truth, beauty, and goodness. But every hour in life, every minute of time increases the extent, the quantity, and the duration of those relations which during his birth were in full harmony, and every step and every hour threaten the impairment of that harmony, and every successive step and every successive hour threaten a new impairment and gives no hope of the restitution of the impaired harmony.

For the most part educators forget that the child's age is the prototype of harmony, and they assume the development of the child, which goes on independently according to immutable laws, as the aim. The development is erroneously taken for the aim because to the educators happens that which takes place with poor sculptors.

Instead of trying to arrest a local exaggerated development or the general development, instead of waiting for a new incident to destroy the irregularity which has arisen, just as a poor sculptor, instead of eradicating that which is superfluous, keeps pasting on more and more,—even thus educators seem to be concerned only about not interrupting the process of development, and if they ever think of the harmony, they try to attain it by approaching an unknown prototype in the future, by departing from the prototype in the present and in the past.

No matter how irregular the development of a child may be, there are always left in him the primitive features of harmony. By moderating, at least by not pushing, the development, we may hope to get a certain approach to regularity and harmony. But we are so sure of ourselves, we are so visionarily devoted to the false ideal of manhood perfection, we are so impatient with irregularities which are near to us and so firmly believe in our ability to correct them, we are so little able to comprehend and value the primitive beauty of a child, that we, as fast as we can, magnify and paste up the irregularities that strike our vision,—we correct, we educate the child. Now one side has to be equalized with the other, now the other has to be equalized with the first. The child is developed more and more, and all the time departs more and more from the former shattered prototype, and the attainment of the imaginary prototype of the perfection of manhood becomes ever more impossible. Our ideal is behind us, not before us. Education spoils, it does not correct men. The more a child is spoiled, the less he ought to be educated, the more liberty he needs.

It is impossible and absurd to teach and educate a child, for the simple reason that the child stands nearer than I do, than any grown-up man does, to that ideal of harmony, truth, beauty, and goodness, to which I, in my pride, wish to raise him. The consciousness of this ideal is more powerful in him than in me. All he needs of me is the material, in order to fill out harmoniously and on all sides. The moment I gave him full liberty and stopped teaching him, he wrote a poetical production, the like of which cannot be found in Russian literature. Therefore, it is my conviction that we cannot teach children in general, and peasant children in particular, to write and compose. All that we can do is to teach them how to go about writing.

If what I did in order to obtain this result may be called method, this method consisted in the following:

(1) Give a great variety of themes, not inventing them specially for the children, but propose such as appear most serious and interesting to the teacher himself.

(2) Give the children children's compositions to read, and give them only children's compositions as models, for children's compositions are always more correct, more artistic, and more moral than the compositions of grown people.

(3) (Most important.) When looking through a pupil's composition, never make any remarks to him about the cleanliness of the copy-book, nor about penmanship, nor orthography, nor, above all, about the structure of the sentences and about logic.

(4) Since the difficulty of composition does not lie in the volume, nor the contents, nor the artistic quality of the theme, the sequence of the themes is not to be based on volume, nor on the contents, nor on the language, but in the mechanism of the work, which consists, first, in selecting one out of a large number of ideas and images presented; secondly, in choosing words for it and clothing it in words; thirdly, in remembering it and finding a place for it; fourthly, in not repeating nor leaving out anything, and in the ability of combining what follows with that which precedes, all the time keeping in mind what is already

written down; fifthly, and finally, in thinking and writing at the same time, without having one of these acts interfere with the other. To obtain this end, I did as follows: A few of those sides of the labour I at first took upon myself, by degrees transferring them to their care. At first I chose from the ideas and images that presented themselves to them such as I considered best, and retained them, and pointed out the place, and consulted what had already been written, keeping them from repetitions, and myself wrote, leaving to them only the clothing of the images and ideas in words; then I allowed them to make their own choice, and later to consult that which had been written down, until, at last, as in the case of "A Soldier's Life," they took the whole matter into their own hands.

4

ALFRED NORTH WHITEHEAD

Alfred North Whitehead (1861–1947) wrote extensively in the fields of mathematics, philosophy of science, metaphysics, physics, and education. Most famously, he co-authored the classic text *Principia Mathematica* with his former student, Bertrand Russell, who would go on to become one of the seminal philosophers of the 20th century. But for this volume, what are most important are his reflections on education and its connections with what Whitehead would later term process philosophy. But it is important to note that Whitehead wrote about education while still a mathematics professor and before he became a speculative philosopher. While the topic of education dropped out of his later philosophical work, we can perhaps argue that his reflections on pedagogy formed a backdrop for later theories of process philosophy. As such, unlike other philosophers of education, such as Dewey (see this volume), Whitehead's philosophical orientation *grew out of* his reflections on education rather than the reverse.

In his text *Process and Reality* (1929), Whitehead argued that real-life objects are process objects composed of events rather than of static, definitive material. As opposed to the classic philosophical argument that substance is the basis for metaphysics, Whitehead thus argued that process is the major constituent of the world. Substance is seen as a continual process of becoming, and the world is reconceptualized as a dynamic world of change, transformation, and unfinishedness. He also criticized traditional categories of philosophy for their failure to realize the interrelation of matter, space, and time. Correcting this fundamental oversight, Whitehead developed a new philosophy of the organism which emphasized relations and interconnectedness.

What do these metaphysical views have to do with education? In education, ideas are often presented as discrete facts, commodities, or static bundles of information to be memorized, yet for Whitehead, reality is always in motion, is always changing. As such, our ideas must be thought of as fluid, open-ended, and dynamic processes. Education as a process-relations must therefore have certain qualities that embrace change and interconnectedness within and between ideas and our sense experiences. Therefore, education should first and foremost impart to children a sense of learning as a process of self-discovery and self-transformation rather than of rote memorization. Second, education should tap into the present interconnectedness of self, community, environment, and social traditions. Third, for ideas to be useful they must connect with the "stream" of events that compose the life of students. Rather than present detached and abstract concepts, education should strive to integrate life and learning. Fourth, as opposed to standardization, Whitehead sees education as deeply personal, intimate, and idiosyncratic. Finally, education is to be religious in the sense that it invokes duty and reverence.

Rounding out Whitehead's philosophy of education is his unique approach to the "rhythm" of educational development and self-transformation through learning. In the essay reproduced here, Whitehead suggests there are three stages rhythmic progression within a learning situation: romance, precision, and generalization. The romance stage is the initial experience of learning a new subject and is supported with feelings of excitement and curiosity. This is a time of intense and playful interest in the subject matter at hand. Following Romance, Whitehead describes the Precision Stage, in which the student learns specific details pertaining to the subject matter. In the sciences this is a time for learning proper procedures and methods of investigation and for artists it is a time for honing one's aesthetic skills and techniques. The final stage concerns generalization, which returns to the previous romance only now with a deeper, more generalized sense of interconnectedness and understanding of the subject. Throughout, continual movement is emphasized, with the teacher regulating the speed of the rhythm of education. Here, we see both Whitehead's emphasis on process and on the organic unity of thought and action with the world of events.

Bearing in mind Whitehead's philosophy of education, we might pose a series of questions: Can you describe the "rhythm" of your own educational experience? If education is highly personal, what types of evaluations can a teacher use to measure educational transformation? What would Whitehead have to say about national standards, such as No Child Left Behind?

REFERENCES

Gershman, Kathleen. "Articulated Memories: The Influence of His Life on the Educational Theory of Alfred North Whitehead." *Educational Theory* 36, no. 2 (1986): 195–204.

Morgan, Kathryn Pauly. "Desperately Seeking Evelyn, or, Alternatively, Exploring Pedagogies of the Personal in Alfred Lord Whitehead and Feminist Theory." In *Philosophy of Education Yearbook, 2002* (pp. 369–77). Urbana-Champaign: University of Illinois, 2002.

Special Issue on Whitehead's Philosophy of Education (2005). *Interchange* 36(1/2).

Whitehead, Alfred North. *Aims of Education and Other Essays*. New York: Macmillan, 1929.

Whitehead, Alfred North. *Process and Reality*. New York: Macmillan, 1929.

THE AIMS OF EDUCATION

3. The Rhythmic Claims of Freedom and Discipline

The fading of ideals is sad evidence of the defeat of human endeavour. In the schools of antiquity philosophers aspired to impart wisdom, in modern colleges our humbler aim is to teach subjects. The drop from the divine wisdom, which was the goal of the ancients, to text-book knowledge of subjects, which is achieved by the moderns, marks an educational failure, sustained through the ages. I am not maintaining that in the practice of education the ancient were more successful than ourselves. You have only to read Lucian, and to note his satiric dramatizations of the pretentious claims of philosophers, to see that in this respect the ancients can boast over us no superiority. My point is that, at the dawn of our European civilisation, men started with the full ideals which should inspire education, and that gradually our ideals have sunk to square with our practice.

But when ideals have sunk to the level of practice, the result is stagnation. In particular, so long as we conceive intellectual education as merely consisting in the acquirement of mechanical mental aptitudes, and of formulated statements of useful truths, there can be no progress; though there will be much activity, amid aimless re-arrangement of syllabuses, in the fruitless endeavour to dodge the inevitable lack of time. We must take it as an unavoidable fact, that God has so made the world that there are more topics desirable for knowledge than any one person can possibly acquire. It is hopeless to approach the problem by the way of the enumeration of subjects which every one ought to have mastered. There are too many of them, all with excellent title-deeds. Perhaps, after all, this plethora of material is fortunate; for the world is made interesting by a delightful ignorance of important truths. What I am anxious to impress on you is that though knowledge is one chief aim of intellectual education, there is another ingredient, vaguer but greater, and more dominating in its importance. The ancients called it "wisdom." You cannot be wise without some basis of knowledge; but you may easily acquire knowledge and remain bare of wisdom.

Now wisdom is the way in which knowledge is held. It concerns the handling of knowledge, its selection for the determination of relevant issues, its employment to add value to our immediate experience. This mastery of knowledge, which is wisdom, is the most intimate freedom obtainable. The ancients saw clearly—more clearly than we do—the necessity for dominating knowledge by wisdom. But, in the pursuit of wisdom in the region of practical education, they erred sadly. To put the matter simply, their popular practice assumed that wisdom could be imparted to the young by procuring philosophers to spout at them. Hence the crop of shady philosophers in the schools of the ancient world. The only avenue towards wisdom is by freedom in the presence of knowledge. But the only avenue towards knowledge is by discipline in the acquirement of ordered fact. Freedom and discipline are the two essentials of education, and hence the title of my discourse to-day, "The Rhythmic Claims of Freedom and Discipline."

The antithesis in education between freedom and discipline is not so sharp as a logical analysis of the meanings of the terms might lead us to imagine. The pupil's mind is a growing organism. On the one hand, it is not a box to be ruthlessly packed with alien ideas: and, on the other hand, the ordered acquirement of knowledge is the natural food for a developing intelligence. Accordingly, it should be the aim of an ideally constructed education that the discipline should be the voluntary issue of free choice, and that the freedom should gain an enrichment of possibility as the issue of discipline. The two principles, freedom and discipline, are not antagonists, but should be so adjusted in the child's life that they correspond to a natural sway, to and fro of the developing personality. It is this adaptation of freedom and discipline to the natural sway of development that I have elsewhere called The Rhythm of Education. I am convinced that much disappointing failure in the past has been due to neglect of attention to the importance of this rhythm. My main position is that the dominant note of education at its beginning and at its end is freedom, but that there is an intermediate stage of discipline with freedom in subordination: Furthermore, that there is not one unique threefold cycle of freedom, discipline, and freedom; but that all mental development is composed of such cycles, and of cycles of such cycles. Such a cycle is a unit cell, or brick; and the complete stage of growth is an organic structure of such cells. In analysing any one such cell, I call the first period of freedom the "stage of Romance," the intermediate period of discipline I call the "stage of Precision," and the final period of freedom is the "stage of Generalisation."

Let me now explain myself in more detail. There can be no mental development without interest. Interest is the *sine qua non* for attention and apprehension. You may endeavour to excite interest by means of birch rods, or you may coax it by the incitement of pleasurable activity. But without interest there will be no progress. Now the natural mode by which living organisms are excited towards suitable self-development is enjoyment. The infant is lured to adapt itself to its environment by its love of its mother and its nurse; we eat because we like a good dinner: we subdue the forces of nature because we have been lured to discovery by an insatiable curiosity: we enjoy exercise: and we enjoy the unchristian passion of hating our dangerous enemies. Undoubtedly pain is one subordinate means of arousing an organism to action. But it only supervenes on the failure of pleasure. Joy is the normal healthy spur for the *élan vital*. I am not maintaining that we can safely abandon ourselves to the allurement of the greater immediate joys. What I do mean is that we should seek to arrange the development of character along a path of natural activity, in itself pleasurable. The subordinate stiffening of discipline must be directed to secure some long-time good; although an adequate object must not be too far below the horizon, if the necessary interest is to be retained.

The second preliminary point which I wish to make, is the unimportance—indeed the evil—of barren knowledge. The importance of knowledge lies in its use, in our active mastery of it—that is to say, it lies in wisdom. It is a convention to speak of mere knowledge, apart from wisdom, as of itself imparting a peculiar dignity to its possessor. I do not share in this reverence for knowledge as such. It all depends on who has the knowledge and what he does with it. That knowledge which adds greatness to character is knowledge so handled as to transform every phase of immediate experience. It is in respect to the activity of knowledge that an over-vigorous discipline in education is so harmful. The habit of active thought, with freshness, can only be generated by adequate freedom. Undiscriminating discipline defeats its own objects by dulling the mind. If you have much to do with the young as they emerge from school and from the university, you soon note the dulled minds of those whose education has consisted in the acquirement of inert knowledge. Also the deplorable tone of English society in respect to learning is a tribute to our educational failure. Furthermore, this overhaste to impart mere knowledge defeats itself. The human mind rejects knowledge imparted in this way. The craving for expansion, for activity, inherent in youth is disgusted by a dry imposition of disciplined knowledge. The discipline, when it comes, should satisfy a natural craving for the wisdom which adds value to bare experience.

But let us now examine more closely the rhythm of these natural cravings of the human intelligence. The first procedure of the mind in a new environment is a somewhat discursive activity amid a welter of ideas and experience. It is a process of discovery, a process of becoming used to curious thoughts, of shaping questions, of seeking for answers, of devising new experiences, of noticing what happens as the result of new ventures. This general process is both natural and of absorbing interest. We must often have noticed children between the ages of eight and thirteen absorbed in its ferment. It is dominated by wonder, and cursed be the dullard who destroys wonder. Now undoubtedly this stage of development requires help, and even discipline. The environment within which the mind is working must be carefully selected. It must, of course, be chosen to suit the child's stage of growth, and must be adapted to individual needs. In a sense it is an imposition from without; but in a deeper sense it answers to the call of life within the child. In the teacher's consciousness the child has been sent to his telescope to look at the stars, in the child's consciousness he has been given free access to the glory of the heavens. Unless, working somewhere, however obscurely, even in the dullest child, there is this transfiguration of imposed routine, the child's nature will refuse to assimilate the alien material. It must never be forgotten that education is not a process of packing articles in a trunk. Such a simile is entirely inapplicable. It is, of course, a process completely of its own peculiar genus. Its nearest analogue is the assimilation of food by a living organism: and we all know how necessary to health is palatable food under suitable conditions. When you have put your boots in a trunk, they will stay there till you take them out again; but this is not at all the case if you feed a child with the wrong food.

This initial stage of romance requires guidance in another way. After all the child is the heir to long ages of civilisation, and it is absurd to let him wander in the intellectual maze of men in the Glacial Epoch. Accordingly, a certain pointing out of important acts, and of simplifying ideas, and of usual names, really strengthens the natural impetus of the pupil. In no part of education can you do without discipline or can you do without freedom; but in the stage of romance the emphasis must always be on freedom, to allow the child to see for itself and to act for itself. My point is that a block in the assimilation of ideas inevitably arises when a discipline of precision is imposed before a stage of romance has run its course in the growing mind. There is no comprehension apart from romance. It is my strong belief that the cause of so much failure in the past has been due to the lack of careful study of the due place of romance. Without the adventure of romance, at the best you get inert knowledge without initiative, and at the worst you get contempt of ideas—without knowledge.

But when this stage of romance has been properly guided another craving grows. The freshness of inexperience has worn off; there is general knowledge of the groundwork of fact and theory: and, above all, there has been plenty of independent browsing amid first-hand experiences, involving adventures of thought and of action. The enlightenment which comes from precise knowledge can now be understood. It corresponds to the obvious requirements of common sense, and deals with familiar material. Now is the time for pushing on, for knowing the subject exactly, and for retaining in the memory its salient features. This is the stage of precision. This stage is the sole stage of learning in the traditional scheme of education, either at school or university. You had to learn your subject; and there was nothing more to be said on the topic of education. The result of such an undue extension of a most necessary period of development was the production of a plentiful array of dunces, and of a few scholars whose natural interest had survived the car of Juggernaut. There is, indeed, always the temptation to teach pupils a little more of fact and of precise theory than at that stage they are fitted to assimilate. If only they could, it would be so useful. We—I am talking of schoolmasters and of university dons—are apt to forget that we are only subordinate elements in the education of a grown man; and that, in their own good time, in later life our pupils will learn for themselves. The phenomena of growth cannot be hurried beyond certain very narrow limits. But an unskilful practitioner can easily damage a sensitive organism. Yet, when all has been said in the way of caution, there is such a thing as pushing on, of getting to know the fundamental details and the main exact generalisations, and of acquiring an easy mastery of technique. There is no getting away from the fact that things have been found out, and that to be effective in the modern world you must have a store of definite acquirement of the best practice. To write poetry you must study metre; and to build bridges you must be learned in the strength of material. Even the Hebrew prophets had learned to write, probably in those days requiring no mean effort. The untutored art of genius is—in the words of the Prayer Book—a vain thing, fondly invented.

During the stage of precision, romance is the background. The stage is dominated by the inescapable fact that there are right ways and wrong ways, and definite truths to be known. But romance is not dead, and it is the art of teaching to foster it amidst definite application to appointed task. It must be fostered for one reason, because romance is after all a necessary ingredient of that balanced wisdom which is the goal to be attained. But there is another reason: The organism will not absorb the fruits of the task unless its powers or apprehension are kept fresh by romance. The real point is to discover in practice that exact balance between freedom and discipline which will give the greatest rate of progress over the things to be known. I do not believe that there is any abstract formula which will give information applicable to all subjects, to all types of pupils, or to each individual pupil; except indeed the formula of rhythmic sway which I have been insisting on, namely, that in the earlier stage the progress requires that the emphasis be laid on freedom, and that in the later middle stage the emphasis be laid on the definite acquirement of allotted tasks. I freely admit that if the stage of romance has been properly managed, the discipline of the second stage is much less apparent, that the children know how to go about their work, want to make a good job of it, and can be safely trusted with the details. Furthermore, I hold that the only discipline, important for its own sake, is self-discipline, and that this can only be acquired by a wide use of freedom. But yet—so many are the delicate points to be considered in education—it is necessary in life to have acquired the habit of cheerfully undertaking imposed tasks. The conditions can be satisfied if the tasks correspond to the natural cravings of the pupil at his stage of progress, if they keep his powers at full stretch, and if they attain an obviously sensible result, and if reasonable freedom is allowed in the mode of execution.

The difficulty of speaking about the way a skilful teacher will keep romance alive in his pupils arises from the fact that what takes a long time to describe, takes a short time to do. The beauty of a passage of Virgil may be rendered by insisting on beauty of verbal enunciation, taking no longer than prosy utterance. The emphasis on the beauty or a mathematical argument, in its marshalling of general considerations to unravel complex fact, is the speediest mode of procedure. The responsibility of the teacher at this stage is immense. To speak the truth, except in the rare case of genius in the teacher, I do not think that it is possible to take a whole class very far along the road of precision without some dulling of the interest. It is the unfortunate dilemma that initiative and training are both necessary, and that training is apt to kill initiative.

But this admission is not to condone a brutal ignorance of methods of mitigating this untoward fact. It is not a theoretical necessity, but arises because perfect tact is unattainable in the treatment of each individual case. In the past the methods employed assassinated interest; we are discussing how to reduce the evil to its smallest dimensions. I merely utter the warning that education is a difficult problem, to be solved by no one simple formula.

In this connection there is, however, one practical consideration which is largely neglected. The territory of romantic interest is large, ill-defined, and not to be controlled by any explicit boundary. It depends on the chance flashes of insight. But the area of precise knowledge, as exacted in any general educational system, can be, and should be, definitely determined. If you make it too wide you will kill interest and defeat your own object: if you make it too narrow your pupils will lack effective grip. Surely, in every subject in each type of curriculum, the precise knowledge required should be determined after the most anxious inquiry. This does not now seem to be the case in any effective way. For example, in the classical studies of boys destined for a scientific career—a class of pupils in whom I am greatly interested—What is the Latin vocabulary which they ought definitely to know? Also what are the grammatical rules and constructions which they ought to have mastered? Why not determine these once and for all, and then bend every exercise to impress just these on the memory, and to understand their derivatives, both in Latin and also in French and English. Then, as to other constructions and words which occur in the reading of texts, supply full information in the easiest manner. A certain ruthless definiteness is essential in education. I am sure that one secret of a successful teacher is that he has formulated quite clearly in his mind what the pupil has got to know in precise fashion. He will then cease from half-hearted attempts to worry his pupils with memorising a lot of irrelevant stuff of inferior importance. The secret of success is pace, and the secret of pace is concentration. But, in respect to precise knowledge, the watchword is pace, pace, pace. Get your knowledge quickly, and then use it. If you can use it, you will retain it.

We have now come to the third stage of the rhythmic cycle, the stage of generalisation. There is here a reaction towards romance. Something definite is now known; aptitudes have been acquired: and general rules and laws are clearly apprehended both in their formulation and then detailed exemplification. The pupil now wants to use his new weapons. He is an effective individual, and it is effects that he wants to produce. He relapses into the discursive adventures of the romantic stage, with the advantage that his mind is now a disciplined regiment instead of a rabble. In this sense, education should begin in research and end in research. After all, the whole affair is merely a preparation for battling with the immediate experiences of life, a preparation by which to qualify each immediate moment with relevant ideas and appropriate actions. An education which does not begin by evoking initiative and end by encouraging it must be wrong. For its whole aim is the production of active wisdom.

In my own work at universities I have been much struck by the paralysis of thought induced in pupils by the aimless accumulation of precise knowledge, inert and unutilised. It should be the chief aim of a university professor to exhibit himself in his own true character—that is, as an ignorant man thinking, actively utilising this small share of knowledge. In a sense, knowledge shrinks as wisdom grows: for details are swallowed up in principles. The details of knowledge which are important will be picked up *ad hoc* in each avocation of life, but the habit of the active utilisation of well-understood principles is the final possession of wisdom. The stage of precision is the stage of growing into the apprehension of principles by the acquisition of a precise knowledge of details. The stage of generalisations is the stage of shedding details in favour of the active application of principles, the details retreating into subconscious habits. We don't go about explicitly retaining in our own minds that two and two make four, though once we had to learn it by heart. We trust to habit for our elementary arithmetic. But the essence of this stage is the emergence from the comparative passivity of being trained into the active freedom of application. Of course, during this stage, precise knowledge will grow, and more actively than ever before, because the mind has experienced the power of definiteness, and responds to the acquisition of general truth, and of richness of illustration. But the growth of knowledge becomes progressively unconscious, as being an incident derived from some active adventure of thought.

So much for the three stages of the rhythmic unit of development. In a general way the whole period of education is dominated by this threefold rhythm. Till the age of thirteen or fourteen there is the romantic stage, from fourteen to eighteen the stage of precision, and from eighteen to two and twenty the stage of generalisation. But these are only average characters, tinging the mode of development as a whole. I do not think that any pupil completes his stages simultaneously in all subjects. For example, I should plead that while language is initiating its stage of precision in the way of acquisition of vocabulary and of grammar, science should be in its full romantic stage. The romantic stage of language begins in infancy with the acquisition of speech, so that it passes early towards a stage of precision; while science is a late comer. Accordingly a precise inculcation of science at an early age wipes out initiative and interest, and destroys any chance of the topic having any richness of content in the child's apprehension. Thus, the romantic stage of science should persist for years after the precise study of language has commenced.

There are minor eddies, each in itself a threefold cycle, running its course in each day, in each week, and in each term. There is the general apprehension of some topic in its vague possibilities, the mastery of the relevant details, and finally the putting of the whole subject together in the light of the relevant knowledge. Unless the pupils are continually sustained by the evocation of interest, the acquirement of technique, and the excitement of success, they can never make progress, and will certainly lose heart. Speaking generally, during the last thirty years the schools of England have been sending up to the universities a disheartened crowd of young folk, inoculated against any outbreak of intellectual zeal. The universities have seconded the efforts of the schools and emphasised the failure. Accordingly, the cheerful gaiety of the young turns to other topics, and thus educated England is not hospitable to ideas. When we can point to some great achievement of our nation—let us hope that it may be something other than a war—which has been won in the class-room of our schools, and not in their playing-fields, then we may feel content with our modes of education.

So far I have been discussing intellectual education and my argument has been cramped on too narrow a basis. After all, our pupils are alive, and cannot be chopped into separate bits, like the pieces of a jigsaw puzzle. In the production of a mechanism the constructive energy lies outside it, and adds discrete parts to discrete parts. The case is far different for a living organism which grows by its own impulse towards self-development. This impulse can be stimulated and guided from outside the organism, and it can also be killed. But for all your stimulation and guidance the creative impulse towards growth comes from within, and is intensely characteristic of the individual. Education is the guidance of the individual towards a comprehension of the art of life; and by the art of life I mean the most complete achievement of varied activity expressing the potentialities of that living creature in the face of its actual environment. This completeness of achievement involves an artistic sense, subordinating the lower to the higher possibilities of the indivisible personality. Science, art, religion, morality, take their rise from this sense of values within the structure of being. Each individual embodies an adventure of existence. The art of life is the guidance of this adventure. The great religions of civilisation include among their original elements revolts against the inculcation of morals as a set of isolated prohibitions. Morality, in the petty negative sense of the term, is the deadly enemy of religion. Paul denounces the Law, and the Gospels are vehement against the Pharisees. Every outbreak of religion exhibits the same intensity of antagonism—an antagonism diminishing as religion fades. No part of education has more to gain from attention to the rhythmic law of growth than has moral and religious education. Whatever be the right way to formulate religious truths, it is death to religion to insist on a premature stage of precision. The vitality of religion is shown by the way in which the religious spirit has survived the ordeal of religious education.

The problem of religion in education is too large to be discussed at this stage of my address. I have referred to it to guard against the suspicion that the principles here advocated are to be conceived in a narrow sense. We are analysing the general law of rhythmic progress in the higher stages of life, embodying the initial awakening, the discipline, and the fruition on the higher plane. What I am now insisting is that the principle of progress is from within: the discovery is made by ourselves, the discipline is self-discipline, and the fruition is the outcome of our own initiative. The teacher has a double function. It is for him to elicit the enthusiasm by resonance from his own personality, and to create the environment of a larger knowledge and a firmer purpose. He is there to avoid the waste, which in the lower stages of existence is nature's way of evolution. The ultimate motive power, alike in science, in morality, and in religion, is the sense of value, the sense of importance. It takes the various forms of wonder, of curiosity, of reverence, or worship, of tumultuous desire for merging personality in something beyond itself. This sense of value imposes on life incredible labours, and apart from it life sinks back into the passivity of its lower types. The most penetrating exhibition of this force is the sense of beauty, the æsthetic sense of realised perfection. This thought leads me to ask, whether in our modern education we emphasise sufficiently the functions of art.

The typical education of our public schools was devised for boys from well-to-do cultivated homes. They travelled in Italy, in Greece, and in France, and often their own homes were set amid beauty. None of these circumstances hold for modern national education in primary or secondary schools, or even for the majority of boys and girls in our enlarged system of public schools. You cannot, without loss, ignore in the life of the spirit so great a factor as art. Our æsthetic emotions provide us with vivid apprehensions of value. If you maim these, you weaken the force of the whole system of spiritual apprehensions. The claim for freedom in education carries with it the corollary that the development of the whole personality must be attended to. You must not arbitrarily refuse its urgent demands. In these days of economy, we hear much of the futility of our educational efforts and of the possibility of curtailing them. The endeavour to develop a bare intellectuality is bound to issue in a large crop of failure. This is just what we have done in our national schools. We do just enough to excite and not enough to satisfy. History shows us that an efflorescence of art is the first activity of nations on the road to civilisation. Yet, in the face of this plain fact, we practically shut out art from the masses of the population. Can we wonder that such an education, evoking and defeating cravings, leads to failure and discontent? The stupidity of the whole procedure is, that art in simple popular forms is just what we can give to the nation without undue strain on our resources. You may, perhaps, by some great reforms, obviate the worst kind of sweated labour and the insecurity of employment. But you can never greatly increase average incomes. On that side all hope of Utopia is closed to you. It would, however, require no very great effort to use our schools to produce a population with some love of music, some enjoyment of drama, and some joy in beauty of form and colour. We could also provide means for the satisfaction of these emotions in the general life of the population. If you think of the simplest ways, you will see that the strain on material resources would be negligible; and when you have done that, and when your population widely appreciates what art can give—its joys and its terrors—do you not think that your prophets and your clergy and your statesmen will be in a stronger position when they speak to the population of the love of God, of the inexorableness of duty, and of the call of patriotism?

Shakespeare wrote his plays for English people reared in the beauty of the country, amid the pageant of life as the Middle Age merged into the Renaissance, and with a new world across the ocean to make vivid the call of romance. Today we deal with herded town populations, reared in a scientific age. I have no doubt that unless we can meet the new age with new methods, to sustain for our populations the life of the spirit, sooner or later, amid some savage outbreak of defeated longings, the fate of Russia will be the fate of England. Historians will write as her epitaph that her fall issued from the spiritual blindness of her governing classes, from their dull materialism, and from their Pharisaic attachment to petty formulæ of statesmanship.

5

FRIEDRICH NIETZSCHE

In January 1889, Friedrich Nietzsche (1844–1900) collapsed on the streets of Turin, Germany, after witnessing the flogging of a horse by a coachman. Although returning to consciousness, Nietzsche drifted into madness and spent the last years of his life suffering from partial paralysis. While there is much debate concerning the causes of this bizarre episode, there is no doubt that Nietzsche had suffered immensely during his life from horrible headaches and spells of extreme nausea and vomiting—perhaps related to injuries suffered from his work as a medic in the Franco-Prussian War. It was this ongoing illness that ultimately made him retire prematurely from his position as professor of classical philology at Basel, which he had held for ten years from 1869–1879.

Why start the introduction to Nietzsche philosophy with this surreal tale of madness and illness? One cannot understand Nietzsche's life or his philosophy without recognizing the pain and suffering he physically endured. For Nietzsche, a major philosophical theme is that of overcoming the limitations of oneself, one's culture, and one's historical moment. While many might have seen his sickness as debilitating, Nietzsche turned it into a strength. Famously, Nietzsche wrote, "Whatever does not destroy me makes me stronger." In fact, health is the ability to triumph over disease and say "Yes!" to life. Thus, sickness became a philosophical perspective, enabling Nietzsche to delve into the deepest recesses of human psychological and physical suffering in order to celebrate the will to overcome.

Another key to understanding Nietzsche's philosophy is his turbulent relationship with the great German composer Richard Wagner (1813–1883). At first, Nietzsche saw in Wagner the possibility for a rebirth of German culture, which was suffering from a sickness of conformity, standardization, resentment, and massification. Whereas the German educational system emphasized greed, careerism, and patriotism, Nietzsche was searching for a new teacher, someone who would cultivate great philosophers, artists, and saints rather than bureaucrats and passive citizens, yet after an intimate friendship, Nietzsche realized that the devotion that Wagner demanded of his inner circle of friends and allies was too restrictive for Nietzsche, whose own philosophical project was beginning to take shape in his young mind. If he turned to Wagner as a teacher leading the way out of "cultural philistinism" and dogmatic education of Germany, then ultimately Nietzsche came to see Wagner as nothing more than a "false prophet" of a cultural romanticism that was no less vulgar and corrupt than the status quo. To stay a devotee of Wagner's meant sacrificing Nietzsche's own will to greatness, which in the end could not be compromised. Thus, Nietzsche turned on his teacher, overcoming his reliance on Wagner to strike out on his own, unique path. For Nietzsche, one's idols must be continually overthrown in an act of intellectual independence. Later in Nietzsche's life he argued, "One repays a teacher badly if one always remains a pupil only." The greatest honor to one's master is to become a free thinker and free spirit. In other words, the ultimate teacher is oneself.

By analyzing Nietzsche's own relationship to his former teacher, we can thus derive a clear picture of Nietzsche's overall philosophy of education. As young and impressionable youth, we seek out a teacher who enables us to overcome the culture of the age through a relentless criticism of all hypocrisy, resentment, and nihilism. In the following reading, Nietzsche turns to the German philosopher Schopenhauer as a symbol of health, joy, and genius. Such a teacher embodies those traits which the student strives to achieve, yet this teacher must also be overcome as the student forges a path of free and independent thinking. And finally one must overcome the limits of oneself, transforming all weaknesses into strength, all doubts into courage, all resentment into joy, all dependencies into independence, etc. Here the student emerges as a strong individual with the will to constantly improve and create new values.

If this essay is an introduction to Nietzsche's work on education, then it must clarify a major misconception that students often associate with Nietzsche's thought. If one is at all familiar with the name Nietzsche it is most likely in relation to Nazi Germany. It can be stated with absolute certainty that Nietzsche was not a proto-Nazi. The origins of this slanderous interpretation can be traced back to Nietzsche's sister, who was married to the infamous anti-Semitic propagandist Bernhard Forster. After Nietzsche's slide into madness, his sister took full control over the publishing rights to Nietzsche's works. She edited them liberally, highlighting and misconstruing certain passages that supported her racist agenda against the Jews. If Nietzsche critiqued the Jewish religion, he equally critiqued Christianity. Ironically, Nietzsche's most vehement criticisms were reserved for Germany itself! Also, in relation to Nietzsche's overall philosophical system, he continually rejected any notion of collective politics (fascist, socialist, or democratic), opting instead to champion the lone, isolated genius. Because Nazism is at its base a collective movement against individualism, it flies in the face of much of Nietzsche's most highly prized ideals. As such, it is a historical and philosophical mistake to read Nazism into Nietzsche's work.

When reading the following excerpt bear these questions in mind: Does Nietzsche's critique of the school system still hold true today? In other words, is there room for a free spirit within national standardization? What advice does Nietzsche give to teachers who are concerned with the freedom of expression and the cultivation of the creativity of students?

REFERENCES

Aloni, N. "Three Pedagogical Dimensions of Nietzsche's Philosophy." *Educational Theory* 39, no. 4 (1989): 301–6.

Bingham, C. "What Nietzsche Cannot Stand About Education." *Educational Theory* 51, no. 3 (2001): 337–52.

Johnston, J. S. "Nietzsche as Educator: A Reexamination." *Educational Theory* 48, no. 1 (1998): 67–82.

Kaufmann, W. *Nietzsche: Philosopher, Psychologist, Antichrist.* Princeton: Princeton University Press, 1974.

Mintz, A. "The Disciplined Schooling of the Free Spirit: Educational Theory in Nietzsche's Middle Period." In Chris Higgins, ed., *Philosophy of Education Society Yearbook, 2004* (pp. 163–70). Urbana-Champaign: University of Illinois at Urbana-Champaign, 2005.

Rosenow, E. "Nietzsche's Educational Legacy." *Journal of Philosophy of Education* 35, no. 4 (2000): 673–85.

SCHOPENHAUER AS EDUCATOR

How can man know himself? He is a thing dark and veiled; and if the hare has seven skins, man can slough off seventy times seven and still not be able to say: 'this is really you, this is no longer outer shell'. Moreover, it is a painful and dangerous undertaking thus to tunnel into oneself and to force one's way down into the shaft of one's being by the nearest path. A man who does it can easily so hurt himself that no physician can cure him. And, moreover again, what need should there be for it, since everything bears witness to what we are, our friendships and enmities, our glance and the clasp of our hand, our memory and that which we do not remember, our books and our handwriting. This, however, is the means by which an inquiry into the most important aspect can be initiated. Let the youthful soul look back on life with the question: what have you truly loved up to now, what has drawn your soul aloft, what has mastered it and at the same time blessed it? Set up these revered objects before you and perhaps their nature and their sequence will give you a law, the fundamental law of your own true self. Compare these objects one with another, see how one completes, expands, surpasses, transfigures another, how they constitute a stepladder upon which you have clambered up to yourself as you are now; for your true nature lies, not concealed deep within you, but immeasurably high above you, or at least above that which you usually take yourself to be. Your true educators and formative teachers reveal to you that the true, original meaning and basic stuff of your nature is something completely incapable of being educated or formed and is in any case something difficult of access, bound and paralysed; your educators can be only your liberators. And that is the secret of all culture: it does not provide artificial limbs, wax noses or spectacles—that which can provide these things is, rather, only sham education. Culture is liberation, the removal of all the weeds, rubble and vermin that want to attack the tender buds of the plant, an outstreaming of light and warmth, the gentle rustling of nocturnal rain, it is imitation and worship of nature where nature is in her motherly and merciful mood, it is the perfecting of nature when it deflects her cruel and merciless assaults and turns them to good, and when it draws a veil over the expressions of nature's step-motherly mood and her sad lack of understanding.

Certainly there may be other means of finding oneself, of coming to oneself out of the bewilderment in which one usually wanders as in a dark cloud, but I know of none better than to think on one's true educators and cultivators. And so today I shall remember one of the teachers and taskmasters of whom I can boast, *Arthur Schopenhauer*—and later on I shall recall others.

If I am to describe what an event my first glance at Schopenhauer's writings was for me, I must dwell for a moment on an idea which used to come to me in my youth more pressingly, and more frequently, than perhaps any other. When in those days I roved as I pleased through wishes of all kinds, I always believed that at some time fate would take from me the terrible effort and duty of educating myself: I believed that, when the time came, I would discover a philosopher to educate me, a true philosopher whom one could follow without any misgiving because one would have more faith in him than one had in oneself. Then I asked myself: what would be the principles by which he would educate you?—and I reflected on what he might say about the two educational maxims which are being hatched in our time. One of them demands that the educator should quickly recognize the real strength of his pupil and then direct all his efforts and energy and heat at them so as to help that one virtue to attain true maturity and fruitfulness. The other maxim, on the contrary, requires that the educator should draw forth and nourish *all* the forces which exist in his pupil and bring them to a harmonious relationship with one another. But should he who has a decided inclination to be a goldsmith for that reason be forcibly compelled to study music? Is one to agree that Benvenuto Cellini's father was right continually to force him to play the 'dear little horn''—that accursed piping', as his son called it? In the case of such strong and definite talents one would not agree: so could it perhaps be that that maxim advocating a harmonious development should be applied only to more mediocre natures in which, though there may reside a congeries of needs and inclinations, none of them amounts to very much taken individually? But where do we discover a harmonious whole at all, a simultaneous sounding of many voices in one nature, if not in such men as Cellini, men in whom everything, knowledge, desire, love, hate, strives towards a central point, a root force, and where a harmonious system is constructed through the compelling domination of this living centre? And so perhaps these two maxims are not opposites at all? Perhaps the one simply says that man should have a centre and the other that he should also have a periphery? That educating philosopher of whom I dreamed would, I came to think, not only discover the central force, he would also know how to prevent its acting destructively on the other forces: his educational task would, it seemed to me, be to mould the whole man into a living solar and planetary system and to understand its higher laws of motion.

In the meantime I still lacked this philosopher, and I tried this one and that one; I discovered how wretched we modern men appear when compared with the Greeks and Romans even merely in the matter of a serious understanding of the tasks of education. With the need for this in one's heart one can run through all Germany, especially its universities, and fail to find what one is seeking; for many far simpler and more basic desires are still unfulfilled there. Anyone who seriously wanted to train in Germany as an orator, for example, or intended to enter a school for writers, would find that school nowhere; it seems not to have been realized that speaking and writing are arts which cannot be acquired without the most careful instruction and arduous apprenticeship. Nothing, however, displays the arrogant self-satisfaction of our contemporaries more clearly or shamefully than their half niggardly, half thoughtless undemandingness in regard to teachers and educators. What will not suffice, even among our noblest and best-instructed families, under the name of family tutor; what a collection of antiques and eccentrics is designated a grammar school and not found wanting; what are we not content with for a university—what leaders, what institutions, in comparison with the difficulty of the task of educating a man to be a man! Even the much admired way in which our German men of learning set about their scientific pursuits reveals above all that they are thinking more of science than they are of mankind, that they have been trained to sacrifice themselves to it like a legion of the lost, so as in turn to draw new generations on to the same sacrifice. If it is not directed and kept within bounds by a higher maxim of education, but on the contrary allowed to run wilder and wilder on the principle 'the more the better', traffic with science is certainly as harmful to men of learning as the economic principle of *laissez faire* is to the morality of whole nations. Who is there that still remembers that the education of the scholar is an extremely difficult problem, if his humanity is not to be sacrificed in the process—and yet this difficulty is plainly obvious when one regards the numerous examples of those who through an unthinking and premature devotion to science have become crook-backed and humped. But there is an even weightier witness to the absence of all higher education, weightier and more perilous and above all much more common. If it is at once obvious why an orator or a writer cannot now be educated in these arts—because there are no educators for them—; if it is almost as obvious why a scholar must now become distorted and contorted—because he is supposed to be educated by science, that is to say by an inhuman abstraction—then one finally asks oneself: where are we, scholars and unscholarly, high placed and low, to find the moral exemplars and models among our contemporaries, the visible epitome of morality for our time? What has become of any reflection on questions of morality—questions that have at all times engaged every more highly civilized society? There is no longer any model or any reflection of any kind; what we are in fact doing is consuming the moral capital we have inherited from our forefathers, which we are incapable of increasing but know only how to squander; in our society one either remains silent about such things or speaks of them in a way that reveals an utter lack of acquaintance with or experience of them and that can only excite revulsion. Thus it has come about that our schools and teachers simply abstain from an education in morality or make do with mere formalities: and virtue is a word that no longer means anything to our teachers or pupils, an old-fashioned word that makes one smile—and it is worse if one does not smile, for then one is being a hypocrite.

Never have moral educators been more needed, and never has it seemed less likely they would be found; in the times when physicians are required the most, in times of great plagues, they are also most in peril. For where are the physicians for modern mankind who themselves stand so firmly and soundly on their feet that they are able to support others and lead them by the hand? A certain gloominess and torpor lies upon even the finest personalities of our time, a feeling of ill-humour at the everlasting struggle between dissimulation and honesty which is being fought out within them, a lack of steady confidence in themselves—whereby they become quite incapable of being signposts and at the same time taskmasters for others.

It was thus truly roving through wishes to imagine I might discover a true philosopher as an educator who could raise me above my insufficiencies insofar as these originated in the age and teach me again to be *simple* and *honest* in thought and life, that is to say to be untimely, that word understood in the profoundest sense; for men have now become so complex and many-sided they are bound to become dishonest whenever they speak at all, make assertions and try to act in accordance with them.

It was in this condition of need, distress and desire that I came to know Schopenhauer.

I am describing nothing but the first, as it were physiological, impression Schopenhauer produced upon me, that magical out-pouring of the inner strength of one natural creature on to another that follows the first and most fleeting encounter; and when I subsequently analyse that impression I discover it to be compounded of three elements, the elements of his honesty, his cheerfulness and his steadfastness. He is honest because he speaks and writes to himself and for himself, cheerful because he has conquered the hardest task by thinking, and steadfast because he has to be. His strength rises straight and calmly upwards like a flame when there is no wind, imperturbably, without restless wavering. He finds his way every time before we have so much as noticed that he has been seeking it; as though compelled by a law of gravity he runs on ahead, so firm and agile, so inevitably. And whoever has felt what it means to discover among our tragelaphine men[†] of today a whole, complete, self-moving, unconstrained and unhampered natural being will understand my joy and amazement when I discovered Schopenhauer: I sensed that in him I had discovered that educator and philosopher I had sought for so long. But I had discovered him only in the form of a book, and that was a great deficiency. So I strove all the harder to see through the book and to imagine the living man whose great testament I had to read and who promised to make his heirs only those who would and could be more than merely his readers: namely his sons and pupils.

I profit from a philosopher only insofar as he can be an example. That he is capable of drawing whole nations after him through this example is beyond doubt; the history of India, which is almost the history of Indian philosophy, proves it. But this example must be supplied by his outward life and not merely in his books—in the way, that is, in which

---

[†]'Tragelaphen-Menschheit'. A 'tragelaph' is a 'goat-stag', i.e. a 'horned beast'.

the philosophers of Greece taught, through their bearing, what they wore and ate, and their morals, rather than by what they said, let alone by what they wrote. How completely this courageous visibility of the philosophical life is lacking in Germany!

Schopenhauer had little patience with the scholarly castes, separated himself from them, strove to be independent of state and society—this is his example, the model he provides—to begin with the most superficial things. But many stages in the liberation of the philosophical life are still unknown among the Germans, though they will not always be able to remain unknown.

An Englishman recently described the most general danger facing uncommon men who live in a society tied to convention: 'Such alien characters at first become submissive, then melancholic, then ill and finally they die. A Shelley would not have been able to live in England, and a race of Shelleys would have been impossible.'* Our Hölderlin and Kleist, and who knows who else besides, were ruined by their uncommonness and could not endure the climate of so-called German culture; and only natures of iron, such as Beethoven, Goethe, Schopenhauer and Wagner are able to stand firm. But these too exhibit many of the effects of the wearying struggle they have had to engage in: they breathe heavily and their voice can easily become too loud.

They know, these solitaries, free in spirit, that they continually seem other than what they think: while they desire nothing but truth and honesty, they are encompassed by a net of misunderstandings; and however vehemently they may desire, they cannot prevent a cloud of false opinions, approximations, half-admissions, indulgent silence, erroneous interpretation from gathering about their actions. Because of this a cloud of melancholy gathers on their brows.

Every human being is accustomed to discovering in himself some limitation, of his talent or of his moral will, which fills him with melancholy and longing; and just as his feeling of sinfulness makes him long for the saint in him, so as an intellectual being he harbours a profound desire for the genius in him. This is the root of all true culture; and if I understand by this the longing of man to be *reborn* as saint and genius, I know that one does not have to be a Buddhist to understand this myth.

---

*Quoted, possibly from memory for it is not entirely accurate, from Walter Bagehot's *Physics and Politics*. Bagehot refers to New England, not England.

Where we discover talent devoid of that longing, in the world of scholars or that of the so-called cultivated, we are repelled and disgusted by it; for we sense that, with all their intellect, such people do not promote an evolving culture and the procreation of genius—which is the goal of all culture—but hinder it. It is a state of petrifaction, equivalent in value to that routine, cold and self-laudatory virtuousness which is also farthest, and keeps itself far, from true saintliness. Now, Schopenhauer's nature contained a strange and extremely dangerous dualism. Few thinkers have felt with a comparable intensity and certainty that genius moved within them; and his genius promised him the highest—that there would be no deeper furrow than that which his ploughshare was digging in the ground of modern mankind.

Each of us bears a productive uniqueness within him as the core of his being; and when he becomes aware of it, there appears around him a strange penumbra which is the mark of his singularity. Most find this something unendurable, because they are, as aforesaid, lazy, and because a chain of toil and burdens is suspended from this uniqueness. There can be no doubt that, for the singular man who encumbers himself with this chain, life withholds almost everything—cheerfulness, security, ease, honour—that he desired of it in his youth; solitude is the gift his fellow men present to him; let him live where he will, he will always find there the desert and the cave. Let him see to it that he does not become subjugated, that he does not become depressed and melancholic. And to that end let him surround himself with pictures of good and brave fighters, such as Schopenhauer was.

A modern thinker will, to repeat, always suffer from an unfulfilled desire: he will want first to be shown life again, true, red-blooded, healthy life, so that he may then pronounce his judgment on it. To himself at least he will regard it as necessary that he should be a living human being if he is to believe he can be a just judge. This is the reason it is precisely the more modern philosophers who are among the mightiest promoters of life, of the will to live and why from out of their own exhausted age they long for a culture, for a transfigured physis. But this longing also constitutes their *danger:* there is struggle within them between the reformer of life and the philosopher, that is to say the judge of life. Wherever the victory may incline, it is a victory that will involve a loss. And how, then, did Schopenhauer elude this danger too?

If it is commonly accepted that the great man is the genuine child of his age, if he in any event suffers from the deficiencies of his age more acutely than do smaller men, then a struggle by such a great man *against* his age seems to be only a senseless and destructive attack on himself. But only seems so; for he is contending against those aspects of his age that prevent him from being great, which means, in his case, being free and entirely himself. From which it follows that his hostility is at bottom directed against that which, though he finds it in himself, is not truly himself: against the indecent compounding and confusing of things eternally incompatible, against the soldering of time-bound things on to his own untimeliness; and in the end the supposed child of his time proves to be only its stepchild. Thus Schopenhauer strove from his early youth against that false, idle and unworthy mother, his age, and by as it were expelling her from him, he healed and purified his being and rediscovered himself in the health and purity native to him. That is why Schopenhauer's writings can be used as a mirror of his age; and it is certainly not due to a fault in the mirror if everything time-bound in his age appears as a disfiguring illness, as thin and pale, as enervated and hollow eyed, as the recognizable sufferings of his stepchildhood. The longing for a stronger nature, for a healthier and simpler humanity, was in his case a longing for himself; and when he had conquered his age in himself he beheld with astonished eyes the genius in himself. The secret of his being was revealed to him the intention of his stepmother age to conceal his genius from him was frustrated, the realm of transfigured *physis* was disclosed. When he now turned his fearless eye upon the question: 'What is life worth as such?'—it was no longer a confused and pallid age and its hypocritical, uncertain life upon which he had to pass judgment. He knew well that there is something higher and purer to be found and attained on this earth than the life of his own time.

But I have undertaken to exhibit my experience of Schopenhauer as an *educator,* and it is thus not early sufficient for me to paint, and to paint imperfectly, that ideal man who, as his Platonic ideal as it were, holds sway in and around him. The hardest task still remains: to say how a new circle of duties may be derived from this ideal and how one can proceed towards so extravagant a goal through a practical activity—in short, to demonstrate that his ideal *educates.*

Here I have arrived at an answer to the question whether it is possible to pursue the great ideal of the Schopenhauerean man by means of a practical activity: One thing above all is certain: these new duties are not the duties of a solitary; on the contrary, they set one in the midst of a mighty community held together, not by external forms and regulations, but by a fundamental idea. It is the fundamental idea of *culture*, insofar as it sets for each one of us but one task: *to promote the production of the philosopher, the artist and the saint within us and without us and thereby to work at the perfecting of nature.*

For we know what culture is. Applied to the Schopenhauerean man, it demands that we prepare and promote his repeated production by getting to know what is inimical to it and removing it—in short, that we unwearyingly combat that which would deprive *us* of the supreme fulfillment of our existence by preventing us from becoming such Schopenhaurean men ourselves.

However loudly the state may proclaim its service to culture, it furthers culture in order to further itself and cannot conceive of a goal higher than its own welfare and continued existence. What the money-makers really want when they ceaselessly demand instruction and education is in the last resort precisely money. When those who require form ascribe to themselves the actual labour on behalf of culture and opine, for instance, that all art belongs to them and must stand in the service of their requirements, what is quite clear is that by affirming culture they are merely affirming themselves: that they too are therefore still involved in a misunderstanding. And so we see that, however zealous all four powers together may be in promoting their *own* interests with the aid of culture, they are dull and without inspiration when these interests are not involved. And that is why the conditions for the production of the genius have *not improved* in modern times, and why antipathy for original men has increased to such an extent that Socrates could not have lived among us and would in any event not have attained seventy.

It demands, to be sure, a quite exceptional reflective capacity to be able to see beyond the educational institutions of the present to those altogether strange and different institutions which may perhaps be required only two or three generations hence. For while the efforts of our present-day higher educators serve to produce either the scholar or the civil servant or the money-maker or the cultural philistine or, finally and more usually, a compound of them all, those institutions still to be invented would have a more difficult task—though not one more difficult as such, since it would be in any event a more natural and to that extent also easier task; and can anything be more difficult than, for example, to train a young man to be a scholar, a thing contrary to nature by the methods at present employed? The difficulty, however, lies for mankind in relearning and envisaging a new goal; and it will cost an unspeakable amount of effort to exchange the fundamental idea behind our present system of education, which has its roots in the Middle Ages and the ideal of which is actually the production of the medieval scholar, for a new fundamental idea. It is already time we took a clear view of these antitheses, for some generation has to commence the struggle if another is to win it. The individual who has grasped this new fundamental idea of culture already finds himself at the crossroads; if he takes one path he will be welcome to his own age, it will not fail to offer him laurels and rewards, powerful parties will bear him along, behind him there will be as many likeminded men as there will be before him, and when the man in the front line gives the word of command it will re-echo through all the ranks. Here the first duty is 'to fight in rank and file', the second to treat as enemies all who refuse to fall in. The other path will offer him companions more seldom, it will be more difficult, more tortuous, steeper; those who have taken the first path will mock at him because his path is more wearisome and more often dangerous, and will try to entice him over to themselves. If the two paths happen to cross he will be mishandled, thrown aside or isolated by being cautiously walked around. Now, what does a cultural institution mean to these dissimilar wanderers on differing paths? The tremendous crowd that presses towards its goal along the first path understands by it the rules and arrangements by means of which it itself is brought to order and marches forward and through which all the solitary and recalcitrant, all who are looking for higher and more remote goals, are excommunicated. For the smaller band on the other path an institution would have a quite different purpose to fulfill: it wants the protection of a firm organization so as to prevent itself from being washed away and dispersed by that tremendous crowd, and so that the individuals that comprise it shall not die from premature exhaustion or even become alienated from their great task. These individuals have to complete their work—that is the sense of their staying together; and all who participate in the institution have, through continual purification and mutual support, to help to prepare within themselves and around them for the birth of the genius and the ripening of his work. Not a few, including some from the ranks of the second- and third-rate talents, are destined for the task of rendering this assistance and only in subjection to such a destiny do they come to feel they have a duty and that their lives possess significance and a goal.

He who has recognized the unreason in the nature of this age, then, will have to think of means of rendering it a little assistance; his task, however, will be to make the free spirits and those who suffer profoundly from our age acquainted with Schopenhauer, assemble them together and through them to engender a current capable of overcoming the ineptitude with which nature employs the philosopher. Such men will come to realize that the forces which blunt the effect of a great philosophy are the same as those which stand in the way of the production of a philosopher; which is why they are entitled to regard it as their goal to prepare the way for the reproduction of Schopenhauer, that is to say of the philosophical genius.

6

JOHN DEWEY

Professor John Dewey was one of the most influential American philosophers and educational thinkers. Born in 1859 in Vermont, he studied at the University of Vermont and obtained his Ph.D. from Johns Hopkins University in 1884. His first academic appointment was at the University of Michigan in "Pedagogy." Subsequently, he was a professor at the University of Chicago in 1894, where he created the famous "Lab School," which still exists. His book *The School and Society* was published in 1899 and is recognized as an important contribution to rethink the role of schools at the time.

In 1904 he became a professor of philosophy at Columbia University in New York, which also included teaching at Teachers College. Influenced by the work of his contemporaries Pierce and James, among others, he became one of the leading voices of pragmatism, an American philosophical school of thought. In a nutshell, his view of pragmatism can be summarized as judging the merits of an argument or a practice in light of their consequences, thus the need for experimentation in education. This view had an impact on his educational arguments. Although he has been associated with progressivism and progressive education, he grew in discontent with educational progressive practices that were unreflective, superficial, and wrongfully guided, resulting in an anti-intellectual experience.

A prolific writer, Dewey wrote about philosophy, art, culture, psychology, and, of course, education. Some of his books are *Experience and Nature,* published in 1925; *Art as Experience,* published in 1934; *Logic: The Theory of Inquiry,* published in 1938; and *Freedom and Culture,* published in 1939. In education some of his major contributions are *Democracy and Education,* published in 1916, and *Experience and Education,* published in 1938. Some important essays he wrote on educational matters are "The Child and the Curriculum," which is included in the selections in this chapter, and "The Relationship of Theory to Practice," which outlines his ideas of a field-based teacher education program.

In his writings about education he advocated for a student- and community-centered curriculum that acknowledges the here and now—education is not about the future but about students who are living now. Furthermore, he wanted active minds and active involvement utilizing well-designed environments that will stimulate learning. Mere facts, in his view, did not count as an education. It would be the job of the teacher to create these environments by understanding students, subject matter, and the wise use of resources. He advocated the active construction of knowledge by also engaging in a learning community. Such learning communities also included in his view the learning to interact with each other and the opportunity to experience and to learn to live in a democracy.

Democracy for Dewey was not just a political system of rules, laws, elections, and representation but also a system of interactions. Such a system incorporates the ways in which we relate to and interact with each other in multiple events and communities in everyday life. Thus, the classroom provided an ideal place to learn to interact and participate democratically. However, the development of habits of mind and habits of human interaction depended on the reflective action upon the experiences stimulated in the educational setting. Fostering critical thinking would be a sine qua non for learning.

In spite of his popularity, his progressive ideas in education seldom were implemented or tested, with the exception of some private schools and a few school districts for short periods of time. Although it can be exiting and rewarding, teaching in the ways he suggested is complex, difficult, and demanding and requires intellectual dedication. A few vulgar versions of progressivism further contributed to the rejection of this practice, particularly by the middle of the 20th century. By then, Dewey was already very critical of how progressive education had developed away from the conceptual and practical proposals he advanced. His contributions, however, are still studied, and scholars in many fields in many parts of the world cite him widely. He died in 1952 at the age of ninety-two.

REFERENCES

Archabault, R. D. *John Dewey on Education: Selected Writings.* Chicago: The University of Chicago Press, 1964.

Dewey, J. *Experience and Education.* New York: Kappa Delta Pi, 1938.

Dewey, J. *Democracy and Education: An Introduction to the Philosophy of Education.* New York: Free Press, 1997.

Dewey, J., and E. Dewey. *Schools of Tomorrow.* New York: Dutton, 1915.

THE SCHOOL AND SOCIAL PROGRESS

We are apt to look at the school from an individualistic standpoint, as something between teacher and pupil, or between teacher and parent. That which interests us most is naturally the progress made by the individual child of our acquaintance, his normal physical development, his advance in ability to read, write, and figure, his growth in the knowledge of geography and history, improvement in manners, habits of promptness, order, and industry—it is from such standards as these that we judge the work of the school. And rightly so. Yet the range of the outlook needs to be enlarged. (What the best and wisest parent wants for his own child, that must the community want for all of its children.) Any other ideal for our schools is narrow and unlovely; acted upon, it destroys our democracy. All that society has accomplished for itself is put, through the agency of the school, at the disposal of its future members. All its better thoughts of itself it hopes to realize through the new possibilities thus opened to its future self. Here individualism and socialism are at one. Only by being true to the full growth of all the individuals who make it up, can society by any chance be true to itself. And in the self-direction thus given, nothing counts as much as the school, for, as Horace Mann said, "Where anything is growing, one former is worth a thousand re-formers."

Whenever we have in mind the discussion of a new movement in education, it is especially necessary to take the broader, or social, view. Otherwise, changes in the school institution and tradition will be looked at as the arbitrary inventions of particular teachers, at the worst transitory fads, and at the best merely improvements in certain details—and this is the plane upon which it is too customary to consider school changes. It is as rational to conceive of the locomotive or the telegraph as personal devices. The modification going on in the method and curriculum of education is as much a product of the changed social situation, and as much an effort to meet the needs of the new society that is forming, as are changes in modes of industry and commerce.

It is to this, then, that I especially ask your attention: the effort to conceive what roughly may be termed the "New Education" in the light of larger changes in society. Can we connect this "New Educa-

"The School and Social Progress" and "The Child and the Curriculum" from *The School and Society* by John Dewey, 1990. Reprinted by permission of the University of Chicago Press.

tion" with the general march of events? If we can, it will lose its isolated character; it will cease to be an affair which proceeds only from the over-ingenious minds of pedagogues dealing with particular pupils. It will appear as part and parcel of the whole social evolution, and, in its more general features at least, as inevitable. Let us then ask after the main aspects of the social movement; and afterward turn to the school to find what witness it gives of effort to put itself in line. And since it is quite impossible to cover the whole ground, I shall for the most part confine myself in this chapter to one typical thing in the modern school movement—that which passes under the name of manual training—hoping, if the relation of that to changed social conditions appears, we shall be ready to concede the point as well regarding other educational innovations.

I make no apology for not dwelling at length upon the social changes in question. Those I shall mention are writ so large that he who runs may read. The change that comes first to mind, the one that overshadows and even controls all others, is the industrial one—the application of science resulting in the great inventions that have utilized the forces of nature on a vast and inexpensive scale: the growth of a worldwide market as the object of production, of vast manufacturing centers to supply this market, of cheap and rapid means of communication and distribution between all its parts. Even as to its feebler beginnings, this change is not much more than a century old; in many of its most important aspects it falls within the short span of those now living. One can hardly believe there has been a revolution in all history so rapid, so extensive, so complete. Through it the face of the earth is making over, even as to its physical forms; political boundaries are wiped out and moved about, as if they were indeed only lines on a paper map; population is hurriedly gathered into cities from the ends of the earth; habits of living are altered with startling abruptness and thoroughness; the search for the truths of nature is infinitely stimulated and facilitated, and their application to life made not only practicable, but commercially necessary. Even our moral and religious ideas and interests, the most conservative because the deepest-lying things in our nature, are profoundly affected. That this revolution should not affect education in some other than a formal and superficial fashion is inconceivable.

Back of the factory system lies the household and neighborhood system. Those of us who are here today need go back only one, two, or at most three generations, to find a time when the household was practically the center in which were carried on, or about which were clustered, all the typical forms of industrial occupation. The clothing worn was for the most part made in the house; the members of the household were usually familiar also with the shearing of the sheep, the carding and spinning of the wool, and the plying of the loom. Instead of pressing a button and flooding the house with electric light, the whole process of getting illumination was followed in its toilsome length from the killing of the animal and the trying of fat to the making of wicks and dipping of candles. The supply of flour, of lumber, of foods, of building materials, of household furniture, even of metal ware, of nails, hinges, hammers, etc., was produced in the immediate neighborhood, in shops which were constantly open to inspection and often centers of neighborhood congregation. The entire industrial process stood revealed, from the production on the farm of the raw materials till the finished article was actually put to use. Not only this, but practically every member of the household had his own share in the work. The children, as they gained in strength and capacity, were gradually initiated into the mysteries of the several processes. It was a matter of immediate and personal concern, even to the point of actual participation.

We cannot overlook the factors of discipline and of character-building involved in this kind of life: training in habits of order and of industry, and in the idea of responsibility, of obligation to do something, to produce something, in the world. There was always something which really needed to be done, and a real necessity that each member of the household should do his own part faithfully and in co-operation with others. Personalities which became effective in action were bred and tested in the medium of action. Again, we cannot overlook the importance for educational purposes of the close and intimate acquaintance got with nature at first hand, with real things and materials, with the actual processes of their manipulation, and the knowledge of their social necessities and uses. In all this there was continual training of observation, of ingenuity, constructive imagination, of logical thought, and of the sense of reality acquired through first-hand contact with actualities. The educative forces of the domestic spinning and weaving, of the sawmill, the gristmill, the cooper shop, and the blacksmith forge, were continuously operative.

No number of object-lessons, got up as object-lessons for the sake of giving information, can afford even the shadow of a substitute for acquaintance with the plants and animals of the farm and garden acquired through actual living among them and caring for them. No training of sense-organs in school, introduced for the sake of training, can begin to compete with the alertness and fulness of sense-life that comes through daily intimacy and interest in familiar occupations. Verbal memory can be trained in committing tasks, a certain discipline of the reasoning powers can be acquired through lessons in science and mathematics; but, after all, this is somewhat remote and shadowy compared with the training of attention and of judgment that is acquired in having to do things with a real motive behind and a real outcome ahead. At present, concentration of industry and division of labor have practically eliminated household and neighborhood occupations—at least for educational purposes. But it is useless to bemoan the departure of the good old days of children's modesty, reverence, and implicit obedience, if we expect merely by bemoaning and by exhortation to bring them back. It is radical conditions which have changed, and only an equally radical change in education suffices. We must recognize our compensations—the increase in toleration, in breadth of social judgment, the larger acquaintance with human nature, the sharpened alertness in reading signs of character and interpreting social situations, greater accuracy of adaptation to differing personalities, contact with greater commercial activities. These considerations mean much to the city-bred child of today. Yet there is a real problem: how shall we retain these advantages, and yet introduce into the school something representing the other side of life—occupations which exact personal responsibilities and which train the child in relation to the physical realities of life?

When we turn to the school, we find that one of the most striking tendencies at present is toward the introduction of so-called manual training, shopwork, and the household arts—sewing and cooking.

This has not been done "on purpose," with a full consciousness that the school must now supply that factor of training formerly taken care of in the home, but rather by instinct, by experimenting and finding that such work takes a vital hold of pupils and gives them something which was not to be got in any other way. Consciousness of its real import is still so weak that the work is often done in a half-hearted, confused, and unrelated way. The reasons assigned to justify it are painfully inadequate or sometimes even positively wrong.

If we were to cross-examine even those who are most favorably disposed to the introduction of this work into our school system, we should, I imagine, generally find the main reasons to be that such work engages the full spontaneous interest and attention of the children. It keeps them alert and active, instead of passive and receptive; it makes them more useful, more capable, and hence more inclined to be helpful at home; it prepares them to some extent for the practical duties of later life—the girls to be more efficient house managers, if not actually cooks and seamstresses; the boys (were our educational system only adequately rounded out into trade schools) for their future vocations. I do not underestimate the worth of these reasons. Of those indicated by the changed attitude of the children I shall indeed have something to say in the next chapter, when speaking directly of the relationship of the school to the child. But the point of view is, upon the whole, unnecessarily narrow. We must conceive of work in wood and metal, of weaving, sewing, and cooking, as methods of living and learning, not as distinct studies.

We must conceive of them in their social significance, as types of the processes by which society keeps itself going, as agencies for bringing home to the child some of the primal necessities of community life, and as ways in which these needs have been met by the growing insight and ingenuity of man; in short, as instrumentalities through which the school itself shall be made a genuine form of active community life, instead of a place set apart in which to learn lessons.

A society is a number of people held together because they are working along common lines, in a common spirit, and with reference to common aims. The common needs and aims demand a growing interchange of thought and growing unity of sympathetic feeling. The radical reason that the present school cannot organize itself as a natural social unit is because just this element of common and productive activity is absent. Upon the playground, in game and sport, social organization takes place spontaneously and inevitably. There is something to do, some activity to be carried on, requiring natural divisions of labor, selection of leaders and followers, mutual co-operation and emulation. In the school-room the motive and the cement of social organization are alike wanting. Upon the ethical side, the tragic weakness of the present school is that it endeavors to prepare future members of the social order in a medium in which the conditions of the social spirit are eminently wanting.

The difference that appears when occupations are made the articulating centers of school life is not easy to describe in words; it is a difference in motive, of spirit and atmosphere. As one enters a busy kitchen in which a group of children are actively engaged in the preparation of food, the psychological difference, the change from more or less passive and inert recipiency and restraint to one of buoyant outgoing energy, is so obvious as fairly to strike one in the face. Indeed, to those whose image of the school is rigidly set the change is sure to give a shock. But the change in the social attitude is equally marked. The mere absorbing of facts and truths is so exclusively individual an affair that it tends very naturally to pass into selfishness. There is no obvious social motive for the acquirement of mere learning, there is no clear social gain in success thereat. Indeed, almost the only measure for success is a competitive one, in the bad sense of that term—a comparison of results in the recitation or in the examination to see which child has succeeded in getting ahead of others in storing up, in accumulating, the maximum of information. So thoroughly is this the prevailing atmosphere that for one child to help another in his task has become a school crime. Where the school work consists in simply learning lessons, mutual assistance, instead of being the most natural form of co-operation and association, becomes a clandestine effort to relieve one's neighbor of his proper duties. Where active work is going on, all this is changed. Helping others, instead of being a form of charity which impoverishes the recipient, is simply an aid in setting free the powers and furthering the impulse of the one helped. A spirit of free communication, of interchange of ideas, suggestions, results, both successes and failures of previous experiences, becomes the dominating note of the recitation. So far as emulation enters in, it is in the comparison of individuals, not with regard to the quantity of information personally absorbed, but with reference to the quality of work done—the genuine community standard of value. In an informal but all the more pervasive way, the school life organizes itself on a social basis.

Within this organization is found the principle of school discipline or order. Of course, order is simply a thing which is relative to an end. If you have the end in view of forty or fifty children learning certain set lessons, to be recited to a teacher, your discipline must be devoted to securing that result. But if the end in view is the development of a spirit of social co-operation and community life, discipline must grow out of and be relative to such an aim. There is little of one sort of order where things are in process of construction; there is a certain disorder in any busy workshop; there is not silence; persons are not engaged in maintaining certain fixed physical postures; their arms are not folded; they are not holding their books thus and so. They are doing a variety of things, and there is the confusion, the bustle, that results from activity. But out of the occupation, out of doing things that are to produce results, and out of doing these in a social and co-operative way, there is born a discipline of its own kind and type. Our whole conception of school discipline changes when we get this point of view. In critical moments we all realize that the only discipline that stands by us, the only training that becomes intuition, is that got through life itself. That we learn from experience, and from books or the sayings of others *only* as they are related to experience, are not mere phrases. But the school has been so set apart, so isolated from the ordinary conditions and motives of life, that the place where children are sent for discipline is the one place in the world where it is most difficult to get experience—the mother of all discipline worth the name. It is only when a narrow and fixed image of traditional school discipline dominates that one is in any danger of overlooking that deeper and infinitely wider discipline that comes from having a part to do in constructive work, in contributing to a result which, social in spirit, is none the less obvious and tangible in form—and hence in a form with reference to which responsibility may be exacted and accurate judgment passed.

The great thing to keep in mind, then, regarding the introduction into the school of various forms of active occupation, is that through them the entire spirit of the school is renewed. It has a chance to affiliate itself with life, to become the child's habitat, where he learns through directed living, instead of being only a place to learn lessons having an abstract and remote reference to some possible living to be done in the future. It gets a chance to be a miniature community, an embryonic society. This is the fundamental fact, and from this arise continuous and orderly streams of instruction. Under the industrial régime described, the child, after all, shared in the work, not for the sake of the sharing, but for the sake of the product. The educational results secured were real, yet incidental and dependent. But in the school the typical occupations followed are freed from all economic stress. The aim is not the economic value of the products, but the development of social power and insight. It is this liberation from narrow utilities, this openness to the possibilities of the human spirit, that makes these practical activities in the school allies of art and centers of science and history.

THE CHILD AND THE CURRICULUM

Profound differences in theory are never gratuitous or invented. They grow out of conflicting elements in a genuine problem—a problem which is genuine just because the elements, taken as they stand, are conflicting. Any significant problem involves conditions that for the moment contradict each other. Solution comes only by getting away from the meaning of terms that is already fixed upon and coming to see the conditions from another point of view, and hence in a fresh light. But this reconstruction means travail of thought. Easier than thinking with surrender of already formed ideas and detachment from facts already learned is just to stick by what is already said, looking about for something with which to buttress it against attack.

Thus sects arise: schools of opinion. Each selects that set of conditions that appeals to it; and then erects them into a complete and independent truth, instead of treating them as a factor in a problem, needing adjustment.

The fundamental factors in the educative process are an immature, undeveloped being; and certain social aims, meanings, values incarnate in the matured experience of the adult. The educative process is the due interaction of these forces. Such a conception of each in relation to the other as facilitates completest and freest interaction is the essence of educational theory.

But here comes the effort of thought. It is easier to see the conditions in their separateness, to insist upon one at the expense of the other, to make antagonists of them, than to discover a reality to which each belongs. The easy thing is to seize upon something in the nature of the child, or upon something in the developed consciousness of the adult, and insist upon *that* as the key to the whole problem. When this happens a really serious practical problem—that of interaction—is transformed into an unreal, and hence insoluble, theoretic problem. Instead of seeing the educative steadily and as a whole, we see conflicting terms. We get the case of the child *vs.* the curriculum; of the individual nature *vs.* social culture. Below all other divisions in pedagogic opinion lies this opposition.

The child lives in a somewhat narrow world of personal contacts. Things hardly come within his experience unless they touch, intimately and obviously, his own well-being, or that of his family and friends. His world is a world of persons with their personal interests, rather than a realm of facts and laws. Not truth, in the sense of conformity to external fact, but affection and sympathy, is its keynote. As against this, the course of study met in the school presents material stretching back indefinitely in time, and extending outward indefinitely into space. The child is taken out of his familiar physical environment, hardly more than a square mile or so in area, into the wide world—yes, and even to the bounds of the solar system. His little span of personal memory and tradition is overlaid with the long centuries of the history of all peoples.

Again, the child's life is an integral, a total one. He passes quickly and readily from one topic to another, as from one spot to another, but is not conscious of transition or break. There is no conscious isolation, hardly conscious distinction. The things that occupy him are held together by the unity of the personal and social interests which his life carries along. Whatever is uppermost in his mind constitutes to him, for the time being, the whole universe. That universe is fluid and fluent; its contents dissolve and re-form with amazing rapidity. But, after all, it is the child's own world. It has the unity and completeness of his own life. He goes to school, and various studies divide and fractionize the world for him. Geography selects, it abstracts and analyzes one set of facts, and from one particular point of view. Arithmetic is another division, grammar another department, and so on indefinitely.

Again, in school each of these subjects is classified. Facts are torn away from their original place in experience and rearranged with reference to some general principle. Classification is not a matter of child experience; things do not come to the individual pigeonholed. The vital ties of affection, the connecting bonds of activity, hold together the variety of his personal experiences. The adult mind is so familiar with the notion of logically ordered facts that it does not recognize—it cannot realize—the amount of separating and reformulating which the facts of direct experience have to undergo before they can appear as a "study," or branch of learning. A principle, for the intellect, has had to be distinguished and defined; facts have had to be interpreted in relation to this principle, not as they are in themselves. They have had to be regathered about a new center which is wholly abstract and ideal. All this means a development of a special intellectual interest. It means ability to view facts impartially and objectively; that is, without reference to their place and meaning in one's own experience. It means capacity to analyze and to synthesize. It means highly matured intellectual habits and the command of a definite technique and apparatus of scientific inquiry.

The studies as classified are the product, in a word, of the science of the ages, not of the experience of the child.

These apparent deviations and differences between child and curriculum might be almost indefinitely widened. But we have here sufficiently fundamental divergences: first, the narrow but personal world of the child against the impersonal but infinitely extended world of space and time; second, the unity, the single wholeheartedness of the child's life, and the specializations and divisions of the curriculum; third, an abstract principle of logical classification and arrangement, and the practical and emotional bonds of child life.

From these elements of conflict grow up different educational sects. One school fixes its attention upon the importance of the subject-matter of the curriculum as compared with the contents of the child's own experience. It is as if they said: Is life petty, narrow, and crude? Then studies reveal the great, wide universe with all its fulness and complexity of meaning. Is the life of the child egoistic, self-centered, impulsive? Then in these studies is found an objective universe of truth, law, and order. Is his experience confused, vague, uncertain, at the mercy of the moment's caprice and circumstance? Then studies introduce a world arranged on the basis of eternal and general truth; a world where all is measured and defined. Hence the moral: ignore and minimize the child's individual peculiarities, whims, and experiences. They are what we need to get away from. They are to be obscured or eliminated. As educators our work is precisely to substitute for these superficial and casual affairs stable and well-ordered realities; and these are found in studies and lessons.

Subdivide each topic into studies; each study into lessons; each lesson into specific facts and formulae. Let the child proceed step by step to master each one of these separate parts, and at last he will have covered the entire ground. The road which looks so long when viewed in its entirety is easily traveled, considered as a series of particular steps. Thus emphasis is put upon the logical subdivisions and consecutions of the subject-matter. Problems of instruction are problems of procuring texts giving logical parts and sequences, and of presenting these portions in class in a similar definite and graded way. Subject-matter furnishes the end, and it determines method. The child is simply the immature being who is to be matured; he is the superficial being who is to be deepened; his is narrow experience which is to be widened. It is his to receive, to accept. His part is fulfilled when he is ductile and docile.

Not so, says the other sect. The child is the starting-point, the center, and the end. His development, his growth, is the ideal. It alone furnishes the standard. To the growth of the child all studies are subservient; they are instruments valued as they serve the needs of growth. Personality, character, is more than subject-matter. Not knowledge or information, but self-realization, is the goal. To possess all the world of knowledge and lose one's own self is as awful a fate in education as in religion. Moreover, subject-matter never can be got into the child from without. Learning is active. It involves reaching out of the mind. It involves organic assimilation starting from within. Literally, we must take our stand with the child and our departure from him. It is he and not the subject-matter which determines both quality and quantity of learning.

The only significant method is the method of the mind as it reaches out and assimilates. Subject-matter is but spiritual food, possible nutritive material. It cannot digest itself; it cannot of its own accord turn into bone and muscle and blood. The source of whatever is dead, mechanical, and formal in schools is found precisely in the subordination of the life and experience of the child to the curriculum. It is because of this that "study" has become a synonym for what is irksome, and a lesson identical with a task.

This fundamental opposition of child and curriculum set up by these two modes of doctrine can be duplicated in a series of other terms. "Discipline" is the watchword of those who magnify the course of study; "interest" that of those who blazon "The Child" upon their banner. The standpoint of the former is logical; that of the latter psychological. The first emphasizes the necessity of adequate training and scholarship on the part of the teacher; the latter that of need of sympathy with the child, and knowledge of his natural instincts. "Guidance and control" are the catchwords of one school; "freedom and initiative" of the other. Law is asserted here; spontaneity proclaimed there. The old, the conservation of what has been achieved in the pain and toil of the ages, is dear to the one; the new, change, progress, wins the affection of the other. Inertness and routine, chaos and anarchism, are accusations bandied back and forth. Neglect of the sacred authority of duty is charged by one side, only to be met by counter-charges of suppression of individuality through tyrannical despotism.

Such oppositions are rarely carried to their logical conclusion. Common-sense recoils at the extreme character of these results. They are left to theorists, while common-sense vibrates back and forward in a maze of inconsistent compromise. The need of getting theory and practical common-sense into closer connection suggests a return to our original thesis: that we have here conditions which are necessarily related to each other in the educative process, since this is precisely one of interaction and adjustment.

What, then, is the problem? It is just to get rid of the prejudicial notion that there is some gap in kind (as distinct from degree) between the child's experience and the various forms of subject-matter that make up the course of study. From the side of the child, it is a question of seeing how his experience already contains within itself elements—facts and truths—of just the same sort as those entering into the formulated study; and, what is of more importance, of how it contains within itself the attitudes, the motives, and the interests which have operated in developing and organizing the subject-matter to the plane which it now occupies. From the side of the studies, it is a question of interpreting them as outgrowths of forces operating in the child's life, and of discovering the steps that intervene between the child's present experience and their richer maturity.

Abandon the notion of subject-matter as something fixed and ready-made in itself, outside the child's experience; cease thinking of the child's experience as also something hard and fast; see it as something fluent, embryonic, vital; and we realize that the child and the curriculum are simply two limits which define a single process. Just as two points define a straight line, so the present standpoint of the child and the facts and truths of studies define instruction. It is continuous reconstruction, moving from the child's present experience out into that represented by the organized bodies of truth that we call studies.

On the face of it, the various studies, arithmetic, geography, language, botany, etc., are themselves experience—they are that of the race. They embody the cumulative outcome of the efforts, the strivings, and the successes of the human race generation after generation. They present this, not as a mere accumulation, not as a miscellaneous heap of separate bits of experience, but in some organized and systematized way—that is, as reflectively formulated.

Hence, the facts and truths that enter into the child's present experience, and those contained in the subject-matter of studies, are the initial and final terms of one reality. To oppose one to the other is to oppose the infancy and maturity of the same growing life; it is to set the moving tendency and the final result of the same process over against each other; it is to hold that the nature and the destiny of the child war with each other.

If such be the case, the problem of the relation of the child and the curriculum presents itself in this guise: Of what use, educationally speaking, is it to be able to see the end in the beginning? How does it assist us in dealing with the early stages of growth to be able to anticipate its later phases? The studies, as we have agreed, represent the possibilities of development inherent in the child's immediate crude experience. But, after all, they are not parts of that present and immediate life. Why, then, or how, make account of them?

Asking such a question suggests its own answer. To see the outcome is to know in what direction the present experience is moving, provided it move normally and soundly. The far-away point, which is of no significance to us simply as far away, becomes of huge importance the moment we take it as defining a present direction of movement. Taken in this way it is no remote and distant result to be achieved, but a guiding method in dealing with the present. The systematized and defined experience of the adult mind, in other words, is of value to us in interpreting the child's life as it immediately shows itself, and in passing on to guidance or direction.

Let us look for a moment at these two ideas: interpretation and guidance. The child's present experience is in no way self-explanatory. It is not final, but transitional. It is nothing complete in itself, but just a sign or index of certain growth-tendencies. As long as we confine our gaze to what the child here and now puts forth, we are confused and misled. We cannot read its meaning. Extreme depreciations of the child morally and intellectually, and sentimental idealizations of him, have their root in a common fallacy. Both spring from taking stages of a growth or movement as something cut off and fixed. The first fails to see the promise contained in feelings and deeds which, taken by themselves, are uncompromising and repellent; the second fails to see that even the most pleasing and beautiful exhibitions are but signs, and that they begin to spoil and rot the moment they are treated as achievements.

What we need is something which will enable us to interpret, to appraise, the elements in the child's present puttings forth and fallings away, his exhibitions of power and weakness, in the light of some larger growth-process in which they have their place. Only in this way can we discriminate. If we isolate the child's present inclinations, purposes, and experiences from the place they occupy and the part they have to perform in a developing experience, all stand upon the same level; all alike are equally good and equally bad. But in the movement of life different elements stand upon different planes of value. Some of the child's deeds are symptoms of a waning tendency; they are survivals in functioning of an organ which has done its part and is passing out of vital use. To give positive attention to such qualities is to arrest development upon a lower level. It is systematically to maintain a rudimentary phase of growth. Other activities are signs of a culminating power and interest; to them applies the maxim of striking while the iron is hot. As regards them, it is perhaps a matter of now or never. Selected, utilized, emphasized, they may mark a turning-point for good in the child's whole career; neglected, an opportunity goes, never to be recalled. Other acts and feelings are prophetic; they represent the dawning of flickering light that will shine steadily only in the far future. As regards them there is little at present to do but give them fair and full chance, waiting for the future for definite direction.

Just as, upon the whole, it was the weakness of the "old education" that it made invidious comparisons between the immaturity of the child and the maturity of the adult, regarding the former as something to be got away from as soon as possible and as much as possible; so it is the danger of the "new education" that it regard the child's present powers and interests as something finally significant in themselves. In truth, his learnings and achievements are fluid and moving. They change from day to day and from hour to hour.

It will do harm if child-study leave in the popular mind the impression that a child of a given age has a positive equipment of purposes and interests to be cultivated just as they stand. Interests in reality are but attitudes toward possible experiences; they are not achievements; their worth is in the leverage they afford, not in the accomplishment they represent. To take the phenomena presented at a given age as in any way self-explanatory or self-contained is inevitably to result in indulgence and spoiling. Any power, whether of child or adult, is indulged when it is taken on its given and present level in consciousness. Its genuine meaning is in the propulsion it affords toward a higher level. It is just something to do with. Appealing to the interest upon the present plane means excitation; it means playing with a power so as continually to stir it up without directing it toward definite achievement. Continuous initiation, continuous starting of activities that do not arrive, is, for all practical purposes, as bad as the continual repression of initiative in conformity with supposed interests of some more perfect thought or will. It is as if the child were forever tasting and never eating; always having his palate tickled upon the emotional side, but never getting the organic satisfaction that comes only with digestion of food and transformation of it into working power.

As against such a view, the subject-matter of science and history and art serves to reveal the real child to us. We do not know the meaning either of his tendencies or of his performances excepting as we take them as germinating seed, or opening bud, of some fruit to be borne. The whole world of visual nature is all too small an answer to the problem of the meaning of the child's instinct for light and form. The entire science of physics is none too much to interpret adequately to us what is involved in some simple demand of the child for explanation of some casual change that has attracted his attention. The art of Raphael or of Corot is none too much to enable us to value the impulses stirring in the child when he draws and daubs.

So much for the use of the subject-matter in interpretation. Its further employment in direction or guidance is but an expansion of the same thought. To interpret the fact is to see it in its vital movement, to see it in its relation to growth. But to view it as a part of a normal growth is to secure the basis for guiding it. Guidance is not external imposition. It is freeing the life-process for its own most adequate fulfilment. What was said about disregard of the child's present experience because of its remoteness from mature experience; and of the sentimental idealization of the child's naive caprices and performances, may be repeated here with slightly altered phrase. There are those who see no alternative between forcing the child from without, or leaving him entirely alone. Seeing no alternative, some choose one mode, some another. Both fall into the same fundamental error. Both fail to see that development is a definite process, having its own law which can be fulfilled only when adequate and normal conditions are provided. Really to interpret the child's present crude impulses in counting, measuring, and arranging things in rhythmic series involves mathematical scholarship—a knowledge of the mathematical formulae and relations which have, in the history of the race, grown out of just such crude beginnings. To see the whole history of development which intervenes between these two terms is simply to see what step the child needs to take just here and now; to what use he needs to put his blind impulse in order that it may get clarity and gain force.

If, once more, the "old education" tended to ignore the dynamic quality, the developing force inherent in the child's present experience, and therefore to assume that direction and control were just matters of arbitrarily putting the child in a given path and compelling him to walk there, the "new education" is in danger of taking the idea of development in altogether too formal and empty a way. The child is expected to "develop" this or that fact or truth out of his own mind. He is told to think things out, or work things out for himself, without being supplied any of the environing conditions which are requisite to start and guide thought. Nothing can be developed from nothing; nothing but the crude can be developed out of the crude—and this is what surely happens when we throw the child back upon his achieved self as a finality, and invite him to spin new truths of nature or of conduct out of that. It is certainly as futile to expect a child to evolve a universe out of his own mere mind as it is for a philosopher to attempt that task. Development does not mean just getting something out of the mind. It is a development of experience and into experience that is really wanted. And this is impossible save as just that educative medium is provided which will enable the powers and interests that have been selected as valuable to function. They must operate, and how they operate will depend almost entirely upon the stimuli which surround them and the material upon which they exercise themselves. The problem of direction is thus the problem of selecting appropriate stimuli for instincts and impulses which it is desired to employ in the gaining of new experience. What new experiences are desirable, and thus what stimuli are needed, it is impossible to tell except as there is some comprehension of the development which is aimed at; except, in a word, as the adult knowledge is drawn upon as revealing the possible career open to the child.

It may be of use to distinguish and to relate to each other the logical and the psychological aspects of experience—the former standing for subject-matter in itself, the latter for it in relation to the child. A psychological statement of experience follows its actual growth; it is historic; it notes steps actually taken, the uncertain and tortuous, as well as the efficient and successful. The logical point of view, on the other hand, assumes that the development has reached a certain positive stage of fulfilment. It neglects the process and considers the outcome. It summarizes and arranges, and thus separates the achieved results from the actual steps by which they were forthcoming in the first instance. We may compare the difference between the logical and the psychological to the difference between the notes which an explorer makes in a new country, blazing a trail and finding his way along as best he may, and the finished map that is constructed after the country has been thoroughly explored. The two are mutually dependent. Without the more or less accidental and devious paths traced by the explorer there would be no facts which could be utilized in the making of the complete and related chart. But no one would get the benefit of the explorer's trip if it was not compared and checked up with similar wanderings undertaken by others; unless the new geographical facts learned, the streams crossed, the mountains climbed, etc., were viewed, not as mere incidents in the journey of the particular traveler, but (quite apart from the individual explorer's life) in relation to other similar facts already known. The map orders individual experiences, connecting them with one another irrespective of the local and temporal circumstances and accidents of their original discovery.

Of what use is this formulated statement of experience? Of what use is the map?

Well, we may first tell what the map is not. The map is not a substitute for a personal experience. The map does not take the place of an actual journey. The logically formulated material of a science or branch of learning, of a study, is no substitute for the having of individual experiences. The mathematical formula for a falling body does not take the place of personal contact and immediate individual experience with the falling thing. But the map, a summary, an arranged and orderly view of previous experiences, serves as a guide to future experience; it gives direction; it facilitates control; it economizes effort, preventing useless wandering, and pointing out the paths which lead most quickly and most certainly to a desired result. Through the map every new traveler may get for his own journey the benefits of the results of others' explorations without the waste of energy and loss of time involved in their wanderings—wanderings which he himself would be obliged to repeat were it not for just the assistance of the objective and generalized record of their performances. That which we call a science or study puts the net product of past experience in the form which makes it most available for the future. It represents a capitalization which may at once be turned to interest. It economizes the workings of the mind in every way. Memory is less taxed because the facts are grouped together about some common principle, instead of being connected solely with the varying incidents of their original discovery. Observation is assisted; we know what to look for and where to look. It is the difference between looking for a needle in a haystack, and searching for a given paper in a well-arranged cabinet. Reasoning is directed, because there is a certain general path or line laid out along which ideas naturally march, instead of moving from one chance association to another.

There is, then, nothing final about a logical rendering of experience. Its value is not contained in itself; its significance is that of standpoint, outlook, method. It intervenes between the more casual, tentative, and roundabout experiences of the past, and more controlled and orderly experiences of the future. It gives past experience in that net form which renders it most available and most significant, most fecund for future experience. The abstractions; generalizations, and classifications which it introduces all have prospective meaning.

The formulated result is then not to be opposed to the process of growth. The logical is not set over against the psychological. The surveyed and arranged result occupies a critical position in the process of growth. It marks a turning-point. It shows how we may get the benefit of past effort in controlling future endeavor. In the largest sense the logical standpoint is itself psychological; it has its meaning as a point in the development of experience, and its justification is in its functioning in the future growth which it insures.

Hence the need of reinstating into experience the subject-matter of the studies, or branches of learning. It must be restored to the experience from which it has been abstracted. It needs to be *psychologized*; turned over, translated into the immediate and individual experiencing within which it has its origin and significance.

Every study or subject thus has two aspects: one for the scientist as a scientist; the other for the teacher as a teacher. These two aspects are in no sense opposed or conflicting. But neither are they immediately identical. For the scientist, the subject-matter represents simply a given body of truth to be employed in locating new problems, instituting new researches, and carrying them through to a verified outcome. To him the subject-matter of the science is self-contained. He refers various portions of it to each other; he connects new facts with it. He is not, as a scientist, called upon to travel outside its particular bounds; if he does, it is only to get more facts of the same general sort. The problem of the teacher is a different one. As a teacher he is not concerned with adding new facts to the science he teaches; in propounding new hypotheses or in verifying them. He is concerned with the subject-matter of the science as *representing a given stage and phase of the development of experience.*

His problem is that of inducing a vital and personal experiencing. Hence, what concerns him, as teacher, is the ways in which that subject may become a part of experience; what there is in the child's present that is usable with reference to it; how such elements are to be used; how his own knowledge of the subject-matter may assist in interpreting the child's needs and doings, and determine the medium in which the child should be placed in order that his growth may be properly directed. He is concerned, not with the subject-matter as such, but with the subject-matter as a related factor in a total and growing experience. Thus to see it is to psychologize it.

It is the failure to keep in mind the double aspect of subject-matter which causes the curriculum and child to be set over against each other as described in our early pages. The subject-matter, just as it is for the scientist, has no direct relationship to the child's present experience. It stands outside of it. The danger here is not a merely theoretical one. We are practically threatened on all sides. Textbook and teacher vie with each other in presenting to the child the subject-matter as it stands to the specialist. Such modification and revision as it undergoes are a mere elimination of certain scientific difficulties, and the general reduction to a lower intellectual level. The material is not translated into life-terms, but is directly offered as a substitute for, or an external annex to, the child's present life.

Three typical evils result: In the first place, the lack of any organic connection with what the child has already seen and felt and loved makes the material purely formal and symbolic. There is a sense in which it is impossible to value too highly the formal and the symbolic. The genuine form, the real symbol, serve as methods in the holding and discovery of truth. They are tools by which the individual pushes out most surely and widely into unexplored areas. They are means by which he brings to bear whatever of reality he has succeeded in gaining in past searchings. But this happens only when the symbol really symbolizes—when it stands for and sums up in shorthand actual experiences which the individual has already gone through. A symbol which is induced from without, which has not been led up to in preliminary activities, is, as we say, a *bare* or *mere* symbol; it is dead and barren. Now, any fact, whether of arithmetic, or geography, or grammar, which is not led up to and into out of something which has previously occupied a significant position in the child's life for its own sake, is forced into this position. It is not a reality, but just the sign of a reality which *might* be experienced if certain conditions were fulfilled. But the abrupt presentation of the fact as something known by others, and requiring only to be studied and learned by the child, rules out such conditions of fulfilment. It condemns the fact to be a hieroglyph: it would mean something if one only had the key. The clue being lacking, it remains an idle curiosity, to fret and obstruct the mind, a dead weight to burden it.

The second evil in this external presentation is lack of motivation. There are not only no facts or truths which have been previously felt as such with which to appropriate and assimilate the new, but there is no craving, no need, no demand. When the subject-matter has been psychologized, that is, viewed as an outgrowth of present tendencies and activities, it is easy to locate in the present some obstacle, intellectual, practical, or ethical, which can be handled more adequately if the truth in question be mastered. This need supplies motive for the learning. An end which is the child's own carries him on to possess the means of its accomplishment. But when material is directly supplied in the form of a lesson to be learned as a lesson, the connecting links of need and aim are conspicuous for their absence. What we mean by the mechanical and dead in instruction is a result of this lack of motivation. The organic and vital mean interaction—they mean play of mental demand and material supply.

The third evil is that even the most scientific matter, arranged in most logical fashion, loses this quality, when presented in external, ready-made fashion, by the time it gets to the child. It has to undergo some modification in order to shut out some phases too hard to grasp, and to reduce some of the attendant difficulties. What happens? Those things which are most significant to the scientific man, and most valuable in the logic of actual inquiry and classification, drop out. The really thought-provoking character is obscured, and the organizing function disappears. Or, as we commonly say, the child's reasoning powers, the faculty of abstraction and generalization, are not adequately developed. So the subject-matter is evacuated of its logical value, and, though it is what it is only from the logical standpoint, is presented as stuff only for "memory." This is the contradiction: the child gets the advantage neither of the adult logical formulation, nor of his own native competencies of apprehension and response. Hence the logic of the child is hampered and mortified, and we are almost fortunate if he does not get actual non-science, flat and common-place residue of what was gaining scientific vitality a generation or two ago—degenerate reminiscence of what someone else once formulated on the basis of the experience that some further person had, once upon a time, experienced.

The train of evils does not cease. It is all too common for opposed erroneous theories to play straight into each other's hands. Psychological considerations may be slurred or shoved one side; they cannot be crowded out. Put out of the door, they come back through the window. Somehow and somewhere motive must be appealed to, connection must be established between the mind and its material. There is no question of getting along without this bond of connection; the only question is whether it be such as grows out of the material itself in relation to the mind, or be imported and hitched on from some outside source. If the subject-matter of the lessons be such as to have an appropriate place within the expanding consciousness of the child, if it grows out of his own past doings, thinkings, and sufferings, and grows into application in further achievements and receptivities, then no device or trick of method has to be resorted to in order to enlist "interest." The psychologized is of interest—that is, it is placed in the whole of conscious life so that it shares the worth of that life. But the externally presented material, conceived and generated in standpoints and attitudes remote from the child, and developed in motives alien to him, has no such place of its own. Hence the recourse to adventitious leverage to push it in, to factitious drill to drive it in, to artificial bribe to lure it in.

Three aspects of this recourse to outside ways for giving the subject matter some psychological meaning may be worth mentioning. Familiarity breeds contempt, but it also breeds something like affection. We get used to the chains we wear, and we miss them when removed. 'Tis an old story that through custom we finally embrace what at first wore a hideous mien. Unpleasant, because meaningless, activities may get agreeable if long enough persisted in. *It is possible for the mind to develop interest in a routine or mechanical procedure it conditions are continually supplied which demand that mode of operation and preclude any other sort.* I frequently hear dulling devices and empty exercises defended and extolled because "the children take such an 'interest' in them." Yes, that is the worst of it; the mind, shut out from worthy employ and missing the taste of adequate performance, comes down to the level of that which is left to it to know and do, and perforce takes an interest in a cabined and cramped experience. To find satisfaction in its own exercise is the normal law of mind, and if large and meaningful business for the mind be denied, it tries to content itself with the formal movements that remain to it—and too often succeeds, save in those cases of more intense activity which cannot accommodate themselves, and that make up the unruly and *declassé* of our school product. An interest in the formal apprehension of symbols and in their memorized reproduction becomes in many pupils a substitute for the original and vital interest in reality; and all because, the subject-matter of the course of study being out of relation to the concrete mind of the individual, some substitute bond to hold it in some kind of working relation to the mind must be discovered and elaborated.

The second substitute for living motivation in the subject-matter is that of contrast-effects; the material of the lesson is rendered interesting, if not in itself, at least in contrast with some alternative experience. To learn the lesson is more interesting than to take a scolding, be held up to general ridicule, stay after school, receive degradingly low marks, or fail to be promoted. And very much of what goes by the name of "discipline," and prides itself upon opposing the doctrines of a soft pedagogy and upon upholding the banner of effort and duty, is nothing more or less than just this appeal to "interest" in its obverse aspect—to fear, to dislike of various kinds of physical, social, and personal pain. The subject-matter does not appeal; it cannot appeal; it lacks origin and bearing in a growing experience. So the appeal is to the thousand and one outside and irrelevant agencies which may serve to throw, by sheer rebuff and rebound, the mind back upon the material from which it is constantly wandering.

Human nature being what it is, however, it tends to seek its motivation in the agreeable rather than in the disagreeable, in direct pleasure rather than in alternative pain. And so has come up the modern theory and practice of the "interesting," in the false sense of that term. The material is still left; so far as its own characteristics are concerned, just material externally selected and formulated. It is still just so much geography and arithmetic and grammar study; not so much potentiality of child-experience with regard to language, earth, and numbered and measured reality. Hence the difficulty of bringing the mind to bear upon it; hence its repulsiveness; the tendency for attention to wander; for other acts and images to crowd in and expel the lesson. The legitimate way out is to transform the material; to psychologize it—that is, once more, to take it and to develop it within the range and scope of the child's life. But it is easier and simpler to leave it as it is, and then by trick of method to *arouse* interest, to *make* it *interesting*; to cover it with sugar-coating; to conceal its barrenness by intermediate and unrelated material; and finally, as it were, to get the child to swallow and digest the unpalatable morsel while he is enjoying tasting something quite different. But alas for the analogy! Mental assimilation is a matter of consciousness; and if the attention has not been playing upon the actual material, that has not been apprehended, nor worked into faculty.

How, then, stands the case of Child *vs.* Curriculum? What shall the verdict be? The radical fallacy in the original pleadings with which we set out is the supposition that we have no choice save either to leave the child to his own unguided spontaneity or to inspire direction upon him from without. Action is response; it is adaptation, adjustment. There is no such thing as sheer self-activity possible—because all activity takes place in a medium, in a situation, and with reference to its conditions. But, again, no such thing as imposition of truth from without, as insertion of truth from without, is possible. All depends upon the activity which the mind itself undergoes in responding to what is presented from without. Now, the value of the formulated wealth of knowledge that makes up the course of study is that it may enable the educator *to determine the environment of the child,* and thus by indirection to direct. Its primary value, its primary indication, is for the teacher, not for the child. It says to the teacher: Such and such are the capacities, the fulfilments, in truth and beauty and behavior, open to these children. Now see to it that day by day the conditions are such that *their own activities* move inevitably in this direction, toward such culmination of themselves. Let the child's nature fulfil its own destiny, revealed to you in whatever of science and art and industry the world now holds as its own.

The case is of Child. It is his present powers which are to assert themselves; his present capacities which are to be exercised; his present attitudes which are to be realized. But save as the teacher knows, knows wisely and thoroughly, the race-expression which is embodied in that thing we call the Curriculum, the teacher knows neither what the present power, capacity, or attitude is, nor yet how it is to be asserted, exercised, and realized.

THE NEED OF A THEORY OF EXPERIENCE

In short, the point I am making is that rejection of the philosophy and practice of traditional education sets a new type of difficult educational problem for those who believe in the new type of education. We shall

From *Experience and Education* by John Dewey, 1997. Reprinted by permission of Kappa Delta Pi, International Honor Society in Education.

operate blindly and in confusion until we recognize this fact; until we thoroughly appreciate that departure from the old solves no problems. What is said in the following pages is, accordingly, intended to indicate some of the main problems with which the newer education is confronted and to suggest the main lines along which their solution is to be sought. I assume that amid all uncertainties there is one permanent frame of reference: namely, the organic connection between education and personal experience; or, that the new philosophy of education is committed to some kind of empirical and experimental philosophy. But experience and experiment are not self-explanatory ideas. Rather, their meaning is part of the problem to be explored. To know the meaning of empiricism we need to understand what experience is.

The belief that all genuine education comes about through experience does not mean that all experiences are genuinely or equally educative. Experience and education cannot be directly equated to each other. For some experiences are mis-educative. Any experience is mis-educative that has the effect of arresting or distorting the growth of further experience. An experience may be such as to engender callousness; it may produce lack of sensitivity and of responsiveness. Then the possibilities of having richer experience in the future are restricted. Again, a given experience may increase a person's automatic skill in a particular direction and yet tend to land him in a groove or rut; the effect again is to narrow the field of further experience. An experience may be immediately enjoyable and yet promote the formation of a slack and careless attitude; this attitude then operates to modify the quality of subsequent experiences so as to prevent a person from getting out of them what they have to give. Again, experiences may be so disconnected from one another that, while each is agreeable or even exciting in itself, they are not linked cumulatively to one another. Energy is then dissipated and a person becomes scatter-brained. Each experience may be lively, vivid, and "interesting," and yet their disconnectedness may artificially generate dispersive, disintegrated, centrifugal habits. The consequence of formation of such habits is inability to control future experiences. They are then taken, either by way of enjoyment or of discontent and revolt, just as they come. Under such circumstances, it is idle to talk of self-control.

Traditional education offers a plethora of examples of experiences of the kinds just mentioned. It is a great mistake to suppose, even tacitly, that the traditional schoolroom was not a place in which pupils had experiences. Yet this is tacitly assumed when progressive

education as a plan of learning by experience is placed in sharp opposition to the old. The proper line of attack is that the experiences which
were had, by pupils and teachers alike, were largely of a wrong kind.
How many students, for example, were rendered callous to ideas, and
how many lost the impetus to learn because of the way in which learning was experienced by them? How many acquired special skills by
means of automatic drill so that their power of judgment and capacity
to act intelligently in new situations was limited? How many came to
associate the learning process with ennui and boredom? How many
found what they did learn so foreign to the situations of life outside the
school as to give them no power of control over the latter? How many
came to associate books with dull drudgery, so that they were "conditioned" to all but flashy reading matter?

If I ask these questions, it is not for the sake of wholesale condemnation of the old education. It is for quite another purpose. It is to
emphasize the fact, first, that young people in traditional schools do
have experiences; and, secondly, that the trouble is not the absence of
experiences, but their defective and wrong character—wrong and
defective from the standpoint of connection with further experience.
The positive side of this point is even more important in connection
with progressive education. It is not enough to insist upon the necessity of experience, nor even of activity in experience. Everything
depends upon the *quality* of the experience which is had. The quality
of any experience has two aspects. There is an immediate aspect of
agreeableness or disagreeableness, and there is its influence upon
later experiences. The first is obvious and easy to judge. The *effect* of
an experience is not borne on its face. It sets a problem to the educator. It is his business to arrange for the kind of experiences which,
while they do not repel the student, but rather engage his activities
are, nevertheless, more than immediately enjoyable since they promote having desirable future experiences. Just as no man lives or dies
to himself, so no experience lives and dies to itself. Wholly independent of desire or intent, every experience lives on in further experiences. Hence the central problem of an education based upon experience is to select the kind of present experiences that live fruitfully and
creatively in subsequent experiences.

Later, I shall discuss in more detail the principle of the continuity of
experience or what may be called the experiential continuum. Here I
wish simply to emphasize the importance of this principle for the phi-

losophy of educative experience. A philosophy of education, like any theory, has to be stated in words, in symbols. But so far as it is more than verbal it is a plan for conducting education. Like any plan, it must be framed with reference to what is to be done and how it is to be done. The more definitely and sincerely it is held that education is a development within, by, and for experience, the more important it is that there shall be clear conceptions of what experience is. Unless experience is so conceived that the result is a plan for deciding upon subject-matter, upon methods of instruction and discipline, and upon material equipment and social organization of the school, it is wholly in the air. It is reduced to a form of words which may be emotionally stirring but for which any other set of words might equally well be substituted unless they indicate operations to be initiated and executed. Just because traditional education was a matter of routine in which the plans and programs were handed down from the past, it does not follow that progressive education is a matter of planless improvisation.

The traditional school could get along without any consistently developed philosophy of education. About all it required in that line was a set of abstract words like culture, discipline, our great cultural heritage, etc., actual guidance being derived not from them but from custom and established routines. Just because progressive schools cannot rely upon established traditions and institutional habits, they must either proceed more or less haphazardly or be directed by ideas which, when they are made articulate and coherent, form a philosophy of education. Revolt against the kind of organization characteristic of the traditional school constitutes a demand for a kind of organization based upon ideas. I think that only slight acquaintance with the history of education is needed to prove that educational reformers and innovators alone have felt the need for a philosophy of education. Those who adhered to the established system needed merely a few fine-sounding words to justify existing practices. The real work was done by habits which were so fixed as to be institutional. The lesson for progressive education is that it requires in an urgent degree, a degree more pressing than was incumbent upon former innovators, a philosophy of education based upon a philosophy of experience.

I remarked incidentally that the philosophy in question is, to paraphrase the saying of Lincoln about democracy, one of education of, by, and for experience. No one of these words, *of, by,* or *for,* names anything which is self-evident. Each of them is a challenge to discover and put into operation a principle of order and organization which follows from understanding what educative experience signifies.

It is, accordingly, a much more difficult task to work out the kinds of materials, of methods, and of social relationships that are appropriate to the new education than is the case with traditional education. I think many of the difficulties experienced in the conduct of progressive schools and many of the criticisms leveled against them arise from this source. The difficulties are aggravated and the criticisms are increased when it is supposed that the new education is somehow easier than the old. This belief is, I imagine, more or less current. Perhaps it illustrates again the *Either-Or* philosophy, springing from the idea that about all which is required is *not* to do what is done in traditional schools.

I admit gladly that the new education is *simpler* in principle than the old. It is in harmony with principles of growth, while there is very much which is artificial in the old selection and arrangement of subjects and methods, and artificiality always leads to unnecessary complexity. But the easy and the simple are not identical. To discover what is really simple and to act upon the discovery is an exceedingly difficult task. After the artificial and complex is once institutionally established and ingrained in custom and routine, it is easier to walk in the paths that have been beaten than it is, after taking a new point of view, to work out what is practically involved in the new point of view. The old Ptolemaic astronomical system was more complicated with its cycles and epicycles than the Copernican system. But until organization of actual astronomical phenomena on the ground of the latter principle had been effected the easiest course was to follow the line of least resistance provided by the old intellectual habit. So we come back to the idea that a coherent *theory* of experience, affording positive direction to selection and organization of appropriate educational methods and materials, is required by the attempt to give new direction to the work of the schools. The process is a slow and arduous one. It is a matter of growth, and there are many obstacles which tend to obstruct growth and to deflect it into wrong lines.

I shall have something to say later about organization. All that is needed, perhaps, at this point is to say that we must escape from the tendency to think of organization in terms of the *kind* of organization, whether of content (or subject-matter), or of methods and social relations, that mark traditional education. I think that a good deal of the current opposition to the idea of organization is due to the fact that it is so hard to get away from the picture of the studies of the old school. The moment "organization" is mentioned imagination goes almost automatically to the kind of organization that is familiar, and in revolting against that we are led to shrink from the very idea of any organization. On the other hand, educational reactionaries, who are now gathering force, use the absence of adequate intellectual and moral organization in the newer type of school as proof not only of the need of organization, but to identify any and every kind of organization with that instituted before the rise of experimental science. Failure to develop a conception of organization upon the empirical and experimental basis gives reactionaries a too easy victory. But the fact that the empirical sciences now offer the best type of intellectual organization which can be found in any field shows that there is no reason why we, who call ourselves emipiricists, should be "pushovers" in the matter of order and organization.

Criteria of Experience

If there is any truth in what has been said about the need of forming a theory of experience in order that education may be intelligently conducted upon the basis of experience, it is clear that the next thing in order in this discussion is to present the principles that are most significant in framing this theory. I shall not, therefore, apologize for engaging in a certain amount of philosophical analysis, which otherwise might be out of place. I may, however, reassure you to some degree by saying that this analysis is not an end in itself but is engaged in for the sake of obtaining criteria to be applied later in discussion of a number of concrete and, to most persons, more interesting issues.

I have already mentioned what I called the category of continuity, or the experiential continuum. This principle is involved, as I pointed out, in every attempt to discriminate between experiences that are worthwhile educationally and those that are not. It may seem superfluous to argue that this discrimination is necessary not only in criticizing the traditional type of education but also in initiating and conducting a different type. Nevertheless, it is advisable to pursue for a little while the idea that it is necessary. One may safely assume, I suppose, that one thing which has recommended the progressive movement is that it seems more in accord with the democratic ideal to which our people is committed than do the procedures of the traditional school, since the latter have so much of the autocratic about them. Another thing which has contributed to its favorable reception is that its methods are humane in comparison with the harshness so often attending the policies of the traditional school.

The question I would raise concerns why we prefer democratic and humane arrangements to those which are autocratic and harsh. And by "why," I mean the *reason* for preferring them, not just the *causes* which lead us to the preference. One *cause* may be that we have been taught not only in the schools but by the press, the pulpit, the platform, and our laws and law-making bodies that democracy is the best of all social institutions. We may have so assimilated this idea from our surroundings that it has become an habitual part of our mental and moral make-up. But similar causes have led other persons in different surroundings to widely varying conclusions—to prefer fascism, for example. The cause for our preference is not the same thing as the reason why we *should* prefer it.

It is not my purpose here to go in detail into the reason. But I would ask a single question: Can we find any reason that does not ultimately come down to the belief that democratic social arrangements promote a better quality of human experience, one which is more widely accessible and enjoyed, than do non-democratic and anti-democratic forms of social life? Does not the principle of regard for individual freedom and for decency and kindliness of human relations come back in the end to the conviction that these things are tributary to a higher quality of experience on the part of a greater number than are methods of repression and coercion or force? Is it not the reason for our preference that we believe that mutual consultation and convictions reached through persuasion, make possible a better quality of experience than can otherwise be provided on any wide scale?

If the answer to these questions is in the affirmative (and personally I do not see how we can justify our preference for democracy and humanity on any other ground), the ultimate reason for hospitality to progressive education, because of its reliance upon and use of humane methods and its kinship to democracy, goes back to the fact that discrimination is made between the inherent values of different experiences. So I come back to the principle of continuity of experience as a criterion of discrimination.

At bottom, this principle rests upon the fact of habit, when *habit* is interpreted biologically. The basic characteristic of habit is that every experience enacted and undergone modifies the one who acts and undergoes, while this modification affects, whether we wish it or not, the quality of subsequent experiences. For it is a somewhat different person who enters into them. The principle of habit so understood obviously goes deeper than the ordinary conception of *a* habit as a more or less fixed way of doing things, although it includes the latter as one of its special cases. It covers the formation of attitudes, attitudes that are emotional and intellectual; it covers our basic sensitivities and ways of meeting and responding to all the conditions which we meet in living. From this point of view, the principle of continuity of experience means that every experience both takes up something from those which have gone before and modifies in some way the quality of those which come after. As the poet states it,

. . . all experience is an arch wherethro'
Gleams that untraveled world, whose margin fades
For ever and for ever when I move.

So far, however, we have no ground for discrimination among experiences. For the principle is of universal application. There is *some* kind of continuity in every case. It is when we note the different forms in which continuity of experience operates that we get the basis of discriminating among experiences. I may illustrate what is meant by an objection which has been brought against an idea which I once put forth— namely, that the educative process can be identified with growth when that is understood in terms of the active participle, *growing*.

Growth, or growing as developing, not only physically but intellectually and morally, is one exemplification of the principle of continuity. The objection made is that growth might take many different directions: a man, for example, who starts out on a career of burglary may grow in that direction, and by practice may grow into a highly expert burglar. Hence it is argued that "growth" is not enough; we must also specify the direction in which growth takes place, the end towards which it tends. Before, however, we decide that the objection is conclusive we must analyze the case a little further.

That a man may grow in efficiency as a burglar, as a gangster, or as a corrupt politician, cannot be doubted. But from the standpoint of growth as education and education as growth the question is whether growth in this direction promotes or retards growth in general. Does this form of growth create conditions for further growth, or does it set up conditions that shut off the person who has grown in this particular direction from the occasions, stimuli, and opportunities for continuing growth in new directions? What is the effect of growth in a special direction upon the attitudes and habits which alone open up avenues for development in other lines? I shall leave you to answer these questions, saying simply that when and *only* when development in a particular line conduces to continuing growth does it answer to the criterion of education as growing. For the conception is one that must find universal and not specialized limited application.

I return now to the question of continuity as a criterion by which to discriminate between experiences which are educative and those which are mis-educative. As we have seen, there is some kind of continuity in any case since every experience affects for better or worse the attitudes which help decide the quality of further experiences, by setting up certain preference and aversion, and making it easier or harder to act for this or that end. Moreover, every experience influences in some degree the objective conditions under which further experiences are had. For example, a child who learns to speak has a new facility and new desire. But he has also widened the external conditions of subsequent learning. When he learns to read, he similarly opens up a new environment. If a person decides to become a teacher, lawyer, physician, or stockbroker, when he executes his intention he thereby necessarily determines to some extent the environment in which he will act in the future. He has rendered himself more sensitive and responsive to certain conditions, and relatively immune to those things about him that would have been stimuli if he had made another choice.

But, while the principle of continuity applies in some way in every case, the quality of the present experience influences the *way* in which the principle applies. We speak of spoiling a child and of the spoilt child. The effect of over-indulging a child is a continuing one. It sets up an attitude which operates as an automatic demand that persons and objects cater to his desires and caprices in the future. It makes him seek the kind of situation that will enable him to do what he feels like doing at the time. It renders him averse to and comparatively incompetent in situations which require effort and perseverance in overcoming obstacles. There is no paradox in the fact that the principle of the continuity of experience may operate so as to leave a person arrested on a low plane of development, in a way which limits later capacity for growth.

On the other hand, if an experience arouses curiosity, strengthens initiative, and sets up desires and purposes that are sufficiently intense to carry a person over dead places in the future, continuity works in a very different way. Every experience is a moving force. Its value can be judged only on the ground of what it moves toward and into. The greater maturity of experience which should belong to the adult as educator puts him in a position to evaluate each experience of the young in a way in which the one having the less mature experience cannot do. It is then the business of the educator to see in what direction an experience is heading. There is no point in his being more mature if, instead of using his greater insight to help organize the conditions of the experience of the immature, he throws away his insight. Failure to take the moving force of an experience into account so as to judge and direct it on the ground of what it is moving into means disloyalty to the principle of experience itself. The disloyalty operates in two directions. The educator is false to the understanding that he should have obtained from his own past experience. He is also unfaithful to the fact that all human experience is ultimately social: that it involves contact and communication. The mature person, to put it in moral terms, has no right to withhold from the young on given occasions whatever capacity for sympathetic understanding his own experience has given him.

No sooner, however, are such things said than there is a tendency to react to the other extreme and take what has been said as a plea for some sort of disguised imposition from outside. It is worth while, accordingly, to say something about the way in which the adult can exercise the wisdom his own wider experience gives him without imposing a merely external control. On one side, it is his business to be on the alert to see what attitudes and habitual tendencies are being created. In this direction he must, if he is an educator, be able to judge what attitudes are actually conducive to continued growth and what are detrimental. He must, in addition, have that sympathetic understanding of individuals as individuals which gives him an idea of what is actually going on in the minds of those who are learning. It is, among other things, the need for these abilities on the part of the parent and teacher which makes a system of education based upon living experience a more difficult affair to conduct successfully than it is to follow the patterns of traditional education.

But there is another aspect of the matter. Experience does not go on simply inside a person. It does go on there, for it influences the formation of attitudes of desire and purpose. But this is not the whole of the story. Every genuine experience has an active side which changes in some degree the objective conditions under which experiences are had. The difference between civilization and savagery, to take an example on a large scale, is found in the degree in which previous experiences have changed the objective conditions under which subsequent experiences take place. The existence of roads, of means of rapid movement and transportation, tools, implements, furniture, electric light and power, are illustrations. Destroy the external conditions of present civilized experience, and for a time our experience would relapse into that of barbaric peoples.

In a word, we live from birth to death in a world of persons and things which in large measure is what it is because of what has been done and transmitted from previous human activities. When this fact is ignored, experience is treated as if it were something which goes on exclusively inside an individual's body and mind. It ought not to be necessary to say that experience does not occur in a vacuum. There are sources outside an individual which give rise to experience. It is constantly fed from these springs. No one would question that a child in a slum tenement has a different experience from that of a child in a cultured home; that the country lad has a different kind of experience from the city boy, or a boy on the seashore one different from the lad who is brought up on inland prairies. Ordinarily we take such facts for granted as too commonplace to record. But when their educational import is recognized, they indicate the second way in which the educator can direct the experience of the young without engaging in imposition. A primary responsibility of educators is that they not only be aware of the general principle of the shaping of actual experience by environing conditions, but that they also recognize in the concrete what surroundings are conducive to having experiences that lead to growth. Above all, they should know how to utilize the surroundings, physical and social, that exist so as to extract from them all that they have to contribute to building up experiences that are worth while.

Traditional education did not have to face this problem; it could systematically dodge this responsibility. The school environment of desks, blackboards, a small school yard, was supposed to suffice. There was no demand that the teacher should become intimately acquainted with the conditions of the local community, physical, historical, economic, occupational, etc., in order to utilize them as educational resources. A system of education based upon the necessary connection of education with experience must, on the contrary, if faithful to its principle, take these things constantly into account. This tax upon the educator is another reason why progressive education is more difficult to carry on than was ever the traditional system.

It is possible to frame schemes of education that pretty systematically subordinate objective conditions to those which reside in the individuals being educated. This happens whenever the place and function of the teacher, of books, of apparatus and equipment, of everything which represents the products of the more mature experience of elders, is systematically subordinated to the immediate inclinations and feelings of the young. Every theory which assumes that importance can be attached to these objective factors only at the expense of imposing external control and of limiting the freedom of individuals rests finally upon the notion that experience is truly experience only when objective conditions are subordinated to what goes on within the individuals having the experience.

I do not mean that it is supposed that objective conditions can be shut out. It is recognized that they must enter in: so much concession is made to the inescapable fact that we live in a world of things and persons. But I think that observation of what goes on in some families and some schools would disclose that some parents and some teachers are acting upon the idea of *subordinating* objective conditions to internal ones. In that case, it is assumed not only that the latter are primary, which in one sense they are, but that just as they temporarily exist they fix the whole educational process.

Let me illustrate from the case of an infant. The needs of a baby for food, rest, and activity are certainly primary and decisive in one respect. Nourishment must be provided; provision must be made for comfortable sleep, and so on. But these facts do not mean that a parent shall feed the baby at any time when the baby is cross or irritable, that there shall not be a program of regular hours of feeding and sleeping, etc. The wise mother takes account of the needs of the infant but not in a way which dispenses with her own responsibility for regulating the objective conditions under which the needs are satisfied. And if she is a wise mother in this respect, she draws upon past experiences of experts as well as her own for the light that these shed upon what experiences are in general most conducive to the normal development of infants. Instead of these conditions being subordinated to the immediate internal condition of the baby, they are definitely ordered so that a particular kind of *interaction* with these immediate internal states may be brought about.

The word "interaction," which has just been used, expresses the second chief principle for interpreting an experience in its educational function and force. It assigns equal rights to both factors in experience—objective and internal conditions. Any normal experience is an interplay of these two sets of conditions. Taken together, or in their interaction, they form what we call a *situation*. The trouble with traditional education was not that it emphasized the external conditions that enter into the control of the experiences but that it paid so little attention to the internal factors which also decide what kind of experience is had. It violated the principle of interaction from one side. But this violation is no reason why the new education should violate the principle from the other side—except upon the basis of the extreme *Either-Or* educational philosophy which has been mentioned.

The illustration drawn from the need for regulation of the objective conditions of a baby's development indicates, first, that the parent has responsibility for arranging the conditions under which an infant's experience of food, sleep, etc., occurs, and, secondly, that the responsibility is fulfilled by utilizing the funded experience of the past, as this is represented, say, by the advice of competent physicians and others who have made a special study of normal physical growth. Does it limit the freedom of the mother when she uses the body of knowledge thus provided to regulate the objective conditions of nourishment and sleep? Or does the enlargement of her intelligence in fulfilling her parental function widen her freedom? Doubtless if a fetish were made of the advice and directions so that they came to be inflexible dictates to be followed under every possible condition, then restriction of freedom of both parent and child would occur. But this restriction would also be a limitation of the intelligence that is exercised in personal judgment.

In what respect does regulation of objective conditions limit the freedom of the baby? Some limitation is certainly placed upon its immediate movements and inclinations when it is put in its crib, at a time when it wants to continue playing, or does not get food at the moment it would like it, or when it isn't picked up and dandled when it cries for attention. Restriction also occurs when mother or nurse snatches a child away from an open fire into which it is about to fall. I shall have more to say later about freedom. Here it is enough to ask whether freedom is to be thought of and adjudged on the basis of relatively momentary incidents or whether its meaning is found in the continuity of developing experience.

The statement that individuals live in a world means, in the concrete, that they live in a series of situations. And when it is said that they live *in* these situations, the meaning of the word "in" is different from its meaning when it is said that pennies are "in" a pocket or paint is "in" a can. It means, once more, that interaction is going on between an individual and objects and other persons. The conceptions of *situation* and of *interaction* are inseparable from each other. An experience is always what it is because of a transaction taking place between an individual and what, at the time, constitutes his environment, whether the latter consists of persons with whom he is talking about some topic or event, the subject talked about being also a part of the situation; or the toys with which he is playing; the book he is reading (in which his environing conditions at the time may be England or ancient Greece or an imaginary region); or the materials of an experiment he is performing. The environment, in other words, is whatever conditions interact with personal needs, desires, purposes, and capacities to create the experience which is had. Even when a person builds a castle in the air he is interacting with the objects which he constructs in fancy.

The two principles of continuity and interaction are not separate from each other. They intercept and unite. They are, so to speak, the longitudinal and lateral aspects of experience. Different situations succeed one another. But because of the principle of continuity something is carried over from the earlier to the later ones. As an individual passes from one situation to another, his world, his environment, expands or contracts. He does not find himself living in another world but in a different part or aspect of one and the same world. What he has learned in the way of knowledge and skill in one situation becomes an instrument of understanding and dealing effectively with the situations which follow. The process goes on as long as life and learning continue. Otherwise the course of experience is disorderly, since the individual factor that enters into making an experience is split. A divided world, a world whose parts and aspects do not hang together, is at once a sign and a cause of a divided personality. When the splitting-up reaches a certain point we call the person insane. A fully integrated personality, on the other hand, exists only when successive experiences are integrated with one another. It can be built up only as a world of related objects is constructed.

Continuity and interaction in their active union with each other provide the measure of the educative significance and value of an experience. The immediate and direct concern of an educator is then with the situations in which interaction takes place. The individual, who enters as a factor into it, is what he is at a given time. It is the other factor, that of objective conditions, which lies to some extent within the possibility of regulation by the educator. As has already been noted, the phrase "objective conditions" covers a wide range. It includes what is done by the educator and the way in which it is done, not only words spoken but the tone of voice in which they are spoken. It includes equipment, books, apparatus, toys, games played. It includes the materials with which an individual interacts, and, most important of all, the total *social* set-up of the situations in which a person is engaged.

When it is said that the objective conditions are those which are within the power of the educator to regulate, it is meant, of course, that his ability to influence directly the experience of others and thereby the education they obtain places upon him the duty of determining that environment which will interact with the existing capacities and needs of those taught to create a worth-while experience. The trouble with traditional education was not that educators took upon themselves the responsibility for providing an environment. The trouble was that they did not consider the other factor in creating an experience; namely, the powers and purposes of those taught. It was assumed that a certain set of conditions was intrinsically desirable, apart from its ability to evoke a certain quality of response in individuals. This lack of mutual adaptation made the process of teaching and learning accidental. Those to whom the provided conditions were suitable managed to learn. Others got on as best they could. Responsibility for selecting objective conditions carries with it, then, the responsibility for understanding the needs and capacities of the individuals who are learning at a given time. It is not enough that certain materials and methods have proved effective with other individuals at other times. There must be a reason for thinking that they will function in generating an experience that has educative quality with particular individuals at a particular time.

It is no reflection upon the nutritive quality of beefsteak that it is not fed to infants. It is not an invidious reflection upon trigonometry that we do not teach it in the first or fifth grade of school. It is not the subject *per se* that is educative or that is conducive to growth. There is no subject that is in and of itself, or without regard to the stage of growth attained by the learner, such that inherent educational value can be attributed to it. Failure to take into account adaptation to the needs and capacities of individuals was the source of the idea that certain subjects and certain methods are intrinsically cultural or intrinsically good for mental discipline. There is no such thing as educational value in the abstract. The notion that some subjects and methods and that acquaintance with certain facts and truths possess educational value in and of themselves is the reason why traditional education reduced the material of education so largely to a diet of predigested materials. According to this notion, it was enough to regulate the quantity and difficulty of the material provided, in a scheme of quantitative grading, from month to month and from year to year. Otherwise a pupil was expected to take it in the doses that were prescribed from without. If the pupil left it instead of taking it, if he engaged in physical truancy, or in the mental truancy of mind-wandering and finally built up an emotional revulsion against the subject, he was held to be at fault. No question was raised as to whether the trouble might not lie in the subject-matter or in the way in which it was offered. The principle of interaction makes it clear that failure of adaptation of material to needs and capacities of individuals may cause an experience to be non-educative quite as much as failure of an individual to adapt himself to the material.

The principle of continuity in its educational application means, nevertheless, that the future has to be taken into account at every stage of the educational process. This idea is easily misunderstood and is badly distorted in traditional education. Its assumption is, that by acquiring certain skills and by learning certain subjects which would be needed later (perhaps in college or perhaps in adult life) pupils are as a matter of course made ready for the needs and circumstances of the future. Now "preparation" is a treacherous idea. In a certain sense every experience should do something to prepare a person for later experiences of a deeper and more expansive quality. That is the very meaning of growth, continuity, reconstruction of experience. But it is a mistake to suppose that the mere acquisition of a certain amount of arithmetic, geography, history, etc., which is taught and studied because it may be useful at some time in the future, has this effect, and it is a mistake to suppose that acquisition of skills in reading and figuring will automatically constitute preparation for their right and effective use under conditions very unlike those in which they were acquired.

Almost everyone has had occasion to look back upon his school days and wonder what has become of the knowledge he was supposed to have amassed during his years of schooling, and why it is that the technical skills he acquired have to be learned over again in changed form in order to stand him in good stead. Indeed, he is lucky who does not find that in order to make progress, in order to go ahead intellectually, he does not have to unlearn much of what he learned in school. These questions cannot be disposed of by saying that the subjects were not actually learned, for they were learned at least sufficiently to enable a pupil to pass examinations in them. One trouble is that the subject-matter in question was learned in isolation; it was put, as it were, in a water-tight compartment. When the question is asked, then, what has become of it, where has it gone to, the right answer is that it is still there in the special compartment in which it was originally stowed away. If exactly the same conditions recurred as those under which it was acquired, it would also recur and be available. But it was segregated when it was acquired and hence is so disconnected from the rest of experience that it is not available under the actual conditions of life. It is contrary to the laws of experience that learning of this kind, no matter how thoroughly engrained at the time, should give genuine preparation.

Nor does failure in preparation end at this point. Perhaps the greatest of all pedagogical fallacies is the notion that a person learns only the particular thing he is studying at the time. Collateral learning in the way of formation of enduring attitudes, of likes and dislikes, may be and often is much more important than the spelling lesson or lesson in geography or history that is learned. For these attitudes are fundamentally what count in the future. The most important attitude that can be formed is that of desire to go on learning. If impetus in this direction is weakened instead of being intensified, something much more than mere lack of preparation takes place. The pupil is actually robbed of native capacities which otherwise would enable him to cope with the circumstances that he meets in the course of his life. We often see persons who have had little schooling and in whose case the absence of set schooling proves to be a positive asset. They have at least retained their native common sense and power of judgment, and its exercise in the actual conditions of living has given them the precious gift of ability to learn from the experiences they have. What avail is it to win prescribed amounts of information about geography and history, to win ability to read and write, if in the process the individual loses his own soul: loses his appreciation of things worth while, of the values to which these things are relative; if he loses desire to apply what he has learned and, above all, loses the ability to extract meaning from his future experiences as they occur?

What, then, is the true meaning of preparation in the educational scheme? In the first place, it means that a person, young or old, gets out of his present experience all that there is in it for him at the time in which he has it. When preparation is made the controlling end, then the potentialities of the present are sacrificed to a suppositious future. When this happens, the actual preparation for the future is missed or distorted. The ideal of using the present simply to get ready for the future contradicts itself. It omits, and even shuts out, the very conditions by which a person can be prepared for his future. We always live at the time we live and not at some other time, and only by extracting at each present time the full meaning of each present experience are we prepared for doing the same thing in the future. This is the only preparation which in the long run amounts to anything.

All this means that attentive care must be devoted to the conditions which give each present experience a worth-while meaning. Instead of inferring that it doesn't make much difference what the present experience is as long as it is enjoyed, the conclusion is the exact opposite. Here is another matter where it is easy to react from one extreme to the other. Because traditional schools tended to sacrifice the present to a remote and more or less unknown future, therefore it comes to be believed that the educator has little responsibility for the kind of present experiences the young undergo. But the relation of the present and the future is not an *Either-Or* affair. The present affects the future anyway. The persons who should have some idea of the connection between the two are those who have achieved maturity. Accordingly, upon them devolves the responsibility for instituting the conditions for the kind of present experience which has a favorable effect upon the future. Education as growth or maturity should be an ever-present process.

Social Control

I have said that educational plans and projects, seeing education in terms of life-experience, are thereby committed to framing and adopting an intelligent theory or, if you please, philosophy of experience. Otherwise they are at the mercy of every intellectual breeze that happens to blow. I have tried to illustrate the need for such a theory by calling attention to two principles which are fundamental in the constitution of experience: the principles of interaction and of continuity. If, then, I am asked why I have spent so much time on expounding a rather abstract philosophy, it is because practical attempts to develop schools based upon the idea that education is found in life-experience are bound to exhibit inconsistencies and confusions unless they are guided by some conception of what experience is, and what marks off educative experience from non-educative and mis-educative experience. I now come to a group of actual educational questions the discussion of which will, I hope, provide topics and material that are more concrete than the discussion up to this point.

The two principles of continuity and interaction as criteria of the value of experience are so intimately connected that it is not easy to tell just what special educational problem to take up first. Even the convenient division into problems of subject-matter or studies and of methods of teaching and learning is likely to fail us in selection and organization of topics to discuss. Consequently, the beginning and sequence of topics is somewhat arbitrary. I shall commence, however, with the old question of individual freedom and social control and pass on to the questions that grow naturally out of it.

It is often well in considering educational problems to get a start by temporarily ignoring the school and thinking of other human situations. I take it that no one would deny that the ordinary good citizen is as a matter of fact subject to a great deal of social control and that a considerable part of this control is not felt to involve restriction of personal freedom. Even the theoretical anarchist, whose philosophy commits him to the idea that state or government control is an unmitigated evil, believes that with abolition of the political state other forms of social control would operate: indeed, his opposition to governmental regulation springs from his belief that other and, to him, more normal modes of control would operate with abolition of the state.

Without taking up this extreme position, let us note some examples of social control that operate in everyday life, and then look for the principle underlying them. Let us begin with the young people themselves. Children at recess or after school play games, from tag and one-old-cat to baseball and football. The games involve rules, and these rules order their conduct. The games do not go on haphazardly or by a succession of improvisations. Without rules there is no game. If disputes arise there is an umpire to appeal to, or discussion and a kind of arbitration are means to a decision; otherwise the game is broken up and comes to an end.

There are certain fairly obvious controlling features of such situations to which I want to call attention. The first is that the rules are a part of the game. They are not outside of it. No rules, then no game; different rules, then a different game. As long as the game goes on with a reasonable smoothness, the players do not feel that they are submitting to external imposition but that they are playing the game. In the second place an individual may at times feel that a decision isn't fair and he may even get angry. But he is not objecting to a rule but to what he claims is a violation of it, to some one-sided and unfair action. In the third place, the rules, and hence the conduct of the game, are fairly standardized. There are recognized ways of counting out, of selection of sides, as well as for positions to be taken, movements to be made, etc. These rules have the sanction of tradition and precedent. Those playing the game have seen, perhaps, professional matches and they want to emulate their elders. An element that is conventional is pretty strong. Usually, a group of youngsters change the rules by which they play only when the adult group to which they look for models have themselves made a change in the rules, while the change made by the elders is at least supposed to conduce to making the game more skillful or more interesting to spectators.

Now, the general conclusion I would draw is that control of individual actions is effected by the whole situation in which individuals are involved, in which they share and of which they are co-operative or interacting parts. For even in a competitive game there is a certain kind of participation, of sharing in a common experience. Stated the other way around, those who take part do not feel that they are bossed by an individual person or are being subjected to the will of some outside superior person. When violent disputes do arise, it is usually on the alleged ground that the umpire or some person on the other side is being unfair; in other words, that in such cases some individual is trying to impose his individual will on someone else.

It may seem to be putting too heavy a load upon a single case to argue that this instance illustrates the general principle of social control of individuals without the violation of freedom. But if the matter were followed out through a number of cases, I think the conclusion that this particular instance does illustrate a general principle would be justified. Games are generally competitive. If we took instances of co-operative activities in which all members of a group take part, as for example in well-ordered family life in which there is mutual confidence, the point would be even clearer. In all such cases it is not the will or desire of any one person which establishes order but the moving spirit of the whole group. The control is social, but individuals are parts of a community, not outside of it.

I do not mean by this that there are no occasions upon which the authority of, say, the parent does not have to intervene and exercise fairly direct control. But I do say that, in the first place, the number of these occasions is slight in comparison with the number of those in which the control is exercised by situations in which all take part. And what is even more important, the authority in question when exercised in a well-regulated household or other community group is not a manifestation of merely personal will; the parent or teacher exercises it as the representative and agent of the interests of the group as a whole. With respect to the first point, in a well-ordered school the main reliance for control of this and that individual is upon the activities carried on and upon the situations in which these activities are maintained. The teacher reduces to a minimum the occasions in which he or she has to exercise authority in a personal way. When it is necessary, in the second place, to speak and act firmly, it is done in behalf of the interest of the group, not as an exhibition of personal power. This makes the difference between action which is arbitrary and that which is just and fair.

Moreover, it is not necessary that the difference should be formulated in words, by either teacher or the young, in order to be felt in experience.

The number of children who do not feel the difference (even if they cannot articulate it and reduce it to an intellectual principle) between action that is motivated by personal power and desire to dictate and action that is fair, because in the interest of all, is small. I should even be willing to say that upon the whole children are more sensitive to the signs and symptoms of this difference than are adults. Children learn the difference when playing with one another. They are willing, often too willing if anything, to take suggestions from one child and let him be a leader if his conduct adds to the experienced value of what they are doing, while they resent the attempt at dictation. Then they often withdraw and when asked why, say that it is because so-and-so "is too bossy."

I do not wish to refer to the traditional school in ways which set up a caricature in lieu of a picture. But I think it is fair to say that one reason the personal commands of the teacher so often played an undue role and a reason why the order which existed was so much a matter of sheer obedience to the will of an adult was because the situation almost forced it upon the teacher. The school was not a group or community held together by participation in common activities. Consequently, the normal, proper conditions of control were lacking. Their absence was made up for, and to a considerable extent had to be made up for, by the direct intervention of the teacher, who, as the saying went, *"kept* order." He kept it because order was in the teacher's keeping, instead of residing in the shared work being done.

The conclusion is that in what are called the new schools, the primary source of social control resides in the very nature of the work done as a social enterprise in which all individuals have an opportunity to contribute and to which all feel a responsibility. Most children are naturally "sociable." Isolation is even more irksome to them than to adults. A genuine community life has its ground in this natural sociability. But community life does not organize itself in an enduring way purely spontaneously. It requires thought and planning ahead. The educator is responsible for a knowledge of individuals and for a knowledge of subject-matter that will enable activities to be selected which lend themselves to social organization, an organization in which all individuals have an opportunity to contribute something, and in which the activities in which all participate are the chief carrier of control.

I am not romantic enough about the young to suppose that every pupil will respond or that any child of normally strong impulses will respond on every occasion. There are likely to be some who, when they come to school, are already victims of injurious conditions outside of the school and who have become so passive and unduly docile that they fail to contribute. There will be others who, because of previous experience, are bumptious and unruly and perhaps downright rebellious. But it is certain that the general principle of social control cannot be predicated upon such cases. It is also true that no general rule can be laid down for dealing with such cases. The teacher has to deal with them individually. They fall into general classes, but no two are exactly alike. The educator has to discover as best he or she can the causes for the recalcitrant attitudes. He or she cannot, if the educational process is to go on, make it a question of pitting one will against another in order to see which is strongest, nor yet allow the unruly and non-participating pupils to stand permanently in the way of the educative activities of others. Exclusion perhaps is the only available measure at a given juncture, but it is no solution. For it may strengthen the very causes which have brought about the undesirable anti-social attitude, such as desire for attention or to show off.

Exceptions rarely prove a rule or give a clew to what the rule should be. I would not, therefore, attach too much importance to these exceptional cases, although it is true at present that progressive schools are likely often to have more than their fair share of these cases, since parents may send children to such schools as a last resort. I do not think weakness in control when it is found in progressive schools arises in any event from these exceptional cases. It is much more likely to arise from failure to arrange in advance for the kind of work (by which I mean all kinds of activities engaged in) which will create situations that of themselves tend to exercise control over what this, that, and the other pupil does and how he does it. This failure most often goes back to lack of sufficiently thoughtful planning in advance. The causes for such lack are varied. The one which is peculiarly important to mention in this connection is the idea that such advance planning is unnecessary and even that it is inherently hostile to the legitimate freedom of those being instructed.

Now, of course, it is quite possible to have preparatory planning by the teacher done in such a rigid and intellectually inflexible fashion that it does result in adult imposition, which is none the less external because executed with tact and the semblance of respect for individual freedom. But this kind of planning does not follow inherently from the principle involved. I do not know what the greater maturity of the teacher and the teacher's greater knowledge of the world, of subject-matters and of individuals, is for unless the teacher can arrange conditions that are conducive to community activity and to organization which exercises control over individual impulses by the mere fact that all are engaged in communal projects. Because the kind of advance planning heretofore engaged in has been so routine as to leave little room for the free play of individual thinking or for contributions due to distinctive individual experience, it does not follow that all planning must be rejected. On the contrary, there is incumbent upon the educator the duty of instituting a much more intelligent, and consequently more difficult, kind of planning. He must survey the capacities and needs of the particular set of individuals with whom he is dealing and must at the same time arrange the conditions which provide the subject-matter or content for experiences that satisfy these needs and develop these capacities. The planning must be flexible enough to permit free play for individuality of experience and yet firm enough to give direction towards continuous development of power.

The present occasion is a suitable one to say something about the province and office of the teacher. The principle that development of experience comes about through interaction means that education is essentially a social process. This quality is realized in the degree in which individuals form a community group. It is absurd to exclude the teacher from membership in the group. As the most mature member of the group he has a peculiar responsibility for the conduct of the interactions and intercommunications which are the very life of the group as a community. That children are individuals whose freedom should be respected while the more mature person should have no freedom as an individual is an idea too absurd to require refutation. The tendency to exclude the teacher from a positive and leading share in the direction of the activities of the community of which he is a member is another instance of reaction from one extreme to another. When pupils were a class rather than a social group, the teacher necessarily acted largely from the outside, not as a director of processes of exchange in which all had a share. When education is based upon experience and educative experience is seen to be a social process, the situation changes radically. The teacher loses the position of external boss or dictator but takes on that of leader of group activities.

In discussing the conduct of games as an example of normal social control, reference was made to the presence of a standardized conventional factor. The counterpart of this factor in school life is found in the question of manners, especially of good manners in the manifestations of politeness and courtesy. The more we know about customs in different parts of the world at different times in the history of mankind, the more we learn how much manners differ from place to place and time to time. This fact proves that there is a large conventional factor involved. But there is no group at any time or place which does not have some code of manners as, for example, with respect to proper ways of greeting other persons. The particular form a convention takes has nothing fixed and absolute about it. But the existence of some form of convention is not itself a convention. It is a uniform attendant of all social relationships. At the very least, it is the oil which prevents or reduces friction.

It is possible, of course, for these social forms to become, as we say, "mere formalities." They may become merely outward show with no meaning behind them. But the avoidance of empty ritualistic forms of social intercourse does not mean the rejection of every formal element. It rather indicates the need for development of forms of intercourse that are inherently appropriate to social situations. Visitors to some progressive schools are shocked by the lack of manners they come across. One who knows the situation better is aware that to some extent their absence is due to the eager interest of children to go on with what they are doing. In their eagerness they may, for example, bump into each other and into visitors with no word of apology. One might say that this condition is better than a display of merely external punctilio accompanying intellectual and emotional lack of interest in school work. But it also represents a failure in education, a failure to learn one of the most important lessons of life, that of mutual accommodation and adaptation. Education is going on in a one-sided way, for attitudes and habits are in process of formation that stand in the way of the future learning that springs from easy and ready contact and communication with others.

7

W. E. B. Du Bois

William Edward Burghardt Du Bois (1868–1963) was one of the most important American intellectuals of the 20th century. Growing up in Great Barrington, Massachusetts, Du Bois's thoughts on race and education in the United States developed early in his life. In 1885 Du Bois entered Fisk University in Nashville and then went on to attend Harvard to earn an M.A. in history and a Ph.D. in social science in 1895 (the first African American to do so). After his graduate work, which included two years of study in Germany at the prestigious Friedrich Wilhelm University in Berlin, Du Bois published his doctoral dissertation "The Suppression of the African Slave Trade to America, 1638–1870" as the first volume of the Harvard Historical Monograph Series. Du Bois went on to be a prolific writer who gracefully moved among writing novels, doing social science research, making theoretical socio-political analyses, and writing political commentary in periodicals. He was also an active member of the Communist party; editor of the NAACP's magazine, *Crisis*; a committed teacher; and one of the most brilliant and productive minds of the 20th century. At the end of his life, Du Bois emigrated to Ghana, Africa (1963), and took over the *Encyclopedia Africana* project while living out the rest of his days.

W. E. B. Du Bois's work on education and U.S. society forms a singular perspective in the history of philosophy of education. Many of his books and essays dealt primarily with education, and much of his other

Author: Clayton Pierce

work spent a good deal of time examining the subject in truly original ways. Because Du Bois was trained in cutting-edge German sociological methods, his early books (*The Suppression of the African Slave Trade to American* and *The Philadelphia Negro*) were superior to the works of any other American sociologist working during his time. The latter is still considered a classic in the field of sociology. His early work very much followed the tenor of standard sociological approaches that utilized empirical analyses and statistical models. Du Bois, however, refrained from introducing political and social critique at this early stage because he believed deeply in science's ability to transcend politics. Departing from this early approach, Du Bois shifted into a more affective and qualitative approach in his most famous work, *The Souls of Black Folk* (1903). In this masterpiece Du Bois produced a highly aestheticized historical work that examined the African American experience, producing the now standard theoretical concepts of "double consciousness" and the "veil."

Du Bois's work on education, in the broadest sense, can be seen as a critique and historical documentation of the ways in which African Americans have been systematically oppressed and denied equality in the very institution that is suppose to promote and cultivate freedom and justice. For Du Bois, slavery may have ended legally with the Emancipation Proclamation but its legacy continued in institutional and social forms throughout Du Bois's lifetime and beyond. His critique of public schooling is thus part of an overall view that institutionalized racism and white supremacy persist despite the dominant rhetoric of freedom, equality, and justice for all.

Segregated schooling, the ruling policy during Du Bois's lifetime, was simply an extension of a social caste system in the United States that facilitated a second life within which African American servitude could be reconstituted. Different from Booker T. Washington, who favored a separate but equal educational system, Du Bois argued vehemently that, if the United States was to deliver and honor the enlightenment principles it was founded on, there could be no compromise that would accept second-class citizenship for African Americans.

Du Bois's analysis of schooling also provides a unique perspective in that it simultaneously illuminates both racial and class inequality in his concept of caste education. This concept is original in the way it can demonstrate how, through racial segregation, educational institutions set in place a structure that guarantees racial domination by whites. This structural feature in Du Bois's educational thought, illuminates how whiteness is privileged and reproduced in schooling while creating a terrain in which democracy is unattainable. Thus, he revealed how the hallmark of public schools, building a democratic and just society through education, is an ideology that obscures the caste education system of the United States.

Du Bois's critique of schooling overlaps with many contemporary progressive critiques of schooling, such as critical pedagogy, which also examines the reproduction of forms of labor and class through schooling. Du Bois's critique and theory of schooling differs, however, in important ways from these because race is not ancillary but, instead, is given equal weight in his analysis. Du Bois's view of education is one that brings to the fore how schools produce not only docile labor for capital but also racist individuals. This analysis of schools offered by Du Bois is as timely today as it was when originally conceived and forces us to ask difficult questions in the face of increasing inequality and decreasing support for public schooling. We might ask the following: In what ways does caste education exist today in the United States? What are some of the major obstacles to realizing democracy through education that Du Bois brings to light? According to Du Bois, what role should education play in society? Finally, does Du Bois remain optimistic about the ability of public schools and education in general to address major social and political problems?

REFERENCES

Alridge, D. P. "Conceptualizing a Du Boisian Philosophy of Education: Toward a Model for African-American Education." *Educational Theory* 49, no. 3 (1999): 359–79.

Du Bois, W. E. B. *The Education of Black People: Ten Critiques 1906–1960*. New York: Monthly Review Press, 2001.

Lewis, D. L. *W. E. B. Du Bois: Biography of a Race 1868–1919*. New York: Henry Holt & Company, 1993.

Lewis, D. L. *W. E. B. Du Bois: The Fight for Equality and the American Century 1919–1963*. New York: Henry Holt & Company, 2000.

Provenzo, E. F. Jr., ed. *Du Bois on Education*. Walnut Creek, CA: AltaMira Press, 2002.

Rabaka, R. "W. E. B. Du Bois's Evolving Africana Philosophy of Education." *Journal of Black Studies* 33, no. 4 (2003): 399–449.

THE IMMORTAL CHILD

If a man die shall he live again? We do not know. But this we do know, that our children's children live forever and grow and develop toward perfection as they are trained. All human problems, then, center in the Immortal Child and his education is the problem of problems.

It is now nineteen years since I first saw Coleridge-Taylor. We were in London in some somber hall where there were many meeting, men and women called chiefly to the beautiful World's Fair at Paris; and then a few slipping over to London to meet Pan-Africa. We were there from Cape Colony and Liberia, from Haiti and the States, and from the Islands of the Sea. I remember the stiff, young officer who came with credentials from Menelik of Abyssinia; I remember the bitter, black American who whispered how an army of the Soudan might some day cross the Alps; I remember Englishmen, like the Colensos, who sat and counseled with us; but above all, I remember Coleridge-Taylor.

He was a little man and nervous, with dark-golden face and hair that bushed and strayed. His fingers were always nervously seeking hidden keys and he was quick with enthusiasm,—instinct with life. His bride of a year or more,—dark, too, in her whiter way,—was of the calm and quiet type. Her soft contralto voice thrilled us often as she sang, while her silences were full of understanding.

Several times we met in public gatherings and then they bade me to their home,—a nest of a cottage, with gate and garden, hidden in London's endless rings of suburbs. I dimly recall through these years a room in cozy disorder, strewn with music—music on the floor and music on the chairs, music in the air as the master rushed to the piano now and again to make some memory melodious—some allusion real.

And then at last, for it was the last, I saw Coleridge-Taylor in a mighty throng of people crowding the Crystal Palace. We came in facing the stage and scarcely dared look around. On the stage were a full orchestra, a chorus of eight hundred voices, and some of the world's famous soloists. He left his wife sitting beside me, and she was very silent as he went forward to lift the conductor's baton. It was one of the earliest renditions of "Hiawatha's Wedding Feast." We sat at rapt attention and when the last, weird music died, the great chorus and

From W. E. B. Du Bois, *Darkwater: Voices from within the Veil*, New York: Dover Publications, 1999 [1920].

orchestra rose as a man to acclaim the master; he turned toward the audience and then we turning for the first time saw that sea of faces behind,—the misty thousands whose voices rose to one strong shout of joy! It was a moment such as one does not often live. It seemed, and was, prophetic.

This young man who stepped forth as one of the most notable of modern English composers had a simple and uneventful career. His father was a black surgeon of Sierra Leone who came to London for study. While there he met an English girl and this son was born, in London, in 1875.

Then came a series of chances. His father failed to succeed and disappeared back to Africa leaving the support of the child to the poor working mother. The child showed evidences of musical talent and a friendly workingman gave him a little violin. A musician glancing from his window saw a little dark boy playing marbles on the street with a tiny violin in one hand; he gave him lessons. He happened to gain entrance into a charity school with a master of understanding mind who recognized genius when he saw it; and finally his beautiful child's treble brought him to the notice of the choirmaster of St. George's, Croyden.

So by happy accident his way was clear. Within his soul was no hesitation. He was one of those fortunate beings who are not called to *Wander-Jahre,* but are born with sails set and seas charted. Already the baby of four little years was a musician, and as choir-boy and violinist he walked unhesitatingly and surely to his life work. He was graduated with honors from the Royal Academy of Music in 1894, and married soon after the daughter of one of his professors. Then his life began, and whatever it lacked of physical adventure in the conventional round of a modern world-city, it more than gained in the almost tempestuous outpouring of his spiritual nature. Life to him was neither meat nor drink,—it was creative flame; ideas, plans, melodies glowed within him. To create, to do, to accomplish; to know the white glory of mighty midnights and the pale Amen of dawns was his day of days. Songs, pianoforte and violin pieces, trios and quintets for strings, incidental music, symphony, orchestral, and choral works rushed from his fingers. Nor were they laboriously contrived or light, thin things made to meet sudden popularity. Rather they were the flaming bits that must be said and sung,—that could not wait the slower birth of years, so hurried to the world as though their young creator knew that God gave him but a day. His whole active life was scarcely more than a decade and a half, and yet in that time, without wealth, friends, or influence, in the face of perhaps the most critical and skeptical and least imaginative civilization of the modern world, he wrote his name so high as a creative artist that it cannot soon be forgotten.

And this was but one side of the man. On the other was the sweet-tempered, sympathetic comrade, always willing to help, never knowing how to refuse, generous with every nerve and fiber of his being. Think of a young musician, father of a family, who at the time of his death held positions as Associate of the Royal College of Music, Professor in Trinity College and Crystal Palace, Conductor of the Handel Choral Society and the Rochester Choral Society, Principal of the Guildhall School of Music, where he had charge of the choral choir, the orchestra, and the opera. He was repeatedly the leader of music festivals all over Great Britain and a judge of contests. And with all this his house was open in cheering hospitality to friends and his hand ever ready with sympathy and help.

When such a man dies, it must bring pause to a reasoning world. We may call his death-sickness pneumonia, but we all know that it was sheer overwork,—the using of a delicately-tuned instrument too commonly and continuously and carelessly to let it last its normal life. We may well talk of the waste of wood and water, of food and fire, but the real and unforgivable waste of modern civilization is the waste of ability and genius,—the killing of useful, indispensable men who have no right to die; who deserve, not for themselves, but for the world, leisure, freedom from distraction, expert medical advice, and intelligent sympathy.

Coleridge-Taylor's life work was not finished,—it was but well begun. He lived only his first period of creative genius, when melody and harmony flashed and fluttered in subtle, compelling, and more than promising profusion. He did not live to do the organized, constructive work in the full, calm power of noonday,—the reflective finishing of evening. In the annals of the future his name must always stand high, but with the priceless gift of years, who can say where it might not have stood.

Why should he have worked so breathlessly, almost furiously? It was, we may be sure, because with unflinching determination and with no thought of surrender he faced the great alternative,—the choice which the cynical, thoughtless, busy, modern world spreads grimly before its greater souls—food or beauty, bread and butter, or ideals. And continually we see worthier men turning to the pettier, cheaper thing—the popular portrait, the sensational novel, the jingling song. The choice is not always between the least and the greatest, the high and the empty, but only too often it is between starvation and something. When, therefore, we see a man, working desperately to earn a living and still stooping to no paltry dickering and to no unworthy work, handing away a "Hiawatha" for less than a song, pausing for glimpses of the stars when a world full of charcoal glowed far more warmly and comfortably, we know that such a man is a hero in a sense never approached by the swashbuckling soldier or the lying patriot.

Deep as was the primal tragedy in the life of Coleridge-Taylor, there lay another still deeper. He smiled at it lightly, as we all do,—we who live within the veil,—to hide the deeper hurt. He had, with us, that divine and African gift of laughter, that echo of a thousand centuries of suns. I mind me how once he told of the bishop, the well-groomed English bishop, who eyed the artist gravely, with his eye-glass—hair and color and figure,—and said quite audibly to his friends, "Quite interesting—looks intelligent,—yes—yes!"

Fortunate was Coleridge-Taylor to be born in Europe and to speak a universal tongue. In America he could hardly have had his career. His genius was, to be sure, recognized (with some palpitation and consternation) when it came full-grown across the seas with an English imprint; but born here, it might never have been permitted to grow. We know in America how to discourage, choke, and murder ability when it so far forgets itself as to choose a dark skin. England, thank God, is slightly more civilized than her colonies; but even there the path of this young man was no way of roses and just a shade thornier than that of whiter men. He did not complain at it,—he did not

"Wince and cry aloud."

Rather the hint here and there of color discrimination in England aroused in him deeper and more poignant sympathy with his people throughout the world. He was one with that great company of mixed-blooded men: Pushkin and Dumas, Hamilton and Douglass, Browning and many others; but he more than most of these men knew the call of the blood when it came and listened and answered. He came to America with strange enthusiasm. He took with quite simple and unconscious grace the conventional congratulations of the musical world. He was used to that. But to his own people —to the sad sweetness of their voices, their inborn sense of music, their broken, half-articulate voices,—he leapt with new enthusiasm. From the fainter shadowings of his own life, he sensed instinctively the vaster tragedy of theirs. His soul yearned to give voice and being to this human thing. He early turned to the sorrow songs. He sat at the faltering feet of Paul Laurence Dunbar and he asked (as we sadly shook our heads) for some masterpiece of this world-tragedy that his soul could set to music. And then, so characteristically, he rushed back to England, composed a half-dozen exquisite harmonies haunted by slave-songs, led the Welsh in their singing, listened to the Scotch, ordered great music festivals in all England, wrote for Beerbohm Tree, took on another music professorship, promised a trip to Germany, and at last, staggering home one night, on his way to his wife and little boy and girl, fell in his tracks and in four days was dead, at the age of thirty-seven. They say that in his death-throe he arose and facing some great, ghostly choir raised his last baton, while all around the massive silence rang with the last mist-music of his dying ears.

He was buried from St. Michael's on September 5, 1912, with the acclaim of kings and music masters and little children and to the majestic melody of his own music. The tributes that followed him to his grave were unusually hearty and sincere. The head of the Royal College calls the first production of "Hiawatha" one of the most remarkable events in modern English musical history and the trilogy one of the most universally-beloved works of modern English music. One critic calls Taylor's a name "which with that of Elgar represented the nation's most individual output" and calls his "Atonement" "perhaps the finest passion music of modern times." Another critic speaks of his originality: "Though surrounded by the influences that are at work in Europe today, he retained his individuality to the end, developing his style, however, and evincing new ideas in each succeeding work. His untimely death at the age of thirty-seven, a short life—like those of Schubert, Mendelssohn, Chopin, and Hugo Wolf—has robbed the world of one of its noblest singers, one of those few men of modern times who found expression in the language of musical song, a lyricist of power and worth."

But the tributes did not rest with the artist; with peculiar unanimity they sought his "sterling character," "the good husband and father," the "staunch and loyal friend." And perhaps I cannot better end these hesitating words than with that tribute from one who called this master, friend, and whose lament cried in the night with more of depth and passion than Alfred Noyes is wont in his self-repression to voice:

"Through him, his race, a moment, lifted up
    Forests of hands to beauty, as in prayer,
Touched through his lips the sacramental cup
    And then sank back, benumbed in our bleak air."

Yet, consider: to many millions of people this man was all wrong. *First*, he ought never to have been born, for he was the mulatto son of a white woman. *Secondly*, he should never have been educated as a musician,—he should have been trained for his "place" in the world and to make him satisfied therewith. *Thirdly*, he should not have married the woman he loved and who loved him, for she was white and the niece of an Oxford professor. *Fourthly*, the children of such a union—but why proceed? You know it all by heart.

If he had been black, like Paul Laurence Dunbar, would the argument have been different? No. He should never have been born, for he is a "problem." He should never be educated, for he cannot be educated. He should never marry, for that means children and there is no place for black children in this world.

In the treatment of the child the world foreshadows its own future and faith. All words and all thinking lead to the child,—to that vast immortality and the wide sweep of infinite possibility which the child represents. Such thought as this it was that made the Master say of old as He saw baby faces:

"And whosoever shall offend one of these little ones, it is better for him that a millstone were hanged about his neck and he were cast into the sea."

And yet the mothers and fathers and the men and women of my race must often pause and ask: Is it worth while? Ought children be born to us? Have we any right to make human souls face what we face today? The answer is clear: If the great battle of human right against poverty, against disease, against color prejudice is to be won, it must be won, not in our day, but in the day of our children's children. Ours is the blood and dust of battle; theirs the rewards of victory. If, then, they are not there because we have not brought them into the world, we have been the guiltiest factor in conquering ourselves. It is our duty, then, to accomplish the immortality of black blood, in order that the day may come in this dark world when poverty shall be abolished, privilege be based on individual desert, and the color of a man's skin be no bar to the outlook of his soul.

If it is our duty as honest colored men and women, battling for a great principle, to bring not aimless rafts of children to the world, but as many as, with reasonable sacrifice, we can train to largest manhood, what in its inner essence shall that training be, particularly in its beginning?

The first temptation is to shield the child,—to hedge it about that it may not know and will not dream of the color line. Then when we can no longer wholly shield, to indulge and pamper and coddle, as though in this dumb way to compensate. From this attitude comes the multitude of our spoiled, wayward, disappointed children. And must we not blame ourselves? For while the motive was pure and the outer menace undoubted, is shielding and indulgence the way to meet it?

Some Negro parents, realizing this, leave their children to sink or swim in this sea of race prejudice. They neither shield nor explain, but thrust them forth grimly into school or street and let them learn as they may from brutal fact. Out of this may come strength, poise, self-dependence, and out of it, too, may come bewilderment, cringing deception, and self-distrust. It is, all said, a brutal, unfair method, and in its way it is as bad as shielding and indulgence. Why not, rather, face the facts and tell the truth? Your child is wiser than you think.

The truth lies ever between extremes. It is wrong to introduce the child to race consciousness prematurely; it is dangerous to let that consciousness grow spontaneously without intelligent guidance. With every step of dawning intelligence, explanation—frank, free, guiding explanation—must come. The day will dawn when mother must explain gently but clearly why the little girls next door do not want to play with "niggers"; what the real cause is of the teacher's unsympathetic attitude; and how people may ride in the backs of street cars and the smoker end of trains and still be people, honest high-minded souls.

Remember, too, that in such frank explanation you are speaking in nine cases out of ten to a good deal clearer understanding than you think and that the child-mind has what your tired soul may have lost faith in,—the Power and the Glory.

Out of little, unspoiled souls rise up wonderful resources and healing balm. Once the colored child understands the white world's attitude and the shameful wrong of it, you have furnished it with a great life motive,—a power and impulse toward good which is the mightiest thing man has. How many white folk would give their own souls if they might graft into their children's souls a great, moving, guiding ideal!

With this Power there comes, in the transfiguring soul of childhood, the Glory: the vision of accomplishment, the lofty ideal. Once let the strength of the motive work, and it becomes the life task of the parent to guide and to shape the ideal; to raise it from resentment and revenge to dignity and self-respect, to breadth and accomplishment, to human service; to beat back every thought of cringing and surrender.

Here, at last, we can speak with no hesitation, with no lack of faith. For we know that as the world grows better there will be realized in our children's lives that for which we fight unfalteringly, but vainly now.

So much for the problem of the home and our own dark children. Now let us look beyond the pale upon the children of the wide world. What is the real lesson of the life of Coleridge-Taylor? It is this: humanly speaking it was sheer accident that this boy developed his genius. We have a right to assume that hundreds and thousands of boys and girls today are missing the chance of developing unusual talents because the chances have been against them; and that indeed the majority of the children of the world are not being systematically fitted for their life work and for life itself. Why?

Many seek the reason in the content of the school program. They feverishly argue the relative values of Greek, mathematics, and manual training, but fail with singular unanimity in pointing out the fundamental cause of our failure in human education: That failure is due to the fact that we aim not at the full development of the child, but that the world regards and always has regarded education first as a means of buttressing the established order of things rather than improving it. And this is the real reason why strife, war, and revolution have marked the onward march of humanity instead of reason and sound reform. Instead of seeking to push the coming generation ahead of our pitiful accomplishment, we insist that it march behind. We say, morally, that high character is conformity to present public opinion; we say industrially that the present order is best and that children must be trained to perpetuate it.

But, it is objected, what else can we do? Can we teach Revolution to the inexperienced in hope that they may discern progress? No, but we may teach frankly that this world is not perfection, but development: that the object of education is manhood and womanhood, clear reason, individual talent and genius and the spirit of service and sacrifice, and not simply a frantic effort to avoid change in present institutions; that industry is for man and not man for industry and that while we must have workers to work, the prime object of our training is not the work but the worker—not the maintenance of present industrial caste but the development of human intelligence by which drudgery may be lessened and beauty widened.

Back of our present educational system is the philosophy that sneers at the foolish Fathers who believed it self-evident, "that all men were created free and equal." Surely the overwhelming evidence is today that men are slaves and unequal. But is it not education that is the creator of this freedom and equality? Most men today cannot conceive of a freedom that does not involve somebody's slavery. They do not want equality because the thrill of their happiness comes from having things that others have not. But may not human education fix the fine ideal of an equal maximum of freedom for every human soul combined with that minimum of slavery for each soul which the inexorable physical facts of the world impose—rather than complete freedom for some and complete slavery for others; and, again, is not the equality toward which the world moves an equality of honor in the assigned human task itself rather than equal facility in doing different tasks? Human equality is not lack of difference, nor do the infinite human differences argue relative superiority and inferiority. And, again, how new an aspect human differences may assume when all men are educated. Today we think of apes, semi-apes, and human beings; tomorrow we may think of Keir Hardies, Roosevelts, and Beethovens—not equals but men. Today we are forcing men into educational slavery in order that others may enjoy life, and excuse ourselves by saying that the world's work must be done. We are degrading some sorts of work by honoring others, and then expressing surprise that most people object to having their children trained solely to take up their father's tasks.

Given as the ideal the utmost possible freedom for every human soul, with slavery for none, and equal honor for all necessary human tasks, then our problem of education is greatly simplified: we aim to develop human souls; to make all intelligent; to discover special talents and genius. With this course of training beginning in early childhood and never ceasing must go the technical training for the present world's work according to carefully studied individual gifts and wishes.

On the other hand, if we arrange our system of education to develop workmen who will not strike and Negroes satisfied with their present place in the world, we have set ourselves a baffling task. We find ourselves compelled to keep the masses ignorant and to curb our own thought and expression so as not to inflame the ignorant. We force moderate reformers and men with new and valuable ideas to become red radicals and revolutionists, since that happens to be the only way to make the world listen to reason. Consider our race problem in the South: the South has invested in Negro ignorance; some Northerners proposed limited education, not, they explained, to better the Negro, but merely to make the investment more profitable to the present beneficiaries. They thus gained wide Southern support for schools like Hampton and Tuskegee. But could this program be expected long to satisfy colored folk? And was this shifty dodging of the real issue the wisest statesmanship? No! The real question in the South is the question of the permanency of present color caste. The problem, then, of the formal training of our colored children has been strangely complicated by the strong feeling of certain persons as to their future in America and the world. And the reaction toward this caste education has strengthened the idea of caste education throughout the world.

Let us then return to fundamental ideals. Children must be trained in a knowledge of what the world is and what it knows and how it does its daily work. These things cannot be separated: we cannot teach pure knowledge apart from actual facts, or separate truth from the human mind. Above all we must not forget that the object of all education is the child itself and not what it does or makes.

It is here that a great movement in America has grievously sinned against the light. There has arisen among us a movement to make the Public School primarily the hand-maiden of production. America is conceived of as existing for the sake of its mines, fields and factories, and not those factories, fields and mines as existing for America. Consequently, the public schools are for training the mass of men as servants and laborers and mechanics to increase the land's industrial efficiency.

Those who oppose this program, especially if they are black, are accused of despising common toil and humble service. In fact, we Negroes are but facing in our own children a world problem: how can we, while maintaining a proper output of goods and furnishing needed services, increase the knowledge of experience of common men and conserve genius for the common weal? Without wider, deeper intelligence among the masses Democracy cannot accomplish its greater ends. Without a more careful conservation of human ability and talent the world cannot secure the services which its greater needs call for. Yet today who goes to college, the Talented or the Rich? Who goes to high school, the Bright or the Well-to-Do? Who does the physical work of the world, those whose muscles need the exercise or those whose souls and minds are stupefied with manual toil? How is the drudgery of the world distributed, by thoughtful justice or the lash of Slavery?

We cannot base the education of future citizens on the present inexcusable inequality of wealth nor on physical differences of race. We must seek not to make men carpenters but to make carpenters men.

Colored Americans must then with deep determination educate their children in the broadest, highest way. They must fill the colleges with the talented and fill the fields and shops with the intelligent. Wisdom is the principal thing. Therefore, get wisdom.

But why am I talking simply of "colored" children? Is not the problem of their education simply an intensification of the problem of educating all children? Look at our plight in the United States, nearly 150 years after the establishment of a government based on human intelligence.

If we take the figures of the Thirteenth Census, we find that there were five and one-half million illiterate Americans of whom 3,184,633 were white. Remembering that illiteracy is a crude and extreme test of ignorance, we may assume that there are in the United States ten million people over ten years of age who are too ignorant either to perform their civic duties or to teach industrial efficiency. Moreover, it does not seem that this illiteracy is disappearing rapidly.

For instance, nine percent of American children between ten and nineteen years of age cannot read and write. Moreover, there are millions of children who, judging by the figures for the school year 1909–10, are not going to learn to read and write, for of the Americans six to fourteen years of age there were 3,125,392 who were not in school a single day during that year. If we take the eleven million youths fifteen to twenty years of age for whom vocational training is particularly adapted, we find that nearly five per cent of these, or 448,414, are absolutely illiterate; it is not too much to assume that a million of them have not acquired enough of the ordinary tools of intelligence to make the most of efficient vocational training.

Confining ourselves to the white people, over fifteen per cent of the white children six to fourteen years of age, or 2,253,198, did not attend school during the school year 1909–10. Of the native white children of native parents ten to fourteen years of age nearly a tenth were not in school during that year; 121,878 native white children of native parents, fifteen to nineteen years of age, were illiterate.

If we continue our attention to the colored children, the case is, of course, much worse.

We cannot hope to make intelligent workmen and intelligent citizens of a group of people, over forty per cent of whose children six to fourteen years of age were not in school a single day during 1909–10; for the other sixty per cent the school term in the majority of cases was probably less than five months. Of the Negro children ten to fourteen years of age 18.9 per cent were illiterate; of those fifteen to nineteen years of age 20.3 per cent were illiterate; of those ten to fourteen years of age 31.4 per cent did not go to school a single day in 1909–10.

What is the trouble? It is simple. We are spending one dollar for education where we should spend ten dollars. If tomorrow we multiplied our effort to educate the next generation ten-fold, we should but begin our bounden duty. The heaven that lies about our infancy is but the ideals come true which every generation of children is capable of bringing; but we, selfish in our own ignorance and incapacity, are making of education a series of miserable compromises: How ignorant can we let a child grow to be in order to make him the best cotton mill operative? What is the least sum that will keep the average youth out of jail? How many months saved on a high school course will make the largest export of wheat?

If we realized that children are the future, that immortality is the present child, that no education which educates can possibly be too costly, then we know that the menace of Kaiserism which called for the expenditure of more than 332 thousand millions of dollars was not a whit more pressing than the menace of ignorance, and that no nation tomorrow will call itself civilized which does not give every single human being college and vocational training free and under the best teaching force procurable for love or money.

This world has never taken the education of children seriously. Misled by selfish dreamings of personal life forever, we have neglected the true and practical immortality through the endless life of children's children. Seeking counsels of our own souls' perfection, we have despised and rejected the possible increasing perfection of unending generations. Or if we are thrown back in pessimistic despair from making living folk decent, we leap to idle speculations of a thousand years hereafter instead of working steadily and persistently for the next generation.

All our problems center in the child. All our hopes, our dreams are for our children. Has our own life failed? Let its lesson save the children's lives from similar failure. Is democracy a failure? Train up citizens that will make it succeed. Is wealth too crude, too foolish in form, and too easily stolen? Train up workers with honor and consciences and brains. Have we degraded service with menials? Abolish the mean spirit and implant sacrifice. Do we despise women? Train them as workers and thinkers and not as playthings, lest future generations ape our worst mistake. Do we despise darker races? Teach the children its fatal cost in spiritual degradation and murder, teach them that to hate "niggers" or "chinks" is to crucify souls like their own. Is there anything we would accomplish with human beings? Do it with the immortal child, with a stretch of endless time for doing it and with infinite possibilities to work on.

Is this our attitude toward education? It is not—neither in England nor America—in France nor Germany—with black nor white nor yellow folk. Education to the modern world is a burden which we are driven to carry. We shirk and complain. We do just as little as possible and only threat or catastrophe induces us to do more than a minimum. If the ignorant mass, panting to know, revolts, we dole them gingerly enough knowledge to pacify them temporarily. If, as in the Great War, we discover soldiers too ignorant to use our machines of murder and destruction, we train them—to use machines of murder and destruction. If mounting wealth calls for intelligent workmen, we rush tumultuously to train workers—in order to increase our wealth. But of great, broad plans to train all men for all things—to make a universe intelligent, busy, good, creative and beautiful—where in this wide world is such an educational program? To announce it is to invite gasps or Brobdingnagian laughter. It cannot be done. It will cost too much.

What has been done with man can be done with men, if the world tries long enough and hard enough. And as to the cost—all the wealth of the world, save that necessary for sheer decent existence and for the maintenance of past civilization, is, and of right ought to be, the property of the children for their education.

I mean it. In one year, 1917, we spent $96,700,000,000 for war. We blew it away to murder, maim, and destroy! Why? Because the blind, brutal crime of powerful and selfish interests made this path through hell the only visible way to heaven. We did it. We had to do it, and we are glad the putrid horror is over. But, now, are we prepared to spend less to make a world in which the resurgence of such devilish power will be impossible?

Do we really want war to cease?

Then educate the children of this generation at a cost no whit less and if necessary a hundred times as great as the cost of the Great War.

Last year, 1917, education cost us $915,000,000.

Next year it ought to cost us at least two thousand million dollars. We should spend enough money to hire the best teaching force possible—the best organizing and directing ability in the land, even if we have to strip the railroads and meat trust. We should dot city and country with the most efficient, sanitary, and beautiful school-houses the world knows and we should give every American child common school, high school, and college training and then vocational guidance in earning a living.

Is this a dream?

Can we afford less?

Consider our so-called educational "problems"; "How may we keep pupils in the high school?" Feed and clothe them. "Shall we teach Latin, Greek, and mathematics to the 'masses'?" If they are worth teaching to anybody, the masses need them most. "Who shall go to college?" Everybody. "When shall culture training give place to technical education for work?" Never.

These questions are not "problems." They are simply "excuses" for spending less time and money on the next generation. Given ten millions of dollars a year, what can we best do with the education of a million children? The real answer is—kill nine hundred and ninety thousand of them quickly and not gradually, and make thoroughly-trained men and women of the other ten thousand. But who set the limit of ten million dollars? Who says it shall not be ten thousand millions, as it ought to be? You and I say it, and in saying it we sin against the Holy Ghost.

We sin because in our befuddled brains we have linked money and education inextricably. We assume that only the wealthy have a real right to education when, in fact, being born is being given a right to college training. Our wealth today is, we all know, distributed mainly by chance inheritance and personal favor and yet we attempt to base the right to education on this foundation. The result is grotesque! We bury genius; we send it to jail; we ridicule and mock it, while we send mediocrity and idiocy to college, gilded and crowned. For three hundred years we have denied black Americans an education and now we exploit them before a gaping world: See how ignorant and degraded they are! All they are fit for is education for cotton-picking and dishwashing. When Dunbar and Taylor happen along, we are torn between something like shamefaced anger or impatient amazement.

A world guilty of this last and mightiest war has no right to enjoy or create until it has made the future safe from another Arkansas or Rheims. To this there is but one patent way, proved and inescapable, Education, and that not for me or for you but for the Immortal Child. And that child is of all races and all colors. All children are the children of all and not of individuals and families and races. The whole generation must be trained and guided and out of it as out of a huge reservoir must be lifted all genius, talent, and intelligence to serve all the world.

8

ANTONIO GRAMSCI

Antonio Gramsci was born in Sardinia, Italy, in 1891 and died in 1937. Because of family difficulties and his health problems, his schooling was irregular, but he managed to complete his secondary education. He was an activist in defense of miners and farmers, a militant in the workers' movement, and a member of the Socialist party. He studied at the University of Turin, an area in the north of Italy with rapid industrial growth in the early part of the 20th century.

Gramsci wrote for socialist newspapers and became one of the editors of "Avanti!"—the Socialist party paper—and a few years later he became the editor of "Il Grido del Popolo." He was known as a clear thinker who explained political theory in accessible ways through his writing. As a militant activist and an ideological leader, he gave numerous public speeches and engaged in educational programs for workers. Influenced by the work of Sorel, an anarchist who advocated for trade unions as a way of disrupting central government powers, Gramsci supported workers' councils, which he thought were an important venue for workers' empowerment during strikes in 1919 and 1920. However, the failure of the councils forced Gramsci to look for alternatives, and he helped create the Communist party of Italy (Partito Comunista d'Italia) in 1921. In his capacity as political leader, he advocated for a united front against fascism. Growing government repression resulted in Gramsci's imprisonment.

Gramsci is one of the most important Marxist thinkers of the 20th century. He was a prolific writer during his years in prison, producing a significant number of essays, many of which have been published in English as a collection titled *Selections from the Prison Notebooks.* He wrote about many topics, including history and politics, as well as some reflections about education. In his writing he explained how cultural hegemony has contributed to maintaining a system of education that serves capitalism, offering the alternative to develop popular education programs for workers supporting the growth of intellectuals from the working class. He also made important distinctions between civil society, which includes schools and unions, and political society, which includes the legal system and the police. While civil society is guided by ideology and agreement, political society is guided by control and domination. The writings of Machiavelli, Sorel, and Marx, as well as several Italian thinkers of his time among others, have influenced his own analysis.

In the following reading selections Gramsci discusses intellectuals and education. He asserted that all people have intellectual abilities in spite of the fact that only a few function as intellectuals in society. Those who work as intellectuals can contribute to the reproduction of hegemonic forces, which in his view served as domination of classes by ideological and cultural means, not by violence, representing the culture of the privileged as the standard, the common sense, and in consequence the working classes accepting the terms of their own conditions. But intellectuals can define their work "organically" to articulate and explain the voice of the marginalized people. Then, he proposes an education system that will enable the development of organic intellectuals and he looks at learning as a form of work. Furthermore, by looking at education in this way, he provoked further thinking about the relationships of social class and schooling, what curriculum is for whom, and what interests and ideas are educational systems serving.

REFERENCE

Gramsci, A. *Selections from the Prison Notebooks.* New York: International, 1971.

THE INTELLECTUALS

The Formation of the Intellectuals

Are intellectuals an autonomous and independent social group, or does every social group have its own particular specialised category of intellectuals? The problem is a complex one, because of the variety of forms assumed to date by the real historical process of formation of the different categories of intellectuals.

The most important of these forms are two:

1. Every social group, coming into existence on the original terrain of an essential function in the world of economic production, creates together with itself, organically, one or more strata[1] of intellectuals which give it homogeneity and an awareness of its own function not only in the economic but also in the social and political fields. The capitalist entrepreneur creates alongside himself the industrial technician, the specialist in political economy, the organisers of a new culture, of a new legal system, etc. It should be noted that the entrepreneur himself represents a higher level of social elaboration, already characterised by a certain directive [*dirigente*][2] and technical (i.e. intellectual) capacity: he must have a certain technical capacity, not only in the limited sphere of his activity and initiative but in other spheres as well, at least in those which are closest to economic production. He must be an organiser of masses of men; he must be an organiser of the "confidence" of investors in his business, of the customers for his product, etc.

If not all entrepreneurs, at least an *élite* amongst them must have the capacity to be an organiser of society in general, including all its complex organism of services, right up to the state organism, because of the need to create the conditions most favourable to the expansion of their own class; or at the least they must possess the capacity to choose the deputies (specialised employees) to whom to entrust this activity of organising the general system of relationships external to the business itself. It can be observed that the "organic" intellectuals which every new class creates alongside itself and elaborates in the course of its development, are for the most part "specialisations" of

From *Prison Notebooks: Selections* by Antonio Gramsci, 1971. Reprinted by permission of International Publishers, New York.

partial aspects of the primitive activity of the new social type which the new class has brought into prominence.*

Even feudal lords were possessors of a particular technical capacity, military capacity, and it is precisely from the moment at which the aristocracy loses its monopoly of technico-military capacity that the crisis of feudalism begins. But the formation of intellectuals in the feudal world and in the preceding classical world is a question to be examined separately: this formation and elaboration follows ways and means which must be studied concretely. Thus it is to be noted that the mass of the peasantry, although it performs an essential function in the world of production, does not elaborate its own "organic" intellectuals, nor does it "assimilate" any stratum of "traditional" intellectuals, although it is from the peasantry that other social groups draw many of their intellectuals and a high proportion of traditional intellectuals are of peasant origin.[4]

2. However, every "essential" social group which emerges into history out of the preceding economic structure, and as an expression of a development of this structure, has found (at least in all of history up to the present) categories of intellectuals already in existence and which seemed indeed to represent an historical continuity uninterrupted even by the most complicated and radical changes in political and social forms.

The most typical of these categories of intellectuals is that of the ecclesiastics, who for a long time (for a whole phase of history, which is partly characterised by this very monopoly) held a monopoly of a number of important services: religious ideology, that is the philosophy and science of the age, together with schools, education, morality, justice, charity, good works, etc. The category of ecclesiastics can be considered the category of intellectuals organically bound to the landed aristocracy. It had equal status juridically with the aristocracy, with which it shared the exercise of feudal ownership of land, and the use of state

---

*Mosca's *Elementi di Scienza Politica* (new expanded edition, 1923) are worth looking at in this connection. Mosca's so-called "political class"[3] is nothing other than the intellectual category of the dominant social group. Mosca's concept of "political class" can be connected with Pareto's concept of the *élite*, which is another attempt to interpret the historical phenomenon of the intellectuals and their function in the life of the state and of society. Mosca's book is an enormous hotch-potch, of a sociological and positivistic character, plus the tendentiousness of immediate politics which makes it less indigestible and livelier from a literary point of view.

privileges connected with property.* But the monopoly held by the ecclesiastics in the superstructural field** was not exercised without a struggle or without limitations, and hence there took place the birth, in various forms (to be gone into and studied concretely), of other categories, favoured and enabled to expand by the growing strength of the central power of the monarch, right up to absolutism. Thus we find the formation of the *noblesse de robe*, with its own privileges, a stratum of administrators, etc., scholars and scientists, theorists, non-ecclesiastical philosophers, etc.

Since these various categories of traditional intellectuals experience through an *"esprit de corps"* their uninterrupted historical continuity and their special qualification, they thus put themselves forward as autonomous and independent of the dominant social group. This self-assessment is not without consequences in the ideological and political field, consequences of wide-ranging import. The whole of idealist philosophy can easily be connected with this position assumed by the social complex of intellectuals and can be defined as the expression of that social utopia by which the intellectuals think of themselves as "independent", autonomous, endowed with a character of their own, etc.

One should note however that if the Pope and the leading hierarchy of the Church consider themselves more linked to Christ and to the apostles than they are to senators Agnelli and Benni,[5] the same does not hold for Gentile and Croce, for example: Croce in particular feels himself closely linked to Aristotle and Plato, but he does not conceal, on the other hand, his links with senators Agnelli and Benni, and it is precisely here that one can discern the most significant character of Croce's philosophy.

---

*For one category of these intellectuals, possibly the most important after the ecclesiastical for its prestige and the social function it performed in primitive societies, the category of *medical men* in the wide sense, that is all those who "struggle" or seem to struggle against death and disease, compare the *Storia della medicina* of Arturo Castiglioni. Note that there has been a connection between religion and medicine, and in certain areas there still is: hospitals in the hands of religious orders for certain organisational functions, apart from the fact that wherever the doctor appears, so does the priest (exorcism, various forms of assistance, etc.). Many great religious figures were and are conceived of as great "healers": the idea of miracles, up to the resurrection of the dead. Even in the case of kings the belief long survived that they could heal with the laying on of hands, etc.

**From this has come the general sense of "intellectual" or "specialist" of the word *"chierico"* (clerk, cleric) in many languages of romance origin or heavily influenced, through church Latin, by the romance languages, together with its correlative *"laico"* (lay, layman) in the sense of profane, non-specialist.

What are the "maximum" limits of acceptance of the term "intellectual"? Can one find a unitary criterion to characterise equally all the diverse and disparate activities of intellectuals and to distinguish these at the same time and in an essential way from the activities of other social groupings? The most widespread error of method seems to me that of having looked for this criterion of distinction in the intrinsic nature of intellectual activities, rather than in the ensemble of the system of relations in which these activities (and therefore the intellectual groups who personify them) have their place within the general complex of social relations. Indeed the worker or proletarian, for example, is not specifically characterised by his manual or instrumental work, but by performing this work in specific conditions and in specific social relations (apart from the consideration that purely physical labour does not exist and that even Taylor's phrase of "trained gorilla"[6] is a metaphor to indicate a limit in a certain direction: in any physical work, even the most degraded and mechanical, there exists a minimum of technical qualification, that is, a minimum of creative intellectual activity.) And we have already observed that the entrepreneur, by virtue of his very function, must have to some degree a certain number of qualifications of an intellectual nature although his part in society is determined not by these, but by the general social relations which specifically characterise the position of the entrepreneur within industry.

All men are intellectuals, one could therefore say: but not all men have in society the function of intellectuals.*

When one distinguishes between intellectuals and non-intellectuals, one is referring in reality only to the immediate social function of the professional category of the intellectuals, that is, one has in mind the direction in which their specific professional activity is weighted, whether towards intellectual elaboration or towards muscular-nervous effort. This means that, although one can speak of intellectuals, one cannot speak of non-intellectuals, because non-intellectuals do not exist. But even the relationship between efforts of intellectual-cerebral elaboration and muscular-nervous effort is not always the same, so that there are varying degrees of specific intellectual activity. There is no human activity from which every form of intellectual participation can be

---

*Thus, because it can happen that everyone at some time fries a couple of eggs or sews up a tear in a jacket, we do not necessarily say that everyone is a cook or a tailor.

excluded: *homo faber* cannot be separated from *homo sapiens*.[7] Each man, finally, outside his professional activity, carries on some form of intellectual activity, that is, he is a "philosopher", an artist, a man of taste, he participates in a particular conception of the world, has a conscious line of moral conduct, and therefore contributes to sustain a conception of the world or to modify it, that is, to bring into being new modes of thought.

The problem of creating a new stratum of intellectuals consists therefore in the critical elaboration of the intellectual activity that exists in everyone at a certain degree of development, modifying its relationship with the muscular-nervous effort towards a new equilibrium, and ensuring that the muscular-nervous effort itself, in so far as it is an element of a general practical activity, which is perpetually innovating the physical and social world, becomes the foundation of a new and integral conception of the world. The traditional and vulgarised type of the intellectual is given by the man of letters, the philosopher, the artist. Therefore journalists, who claim to be men of letters, philosophers, artists, also regard themselves as the "true" intellectuals. In the modern world, technical education, closely bound to industrial labour even at the most primitive and unqualified level, must form the basis of the new type of intellectual.

On this basis the weekly *Ordine Nuovo*[8] worked to develop certain forms of new intellectualism and to determine its new concepts, and this was not the least of the reasons for its success, since such a conception corresponded to latent aspirations and conformed to the development of the real forms of life. The mode of being of the new intellectual can no longer consist in eloquence, which is an exterior and momentary mover of feelings and passions, but in active participation in practical life, as constructor, organiser, "permanent persuader" and not just a simple orator (but superior at the same time to the abstract mathematical spirit); from technique-as-work one proceeds to technique-as-science and to the humanistic conception of history, without which one remains "specialised" and does not become "directive"[9] (specialised and political).

Thus there are historically formed specialised categories for the exercise of the intellectual function. They are formed in connection with all social groups, but especially in connection with the more important, and they undergo more extensive and complex elaboration in connection with the dominant social group. One of the most important characteristics of any group that is developing towards dominance is its struggle to assimilate and to conquer "ideologically" the traditional intellectuals, but this assimilation and conquest is made quicker and more efficacious the more the group in question succeeds in simultaneously elaborating its own organic intellectuals.

The enormous development of activity and organisation of education in the broad sense in the societies that emerged from the medieval world is an index of the importance assumed in the modern world by intellectual functions and categories. Parallel with the attempt to deepen and to broaden the "intellectuality" of each individual, there has also been an attempt to multiply and narrow the various specialisations. This can be seen from educational institutions at all levels, up to and including the organisms that exist to promote so-called "high culture" in all fields of science and technology.

School is the instrument through which intellectuals of various levels are elaborated. The complexity of the intellectual function in different states can be measured objectively by the number and gradation of specialised schools: the more extensive the "area" covered by education and the more numerous the "vertical" "levels" of schooling, the more complex is the cultural world, the civilisation, of a particular state. A point of comparison can be found in the sphere of industrial technology: the industrialisation of a country can be measured by how well equipped it is in the production of machines with which to produce machines, and in the manufacture of ever more accurate instruments for making both machines and further instruments for making machines, etc. The country which is best equipped in the construction of instruments for experimental scientific laboratories and in the construction of instruments with which to test the first instruments, can be regarded as the most complex in the technical-industrial field, with the highest level of civilisation, etc. The same applies to the preparation of intellectuals and to the schools dedicated to this preparation; schools and institutes of high culture can be assimilated to each other. In this field also, quantity cannot be separated from quality. To the most refined technical-cultural specialisation there cannot but correspond the maximum possible diffusion of primary education and the maximum care taken to expand the middle grades numerically as much as possible.

Naturally this need to provide the widest base possible for the selection and elaboration of the top intellectual qualifications—i.e. to give a democratic structure to high culture and top-level technology—is not without its disadvantages: it creates the possibility of vast crises of unemployment for the middle intellectual strata, and in all modern societies this actually takes place.

It is worth noting that the elaboration of intellectual strata in concrete reality does not take place on the terrain of abstract democracy but in accordance with very concrete traditional historical processes. Strata have grown up which traditionally "produce" intellectuals and these strata coincide with those which have specialised in "saving", i.e. the petty and middle landed bourgeoisie and certain strata of the petty and middle urban bourgeoisie. The varying distribution of different types of school (classical and professional)[10] over the "economic" territory and the varying aspirations of different categories within these strata determine, or give form to, the production of various branches of intellectual specialisation. Thus in Italy the rural bourgeoisie produces in particular state functionaries and professional people, whereas the urban bourgeoisie produces technicians for industry. Consequently it is largely northern Italy which produces technicians and the South which produces functionaries and professional men.

The relationship between the intellectuals and the world of production is not as direct as it is with the fundamental social groups but is, in varying degrees, "mediated" by the whole fabric of society and by the complex of superstructures, of which the intellectuals are, precisely, the "functionaries". It should be possible both to measure the "organic quality" [*organicità*] of the various intellectual strata and their degree of connection with a fundamental social group, and to establish a gradation of their functions and of the superstructures from the bottom to the top (from the structural base upwards). What we can do, for the moment, is to fix two major superstructural "levels": the one that can be called "civil society", that is the ensemble of organisms commonly called "private", and that of "political society" or "the State". These two levels correspond on the one hand to the function of "hegemony" which the dominant group exercises throughout society and on the other hand to that of "direct domination" or command exercised through the State and "juridical" government. The functions in question are precisely organisational and connective. The intellectuals are the dominant group's "deputies" exercising the subaltern functions of social hegemony and political government. These comprise:

1. The "spontaneous" consent given by the great masses of the population to the general direction imposed on social life by the dominant fundamental group; this consent is "historically" caused by the prestige (and consequent confidence) which the dominant group enjoys because of its position and function in the world of production.

2. The apparatus of state coercive power which "legally" enforces discipline on those groups who do not "consent" either actively or passively. This apparatus is, however, constituted for the whole of society in anticipation of moments of crisis of command and direction when spontaneous consent has failed.

This way of posing the problem has as a result a considerable extension of the concept of intellectual, but it is the only way which enables one to reach a concrete approximation of reality. It also clashes with preconceptions of caste. The function of organising social hegemony and state domination certainly gives rise to a particular division of labour and therefore to a whole hierarchy of qualifications in some of which there is no apparent attribution of directive or organisational functions. For example, in the apparatus of social and state direction there exist a whole series of jobs of a manual and instrumental character (non-executive work, agents rather than officials or functionaries).[11] It is obvious that such a distinction has to be made just as it is obvious that other distinctions have to be made as well. Indeed, intellectual activity must also be distinguished in terms of its intrinsic characteristics, according to levels which in moments of extreme opposition represent a real qualitative difference—at the highest level would be the creators of the various sciences, philosophy, art, etc., at the lowest the most humble "administrators" and divulgators of pre-existing, traditional, accumulated intellectual wealth.*

In the modern world the category of intellectuals, understood in this sense, has undergone an unprecedented expansion. The democratic-bureaucratic system has given rise to a great mass of functions which

---

*Here again military organisation offers a model of complex gradations between subaltern officers, senior officers and general staff, not to mention the NCO's, whose importance is greater than is generally admitted. It is worth observing that all these parts feel a solidarity and indeed that it is the lower strata that display the most blatant *esprit de corps*, from which they derive a certain "conceit"[12] which is apt to lay them open to jokes and witticisms.

are not all justified by the social necessities of production, though they are justified by the political necessities of the dominant fundamental group. Hence Loria's[13] conception of the unproductive "worker" (but unproductive in relation to whom and to what mode of production?), a conception which could in part be justified if one takes account of the fact that these masses exploit their position to take for themselves a large cut out of the national income. Mass formation has standardised individuals both psychologically and in terms of individual qualification and has produced the same phenomena as with other standardised masses: competition which makes necessary organisations for the defence of professions, unemployment, over-production in the schools, emigration, etc.

Notes

1. The Italian word here is *"ceti"* which does not carry quite the same connotations as "strata", but which we have been forced to translate in that way for lack of alternatives. It should be noted that Gramsci tends, for reasons of censorship, to avoid using the word class in contexts where its Marxist overtones would be apparent, preferring (as for example in this sentence) the more neutral "social group". The word "group", however, is not always a euphemism for "class", and to avoid ambiguity Gramsci uses the phrase "fundamental social group" when he wishes to emphasise the fact that he is referring to one or other of the major social classes (bourgeoisie, proletariat) defined in strict Marxist terms by its position in the fundamental relations of production. Class groupings which do not have this fundamental role are often described as "castes" (aristocracy, etc.). The word "category", on the other hand, which also occurs on this page, Gramsci tends to use in the standard Italian sense of members of a trade or profession, though also more generally. Throughout this edition we have rendered Gramsci's usage as literally as possible (see note on Gramsci's Terminology, p. xiii).
2. See note on Gramsci's Terminology.
3. Usually translated in English as "ruling class", which is also the title of the English version of Mosca's *Elementi* (G. Mosca, *The Ruling Class*, New York 1939). Gaetano Mosca (1858–1941) was, together with Pareto and Michels, one of the major early Italian exponents of the theory of political *élites*. Although sympathetic to fascism, Mosca was basically a conservative, who saw the *élite* in rather more static terms than did some of his fellows.
4. Notably in Southern Italy. See below, "The Different Position of Urban and Rural-type Intellectuals", pp. 14–23. Gramsci's general argument, here as elsewhere in the *Quaderni*, is that the person of peasant origin who becomes an "intellectual" (priest, lawyer, etc.) generally thereby ceases to be organically linked to his class of origin. One of the essential differences

between, say, the Catholic Church and the revolutionary party of the working class lies in the fact that, ideally, the proletariat should be able to generate its own "organic" intellectuals within the class and who remain intellectuals *of* their class.

5. Heads of FIAT and Montecatini (Chemicals) respectively. For Agnelli, of
    whom Gramsci had direct experience during the *Ordine Nuovo* period, see
    note II on p. 286.
6. For Frederick Taylor and his notion of the manual worker as a "trained
    gorilla", see Gramsci's essay *Americanism and Fordism*, pp. 277–318 of this
    volume.
7. i.e. Man the maker (or tool-bearer) and Man the thinker.
8. The *Ordine Nuovo*, the magazine edited by Gramsci during his days as a
    militant in Turin, ran as a "weekly review of Socialist culture" in 1919 and
    1920. See Introduction, pp. xxxv ff.
9. *"Dirigente."* This extremely condensed and elliptical sentence contains a
    number of key Gramscian ideas: on the possibility of proletarian cultural
    hegemony through domination of the work process, on the distinction
    between organic intellectuals of the working class and traditional intellec-
    tuals from outside, on the unity of theory and practice as a basic Marxist
    postulate, etc.
10. The Italian school system above compulsory level is based on a division
    between academic ("classical" and "scientific") education and vocational
    training for professional purposes. Technical and, at the academic level,
    "scientific" colleges tend to be concentrated in the Northern industrial
    areas.
11. *"funzionari"*: in Italian usage the word is applied to the middle and higher
    echelons of the bureaucracy. Conversely "administrators" (*"amministra-
    tori"*) is used here (end of paragraph) to mean people who merely "admin-
    ister" the decisions of others. The phrase "non-executive work" is a transla-
    tion of *"[impiego] di ordine e non di concetto"* which refers to distinctions
    within clerical work.
12. *"boria"*. This is a reference to an idea of Vico (see note 41 on p. 151).
13. For Loria see note 108 on p. 458. The notion of the "unproductive labourer"
    is not in fact an invention of Loria's but has its origins in Marx's definitions
    of productive and unproductive labour in *Capital,* which Loria, in his char-
    acteristic way, both vulgarised and claimed as his own discovery.

ON EDUCATION

The Organisation of Education and of Culture

It may be observed in general that in modern civilisation all practical
activities have become so complex, and the sciences[1] so interwoven
with everyday life, that each practical activity tends to create a new

type of school for its own executives and specialists and hence to create a body of specialist intellectuals at a higher level to teach in these schools. Thus, side by side with the type of school which may be called "humanistic"—the oldest form of traditional school, designed to develop in each individual human being an as yet undifferentiated general culture, the fundamental power to think and ability to find one's way in life—a whole system of specialised schools, at varying levels, has been being created to serve entire professional sectors, or professions which are already specialised and defined within precise boundaries. It may be said, indeed, that the educational crisis raging today is precisely linked to the fact that this process of differentiation and particularisation is taking place chaotically, without clear and precise principles, without a well-studied and consciously established plan. The crisis of the curriculum and organisation of the schools, i.e. of the overall framework of a policy for forming modern intellectual cadres, is to a great extent an aspect and a ramification of the more comprehensive and general organic crisis.

The fundamental division into classical and vocational (professional) schools was a rational formula: the vocational school for the instrumental classes,[2] the classical school for the dominant classes and the intellectuals. The development of an industrial base both in the cities and in the countryside meant a growing need for the new type of urban intellectual. Side by side with the classical school there developed the technical school (vocational, but not manual), and this placed a question-mark over the very principle of a concrete programme of general culture, a humanistic programme of general culture based on the Græco-Roman tradition. This programme, once questioned, can be said to be doomed, since its formative capacity was to a great extent based on the general and traditionally unquestioned prestige of a particular form of civilisation.

The tendency today is to abolish every type of schooling that is "disinterested" (not serving immediate interests) or "formative"—keeping at most only a small-scale version to serve a tiny élite of ladies and gentlemen who do not have to worry about assuring themselves of a future career. Instead, there is a steady growth of specialised vocational schools, in which the pupil's destiny and future activity are determined in advance. A rational solution to the crisis ought to adopt the following lines. First, a common basic education, imparting a general, humanistic, formative culture; this would strike the right balance

between development of the capacity for working manually (technically, industrially) and development of the capacities required for intellectual work. From this type of common schooling, via repeated experiments in vocational orientation, pupils would pass on to one of the
specialised schools or to productive work.

One must bear in mind the developing tendency for every practical activity to create for itself its own specialised school, just as
every intellectual activity tends to create for itself cultural associations of its own; the latter take on the function of post-scholastic
institutions, specialised in organising the conditions in which it is
possible to keep abreast of whatever progress is being made in the
given scientific field.

It may also be observed that deliberative bodies tend to an ever-
increasing extent to distinguish their activity into two "organic"
aspects: into the deliberative activity which is their essence, and into
technical-cultural activity in which the questions upon which they have
to take decisions are first examined by experts and analysed scientifically. This latter activity has already created a whole bureaucratic body,
with a new structure; for apart from the specialised departments of
experts who prepare the technical material for the deliberative bodies, a
second body of functionaries is created—more or less disinterested
"volunteers", selected variously from industry, from the banks, from
finance houses. This is one of the mechanisms by means of which the
career bureaucracy eventually came to control the democratic regimes
and parliaments; now the mechanism is being organically extended,
and is absorbing into its sphere the great specialists of private enterprise, which thus comes to control both régimes and bureaucracies.
What is involved is a necessary, organic development which tends to
integrate the personnel specialised in the technique of politics with personnel specialised in the concrete problems of administering the essential practical activities of the great and complex national societies of
today. Hence every attempt to exorcise these tendencies from the outside produces no result other than moralistic sermons and rhetorical
lamentations.

The question is thus raised of modifying the training of technical-political personnel, completing their culture in accordance with
the new necessities, and of creating specialised functionaries of a
new kind, who as a body will complement deliberative activity. The
traditional type of political "leader", prepared only for formal-

juridical activities, is becoming anachronistic and represents a danger for the life of the State: the leader must have that minimum of general technical culture which will permit him, if not to "create" autonomously the correct solution, at least to know how to adjudicate between the solutions put forward by the experts, and hence to choose the correct one from the "synthetic" viewpoint of political technique.

A type of deliberative body which seeks to incorporate the technical expertise necessary for it to operate realistically has been described elsewhere,[3] in an account of what happens on the editorial committees of some reviews, when these function at the same time both as editorial committees and as cultural groups. The group criticises as a body, and thus helps to define the tasks of the individual editors, whose activity is organised according to a plan and a division of labour which are rationally arranged in advance. By means of collective discussion and criticism (made up of suggestions, advice, comments on method, and criticism which is constructive and aimed at mutual education) in which each individual functions as a specialist in his own field and helps to complete the expertise of the collectivity, the average level of the individual editors is in fact successfully raised so that it reaches the altitude or capacity of the most highly-skilled—thus not merely ensuring an ever more select and organic collaboration for the review, but also creating the conditions for the emergence of a homogeneous group of intellectuals, trained to produce a regular and methodical "writing" activity (not only in terms of occasional publications or short articles, but also of organic, synthetic studies).

Undoubtedly, in this kind of collective activity, each task produces new capacities and possibilities of work, since it creates ever more organic conditions of work: files, bibliographical digests, a library of basic specialised works, etc. Such activity requires an unyielding struggle against habits of dilettantism, of improvisation, of "rhetorical" solutions or those proposed for effect. The work has to be done particularly in written form, just as it is in written form that criticisms have to be made—in the form of terse, succinct notes: this can be achieved if the material is distributed in time, etc.; the writing down of notes and criticisms is a didactic principle rendered necessary by the need to combat the habits formed in public speaking—prolixity, demagogy and paralogism. This type of intellectual work is necessary in order to impart to autodidacts the discipline in study which an orthodox scholastic career provides, in order to Taylorise[4] intellectual work. Hence the usefulness of the principle of the "old men of Santa Zita" of whom De Sanctis speaks in his memoirs of the Neapolitan school of Basilio Puoti:[5] i.e. the usefulness of a certain "stratification" of capabilities and attitudes, and of the formation of work-groups under the guidance of the most highly-skilled and highly-developed, who can accelerate the training of the most backward and untrained.

When one comes to study the practical organisation of the common school, one problem of importance is that of the various phases of the educational process, phases which correspond to the age and intellectual-moral development of the pupils and to the aims which the school sets itself. The common school, or school of humanistic formation (taking the term "humanism" in a broad sense rather than simply in the traditional one) or general culture, should aim to insert young men and women into social activity after bringing them to a certain level of maturity, of capacity for intellectual and practical creativity, and of autonomy of orientation and initiative. The fixing of an age for compulsory school attendance depends on the general economic conditions, since the latter may make it necessary to demand of young men and women, or even of children, a certain immediate productive contribution. The common school necessitates the State's being able to take on the expenditure which at present falls on the family for the maintenance of children at school; in other words, it transforms the budget of the national department from top to bottom, expanding it to an unheard of extent and making it more complex. The entire function of educating and forming the new generations ceases to be private and becomes public; for only thus can it involve them in their entirety, without divisions of group or caste. But this transformation of scholastic activity requires an unprecedented expansion of the practical organisation of the school, i.e. of buildings, scientific material, of the teaching body, etc. The teaching body in particular would have to be increased, since the smaller the ratio between teachers and pupils the greater will be the efficiency of the school—and this presents other problems neither easy nor quick to solve. The question of school buildings is not simple either, since this type of school should be a college, with dormitories, refectories, specialised libraries, rooms designed for seminar work, etc. Hence initially the new type of school will have to be, cannot help being, only for restricted groups, made up of young people selected through competition or recommended by similar institutions.

The common school ought to correspond to the period represented today by the primary and secondary schools, reorganised not only as regards the content and the method of teaching, but also as regards the arrangement of the various phases of the educational process. The first, primary grade should not last longer than three or four years, and in addition to imparting the first "instrumental" notions of schooling—reading, writing, sums, geography, history—ought in particular to deal with an aspect of education that is now neglected—i.e. with "rights and duties", with the first notions of the State and society as primordial elements of a new conception of the world which challenges the conceptions that are imparted by the various traditional social environments, i.e. those conceptions which can be termed folkloristic. The didactic problem is one of mitigating and rendering more fertile the dogmatic approach which must inevitably characterise these first years. The rest of the course should not last more than six years, so that by the age of fifteen or sixteen it should be possible to complete all the grades of the common school.

One may object that such a course is too exhausting because too rapid, if the aim is to attain in effect the results which the present organisation of the classical school aims at but does not attain. Yet the new organisation as a whole will have to contain within itself the general elements which in fact make the course too slow today, at least for a part of the pupils. Which are these elements? In a whole series of families, especially in the intellectual strata, the children find in their family life a preparation, a prolongation and a completion of school life; they "breathe in", as the expression goes, a whole quantity of notions and attitudes which facilitate the educational process properly speaking. They already know and develop their knowledge of the literary language, i.e. the means of expression and of knowledge, which is technically superior to the means possessed by the average member of the school population between the ages of six and twelve. Thus city children, by the very fact of living in a city, have already absorbed by the age of six a quantity of notions and attitudes which make their school careers easier, more profitable, and more rapid. In the basic organisation of the common school, at least the essentials of these conditions must be created—not to speak of the fact, which goes without saying, that parallel to the common school a network of kindergartens and other institutions would develop, in which, even before the school age, children would be habituated to a certain collective discipline and acquire pre-scholastic notions and attitudes. In fact, the common school should be organised like a college, with a collective life by day and by night, freed from the present forms of hypocritical and mechanical discipline; studies should be carried on collectively, with the assistance of the teachers and the best pupils, even during periods of so-called individual study, etc.

The fundamental problem is posed by that phase of the existing school career which is today represented by the *liceo*,[6] and which today does not differ at all, as far as the kind of education is concerned, from the preceding grades—except by the abstract presumption of a greater intellectual and moral maturity of the pupil, matching his greater age and the experience he has already accumulated.

In fact between *liceo* and university, i.e. between the school properly speaking and life, there is now a jump, a real break in continuity, and not a rational passage from quantity (age) to quality (intellectual and moral maturity). From an almost purely dogmatic education, in which learning by heart plays a great part, the pupil passes to the creative phase, the phase of autonomous, independent work. From the school, where his studies are subjected to a discipline that is imposed and controlled by authority, the pupil passes on to a phase of study or of professional work in which intellectual self-discipline and moral independence are theoretically unlimited. And this happens immediately after the crisis of puberty, when the ardour of the instinctive and elementary passions has not yet resolved its struggle with the fetters of the character and of moral conscience which are in the process of being formed. Moreover, in Italy, where the principle of 'seminar' work is not widespread in the universities, this passage is even more brusque and mechanical.

By contrast, therefore, the last phase of the common school must be conceived and structured as the decisive phase, whose aim is to create the fundamental values of "humanism", the intellectual self-discipline and the moral independence which are necessary for subsequent specialisation—whether it be of a scientific character (university studies) or of an immediately practical-productive character (industry, civil service, organisation of commerce, etc.). The study and learning of creative methods in science and in life must begin in this last phase of the school, and no longer be a monopoly of the university or be left to chance in practical life. This phase of the school must already contribute to developing the element of independent responsibility in each individual, must be a creative school. A distinction must be made between creative school and active school, even in the form given to the latter by the Dalton method.[7] The entire common school is an active school, although it is necessary to place limits on libertarian ideologies in this field and to stress with some energy the duty of the adult generations, i.e. of the State, to "mould" the new generations. The active school is still in its romantic phase, in which the elements of struggle against the mechanical and Jesuitical school have become unhealthily exaggerated—through a desire to distinguish themselves sharply from the latter, and for polemical reasons. It is necessary to enter the "classical", rational phase, and to find in the ends to be attained the natural source for developing the appropriate methods and forms.

The creative school is the culmination of the active school. In the first phase the aim is to discipline, hence also to level out—to obtain a certain kind of "conformism" which may be called "dynamic". In the creative phase, on the basis that has been achieved of "collectivisation" of the social type, the aim is to expand the personality—by now autonomous and responsible, but with a solid and homogeneous moral and social conscience. Thus creative school does not mean school of "inventors and discoverers"; it indicates a phase and a method of research and of knowledge, and not a predetermined "programme" with an obligation to originality and innovation at all costs. It indicates that learning takes place especially through a spontaneous and autonomous effort of the pupil, with the teacher only exercising a function of friendly guide—as happens or should happen in the university. To discover a truth oneself, without external suggestions or assistance, is to create—even if the truth is an old one. It demonstrates a mastery of the method, and indicates that in any case one has entered the phase of intellectual maturity in which one may discover new truths. Hence in this phase the fundamental scholastic activity will be carried on in seminars, in libraries, in experimental laboratories; during it, the organic data will be collected for a professional orientation.

The advent of the common school means the beginning of new relations between intellectual and industrial work, not only in the school but in the whole of social life. The comprehensive principle will therefore be reflected in all the organisms of culture, transforming them and giving them a new content.

In Search of the Educational Principle

In the old primary school, there used to be two elements in the educational formation of the children.[8] They were taught the rudiments of natural science, and the idea of civic rights and duties. Scientific ideas were intended to insert the child into the *societas rerum*, the world of things, while lessons in rights and duties were intended to insert him into the State and into civil society. The scientific ideas the children learnt conflicted with the magical conception of the world and nature which they absorbed from an environment steeped in folklore;[9] while the idea of civic rights and duties conflicted with tendencies towards individualistic and localistic barbarism—another dimension of folklore. The school combated folklore, indeed every residue of traditional conceptions of the world. It taught a more modern outlook based essentially on an awareness of the simple and fundamental fact that there exist objective, intractable natural laws to which man must adapt himself if he is to master them in his turn—and that there exist social and state laws which are the product of human activity, which are established by men and can be altered by men in the interests of their collective development. These laws of the State and of society create that human order which historically best enables men to dominate the laws of nature, that is to say which most facilitates their *work*. For work is the specific mode by which man actively participates in natural life in order to transform and socialise it more and more deeply and extensively.

Thus one can say that the educational principle which was the basis of the old primary school was the idea of work. Human work cannot be realised in all its power of expansion and productivity without an exact and realistic knowledge of natural laws and without a legal order which organically regulates men's life in common. Men must respect this legal order through spontaneous assent, and not merely as an external imposition—it must be a necessity recognised and proposed to themselves as freedom, and not simply the result of coercion. The idea and the fact of work (of theoretical and practical activity) was the educational principle latent in the primary school, since it is by means of work that the social and State order (rights and duties) is introduced and identified within the natural order. The discovery that the relations between the social and natural orders are mediated by work, by man's theoretical and practical activity, creates the first elements of an intuition of the world free from all magic and superstition. It provides a basis for the subsequent development of an historical, dialectical conception of the world, which understands movement and change, which appreciates the sum of effort and sacrifice which the present has cost the past and which the future is costing the present, and which conceives the contemporary world as a synthesis of the past, of all past generations, which projects itself into the future. This was the real basis of the primary school. Whether it yielded all its fruits, and whether the actual teachers were aware of the nature and philosophical content of their task, is another question. This requires an analysis of the degree of civic consciousness of the entire nation, of which the teaching body was merely an expression, and rather a poor expression—certainly not an *avant-garde*.

It is not entirely true that "instruction" is something quite different from "education".[10] An excessive emphasis on this distinction has been a serious error of idealist educationalists and its effects can already be seen in the school system as they have reorganised it. For instruction to be wholly distinct from education, the pupil would have to be pure passivity, a "mechanical receiver" of abstract notions—which is absurd and is anyway "abstractly" denied by the supporters of pure educativity precisely in their opposition to mere mechanistic instruction. The "certain" becomes "true" in the child's consciousness.[11] But the child's consciousness is not something "individual" (still less individuated), it reflects the sector of civil society in which the child participates, and the social relations which are formed within his family, his neighbourhood, his village, etc. The individual consciousness of the overwhelming majority of children reflects social and cultural relations which are different from and antagonistic to those which are represented in the school curricula: thus the "certain" of an advanced culture becomes "true" in the framework of a fossilised and anachronistic culture. There is no unity between school and life, and so there is no automatic unity between instruction and education. In the school, the nexus between instruction and education can only be realised by the living work of the teacher. For this he must be aware of the contrast between the type of culture and society which he represents and the type of culture and society represented by his pupils, and conscious of his obligation to accelerate and regulate the child's formation in conformity with the former and in conflict with the latter. If the teaching body is not adequate and the nexus between instruction and education is dissolved, while the problem of teaching is conjured away by cardboard schemata exalting educativity, the teacher's work will as a result become yet more inadequate. We will have rhetorical schools, quite unserious, because the material solidity of what is "certain" will be missing, and what is "true" will be a truth only of words: that is to say, precisely, rhetoric.

This degeneration is even clearer in the secondary school, in the literature and philosophy syllabus. Previously, the pupils at least acquired a certain "baggage" or "equipment" (according to taste) of concrete facts. Now that the teacher must be specifically a philosopher and aesthete, the pupil does not bother with concrete facts and fills his head with formulae and words which usually mean nothing to him, and which are forgotten at once. It was right to struggle against the old school, but reforming it was not so simple as it seemed. The problem was not one of model curricula but of men, and not just of the men who are actually teachers themselves but of the entire social complex which they express. In reality a mediocre teacher may manage to see to it that his pupils become more *informed,* although he will not succeed in making them better educated; he can devote a scrupulous and bureaucratic conscientiousness to the mechanical part of teaching—and the pupil, if he has an active intelligence, will give an order of his own, with the aid of his social background, to the "baggage" he accumulates. With the new curricula, which coincide with a general lowering of the level of the teaching profession, there will no longer be any "baggage" to put in order. The new curricula should have abolished examinations entirely; for to take an examination now must be fearfully more chancy than before. A date is always a date, whoever the examiner is, and a definition is always a definition. But an aesthetic judgement or a philosophical analysis?

The educational efficacy of the old Italian secondary school, as organised by the Casati Act,[12] was not to be sought (or rejected) in its explicit aim as an "educative" system, but in the fact that its structure and its curriculum were the expression of a traditional mode of intellectual and moral life, of a cultural climate diffused throughout Italian society by ancient tradition. It was the fact that this climate and way of life were in their death-throes, and that the school had become cut off from life, which brought about the crisis in education. A criticism of the curricula and disciplinary structure of the old system means less than nothing if one does not keep this situation in mind. Thus we come back to the truly active participation of the pupil in the school, which can only exist if the school is related to life. The more the new curricula nominally affirm and theorise the pupil's activity and working collaboration with the teacher, the more they are actually designed as if the pupil were purely passive.

In the old school the grammatical study of Latin and Greek, together with the study of their respective literatures and political histories, was an educational principle—for the humanistic ideal, symbolised by Athens and Rome, was diffused throughout society, and was an essential element of national life and culture. Even the mechanical character of the study of grammar was enlivened by this cultural perspective. Individual facts were not learnt for an immediate practical or professional end. The end seemed disinterested, because the real interest was the interior development of personality, the formation of character by means of the absorption and assimilation of the whole cultural past of modern European civilisation. Pupils did not learn Latin and Greek in order to speak them, to become waiters, interpreters or commercial letter-writers. They learnt them in order to know at first hand the civilisation of Greece and of Rome—a civilisation that was a necessary precondition of our modern civilisation: in other words, they learnt them in order to be themselves and know themselves consciously. Latin and Greek were learnt through their grammar, mechanically; but the accusation of formalism and aridity is very unjust and inappropriate. In education one is dealing with children in whom one has to inculcate certain habits of diligence, precision, poise (even physical poise), ability to concentrate on specific subjects, which cannot be acquired without the mechanical repetition of disciplined and methodical acts. Would a scholar at the age of forty be able to sit for sixteen hours on end at his work-table if he had not, as a child, compulsorily, through mechanical coercion, acquired the appropriate psycho-physical habits? If one wishes to produce great scholars, one still has to start at this point and apply pressure throughout the educational system in order to succeed in creating those thousands or hundreds or even only dozens of scholars of the highest quality which are necessary to every civilisation. (Of course, one can improve a great deal in this field by the provision of adequate funds for research, without going back to the educational methods of the Jesuits.)

Latin is learnt (or rather studied) by analysing it down to its smallest parts—analysing it like a dead thing, it is true, but all analyses made by children can only be of dead things. Besides, one must not forget that the life of the Romans is a myth which to some extent has already interested the child and continues to interest him, so that in the dead object there is always present a greater living being. Thus, the language is dead, it is analysed as an inert object, as a corpse on the dissecting table, but it continually comes to life again in examples and in stories. Could one study Italian in the same way? Impossible. No living language could be studied like Latin: it would be and *would seem* absurd. No child knows Latin when he starts to study it by these analytical methods. But a living language can be known and it would be enough for a single child to know it, and the spell would be broken: everybody would be off to the Berlitz school at once. Latin (like Greek) appears to the imagination as a myth, even for the teacher. One does not study Latin in order to learn the language. For a long time, as a result of a cultural and scholarly tradition whose origin and development one might investigate, Latin has been studied as an element in an ideal curriculum, an element which combines and satisfies a whole series of pedagogic and psychological requirements. It has been studied in order to accustom children to studying in a specific manner, and to analysing an historical body which can be treated as a corpse which returns continually to life; in order to accustom them to reason, to think abstractly and schematically while remaining able to plunge back from abstraction into real and immediate life, to see in each fact or datum what is general and what is particular, to distinguish the concept from the specific instance.

For what after all is the educational significance of the constant comparison between Latin and the language one speaks? It involves the distinction and the identification of words and concepts; suggests the whole of formal logic, from the contradiction between opposites to the analysis of distincts;[13] reveals the historical movement of the entire language, modified through time, developing and not static. In the eight years of *ginnasio* and *liceo*[14] the entire history of the real language is studied, after it has first been photographed in one abstract moment in the form of grammar. It is studied from Ennius (or rather from the words of the fragments of the twelve tablets) right up to Phaedrus and the Christian writers in Latin: an historical process is analysed from its source until its death in time—or seeming death, since we know that Italian, with which Latin is continually contrasted in school, is modern Latin. Not only the grammar of a certain epoch (which is an abstraction) or its vocabulary are studied, but also, for comparison, the grammar and the vocabulary of each individual author and the meaning of each term in each particular stylistic "period". Thus the child discovers that the grammar and the vocabulary of Phaedrus are not those of Cicero, nor those of Plautus, nor of Lactantius or Tertullian, and that the same nexus of sounds does not have the same meaning in different periods and for different authors. Latin and Italian are continually compared; but each word is a concept, a symbol, which takes on different shades of meaning according to the period and the writer in each of the two languages under comparison. The child studies the literary history of the books written in that language, the political history, the achievements of the men who spoke that language. His education is determined by the whole of this organic complex, by the fact that he has followed that itinerary, if only in a purely literal sense, he has passed through those various stages, etc. He has plunged into history and acquired a historicising understanding of the world and of life, which becomes a second—nearly spontaneous—nature, since it is not inculcated pedantically with an openly educational intention. These studies educated without an explicitly declared aim of doing so, with a minimal "educative" intervention on the part of the teacher: they educated because they gave instruction. Logical, artistic, psychological experience was gained unawares, without a continual self-consciousness. Above all a profound "synthetic", philosophical experience was gained, of an actual historical development. This does not mean—it would be stupid to think so—that Latin and Greek, as such, have intrinsically thaumaturgical qualities in the educational field. It is the whole cultural tradition, which also and particularly lives outside the school, which in a given ambience produces such results. In any case one can see today, with the changes in the traditional idea of culture, the way in which the school is in crisis and with it the study of Latin and Greek.

It will be necessary to replace Latin and Greek as the fulcrum of the formative school, and they will be replaced. But it will not be easy to deploy the new subject or subjects in a didactic form which gives equivalent results in terms of education and general personality-formation, from early childhood to the threshold of the adult choice of career. For in this period what is learnt, or the greater part of it, must be—or appear to the pupils to be—disinterested, i.e. not have immediate or too immediate practical purposes. It must be formative, while being "instructive"—in other words rich in concrete facts. In the present school, the profound crisis in the traditional culture and its conception of life and of man has resulted in a progressive degeneration. Schools of the vocational type, i.e. those designed to satisfy immediate, practical interests, are beginning to predominate over the formative school, which is not immediately "interested". The most paradoxical aspect of it all is that this new type of school appears and is advocated as being democratic, while in fact it is destined not merely to perpetuate social differences but to crystallise them in Chinese complexities.

The traditional school was oligarchic because it was intended for the new generation of the ruling class, destined to rule in its turn: but it was not oligarchic in its mode of teaching. It is not the fact that the pupils learn how to rule there, nor the fact that it tends to produce gifted men, which gives a particular type of school its social character. This social character is determined by the fact that each social group has its own type of school, intended to perpetuate a specific traditional function, ruling or subordinate. If one wishes to break this pattern one needs, instead of multiplying and grading different types of vocational school, to create a single type of formative school (primary-secondary) which would take the child up to the threshold of his choice of job, forming him during this time as a person capable of thinking, studying, and ruling—or controlling those who rule.

The multiplication of types of vocational school thus tends to perpetuate traditional social differences; but since, within these differences, it tends to encourage internal diversification, it gives the impression of being democratic in tendency. The labourer can become a skilled worker, for instance, the peasant a surveyor or petty agronomist. But democracy, by definition, cannot mean merely that an unskilled worker can become skilled. It must mean that every "citizen" can "govern" and that society places him, even if only abstractly, in a general condition to achieve this. Political democracy tends towards a coincidence of the rulers and the ruled (in the sense of government with the consent of the governed), ensuring for each nonruler a free training in the skills and general technical preparation necessary to that end. But the type of school which is now developing as the school for the people does not tend even to keep up this illusion. For it is organised ever more fully in such a way as to restrict recruitment to the technically qualified governing stratum, in a social and political context which makes it increasingly difficult for "personal initiative" to acquire such skills and technical-political preparation. Thus we are really going back to a division into juridically fixed and crystallised estates rather than moving towards the transcendence of class divisions. The multiplication of vocational schools which specialise increasingly from the very beginning of the child's educational career is one of the most notable manifestations of this tendency. It is noticeable that the new pedagogy has concentrated its fire on "dogmatism" in the field of instruction and the learning of concrete facts—i.e. precisely in the field in which a certain dogmatism is practically indispensable and can be reabsorbed and dissolved only in the whole cycle of the educational process (historical grammar could not be taught in *liceo* classes). On the other hand, it has been forced to accept the introduction of dogmatism *par excellence* in the field of religious thought, with the result that the whole history of philosophy is now implicitly seen as a succession of ravings and delusions.[15] In the philosophy course, the new curriculum impoverishes the teaching and in practice lowers its level (at least for the overwhelming majority of pupils who do not receive intellectual help outside the school from their family or home environment, and who have to form themselves solely by means of the knowledge they receive in the class-room)—in spite of seeming very rational and fine, fine as any utopia. The traditional descriptive philosophy, backed by a course in the history of philosophy and by the reading of a certain number of philosophers, in practice seems the best thing. Descriptive, definitional philosophy may be a dogmatic abstraction, just as grammar and mathematics are, but it is an educational and didactive necessity. "One equals one" is an abstraction, but it leads nobody to think that one fly equals one elephant. The rules of formal logic are abstractions of the same kind, they are like the grammar of normal thought; but they still need to be studied, since they are not something innate, but have to be acquired through work and reflection. The new curriculum presupposes that formal logic is something you already possess when you think, but does not explain how it is to be acquired, so that in practice it is assumed to be innate. Formal logic is like grammar: it is assimilated in a "living" way even if the actual learning process has been necessarily schematic and abstract. For the learner is not a passive and mechanical recipient, a gramophone record—even if the liturgical conformity of examinations sometimes makes him appear so. The relation between these educational forms and the child's psychology is always active and creative, just as the relation of the worker to his tools is active and creative. A calibre is likewise a complex of abstractions, but without calibration it is not possible to produce real objects—real objects which are social relations, and which implicitly embody ideas.

The child who sweats at *Barbara, Baralipton*[16] is certainly performing a tiring task, and it is important that he does only what is absolutely necessary and no more. But it is also true that it will always be an effort to learn physical self-discipline and self-control; the pupil has, in effect, to undergo a psycho-physical training. Many people have to be persuaded that studying too is a job, and a very tiring one, with its own particular apprenticeship—involving muscles and nerves as well as intellect. It is a process of adaptation, a habit acquired with effort, tedium and even suffering. Wider participation in secondary education brings with it a tendency to ease off the discipline of studies, and to ask for "relaxations". Many even think that the difficulties of learning are artificial, since they are accustomed to think only of manual work as sweat and toil. The question is a complex one. Undoubtedly the child of a traditionally intellectual family acquires this psycho-physical adaptation more easily. Before he ever enters the class-room he has numerous advantages over his comrades, and is already in possession of attitudes learnt from his family environment: he concentrates more easily, since he is used to "sitting still", etc. Similarly, the son of a city worker suffers less when he goes to work in a factory than does a peasant's child or a young peasant already formed by country life. (Even diet has its importance, etc.) This is why many people think that the difficulty of study conceals some "trick" which handicaps them—that is, when they do not simply believe that they are stupid by nature. They see the "gentleman"[17]—and for many, especially in the country, "gentleman" means intellectual—complete, speedily and with apparent ease, work which costs their sons tears and blood, and they think there is a "trick". In the future, these questions may become extremely acute and it will be necessary to resist the tendency to render easy that which cannot become easy without being distorted. If our aim is to produce a new stratum of intellectuals, including those capable of the highest degree of specialisation, from a social group which has not traditionally developed the appropriate attitudes, then we have unprecedented difficulties to overcome.

Notes

1. "Sciences" in the sense of branches of human knowledge, rather than in the more restricted meaning which the word has taken on since the industrial revolution.

2. *Classi strumentali* is a term used by Gramsci interchangeably with the terms *classi subalterne* or *classi subordinate,* and there seems no alternative to a literal translation of each which leaves the reader free to decide whether there is any different nuance of stress between them. See too the final paragraph of "History of the Subaltern Classes" on pp. 52–5 below.

3. Int., pp. 137 ff.

4. For Gramsci's analysis of Taylorism, see "Americanism and Fordism", below pp. 302 ff.

5. De Sanctis in his memoirs recounts how as a child in Naples he was taken to be taught literary Italian at a school for the aristocracy of the city run in his home by the Marchese Puoti. Puoti used to refer to the elder boys, whose "judgement carried great weight, and when one of them spoke everyone fell silent, the marquis soonest of all, and was filled with admiration", as *gli anziani di Santa Zita,* in reference to Dante, *Inferno* XXI, 38. The "*anziani*" were the magistrates of the city of Lucca, whose patron saint was Zita.

6. Perhaps the nearest English-language equivalents of *ginnasio* and *liceo* are the American junior high school and high school, though in the Italian system they are selective schools (like English grammar schools) leading to a university education.

7. The Dalton Method, a development of Montessori's ideas, is described elsewhere by Gramsci (Int., p. 122): "the pupils are free to attend whichever lessons (whether practical or theoretical) they please, provided that by the end of each month they have completed the programme set for them; discipline is entrusted to the pupils themselves. The system has a serious defect: the pupils generally postpone doing their work until the last days of the month, and this detracts from the seriousness of the education and represents a major difficulty for the teachers who are supposed to help them but are overwhelmed with work—whereas in the first weeks of the month they have little or nothing to do. (The Dalton system is simply an extension to the secondary schools of the methods of study which obtain in the Italian universities, methods which leave the student complete freedom in his

studies: in certain faculties the students sit twenty examinations and their final degree in the fourth and last year, and the lecturer never so much as knows the student.)"

8. i.e. before the Gentile reform—see introduction to this section, and note 14 on p. 132.

9. See above, p. 30, for Gramsci's use of the term "folklore". See too, note 5 on p. 326.

10. For this distinction, popular with educational thinkers influenced by Gentile and by Croce, see the introduction to this section.

11. This distinction was made by Vico, in his *Scienza Nuova* of 1725. Para. 321: "The 'certain' in the laws is an obscurity of judgement backed only by authority, so that we find them harsh in application, yet are obliged to apply them just because they are certain. In good Latin *certum* means particularised, or, as the schools say, individuated; so that, in over-elegant Latin, *certum* and *commune*, the certain and the common, are opposed to each other." Para. 324: "The true in the laws is a certain light and splendour with which natural reason illuminates them; so that jurisconsults are often in the habit of saying *verum est* for *aequum est.*" Para. 137: "Men who do not know what is true of things take care to hold fast to what is certain, so that, if they cannot satisfy their intellects by knowledge *(scienza)*, their wills at least may rest on consciousness *(coscienza).*" The New Science, trans. Bergin and Fisch, Cornell, 1968.

12. The Casati Act, passed in 1859, remained the basis of the Italian educational system until the Gentile Reform of 1923.

13. For Croce's concept of the "analysis of distincts" see Introduction, p. xxiii.

14. See note 6 on p. 31.

15. The Gentile Reform provided for compulsory religious education in Italian schools, and Gentile's justifications of this are criticised by Gramsci in Int., pp. 116–18: ". . . Gentile's thinking . . . is nothing more than an extension of the idea that 'religion is good for the people' (people = child = primitive phase of thought to which religion corresponds, etc.), i.e. a (tendentious) abandonment of the aim of educating the people . . . Gentile's historicism is of a very degenerate kind: it is the historicism of those jurists for whom the knout is not a knout when it is an 'historical' knout. Moreover, its ideas are extremely vague and confused. The fact that a 'dogmatic' exposition of scientific ideas and a certain 'mythology' are necessary in the primary school does not mean that the dogma and the mythology have to be precisely those of religion." Etc. See note 14 on p. 132.

16. *Barbara, Baralipton,* were mnemonic words used to memorise syllogisms in classical logic.

17. *Signore.* On this term, not of course an exact equivalent of "gentleman", see below p. 272.

9

MARTIN HEIDEGGER

Martin Heidegger (1889–1976) is a significant figure in the Western philosophical tradition, but interpreting his work raises a moral dilemma. Heidegger was a member of the German National Socialist party during World War II. He was appointed rector of the University of Freiburg from 1933 to 1945; this was only possible because he was a Nazi party member and a public supporter of Hitler. He was not blind to the nature of the Nazi regime; he did not intervene to stop the forced resignation of his Jewish teacher, Edmund Husserl (1859–1938), and he accepted the self-imposed exile of his Jewish lover, student, and friend, Hannah Arendt (1906–1975). When Germany was defeated in 1945, Heidegger was barred from teaching and stripped of his professorship. Four years later, however, he was reinstated as emeritus professor. The extract included comes from the deposition Heidegger submitted before the committee on de-nazification at the Albert Ludwig University. In it, he intended to answer accusations that he had used his position as professor and rector to unduly influence students by subordinating educational ideals to political ones.

In the deposition, Heidegger outlines the idea of the university, and this outline has a broader application to other forms of schooling. The deposition outlines three models of education. The first is the "banking," or transmission, model of education; it is the most familiar. According to this view, teachers communicate privileged, identity-constituting "facts" which students lack. In the process, the teacher replicates knowledge and knowers. This model has been criticized by progressivists and critical theorists on largely psychological and political grounds. They see it is an inherently unrealistic and oppressive pedagogy. Heidegger objects to the model on epistemic grounds; he argues that its assumption that it is possible to discover "facts" that are not theoretically constituted is mistakenly positivist. Recalling Plato's myth of the cave, it is to mistake the shadows or "facts" for reality.

Heidegger's second model of education, "enframement," reduces all existence or being—truth—to theory, language, and interpretation. This model assumes that humanity appropriates *all* experience to some form of theoretical framework. Here Heidegger unwittingly anticipates the current state of play in contemporary educational discourse. He is worried about the inherent nihilism of this model and the increasing diversification and specialization that it produces. Returning to Plato's myth of the cave, this second model places us at the fire. Having debunked our naïve version of truth as "fact," we are now enraptured by the theories that we know to be constitutive of these facts. Only the third, and final, model of education liberates humanity from the cave.

The third, or genuine, model of education teaches us to dwell in, and with, the phenomenological richness of being. It engages us in a reflexive return to our ontological human existence. For this model, the goal of education is to encourage students to turn away from what is familiar, so that they might turn back and look at the world as a realm in which reality can appear. This process should develop in students a fundamental comportment toward the disclosure of being. According to this picture of education, truth is phenomenological rather than propositional (transmission model) or hermeneutic (enframing model). It is a kind of unknowing joy in what we find unthinkable and yet thought-provoking. For this reason, Heidegger urges the critical examination of those experiences that inspire us to feel joy. This existential receptivity is learned from the observation of learners. In this sense, the teacher is exemplary learner. She learns in public, so that students might learn how to learn. The teacher's silence, faltering articulation, and exposed resourcelessness permits students to wait, listen, and attune themselves to the solicitations of a reality that transcends theoretical understanding. The teacher returns to the cave to inspire the individuals that dwell in it; she shows herself in order to disclose the world.

You may feel that Heidegger does not answer his detractors because he does not address his political allegiance to the Nazi party and its role in his teaching and administration of the university. Perhaps Heidegger's position is that to ask an academic about his or her political affiliations is to miss the point of a university and its educative purpose. In Heidegger's view, a university deserves immunity from any dominant ideology, regardless of whether it is fascism, nationalism, and imperialist expansionism or civil rights, gender equity, and social justice. Universities are not accountable in this sense because their commitment is to thinking, and learning how to think, which involves the intentional transcendence of any prior conceptual understanding. Irrespective of whether you agree with him, Heidegger's philosophy presents a serious challenge to the current educational focus on issues of diversity, inclusion, multiculturalism, environmentalism, and equity—we have certainly lost our way, in his view.

REFERENCES

Heidegger, Martin. *Being and Time.* Translated by John Macquarie and Edward Robinson. New York: Harper and Row, 1962.

———. *Poetry, Language and Thought.* Translations and introduction by Albert Hofstadter. New York: Perennial Classics, 1971.

Malpas, Jeff. "Beginning in Wonder: Placing the Origin of Thinking." In *Philosophical Romanticism*, 282–98 ed. Nikolas Kompridis. London and New York: Routledge, 2006.

Peter, Michael A., ed. *Heidegger, Education and Modernity.* Oxford, England: Rowan and Littlefield, 2002.

HEIDEGGER ON THE ART OF TEACHING

Excerpted from the transcript of the deposition[1] of professor Dr. Martin Heidegger, submitted before the committee on de-nazification of the Albert Ludwig University, Freiburg Im Breisgau, July 23, 1945.

PRESIDING: Constantin von Dietze, President Artur Allgeier, Adolf Lampe, Friedrich Oehlkers, Gerhard Ritter, Members
APPEARING: Martin Heidegger

The undersigned deponent, Professor Dr. Martin Heidegger, having been duly sworn by a Notary Public in and for the State of Baden, deposes and states to this session of the Committee on De-Nazification of the Albert Ludwig University, under penalties of perjury, as follows:

Esteemed President and distinguished Members of the Committee, appointed under the auspices of the Academic Senate of Freiburg University by commission of the Provisional Allied Military Administration for the City of Freiburg, your fellow colleague, Martin Heidegger, hereby respectfully appears before you at your behest to be heard in his own behalf to answer the charges preferred against him. Before you is the issue of whether I shall be allowed to resume the tenure of office of ordinary professor in this learned university or whether I shall be debarred therefrom by reason of unfitness to hold such office and to discharge its duties faithfully and responsibly in a manner consistent with the values and ideals intrinsic to higher education. The gravity of the matter committed to your collective charge for exercise of judgment is of such magnitude, especially to anyone who has dedicated an entire life to higher education, that it must unavoidably be daunting to whomever it befalls to take the stand so untutored in the arts of advocacy. I am sensible how much hangs upon not only the cogency, but also the manner of my speech itself, which has generally been reputed of obscure and impenetrable idiom. I cannot but reflect that if either my pleading be injudicious or its defenses lame, it will cast such damp upon the goodwill you have exhibited toward me as to prejudice my cause. This prospect is even more daunting as I am overwhelmed by how unequal I am to the task at hand, since it is

"Heidegger on the Art of Teaching" edited and translated by Valerie Allen and Ares D. Axiotis from *Heidegger, Education, and Modernity* edited by Michael A. Peters, 2002. Reprinted by permission of Rowman & Littlefield Publishers.

clear that all explanations I have hitherto rendered have fallen short of the mark of persuasion. You will bear with me, therefore, if I abjure the sophistication of the advocate for the halting speech of the beginner from Messkirch.

The bill of indictment, which you have afforded me a reasonable opportunity to examine and to answer, contains two main counts. As and for the first count, it is alleged that during the term of my rectorate I sought willfully to place the University in the service of [*Gleichschaltung*] the state-regime of the National Socialist German Workers Party by conforming the institution of the University to the rule of the National Socialist leader-cult [*Führerprinzip*]. As for the second count, it is alleged that in and through my teaching and research as a member of the philosophy faculty of the University, I willfully propagated the ideas of the National Socialist German Workers Party with a view to indoctrinating students and inciting them to engage in action in conformity therewith.

These allegations are cast in terms of subversion of identities, of crossing the line between education and politics, university and state; of exceeding the limit beyond which philosophy becomes ideology [*Weltanschauung*] and teaching turns into propaganda; of overstepping the bounds between advocacy and action. The delict complained of is, in essence, none other than the vice of intemperance, an unfitness in the direction of excess in respect of the right measure or proper degree. What is adverted to is a deficiency in the mode of rational deliberation that issues in the propensity for immoderation in all things, conduct and thought utterly lacking in self-restraint. Where the intemperate is said to go wrong is precisely in the unwillingness to abide the rule or limit of reason. In the instant case, the accusations impute irreverence toward academe: the province of reason itself, staked in metes and bounds by calls and distances, has been adversely possessed by other than the rightful title-holder. Possession having now been recovered by right reason, an action for ejectment ensues to restore the proper boundaries by summoning the encroachers to renounce any competing claims to the estate.

I am admonished by earnest supporters to seize this occasion publicly to recant any offending words and deeds from the past and to promise to do the same in future lectures and publications in order [*wieder*] to rehabilitate [*habilitieren*] myself. Convincingly reformed in word and work, such a teacher could without risk be placed before the impressionable young minds of today. If anything, an academic of acknowledged renown, it is argued, is more likely to be readmitted into the fold of the postwar university as an exemplar of self-criticism than to be rejected altogether in retribution for alleged past misdeeds. To pray for your clemency by an admission of fault, however expedient, would nevertheless be to perpetrate a fraud upon this tribunal and the institution to which I have devoted myself, if the motive were simply what is good in the way of consequences. So reprehensible would it be to retain one's academic status under such pretenses, irrespective of the question of responsibility, that I am loath to give even the appearance of implementing such a tactic.

Still other well-meaning supporters advise taking an altogether different tack: to defend on procedural grounds that point to the extraordinary nature of this academic disciplinary proceeding, which has no basis in the statutes and ordinances of the University. A proper action [*Prozess*] to discipline a member of the faculty, it is argued, presupposes the distinction between law and fact and involves the application of rule to fact, which issues in a reasoned verdict. As distinguished from an ordinary action, the instant matter, it is held, is a controversy undecidable in principle, because judgment cannot be rendered by appeal to controlling rules, and, therefore, justice cannot be done. Here perhaps only politics prevails. Where the validity of one side's cause does not entail the invalidity of the other's, to submit the dispute to the jurisdiction of an abstract measure, hoisted *ex post facto,* as if it were common to both, commits an injustice of an order equal to the wrong originally complained of. I am told that it is of the nature of this controversy to confound the statutes and ordinances of the University: the cause of action defies being put into legal idiom at the same time as it gains its sense from the very idiom of law. One might therefore say: "I cannot find words to answer charges that institute an idiom that does not yet exist." Here a cause of action demands to be expressed in the law, yet is prejudiced by the inability of the law to give it voice. Silence therefore corresponds [*entspricht*] intrinsically to the nature of the facts as charged. It does not necessarily bear witness to guilt.

There is, however, too much at stake, is there not, to take refuge in what may appear to many to be self-serving distinctions. One cannot but ruminate on the duty of giving utterance to the unspeakable. What is required is to bear witness to the tragedy of our time for posterity, not to testify in favor of one side or the other, *for* or *against*, but to bear witness as such. It is a matter not of giving *testimony*, but of making a *testament*. A testament is by its nature an ambulatory instrument, speaking of the present to the future, binding one to the other in a future past: as an execution of one's purpose, the meaning of the testament is always deferred to some uncertain future date. If I commit these words to you today, it is with such testamentary, rather than apologetic, spirit that I speak, not in order to be exonerated, but to be acknowledged by you and to have my declaration and intent attested for the future by your authority. Indeed, what has to be said, what demands to be asserted, is an *extraordinary* pronouncement of the order of a will. A testament may be oriented to the future, but it also always arises out of and is motivated by the experience of the present as the decisive moment of dispensation in one's life, whether brought about by a shattering crisis or simply a calmer moment of transcendence of the everyday. As I have been immersed in the business of university teaching for so many years, it strikes me now that, in addressing this tribunal, it would be especially fitting that any declaration I should make be in the way of a testament to the postwar university: *Testament*, that is, taken in its original derivation from the Latin rendering of the Greek legal term *diatheke*, meaning "covenant": a compact with the next generation who shall follow in our footsteps, inheritors of the legacy of our words and deeds.

To the postwar German university, I bequeath the principal task [*Aufgabe*] that I set myself many years ago and that has exercised me ceaselessly ever since to one degree or another. It is the task of understanding in ever more radical ways the notion of intentionality. This is what we venture the task of education to be all about, as first articulated by the Greeks with the concept of paideia. Viewed in this general way, the learning process extends without limit before an open horizon of radicalization, as each succeeding generation brings its own fund of experience to bear on interpreting such notions of fundamental import to the leading of a life. The function of the university, as the pinnacle of our educational system, is to assume and to remain faithful to just such a role, regardless of consequence, because, according to the nature of its task, the university finds itself under a categorical imperative to advance the understanding of intentionality before all other service to society, whether in the interest of church, state, or civil society.

Pedagogy, insofar as it remains in touch with and perseveres in its original Greek spirit, eschews the rational imperative of relevance in all the forms that fitness for purpose may take, such as utility and expediency, on the one hand, or conformity to convention and custom, on the other. To grasp the task of education is thus already to know something essential about the structure of the university, that it cannot be an instrument of social engineering or, more generally, simply a *means* to an end, without ceasing to *educate*. Professional training and liberal education, though differing in orientation, both miss the mark in the same respect in that they both seek to perfect the pupil, each after its own fashion, as effective *bourgeois* or universal *citoyen* [*sic*]. Elsewhere,[2] I have, at risk to my reputation, laid great emphasis upon this cardinal point: that the defining trait of the university lies in its *self-assertion* [*Selbstbehauptung*] from the social powers that are bent upon bringing it to heel, insofar as they are ultimately threatened by the institutionalizing of the practice of interpreting intentionality and transcendence in a free and unfettered way.

The youth of tomorrow, born of today's devastation, will one day demand of us an answer to a simple, but profound, question: why attend university? What they are after will be nothing less than an insight into the meaning of education appropriate to the needs of their postwar era, in the same way as the Humboldt-university idea arose out of the national ferment generated in the aftermath of the Napoleonic Wars to dominate higher education for the next century. It will not do then to serve up warmed-over platitudes from the bygone tradition of German Idealism. The way of education leads today to a crossroads [*Scheideweg*]. In my time, I came to realize that the first, faltering step forward must be to release the stranglehold that reason in the form of theory has exercised over higher education since the founding of the Academy by Plato. The idea of the university as it has come down to us has essentially been defined by two moments: an abstraction and a generalization. The abstraction has been to reduce education to theoretical understanding alone, to seeing the world in a contemplative way in order to bring into view general principles that govern the manifold of phenomena. This marks the transition from traditional education as mere socialization into the customs of the tribe to rational education as ascending from the concrete particular to the abstract universal and back again. The generalization has been to hold that theoretical understanding—this way of seeing things *sub specie aeternitatis*—can be had of anything and everything, without exception, including ourselves as human beings. Rational education, insofar as it elevates us to the god's eye view of the world, comes thus to define our highest aspiration—the true good of human life, when we are *kata physin* in our most human relation, means living according to theory. From its very beginning, then, the university got off on the wrong foot by instituting itself as the privileged site of access to what is real, where all things submit to the theoretical gaze. The thought that I have sought to phrase in my writings with varying degrees of success is the recognition of the inherent limitations of the university, imposed by the monopoly of theory over education, which gives primacy to the theoretical relation to the world over other, concrete ways of relating to things. A university cannot truly profess to have its beginning in theory. Its beginning originates in mood [*Stimmung*], springing from the *thaumazein* or astonishment of which Aristotle spoke as the concrete bond between life and thought.

I am acutely aware that I stand at a crossroads [*Scheideweg*] in my career and in my life, just as the German University does. I do not use the metaphor lightly, for the path, the way [*Weg*], has all along been the guiding principle of my thought, not to mention, of education itself. After all, the crossroads [*Kreuzung*] of the trivium (grammar, rhetoric, and dialectic) was precisely the turning-point [*Scheideweg*] where our medieval students in Freiburg began their education.[3] Yet we have repressed the memory that the university is but a chance meeting-place of roads in the open. What is more, today's university has lost the sense in which the threefold divergent way was originally an ominous place, one where all is put at risk. It was where three fatal roads met that Oedipus unwittingly fulfilled the Delphic oracle's prophecy and, at Jocasta's subsequent description of the place, recognized his horrible destiny; it was the place sacred to Hekate, Daughter of Night.[4] But it also bore the meaning of a common place of ill repute, of the gutter.[5] We retain a faint resonance of this derogation in the term "triviality" [*Trivialität*]. However, the university bears acknowledging its bastard pedigree on its escutcheon of pure reason. By the heyday of scholasticism, the three paths had already been cleaned up, their inherent dangers tamed, their mystery withdrawn.

Nevertheless, the way of education ineluctably returns us from the soaring heights of theory to the lowly gutter of our finitude. The way of education constitutes the passage into thought, but not a lifeless conduit connecting us as subject to an object by way of representation. No, where it leads only discloses itself as we venture onto it with the weight of our entire being.

Our professors have forgotten that the three subjects of the trivium were pursued singly, not simultaneously, on the assumption that one "graduated" [*graduiert*] along the path from one to the other: first from grammar, which teaches us to speak aright, then to dialectic, which teaches us to reason aright, and finally to rhetoric, which teaches us to speak and reason well. Trivium, although a singular word, already points to the multiplicity within-*tri-via-ium*, three roads made into one. To translate this as "cross-roads" [*Kreuzung*], as one does and ought to, properly implies that one is *standing* between paths, *inter vias*, looking down each road and debating which to take, for actually to traverse the way requires that one has already moved beyond the cross-roads and committed to a single path. To walk the trivium is in one sense an impossibility, obliging us to recognize that our forward motion comes from standing and deliberating—being undecided or even lost. It is a strange kind of perambulatory progress that requires perpetual hesitation at a turning point. Each step forward is simultaneously a *faux pas* [*sic*] that must be retracted to return us to our crossroads [*Kreuzung*]. Hesitation before possibilities both visible and concealed, itself a kind of unknowing, is how we progress into knowledge. As one is called to account for oneself, one hesitates and does not suppose to know.

Who among the linguists and philologists remembers that grammar, the first way trodden in the liberal curriculum, employed a terminology taken from quotidian life and hence was already dense with pun and metaphor, making apparent the familiarity and strangeness of language? Just as in German, the Latin grammatical term "case" [*casus*] denoted a falling away from the uprightness of the *nomen* into an oblique relation; indeed, the "nominative" is not, strictly speaking, a "case" [*Fall*] at all, and *casus rectus*, literally meaning "the straight obliqueness," is a contradiction. Lucillius makes the innuendo in an epigram that Menander the grammar teacher keeps his pupil's mother Zenonis up all night practicing her declensions. With Christianity, the theological association between Adam's *lapsus* and grammatical declension came to the fore. Labored and arcane as these puns must have appeared, they nonetheless convey a renewed wonder at the abundance of language. The fixed case-options of genitive, dative, accusative and so on that we employ countless times a day in the service of idle chatter assume in these puns a certain unfamiliarity, which obliges us to consider that our relation to the world must always remain, in some larger sense of the word, ethical. As prior, this relation cannot be theorized in the puritan language of science without already begging the question of value [*Wertfrage*]. Now, this ethical aspect of the grammatical art has been quite lost from the modern university. Language occurs as a result of chosen words, and thus grammar is the art of choosing aright; it is, as Boethius declares, the art of right speaking [*recte loquendi*] and any violation of its rules is a deviation of the rectitude of speech, a verbal *vitium*. Properly grounded, the university is home to an indivisible inquiry in which the question of being [*Seinsfrage*], the Parmenidean *ti to on*, and the question of value [*Wertfrage*], the Socratic *ti bioteon*, are brought together again under one roof.

In the grammar of *Dasein*, the declining [*Verfall*] is perpetual value-motion, never coming to rest at any fixed point of case-relation; nor is there any formerly erect, pre-lapsarian subject-position from which it falls in declining relation with objects. Fallenness, relatedness to the everyday things of here and now, is our first condition. That prepositional bridge, that *pons asinorum* we construct between nominative subject and the object, collapses. As I explained in *Being and Time*: "In falling, nothing other than our potentiality-for-Being-in-the-world is the issue, even if in the mode of inauthenticity. *Dasein* can fall only *because* Being-in-the-world understandingly with a state-of-mind is an issue for it. On the other hand, *authentic* existence is not something which floats above falling everydayness; existentially, it is only a modified way in which such everydayness is seized upon."[6] The self-containment expressed in Descartes's postulate *ego cogito ergo sum* asserts both the primacy of the transcendental ego as absolute consciousness intact from the taint of involvement with external objects and existence as prior to all such involvement; but the fallenness of *Dasein* denotes its fundamental condition of being alongside the world and its concern with the here and now, with the ready-to-hand matters that inevitably distract us from asking ourselves where the path we tread is leading. More ominously, it can also take us along the path of the They [*Man*], the public highway of mediocrity where right speaking is mere chatter [*Gerede*] and beautiful writing mere scribbling [*Geschreibe*].

Logic, the art and science of right reasoning, teaches us the proper sense of words, gives us the tools to form concepts and to put them together in a proposition. Philosophical tradition ascribes logic's "birth" to Aristotle, who articulated the syllogistic figures of reasoning and the primary categories under which all entities can be classified. Among these, that of the relation between subject and predicate stands preeminent. The term, in Greek *hypokeimenon* and in Latin *subiectum*, literally means "lying beneath" [*darunter liegende*]. In German, we retain the Latinate term *Subjekt* for application to logic and linguistics, but we transliterate the sense of throwing under into Germanic terminology to achieve a different sense: subjection [*Unterwerfung*]. The meanings point in contrary directions. In its political sense, one is subjugated [*unterworfen*] by a sovereign authority: the word suggests obligation.[7] Aristotle, however, uses it in the sense of substance, that which stands beneath, that of which properties, accidents, and relations are predicated.[8] Here, in the Aristotelian use of the term, *hypokeimenon* or *subiectum* constitutes the very center of one's identity; substantiality is essential, coterminous with and forever present unto the self. The violent sense of throwing [*werfen*] has receded into the background. The original sense of Latin *subicere*, "to place beneath," was applied in the most basic of senses, as in placing a mare beneath a stallion, while *adicere* (from which we get the grammatical *adiectum*) meant "to insert," "to hurl (oneself) on top of."[9] In a curious reversal of fortune from inferior to superior position, the theoretical subject [*Subjekt*], now sovereign, seizes upon the object [*Objekt*], thrown before the mind, to represent it in the abstraction of thought. Likewise, in the university, where logic and argument prevail, the pedagogical relation between teacher and student is understood in homologous terms as a practical instance of the more general relation of subject to object. The teacher gives *eidos*, form and finality, to the student as spiritual material presented for shaping and forming *kata ton logon*, in accordance with an abstract model. The Greek metaphors of formation that provide the basis for our concept of education [*Bildung*] bear out this connection. In the word *morphe*, there is still to be found the potter's poietical [*sic*] hand at work on malleable clay. The teacher stands as *typos*, the mold, from which students will emerge as exemplars. As a verb, *typto* reminds us of the violence of education in subject-object terms, for it has the meaning "to beat" or "to pound," as when combating an adversary or, more to the point, pressing a coin. The student is to be beaten into an image, fashioned [*plattein*] as if he were a drachma coin to be put into circulation. What becomes clear is that the university as pedagogical community is constructed to be hierarchical and authoritarian: the student is subjected to the discipline of the teacher. Implicit in all of this, of course, is that the representation of the teacher is borrowed from *techne* and its relations of production. It is precisely this reduction of education to the instrumental, by analogy with *techne*, that is the source of everything awry with the university today. In truth, Aristotle also points out where one is to look for the solution: pedagogy understood by analogy with *physis*. In this regard, *morphe* is to be paired with self-creating and self-emerging *physis* rather than with technical *hyle*, the raw matter of production. As a mustering into appearance, the essence of education is thus inextricably bound to the meaning of being [*Sinn des Seins*] with the result that the university emerges as a clearing [*Lichtung*] in which the relation between teacher and student takes on different shapes and forms. In a movement of transcendence, *Dasein* is torn and dislocated from its world by entry into the clearing of the university. It loses its substance, which stands constant and sturdy beneath the daily flux of moods and petty duties that preoccupy. The soul, according to custom, is a self-moving principle; by definition, it cannot be moved or thrown. But, within the walls of academe, strange is the self-government [*Selbst-Gouvernement*][10] of the subject whose ship only reaches its harbor when thrown off course.

Although insisting that the category of substance cannot also be a category of relation, Aristotle raises the possibility that "being is the same as being somehow related to something,"[11] only to deny it at once. Yet here precisely is the unthought of the university: that theory is ever only an abstraction from life and must always be referred back to it for meaning. For Aristotle, the category of substance alone escapes the touch of the category of relation; only the subject can be thought of as a self-standing entity. The category of relation, denoted by the Greek accusative *pros ti* or genitive *tinos* (Latin *ad aliquid* and *cuius*), subsumes all oblique positions, all declining and, hence, all relation with the other. But the relatedness of *Dasein* and world, misconstrued by theory, is of an order of relation that can neither be captured by any single preposition of choice nor frozen into any one grammatical *casus*.

Lastly, to rhetoric, to the task of persuasion as the end of speaking and reasoning well. Although it was traditionally to the lot of grammar that the business of reading poetry and appreciating tropes fell, nonetheless it is rhetoric that I here identify as the bastard son of academe, who deserves legitimation. Today, under oath, I am required to speak the truth [*Wahrheit*] before you. In *Being and Time*, I began to rethink the traditional correspondence theory of truth in terms of the rhetorical notion of figuration. I came to see that the idea of truth as adequation of exchange between two things, representation and what is represented, was itself but an instance of figurative disclosure [*Erschlossenheit*] that had become fixed in our imagination. Since Plato there has been a fatal relocation of truth away from concrete things themselves as they naturally show and reveal themselves in the richness of our vernaculars toward the idea of the exchange of equivalents. To be established, however, equivalence, as the word implies, requires a general notion of value, a common denominator by which the equality of the exchange is to be measured. In exchange, formal identity is preserved over material change. Something remains the same and self-identical, while in all other respects it is replaced by something entirely different from itself. Now, this commensuration can only take place by means of abstraction, generalization, and reduction to what is held in common. To advert to Aristotle again, exchange, whether in commerce or in theoretical representation, implies the notion of a general equivalent, a standard measure "which by making things commensurable, renders it possible to make them equal."[12] The truth of theory, being truth as adequation, is thus the abstract, one-sided, and fragmented truth of general equivalence. The genesis of the general equivalent is no more than the invention by the Greeks of conceptual thinking, in which thought sloughs off what is fortuitous, separating essential from inessential in the phenomenon, thereby creating an abstract representation of it. Whereas in intuition we stand in immediate relation to the whole, rich but undifferentiated, thought sunders, allowing us to mediate between many different things, thus bringing them into relation with one another by means of universal representations. The development of the concept is a rising movement from the singular to the particular and, thence, from the particular to the universal as general equivalent. In the process of rising to the concept, theory exiles thought from its prior status, inscribed with a truth more integral than that of the law of exchange, which results only in more and more complex substitutions of equivalents. What I designated by truth as aletheia is this primordial, concrete truth as world disclosure, which does not efface difference and accentuate identity in order to prevail. Against the communism of the concept, to which our universities had succumbed wholesale, I erected a bulwark to the erosion of distinction in life and the flattening out of relief in the world. My interest in the Greek beginnings of education represents a glimpse of the possibility of the Academy on the basis of aletheia, as one of the ways in which truth essences. In the early thirties, I conceived the institution of the university as a possibility of a similar occurrence of truth. Now, my disagreements with the official tenets of National Socialism are a matter of record before you. Any afterthought I might have to add is this: National Socialism has more to do with the replacement of the propositional truth of theory by an equally abstract, voluntarist view of truth than with any affinity to the concrete truth of the Greeks as world disclosure. To think otherwise is to conflate the very real difference in kind between, on the one hand, communism, whether of the concept under reason or of the will under the *Führer* [sic], and on the other, the anarchism of the rhetorical trope.

Great thinking has rarely been a matter of pronouncing upon the pros and cons of a thesis. It is a struggle [*Kampf*] between an entrenched vernacular and one better expressing the demands of the age. The unit of persuasion is the vernacular as a whole rather than this or that compelling enthymeme; the method, translation rather than inference; logic is ancillary to this process. *Elocutio* or *lexis*, the stage of rhetoric in which one chooses the colors to deck out the arguments of invention, has no purchase here, for vernaculars break completely with the notion of an ideal language against which all others are measured for clarity and refinement.

To think of rhetoric's turns [*Wenden*][13] as forerunners of new ways of world disclosure is to consider the trope on a cognitive par with intuition and inference, rather than considering it to be either instrumental or ornamental in function. Theory has aimed to forget its history and to fashion thought as pure presence by freeing us from the language we have inherited from past thinkers; but those thinkers are the rhetors of being. Our relation to tradition must be a hearing, or rather, a rehearing of thought's oration. To me, the business of philosophy is to preserve the force of the most elemental tropes in which *Dasein* expresses itself. We need to hear the words, hear their oratory, hear their metaphors as if for the first time. The relatedness between *Dasein* and the world is not only a question of grammatical preposition; it is also exactly that—a question, a calling [*Anruf*], a response. As subjects, we are in the vocative [*Vokativ*], in the condition of being called. The language of *Dasein* is no *lingua franca* but a vernacular whose words are a matter of sounds altogether untranslatable in the same sense in which poetry and its metaphors are untranslatable. My own "metaphors" have earned me some reproach, for it is as the so-called "philosopher of the Black Forest," with all the figurative baggage that goes with it—the way, foothills, and sublime landscapes—that I am accused of reactionary romanticism in the service of irrational nationalism.

I do tend to eschew the ocular metaphor, whose use is largely due to Platonic idealism. It is the metaphor par excellence of theory, if "metaphor" is even permissible here; call it rather a momentary lapse [*Lapsus*] from abstraction into the material, a metaphor that denies its figuration. It exhorts us to ascend to a point of view from which everything can be seen steadily and whole; it is *theoria*, which sweeps our feet off the ground (dare we call it groundless [*grundlos*]?), takes the long view, maps out all logical space, and stands ready with a pigeonhole for every occurrence. Rhetoric, on the other hand, keeps one's feet on the ground [*Grund*] but also turns [*wenden*] it, such that our falling precludes any safe return to undeclined ideation. No long view here, but myopia [*Myopie*],[14] narrowing the eye to a pinpoint [*Nadelspitze*] in the glare of theory. The metaphor of the way, as ubiquitous in my work as that of the eye in Plato's, differs in that its figurativeness cannot be forgotten. Rhetoric's metaphors get in the way [*den Weg versperren*] of abstract thought.

We think of error [*Irrnis*] as wandering [*verirren*], implying that truth is a matter of traversing most directly the distance between the two termini of idea and thing. It is with our feet that we either stumble or make progress. The foot has long been an important register of the exotic—think of the Queen of Sheba[15] and the Sciapods.[16] But since two-footedness is the common lot of the rational animal, our understanding of mental progress has generally developed around a binarity of some sort. We think not in sciapodal hops but through the interconnected lurches of ambulation. Rational thought is all about taking a walk, for "division," in its arithmetical sense, underlies the meaning of *ratio* as the *differentia* of our species. Where pure reason represents a grasping of the thing in its entirety, the rational animal, as Plato teaches us, first gathers thought into its genus and then "divides" it into its species. Just as we cannot grasp the whole without apprehension of its parts, so our whole body cannot propel itself without the separate motion of its discrete parts, right, left, *sic et non*, thesis, antithesis. Thus, *ratio* thrusts us forward in hopscotch fashion from privation to possession. Dialectic is the name we give to thought's ambulation, and it is a gait that holds its destination in full view before it starts, that cannot stray [*verirren*]. But to ask a question that itself opens up the way by virtue of the asking is to position our feet in a new way.

Philosophy's early form, the Socratic dialogue, is even then resistant to a totally logical mapping, for it meanders around, tells myths, takes detours. Purest of thinkers for writing nothing down, Socrates, shoeless as tradition has it, roved the *agora*, the meeting place of riffraff and of roads. Iconoclastic and impious, he nonetheless went barefoot in perpetual presence of the holy. Refusing to abandon his homeland of Athens, he nonetheless roamed perpetually within the city. A native citizen, Socrates yet was a stranger in his own land, while his student's student, Aristotle the Stagyrite, was a metic, a settled outsider who made foreign Athens his home. Where Socrates would ostracize foreign poetry (and rhetoric) from his Republic, Aristotle, tutor to Alexander the builder of empires, maps a mighty domain in which all human knowledge [*Wissen*] is parceled out to its inhabitants. The inclusive empire, which claims all known terrain for itself, leaves no one out, not even barbarian rhetoric or poetry, which now is civilized and made subject to the higher *scientiae* of dialectic and politics. Socrates' sense of place, whether inside the city-state or outside it, fades in the Aristotelian empire of knowledge, for all places are now within, and the totality of space must become all the space that is. Ironically, it is at this loss of fundamental distinction for Aristotle that smaller distinctions proliferate: here rhetoric must be distinguished from politics, there politics from ethics, this faculty from that; each special *techne* now needs another by which to identify what it is not. In the erasure of fundamental difference, the need to tell each other apart overrides all other concerns. More vehement in his denigration of rhetoric than Aristotle ever was, Socrates nonetheless came closer to its spirit, recognizing the threat it posed to the business of philosophy.

As early as 1919, I alone among academic reformers focused on the presence of theoretical abstraction as a totality within the very idea of the university. By making theory into its principle, the university inevitably conditions the quality of the pedagogic relation. The result is an encounter between teacher and student, mediated by the theoretical abstraction, which regards the terms of this relation as a matter of minds meeting together in an act of speculation. Instead of starting with a conception of the teacher/student relation at once inflected by both head and hand, the university conceives the pedagogic process in conformity with the model of abstract exchange derived from theory, according to which the fundamental relation is that of mind to the world, regarded as a relation of subject to object by way of representation. The exchange abstraction is thus imparted to the learning experience from without to give it the form and substance of a *quid pro quo,* a relation in which the teacher offers something of value in return for something else of value from the student, the result being that pedagogy now becomes regulated by the logic of contract. Teacher and student always stand to each other, first and foremost, as parties to a contract. The contractualizing of pedagogy has, in fact, achieved such an axiomatic status within the university tradition that discussions of educational reform, even supposed radical ones, simply take it for granted, ignoring ways of conceiving pedagogy innocent of contract as counterintuitive. Indeed, one must go back to the figure of Socrates in order to find an example of teaching and learning at odds with the law of exchange.

In a system of higher education in the thrall of theory, we find pedagogy confined within the coordinates set by certain fundamental distinctions, among them the distinction between teacher and student, head and hand, knowledge and opinion, disinterest and interest, earnest and game [*Ernst und Spiel*], and the liberal and the vocational. Through these and other derivative distinctions, the set of priorities definitive of the life of the mind are affirmed, while the values associated with more concrete and integral modes of human expression are denied. The language of the distinctions itself already entails that the first of the terms takes privilege over what it is contrasted with. To the contrary, I have long endeavored to develop concepts and distinctions more nuanced than any such set of stark dichotomies might indicate in order to express the essence of paideia. In particular, what is to be avoided is negative determination: for example, the student defined only in relation to the prior notion of the teacher as what the teacher is not. For such an approach implicitly makes use of the metaphysical distinction between being and becoming by defining the student as on the way to becoming *like* the teacher, as aiming to be that which the teacher *is*. Early on, this seemed to me to be utterly misguided. Once again, the figure of Socrates points the way forward. In the *Symposium*, Socrates purports to show how head and heart are not to be radically separated, but belong together as integral moments of education. Likewise, Socrates' self-referential paradox "I know that I know nothing"[17] gestures towards a pedagogy in which ignorance lies at the foot of knowledge and contradiction at the font of truth. In a similar vein, it occurred to me unexpectedly as a result of the decisive turn in our history that there were vital prescriptions for the future of the university to be gleaned by going against the grain of our idealist Humboldtian heritage of higher education. At a stroke, the hackneyed representations of teaching and learning fell by the wayside, opening a new horizon to be charted with the compass of Greek paideia to hand.

Characteristic of paideia, as it has come down to us from antiquity, has always been the Socratic injunction against receiving payment for one's teaching. That this is original to the concept, and not simply some Socratic innovation, can be surmised from Socrates' telling anachronism that the Seven Sages, unlike the sophists of his day, never charged their pupils fees for tuition.[18] What Socrates decries as inimical to paideia is the reduction of education by the logic of contract to the status of commodity to be exchanged for consideration according to the law of equivalence. There is an internal connection to be drawn between centralization in the life of the university and theory's rise to the level of the general equivalent. What becomes apparent in the lecture and the seminar is the division between the many, the particular manifold, and the one, the general equivalent that dominates and governs it. The teacher's role in the pedagogic exchange is to represent the general equivalent, administering equivalences among the students, who participate in his unity by subsuming themselves under his generality. Before the teacher, there is formal equality within the collective of students. Instruction is thus modeled on exchange: to teach, the teacher disregards the differences and distinctions within the concrete student manifold and addresses himself to the faceless, abstract student that is his counterpart. Likewise, to learn, the student abandons the idiosyncratic expressions of his life for a generic way of thinking that raises him to the level of the teacher.

As a teacher, I have strived to confound commodity exchange in the classroom. For this reason, my lectures and seminars have appeared odd to many, who are accustomed to the norm of generic education. My paradigm of teaching and learning is the Socratic conversation, the question and answer between individuals who embody the pedagogical scene concretely in ever shifting and undefined ways, such that their respective identities may be thrown into doubt. The desire to know does not arise from lack *per se*, but is engendered upon the realization that one lacks what is good. One utterly ignorant cannot desire to become wise, as his condition prevents him from recognizing his deficiency. Ignorance is thus never simple and unqualified, and the knowledge of one's ignorance results in *eros* or the desire to know. The philosopher, lover of wisdom, is neither actually wise nor entirely ignorant. Ignorance is a condition of knowledge and wisdom. The claim then to know that one does not know is not so much a self-contradiction as it is a sense of what conceals itself in the revealing.

The Socratic encounter employs various techniques of discourse in the service of concrete pedagogy. With his needling remarks [*Nadelstiche*], Socrates questions his interlocutors into contradiction and confusion, reducing them to *aporia*, lack of resource. *Aporia* is a specific kind of lack or want, a perplexity achieved by encounter with the previously unthought, an uncertainty about where to go next driven by a desire to progress. The institution of the university as such confers upon the teacher a recognition of status, an authority that can impede communication. A pedagogy that regards the teacher as the authoritative repository and dispenser of knowledge and wisdom inevitably averts desire. Tyranny in the pedagogical scenario is counterproductive. If the pose of teacherly omniscience and the authority that this pose articulates are disincentives to learn, then the question of education is the question not of how to transmit knowledge but of how to suspend it. The concrete teacher is one who temporarily stages the scene of resourcelessness. Education is not a passing on of knowledge and skills either in the medieval paradigm of master/apprentice or in the modern of seller/consumer. Rather call it a withholding, a delaying of articulation, in order that the student may attain an answer. Ignorance as a mode of suspension interrogates the role of the teacher as the one who knows and of the student as the one who does not. The teacher's silence is finally what has to be heard. Yet it is precisely as teacher that I here must speak.

The university has always focused on the theoretical over the practical, implying that the detached, contemplative point of view is prior to and independent of the background practices of involvement and concern with people and things. Human actions—excluding our involuntary actions, such as blinking and the beating of the heart—cannot count as the stuff of practical virtue unless at every step they apply and are informed by consciousness and intention. Hitherto, intention and intentionality have been understood as aspects of consciousness, as a subject to be studied in epistemology. Medieval philosophy left us with the distinction between an object in its unobserved, natural being *(in esse naturali)* and that same object in its significant being *(in esse intentionali)* as apprehended by the individual knower. It is through the concept, the that-by-which or *medium quo*, that brute matter, which itself has no intelligence, can be rendered intelligible. By positing a concept to be always a concept *of* something, the theory of the intentional existence of forms bridged the gap for the medieval world between the knowing subject and the external world, and as such, it remained within the domain of cognition. Likewise for Brentano and Husserl, intentionality formed the backdrop which conditioned and relativized the gap between subject and object. As a psychical phenomenon, intentionality is attributed to consciousness [*Bewußtsein*], and, in accord with the tradition of Western philosophy, privileges theoretical directedness over the practical. To break the tradition entails surpassing the subject/object distinction in all its domains, including action. The task is not to decide which kind of intentionality, practical or theoretical, is prior, but to get beyond the terms altogether. Displacing the priority of *theoria* is not achieved by simply inverting its relation with *praxis*. The traditional account of both these ways of relating, knowing and doing, contemplation and action, the head and the hand, presupposes a more fundamental sort of intentionality. I do not deny Husserl's great insight that intentional directedness is essential, but I question that it is to be understood primarily in mental terms. Intentionality is first and foremost to be attributed to *Dasein*, not to consciousness [*Bewußtsein*]. Echoing its immediate Latin source *intendere* and the more distant Greek *teino*, intentionality has more to do with an initial act of stretching out, with a hand reaching for something, with tendons tautening purposefully. Intentionality involves doing something for a purpose, rather than being conscious of something, and hence its meaning as mental directedness is derivative and abstracted from a more concrete, nonrepresentational relatedness to things. The bare object of pure, disinterested contemplation, instead of being that which is, is an impoverished residue of what we already handle, what already is of significance and concern to us in a world organized in terms of purposes. The way we relate to things is by comportment [*Verhalten*]. Comportment is nondeliberate, concrete involvement with people and things, practices and institutions, economy and nation.

Intentionality as comportment and truth as world disclosure go hand in hand. Without radically rethinking intentionality, the university's attempts to lay claim to its much vaunted neutrality, to evade being the organ of the nation-state and of the market, is quite futile. The religious particularity of the premodern university was eroded from two sides: nascent nationalism and economic utility. Despite the university's efforts to maintain a theoretical detachment from state and market interest, secularization does not result in independence from values [*Wertfreiheit*] but in replacement of one set of religious values with other, more abstract ones.

How then have I comported myself as I stand here before you, a legal subject asked to render account of my philosophical concepts, my political opinions, my actions, and my relatedness to the students and teachers of this university—experiences that were at no point not already cancelled [*durchkreuzt*] even as they were asserted [*behauptet*]?[19] Those who sought herein for the entry of a plea of guilty or not guilty will have been disappointed by what they found. Under seal of this tribunal, mine have been rather words of bequeathal, however untimely, by a tragic educator, divided between a *not-yet* and a *no-longer*.

Editors' Afterword

What do we do when we expound a sustained theme in someone's writing? We speak, as it were, on their behalf, staying faithful to the testimony of their words, but representing them systematically and in the language of the court of philosophy. We attorn for them. What do we do when we expound a theme in someone's writing that is present only in an *ad hoc* and unsustained manner? We do exactly the same thing.

As early as summer semester 1919, Heidegger was thinking about education in his lectures "On the Essence of the University and Academic Study." It is no accident that almost all his publications since *Being and Time* were first lectures or seminars. Winter 1929–30, and Heidegger once again linked the possibility of philosophy to the question of the role of the university, in the Freiburg Inaugural Lecture and in the lecture course "Introduction to Academic Study." Heidegger's understanding of the role of the philosopher changed, in that he came to make a conscious break with strictly academic philosophy in order henceforth to philosophize in another, nonprofessional way, in immediate confrontation with problems of the time perceived as urgent. His Rectoral Address to the University in 1933 epitomizes this gesture. His consciousness of crisis of the present moment, his interpretation of the German situation at the beginning of the thirties, must always be balanced against his fascination with the past, against an apparent disregard for *Historie,* which refers to undisputed "factual" events, in favor of *Geschichte,* which designates an authentic relation with the past. His search was for a third way irreducible to either of the two then predominant educational alternatives—liberal education and vocational training.

In view of the absence of some definitive text on education written by Heidegger, and in the spirit of improvisation and of imitation, we wrote one for him. We present here Heidegger's apology. Apologetic writing was itself a renowned literary genre in antiquity. An aspiring rhetor was put through his paces by inventing his own defense of Helen of Troy or of Socrates at his trial. The apology presented itself as a formidable test of rhetorical virtuosity. Numerous Socratic apologies existed, of which only three survive, by Xenophon, Plato, and Libanius in the fourth century A.D.

Notes

1. [Ed.] This abridged text of Martin Heidegger's deposition before the Committee on De-Nazification of Freiburg University, translated for the first time into English, has been rendered from the official typewritten transcript of the record of the Committee's proceedings, preserved in the archives of the University. Heidegger read from a handwritten draft, no longer extant, composed specifically for the occasion. The charge of the Committee was to conduct an inquiry into whether Heidegger should be debarred as a faculty member from the University for the nature and manner of his teaching, research, and administration during the Nazi period. The investigation came to focus on the twin issues of violating academic freedom by turning the University into an instrument of Nazi propaganda, and of being an ideologically corrupting influence on students. Although the Committee's predilection was to allow Heidegger to continue in the University in some faculty capacity, upon the insistence of the Allied military government, which saw the internationally renowned philosopher's case as exemplary, the Committee came out in favor of a compromise: suspension. The suspension was only rescinded when Heidegger was allowed to resume university teaching again in 1951.

   Apart from its historical merit, the deposition is of interest for its exposition of Heidegger's views on higher education and pedagogy in general, which are not to be found elsewhere in any of his philosophical works, at least in such a sustained manner. Purposely departing from his signature style, Heidegger adopts a plainer idiom, less immersed in the characteristic philosophical jargon, and provides a unique glimpse into the man himself *in extremis.*

2. [Ed.] See Heidegger's 1933 Rectoral Address, "The Self-Assertion of the German University." In *Review of Metaphysics*, 38 (March): 467–502.

3. [Ed.] The University of Freiburg was founded in 1457.

4. [Ed.] See Virgil, *Aeneid*, trans. R. Fitzgerald, New York: Random House (1983), IV, 609.

5. [Ed.] See Horace, *Ars Poetica*, edited by E. H. Blakeney, Freeport, N.Y.: Books for Libraries Press, (1970), 245. As Phaedrus says in his *Fabulae*, "conceived in the gutter *[trivio]*, educated in dung" (1.27.11).

6. [Ed.] Martin Heidegger, *Being and Time*, trans. J. Macquarrie and E. Robinson, London: SCM Press, (1962), 179.

7. [Ed.] Plato uses *hypokeisthai*, "to underlie," in this political sense (*Gorgias* 510c).

8. [Ed.] See Aristotle, *Metaphysics*, Oxford: Clarendon, (1980), 1017b, 13.

9. [Ed.] The *double entendre* in "subject" meaning "placed under" and "adjective" meaning "inserted" is part of an array of grammatical puns in the Middle Ages. See Alan of Lille's *Complaint of Nature*, trans. J. Sheridan, Toronto: Pontifical Institute of Mediaeval Studies, (1980), Pr.v.

10. [Trans.] Latin *gubernare* means originally to "steer a ship" and then, by extension, "to govern."

11. [Ed.] Aristotle, *Categories*, trans. J. Dillon, London: Duckworth, (1990), 8a.

12. [Ed.] Aristotle, *The Nicomachean Ethics*, trans. and introduction by D. Ross, revised by J. A. Ackrill and J. O. Urmson, Oxford, Oxford University Press, (1980), V, 5.

13. [Trans.] In "turns" [*Wenden*], Heidegger brings together the ideas of rhetorical trope, the "fall" of grammatical case, and the "lapse" of philosophy into metaphor.

14. [Trans.] Heidegger here chooses the word with the Greek root, *Myopie*, rather than the Germanic word for shortsightedness, *Kurzsichtigkeit*. This is not casually done, as is made clear by its juxtaposition with "pinpoint" [*Nadelspitze*] and by a subsequent reference to Socrates goading the Athenians with "needling comments" [*Nadelstiche*]. Plato describes Socrates as a sharp stinging insect *(muops)*, the same word for shortsightedness, the condition of myopia.

15. [Ed.] The Queen of Sheba is traditionally depicted with webbed feet. See *The Book of Hours of Catherine of Cleves*, ed. John Plummer (New York: Pierpoint Morgan Library, 1964), plate 21, p. 49.

16. [Ed.] Mentioned in Pliny and numerous later writings, the Sciapods were alleged to have one huge foot, and they are depicted lying on their back with their foot shielding them from the sun's rays.

17. [Ed.] Plato's *Apology of Socrates*, trans. T. G. West, Ithaca, New York: Cornell University Press, (1979), [21b–e, 29b].

18. [Ed.] Plato, *Hippías Major*, trans. with commentary by P. Woodruff, Oxford, Blackwell, (1982), [282c–d].

19. [Trans.] The word recalls the crossroads [*Kreuzung*] of the trivium and anticipates Heidegger's move in a later essay, "On the Question of Being," to place *Sein* beneath the "mark of crossing out" [*Zeichen der Durchkreuzung*].

10

GEORGE COUNTS

Between 1890 and 1940 there was a major shift in education in the United States. Urban centers saw the rise of centralized school systems run by boards of elite, corporate men who were well schooled in business administration. Schools began to cater to the interests of big business and school boards became dominated by rich members who were not elected but appointed. Some critics began to see a distinct contradiction emerging in this newly unified and increasingly standardized system of public education: elites praised democracy yet increasingly removed the control of schools from the hands of the parents and teachers. Furthermore, these business leaders believed in a scientific form of school administration yet did not realize that their business interests were guiding their decisions.

At the same time, there were new, progressive schools that called into question many of the foundational educational assumptions of the new public schooling system. Drawing inspiration from Dewey's laboratory schools, progressive reformers argued for less business interference and more local control by teachers, yet there appeared to be a contradiction here as well: these schools supported democracy yet they were only available to the wealthy middle class. The progressive movement said it supported social welfare, but really it only supported middle-class notions of the free individual, hence the fact that such schools appealed to middle-class parents. Because of this, progressive education in the end was conservative, supporting class inequalities.

George Counts (1889–1974) emerged from these debates as a critic of both the corporate model of hierarchical control and progressive school reform. He proposed "reconstructionism" as the real inheritor of Dewey's progressivism (society-centered education as opposed to more middle-class notions of child-centered learning). Schools are social institutions and as such must reconstruct society. While Dewey was committed in a general sense to democracy and community, Counts was more radical, arguing for a drastic if not revolutionary shift from capitalist competition and liberal individualism toward a more or less socialist-inspired vision of democratic and collective enterprise.

Counts's question is to this day an important one to remember. Instead of asking if schools *can* rebuild society, he accepts that schools have sufficient influence within society to affect widespread social transformation. Likewise, he does not ask if schools *should* rebuild society. For Counts, it is presupposed that schools are democratic institutions and thus should act to fulfill their democratic mandate. Thus, Count poses a new question: *dare* schools build a new social order? Here he questions the determination and political will of teachers and administrators to use the power invested in the school to solve pressing social issues, such as the anti-democratic plundering that led to the stock market crash in 1929. Teachers should become leaders in social transformation and align themselves with progressive social movements, such as labor unions, in order to address large-scale political and economic issues. In addition, educators should impose democratic values onto students. If all education is political, then teachers should dare to consciously select the most progressive character traits to help produce civic-minded, democratic citizens.

Counts's influence is still felt today, and in many ways current critical pedagogues, such as Henry Giroux (who has argued that teachers should be seen as intellectual cultural workers) and Peter McLaren (who argues that educators should dare to call into question global capitalism in the name of socialist values), are directly or indirectly inheritors of Counts's challenge and his social vision, yet when reading Counts's impassioned work, we must take pause and ask some key questions. What is the difference between indoctrination and imposition, or is there a difference? Can one impose democratic ideals and values onto children, or is this a performative contradiction? What is the relationship between education and politics?

REFERENCES

Gutek, Gerald. *The Educational Theory of George S. Counts.* Ohio State University Press, 1970.

Niece, Richard, and Karen Viechnicki. "Recounting Counts: A Review of George S. Counts' Challenge and the Reactions to 'Dare Progressive Education Be Progressive?'" *Journal of Educational Thought* 21 (1987): 149–54.

Sewell, W.C. "Affecting Social Change: The Struggle for Educators to Transform Society." *Educational Foundations* 19, no. 3/4 (2005): 5–14.

DARE THE SCHOOL BUILD A NEW SOCIAL ORDER?

If an educational movement, or any other movement, calls itself progressive, it must have orientation; it must possess direction. The word itself implies moving forward, and moving forward can have little meaning in the absence of clearly defined purposes. We cannot, like Stephen Leacock's horseman, dash off in all directions at once. Nor should we, like our presidential candidates, evade every disturbing issue and be all things to all men. Also we must beware lest we become so devoted to motion that we neglect the question of direction and be entirely satisfied with movement in circles. Here, I think, we find the fundamental weakness, not only of Progressive Education, but also of American education generally. Like a baby shaking a rattle, we seem to be utterly content with action, provided it is sufficiently vigorous and noisy. In the last analysis a very large part of American educational thought, inquiry, and experimentation is much ado about nothing. And if we are permitted to push the analogy of the rattle a bit further, our consecration to motion is encouraged and supported in order to keep us out of mischief. At least we know that so long as we thus busy ourselves we shall not incur the serious displeasure of our social elders.

The weakness of Progressive Education thus lies in the fact that it has elaborated no theory of social welfare, unless it be that of anarchy or extreme individualism. In this, of course, it is but reflecting the viewpoint of the members of the liberal-minded upper middle class who send their children to the Progressive schools—persons who are fairly well-off, who have abandoned the faiths of their fathers, who assume an agnostic attitude towards all important questions, who pride themselves on their open-mindedness and tolerance, who favor in a mild sort of way fairly liberal programs of social reconstruction, who are full of good will and humane sentiment, who have vague aspirations for world peace and human brotherhood, who can be counted upon to respond moderately to any appeal made in the name of charity, who are genuinely distressed at the sight of *unwonted* forms of cruelty, misery, and suffering, and who perhaps serve to soften somewhat the bitter clashes of those real forces that govern the world; but who, in spite of all their good qualities, have no deep and abiding

From *Dare the School Build a New Social Order?* by George S. Counts, 1978. Reprinted by permission of Martha L. Counts.

loyalties, possess no convictions for which they would sacrifice over-much, would find it hard to live without their customary material comforts, are rather insensitive to the accepted forms of social injustice, are content to play the role of interested spectator in the drama of human history, refuse to see reality in its harsher and more disagreeable forms, rarely move outside the pleasant circles of the class to which they belong, and in the day of severe trial will follow the lead of the most powerful and respectable forces in society and at the same time find good reasons for so doing. These people have shown themselves entirely incapable of dealing with any of the great crises of our time—war, prosperity, or depression. At bottom they are romantic sentimentalists, but with a sharp eye on the main chance. That they can be trusted to write our educational theories and shape our educational programs is highly improbable.

Among the members of this class the number of children is small, the income relatively high, and the economic functions of the home greatly reduced. For these reasons an inordinate emphasis on the child and child interests is entirely welcome to them. They wish to guard their offspring from too strenuous endeavor and from coming into too intimate contact with the grimmer aspects of industrial society. They wish their sons and daughters to succeed according to the standards of their class and to be a credit to their parents. At heart feeling themselves members of a superior human strain, they do not want their children to mix too freely with the children of the poor or of the less fortunate races. Nor do they want them to accept radical social doctrines, espouse unpopular causes, or lose themselves in quest of any Holy Grail. According to their views education should deal with life, but with life at a distance or in a highly diluted form. They would generally maintain that life should be kept at arm's length, if it should not be handled with a poker.

If Progressive Education is to be genuinely progressive, it must emancipate itself from the influence of this class, face squarely and courageously every social issue, come to grips with life in all of its stark reality, establish an organic relation the community, develop a realistic and comprehensive theory of welfare, fashion a compelling and challenging vision of human destiny, and become less frightened than it is today at the bogies of *imposition* and *indoctrination*. In a word, Progressive Education cannot place its trust in a child-centered school.

This brings us to the most crucial issue in education—the question of the nature and extent of the influence which the school should exercise over the development of the child. The advocates of extreme freedom have been so successful in championing what they call the rights of the child that even the most skillful practitioners of the art of converting others to their opinions disclaim all intention of molding the learner. And when the word indoctrination is coupled with education there is scarcely one among us possessing the hardihood to refuse to horrified.

The issue is no doubt badly confused by historical causes. The champions of freedom are obviously the product of an age that has broken very fundamentally with the past and is equally uncertain about the future. In many cases they feel themselves victims of narrow orthodoxies which were imposed upon them during childhood and which have severely cramped their lives. At any suggestion that the child should be influenced by his elders they therefore envisage the establishment of a state church, the formulation of a body of sacred doctrine, and the teaching of this doctrine as fixed and final. If we are forced to choose between such an unenlightened form of pedagogical influence and a condition of complete freedom for the child, most of us would in all probability choose the latter as the lesser of two evils. But this is to create a wholly artificial situation: the choice should not be limited to these two extremes. Indeed today neither extreme is possible.

I believe firmly that a critical factor must play an important role in any adequate educational program, at least in any such program fashioned for the modern world. An education that does not strive to promote the fullest and most thorough understanding of the world is not worthy of the name. Also there must be no deliberate distortion or suppression of facts to support any theory or point of view. On the other hand, I am prepared to defend the thesis that all education contains a large element of imposition, that in the very nature of the case this is inevitable, that the existence and evolution of society depend upon it, that it is consequently* eminently desirable, and that the frank acceptance of this fact by the educator is a major professional obligation. I even contend that failure to do this involves the clothing of one's own

---

*Some persons would no doubt regard this as a *non sequitur,* but the great majority of the members of the human race would, I think, accept the argument.

deepest prejudices in the garb of universal truth and the introduction into the theory and practice of education of an element of obscurantism.

If we may now assume that the child will be imposed upon in some fashion by the various elements in his environment, the real question is not whether imposition will take place, but rather from what source it will come. If we were to answer this question in terms of the past, there could, I think, be but one answer: on all genuinely crucial matters the school follows the wishes of the groups or classes that actually rule society; on minor matters the school is sometimes allowed a certain measure of freedom. But the future may be unlike the past. Or perhaps I should say that teachers, if they could increase sufficiently their stock of courage, intelligence, and vision, might become a social force of some magnitude. About this eventuality I am not over sanguine, but a society lacking leadership as ours does, might even accept the guidance of teachers. Through powerful organizations they might at least reach the public conscience and come to exercise a larger measure of control over the schools than hitherto. They would then have to assume some responsibility for the more fundamental mental forms of imposition which, according to my argument, cannot be avoided.

That the teachers should deliberately reach for power and then make the most of their conquest is my firm conviction. To the extent that they are permitted to fashion the curriculum and the procedures of the school they will definitely and positively influence the social attitudes, ideals, and behavior of the coming generation. In doing this they should resort to no subterfuge or false modesty. They should say neither that they are merely teaching the truth nor that they are unwilling to wield power in their own right. The first position is false and the second is a confession of incompetence. It is my observation that the men and women who have affected the course of human events are those who have not hesitated to use the power that has come to them. Representing as they do, not the interests of the moment or of any special class, but rather the common and abiding interests of the people, teachers are under heavy social obligation to protect and further those interests. In this they occupy a relatively unique position in society. Also since the profession should embrace scientists and scholars of the highest rank, as well as teachers working at all levels of the educational system, it has at its disposal, as no other group, the knowledge and wisdom of the ages. It is scarcely thinkable that these men and women would ever act as selfishly or bungle as badly as have the so-called "practical" men of our generation—the politicians, the financiers, the industrialists. If all of these facts are taken into account, instead of shunning power, the profession should rather seek power and then strive to use that power fully and wisely and in the interests of the great masses of the people.

This brings us to the question of the kind of imposition in which teachers should engage, if they had the power. Our obligations, I think, grow out of the social situation. We live in troublous times; we live in an age of profound change; we live in an age of revolution. Indeed it is highly doubtful whether man ever lived in a more eventful period than the present. In order to match our epoch we would probably have to go back to the fall of the ancient empires or even to that unrecorded age when men first abandoned the natural arts of hunting and fishing and trapping and began to experiment with agriculture and the settled life. Today we are witnessing the rise of a civilization quite without precedent in human history—a civilization founded on science, technology, and machinery, possessing the most extraordinary power, and rapidly making of the entire world a single great society. Because of forces already released, whether in the field of economics, politics, morals, religion, or art, the old molds are being broken. And the peoples of the earth are everywhere seething with strange ideas and passions. If life were peaceful and quiet and undisturbed by great issues, we might with some show of wisdom center our attention on the nature of the child. But with the world as it is, we cannot afford for a single instant to remove our eyes from the social scene or shift our attention from the peculiar needs of the age.

The ideal foundations on which we must build are easily discernible. Until recently the very word America has been synonymous throughout the world with democracy and symbolic to the oppressed classes of all lands of hope and opportunity. Child of the revolutionary ideas and impulses of the eighteenth century, the American nation became the embodiment of bold social experimentation and a champion of the power of environment to develop the capacities and redeem the souls of common men and women. And as her stature grew, her lengthening shadow reached to the four corners of the earth and everywhere impelled the human will to rebel against ancient wrongs. Here undoubtedly is the finest jewel in our heritage and the thing that is most worthy of preservation. If America should lose her honest devotion to democracy, or if she should lose her revolutionary temper, she will no longer be America. In that day, if it has not already arrived, her spirit will have fled and she will be known merely as the richest and most powerful of the nations. If America is not to be false to the promise of her youth, she must do more than simply perpetuate the democratic ideal of human relationships: she must make an intelligent and determined effort to fulfill it. The democracy of the past was the chance fruit of a strange conjunction of forces on the new continent; the democracy of the future can only be the intended offspring of the union of human reason, purpose, and will. The conscious and deliberate achievement of democracy under novel circumstances is the task of our generation.

The fact that other groups refuse to deal boldly and realistically with the present situation does not justify the teachers of the country in their customary policy of hesitation and equivocation. The times are literally crying for a new vision of American destiny. The teaching profession, or at least its progressive elements, should eagerly grasp the opportunity which the fates have placed in their hands.

Such a vision of what America might become in the industrial age I would introduce into our schools as the supreme imposition, but one to which our children are entitled—a priceless legacy which it should be the first concern of our profession to fashion and bequeath. The objection will of course be raised that this is asking teachers to assume unprecedented social responsibilities. But we live in difficult and dangerous times—times when precedents lose their significance. If we are content to remain where all is safe and quiet and serene, we shall dedicate ourselves, as teachers have commonly done in the past, to a role of futility, if not of positive social reaction. Neutrality with respect to the great issues that agitate society, while perhaps theoretically possible, is practically tantamount to giving support to the forces of conservatism. As Justice Holmes has candidly said in his essay on Natural Law, "we all, whether we know it or not, are fighting to make the kind of world that we should like." If neutrality is impossible even in the dispensation of justice, whose emblem is the blindfolded goddess, how is it to be achieved in education? To ask the question is to answer it.

To refuse to face the task of creating a vision of a future America immeasurably more just and noble and beautiful than the America of today is to evade the most crucial, difficult, and important educational task.

11

THEODOR ADORNO

Theodor Ludwig Wiesengrund Adorno (1903–1969) was an influential social philosopher and member of the Frankfurt Institute for Social Research. Born in Frankfurt am Main, Germany, Adorno would become one of the most well known proponents of "late Marxism," also referred to as "critical theory." Throughout his life, Adorno was a passionate music critic, composer, sociologist, and philosopher, embodying the metatheoretical and totalizing materialist social theory endorsed by the Frankfurt School. While many view his writing as eclectic and highly difficult (if not elitist), Adorno was always interested in revitalizing and rethinking philosophical concepts in relation to pressing realities of industrial capitalism, mass culture, consumerism, fascist genocide, and the crisis in education.

While close friends with many of the key members of the Institute for Social Research, it was not until his emigration to New York in 1938 that Adorno became an official member. From the unique perspective of a recent emigrant, Adorno utilized a challenging synthesis of Freudian psychoanalysis, Kantian philosophy, aesthetic theory, and Marxism to analyze the rise of the culture industry in the United States. In particular, he was a consultant on "The Radio Project" in New York, which analyzed the social impact of radio, and later in Los Angeles, Adorno contributed to the *Studies in Anti-Semitic Prejudice* in order to uncover the hidden authoritarian character of U.S. test subjects.

Overall, Adorno's scholarship embodies a critical theory of society. Critical theory has several key features which differentiate it from traditional theory. For instance, it is always transdisciplinary, refusing to be bound by academic disciplines. Second, it is comprehensive, always searching for the relations between individual phenomena (particulars) and social forces (generalities). Third, critical theory is dialectic. Here dialectical thinking involves the analysis of ambiguity—the socially progressive and regressive, oppressive, and emancipatory aspects of current social life. Because critical theory is so closely linked with emergent social trends, the theory itself precludes any orthodox position and must change as history changes. Finally, the goal of critical theory is to resist oppression, exploitation, and subjugation in the name of emancipation.

In the influential book *Dialectic of Enlightenment* (1949), co-written with Max Horkheimer, Adorno utilized critical theory in order to understand the disturbing tendency for enlightenment reason to self-destruct (most clearly witnessed in the Jewish Holocaust). Through a variety of essays, Horkheimer and Adorno detailed the birth of irrationality from within the very core of rationality. The final logic of enlightenment organization, systematization, quantification, calculation, and control is exhibited in (a) the concentration camp of Auschwitz where individuals were turned into faceless numbers devoid of human value and (b) the U.S. culture industry where massification, standardization, and administration of art, culture, and social relations have come to dominate. Thus, while "official" narratives read history as a progress of reason, liberation, and freedom, Adorno tends to emphasize those aspects of the enlightenment left out of this story: the dark, brutal, and violent side of history. In short, Adorno had an amazingly acute ability to find the nonidentical within the identical (i.e., the irrational within the rational).

Upon returning to Germany in 1949, Adorno became concerned with the possibility that fascism remained a strong psychological tendency within the recently democratized West German citizenry. In order to combat these ominous tendencies, Adorno became a public intellectual, appearing in 160 radio programs. His writings and lectures on education as an important means of overcoming the hardness and coldness of fascism are part of this concerted political agenda. While his influence on educational philosophy in the United States has yet to be fully realized, Adorno's influence on German education is not to be underestimated. In light of ongoing genocides in Africa and Asia, we cannot easily forget Adorno's clarion call that the goal of education should be to prevent such widespread human catastrophes.

REFERENCES

Buck-Morss, Susan. *The Origin of Negative Dialectics: Theodor W. Adorno, Walter Benjamin, and the Frankfurt Institute.* New York: Free Press, 1979.

Kellner, Douglas. *Critical Theory, Marxism, and Modernity.* Baltimore: Johns Hopkins University Press, 1992.

Papastephanou, Marianna. "Aesthetics, Education, the Critical Autonomous Self, and the Culture Industry." *Journal of Aesthetic Education* 40, no. 3 (2006): 75–91.

Scherr, Albert. "Critical Theory and Pedagogy: Theodor W. Adorno and Max Horkheimer's Contemporary Significance for a Critical Pedagogy." In Gustavo Fischman, Peter McLaren, Heinz Sunker, and Colin Lankshear, eds. *Critical Theories, Radical Pedagogies, and Global Conflicts* (pp. 154–63). Lanham: Rowman and Littlefield, 2005.

Thompson, Christiane. "Adorno and the Borders of Experience: The Significance of the Nonidentical for a 'Different' Theory of *Bildung*." *Educational Theory* 56, no. 1 (2006): 69–87.

EDUCATION AFTER AUSCHWITZ

The premier demand upon all education is that Auschwitz not happen again. Its priority before any other requirement is such that I believe I need not and should not justify it. I cannot understand why it has been given so little concern until now. To justify it would be monstrous in the face of the monstrosity that took place. Yet the fact that one is so barely conscious of this demand and the questions it raises shows that the monstrosity has not penetrated people's minds deeply, itself a symptom of the continuing potential for its recurrence as far as peoples' conscious and unconscious is concerned. Every debate about the ideals of education is trivial and inconsequential compared to this single ideal: never again Auschwitz. It was the barbarism all education strive against. One speaks of the threat of a relapse into barbarism. But it is not a threat—Auschwitz *was* this relapse, and barbarism continues as long as the fundamental conditions that favored that relapse continue largely unchanged. That is the whole horror. The societal pressure still bears down, although the danger remains invisible nowadays. It drives people toward the unspeakable, which culminated on a world-historical scale in Auschwitz. Among the insights of Freud that truly extend even into culture and sociology, one of the most profound seems to me to be that civilization itself produces anti-civilization and increasingly reinforces it. His writings *Civilization and its Discontents* and *Group Psychology and the Analysis of the Ego* deserve the widest possible diffusion, especially in connection with Auschwitz. If barbarism itself is inscribed within the principle of civilization, then there is something desperate in the attempt to rise up against it.

Since the possibility of changing the objective—namely societal and political—conditions is extremely limited today, attempts to work against the repetition of Auschwitz are necessarily restricted to the subjective dimension. By this I also mean essentially the psychology of people who do such things. I do not believe it would help much to appeal to eternal values, at which the very people who are prone to commit such atrocities would merely shrug their shoulders. I also do not believe that enlightenment about the positive qualities possessed by persecuted minorities would be of much use. The roots must be sought in the persecutors, not in the victims who are murdered under the paltriest of pretenses. What is necessary is what I once in this respect called the turn to the subject. One must come to know the mechanisms that render people capable of such deeds, must reveal these mechanisms to them, and strive, by awakening a general awareness of those mechanisms, to prevent people from becoming so again. It is not the victims who are guilty, not even in the sophistic and caricatured sense in which still today many like to construe it. Only those who unreflectingly vented their hate and aggression upon them are guilty. One must labor against this lack of reflection, must dissuade people from striking outward without reflecting upon themselves. The only education that has any sense at all is an education toward critical self-reflection. But since according to the findings of depth psychology, all personalities, even those who commit atrocities in later life, are formed in early childhood, education seeking to prevent the repetition must concentrate upon early childhood. I mentioned Freud's thesis on discontent in culture. Yet the phenomenon extends even further than he understood it, above all, because the pressure of civilization he had observed has in the meantime multiplied to an unbearable degree. At the same time the explosive tendencies he first drew attention to have assumed a violence he could hardly have foreseen. The discontent in culture, however, also has its social dimension, which Freud did not overlook though he did not explore it concretely. One can speak of the claustrophobia of humanity in the administered world, of a feeling of being incarcerated in a thoroughly societalized, closely woven, netlike environment. The denser the weave, the more one wants to escape it, whereas it is precisely its close weave that prevents any escape. This intensifies the fury against civilization. The revolt against it is violent and irrational.

When I speak of education after Auschwitz, then, I mean two areas: first children's education, especially in early childhood; then general enlightenment that provides an intellectual, cultural, and social climate in which a recurrence would no longer be possible, a climate, therefore, in which the motives that led to the horror would become relatively conscious. Naturally, I cannot presume to sketch out the plan of such an education even in rough outline. Yet I would like at least to indicate some of it nerve centers.

Very often well-meaning people who don't want it to happen again, invoke the concept of bonds. According to them, the fact that people no longer had any bonds is responsible for what took place. In fact, the loss of authority, one of the conditions of the sadistic-authoritarian horror, is connected with this state of affairs. To normal common sense it is plausible to appeal to bonds that check the sadistic, destructive, and ruinous impulse with an emphatic "You must not." Nevertheless I consider it an illusion to think that the appeal to bonds—let alone the demand that everyone should again embrace social ties so that things will look up for the world and for people—would help in any serious way. One senses very quickly the untruth of bonds that are required only so that they produce a result—even if it be good—without the bonds being experienced by people as something substantial in themselves. It is surprising how swiftly even the most foolish and naive people react when it comes to detecting the weaknesses of their betters. The so-called bonds easily become either a ready badge of shared convictions—one enters into them to prove oneself a good citizen—or they produce spiteful resentment, psychologically the opposite of the purpose for which they were drummed up. They amount to heteronomy, a dependence on rules, on norms that cannot be justified by the individual's own reason. What psychology calls the superego, the conscience, is replaced in the name of bonds by external, unbinding, and interchangeable authorities, as one could observe quite clearly in Germany after the collapse of the Third Reich. Yet the very willingness to connive with power and to submit outwardly to what is stronger, under the guise of a norm, is the attitude of the tormentors that should not arise again. It is for this reason that the advocacy of bonds is so fatal. People who adopt them more or less voluntarily are placed under a kind of permanent compulsion to obey orders. The single genuine power standing against the principle of Auschwitz is autonomy, if I might use the Kantian expression: the power of reflection, of self-determination of not cooperating.

What Auschwitz produced, the characteristic personality types of the world of Auschwitz, presumably represents something new. On the one hand, those personality types epitomize the blind identification with the collective. On the other hand, they are fashioned in order to manipulate masses, collectives, as Himmler, Höss, and Eichmann did. I think the most important way to confront the danger of recurrence is to work against the brute predominance of all collectives, to intensify the resistance to it by concentrating on the problem of collectivization. That is not as abstract as it sounds in view of the passion with which especially young and progressively minded people desire to integrate themselves into something or other. One could start with the suffering the collective first inflicts upon all the individuals it accepts. One has only to think of one's own first experiences in school. One must fight against the type of *folkways* [*Volkssitten*], initiation rites of all shapes, that inflict physical pain—upon a person as the price that must be paid in order to consider oneself a member, one of the collective. The evil of customs such as the *Rauhnächte* and the *Haberfeldtreiben* and whatever else such long-rooted practices might be called is a direct anticipation of National Socialist acts of violence. It is no coincidence that the Nazis glorified and cultivated such monstrosities in the name of "customs." Science here has one of its most relevant tasks. It could vigorously redirect the tendencies of folk-studies [*Volkskunde*] that were enthusiastically appropriated by the Nazis in order to prevent the survival, at once brutal and ghostly, of these folk-pleasures.

This entire sphere is animated by an alleged ideal that also plays a considerable role in the traditional education: the ideal of being hard. This ideal can also, ignominiously enough, invoke a remark of Nietzsche, although he truly meant something else. I remember how the dreadful Boger during the Auschwitz trial had an outburst that culminated in a panegyric to education instilling discipline through hardness. He thought hardness necessary to produce what he considered to be the correct type of person. This educational ideal of hardness, in which many may believe without reflecting about it, is utterly wrong. The idea that virility consists in the maximum degree of endurance long ago became a screen-image for masochism that, as psychology has demonstrated, aligns itself all too easily with sadism. Being hard, the vaunted quality education should inculcate, means absolute indifference toward pain as such. In this the distinction between one's own pain and that of another is not so stringently maintained. Whoever is hard with himself earns the right to be hard with others as well and avenges himself for the pain whose manifestations he was not allowed to show and had to repress. This mechanism must be made conscious, just as an education must be promoted that no longer sets a premium on pain and the ability to endure pain. In other words: education must take seriously an idea in no wise unfamiliar to philosophy: that anxiety must not be repressed. When anxiety is not repressed, when one permits oneself to have, in fact, all the anxiety that this reality warrants, then precisely by doing that, much of the destructive effect of unconscious and displaced anxiety will probably disappear.

People who blindly slot themselves into the collective already make themselves into something like inert material, extinguish themselves as self-determined beings. With this comes the willingness to treat others as an amorphous mass. I called those who behave in this way "the manipulative character" in the *Authoritarian Personality*, indeed at a time when the diary of Höss or the recordings of Eichmann were not yet known. My descriptions of the manipulative character date back to the last years of the Second World War. Sometimes social psychology and sociology are able to construct concepts that only later are empirically verified. The manipulative character—as anyone can confirm in the sources available about those Nazi leaders—is distinguished by a rage for organization, by the inability to have any immediate human experiences at all, by a certain lack of emotion, by an overvalued realism. At any cost he wants to conduct supposed, even if delusional, *Realpolitik*. He does not for one second think or wish that the world were any different than it is, he obsessed by the desire *of doing things* [*Dinge zu tun*], indifferent to the consent of such action. He makes a cult action, activity, of so-called *efficiency* as such, which reappears in the advertising image of the active person. If my observations do not deceive me and if several sociological investigations permit generalization, then this type has become much more prevalent today than one would think. What at that time was exemplified in only a few Nazi monsters could be confirmed today in numerous people, for instance, in juvenile criminals, gang leaders, and the like, about whom one reads in the newspapers every day. If I had to reduce this type of manipulative character to a formula—perhaps one should not do it, but it could also contribute to understanding—then I would call it the type of *reified consciousness*. People of such a nature have, as it were, assimilated themselves to things. And then, when possible, they assimilate others to things. This is conveyed very precisely in the expression "to finish off" [*"fertig-machen"*], just as popular in the world of juvenile rowdies as in the world of the Nazis. This expression defines people as finished or prepared things in a doubled sense. Accordingly to the insight of Max Horkheimer, torture is a manipulated and somewhat accelerated adaptation of people to collectives. There is something of this in the spirit of the age, though it has little to do with spirit. I merely cite the saying of Paul Valéry before the last war, that inhumanity has a great future. It is especially difficult to fight against it because those manipulative people, who actually are incapable of true experience, for that very reason manifest an unresponsiveness that associates them with certain mentally ill or psychotic characters, namely schizoids.

I mentioned the concept of reified consciousness. Above all this is a consciousness blinded to all historical past, all insight into one's own conditionedness, and posits as absolute what exists contingently. If this coercive mechanism were once ruptured, then, I think, something would indeed be gained.

Furthermore, in connection with reified consciousness one should also observe closely the relationship to technology, and certainly not only within small groups. The relationship here is just as ambiguous as in sports, to which it is related, incidentally. On the one hand, each epoch produces those personalities—types varying according to their distribution of psychic energy—it needs societally. A world where technology occupies such a key position as it does nowadays produces technological people, who are attuned to technology. This has its good reason: in their own narrow filed they will be less likely to be fooled and that can also affect the overall situation. On the other hand, there is something exaggerated, irrational, pathogenic in the present-day relationship to technology. This is connected with the "veil of technology." People are inclined to take technology to be the thing itself, as an end in itself, a force of its own, and they forget that it is an extension of human dexterity. The means—and technology is the epitome of the means of self-preservation of the human species—are fetishized, because the ends—a life of human dignity—are concealed and removed from the consciousness of people. As long as one formulates this as generally as I just did, it should provide insight. But such a hypothesis is still much too abstract. It is by no means clear precisely how the fetishization of technology establishes itself within the individual psychology of particular people, or where the threshold lies between a rational relationship to technology and the overvaluation that finally leads to the point where one who cleverly devises a train system that brings the victims to Auschwitz as quickly and smoothly as possible forgets about what happens to them there. With this type, who tends to fetishize technology, we are concerned—badly put, with people who cannot love. This is not meant to be sentimental or moralistic but rather describes a deficient libidinal relationship to other persons. Those people are thoroughly cold; deep within themselves they must deny the possibility of love, must withdraw their love from other people initially, before it can even unfold. And whatever of the ability to love somehow survives in them they must expend on devices. Those prejudiced, authoritarian characters whom we examined at Berkeley in the *Authoritarian Personality*, provided us with much proof of this. A test subject—the expression itself comes from reified consciousness—said of himself: *"I like nice equipment"* [*Ich habe hübsche Ausstattungen, hübsche Apparaturen gern*], completely indifferent about what equipment it was. His love was absorbed by things, machines as such. The alarming thing about this— alarming, because it can seem so hopeless to combat it—is that this trend goes hand in hand with that of the entire civilization. To struggle against it means as much as to stand against the world spirit; but with this I am only repeating what I mentioned at the outset as the darkest aspect of an education opposed to Auschwitz.

As I said, those people are cold in a specific way. Surely a few words about coldness in general are permitted. If coldness were not a fundamental trait of anthropology, that is, the constitution of people as they in fact exist in our society, if people were not profoundly indifferent toward whatever happens to everyone else except for a few to whom they are closely bound and, if possible, by tangible interests, then Auschwitz would not have been possible, people would not have accepted it. Society in its present form—and no doubt as it has been for centuries already—is based not, as was ideologically assumed since Aristotle, on appeal, on attraction, but rather on the pursuit of one's own interests against the interests of everyone else. This has settled into the character of people to their innermost center. What contradicts my observations, the herd drive of the so-called *lonely crowd* [*die einsame Menge*], is a reaction to this process, a banding together of people completely cold who cannot endure their own coldness and yet cannot change it. Every person today, without exception, feels too little loved, because every person cannot love enough. The inability to identify with others was unquestionably the most important psychological condition for the fact that something like Auschwitz could have occurred in the midst of more or less civilized and innocent people. What is called fellow traveling was primarily business interest: one pursue one's own advantage before all else and, simply not to endanger oneself, does not talk too much. That is a general law of the status quo. The silence under the terror was only its consequence. The coldness of the societal monad, the isolated competitor, was the precondition, as indifference to the fate of others, for the fact that only very few people reacted. The torturers know this, and they put it to the test ever anew.

Understand me correctly. I do not want to preach love. I consider it futile to preach it; no one has the right to preach it since the lack of love, as I have already said, is a lack belonging to *all* people without exception as they exist today. To preach love already presupposes in those to whom one appeals a character structure different from the one that needs to be changed. For the people whom one should love are themselves such that they cannot love, and therefore in turn are not at all that lovable. One of the greatest impulses of Christianity, not immediately identical with its dogma, was to eradicate the coldness that permeates everything. But this attempt failed; surely because it did not reach into the societal order that produces and reproduces that coldness. Probably that warmth among people, which everyone longs for, has never been present at all, except during short periods and in very small groups, perhaps even among peaceful savages. The much maligned utopians saw this. Thus Charles Fourier defined attraction as something that first must be produced through a humane societal order; he also recognized that this condition would be possible only when the drives of people are no longer repressed, but fulfilled and released. If anything can help against coldness as the condition for disaster, then it is the insight into the conditions that determine it and the attempt to combat those conditions, initially in the domain of the individual. One might think that the less is denied to children, the better they are treated, the greater would be the chance of success. But here too illusions threaten. Children who have no idea of the cruelty and hardness of life are then truly exposed to barbarism when they must leave their protected environment. Above all, however, it is impossible to awaken warmth in the parents, who are themselves products of this society and who bear its marks. The exhortation to give more warmth to children amounts to pumping out warmth artificially, thereby negating it. Moreover, love cannot be summoned in professionally mediated relations like that of teacher and student, doctor and patient, lawyer and client. Love is something immediate and in essence contradicts mediated relationships. The exhortation to love—even in its imperative form, that one *should* do it—is itself part of the ideology coldness perpetuates. It bears the compulsive, oppressive quality that counteracts the ability to love. The first thing therefore is to bring coldness to the consciousness of itself, of the reasons why it arose.

In conclusion, permit me to say a few words about some possibilities for making conscious the general subjective mechanisms without which Auschwitz would hardly have been possible. Knowledge of these mechanisms is necessary, as is knowledge of the stereotypical defense mechanisms that block such a consciousness. Whoever still says today that it did not happen or was not all that bad already defends what took place and unquestionably would be prepared to look on or join in if it happens again. Even if rational enlightenment, as psychology well knows, does not straightaway eliminate the unconscious mechanisms, then it reinforces, at least in the preconscious, certain counter-impulses and helps prepare a climate that does not favor the uttermost extreme. If the entire cultural consciousness really became permeated with the idea of the pathogenic character of the tendencies that came into their own at Auschwitz, then perhaps people would better control those tendencies.

Furthermore, one should work to raise awareness about the possible displacement of what broke out in Auschwitz. Tomorrow a group other than the Jews may come along, say the elderly, who indeed were still spared in the Third Reich, or the intellectuals, or simply deviant groups. As I indicated, the climate that most promotes such a resurrection is the revival of nationalism. It is so evil because, in the age of international communication and supernational blocs, nationalism cannot really believe in itself anymore and must exaggerate itself to the extreme in order to persuade itself and others that it is still substantial.

All political instruction finally should be centered upon the idea that Auschwitz should never happen again. This would be possible only when it devotes itself openly, without fear of offending any authorities, to this most important of problems. To do this education must transform itself into sociology, that is, it must teach about the societal play of forces that operates beneath the surface of political forms.

One must submit to critical treatment—to provide just one model— such a respectable concept as that of "reason of state"; in placing the right of the state over that of its members, the horror is potentially already posited.

Walter Benjamin asked me once in Paris during his emigration, when I was still returning to Germany sporadically, whether there were really enough torturers back there to carry out the orders of the Nazis. There were enough. Nevertheless the question has its profound legitimacy. Benjamin sensed that the people who *do* it, as opposed to the bureaucratic desktop murderers and ideologues, operate contrary to their own immediate interests, are murderers of themselves while they murder others. I fear that the measures of even such an elaborate education will hardly hinder the renewed growth of desktop murderers. But that the are people who do it down below, indeed as servants, through which they perpetuate their own servitude and degrade themselves, that there are more Bogers and Kaduks: against this, however, education and enlightenment can still manage a little something.

12

ERICH FROMM

Erich Fromm (1900–1980) was an important social psychologist linked to the now famous Frankfurt Institute for Social Research in Germany. After he received a Ph.D. from Heidelberg, Fromm began to practice psychoanalysis in 1922. Although his work with the Institute for Social Research was based in Germany, he later became an international figure, moving to New York City in 1934, and then later in his life moving to Mexico City, where he met with Paulo Freire, another important educational philosopher. From Fromm, Freire learned key concepts such as "humanization."

As a member of the "Frankfurt School," Fromm was interested in developing a multidisciplinary and comprehensive materialist social psychology that could explain the individual psychology of the new consumer society in advanced capitalist countries. In particular, Fromm was searching for answers to some of the most pressing questions of the day, including psychological reasons for the rise of fascist authoritarianism throughout Europe. Why did the working class opt for fascist leaders rather than socialism? Such questions seemed to demand a more complex model of the relationship between consciousness and society than had been offered previously by social scientists or by philosophers.

The theory of "social character" that Fromm developed in response to these questions was a synthesis of Marxist philosophy and Freudian psychoanalysis. On the surface, these two theories seemed to be radically opposed to one another. Marx, for instance, believed that the individual

233

is largely a reflection of larger social relations, while Freud believed that society was a reflection of individual psychological drives, yet, where others had seen only oppositions, Fromm discovered a more important similarity between the two: both were materialist theories in that they started not from abstract ideas but rather from life, needs, and social relations. This observation formed the base for a very complex synthesis between the two theories, leading to Fromm's unique notion of "Marxist Humanism." For Fromm, a person's character mediates between individual drives, desires, and needs and larger social and economic forces, hence the term "social character." Social character is therefore molded by the necessities of the social system, but in turn this character is a productive force that comes to shape social processes.

A major example of Fromm's approach appeared in his work at the Institute for Social Research concerning the connections between the family and social authority (1936). In this study, Fromm and others carefully examined how the irrational psychological disposition toward submission to authority arose from family socialization. Ideally, a child is able to develop inner strength, an ability to love, and the capacity to labor collectively with others, yet, due to the structure of the family within advanced capitalism, child development often takes a turn away from freedom and escapes into submission to authority. Thus, the social character structure of advanced capitalism is authoritarian. This means that our abilities to think critically, love others, and be in the world rather than lust to own it are sacrificed for the false security of conformity in accordance with authoritarian rule.

While Fromm has been largely ignored in educational research in the United States, his theory is provocative for educational philosophers and social researchers. For instance, we might ask what type of social character education produces today. Does education promote ways of being in the world that encourage submission to authority rather than an embrace of freedom? How does learning reproduce social and economic inequality through the teaching of social psychology?

REFERENCES

Fromm, Erich. *Escape from Freedom.* New York: Henry Holt and Company, 1994.

Kellner, Douglas. *Critical Theory, Marxism, and Modernity.* Baltimore: Johns Hopkins University Press, 1992.

McLaughlin, Neil. "Nazism, Nationalism, and the Sociology of Emotions: *Escape from Freedom* Revisited." *Theory and Society* 15, no. 3 (1986): 351–400.

TO HAVE OR TO BE?

Origin of the Terms

"To have" is a deceptively simple expression. Every human being *has* something: a body,* clothes, shelter—on up to the modern man or woman who has a car, a television set, a washing machine, etc. Living without having something is virtually impossible. Why, then, should having be a problem? Yet the linguistic history of "having" indicates that the word is indeed a problem. To those who believe that to have is a most natural category of human existence it may come as a surprise to learn that many languages have no word for "to have." In Hebrew, for instance, "I have" must be expressed by the indirect form *jesh li* ("it is to me"). In fact, languages that express possession in this way, rather than by "I have," predominate. It is interesting to note that in the development of many languages the construction "it is to me" is followed later on by the construction "I have," but as Emile Benveniste has pointed out, the evolution does not occur in the reverse direction.** This fact suggests that the word for *to have* develops in connection with the development of private property, while it is absent in societies with predominantly functional property, that is, possession for use. Further sociolinguistic studies should be able to show if and to what extent this hypothesis is valid.

If *having* seems to be a relatively simple concept, *being*, or the form "to be," is all the more complicated and difficult. "Being" is used in several different ways: (1) as a copula—such as "I am tall," "I am white," "I am poor," i.e., a grammatical denotation of identity (many languages do not have a word for "to be" in this sense; Spanish distinguishes between permanent qualities, *ser*, which belong to the essence of the subject, and contingent qualities, *estar*, which are not of the essence); (2) as the passive, suffering form of a verb—for example, "I am beaten" means I am the object of another's activity, not the subject of my activity, as in "I beat"; (3) as meaning to exist—wherein, as Beneveniste has shown, the "to be" of existence is a different term from "to be" as a

From *To Have or To Be?* by Eric Fromm, 1988. Reprinted by permission of The Continuum International Publishing Group.

*It should be mentioned here, at least in passing, that there also exists a being relationship to one's body that experiences the body as alive, and that can be expressed by saying "I am my body," rather than "I have my body"; all practices of sensory awareness attempt this being experience of the body.
**This and the following linguistic quotations are taken from Benveniste.

copula stating identity: "The two words have coexisted and can still coexist, although they are entirely different."

Benveniste's study throws new light on the meaning of "to be" as a verb in its own right rather than as a copula. "To be," in Indo-European languages, is expressed by the root *es*, the meaning of which is "to have existence, to be found in reality." Existence and reality are defined as "that which is authentic, consistent, "true." (In Sanskrit, *sant*, "existent," "actual good," "true"; superlative *Sattama*, "the best.") "Being" in its etymological root is thus more than a statement of identity between subject and attribute; it is more than a *descriptive* term for a phenomenon. It denotes the reality of existence of who or what *is*; it states his/her/its authenticity and truth. Stating that somebody or something *is* refers to the person's or the thing's essence, not to his/her/its appearance.

This preliminary survey of the meaning of having and being leads to these conclusions:

1. By being or having I do not refer to certain separate qualities of a subject as illustrated in such statements as "I have a car" or "I am white" or "I am happy." I refer to two fundamental modes of existence, to two different kinds of orientation toward self and the world, to two different kinds of character structure the respective predominance of which determines the totality of a person's thinking, feeling, and acting.

2. In the having mode of existence my relationship to the world is one of possessing and owning, one in which I want to make everybody and everything, including myself, my property.

3. In the being mode of existence, we must identify two forms of being. One is in contrast to *having*, as exemplified in the Du Marais statement, and means aliveness and authentic relatedness to the world. The other form of being is in contrast to *appearing* and refers to the true nature, the true reality, of a person or a thing in contrast to deceptive appearances as exemplified in the etymology of being (Benveniste).

In order to fully appreciate the mode of having that we are dealing with here, yet another qualification seems necessary, that of the function of *existential having*; human existence requires that we have, keep, take care of, and use certain things in order to survive. This holds true for our bodies, for food, shelter, clothing, and for the tools necessary to produce our needs. This form of having may be called existential having because it is rooted in human existence. It is a rationally directed impulse in the pursuit of staying alive—in contrast to the *characterological having* we have been dealing with so far, which is a passionate drive to retain and keep that is not innate, but that has developed as the result of the impact of social conditions on the human species as it is biological given.

Existential having is not in conflict with being; characterological having necessarily is. Even the "just" and the "saintly," inasmuch as they are human, must want to have in the existential sense—while the average person wants to have in the existential *and* in the characterological sense. (See the earlier discussion of existential and characterological dichotomies in *Man for Himself.*)

Having and Being in Daily Experience

Because the society we live in is devoted to acquiring property and making a profit, we rarely see any evidence of the being mode of existence and most people see the having mode as the most natural mode of existence, even the only acceptable way of life. All of which makes it especially difficult for people to comprehend the nature of the being mode, and even to understand that having is only one possible orientation. Nevertheless, these two concepts are rooted in human experience. Neither one should be, or can be, examined in an abstract, purely cerebral way; both are reflected in our daily life and must be dealt with concretely. The following simple examples of how having and being are demonstrated in everyday life may help readers to understand these two alternative modes of existence

Learning   Students in the having mode of existence will listen to a lecture, hearing the words and understanding their logical structure and their meaning and, as best they can, will write down every word in their looseleaf notebooks—so that, later on, they can memorize their notes and thus pass an examination. But the content does not become part of their own individual system of thought, enriching and widening it. Instead, they transform the words they hear into fixed clusters of thought, or whole theories, which they store up. The students and the content of the lectures remain strangers to each other, except that each student has become the owner of a collection of statements made by somebody else (who had either created them or taken them over from another source).

Students in the having mode have but one aim: to hold onto what they "learned," either by entrusting it firmly to their memories or by carefully guarding their notes. They do not have to produce or create something new. In fact, the *having*-type individuals feel rather disturbed by new thoughts or ideas about a subject, because the new puts into question the fixed sum of information they have. Indeed, to one for whom having is the main form of relatedness to the world, ideas that cannot easily be pinned down (or penned down) are frightening—like everything else that grows and changes, and thus is not controllable.

The process of learning has an entirely different quality for students in the being mode of relatedness *to* the world. To begin with, they do not go to the course of lectures, even to the first one in a course, as *tabulae rasae*. They have thought beforehand about the problems the lectures will be dealing with and have in mind certain questions and problems of their own. They have been occupied with the topic and it interests them. Instead of being passive receptacles of words and ideas, they listen, they *hear*, and most important, they *receive* and they *respond* in an active, productive way. What they listen to stimulates their own thinking processes. New questions, new ideas, new perspectives arise in their minds. Their listening is an alive process. They listen with interest, hear what the lecturer says, and spontaneously come to life in response to what they hear. They do not simply acquire knowledge that they can take home and memorize. Each student has been affected and has changed: each is different after the lecture than he or she was before it. Of course, this mode of learning can prevail only if the lecture offers stimulating material. Empty talk cannot be responded to in the being mode, and in such circumstances, students in the being mode find it best not to listen at all, but to concentrate on their own thought processes.

At least a passing reference should be made here to the word "interests," which in current usage has become a pallid, worn-out expression. Yet its essential meaning is contained in its root: Latin, *interesse*, "to be in [or] among" it. This active interest was expressed in Middle English by the term "to list" (adjective, listy; adverb, listily). In modern English, "to list" is only used in a spatial sense: "a ship lists"; the original meaning in a psychical sense we have only in the negative "listless." "To list" once meant "to be actively striving for," "to be genuinely interested in." The root is the same as that of "lust," but "to list" is not a lust one is *driven by,* but the *free and active interest in, or striving for.* "To list" is one of the key expressions of the anonymous author (mid-fourteenth century) of *The Cloud of Unknowing* (Evelyn Underhill, ed.). That the language has retained the word only in its negative sense is characteristic of the change of spirit in society from the thirteenth to the twentieth century.

Remembering Remembering can occur in either the having or the being mode. What matters most for the difference between the two forms of remembering is the *kind* of connection that is made. In the having mode of remembering, the connection is entirely *mechanical,* as when the connection between one word and the next becomes firmly established by the frequency with which it is made. Or the connections may be purely *logical,* such as the connection between opposites, or between converging concepts, or with time, space, size, color, or within a given system of thought.

In the being mode, remembering is *actively* recalling words, ideas, sights, paintings, music; that is, connecting the single datum to be remembered and the many other data that it is connected with. The connections in the case of being are neither mechanical nor purely logical, but alive. One concept is connected with another by a productive act of thinking (or feeling) that is mobilized when one searches for the right word. A simple example: If I associate the word "headache" with the word "aspirin," I form a logical, conventional association. But if I associate the word "headache" with "stress" or "anger," I connect the given datum with its possible causes, an insight I have arrived at in studying the phenomenon. This latter type of remembering constitutes in itself an act of productive thinking. The most striking examples of this kind of alive remembering are the "free associations" devised by Freud.

Persons not mainly inclined toward storing up data will find that their memories, in order to function well, need a strong and immediate *interest.* For example, individuals have been known to remember words of a long-forgotten foreign language when it has been of vital importance to do so. And in my own experience, while I am not endowed with a particularly good memory, I have remembered the dream of a person I analyzed, be it two weeks or five years ago, when I again come face to face with and concentrate on the whole personality of that person. Yet not five minutes before, in the cold as it were, I was quite unable to remember that dream.

Remembering in the mode of being implies bringing to life something one saw or heard before. We can experience this productive remembering by trying to envision a person's face or scenery that we had once seen. We will not be able to remember instantly in either case; we must re-create the subject, bring it to life in our mind. This kind of remembering is not always easy; to be able to fully recall the face or the scenery one must once have seen it with sufficient concentration. When such remembering is fully achieved, the person whose face is recalled is as alive, the remembered scenery as vivid, as if that person or that scenery were actually physically before one.

The way those in the having mode remember a face or scenery is typified by the way most people look at a photograph. The photograph serves only as an aid to their memory in identifying a person or a scene, and the usual reaction it elicits is: "Yes, that's him"; or "Yes, I've been there." The photograph becomes, for most people, an *alienated* memory.

Memory entrusted to paper is another form of alienated remembering. By writing down what I want to remember I am sure to *have* that information, and I do not try to engrave it on my brain. I am sure of my possession—except that when I have lost my notes, I have lost my memory of the information, too. My capacity to remember has left me, for my memory bank had become an externalized part of me, in the form of my notes.

Considering the multitude of data that people in contemporary society need to remember, a certain amount of notemaking and information deposited in books is unavoidable. One can easily and best observe in oneself that writing down things diminishes one's power of remembering, but some typical examples may prove helpful.

An everyday example occurs in stores. Today a salesclerk will rarely do a simple addition of two or three items in his or her head, but will immediately use a machine. The classroom provides another example. Teachers can observe that the students who carefully write down every sentence of the lecture will, in all likelihood, understand and remember less than the students who trusted their capacity to understand and, hence, remember at least the essentials. Further, musicians know that those who most easily sight-read a score have more difficulty in remembering the music without the score.* (Toscanini, whose

---

*This information was provided by Dr. Moshe Budmor.

memory was known to be extraordinary, is a good example of a musician in the being mode.) For a final example, in Mexico I have observed that people who are illiterate or who write little have memories far superior to the fluently literate inhabitants of the industrialized countries. Among other facts, this suggests that literacy is by no means the blessing it is advertised to be, especially when people use it merely to read material that impoverishes their capacity to experience and to imagine.

Conversing   The difference between having and being modes can be easily observed in two examples of conversations. Let us take a typical conversational debate between two men in which A *has* opinion X and B *has* opinion Y. Each identifies with his own opinion. What matters to each is to find better, i.e., more reasonable, arguments to defend his opinion. Neither expects to change his own opinion, or that his opponent's opinion will change. Each is afraid of changing his own opinion, precisely because it is one of his possessions, and hence its loss would mean an impoverishment.

The situation is somewhat different in a conversation that is not meant to be a debate. Who has not experienced meeting a person distinguished by prominence or fame or even by real qualities, or a person of whom one wants something; a good job, to be loved, to be admired? In any such circumstances many people tend to be at least mildly anxious, and often they "prepare" themselves for the important meeting. They think of topics that might interest the other; they think in advance how they might begin the conversation; some even map out the whole conversation, as far as their own part is concerned. Or they may bolster themselves up by thinking about what they *have:* their past successes, their charming personality (or their intimidating personality if this role is more effective), their social position, their connections, their appearance and dress. In a word, they mentally balance their worth, and based on this evaluation, they display their wares in the ensuing conversation. The person who is very good at this will indeed impress many people, although the created impression is only partly due to the individual's performance and largely due to the poverty of most people's judgment. If the performer is not so clever, however, the performance will appear wooden, contrived, boring and will not elicit much interest.

In contrast are those who approach a situation by preparing nothing in advance, not bolstering themselves up in any way. Instead, they respond spontaneously and productively; they forget about themselves, about the knowledge, the positions they have. Their egos do not stand in their own way, and it is precisely for this reason that they can fully respond to the other person and that person's ideas. They gave birth to new ideas, because they are not holding onto anything. While the having persons rely on what they *have*, the being persons rely on the fact that they *are*, that they are alive and that something new will be born if only they have the courage to let go and to respond. They come fully alive in the conversation, because they do not stifle themselves by anxious concern with what they have. Their own aliveness is infectious and often helps the other person to transcend his or her egocentricity. Thus the conversation ceases to be an exchange of commodities (information, knowledge, status) and becomes a dialogue in which it does not matter any more who is right. The duelists begin to dance together, and they part not with triumph or sorrow—which are equally sterile—but with joy. (The essential factor in psychoanalytic therapy is this enlivening quality of the therapist. No amount of psychoanalytic interpretation will have an effect if the therapeutic atmosphere is heavy, unalive, and boring.)

Reading   What holds true for a conversation holds equally true for reading, which is—or should be—a conversation between the author and the reader. Of course, in reading (as well as in a personal conversation) *whom* I read from (or talk with) is important. Reading an artless, cheap novel is a form of day-dreaming. It does not permit productive response; the text is swallowed like a television show, or the potato chips one munches while watching TV. But a novel, say by Balzac, can be read with inner participation, productively—that is, in the mode of being. Yet probably most of the time it is also read in the mode of consuming—of having. Their curiosity having been aroused, the readers want to know the plot: whether the hero dies or lives, whether the heroine is seduced or resists; they want to know the answers. The novel serves as a kind of foreplay to excite them: the happy or unhappy end culminates their experience: when they know the end, they *have* the whole story, almost as real as if they rummaged in their own memories. But they have not enhanced their knowledge; they have not understood the person in the novel and thus have not deepened their insight into human nature, or gained knowledge about themselves.

The modes of reading are the same with regard to a book whose theme is philosophy or history. The way one reads a philosophy or history book is formed—or better, deformed—by education. The school aims to give each student a certain amount of "cultural property," and at the end of their schooling certifies the students as *having* at least the minimum amount. Students are taught to read a book so that they can repeat the author's main thoughts. This is how the students "know" Plato, Aristotle, Descartes, Spinoza, Leibniz, Kant, Heidegger, Sartre. The difference between various levels of education from high school to graduate school is mainly in the amount of cultural property that is acquired, which corresponds roughly to the amount of material property the students may be expected to own in later life. The so-called excellent students are the ones who can most accurately repeat what each of the various philosophers had to say. They are like a well-informed guide at a museum. What they do not learn is that which goes beyond this kind of property knowledge. They do not learn to question the philosophers, to talk to them; they do not learn to be aware of the philosophers' own contradictions, of their leaving out certain problems or evading issues; they do not learn to distinguish between what was new and what the authors could not help thinking because it was the "common sense" of their time; they do not learn to hear so that they are able to distinguish when the authors speak only from their brain and when their brain and heart speak together; they do not learn to discover whether the authors are authentic or fake; and many more things.

The mode of being readers will often come to the conclusion that even a highly praised book is entirely without or of very limited value. Or they may have fully understood a book, sometimes better than had the author, who may have considered everything he or she wrote as being equally important.

Exercising Authority   Another example of the difference between the modes of having and being is the exercise of authority. The crucial point is expressed in the difference between *having* authority and *being* an authority. Almost all of us exercise authority at least at some stage of our lives. Those who bring up children must exercise authority—whether they want to or not—in order to protect their children from dangers and give them at least minimal advice on how to act in various situations. In a patriarchal society women, too, are objects of authority, for most men. Most members of a bureaucratic, hierarchically organized society like ours exercise authority, except the people on the lowest social level, who are only objects of authority.

Our understanding of authority in the two modes depends on our recognizing that "authority" is a broad term with two entirely different meanings: it can be either "rational" or "irrational" authority. Rational authority is based on competence, and it helps the person who leans on it to grow. Irrational authority is based on power and serves to exploit the person subjected to it. (I have discussed this distinction in *Escape from Freedom*.)

Among the most primitive societies, i.e., the hunters and food gatherers, authority is exercised by the person who is generally recognized as being competent for the task. What qualities this competence rests on depends much on the specific circumstances; generally they would include experience, wisdom, generosity, skill, "presence," courage. No permanent authority exists in many of these tribes, but an authority emerges in the case of need. Or there are different authorities for different occasions: war, religious practice, adjustment of quarrels. When the qualities on which the authority rests disappear or weaken, the authority itself ends. A very similar form of authority may be observed among many primate societies, in which competence is often established not by physical strength but by such qualities as experience and "wisdom." In a very ingenious experiment with monkeys, J. M. R. Delgado (1967) has shown that if the dominant animal even momentarily loses the qualities that constitute its competence, its authority ends.

Being-authority is grounded not only in the individual's competence to fulfill certain social functions, but equally so in the very essence of a personality that has achieved a high degree of growth and integration. Such persons radiate authority and do not have to give orders, threaten, bribe. They are highly developed individuals who demonstrate by what they are—and not mainly by what they do or say—what human beings can be. The great Masters of Living were such authorities, and to a lesser degree of perfection, such individuals may be found on all educational levels and in the most diverse cultures. (The problem of education hinges on this point. If parents were more developed themselves and rested in their own center, the opposition between authoritarian and laissez-faire education would hardly exist. Needing this being-authority, the child reacts to it with great eagerness; on the other hand, the child rebels against pressure or neglect by people who show by their own behavior that they themselves have not made the effort they expect from the growing child.)

With the formation of societies based on a hierarchical order and much larger and more complex than those of the hunters and food gatherers, authority by competence yields to authority by social status. This does not mean that the existing authority is necessarily incompetent; it does mean that competence is not an essential element of authority. Whether we deal with monarchical authority—where the lottery of genes decides qualities of competence—or with an unscrupulous criminal who succeeds in becoming an authority by murder or treachery, or, as frequently in modern democracy, with authorities elected on the basis of their photogenic physiognomy or the amount of money they can spend on their election, in all these cases there may be almost no relation between competence and authority.

But there are even serious problems in the cases of authority established on the basis of some competence: a leader may have been competent in one field, incompetent in another—for instance, a statesman may be competent in conducting war and incompetent in the situation of peace; or a leader who is honest and courageous at the beginning of his or her career loses these qualities by the seduction of power; or age or physical troubles may lead to a certain deterioration. Finally, one must consider that it is much easier for the members of a small tribe to judge the behavior of an authority than it is for the millions of people in our system, who know their candidate only by the artificial image created by public relations specialists.

Whatever the reasons for the loss of the competence-forming qualities, in most larger and hierarchically organized societies the process of alienation of authority occurs. The real or alleged initial competence is transferred to the uniform or to the title of the authority. If the authority wears the proper uniform or has the proper title, this external sign of competence replaces the real competence and its qualities. The king—to use this title as a symbol for this type of authority—can be stupid, vicious, evil, i.e., utterly incompetent to *be* an authority, yet he *has* authority. As long as he has the title, he is supposed to have the qualities of competence. Even if the emperor is naked, everybody believes he wears beautiful clothes.

That people take uniforms and titles for the real qualities of competence is not something that happens quite of itself. Those who have these symbols of authority and those who benefit therefrom must dull their subject people's realistic, i.e., critical, thinking and make them believe the fiction. Anybody who will think about it knows the machinations of propaganda, the methods by which critical judgment is destroyed, how the mind is lulled into submission by clichés, how people are made dumb because they become dependent and lose their capacity to trust their eyes and judgment. They are blinded to reality by the fiction they believe.

Having Knowledge and Knowing   The difference between the mode of having and the mode of being in the sphere of *knowing* is expressed in two formulations: "I have knowledge" and "I know." *Having* knowledge is taking and keeping possession of available knowledge (information); *knowing* is functional and part of the process of productive thinking.

Our understanding of the quality of knowing in the being mode of existence can be enhanced by the insights of such thinkers as the Buddha, the Hebrew prophets, Jesus, Master Eckhart, Sigmund Freud, and Karl Marx. In their view, knowing begins with the awareness of the deceptiveness of our common sense perceptions, in the sense that our picture of physical reality does not correspond to what is "really real" and, mainly, in the sense that most people are half-awake, half-dreaming, and are unaware that most of what they hold to be true and self-evident is illusion produced by the suggestive influence of the social world in which they live. Knowing, then, begins with shattering of illusions, with disillusionment *(Ent-täuschung)*. Knowing means to penetrate through the surface, in order to arrive at the roots, and hence the causes; knowing means to "see" reality in its nakedness. Knowing does not mean to be in possession of the truth; it means to penetrate the surface and to strive critically and actively in order to approach truth ever more closely.

This quality of creative penetration is expressed in the Hebrew *jadoa,* which means to know and to love, in the sense of male sexual penetration. The Buddha, the Awakened One, calls on people to wake up and liberate themselves from the illusion that craving for things leads to happiness. The Hebrew prophets appeal to the people to wake up and know that their idols are nothing but the work of their own hands, are illusions. Jesus says: "The truth shall make you free!" Master

Eckhart expressed his concept of knowing many times; for instance, when speaking of God he says: "Knowledge is no particular thought but rather it peels off [all coverings] and is disinterested and runs naked to God, until it touches him and grasps him" (Blakney, p. 243). ("Nakedness" and "naked" are favorite expressions of Master Eckhart as well as of his contemporary, the anonymous author of *The Cloud of Unknowing*.) According to Marx, one needs to destroy illusions in order to create the conditions that make illusions unnecessary. Freud's concept of self-knowledge is based on the idea of destroying illusions ("rationalizations") in order to become aware of the unconscious reality. (The last of the Enlightenment thinkers, Freud can be called a revolutionary thinker in terms of the eighteenth-century Enlightenment philosophy, not in terms of the twentieth century.)

All these thinkers were concerned with human salvation; they were all critical of socially accepted thought patterns. To them the aim of knowing is not the certainty of "absolute truth," something one can feel secure with, but *the self-affirming process of human reason.* Ignorance, for the one who *knows,* is as good as knowledge, since both are part of the process of knowing, even though ignorance of this kind is different from the ignorance of the unthinking. Optimum knowledge in the being mode is *to know more deeply.* In the having mode it is *to have more knowledge.*

Our education generally tries to train people to *have* knowledge as a possession, by and large commensurate with the amount of property or social prestige they are likely to have in later life. The minimum they receive is the amount they will need in order to function properly in their work. In addition they are each given a "luxury-knowledge package" to enhance their feeling of worth, the size of each such package being in accord with the person's probable social prestige. The schools are the factories in which these overall knowledge packages are produced—although schools usually claim they mean to bring the students in touch with the highest achievements of the human mind. Many undergraduate colleges are particularly adroit in nurturing these illusions. From Indian thought and art to existentialism and surrealism, a vast smörgåsbord of knowledge is offered from which students pick a little here, a little there, and in the name of spontaneity and freedom are not urged to concentrate on one subject, not even ever to finish reading an entire book. (Ivan Illich's radical critique of the school system brings many of its failings into focus.)

13

MICHEL FOUCAULT

Michel Foucault was born in France in 1926. He studied in the Normal School Superior (École Normale Supérieure) and in 1951 obtained his degree in philosophy. In 1961 he completed his doctoral dissertation, published as "Madness and Civilization: A History of Insanity in the Age of Reason." He taught in several French universities and published widely, utilizing a combination of methods derived from philosophy, history, and the social sciences. As a young scholar, he had already rejected some of the work of many of the French and European thinkers of the time, including dogmatic Marxist interpretations of social and cultural relations, rigid structuralism, and existentialism. He published in 1966 *The Order of Things: An Archaeology of the Human Sciences,* and one of his most important contributions was published in 1969, *The Archaeology of Knowledge.* Some of the selections presented in this book come from his influential work published in English in 1975, *Discipline and Punish: The Birth of the Prison.* Between 1976 and 1984 he produced three volumes called *History of Sexuality.* Numerous interviews with him and commentaries that have been published help us further understand his unique and original thinking. Foucault died of complications of AIDS in 1984.

Foucault explained how power works within social institutions, formal and informal, and how relationships within these institutions can serve to control behavior and thought of individuals and groups. Paradoxically, power within these institutions could also generate alternatives to dominant and accepted norms. In addition, he looked at power in a different way by investigating how opposition, behavioral and/or ideological, can be controlled and neutralized within organizations, which includes schools. His view of power is illustrated by the use of the panopticon in the design of prisons. Such structure consists of a tower surrounded by a building containing cells for the inmates. The activities of the individuals in the cells can be easily observed from the tower. However, the occupants of these cells cannot know if someone in the tower is observing them; thus, their behavior is controlled all the time, regardless of being observed or not, because they do not know. This system of control symbolizes how control is internalized by invisible modes of power. Such an approach to analyzing power has helped educational analysts understand classroom relationships, pedagogies, and school organization, among other topics.

In Foucault's view, power is exercised through institutional relations that enable us to self-regulate our ways of thinking and acting. In schools, for instance, the internalization of norms of correct behavior and accepted ways of thinking is accomplished through various disciplinary practices—such as a curriculum of subjects (disciplines) that teach how to think within a defined area of study, and enforcement of explicit rules of behavior—as well as through the reinforcement of cultural norms. Internalizing what is correct or not and the conditions and consequences of one's actions is what Foucault called normalization. The relevance of Foucault's work for schools is that even educational practices that are progressive and democratic, including discussions and inquiries, are forms of disciplinary power. However, control and discipline are not necessarily negative because schools cannot operate without some system of rights and duties. These systems take form in discourse (articulation of coherent and connected statements that represent some form of common sense and truth) and practices that happen routinely and are taken for granted, since they follow the norms, which are accepted because they have been practiced without interrogation.

In Foucault's opinion, discourses and practices of teaching, counseling, and administration construct a "regime of truth," a set of unified and cohesive beliefs about what is right to do. However, Foucault argued that practices and discourses could have been different—that what they are does not obligate us to accept them as the only alternative. Grading, as an example of evaluation, can point out students' problems as well as students' strengths or improvement. Depending on how this is done, it can be oppressive and controlling or constructive and liberating.

Foucault's role as an intellectual innovator and provocateur, as someone who has challenged the status quo and who has dared to interrogate and seek alternative explanations utilizing alternative methods of inquiry, are reflected in the following reading selections.

REFERENCES

Foucault, M. *The Archeology of Knowledge.* London: Tavistock, 1972.

Foucault, M. *Madness and Civilization: A History of Insanity in the Age of Reason.* New York: Vintage, 1973.

Foucault, M. *Discipline and Punish: The Birth of the Prison.* New York: Vintage, 1979.

Foucault, M. *Power/Knowledge: Selected Interviews and Other Writings by Michel Foucault, 1972–1977.* New York: Pantheon, 1980.

Foucault, M. *Power: Essential Works of Foucault, 1854–1984, Volume III* New York: New Press, 2000.

I. DOCILE BODIES

Let us take the ideal figure of the soldier as it was still seen in the early seventeenth century. To begin with, the soldier was someone who could be recognized from afar; he bore certain signs: the natural signs of his strength and his courage, the marks, too, of his pride; his body was the blazon of his strength and valour; and although it is true that he had to learn the profession of arms little by little—generally in actual fighting—movements like marching and attitudes like the bearing of the head belonged for the most part to a bodily rhetoric of honour; 'The signs for recognizing those most suited to this profession are a lively, alert manner, an erect head, a taut stomach, broad shoulders, long arms, strong fingers, a small belly, thick thighs, slender legs and dry feet, because a man of such a figure could not fail to be agile and strong'; when he becomes a pike-bearer, the soldier 'will have to march in step in order to have as much grace and gravity as possible, for the pike is an honourable weapon, worthy to be borne with gravity and boldness' (Montgommery, 6 and 7). By the late eighteenth century, the soldier has become something that can be made; out of a formless clay, an inapt body, the machine required can be constructed; posture is gradually corrected; a calculated constraint runs slowly through each part of the body, mastering it, making it pliable, ready at all times, turning silently into the automatism of habit; in short, one has 'got rid of the peasant' and given him 'the air of a soldier' (ordinance of 20 March 1764). Recruits become accustomed to 'holding their heads high and erect; to standing upright, without bending the back, to sticking out the belly, throwing out the chest and throwing back the shoulders; and, to help them acquire the habit, they are given this position while standing against a wall in such a way that the heels, the thighs, the waist and the shoulders touch it, as also do the backs of the hands, as one turns the arms outwards, without moving them away from the body . . . Likewise, they will be taught never to fix their eyes on the ground, but to look straight at those they pass . . . to remain motionless until the order is given, without moving the head, the hands or the feet . . .

lastly to march with a bold step, with knee and ham taut, on the points of the feet, which should face outwards' (ordinance of 20 March 1764).

The classical age discovered the body as object and target of power. It is easy enough to find signs of the attention then paid to the body—to the body that is manipulated, shaped, trained, which obeys, responds, becomes skilful and increases its forces. The great book of Man-the-Machine was written simultaneously on two registers: the anatomico-metaphysical register, of which Descartes wrote the first pages and which the physicians and philosophers continued, and the technico-political register, which was constituted by a whole set of regulations and by empirical and calculated methods relating to the army, the school and the hospital, for controlling or correcting the operations of the body. These two registers are quite distinct, since it was a question, on the one hand, of submission and use and, on the other, of functioning and explanation: there was a useful body and an intelligible body. And yet there are points of overlap from one to the other. La Mettrie's *L'Homme-machine* is both a materialist reduction of the soul and a general theory of *dressage*, at the centre of which reigns the notion of 'docility', which joins the analysable body to the manipulable body. A body is docile that may be subjected, used, transformed and improved. The celebrated automata, on the other hand, were not only a way of illustrating an organism, they were also political puppets, small-scale models of power: Frederick II, the meticulous king of small machines, well-trained regiments and long exercises, was obsessed with them.

What was so new in these projects of docility that interested the eighteenth century so much? It was certainly not the first time that the body had become the object of such imperious and pressing investments; in every society, the body was in the grip of very strict powers, which imposed on it constraints, prohibitions or obligations. However, there were several new things in these techniques. To begin with, there was the scale of the control: it was a question not of treating the body, *en masse*, 'wholesale', as if it were an indissociable unity, but of working it 'retail', individually; of exercising upon it a subtle coercion, of obtaining holds upon it at the level of the mechanism itself—movements, gestures, attitudes, rapidity: an infinitesimal power over the active body. Then there was the object of the control: it was not or was no longer the signifying elements of behaviour or the language of the body, but the economy, the efficiency of movements, their internal organization; constraint bears upon the forces rather than upon the signs; the only truly important ceremony is that of exercise. Lastly, there is the modality: it implies an uninterrupted, constant coercion, supervising the processes of the activity rather than its result and it is exercised according to a codification that partitions as closely as possible time, space, movement. These methods, which made possible the meticulous control of the operations of the body, which assured the constant subjection of its forces and imposed upon them a relation of docility-utility, might be called 'disciplines'. Many disciplinary methods had long been in existence—in monasteries, armies, workshops. But in the course of the seventeenth and eighteenth centuries the disciplines became general formulas of domination. They were different from slavery because they were not based on a relation of appropriation of bodies; indeed, the elegance of the discipline lay in the fact that it could dispense with this costly and violent relation by obtaining effects of utility at least as great. They were different, too, from 'service', which was a constant, total, massive, non-analytical, unlimited relation of domination, established in the form of the individual will of the master, his 'caprice'. They were different from vassalage, which was a highly coded, but distant relation of submission, which bore less on the operations of the body than on the products of labour and the ritual marks of allegiance. Again, they were different from asceticism and from 'disciplines' of a monastic type, whose function was to obtain renunciations rather than increases of utility and which, although they involved obedience to others, had as their principal aim an increase of the mastery of each individual over his own body. The historical moment of the disciplines was the moment when an art of the human body was born, which was directed not only at the growth of its skills, nor at the intensification of its subjection, but at the formation of a relation that in the mechanism itself makes it more obedient as it becomes more useful, and conversely. What was then being formed was a policy of coercions that act upon the body, a calculated manipulation of its elements, its gestures, its behaviour. The human body was entering a machinery of power that explores it, breaks it down and rearranges it. A 'political anatomy', which was also a 'mechanics of power', was being born; it defined how one may have a hold over others' bodies, not only so that they may do what one wishes, but so that they may operate as one wishes, with the techniques, the speed and the efficiency that one determines. Thus discipline produces subjected and practised bodies, 'docile' bodies. Discipline increases the forces of the body (in economic terms of utility) and diminishes these same forces (in political terms of obedience). In short, it dissociates power from the body; on the one hand, it turns it into an 'aptitude', a 'capacity', which it seeks to increase; on the other hand, it reverses the course of the energy, the power that might result from it, and turns it into a relation of strict subjection. If economic exploitation separates the force and the product of labour, let us say that disciplinary coercion establishes in the body the constricting link between an increased aptitude and an increased domination.

The 'invention' of this new political anatomy must not be seen as a sudden discovery. It is rather a multiplicity of often minor processes, of different origin and scattered location, which overlap, repeat, or imitate one another, support one another, distinguish themselves from one another according to their domain of application, converge and gradually produce the blueprint of a general method. They were at work in secondary education at a very early date, later in primary schools; they slowly invested the space of the hospital; and, in a few decades, they restructured the military organization. They sometimes circulated very rapidly from one point to another (between the army and the technical schools or secondary schools), sometimes slowly and discreetly (the insidious militarization of the large workshops). On almost every occasion, they were adopted in response to particular needs: an industrial innovation, a renewed outbreak of certain epidemic diseases, the invention of the rifle or the victories of Prussia. This did not prevent them being totally inscribed in general and essential transformations, which we must now try to delineate.

There can be no question here of writing the history of the different disciplinary institutions, with all their individual differences. I simply intend to map on a series of examples some of the essential techniques that most easily spread from one to another. These were always meticulous, often minute, techniques, but they had their importance: because they defined a certain mode of detailed political investment of the body, a 'new micro-physics' of power; and because, since the seventeenth century, they had constantly reached out to ever broader domains, as if they tended to cover the entire social body. Small acts of cunning endowed with a great power of diffusion, subtle arrangements, apparently innocent, but profoundly suspicious, mechanisms that obeyed economies too shameful to be acknowledged, or pursued petty forms of coercion—it was nevertheless they that brought about the mutation of the punitive system, at the threshold of the contemporary period. Describing them will require great attention to detail:

beneath every set of figures, we must seek not a meaning, but a precaution; we must situate them not only in the inextricability of a functioning, but in the coherence of a tactic. They are the acts of cunning, not so
much of the greater reason that works even in its sleep and gives meaning to the insignificant, as of the attentive 'malevolence' that turns
everything to account. Discipline is a political anatomy of detail.

Before we lose patience we would do well to recall the words of
Marshal de Saxe: 'Although those who concern themselves with details
are regarded as folk of limited intelligence, it seems to me that this part
is essential, because it is the foundation, and it is impossible to erect
any building or establish any method without understanding its principles. It is not enough to have a liking for architecture. One must also
know stone-cutting' (Saxe, 5). There is a whole history to be written
about such 'stone-cutting'—a history of the utilitarian rationalization of
detail in moral accountability and political control. The classical age did
not initiate it; rather it accelerated it, changed its scale, gave it precise
instruments, and perhaps found some echoes for it in the calculation of
the infinitely small or in the description of the most detailed characteristics of natural beings. In any case, 'detail' had long been a category of
theology and asceticism: every detail is important since, in the sight of
God, no immensity is greater than a detail, nor is anything so small that
it was not willed by one of his individual wishes. In this great tradition
of the eminence of detail, all the minutiae of Christian education, of
scholastic or military pedagogy, all forms of 'training' found their place
easily enough. For the disciplined man, as for the true believer, no
detail is unimportant, but not so much for the meaning that it conceals
within it as for the hold it provides for the power that wishes to seize it.
Characteristic is the great hymn to the 'little things' and to their eternal
importance, sung by Jean-Baptiste de La Salle, in his *Traité sur les obligations des frères des Écoles chrétiennes*. The mystique of the everyday is
joined here with the discipline of the minute. 'How dangerous it is to
neglect little things. It is a very consoling reflection for a soul like mine,
little disposed to great actions, to think that fidelity to little things may,
by an imperceptible progress, raise us to the most eminent sanctity:
because little things lead to greater . . . Little things; it will be said,
alas, my God, what can we do that is great for you, weak and mortal
creatures that we are. Little things; if great things presented themselves
would we perform them? Would we not think them beyond our

strength? Little things; and if God accepts them and wishes to receive them as great things? Little things; has one ever felt this? Does one judge according to experience? Little things; one is certainly guilty, therefore, if seeing them as such, one refuses them? Little things; yet it is they that in the end have made great saints! Yes, little things; but great motives, great feelings, great fervour, great ardour, and consequently great merits, great treasures, great rewards' (La Salle, *Traité* . . ., 238–9). The meticulousness of the regulations, the fussiness of the inspections, the supervision of the smallest fragment of life and of the body will soon provide, in the context of the school, the barracks, the hospital or the workshop, a laicized content, an economic or technical rationality for this mystical calculus of the infinitesimal and the infinite. And a History of Detail in the eighteenth century, presided over by Jean-Baptiste de La Salle, touching on Leibniz and Buffon, via Frederick II, covering pedagogy, medicine, military tactics and economics, should bring us, at the end of the century, to the man who dreamt of being another Newton, not the Newton of the immensities of the heavens and the planetary masses, but a Newton of 'small bodies', small movements, small actions; to the man who replied to Monge's remark, 'there was only one world to discover': 'What do I hear? But the world of details, who has never dreamt of that other world, what of that world? I have believed in it ever since I was fifteen. I was concerned with it then, and this memory lives within me, as an obsession never to be abandoned . . . That other world is the most important of all that I flatter myself I have discovered: when I think of it, my heart aches' (these words are attributed to Bonaparte in the Introduction to Saint-Hilaire's *Notions synthétiques et historiques de philosophie naturelle*). Napoleon did not discover this world; but we know that he set out to organize it; and he wished to arrange around him a mechanism of power that would enable him to see the smallest event that occurred in the state he governed; he intended, by means of the rigorous discipline that he imposed, 'to embrace the whole of this vast machine without the slightest detail escaping his attention' (Treilhard, 14).

A meticulous observation of detail, and at the same time a political awareness of these small things, for the control and use of men, emerge through the classical age bearing with them a whole set of techniques, a whole corpus of methods and knowledge, descriptions, plans and data. And from such trifles, no doubt, the man of modern humanism was born.

The art of distributions

In the first instance, discipline proceeds from the distribution of individuals in space. To achieve this end, it employs several techniques.

1. Discipline sometimes requires *enclosure*, the specification of a place heterogeneous to all others and closed in upon itself. It is the protected place of disciplinary monotony. There was the great 'confinement' of vagabonds and paupers; there were other more discreet, but insidious and effective ones. There were the *collèges*, or secondary schools: the monastic model was gradually imposed; boarding appeared as the most perfect, if not the most frequent, educational régime; it became obligatory at Louis-le-Grand when, after the departure of the Jesuits, it was turned into a model school (cf. Ariès, 308–13 and Snyders, 35–41). There were the military barracks: the army, that vagabond mass, has to be held in place; looting and violence must be prevented; the fears of local inhabitants, who do not care for troops passing through their towns, must be calmed; conflicts with the civil authorities must be avoided; desertion must be stopped, expenditure controlled. The ordinance of 1719 envisaged the construction of several hundred barracks, on the model of those already set up in the south of the country; there would be strict confinements: 'The whole will be enclosed by an outer wall ten feet high, which will surround the said houses, at a distance of thirty feet from all the sides'; this will have the effect of maintaining the troops in 'order and discipline, so that an officer will be in a position to answer for them' (*L'Ordonnance militaire*, IXL, 25 September 1719). In 1745, there were barracks in about 320 towns; and it was estimated that the total capacity of the barracks in 1775 was approximately 200,000 men (Daisy, 201–9; an anonymous memoir of 1775, in Dépôt de la guerre, 3689, f. 156; Navereau, 132–5). Side by side with the spread of workshops, there also developed great manufacturing spaces, both homogeneous and well defined: first, the combined manufactories, then, in the second half of the eighteenth century, the works or factories proper (the Chaussade ironworks occupied almost the whole of the Médine peninsula, between Nièvre and Loire; in order to set up the Indret factory in 1777, Wilkinson, by means of embankments and dikes, constructed an island on the Loire; Toufait built Le Creusot in the valley of the Charbonnière, which he transformed, and he had workers' accommodation built in the factory itself); it was a change of scale, but it was also a new type of control. The factory was

explicitly compared with the monastery, the fortress, a walled town; the guardian 'will open the gates only on the return of the workers, and after the bell that announces the resumption of work has been rung'; a quarter of an hour later no one will be admitted; at the end of the day, the workshops' heads will hand back the keys to the Swiss guard of the factory, who will then open the gates (*Amboise*, f. 12, 1301). The aim is to derive the maximum advantages and to neutralize the inconveniences (thefts, interruptions of work, disturbances and 'cabals'), as the forces of production become more concentrated; to protect materials and tools and to master the labour force: 'The order and inspection that must be maintained require that all workers be assembled under the same roof, so that the partner who is entrusted with the management of the manufactory may prevent and remedy abuses that may arise among the workers and arrest their progress at the outset' (Dauphin, 199).

2. But the principle of 'enclosure' is neither constant, nor indispensable, nor sufficient in disciplinary machinery. This machinery works space in a much more flexible and detailed way. It does this first of all on the principle of elementary location or *partitioning*. Each individual has his own place; and each place its individual. Avoid distributions in groups; break up collective dispositions; analyse confused, massive or transient pluralities. Disciplinary space tends to be divided into as many sections as there are bodies or elements to be distributed. One must eliminate the effects of imprecise distributions, the uncontrolled disappearance of individuals, their diffuse circulation, their unusable and dangerous coagulation; it was a tactic of anti-desertion, anti-vagabondage, anti-concentration. Its aim was to establish presences and absences, to know where and how to locate individuals, to set up useful communications, to interrupt others, to be able at each moment to supervise the conduct of each individual, to assess it, to judge it, to calculate its qualities or merits. It was a procedure, therefore, aimed at knowing, mastering and using. Discipline organizes an analytical space.

And there, too, it encountered an old architectural and religious method: the monastic cell. Even if the compartments it assigns become purely ideal, the disciplinary space is always, basically, cellular. Solitude was necessary to both body and soul, according to a certain asceticism: they must, at certain moments at least, confront temptation and perhaps the severity of God alone. 'Sleep is the image of death, the dormitory is the image of the sepulchre . . . although the dormitories are shared, the beds are nevertheless arranged in such a way and closed so exactly by means of curtains that the girls may rise and retire without being seen' (*Règlement pour la communauté des filles du Bon Pasteur*, in Delamare, 507). But this is still a very crude form.

3. The rule of *functional sites* would gradually, in the disciplinary institutions, code a space that architecture generally left at the disposal of several different uses. Particular places were defined to correspond not only to the need to supervise, to break dangerous communications, but also to create a useful space. The process appeared clearly in the hospitals., especially in the military and naval hospitals. In France, it seems that Rochefort served both as experiment and model. A port, and a military port is—with its circulation of goods, men signed up willingly or by force, sailors embarking and disembarking, diseases and epidemics—a place of desertion, smuggling, contagion: it is a crossroads for dangerous mixtures, a meeting-place for forbidden circulations. The naval hospital must therefore treat, but in order to do this it must be a filter, a mechanism that pins down and partitions; it must provide a hold over this whole mobile, swarming mass, by dissipating the confusion of illegality and evil. The medical supervision of diseases and contagions is inseparable from a whole series of other controls: the military control over deserters, fiscal control over commodities, administrative control over remedies, rations, disappearances, cures, deaths, simulations. Hence the need to distribute and partition off space in a rigorous manner. The first steps taken at Rochefort concerned things rather than men, precious commodities, rather than patients. The arrangements of fiscal and economic supervision preceded the techniques of medical observation: placing of medicines under lock and key, recording their use; a little later, a system was worked out to verify the real number of patients, their identity, the units to which they belonged; then one began to regulate their comings and goings; they were forced to remain in their wards; to each bed was attached the name of its occupant; each individual treated was entered in a register that the doctor had to consult during the visit; later came the isolation of contagious patients and separate beds. Gradually, an administrative and political space was articulated upon a therapeutic space; it tended to individualize bodies, diseases, symptoms, lives and deaths; it constituted a real table of juxtaposed and carefully distinct singularities. Out of discipline, a medically useful space was born.

In the factories that appeared at the end of the eighteenth century, the principle of individualizing partitioning became more complicated. It was a question of distributing individuals in a space in which one might isolate them and map them; but also of articulating this distribution on a production machinery that had its own requirements. The distribution of bodies, the spatial arrangement of production machinery and the different forms of activity in the distribution of 'posts' had to be linked together. The Oberkampf manufactory at Jouy obeyed this principle. It was made up of a series of workshops specified according to each broad type of operation: for the printers, the handlers, the colourists, the women who touched up the design, the engravers, the dyers. The largest of the buildings, built in 1791, by Toussaint Barré, was 110 metres long and had three storeys. The ground floor was devoted mainly to block printing; it contained 132 tables arranged in two rows, the length of the workshop, which had eighty-eight windows; each printer worked at a table with his 'puller', who prepared and spread the colours. There were 264 persons in all. At the end of each table was a sort of rack on which the material that had just been printed was left to dry (Saint-Maur). By walking up and down the central aisle of the workshop, it was possible to carry out a supervision that was both general and individual: to observe the worker's presence and application, and the quality of his work; to compare workers with one another, to classify them according to skill and speed; to follow the successive stages of the production process. All these serializations formed a permanent grid: confusion was eliminated: that is to say, production was divided up and the labour process was articulated, on the one hand, according to its stages or elementary operations, and, on the other hand, according to the individuals, the particular bodies, that carried it out: each variable of this force—strength, promptness, skill, constancy—would be observed, and therefore characterized, assessed, computed and related to the individual who was its particular agent. Thus, spread out in a perfectly legible way over the whole series of individual bodies, the work force may be analysed in individual units. At the emergence of large-scale industry, one finds, beneath the division of the production process, the individualizing fragmentation of labour power; the distributions of the disciplinary space often assured both.

4. In discipline, the elements are interchangeable, since each is defined by the place it occupies in a series, and by the gap that separates it from the others. The unit is, therefore, neither the territory (unit

of domination), nor the place (unit of residence), but the *rank:* the place one occupies in a classification, the point at which a line and a column intersect, the interval in a series of intervals that one may traverse one after the other. Discipline is an art of rank, a technique for the transformation of arrangements. It individualizes bodies by a location that does not give them a fixed position, but distributes them and circulates them in a network of relations.

Take the example of the 'class'. In the Jesuit colleges, one still found an organization that was at once binary and unified; the classes, which might comprise up to two or three hundred pupils, were subdivided into groups of ten; each of these groups, with its 'decurion', was placed in a camp, Roman or Carthaginian; each 'decury' had its counterpart in the opposing camp. The general form was that of war and rivalry; work, apprenticeship and classification were carried out in the form of the joust, through the confrontation of two armies; the contribution of each pupil was inscribed in this general duel; it contributed to the victory or the defeat of a whole camp; and the pupils were assigned a place that corresponded to the function of each individual and to his value as a combatant in the unitary group of his 'decury' (Rochemonteix, 51ff). It should be observed moreover that this Roman comedy made it possible to link, to the binary exercises of rivalry, a spatial disposition inspired by the legion, with rank, hierarchy, pyramidal supervision. One should not forget that, generally speaking, the Roman model, at the Enlightenment, played a dual role: in its republican aspect, it was the very embodiment of liberty; in its military aspect, it was the ideal schema of discipline. The Rome of the eighteenth century and of the Revolution was the Rome of the Senate, but it was also that of the legion; it was the Rome of the Forum, but it was also that of the camps. Up to the empire, the Roman reference transmitted, somewhat ambiguously, the juridical ideal of citizenship and the technique of disciplinary methods. In any case, the strictly disciplinary element in the ancient fable used by the Jesuit colleges came to dominate the element of joust and mock warfare. Gradually—but especially after 1762—the educational space unfolds; the class becomes homogeneous, it is no longer made up of individual elements arranged side by side under the master's eye. In the eighteenth century, 'rank' begins to define the great form of distribution of individuals in the educational order: rows or ranks of pupils in the class, corridors, courtyards; rank attributed to each pupil at the end of each task and each examination; the rank he obtains from week to week, month to month, year to year; an alignment of age groups, one after another; a succession of subjects taught and questions treated, according to an order of increasing difficulty. And, in this ensemble of compulsory alignments, each pupil, according to his age, his performance, his behaviour, occupies sometimes one rank, sometimes another; he moves constantly over a series of compartments—some of these are 'ideal' compartments, marking a hierarchy of knowledge or ability, others express the distribution of values or merits in material terms in the space of the college or classroom. It is a perpetual movement in which individuals replace one another in a space marked off by aligned intervals.

The organization of a serial space was one of the great technical mutations of elementary education. It made it possible to supersede the traditional system (a pupil working for a few minutes with the master, while the rest of the heterogeneous group remained idle and unattended). By assigning individual places it made possible the supervision of each individual and the simultaneous work of all. It organized a new economy of the time of apprenticeship. It made the educational space function like a learning machine, but also as a machine for supervising, hierarchizing, rewarding. Jean-Baptiste de La Salle dreamt of a classroom in which the spatial distribution might provide a whole series of distinctions at once: according to the pupils' progress, worth, character, application, cleanliness and parents' fortune. Thus, the classroom would form a single great table, with many different entries, under the scrupulously 'classificatory' eye of the master: 'In every class there will be places assigned for all the pupils of all the lessons, so that all those attending the same lesson will always occupy the same place. Pupils attending the highest lessons will be placed in the benches closest to the wall, followed by the others according to the order of the lessons moving towards the middle of the classroom . . . Each of the pupils will have his place assigned to him and none of them will leave it or change it except on the order or with the consent of the school inspector.' Things must be so arranged that 'those whose parents are neglectful and verminous must be separated from those who are careful and clean; that an unruly and frivolous pupil should be placed between two who are well behaved and serious, a libertine either alone or between two pious pupils'.

In organizing 'cells', 'places' and 'ranks', the disciplines create complex spaces that are at once architectural, functional and hierarchical. It is spaces that provide fixed positions and permit circulation; they carve out individual segments and establish operational links; they mark places and indicate values; they guarantee the obedience of individuals, but also a better economy of time and gesture. They are mixed spaces: real because they govern the disposition of buildings, rooms, furniture, but also ideal, because they are projected over this arrangement of characterizations, assessments, hierarchies. The first of the great operations of discipline is, therefore, the constitution of 'tableaux vivants', which transform the confused, useless or dangerous multitudes into ordered multiplicities. The drawing up of 'tables' was one of the great problems of the scientific, political and economic technology of the eighteenth century: how one was to arrange botanical and zoological gardens, and construct at the same time rational classifications of living beings; how one was to observe, supervise, regularize the circulation of commodities and money and thus build up an economic table that might serve as the principle of the increase of wealth; how one was to inspect men, observe their presence and absence and constitute a general and permanent register of the armed forces; how one was to distribute patients, separate them from one another, divide up the hospital space and make a systematic classification of diseases: these were all twin operations in which the two elements—distribution and analysis, supervision and intelligibility—are inextricably bound up. In the eighteenth century, the table was both a technique of power and a procedure of knowledge. It was a question of organizing the multiple, of providing oneself with an instrument to cover it and to master it; it was a question of imposing upon it an 'order'. Like the army general of whom Guibert spoke, the naturalist, the physician, the economist was 'blinded by the immensity, dazed by the multitude . . . the innumerable combinations that result from the multiplicity of objects, so many concerns together form a burden above his strength. In perfecting itself, in approaching true principles, the science of modern warfare might become simpler and less difficult'; armies 'with simple, similar tactics, capable of being adapted to every movement . . . would be easier to move and lead' (Guibert, xxxvi). Tactics, the spatial ordering of men; taxonomy, the disciplinary space of natural beings; the economic table, the regulated movement of wealth.

But the table does not have the same function in these different registers. In the order of the economy, it makes possible the measurement of quantities and the analysis of movements. In the form of taxonomy, it has the function of characterizing (and consequently reducing individual singularities) and constituting classes (and therefore of excluding considerations of number). But in the form of the disciplinary distribution, on the other hand, the table has the function of treating multiplicity itself, distributing it and deriving from it as many effects as possible. Whereas natural taxonomy is situated on the axis that links character and categorical disciplinary tactics is situated on the axis that links the singular and the multiple. It allows both the characterization of the individual as individual and the ordering of a given multiplicity. It is the first condition for the control and use of an ensemble of distinct elements, the base for a micro-physics of what might be called a 'cellular' power.

The control of activity

1. The *time-table* is an old inheritance. The strict model was no doubt suggested by the monastic communities. It soon spread. Its three great methods—establish rhythms, impose particular occupations, regulate the cycles of repetition—were soon to be found in schools, workshops and hospitals. The new disciplines had no difficulty in taking up their place in the old forms; the schools and poor houses extended the life and the regularity of the monastic communities to which they were often attached. The rigours of the industrial period long retained a religious air; in the seventeenth century, the regulations of the great manufactories laid down the exercises that would divide up the working day: 'On arrival in the morning, before beginning their work, all persons shall wash their hands, offer up their work to God and make the sign of the cross (Saint-Maur, article 1); but even in the nineteenth century, when the rural populations were needed in industry, they were sometimes formed into 'congregations', in an attempt to inure them to work in the workshops; the framework of the 'factory-monastery' was imposed upon the workers. In the Protestant armies of Maurice of Orange and Gustavus Adolphus, military discipline was achieved through a rhythmics of time punctuated by pious exercises; army life, Boussanelle was later to say, should have some of the 'perfections of the cloister itself' (Boussanelle, 2; on the religious character of discipline in the Swedish army, cf. *The Swedish Discipline*, London, 1632). For centuries, the religious orders had been masters of discipline: they were the specialists of time, the great technicians of rhythm and regular

activities. But the disciplines altered these methods of temporal regulation from which they derived. They altered them first by refining them. One began to count in quarter hours, in minutes, in seconds. This happened in the army, of course: Guibert systematically implemented the chronometric measurement of shooting that had been suggested earlier by Vauban. In the elementary schools, the division of time became increasingly minute; activities were governed in detail by orders that had to be obeyed immediately: 'At the last stroke of the hour, a pupil will ring the bell, and at the first sound of the bell all the pupils will kneel, with their arms crossed and their eyes lowered. When the prayer has been said, the teacher will strike the signal once to indicate that the pupils should get up, a second time as a sign that they should salute Christ, and a third that they should sit down' (La Salle, *Conduite . . .*, 27—8). In the early nineteenth century, the following time-table was suggested for the *Écoles mutuelles*, or 'mutual improvement schools': 8.45 entrance of the monitor, 8.52 the monitor's summons, 8.56 entrance of the children and prayer, 9.00 the children go to their benches, 9.04 first slate, 9.08 end of dictation, 9.12 second slate, etc. (Tronchot, 221). The gradual extension of the wage-earning class brought with it a more detailed partitioning of time: 'If workers arrive later than a quarter of an hour after the ringing of the bell . . .' (Amboise, article 2); 'if any one of the companions is asked for during work and loses more than five minutes . . .', 'anyone who is not at his work at the correct time . . .' (Oppenheim, article 7—8). But an attempt is also made to assure the quality of the time used: constant supervision, the pressure of supervisors, the elimination of anything that might disturb or distract; it is a question of constituting a totally useful time: 'It is expressly forbidden during work to amuse one's companions by gestures or in any other way, to play at any game whatsoever, to eat, to sleep, to tell stories and comedies' (Oppenheim, article 16); and even during the meal-break, 'there will be no telling of stories, adventures or other such talk that distracts the workers from their work'; 'it is expressly forbidden for any worker, under any pretext, to bring wine into the manufactory and to drink in the workshops' (*Amboise*, article 4). Time measured and paid must also be a time without impurities or defects; a time of good quality, throughout which the body is constantly applied to its exercise. Precision and application are, with regularity, the fundamental virtues of disciplinary time. But this is not the newest thing about it. Other methods are more characteristic of the disciplines.

2. *The temporal elaboration of the act.* There are, for example, two ways of controlling marching troops. In the early seventeenth century, we have: 'Accustomed soldiers marching in file or in battalion to march to the rhythm of the drum. And to do this, one must begin with the right foot so that the whole troop raises the same foot at the same time' (Montgommery, 86). In the mid-eighteenth century, there are four sorts of steps: 'The length of the the short step will be a foot, that of the ordinary step, the double step and the marching step will be two feet, the whole measured from one heel to the next; as for the duration, that of the small step and the ordinary step will last one second, during which two double steps would be performed; the duration of the marching step will be a little longer than one second. The oblique step will take one second; it will be at most eighteen inches from one heel to the next. . . . The ordinary step will be executed forwards, holding the head up high and the body erect, holding oneself in balance successively on a single leg, and bringing the other forwards, the ham taut, the point of the foot a little turned outwards and low, so that one may without affectation brush the ground on which one must walk and place one's foot, in such a way that each part may come to rest there at the same time without striking the ground' ('Ordonnance du 1er janvier 1766, pour régler l'exercise de l'infanterie'). Between these two instructions, a new set of restraints had been brought into play, another degree of precision in the breakdown of gestures and movements, another way of adjusting the body to temporal imperatives.

What the ordinance of 1766 defines is not a time-table—the general framework for an activity; it is rather a collective and obligatory rhythm, imposed from the outside; it is a 'programme'; it assures the elaboration of the act itself; it controls its development and its stages from the inside. We have passed from a form of injunction that measured or punctuated gestures to a web that constrains them or sustains them throughout their entire succession. A sort of anatomo-chronological schema of behaviour is defined. The act is broken down into its elements; the position of the body, limbs, articulations is defined; to each movement are assigned a direction, an aptitude, a duration; their order of succession is prescribed. Time penetrates the body and with it all the meticulous controls of power.

3. Hence *the correlation of the body and the gesture*. Disciplinary control does not consist simply in teaching or imposing a series of particular gestures; it imposes the best relation between a gesture and the

overall position of the body, which is its condition of efficiency and speed. In the correct use of the body, which makes possible a correct use of time, nothing must remain idle or useless: everything must be called upon to form the support of the act required. A well-disciplined body forms the operational context of the slightest gesture. Good handwriting, for example, presupposes a gymnastics—a whole routine whose rigorous code invests the body in its entirety, from the points of the feet to the tip of the index finger. The pupils must always 'hold their bodies erect, somewhat turned and free on the left side, slightly inclined, so that, with the elbow placed on the table, the chin can be rested upon the hand, unless this were to interfere with the view; the left leg must be somewhat more forward under the table than the right. A distance of two fingers must be left between the body and the table; for not only does one write with more alertness, but nothing is more harmful to the health than to acquire the habit of pressing one's stomach against the table; the part of the left arm from the elbow to the hand must be placed on the table. The right arm must be at a distance from the body of about three fingers and be about five fingers from the table, on which it must rest lightly. The teacher will place the pupils in the posture that they should maintain when writing, and will correct it either by sign or otherwise, when they change this position' (La Salle, *Conduite* . . ., 63–4). A disciplined body is the prerequisite of an efficient gesture.

4. *The body-object articulation.* Discipline defines each of the relations that the body must have with the object that it manipulates. Between them, it outlines a meticulous meshing. 'Bring the weapon forward. In three stages. Raise the rifle with the right hand, bringing it close to the body so as to hold it perpendicular with the right knee, the end of the barrel at eye level, grasping it by striking it with the right hand, the arm held close to the body at waist height. At the second stage, bring the rifle in front of you with the left hand, the barrel in the middle between the two eyes, vertical, the right hand grasping it at the small of the butt, the arm outstretched, the trigger-guard resting on the first finger, the left hand at the height of the notch, the thumb lying along the barrel against the moulding. At the third stage, let go of the rifle with the left hand, which falls along the thigh, raising the rifle with the right hand, the lock outwards and opposite the chest, the right arm half flexed, the elbow close to the body, the thumb lying against the lock, resting

against the first screw, the hammer resting on the first finger, the barrel perpendicular' ('Ordonnance du 1er janvier 1766 . . ., titre XI, article 2'). This is an example of what might be called the instrumental coding of the body. It consists of a breakdown of the total gesture into two parallel series: that of the parts of the body to be used (right hand, left hand, different fingers of the hand, knee, eye, elbow, etc.) and that of the parts of the object manipulated (barrel, notch, hammer, screw, etc.); then the two sets of parts are correlated together according to a number of simple gestures (rest, bend); lastly, it fixes the canonical succession in which each of these correlations occupies a particular place. This obligatory syntax is what the military theoreticians of the eighteenth century called '*manoeuvre*'. The traditional recipe gives place to explicit and obligatory prescriptions. Over the whole surface of contact between the body and the object it handles, power is introduced, fastening them to one another. It constitutes a body-weapon, body-tool, body-machine complex. One is as far as possible from those forms of subjection that demanded of the body only signs or products, forms of expression or the result of labour. The regulation imposed by power is at the same time the law of construction of the operation. Thus disciplinary power appears to have the function not so much of deduction as of synthesis, not so much of exploitation of the product as of coercive link with the apparatus of production.

5. *Exhaustive use.* The principle that underlay the time-table in its traditional form was essentially negative; it was the principle of non-idleness: it was forbidden to waste time, which was counted by God and paid for by men; the time-table was to eliminate the danger of wasting it—a moral offence and economic dishonesty. Discipline, on the other hand, arranges a positive economy; it poses the principle of a theoretically ever-growing use of time: exhaustion rather than use; it is a question of extracting, from time, ever more available moments and, from each moment, ever more useful forces. This means that one must seek to intensify the use of the slightest moment, as if time, in its very fragmentation, were inexhaustible or as if, at least by an ever more detailed internal arrangement, one could tend towards an ideal point at which one maintained maximum speed and maximum efficiency. It was precisely this that was implemented in the celebrated regulations of the Prussian infantry that the whole of Europe imitated after the victories of Frederick II: the more time is broken down, the

more its subdivisions multiply, the better one disarticulates it by deploying its internal elements under a gaze that supervises them, the more one can accelerate an operation, or at least regulate it according to an optimum speed; hence this regulation of the time of an action that was so important in the army and which was to be so throughout the entire technology of human activity: the Prussian regulations of 1743 laid down six stages to bring the weapon to one's foot, four to extend it, thirteen to raise it to the shoulder, etc. By other means, the 'mutual improvement school' was also arranged as a machine to intensify the use of time; its organization made it possible to obviate the linear, successive character of the master's teaching: it regulated the counterpoint of operations performed, at the same moment, by different groups of pupils under the direction of monitors and assistants, so that each passing moment was filled with many different, but ordered activities; and, on the other hand, the rhythm imposed by signals, whistles, orders imposed on everyone temporal norms that were intended both to accelerate the process of learning and to teach speed as a virtue; 'the sole aim of these commands . . . is to accustom the children to executing well and quickly the same operations, to diminish as far as possible by speed the loss of time caused by moving from one operation to another' (Bernard).

Through this technique of subjection a new object was being formed; slowly, it superseded the mechanical body—the body composed of solids and assigned movements, the image of which had for so long haunted those who dreamt of disciplinary perfection. This new object is the natural body, the bearer of forces and the seat of duration; it is the body susceptible to specified operations, which have their order, their stages, their internal conditions, their constituent elements. In becoming the target for new mechanisms of power, the body is offered up to new forms of knowledge. It is the body of exercise, rather than of speculative physics; a body manipulated by authority, rather than imbued with animal spirits; a body of useful training and not of rational mechanics, but one in which, by virtue of that very fact, a number of natural requirements and functional constraints are beginning to emerge. This is the body that Guibert discovered in his critique of excessively artificial movements. In the exercise that is imposed upon it and which it resists, the body brings out its essential correlations and spontaneously rejects the incompatible: 'On entering most of our training schools, one sees all those unfortunate soldiers in constricting and forced attitudes, one sees all their muscles contracted, the circulation of their blood interrupted . . . If we studied the intention of nature and the construction of the human body, we would find the position and the bearing that nature clearly prescribes for the soldier. The head must be erect, standing out from the shoulders, sitting perpendicularly between them. It must be turned neither to left nor to right, because, in view of the correspondence between the vertebrae of the neck and the shoulder-blade to which they are attached, none of them may move in a circular manner without slightly bringing with it from the same side that it moves one of the shoulders and because, the body no longer being placed squarely, the soldier can no longer walk straight in front of him or serve as a point of alignment . . . Since the hip-bone, which the ordinance indicates as the point against which the butt end should rest, is not situated the same in all men, the rifle must be placed more to the right for some, and more to the left for others. For the same reason of inequality of structure, the trigger-guard is more or less pressed against the body, depending on whether the outer parts of a man's shoulder is more or less fleshy' (Guibert, 21–2).

We have seen how the procedures of disciplinary distribution had their place among the contemporary techniques of classification and tabulation; but also how they introduced into them the specific problem of individuals and multiplicity. Similarly, the disciplinary controls of activity belonged to a whole series of researches, theoretical or practical, into the natural machinery of bodies; but they began to discover in them specific processes; behaviour and its organized requirements gradually replaced the simple physics of movement. The body, required to be docile in its minutest operations, opposes and shows the conditions of functioning proper to an organism. Disciplinary power has as its correlative an individuality that is not only analytical and 'cellular', but also natural and 'organic'.

The organization of geneses

In 1667, the edict that set up the manufactory of the Gobelins envisaged the organization of a school. Sixty scholarship children were to be chosen by the superintendent of royal buildings, entrusted for a time to a master whose task it would be to provide them with 'upbringing and instruction', then apprenticed to the various master tapestry makers of the manufactory (who by virtue of this fact received compensation deducted from the pupils' scholarships); after six years' apprenticeship, four years of service and a qualifying examination, they were given the right to 'set up and run a shop' in any town of the kingdom. We find here the characteristics of guild apprenticeship: the relation of dependence on the master that is both individual and total; the statutory duration of the training, which is concluded by a qualifying examination, but which is not broken down according to a precise programme; an overall exchange between the master who must give his knowledge and the apprentice who must offer his services, his assistance and often some payment. The form of domestic service is mixed with a transference of knowledge. In 1737, an edict organized a school of drawing for the apprentices of the Gobelins; it was not intended to replace the training given by the master workers, but to complement it. It involved a quite different arrangement of time. Two hours a day, except on Sundays and feast days, the pupils met in the school. A roll-call was taken, from a list on the wall; the absentees were noted down in a register. The school was divided into three classes. The first for those who had no notion of drawing; they were made to copy models, which were more or less difficult according to the abilities of each pupil. The second 'for those who already have some principles', or who had passed through the first class; they had to reproduce pictures 'at sight, without tracing', but considering only the drawing. In the third class, they learnt colouring and pastel drawing, and were introduced to the theory and practice of dyeing. The pupils performed individual tasks at regular intervals; each of these exercises, signed with the name of its author and date of execution, was handed in to the teacher; the best were rewarded; assembled together at the end of the year and compared, they made it possible to establish the progress, the present ability and the relative place of each pupil; it was then decided which of them could pass into the next class. A general book, kept by the teachers and their assistants, recorded from day to day the behaviour of the pupils and everything that happened in the school; it was periodically shown to an inspector (Gerspach, 1892).

The Gobelins school is only one example of an important phenomenon: the development, in the classical period, of a new technique for taking charge of the time of individual existences; for regulating the relations of time, bodies and forces; for assuring an accumulation of duration; and for turning to ever-increased profit or use the movement of passing time. How can one capitalize the time of individuals, accumulate it in each of them, in their bodies, in their forces or in their abilities, in a way that is susceptible of use and control? How can one organize profitable durations? The disciplines, which analyse space, break up and rearrange activities, must also be understood as machinery for adding up and capitalizing time. This was done in four ways, which emerge most clearly in military organization.

1. Divide duration into successive or parallel segments, each of which must end at a specific time. For example, isolate the period of training and the period of practice; do not mix the instruction of recruits and the exercise of veterans; open separate military schools for the armed service (in 1764, the creation of the École Militaire in Paris, in 1776 the creation of twelve schools in the provinces); recruit professional soldiers at the youngest possible age, take children, 'have them adopted by the nation, and brought up in special schools' (Servan, J., 456); teach in turn posture, marching, the handling of weapons, shooting, and do not pass to another activity until the first has been completely mastered: 'One of the principal mistakes is to show a soldier every exercise at once' ('Règlement de 1743 . . .'); in short, break down time into separate and adjusted threads. 2. Organize these threads according to an analytical plan—successions of elements as simple as possible, combining according to increasing complexity. This presupposes that instruction should abandon the principle of analogical repetition. In the sixteenth century, military exercise consisted above all in copying all or part of the action, and of generally increasing the soldier's skill or strength; in the eighteenth century, the instruction of the 'manual' followed the principle of the 'elementary' and not of the 'exemplary': simple gestures—the position of the fingers, the bend of the leg, the movement of the arms—basic elements for useful actions that also provide a general training in strength, skill, docility. 3. Finalize these temporal segments, decide on how long each will last and conclude it with an examination, which will have the triple function of showing whether the subject has reached the level required, of guaranteeing that each subject undergoes the same apprenticeship and of differentiating the abilities of each individual. When the sergeants, corporals, etc. 'entrusted with the task of instructing the others, are of the opinion that a particular soldier is ready to pass into the first class, they

will present him first to the officers of their company, who will carefully examine him; if they do not find him sufficiently practised, they will refuse to admit him; if, on the other hand, the man presented seems to them to be ready, the said officers will themselves propose him to the commanding officer of the regiment, who will see him if he thinks it necessary, and will have him examined by the senior officers. The slightest mistakes will be enough to have him rejected, and no one will be able to pass from the second class to the first until he has undergone this first examination' (*Instruction par l'exercise de l'infanterie*, 14 mai 1754). 4. Draw up series of series; lay down for each individual, according to his level, his seniority, his rank, the exercises that are suited to him; common exercises have a differing role and each difference involves specific exercises. At the end of each series, others begin, branch off and subdivide in turn. Thus each individual is caught up in a temporal series which specifically defines his level or his rank. It is a disciplinary polyphony of exercises: 'Soldiers of the second class will be exercised every morning by sergeants, corporals, *anspessades,* lance-corporals . . . The lance-corporals will be exercised every Sunday by the head of the section . . .; the corporals and *anspessades* will be exercised every Tuesday afternoon by the sergeants and their company and these in turn on the afternoons of every second, twelfth and twenty-second day of each month by senior officers' (*Instruction . . .*).

It is this disciplinary time that was gradually imposed on pedagogical practice—specializing the time of training and detaching it from the adult time, from the time of mastery; arranging different stages, separated from one another by graded examinations; drawing up programmes, each of which must take place during a particular stage and which involves exercises of increasing difficulty; qualifying individuals according to the way in which they progress through these series. For the 'initiatory' time of traditional training (an overall time, supervised by the master alone, authorized by a single examination), disciplinary time had substituted its multiple and progressive series. A whole analytical pedagogy was being formed, meticulous in its detail (it broke down the subject being taught into its simplest elements, it hierarchized each stage of development into small steps) and also very precocious in its history (it largely anticipated the genetic analyses of the *idéologues,* whose technical model it appears to have been). At the beginning of the eighteenth century, Demia suggested a division of the process of learning to read into seven levels: the first for those who are beginning to learn the letters, the second for those who are learning to spell, the third for those who are learning to join syllables together to make words, the fourth for those who are reading Latin in sentences or from punctuation to punctuation, the fifth for those who are beginning to read French, the sixth for the best readers, the seventh for those who can read manuscripts. But, where there are a great many pupils, further subdivisions would have to be introduced; the first class would comprise four streams: one for those who are learning the 'simple letters'; a second for those who are learning the 'mixed' letters; a third for those who are learning the abbreviated letters (*â, ê* . . .); a fourth for those who are learning the double letters (*ff, ss, tt, st*). The second class would be divided into three streams: for those who 'count each letter aloud before spelling the syllable, *D.O., DO*'; for those 'who spell the most difficult syllables, such as *bant, brand, spinx*', etc. (Demia, 19–20). Each stage in the combinatory of elements must be inscribed within a great temporal series, which is both a natural progress of the mind and a code for educative procedures.

The 'seriation' of successive activities makes possible a whole investment of duration by power: the possibility of a detailed control and a regular intervention (of differentiation, correction, punishment, elimination) in each moment of time; the possibility of characterizing, and therefore of using individuals according to the level in the series that they are moving through; the possibility of accumulating time and activity, of rediscovering them, totalized and usable in a final result, which is the ultimate capacity of an individual. Temporal dispersal is brought together to produce a profit, thus mastering a duration that would otherwise elude one's grasp. Power is articulated directly onto time; it assures its control and guarantees its use.

The disciplinary methods reveal a linear time whose moments are integrated, one upon another, and which is orientated towards a terminal, stable point; in short, an 'evolutive' time. But it must be recalled that, at the same moment, the administrative and economic techniques of control reveal a social time of a serial, orientated, cumulative type: the discovery of an evolution in terms of 'progress'. The disciplinary techniques reveal individual series: the discovery of an evolution in terms of 'genesis'. These two great 'discoveries' of the eighteenth century—the progress of societies and the geneses of individuals—were perhaps correlative with the new techniques of power, and more specifically, with a new way of administering time and making it useful, by segmentation, seriation, synthesis and totalization. A macro- and a micro-physics of power made possible, not the invention of history (it had long had no need of that), but the integration of a temporal, unitary, continuous, cumulative dimension in the exercise of controls and the practice of dominations. 'Evolutive' historicity, as it was then constituted—and so profoundly that it is still self-evident for many today—is bound up with a mode of functioning of power. No doubt it is as if the 'history-remembering' of the chronicles, genealogies, exploits, reigns and deeds had long been linked to a modality of power. With the new techniques of subjection, the 'dynamics' of continuous evolutions tends to replace the 'dynasties' of solemn events.

In any case, the small temporal continuum of individuality-genesis certainly seems to be, like the individuality-cell or the individuality-organism, an effect and an object of discipline. And, at the centre of this seriation of time, one finds a procedure that is, for it, what the drawing up of 'tables' was for the distribution of individuals and cellular segmentation, or, again, what *'manoeuvre'* was for the economy of activities and organic control. This procedure is 'exercise'. Exercise is that technique by which one imposes on the body tasks that are both repetitive and different, but always graduated. By bending behaviour towards a terminal state, exercise makes possible a perpetual characterization of the individual either in relation to this term, in relation to other individuals, or in relation to a type of itinerary. It thus assures, in the form of continuity and constraint, a growth, an observation, a qualification. Before adopting this strictly disciplinary form, exercise had a long history: it is to be found in military, religious and university practices either as initiation ritual, preparatory ceremony, theatrical rehearsal or examination. Its linear, continuously progressive organization, its genetic development in time were, at least in the army and the school, introduced at a later date—and were no doubt of religious origin. In any case, the idea of an educational 'programme' that would follow the child to the end of his schooling and which would involve from year to year, month to month, exercises of increasing complexity, first appeared, it seems, in a religious group, the Brothers of the Common Life (cf. Meir, 160 ff). Strongly inspired by Ruysbroek and Rhenish mysticism, they transposed certain of the spiritual techniques to education—and to the education not only of clerks, but also of magistrates and merchants: the theme of a perfection towards which the exemplary master guides the pupil became with them that of an authoritarian perfection of the pupils by the teacher; the ever-increasing rigorous exercises that the ascetic life proposed became tasks of increasing complexity that marked the gradual acquisition of knowledge and good behaviour; the striving of the whole community towards salvation became the collective, permanent competition of individuals being classified in relation to one another. Perhaps it was these procedures of community life and salvation that were the first nucleus of methods intended to produce individually characterized, but collectively useful aptitudes. In its mystical or ascetic form, exercise was a way of ordering earthly time for the conquest of salvation. It was gradually, in the history of the West, to change direction while preserving certain of its characteristics; it served to economize the time of life, to accumulate it in a useful form and to exercise power over men through the mediation of time arranged in this way. Exercise, having become an element in the political technology of the body and of duration, does not culminate in a beyond, but tends towards a subjection that has never reached its limit.

The composition of forces

'Let us begin by destroying the old prejudice, according to which one believed one was increasing the strength of a troop by increasing its depth. All the physical laws of movement become chimeras when one wishes to adapt them to tactics.' From the end of the seventeenth century, the technical problem of infantry had been freed from the physical model of mass. In an army of pikes and muskets—slow, imprecise, practically incapable of selecting a target and taking aim—troops were used as a projectile, a wall or a fortress: 'the formidable infantry of the army of Spain'; the distribution of soldiers in this mass was carried out above all according to their seniority and their bravery; at the centre, with the task of providing weight and volume, of giving density to the body, were the least experienced; in front, at the angles and on the flanks, were the bravest or reputedly most skilful soldiers. In the course of the classical period, one passed over to a whole set of delicate articulations. The unit—regiment, battalion, section and, later, 'division'—became a sort of machine with many parts, moving in relation to one another, in order to arrive at a configuration and to obtain a specific result. What were the reasons for this mutation? Some were economic: to make each individual useful and the training, maintenance, and arming of troops profitable; to give to each soldier, a precious unit, maximum efficiency. But these economic reasons could become determinant only with a technical transformation: the invention of the rifle: more accurate, more rapid than the musket, it gave greater value to the soldier's skill; more capable of reaching a particular target, it made it possible to exploit fire-power at an individual level; and, conversely, it turned every soldier into a possible target, requiring by the same token greater mobility; it involved therefore the disappearance of a technique of masses in favour of an art that distributed units and men along extended, relatively flexible, mobile lines. Hence the need to find a whole calculated practice of individual and collective dispositions, movements of groups or isolated elements, changes of position, of movement from one disposition to another; in short, the need to invent a machinery whose principle would no longer be the mobile or immobile mass, but a geometry of divisible segments whose basic unity was the mobile soldier with his rifle; and, no doubt, below the soldier himself, the minimal gestures, the elementary stages of actions, the fragments of spaces occupied or traversed.

The same problems arose when it was a question of constituting a productive force whose effect had to be superior to the sum of elementary forces that composed it: 'The combined working-day produces, relatively to an equal sum of working-days, a greater quantity of use-values, and, consequently, diminishes the labour-time necessary for the production of a given useful effect. Whether the combined working-day, in a given case, acquires this increased productive power, because it heightens the mechanical force of labour, or extends its sphere of action over a greater space, or contracts the field of production relatively to the scale of production, or at the critical moment sets large masses of labour to work . . . the special productive power of the combined working-day is, under all circumstances, the social productive power of labour, or the productive power of social labour. This power is due to cooperation itself' (Marx, *Capital*, vol. 1, 311–12). On several occasions, Marx stresses the analogy between the problems of the division of labour and those of military tactics. For example: 'Just as the offensive power of a squadron of cavalry, or the defensive power of a regiment of infantry, is essentially different from the sum of the offensive or defensive powers of the individual cavalry or infantry soldiers taken separately, so the sum total of the mechanical forces exerted by isolated workmen differs from the social force that is developed, when many hands take part simultaneously in one and the same undivided operation' (Marx, *Capital*, vol. 1, 308).

Thus a new demand appears to which discipline must respond: to construct a machine whose effect will be maximized by the concerted articulation of the elementary parts of which it is composed. Discipline is no longer simply an art of distributing bodies, of extracting time from them and accumulating it, but of composing forces in order to obtain an efficient machine. This demand is expressed in several ways.

1. The individual body becomes an element that may be placed, moved, articulated on others. Its bravery or its strength are no longer the principal variables that define it; but the place it occupies, the interval it covers, the regularity, the good order according to which it operates its movements. The soldier is above all a fragment of mobile space, before he is courage or honour. Guibert describes the soldier in the following way: 'When he is under arms, he occupies two feet along his greatest diameter, that is to say, taking him from one end to the other, and about one foot in his greatest thickness taken from the chest to the shoulders, to which one must add an interval of a foot between him and the next man; this gives two feet in all directions per soldier and indicates that a troop of infantry in battle occupies, either in its front or in its depth, as many steps as it has ranks' (Guibert, 27). This is a functional reduction of the body. But it is also an insertion of this body-segment in a whole ensemble over which it is articulated. The soldier whose body has been trained to function part by part for particular operations must in turn form an element in a mechanism at another level. The soldiers will be instructed first 'one by one, then two by two, then in greater numbers . . . For the handling of weapons, one will ascertain that, when the soldiers have been separately instructed, they will carry it out two by two, and then change places alternately, so that the one on the left may learn to adapt himself to the one on the right' ('Ordonnance . . .'). The body is constituted as a part of a multi-segmentary machine.

2. The various chronological series that discipline must combine to form a composite time are also pieces of machinery. The time of each

must be adjusted to the time of the others in such a way that the maximum quantity of forces may be extracted from each and combined with the optimum result. Thus Servan dreamt of a military machine that would cover the whole territory of the nation and in which each individual would be occupied without interruption but in a different way according to the evolutive segment, the genetic sequence in which he finds himself. Military life would begin in childhood, when young children would be taught the profession of arms in 'military manors'; it would end in these same manors when the veterans, right up to their last day, would teach the children, exercise the recruits, preside over the soldiers' exercises, supervise them when they were carrying out works in the public interest, and finally make order reign in the country, when the troops were fighting at the frontiers. There is not a single moment of life from which one cannot extract forces, providing one knows how to differentiate it and combine it with others. Similarly, one uses the labour of children and of old people in the great workshops; this is because they have certain elementary capacities for which it is not necessary to use workers who have many other aptitudes; furthermore, they constitute a cheap labour force; lastly, if they work, they are no longer at anyone's charge: 'Labouring mankind', said a tax collector of an enterprise at Angers, 'may find in this manufactory, from the age of ten to old age, resources against idleness and the penury that follows from it' (Marchegay, 360). But it was probably in primary education that this adjustment of different chronologies was to be carried out with most subtlety. From the seventeenth century to the introduction, at the beginning of the nineteenth, of the Lancaster method, the complex clockwork of the mutual improvement school was built up cog by cog: first the oldest pupils were entrusted with tasks involving simple supervision, then of checking work, then of teaching; in the end, all the time of all the pupils was occupied either with teaching or with being taught. The school became a machine for learning, in which each pupil, each level and each moment, if correctly combined, were permanently utilized in the general process of teaching. One of the great advocates of the mutual improvement schools gives us some idea of this progress: 'In a school of 360 children, the master who would like to instruct each pupil in turn for a session of three hours would not be able to give half a minute to each. By the new method, each of the 360 pupils writes, reads or counts for two and a half hours' (cf. Bernard).

3. This carefully measured combination of forces requires a precise system of command. All the activity of the disciplined individual must be punctuated and sustained by injunctions whose efficacity rests on brevity and clarity; the order does not need to be explained or formulated; it must trigger off the required behaviour and that is enough. From the master of discipline to him who is subjected to it the relation is one of signalization: it is a question not of understanding the injunction but of perceiving the signal and reacting to it immediately, according to a more or less artificial, prearranged code. Place the bodies in a little world of signals to each of which is attached a single, obligatory response: it is a technique of training, of *dressage*, that 'despotically excludes in everything the least representation, and the smallest murmur'; the disciplined soldier 'begins to obey whatever he is ordered to do; his obedience is prompt and blind; an appearance of indocility, the least delay would be a crime' (Boussanelle, 2). The training of schoolchildren was to be carried out in the same way: few words, no explanation, a total silence interrupted only by signals—bells, clapping of hands, gestures, a mere glance from the teacher, or that little wooden apparatus used by the Brothers of the Christian Schools; it was called *par excellence* the 'Signal' and it contained in its mechanical brevity both the technique of command and the morality of obedience. 'The first and principal use of the signal is to attract at once the attention of all the pupils to the teacher and to make them attentive to what he wishes to impart to them. Thus, whenever he wishes to attract the attention of the children, and to bring the exercise to an end, he will strike the signal once. Whenever a good pupil hears the noise of the signal, he will imagine that he is hearing the voice of the teacher or rather the voice of God himself calling him by his name. He will then partake of the feelings of the young Samuel, saying with him in the depths of his soul: "Lord, I am here." ' The pupil will have to have learnt the code of the signals and respond automatically to them. 'When prayer has been said, the teacher will strike the signal at once and, turning to the child whom he wishes to read, he will make the sign to begin. To make a sign to stop to a pupil who is reading, he will strike the signal once . . . To make a sign to a pupil to repeat when he has read badly or mispronounced a letter, a syllable or a word, he will strike the signal twice in rapid succession. If, after the sign had been made two or three times, the pupil who is reading does not find and repeat the word that he has

badly read or mispronounced—because he has read several words beyond it before being called to order—the teacher will strike three times in rapid succession, as a sign to him to begin to read farther back; and he will continue to make the sign till the pupil finds the word which he has said incorrectly' (La Salle, *Conduite* . . . 137–8; cf. also Demia, 21). The mutual improvement school was to exploit still further this control of behaviour by the system of signals to which one had to react immediately. Even verbal orders were to function as elements of signalization: 'Enter your benches. At the word *enter*, the children bring their right hands down on the table with a resounding thud and at the same time put one leg into the bench; at the words *your benches* they put the other leg in and sit down opposite their slates . . . *Take your slates.* At the word *take*, the children, with their right hands, take hold of the string by which the slate is suspended from the nail before them, and, with their left hands, they grasp the slate in the middle; at the word *slates*, they unhook it and place it on the table'.

To sum up, it might be said that discipline creates out of the bodies it controls four types of individuality, or rather an individuality that is endowed with four characteristics: it is cellular (by the play of spatial distribution), it is organic (by the coding of activities), it is genetic (by the accumulation of time), it is combinatory (by the composition of forces). And, in doing so, it operates four great techniques: it draws up tables; it prescribes movements; it imposes exercises; lastly, in order to obtain the combination of forces, it arranges 'tactics'. Tactics, the art of constructing, with located bodies, coded activities and trained apti-tudes, mechanisms in which the product of the various forces is increased by their calculated combination are no doubt the highest form of disciplinary practice. In this knowledge, the eighteenth-century theoreticians saw the general foundation of all military practice, from the control and exercise of individual bodies to the use of forces specific to the most complex multiplicities. The architecture, anatomy, mechan-ics, economy of the disciplinary body: 'In the eyes of most soldiers, tac-tics are only a branch of the vast science of war; for me, they are the base of this science; they are this science itself, because they teach how to constitute troops, order them, move them, get them to fight; because tactics alone may make up for numbers, and handle the multitude; lastly, it will include knowledge of men, weapons, tensions, circum-stances, because it is all these kinds of knowledge brought together that must determine those movements' (Guibert, 4). Or again: 'The term tactics . . . gives some idea of the respective position of the men who make up a particular troop in relation to that of the different troops that make up an army, their movements and their actions, their relations with one another' (Joly de Maizeroy, 2).

It may be that war as strategy is a continuation of politics. But it must not be forgotten that 'politics' has been conceived as a continuation, if not exactly and directly of war, at least of the military model as a fundamental means of preventing civil disorder. Politics, as a technique of internal peace and order, sought to implement the mechanism of the perfect army, of the disciplined mass, of the docile, useful troop, of the regiment in camp and in the field, on manoeuvres and on exercises. In the great eighteenth-century states, the army guaranteed civil peace no doubt because it was a real force, an ever-threatening sword, but also because it was a technique and a body of knowledge that could project their schema over the social body. If there is a politics-war series that passes through strategy, there is an army-politics series that passes through tactics. It is strategy that makes it possible to understand warfare as a way of conducting politics between states; it is tactics that makes it possible to understand the army as a principle for maintaining the absence of warfare in civil society. The classical age saw the birth of the great political and military strategy by which nations confronted each other's economic and demographic forces; but it also saw the birth of meticulous military and political tactics by which the control of bodies and individual forces was exercised within states. The '*militaire*'—the military institution, military science, the *militaire* himself, so different from what was formerly characterized by the term '*homme de guerre*'—was specified, during this period, at the point of junction between war and the noise of battle on the one hand, and order and silence, subservient to peace, on the other. Historians of ideas usually attribute the dream of a perfect society to the philosophers and jurists of the eighteenth century; but there was also a military dream of society; its fundamental reference was not to the state of nature, but to the meticulously subordinated cogs of a machine, not to the primal social contract, but to permanent coercions, not to fundamental rights, but to indefinitely progressive forms of training, not to the general will but to automatic docility.

'Discipline must be made national,' said Guibert. 'The state that I depict will have a simple, reliable, easily controlled administration. It will resemble those huge machines, which by quite uncomplicated means produce great effects; the strength of this state will spring from its own strength, its prosperity from its own prosperity. Time, which destroys all, will increase its power. It will disprove that vulgar prejudice by which we are made to imagine that empires are subjected to an imperious law of decline and ruin' (Guibert, xxiii–xxiv; cf. what Marx says about the army and forms of bourgeois society in his letter to Engels, 25 September 1857). The Napoleonic régime was not far off and with it the form of state that was to survive it and, we must not forget, the foundations of which were laid not only by jurists, but also by soldiers, not only councillors of state, but also junior officers, not only the men of the courts, but also the men of the camps. The Roman reference that accompanied this formation certainly bears with it this double index: citizens and legionaries, law and manoeuvres. While jurists or philosophers were seeking in the pact a primal model for the construction or reconstruction of the social body, the soldiers and with them the technicians of discipline were elaborating procedures for the individual and collective coercion of bodies.

14

PAULO FREIRE

Paulo Freire was born in 1921 in the city of Recife. Raised and educated in Brazil, he completed his Ph.D. in 1959 at the University of Recife. He was one of the most influential educational thinkers of the 20th century, and his ideas and programs have had an impact in many countries, including the United States. While some of his early work focused on adult literacy programs among marginalized populations in Brazil, his analysis of the conditions of education and pedagogical practices vis-à-vis the conditions of oppression and exploitation were read and discussed widely by educators, philosophers, social scientists, activists, and policy makers. A close reading of classic philosophy and modern critical theory, including Marxism and postcolonial theories, as well as Catholicism and theology of liberation, has influenced his own ideas. His book *Pedagogy of the Oppressed* (1972) has been translated to many languages, including English, and sold millions of copies.

His successful adult literacy programs used critical dialogues among participants about the conditions of everyday life. However, these dialogues were received with suspicion by military governments. He was exiled in the early 1960s, but his work continued in Chile and other parts of the world. He lived and taught in Africa, Mexico, Switzerland, and the United States, among other places. When he returned to Brazil in the 1980s, he became Minister of Education for the state of Sao Paulo, which includes the city of the same name—one of the largest cities in the world, with more than 20 million people. He captured some of his reflections about that work in the book *Pedagogy of the City* (1993), and he authored *Pedagogy of Hope* (1994).

Freire offered us a reason for hope. His critiques of pedagogy, curriculum, and schooling not only name what has been wrong with systems and practices that perpetuated marginality for many students but also offer alternative visions and examples for educators, which invite them to dream and hope for change. Furthermore, he wanted us to understand teaching as a political act in the sense that teachers have the power to create or to deny opportunities to students—that teachers must question who benefits from the chosen pedagogies: who would learn what, under what conditions, how, and/or for what purposes?

His humanistic and critical writing challenges teachers to interrogate who they are and who their students are, problematizing institutional organizations, rules, content, and pedagogy. In turn, interrogation and problematization are habits of mind that prompt action. Furthermore, as some of the pages in these reading selections suggest, teaching is a humanizing act and dialogical pedagogies can lead to freedom from oppression, some type of liberatory experience in the traditions of classic and modern thought when designed to "read the word and the world," to question the routines of what he named "banking pedagogies" and classrooms' "culture of silence." Critical pedagogy engages teachers, students, and others to analyze how power works in a classroom, who has power to do things, for what purposes these things are done, and who participates and in what ways. Furthermore, in Freire's view, teachers and students engage in active listening, participatory dialogues, active involvement in learning experiences, and mutual inquiry, thus gaining collective ownership in a process of gaining awareness about themselves and the multiple communities to which they belong, with the purpose of individual and social transformation. Teaching this way requires courage and daring. Freire passed away in 1997, but his ideas and practices continue to influence educators all over the world.

His publications in English also include *Letters to Cristina* (1996), *The Politics of Education* (1985), *Teachers as Cultural Workers* (1998), *Pedagogy of the Heart* (1998), and *Pedagogy of Freedom* (1993), among many other books and articles.

REFERENCES

Freire, P. *Pedagogy of the Oppressed.* New York: Seabury, 1970.

Freire, P. *Pedagogy of Freedom: Ethics, Democracy, and Civic Courage.* Lanham, MD: Rowman and Littlefield, 1998.

Freire, P. *Pedagogy of the Heart.* New York: Continuum, 1998.

Freire, P. *Teachers as Cultural Workers: Letters to Those Who Dare to Teach.* Boulder, CO: Westview, 1998.

UNDER THE SHADE OF A MANGO TREE

Solitude–Communion

The search that brings me to the comforting shade of this mango tree*
could be of little interest to most people. I find refuge under its shade
when I am there alone, secluded from the world and others, asking
myself questions, or talking to myself. My talks are not always triggered by my questions.

There has to be an a priori reason that has been lost in the pleasure
of finding refuge under the shade of this tree. What I should do is to
totally let myself be taken by the feelings of being under it, to live it,
and to make this experience more and more intense to the extent that I
prove its existence.

To come under the shade of this mango tree with such deliberateness and to experience the fulfillment of solitude emphasize my need
for communion. While I am physically alone proves that I understand
the essentiality of to be *with*. It is interesting for me to think now how
important, even indispensable, it is to be *with*. To be alone has represented for me throughout my lifetime a form of being *with*. I never
avoid being with others as if I am afraid of company, as if I do not need
others to feel fulfilled, or as if I feel awkward in the world. On the contrary, by isolating myself I get to know myself better while I recognize
my limits, and the needs that involve me in a permanent search that
would not be viable through isolation. I need the world as the world
needs me. Isolation can only make sense when, instead of rejecting
communion, it confirms it as a moment of its existence.

A negative isolation is to be found in those who timidly or methodically look to find some refuge in being alone. A negative isolation is
characterized by those who selfishly require that everything revolves
around them so as to meet their needs. This form of solitude is often
required by those who only see themselves even when they are surrounded by a multitude of people. These individuals can only see
themselves, their class, or their group due to their greed, which suffo-
cates the rights of others. These types of people are characterized by the

*An allusion to the Portuguese title of this volume. Cf. footnote page 8, in the fore-
word, as well as the preface, page 26.

feeling that the more they have, the more they *want* to have—and it does not matter what means they use to achieve their ends. These are insensitive people who add arrogance and meanness to their insensitivity. These are the people who when they are in a good mood, call the popular classes "those people," and when they are in bad mood, refer to them as "trashy people."

Let me first make it clear that I refuse to accept a certain type of scientistic criticism that insinuates that I lack rigor in the way I deal with these issues or the overaffective language I use in this process. The passion with which I know, I speak, or I write does not, in any way, diminish the commitment with which I announce or denounce. I am a totality and not a dichotomy. I do not have a side of me that is schematic, meticulous, nationalist, and another side that is disarticulated or imprecise, which simply likes the world. I know with my entire body, with feelings, with passion, and also with reason.

I have been always engaged with many thoughts concerning the challenges that draw me to this or that issue or to the doubts that make me unquiet. These doubts take me to uncertainties, the only place where it is possible to work toward the necessary provisional certainties. It is not the case that it is impossible to be certain about some things. What is impossible is to be absolutely certain, as if the certainty of today were the same as that of yesterday and will continue to be the same as that of tomorrow.

In being methodical concerning the certainty of uncertainties does not deny the isolation of the cognitive possibility. The fundamental certainty is that I can know. *I know that I know.* In the same way, I also know that I do not know, which predisposes me to know the following: first, that I can know better what I know; second, that I can know what I do not know yet; third, that I can produce forms of knowledge that do not exist yet.

In being conscious that I can know socially and historically, I also know that what I know cannot be divorced from the historical continuity. Knowledge has historicity. It never is, it is always in the process of being. But this does not at all diminish, on the one hand, the fundamental certainty that I can know; on the other hand, it does not diminish the possibility of knowing with more methodological rigor that would enhance the level of the accuracy of the findings.

In order to know better what I already know implies, sometimes, to know what before was not possible to know. Thus, the important thing is to educate the curiosity through which knowledge is constituted as it grows and refines itself through the very exercise of knowing.

An education of answers does not at all help the curiosity that is indispensable in the cognitive process. On the contrary, this form of education emphasizes the mechanical memorization of contents. Only an education of question can trigger, motivate, and reinforce curiosity.

It is obvious that the mistake inherent in an education that forms only in giving answers does not reside in the answer itself but in the rupture between the answer and the question. The mistake lies in the fact that the answer is given independently from the question that triggers it. By the same token, an education of answer would be wrong if the answer is not perceived as part of the question. To question and to answer represent a constitutive path to curiosity.

It is necessary that we should always be expecting that a new knowledge will arise, transcending another that, in being new, would became old.

History, like us, is a process of being limited and conditioned by the knowledge that we produce. Nothing that we engender, live, think, and make explicit takes place outside of time and history. To be certain or to doubt would represent historical forms of being.

Life Support and the World

It would be unthinkable to have a world where the human experience took place outside of a continuity, that is, outside of history. The often-proclaimed "death of history" implies the death of women and men. We cannot survive the death of history: while it is constituted by us, it makes and remakes us. What occurs is the transcendence of a historical phase for another that does not eliminate the continuity of history in the depth of change itself.

It is impossible to change the world into something that is unappealingly immobile, within which nothing happens outside of what has been preestablished, to thereby create a world that is plane, horizontal, and timeless. The world, in order to be, must be in *the process of being*. A world that is plane, horizontal, and timeless could even be compatible with animal life but it remains incompatible with human existence. In this sense, the animals usually adapt to the life-support world, while human beings, in integrating themselves to their contexts so that they can intervene in them, transform the world. It is for this reason that we can tell stories about what happens in the life-support world, we talk about various forms of life that are formed in it. However, the history that is processed in the world is what is made by human beings.

If communication and intercommunication represent processes that speak to life about the support system, in the existential experience they acquire a special connotation. In this instance, both communication and intercommunication involve the comprehension of the world. The life-support world does not imply a language or the erect posture that permitted the liberation of the hands. The life-support becomes world and life becomes existence to the degree that there is an increasing solidarity between the mind and the hands. In other words, this change depends upon the proportion to which the human body becomes a conscient body that can capture, apprehend, and transform the world so it ceases being an empty space to be filled by contents.*

The process through which humans became erect, produced instruments, spoke, developed understanding, and began to communicate with one another represents tasks that involve solidarity and, simultaneously, imply cause and effect due to the presence of humans and their invention of the world as well as their domination over the life support. To be in the world necessarily implies being *with* the world and *with* others. For those beings who are simply in the life support, their activities in the life support represent a mere meddling; in the world with its social, historical, and cultural context, human beings interfere more than just merely meddle with the world.

In this sense, the shift from life support to world implies technical inventions and instruments that make the intervention in the world easier. Once these instruments are invented, men and women never stop the process of creating and reinventing new techniques with which they perfect their presence in the world. All operations in the world necessarily involve their comprehension, a knowledge about the process to operate in the world, an inventory about the findings but, above all, a vision with respect to the ends proposed in these operations. The creation intensifies to the degree that the rhythm of change is accelerated by developed techniques, which become more and more adequate to deal with these challenges.

---

*See *The Cambridge Encyclopedia of Language*. Cambridge: Cambridge University Press, 1987.

The time period between significant changes in the world diminishes increasingly. In certain fields of science and the present technology, it takes a mere few months for the procedure to become obsolete. Sometimes, for reasons that are purely economic, these procedures have "a longer shelf life." This has to do with the resources spent in the development of a particular technological procedure or instruments that have not yet been operated, and, even though these procedures or instruments become obsolete, they continue to be considered efficient.

The ability to reflect, to evaluate, to program, to investigate, and to transform is unique to human beings in the world and with the world. Life becomes existence and life support becomes world when the conscience about the world, which also implies the conscience of the self, emerges and establishes a dialectical relationship with the world. The question between conscience/world that involves their mutual relations led Sartre to observe that "conscience and world take place at the same time." The relations between them are naturally dialectical, regardless of the school of thought and the philosophy that one studies. If one is a mechanist or an idealist, one cannot alter the dialectic conscience/world and subjectivity/objectivity. This does not mean that one mechanistic or idealistic practice is freed from its fundamental error. The plans of action that are based on the conception that conscience is the arbitrary maker of the world, and that defend the idea that before changing the world the moral conscience must be purified, will usually end up in a great failure. By the same token, projects that are based on a mechanistic vision in which the conscience is a mere reflex of the objective materiality cannot escape the punishment of history.

Many possible dreams end up not being viable due to the excess of certainty of their agents; and the capriciousness with which they pretended to mold history instead of making it with others would lead to a remaking of one another in the process. If history is not a superior entity that is above our heads and possesses us, it also cannot be reduced to an object to be manipulated.

By rejecting the dialectical tension between conscience/world, both idealists and mechanists, in their own way, become obstacles to connect intelligence of the world. This has been a theme that has always challenged me, one I have always attempted to address coherently with my democratic dream. Rarely do I find myself under the shadow of my mango tree without feeling unquiet and not thinking about this.

I am not a being in the life support but a being in the world, with the world, and with others; I am a being who makes things, knows and ignores, speaks, fears and takes risks, dreams and loves, becomes angry and is enchanted. I am a being who rejects the condition of being a mere object. I am a being who does not bow before the indisputable power accumulated by technology because, in knowing that it is a human production, I do not accept that it is, in and of itself, bad. I am a being who rejects a view of technology as a demon's deed designed to throw out God's work.*

It is not enough for me to ask: "What can one do? Technology necessarily engenders automatism, which leads to unemployment. The unemployed must change: they should seek leisure, a fundamental theme of postmodernity." No: I do not accept this form of fatalism.

The state cannot be so liberal as the neoliberals would like it to be. It behooves the progressive political parties to fight in favor of economic development and the limitation of the size of the state. The state should neither be an almighty entity nor a lackey that obeys the orders of those who live well. The projects of economic development cannot exclude men and women of history in the name of any fatalism.

My radical posture requires of me an absolute loyalty to all men and women. An economy that is incapable of developing programs according to human needs, and that coexists indifferently with the hunger of millions of people to whom everything is denied, does not deserve my respect as an educator. Above all, it does not deserve my respect as a human being. And it is not well to say, "Things are the way they are because they cannot be different." They cannot be different because if they were, they would be in conflict with the interests of the ruling class. This cannot, however, be the determining essence of the economic practice. I cannot become fatalistic in order to meet the interests of the ruling class. Neither can I invent a "scientific" explanation to cover up a lie.

---

*See Neil Postman. *Technology: The Surrender of Culture to Technology.* New York: Alfred A. Knopf, 1992.

The power of those in power always aims to decimate the power-less. But, alongside material power, there was always mother force—ideology—which is also material and strengthens the power structure. Technological advances enhance with great efficiency the ideological support of material power.

One of the most important tasks for progressive intellectuals is to demystify postmodern discourses with respect to the inexorability of this situation. I vehemently reject such immobilization of history.

The affirmation that "Things are the way they are because they cannot be otherwise" is hatefully fatalistic since it decrees that happiness only belongs to those in power. The poor people, the disinherited, and those who have been excluded, were destined to die of cold no matter if they are from the South or the North of the world.

If the economic and political power of the ruling class denies the powerless the minimum space to survive, it is not because it should be that way. It is necessary that the weakness of the powerless is trans-formed into a force capable of announcing justice. For this to happen, a total denouncement of fatalism is necessary. We are transformative beings and not beings for accommodation.

We cannot reject the struggle for the exercise of our capacities and our rights to decide. In this way, I insist that *history is possibility and not determinism.* We are conditioned beings but not determined beings. It is impossible to understand history as possibility if we do not recognize human beings as beings who make free decisions. Without this form of exercise it is not worth speaking about ethics.

Dialogism

I now return to the discussion of a dialogic relationship, while a funda-mental practice to human nature and to democracy on the one hand, and on the other, as an epistemological requirement.

As a matter of method, I never directly focus my attention on the object that challenges me in the process of knowledge discovery. On the contrary, by taking epistemological distance from the object, I proceed to approach it by encircling it. "Taking epistemological distance" means taking the object in hand in order to get to know it; in my "epis-temological encircling" of it, I seek to decipher some of its reasons for being in order to appropriate its substantiveness better. In the episte-mological encircling, I do not intend to isolate the object to apprehend it; in this operation, I try to understand the object, the interior of its relationship with others.

This is how I will work through the issue of *dialogism*. Instead of describing a profile of the concept of dialogism, I will begin by attempting to comprehend its foundation, what makes of it a strategic requirement, rather than solely the tactics of "smart" subjects toward reaching results. Dialogism must not be understood as a tool used by the educator, at times, in keeping with his or her political choices. Dialogism is a requirement of human nature and also a sign of the educator's democratic stand.

There is no communication without dialogism, and communication lies at the core of the vital phenomenon. In this sense, communication is life and a vector for *more-life*. But, if communication and information occur on the level of life upon its support, let us imagine its importance and, thus, that of dialogism for human existence in the world. On this level, communication and information are served by sophisticated languages and by technological instruments that "shorten" space and time. The social production of language and of instruments with which human beings can better interfere in the world announce what technology will be.

Not too long ago, my grandson, Alexandre Dowbor, called me to say that his computer, connected to the Internet, had "picked up" a message from a German scholar requesting my address. He responded to her request and also provided my fax number. Fifteen minutes later, I was talking with the German professor: thanks to technology.

If my mother, who died in 1978, had been back to the earth for a moment and listened to my conversation with Alexandre, she would have understood nothing.

I have called attention to human nature as *being* socially and historically *constituted*, rather than as preexisting. The trajectory through which we make ourselves conscious is marked by finiteness, by inconclusion, and it characterizes us as historical beings.

Not only have we been unfinished, but we have made ourselves capable of knowing ourselves as such. Here, an opportunity is open for us to become immersed in a permanent search. One of the roots of education, which makes it specifically human, lies in the radicalness of an inconclusion that is perceived as such. The permanence of education also lies in the constant character of the search, perceived as necessary. Likewise, here lie also roots of the metaphysical foundation of hope. How would it be possible for a consciously inconclusive being to become immersed in a permanent search without hope? My hope starts from my nature as a project. For this reason I am hopeful, and not for pure stubbornness.

In order for finiteness, which implies a process, a claim for education, it is necessary that the being involved becomes aware of it. Consciousness of one's inconclusiveness makes that being educable. Unfinishedness in the absence of consciousness about it engenders *domestication* and *cultivation*. Animals are domesticated; plants are cultivated; men and women educate themselves.

Consciousness of, an intentionality of consciousness does not end with rationality. Consciousness about the world, which implies consciousness about myself in the world, with it and with others, which also implies our ability to realize the world, to understand it, is not limited to a rationalistic experience. This consciousness is a totality—reason, feelings, emotions, desires; my body, conscious of the world and myself, seizes the world toward which it has an intention.

My *conscious body's* constant exercise in releasing itself *even to* or *from* my consciousness intending toward the world brings or contains in itself a certain quality of life that, in the human existence, becomes more intense and richer. I am referring to the need for *relational* experience on the level of *existence* and of *interactions,* the level of *living.*

There is a fundamental element in *interaction,* which takes on greater complexity in *relationship,* I am referring to *curiosity,* some sort of openness to comprehending what is in the orbit of the challenged being's sensibility. It is this human disposition to be surprised before people, what they do, say, seem like, before facts and phenomena, before beauty and ugliness, this unrefrainable need to understand in order to explain, to seek the reason for being of facts. It is this desire, always alive, of feeling, living, realizing what lies in the realm of one's "visions of depth" (see *Pedagogy of the Oppressed,* New Revised 20th-Anniversary Edition, New York: Continuum, 1993).

Without the curiosity that makes us beings in permanent availability for questioning—be the questioning well constructed or poorly founded, it does not matter—there would be no gnoseologic activity, a concrete expression of our possibility of knowing.

Concern with the mechanical memorization of content is curious, the use of repetitive exercises that surpass a reasonable limit while leaving out *a critical education about curiosity* (see Paulo Freire and Antonio Faundez, *Learning to Question,* New York: Continuum, 1989). We continue to discourse about answers and questions that were not posed to us, without emphasizing the importance of curiosity to the students.

Let us take half a day in Pedro's life as the object of our curiosity. Let us follow his main movements: he awakes, showers, eats breakfast. He skims the first pages of the newspaper, and since he lives near the university where he works, he walks over there. He leaves the house, greets some people, walks past others; carefree, he observes the rushed movement of those coming and going; he says good morning to some, smiles at others. At the sight of a walk sign, he walks across to the other side. He runs into a friend, detains himself. It is a short conversation, promises of meeting again, who knows, maybe next Wednesday. They know they are not going to meet then. The promises will not hurt either one. They will not expect each other next Wednesday.

Peter gets to the university. He greets some coworkers and students. He heads over to the room where the Tuesday seminars are held.

So far, from the moment of his morning shower to his arrival at the seminar room, Pedro has not once questioned himself about this or that action of his. His mind is not epistemologically operating. This is what characterizes our movement through the world of day-to-day life.

That does not mean to say that there may not be curiosity in day-to-day life. It exists and it could not not exist: there we have it, human life, existence. In this domain, however, our curiosity is *unguarded,* spontaneous, without any methodical rigor. It does not lack method, for there cannot be curiosity without method: it is methodical in itself.

There is another way to immerse ourselves pleasurably in a challenge. It is a matter of aesthetic curiosity. It is what makes me stop and gaze upon the sunset. It is what detains me, lost in my contemplation of the speed and elegance with which the clouds move across the blue depth of the sky. It is what touches me when faced with a work of art that centers me in beauty.

Unguarded curiosity must not be the way for Pedro to behave in the classroom. The seminar room is a *theoretical context,* which is in a contradictory relationship with a *concrete context,* where facts occur; thus, it demands epistemological curiosity. This curiosity, however, does not refuse to consider the aesthetic. On the contrary, it avails itself of it.

In a theoretical context, we take distance from the concrete one in order, while objectifying it, to examine what takes place in it critically. In a concrete context, there is always the possibility of its subjects' adopting a reflective-critical position; in it, spontaneous curiosity may come to be epistemological.

If, while engaged in concreteness, I could not distance myself from it in order to understand it better only because I found myself in action, the relationship between the concrete context and the theoretical one would be solely mechanical. In order to reflect theoretically upon my practice, it is not required that I change physical contexts. It is required that my curiosity become epistemological. The appropriate context for the exercise of epistemological curiosity is the theoretical one. But physical space is not what makes a context theoretical, the state of the mind is. That being, hence, how we may convert a given moment in the concrete context into a theoretical moment.

Likewise, the space of the concrete context does not necessarily make it theoretical, but the epistemologically curious posture with which we may operate in it does. In the same way, the methodological rigor indispensable to the theoretical context may be twisted, leading one to operate mechanically in that context. The *banking* model of educational practice is of this kind.

Spontaneous curiosity is not what makes it possible to take epistemological distance. This task belongs to epistemological curiosity— overcoming naive curiosity, it makes itself more methodically rigorous. It is this methodical rigor that takes knowledge from the level of *common sense* to that of scientific knowledge. Scientific knowledge is not what is rigorous. Rigor lies in the method applied in an approach to the object. This rigor allows for a greater or lesser *precision* in the knowledge produced or found through our epistemological quest.

As we emphasize an epistemologically curious posture as fundamental in constituting the theoretical context, the importance of this space should be clear. Due attention to the educational space, while it is a context open to the exercise of epistemological curiosity, should be a concern of every serious educational project.

Attention should go into every detail of the school space: hygiene, wall furnishings, cleanliness of desks, the teacher's desk setup, educational materials, books, magazines, newspapers, dictionaries, encyclopedias, and little by little, the introduction of projectors, video, fax, computers. By making clear that the educational space is valuable, the administration is able to demand the due respect for it from learners. Further, this is the way to facilitating the exercise of epistemological curiosity. Without that, the progressive educational practice deteriorates.

While a practice of learning and teaching, educational practice is gnoseologic by nature. The role of the progressive educator is to challenge the learner's naive curiosity in order that they can both share criticalness. That is how an educational practice can affirm itself as the unveiling of hidden truths.

I have previously mentioned the mistake of the postmodernist, who before such contemporary demands as responsiveness to different situations, must defend a certain variety of critical education. To them, however, such education must not go beyond the administrative and technical domains, which are seen as neutral.

The pragmatic reactionary educator who teaches biology, for example, sees no reason to challenge the learner to discuss the vital phenomenon from a social, ideological, or political point of view. What is strictly necessary for them is to deposit contents about the vital phenomenon in the learner.

A technicistic vision of education, which renders it purely technical, or worse yet neutral, works toward the instrumental *training* of the learner. It assumes that there is no longer any antagonism between interests, that everything is more or less the same, and that all that really matters is solely technical training, the standardization of content, and the transfer of a well-behaved *knowledge of results.*

Within such political vision, the permanent development of educators will adhere too much to the *banking* model. The enlightened professional development committees will be interested in training front-line educators—reduced to the role of subordinate intellectuals—into using teaching techniques and materials designed to transfer the "indispensable" content (see Henry Giroux, *Teachers as Intellectuals—Toward a Critical Pedagogy*).

Well to the liking of the World Bank, this political vision necessarily ignores the intelligence and judgment and creative abilities of teachers. Teachers need to be respected, decently paid, called into discussions of their problems, the local, regional, and national problems woven into the problems of education. They must not be diminished and blamed for the gaps in their professional development.

Let us overcome the gaps, but not from the starting point of raising the proclaimed incompetence of teachers. It would be extraordinary if—given our historic situation of disrespect toward public problems, toward teachers, with the starving salaries that they receive—the majority of them *did not* result in desperation.

We shall overcome the gaps by redirecting public spending, eliminating wasteful spending, and eradicating contempt for public property, through an effective fiscal policy, and by revising the role of the state. From all that, the concrete possibility will result in a pedagogical policy based on the decent treatment of teachers and on the exercise of their legitimate development. Only from this point on will it be possible to demand effectiveness from teachers.

Let us return to the issue of dialogism in relation to naive and epistemological curiosity. A dialogic relationship—communication and intercommunication among active subjects who are immune to the bureaucratization of their minds and open to discovery and to knowing more—is indispensable to knowledge. The social nature of this process makes a dialogical relationship a natural element of it. In that sense, authoritarian antidialogue violates the nature of human beings, their process of discovery, and it contradicts democracy.

Authoritarian regimes are enemies of curiosity. They punish citizens for displaying it. Authoritarian power is prying, not curious or questioning. Dialogue, on the other hand, is full of curiosity and unrest. It is full of mutual respect between the dialoging subjects. Dialogism presupposes maturity, a spirit of adventure, confidence in questioning, and seriousness in providing answers. In a dialogic atmosphere, the questioning subject knows the reason for being the questioner. They do not ask questions just for asking or just to seem *alive* to the listener.

A dialogic relationship is the mark of a gnoseologic process: it is not a favor or kindness. Dialogic seriousness and surrender to a critical quest must not be confused with *babbling*. To dialogue is not to babble. That is why there may be dialogue in a professor's critical, rigorously methodical exposition, to which the learners' listen as if *to eat up* the discourse, but also to understand its intellection.

Even though things are never just their atmosphere, but are things themselves, we may speak of a *dialogic atmosphere*. There is an invisible, previous dialogue where one does not need *to make up* questions. Truly democratic educators *are not* for the moment, but *are* by nature dialogic. One of their substantive tasks in our society is to gestate this dialogic atmosphere.

Dialogic experience is fundamental for building epistemological curiosity. Dialogue also implies a critical posture; it implies a preoccupation with the raison d'être of the objects that mediates the subjects of the dialogue.

The growing gap between educational practice and the epistemological curiosity exercise is of concern to me. I fear the curiosity achieved by an educational practice reduced to pure technique may be an anesthetized curiosity, one that does not go past a *scientificist* position before the world.

This is what lies at the core of the "pragmatic" discourse about education. The utopia of solidarity makes way for technical training directed toward survival in a world without dreams, "which have created enough problems." In this case, what matters is training learners just so they can *manage* well.

What counts is training them so that they can adapt without protest. Protest agitates, undermines, twists the truth; it disrupts and moves against order, against the *silence* needed from those who produce.

I reject this fatalism in the name of my understanding of the human being and of history, of my ethical point of view and, because I cannot deny it, of my faith. Here and in other writings, I have spoken about how I understand the human being and history. I would like to emphasize the *finiteness* we are aware of that makes us beings inserted in a permanent search for *being more*—both the natural inclination and the risk of losing *direction* at the same time. Our historical inclination is not fate, but rather possibility. And there cannot be possibility that is not exposed to its negation, to impossibility. Conversely, something impossible today may come to be possible some day. In history as possibility we cannot be but responsible, thus ethical. Such responsibility implies an equally ethical struggle so that we can live up to it. The fact that we are ontologically responsible is not something that can be experienced without search, without fighting against those who irresponsibly prohibit us from being responsible for our own freedom. For this reason, the struggle for liberation implies a previous task, that of accepting the very struggle only as we stand for it. That is how we liberate ourselves, or fail to. Freedom, without which we cannot be, is not a gift but a conquest.

The statement, "Things are as they are because they cannot be any other way," is one of the many instruments used by the dominant in an attempt to abort the dominated's *resistance*. The more historically anesthetized, the more fatalistically immersed in a reality impossible to be touched, let alone transformed, the less of a future we have. Hope is pulverized in the immobility of a crushing present, some sort of final stop beyond which nothing is possible *(Pedagogy of Hope).*

THERE IS NO TEACHING WITHOUT LEARNING

Although my main interest in this book is to look at the kind of knowledge that is indispensable to educators who consider themselves to be critical progressives, such knowledge may be indispensable to educators who regard themselves as conservatives. I refer here to the kind of knowledge that belongs inherently to educative practice itself, whatever the political persuasion of the educator.

As the chapters unfold, the reader can make up his or her own mind as to whether the knowledge I discuss is part of progressive or conservative educative practice or is an intrinsic requirement of educational practice itself, independent of political or ideological coloring. In previous writings, I have referred to various aspects of this kind of knowledge, though not in any systematic way. Even so, it seems to me legitimate to continue this kind of reflection in the context of teacher preparation and in critical educational practice.

Let us take, for example, the practice of cooking. Cooking presupposes certain kinds of knowledge regarding the use of the cooking stove. How to light it. How to turn the heat up and down. How to deal with the possibility of fire. How to balance the ingredients in a harmonious and pleasing synthesis. With practice newcomers to the kitchen will confirm some of the things they already know, correct others that they do not know so well, and gradually open up the way to become cooks. The practice of sailing requires some fundamental knowledge about the control of the boat, the parts of which it is made, and the function of each of them. It requires, in addition, a capacity to measure and interpret the strength and direction of the winds, to gauge the interaction between the wind and sail, and to

"There is No Teaching Without Learning" and "Teaching is a Human Act" from *Pedagogy of Freedom: Ethics, Democracy & Civic Courage* by Paulo Freire, 1998. Reprinted by permission of Rowman & Littlefield Publishers.

position the sails themselves. It requires, too, some knowledge of the motor and the relationship between it and the sails. And, in the practice of sailing, all these kinds of knowledge are either confirmed, modified, or amplified.

Critical reflection on practice is a requirement of the relationship between theory and practice. Otherwise theory becomes simply "blah, blah, blah," and practice, pure activism.

But let me return to what interests me here. I want to focus on and discuss some of the kinds of knowledge that are fundamental to what I call critical (or progressive) educative practice and that, for that reason, ought to be considered essential in the teacher preparation program. Essential in their comprehension and lucid clarity. The very first of these types of knowledge, indispensable from the beginning to the teacher (that is, to the teacher who considers him- or herself to be an agent in the production of knowledge), is that to teach is not *to transfer knowledge* but to create the possibilities for the production or construction of knowledge.

If, during the time of my education, which in any case should be ongoing, I begin believing that my teacher is the "subject" in relation to whom I consider myself to be the "object" (if, in other words, he/she is the subject who forms me, and I, the object shaped by him or her), then I put myself in the passive role of one who receives quantities of accumulated knowledge, transferred to me by a "subject" who "knows." Living and understanding my educational process in this way, I, as "object," will become in my turn a false subject, responsible for the reproduction of further objects. It is essential therefore, from the very beginning of the process, that the following principle be clear: namely, that although the teachers or the students are not the same, the person in charge of education is being formed or re-formed as he/she teaches, and the person who is being taught forms him/herself in this process. In this sense teaching is not about transferring knowledge or contents. Nor is it an act whereby a creator-subject gives shape, style, or soul to an indecisive and complacent body. There is, in fact, no teaching without learning. One requires the other. And the subject of each, despite their obvious differences, cannot be educated to the status of object. Whoever teaches learns in the act of teaching, and whoever learns teaches in the act of learning. From the grammatical point of view, the verb to teach is a "transitive-relative" verb, that is, a verb that requires a direct object (something) and an indirect object (to someone). In this sense, to teach is teaching something to someone. But to teach is much more than a transitive-relative verb. And this is clear not only from the context of democratic thought in which I place myself but also from an essentially meta-physical point of view in which my comprehension of the cognitive process is grounded. In other words, simply "to teach" is not possible in the context of human historical unfinishedness. Socially and histor-ically, women and men discovered that it was the process of learning that made (and makes) teaching possible. Learning in social contexts through the ages, people discovered that it was possible to develop ways, paths, and methods of teaching. To learn, then, logically pre-cedes to teach. In other words, to teach is part of the very fabric of learning. This is true to such an extent that I do not hesitate to say that there is no valid teaching from which there does not emerge some-thing learned and through which the learner does not become capable of recreating and remaking what has been thought. In essence, teach-ing that does not emerge from the experience of learning cannot be learned by anyone.

When we live our lives with the authenticity demanded by the practice of teaching that is also learning and learning that is also teach-ing, we are participating in a total experience that is simultaneously directive, political, ideological, gnostic, pedagogical, aesthetic, and ethi-cal. In this experience the beautiful, the decent, and the serious form a circle with hands joined.

At times, in moments of silence when I seem to be lost, floating, almost disconnected, I reflect on the way that women and men are and have become "programmed for learning," in the words of François Jacob. In other words, the process of learning, through which histori-cally we have discovered that teaching is a task not only inherent to the learning process but is also characterized by it, can set off in the learner an ever-increasing creative curiosity. What I'm really saying is this: The more critically one exercises one's capacity for learning, the greater is one's capacity for constructing and developing what I call "epistemo-logical curiosity," without which it is not possible to obtain a complete grasp of the object of our knowledge.

This understanding of epistemological curiosity brings us, on the one hand, to a critique and a refusal of the "banking system" of edu-cation, and, on the other hand, to an understanding that, even when submitted to this system that is a deformation of the creativity of both

learners and teachers, the learners are not necessarily fated to stagnate. Not because of the "teaching" they have received but because of
the very process of learning itself, learners can circumvent and out-
maneuver the authoritarianism and the epistemological error of this
"banking system."

What is essential is that learners, though subjected to the praxis of
the "banking system," maintain alive the flame of resistance that sharp-
ens their curiosity and stimulates their capacity for risk, for adventure,
so as to immunize themselves against the banking system. In this sense,
the creative force of the learning process, which encompasses comparison, repetition, observation, indomitable doubt, and curiosity not easily
satisfied, overcomes the negative effects of false teaching. This capacity
to go beyond the factors of conditioning is one of the obvious advantages of the human person. Of course, this capacity does not mean that
it is a matter of indifference to us whether we become a "banking system" educator or one whose role is essentially to "problematize," to use
the critical faculty.

Methodological Rigor

The educator with a democratic vision or posture cannot avoid in his
teaching praxis insisting on the critical capacity, curiosity, and autonomy of the learner. One of the essential tasks of the teaching process is
to introduce the learners to the methodological exactitude with which
they should approach the learning process, through which the objects
of learning are knowable. And this methodological exactitude has
nothing to do with the discourse of the "banking system," something
that merely touches the surface of the object or its contents. It's exactly
in this sense that to teach cannot be reduced to a superficial or externalized contact with the object or its content but extends to the production of the conditions in which critical learning is possible. These
conditions imply and demand the presence of teaching and learning
simultaneously in the context of a rigorous methodological curiosity
anxious to explore the limits of creativity, persistent in the search, and
courageously humble in the adventure. In these conditions, those who
are engaged in critical learning know that their teachers are continuously in the process of acquiring new knowledge and that this new
knowledge cannot simply be transferred to them, the learners. At the
same time, in the context of true learning, the learners will be engaged

in a continuous transformation through which they become authentic subjects of the construction and reconstruction of what is being taught, side by side with the teacher, who is equally subject to the same process. Only in this way can we speak authentically of knowledge that is taught, in which the taught is grasped in its very essence and, therefore, learned by those who are learning.

Thus it becomes clear that the role of the educator is one of a tranquil possession of certitude in regard to the teaching not only of contents but also of "correct thinking." Therefore, it becomes obvious that she/he will never develop a truly "critical" perspective as a teacher by indulging in mechanical memorization or the rhythmic repetition of phrases and ideas at the expense of creative challenge. Intellectuals who memorize everything, reading for hours on end, slaves to the text, fearful of taking a risk, speaking as if they were reciting from memory, fail to make any concrete connections between what they have read and what is happening in the world, the country, or the local community. They repeat what has been read with precision but rarely teach anything of personal value. They speak correctly about dialectical thought but think mechanistically. Such teachers inhabit an idealized world, a world of mere data, disconnected from the one most people inhabit.

It's not possible to read critically if one treats reading as if it were a similar operation to buying in bulk. What's the point of boasting of having read twenty books—twenty books! Really reading involves a kind of relationship with the text, which offers itself to me and to which I give myself and through the fundamental comprehension of which I undergo the process of becoming a subject. While reading, I'm not just a captive of the mind of the text as if it were simply a product of its author. This is a vitiated form of reading that has nothing to do with thinking or teaching correctly.

In fact, the person who thinks "correctly," even if at times she/he thinks wrongly, is the only one capable of teaching "correct" thinking. For one of the necessary requirements for correct thinking is a capacity for not being overly convinced of one's own certitudes. Taking into account the need for a rigorous ethical purity totally distinct from Puritanism (in other words, an ethical purity that generates beauty), correct thinking is in this sense irreconcilable with self-conceited arrogance.

The teacher who thinks "correctly" transmits to the students the beauty of our way of existing in the world as historical beings, capable of intervening in and knowing this world. Historical as we are, our knowledge of the world has historicity. It transmits, in addition, that our knowing and our knowledge are the fruit of historicity. And that knowledge, when newly produced, replaces what before was new but is now old and ready to be surpassed by the coming of a new dawn. Therefore, it is as necessary to be immersed in existing knowledge as it is to be open and capable of producing something that does not yet exist. And these two moments of the epistemological process are accounted for in teaching, learning, and doing research. The one moment, in which knowledge that already exists is taught and learned, and the other, in which the production of what is not yet known is the object of research. Thus, the teaching-learning process, together with the work of research, is essential and an inseparable aspect of the gnostic cycle.

Research

Once again, there is no such thing as teaching without research and research without teaching. One inhabits the body of the other. As I teach, I continue to search and re-search. I teach because I search, because I question, and because I submit myself to questioning. I research because I notice things, take cognizance of them. And in so doing, I intervene. And intervening, I educate and educate myself. I do research so as to know what I do not yet know and to communicate and proclaim what I discover.

To think correctly, in critical terms, is a requirement imposed by the rhythms of the gnostic circle on our curiosity, which, as it becomes more methodologically rigorous, progresses from ingenuity to what I have called "epistemological curiosity." Ingenuous curiosity, from which there results, without doubt, a certain kind of knowledge (even though not methodologically rigorous) is what characterizes "common sense" knowing. It is knowledge extracted from pure experience. To think correctly, from the teacher's point of view, implies respect for "common sense" knowing as it progresses from "common sense" to its higher stage. It also implies respect and stimulus for the creative capacity of the learner. It further implies a commitment on the part of educators and teachers that respects the critical consciousness of the learner, in the knowledge that the ingenuous consciousness of the learner will not be overcome automatically.

Respect for What Students Know

For this reason, thinking correctly puts the responsibility on the teacher, or, more correctly, on the school, not only to respect the kinds of knowledge that exist especially among the popular classes—knowledge socially constructed in communitarian praxis—but also (as I've been saying for thirty years) to discuss with the students the logic of these kinds of knowledge in relation to their contents.

Why not, for example, take advantage of the students' experience of life in those parts of the city neglected by the authorities to discuss the problems of pollution in the rivers and the question of poverty and the risks to health from the rubbish heaps in such areas? Why are there no rubbish heaps in the heart of the rich areas of the city? This question is considered "in bad taste." Pure demagogy. Almost subversive, say the defenders of democracy.

Why not discuss with the students the concrete reality of their lives and that aggressive reality in which violence is permanent and where people are much more familiar with death than with life? Why not establish an "intimate" connection between knowledge considered basic to any school curriculum and knowledge that is the fruit of the lived experience of these students as individuals? Why not discuss the implications, political and ideological, of the neglect of the poor areas of the city by the constituted authorities? Are there class-related ethical questions that need to be looked at here? A pragmatic reactionary educator would probably say that there is no connection between one thing and the other. That the school is not the Party. That the function of the school is to teach and transfer contents—packages—to the students, which, once learned, will operate automatically.

A Capacity to Be Critical

It is my conviction that the difference and the distance between ingenuity and critical thinking, between knowledge resulting from pure experience and that resulting from rigorous methodological procedure, do not constitute a rupture but a sort of further stage in the knowing process. This further stage, which is a continuity rather than a rupture, happens when ingenuous curiosity, while remaining curious, becomes capable of self-criticism. In criticizing itself, ingenuous curiosity becomes "epistemological curiosity," as through greater methodological exactitude it appropriates the object of its knowing.

In truth, ingenuous, "unarmed" curiosity, which is associated with common sense knowledge, is the same curiosity that, as it develops its critical possibilities through a more rigorous methodological approximation of the known object, becomes epistemological curiosity. It changes in quality but not in essence. The curiosity of simple rural people with whom I have been in dialogue throughout my politico-pedagogical career, whether fatalist or rebellious in the face of the violence of injustice, is the same curiosity, in the sense of a kind of awe or wonder in the presence of the "not I," common to scientists or philosophers as they contemplate the world. Scientists and philosophers, however, overcome the ingenuous curiosity of simple folk and become "epistemologically" curious.

Curiosity as restless questioning, as movement toward the revelation of something hidden, as a question verbalized or not, as search for clarity, as a moment of attention, suggestion, and vigilance, constitutes an integral part of the phenomenon of being alive. There could be no creativity without the curiosity that moves us and sets us patiently impatient before a world that we did not make, to add to it something of our own making.

In fact, human curiosity, as a phenomenon present to all vital experience, is in a permanent process of social and historical construction and reconstruction. It's precisely because ingenuous curiosity does not automatically become critical that one of the essential tasks of progressive educational praxis is the promotion of a curiosity that is critical, bold, and adventurous. A type of curiosity that can defend us from the excess of a rationality that now inundates our highly technologized world. Which does not mean that we are to adopt a false humanist posture of denying the value of technology and science. On the contrary, it's a posture of balance that neither deifies nor demonizes technology. A posture that is from those who consider technology from a critically curious standpoint.

Ethics and Aesthetics

Further, the necessary process from ingenuous to critical curiosity should also be accompanied by a rigorous ethical formation side by side with an aesthetic appreciation. Beauty and decency, hand in hand. I am more and more convinced that educational praxis, while avoiding the trap of puritanical moralism, cannot avoid the task of becoming a clear witness to decency and purity. That is, it cannot avoid the task of being a permanent critique of the easy solutions that tempt us away from the true path that we need to construct and follow. As men and women inserted in and formed by a socio-historical context of relations, we become capable of comparing, evaluating, intervening, deciding, taking new directions, and thereby constituting ourselves as ethical beings. It is in our becoming that we constitute our being so. Because the condition of becoming is the condition of being. In addition, it is not possible to imagine the human condition disconnected from the ethical condition. Because to be disconnected from it or to regard it as irrelevant constitutes for us women and men a transgression. For this reason, to transform the experience of educating into a matter of simple technique is to impoverish what is fundamentally human in this experience: namely, its capacity to form the human person. If we have any serious regard for what it means to be human, the teaching of contents cannot be separated from the moral formation of the learners. To educate is essentially to form. To deify or demonize technology or science is an extremely negative way of thinking incorrectly. To act in front of students as if the truth belongs only to the teacher is not only preposterous but also false. To think correctly demands profundity and not superficiality in the comprehension and interpretation of the facts. It presupposes an openness that allows for the revision of conclusions; it recognizes not only the possibility of making a new choice or a new evaluation but also the *right* to do so. However, since there can be no "right thinking" disconnected from ethical principles, it is also clear that the demands of "right thinking" require that the possibility or the right to change be not simply rhetorical. In other words, to claim the right to change requires a coherence that makes a difference. There is no point in making such a claim and continuing as if nothing had changed.

Words Incarnated in Example

The teacher who really teaches, that is, who really works with contents within the context of methodological exactitude, will deny as false the hypocritical formula, "do as I say, not as I do." Whoever is engaged in "right thinking" knows only too well that words not given body (made flesh) have little or no value. Right thinking is right doing.

What are serious students to think of a teacher who for two semesters spoke passionately about the necessity for popular movements to struggle for their autonomy and who today, denying that he has changed, indulges in pragmatic attacks against these same popular classes, attributing little or no value to their utopias, and who himself fully engaged in transferring his own knowledge to his students à la banking system. What can be said of the teacher who until recently, as a member of a leftist party, defended the necessity of education for the working classes and who now, resigned fatalistically to neoliberal pragmatism, is satisfied with the simple professional training of the unemployed, while considering that he is still "progressive" pedagogically and politically?

There is no right thinking that can be separated from a kind of coherent, lived practice that is capable of reformulating contents and paradigms instead of simply negating what is no longer regarded as relevant. It is absurd for teachers to imagine that they are engaged in right thinking and at the same time to relate to the student in a patronizing way.

The attitude, which is a way of being and not just an occasional phase, of the teacher engaged in right thinking demands a seriousness in the search for secure and solid bases for his/her positions. A teacher with such an attitude, while capable of disagreeing with an opponent, does not harbor rancor against that person in such a way that the rancor assumes proportions greater than the reasons for the original disagreement. Once, one such rancorous person forbade a student who was doing a dissertation on literacy and citizenship from reading any of my works. "He is old hat," was the rigorously "neutral" way that he dismissed the "object" that was myself. "If you read his work you will end up the worse for it," was his concluding remark to the student. That is no way to be engaged in right thinking or in right teaching. Integral to right thinking is a generous heart, one that, while not denying the right to anger, can distinguish it from cynicism or unbalanced fury.

Risk, Acceptance of What Is New, and Rejection of Discrimination

Proper to right thinking is a willingness to risk, to welcome the new, which cannot be rejected simply because it is new no more than the old can be rejected because chronologically it is no longer new. The old is capable of remaining new when it remains faithful through time to the experience of original and founding intuitions and inspirations.

It is equally part of right thinking to reject decidedly any and every form of discrimination. Preconceptions of race, class, or sex offend the essence of human dignity and constitute a radical negation of democracy. How far from these values we are when we tolerate the impunity of those who kill a street child; those who murder peasants who struggle for a minimum of justice; those who discriminate on the basis of color, burning churches where blacks pray because prayer is only white; those who treat women as inferior beings; and so on. I feel more pity than rage at the absurd arrogance of this kind of white supremacy, passing itself off to the world as democracy. In fact, this form of thinking and doing is far removed from the humility demanded by "right" thinking. Nor has it anything to do with the good sense that keeps our exaggerations in check and helps us avoid falling into the ridiculous and the senseless.

There are times when I fear that someone reading this, even if not yet totally converted to neoliberal pragmatism but perhaps somewhat contaminated by it, may think that there is no more place among us for the dreamer and the believer in utopia. Yet what I have been saying up to now is not the stuff of inconsequential dreamers. It has to do with the very nature of men and women as makers and dreamers of history and not simply as casualties of an a priori vision of the world.

Given my understanding of human nature, I have no option but to defend the position I have been defending all along. It's a demand about right thinking that I make on myself as I write this text. The demand, that is, that right thinking belongs intimately to right doing. In this sense, to teach right thinking is not something that is simply spoken of or an experience that is merely described. But something that is done and lived while it is being spoken of, as if the doing and living of it constituted a kind of irrefutable witness of its truth. To think correctly implies the existence of subjects whose thinking is mediated by objects that provoke and modify the thinking subject. Thinking correctly is, in other words, not an isolated act or something to draw near in isolation but an act of communication. For this reason, there is no right thinking without understanding, and this understanding, from a correct thinking point of view, is not something transferred but something that belongs essentially to the process of coparticipation. If, from the grammatical point of view, the verb to understand is "transitive," in relation to a correct way of thinking it is also a verb whose subject is always a coparticipant with the other. All understanding, if it is not mechanistically treated, that is, submitted to the alienating care that threatens the mind and that I have been designating as a "bureaucratized" mind, necessarily implies communicability. There is no knowing (that is, connecting one thing to another) something that is not at the same time a "communication" of the something known (unless, of course, the process of knowing has broken down). The act of a correct way of thinking does not "transfer," "deposit," "offer," or "donate" to the other as if the receiver were a passive object of facts, concepts, and intelligibility. To be coherent, the educator who thinks correctly, exercising as a human subject the incontestable practice of comprehension, challenges the learner with whom and to whom she/he communicates to produce her or his understanding of what is being communicated. There is no intelligibility that is not at the same time communication and intercommunication, and that is not grounded in dialogue. For this reason, a correct way of thinking is dialogical and not polemical.

Critical Reflection on Practice

A correct way of thinking knows, for example, that the practice of critical teaching is not built as if thinking correctly were a mere given. However, it knows that without a correct way of thinking, there can be no critical practice. In other words, the practice of critical teaching, implicit in a correct way of thinking, involves a dynamic and dialectical movement between "doing" and "reflecting on doing." The knowledge produced by spontaneous or almost spontaneous teaching practice is ingenuous in the sense that it lacks the methodological rigor that characterizes the epistemological curiosity of a reflecting subject. Such knowledge is not what disciplined, correct thinking seeks. For this reason it is essential that during the experience of teaching preparation, the prospective teacher must realize that a correct way of thinking is not a gift from heaven, nor is it to be found in teachers' guide books, put there by illuminated intellectuals who occupy the center of power. On the contrary, a correct way of thinking that goes beyond the ingenuous must be produced by the learners in communion with the teacher responsible for their education. At the same time, it is necessary to insist that the matrix both of ingenuous and critical thinking is the same curiosity that characterizes all human vitality. In this sense, the untrained teachers in rural areas around Pernambuco, Brazil, or in any of the world's "remote" places, are as curious as the professor of philosophy of education in any university. All that is necessary is that, through reflection on a given practice, ingenuous curiosity perceive itself as such so as to advance to the critical stage.

For this reason, in the process of the ongoing education of teachers, the essential moment is that of critical reflection on one's practice. Thinking critically about practice, of today or yesterday, makes possible the improvement of tomorrow's practice. Even theoretical discourse itself, necessary as it is to critical reflection, must be concrete enough to be clearly identifiable with practice. Its epistemological "distance" from practice as an object of analysis ought to be compensated for by an even greater proximity to the object of analysis, in terms of lived experience. The better this process is accomplished, the greater is the gain in intelligence and the greater the possibility of communicability in overcoming an ingenuous attitude toward knowledge. In addition, the more I acknowledge my own process and attitudes and perceive the reasons behind these, the more I am capable of changing and advancing from the stage of ingenuous curiosity to epistemological curiosity. It's really not possible for someone to imagine himself/herself as a subject in the process of becoming without having at the same time a disposition for change. And change of which she/he is not merely the victim but the subject.

It is an idealistic exaggeration, for example, to imagine that the objective threat that smoking poses to anyone's health and to my life is enough to make me stop smoking. Of course, the objective threat is contextually essential if I am to take any steps at all. But such a threat will only become a "subjective" decision to the degree that it generates new options that can provoke a break with past habits and an acceptance of new commitments: When I assume consciously the danger represented by smoking, I am then moved to reflect on its consequences and to engage in a decision-making process, leading to a break, an option, which becomes concretized, materially speaking, in the practice of "not smoking," a practice grounded on the risk to health and life implicit in smoking.

There is another fundamental element here too: the emotional one. In other words, in addition to the knowledge I have of the harm smoking does to me, I now have, through the consciousness I have acquired of this harm, a sense of legitimate anger. In addition, I have a sense of joy that I was able to be angry because it means that I can continue to live a while longer in the world. The kind of education that does not recognize the right to express appropriate anger against injustice, against disloyalty, against the negation of love, against exploitation, and against violence fails to see the educational role implicit in the expression of these feelings. One thinks of Christ's anger against the merchants in the temple. Of those who struggle for agrarian reform against the enemies of agrarian reform. Of the victims of violence and of discrimination based on class, race, and sex. Of those whose victimization cannot be vindicated because of the perpetrator's impunity. Of those who go hungry against those who not only eat well but also waste food, as if life belonged to them alone. However, it's important to stress the "appropriateness" of this anger; otherwise it simply degenerates into rage and even hatred.

Cultural Identity

It's interesting to take a close look at the verb "to assume," which is a transitive verb and can have as its object the person who assumes his or herself. For example, I can assume the risk inherent in smoking just as much as I can assume myself (what I am) as the subject and object of that assumption. When I say that in order to stop smoking it is essential that I assume that smoking constitutes a risk to my life, what I am really saying is that I have acquired a complete and clear picture of what smoking is and what its consequences are. A more radical sense of "to assume" is when I say: One of the most important tasks of critical educational practice is to make possible the conditions in which the learners, in their interaction with one another and with their teachers, engage in the experience of assuming themselves as social, historical, thinking, communicating, transformative, creative persons; dreamers of possible utopias, capable of being angry because of a capacity to love. Capable of assuming themselves as "subject" because of the capacity to recognize themselves as "object." All this, while bearing in mind that the assumption of oneself does not signify the exclusion of others. Because it is the otherness of the "not I" or the "you" that makes me assume the radicality of the "I." There's another question that cannot be overlooked either, namely, the question of cultural identity in relation to both individuals and classes among the learners and for which (in the context of forward-looking educational practice) respect is absolutely fundamental. It is connected directly to the challenge of assuming who we are, which is what a purely technical, objective, and grammatical vision of education cannot do or be.

The historical, political, social, and cultural experience of men and women can never be acquired outside of the conflict between those forces that are dedicated to the prevention of self-assumption on the part of individuals and groups and those forces that work in favor of such an assumption. Teaching preparation that considers itself to be above such "intrigues" does nothing less than work in favor of the obstacles to self-assumption. The socio-political solidarity that we need today to build a less ugly and less intolerant human community where we can be really what we are cannot neglect the importance of democratic practice. Purely pragmatic training, with its implicit or openly expressed elitist authoritarianism, is incompatible with the learning and practice of becoming a "subject."

Sometimes a simple, almost insignificant gesture on the part of a teacher can have a profound formative effect on the life of a student. I will always remember one such gesture in my life when I was an adolescent. A gesture that marks me profoundly but whose significance on my life was almost certainly not noticed or known by my teacher. At that time I experienced myself as an insecure adolescent, not at home with a body perceived as more bone than beauty, feeling myself to be less capable than the other students, insecure about my own creative possibilities, easily riled, and not very much at peace with the world. The slightest gesture by any of the better-off students in the class was capable of highlighting my insecurity and my fragility.

On this occasion our teacher had brought our homework to school after correcting it and was calling us one by one to comment on it. When my turn came, I noticed he was looking over my text with great attention, nodding his head in an attitude of respect and consideration. His respectful and appreciative attitude had a much greater effect on me than the high classification that he gave me for my work. The gesture of the teacher affirmed in me a self-confidence that obviously still had much room to grow. But it inspired in me a belief that I too had value and could work and produce results—results that clearly had their limits but that were a demonstration of my capacity, which up until that moment I would have been inclined to hide or not fully believe in. And the greatest proof of the importance of that gesture is that I can speak of it now as if it had happened only today.

The importance of the kind of knowledge transmitted by gestures such as these, which are part and parcel of daily school life, needs serious reflection. It's a pity that the socializing character of the school, with its multiple possibilities for formation or deformation, especially in the context of the ordinary informality of the day to day, is so much neglected. What we mostly hear about is the teaching of contents, understood almost always, unfortunately, as the transference of knowledge. One of the reasons, in my view, for this negligence is a too narrow understanding of what education and learning are. Really, it has not yet dawned on us that education is something that women and men discovered experimentally, in the course of history. If it were clear to us that our capacity to teach arose from our capacity to learn, we would easily have understood the importance of informal experiences in the street, in the square, in the work place, in the classroom, in the playground, among the school staff of both teachers and administrative personnel. There is strong "witness" potential in all of these informal situations, but it is, practically speaking, unexplored territory. In "Education in the City," I drew attention to this fact when I discovered the calamitous state of the education system that Luíza Erundina encountered when she took up office in 1989 as mayor of São Paulo, Brazil. On my first visits to the city schools, I saw the calamity with my own eyes and I was terrified. The whole system was a disaster, from the state of the buildings and the classrooms to the quality of the teaching. How was it possible to ask of the children the minimum of respect for their material surroundings when the authorities demonstrated such absolute neglect of and indifference to the public institutions under their care? It's really unbelievable that we are unable to include all these elements in our "rhetoric" about education. Why does such "rhetoric" not include hygiene, cleanliness, beauty? Why does it neglect the indisputable pedagogical value of the "materiality" of the school environment?

Yet, it is such detail in the daily life both of teacher and student, to which so little attention is given, that in fact possesses significant weight in the evaluation of teaching practice. What is important in teaching is not the mechanical repetition of this or that gesture but a comprehension of the value of sentiments, emotions, and desires. Of the insecurity that can only be overcome by inspiring confidence. Of the fear that can only be abated to the degree that courage takes its place.

There is no true teaching preparation possible separated from a critical attitude that spurs ingenuous curiosity to become epistemological curiosity, together with a recognition of the value of emotions, sensibility, affectivity, and intuition. To know is not simply to intuit or to have a hunch, though there is an intimate connection between them. We must build on our intuitions and submit them to methodical and rigorous analysis so that our curiosity becomes epistemological.

TEACHING IS A HUMAN ACT

Commitment

Another type of knowledge that I ought to possess and that has to do with almost all of the others that I have so far spoken of is the understanding that the exercise of my teaching activity does not leave me untouched. No more than I could be out in the rain with no protection and expect not to get wet. We must understand the meaning of a moment of silence, of a smile, or even of an instance in which someone needs to leave the room. Or the fact that a question was asked perhaps a little discourteously. After all, our teaching space is a text that has to be constantly read, interpreted, written, and rewritten. In this sense, the more solidarity there is between teacher and student in the way this space is mutually used, the more possibilities for democratic learning will be opened up in the school.

It is my belief that today the progressive kind of teacher needs to watch out as never before for the clever uses of the dominant ideology of our time, especially its insidious capacity for spreading the idea that it is possible for education to be neutral. This is an extremely reactionary philosophy, which uses the classroom to inculcate in the students political attitudes and practices, as if it were possible to exist as a human being in the world and at the same time be neutral.

My very presence in the school as a teacher is intrinsically a political presence, something that students cannot possibly ignore. In this sense, I ought to transmit to the students my capacity to analyze, to compare, to evaluate, to decide, to opt, to break with. My capacity to be just, to practice justice, and to have a political presence. And as a presence, I cannot sin by omission. I am, by definition, a subject "destined" to choose. To have options. I honor truth. And all that means being ethical. It may help me or hinder me as a teacher, to know that I cannot escape the attention and evaluation of the students. Even so, it ought to make me aware of the care I need to take in carrying out my teaching activity. If I have made a choice for open-minded, democratic practice, then obviously this excludes reactionary, authoritarian, elitist attitudes and actions. Under no circumstances, therefore, may I discriminate against a student. In addition, the perception the student has of my teaching is not exclusively the result of how I act but also of how the student understands my action. Obviously, I cannot spend my life as a teacher asking the students what they think of me and my teaching activity. Even so, I ought to be attentive to their reading of my activity and interaction with them. Furthermore, we need to learn the significance of being ethical. It becomes a way of life.

Education as a Form of Intervention in the World

Another kind of knowledge whose existence I cannot doubt for a moment in my critical educative practice is that education, as a specifically human experience, is a form of intervention in the world. In addition to contents either well or badly taught, this type of intervention also implies both the reproduction of the dominant ideology and its unmasking. The dialectical nature of the educational process does not allow it to be only one or the other of these things.

Education never was, is not, and never can be neutral or indifferent in regard to the reproduction of the dominant ideology or the interrogation of it. It is a fundamental error to state that education is simply an instrument for the reproduction of the dominant ideology, as it is an error to consider it no more than an instrument for unmasking that ideology, as if such a task were something that could be accomplished simplistically, fundamentally, without obstacles and difficult struggles. These attitudes are serious errors, and they indicate a defective vision of both history and consciousness. On the one hand, we have a mechanistic comprehension of history that reduces consciousness to a simple reflex of matter, and on the other, we have a subjective idealism that tries to make the role of consciousness fit into the facts of history. As women and men, we are not simply determined by facts and events. At the same time, we are subject to genetic, cultural, social, class, sexual, and historical conditionings that mark us profoundly and that constitute for us a center of reference.

From the perspective of the dominant classes, there is no doubt of course that educational practice ought to cover up the truth and immobilize the classes. Conversely, these same interests are capable of being "progressive" when it suits them. Progressive by half, so to speak. They are able to bring into being technical advances that are understood and often carried out in a "neutral" way. It would be extremely naive on our part to believe that the ranchers' lobby would agree that our schools, both rural and urban, should discuss the questions of agrarian reform as an economic, political, and ethical problem of the greatest importance for the development of the country. This task falls to progressive-minded educators, both inside and outside the schools. It's a task also for nongovernmental organizations and democratic-minded unions. On the one hand, we might expect modern-minded business with urban roots to be sympathetic to the cause of agrarian reform, because its interests in the expansion of the market seem "progressive" in the face of rural conservatism. On the other hand, the "progressiveness" of modern business, welcome as it is in contrast to the retrograde truculence of the ranchers, does not have to think twice about where its loyalty lies when confronted with a clash between human interests and the interests of the market.

I continue to ponder Marx's observation about the necessary radicality that enables me to be permanently aware of everything that has to do with the defense of human interests, which are superior to those of particular groups or classes of people.

Recognizing that precisely because we are constantly in the process of becoming and, therefore, are capable of observing, comparing, evaluating, choosing, deciding, intervening, breaking with, and making options, we are ethical beings, capable of transgressing our ethical grounding. However, though transgression of this grounding exists as a possibility, we can never claim transgression as a right. And, of course, we cannot sit idly by and fold our arms in the face of such a possibility. Hence my categorical refusal of fatalistic quietude, which, instead of condemning ethical transgression, tries to absorb it as if it belonged to "right" thinking. I cannot be complicit with a perverse system, exempting it from responsibility for its malice, by attributing to "blind forces" the damage caused to human beings.

Of course (and I restate my belief), modern business leaders accept, stimulate, and support technical training courses for their workers.

What they obviously refuse is an education that both includes technical and scientific preparation and speaks of the workers' presence in the world. A human and ethical presence, debased every time it is transformed into pure shadow.

I cannot be a teacher if I do not perceive with ever greater clarity that my practice demands of me a definition about where I stand. A break with what is not right ethically. I must choose between one thing and another thing. I cannot be a teacher and be in favor of everyone and everything. I cannot be in favor merely of people, humanity, vague phrases far from the concrete nature of educative practice. Mass hunger and unemployment, side by side with opulence, are not the result of destiny, as certain reactionary circles would have us believe, claiming that people suffer because they can do nothing about the situation. The question here is not "destiny." It is immorality. Here I want to repeat—forcefully—that nothing can justify the degradation of human beings. Nothing. The advance of science or technology cannot legitimate "class" and call it "order" so that a minority who holds power may use and squander the fruits of the earth while the vast majority are hard pressed even to survive and often justify their own misery as the will of God. I refuse to add my voice to that of the "peacemakers" who call upon the wretched of the earth to be resigned to their fate. My voice is in tune with a different language, another kind of music. It speaks of resistance, indignation, the just anger of those who are deceived and betrayed. It speaks, too, of their right to rebel against the ethical transgressions of which they are the long-suffering victims.

The fatalistic philosophy of neoliberal politics of which I have been speaking is a case in point of how human interests are abandoned whenever they threaten the values of the market.

I cannot imagine, for example, a modern manager allowing one of his workers the right to discuss, during a literacy class or during an in-service training course in the factory, the pros and cons of the dominant ideology. For example, to discuss the question "unemployment today is an end-of-the-century inevitability." And, in that context, to ask: Why is agrarian reform not also an inevitability? And why not make putting an end to hunger and misery inevitable as well?

It's extremely reactionary to say that what only interests workers is achieving the highest grade of technical efficiency and that they do not want to get involved in ideological debates that, in any case, lead nowhere. It is in the context of the work situation that the worker needs to engage in the process of becoming a citizen, something that does not happen as a consequence of "technical efficiency." It is the result of a political struggle to re-creation of a kind of society that is both humane and just.

Thus, since I cannot be a teacher without considering myself prepared to teach well and correctly the contents of my discipline, I cannot reduce my teaching practice to the mere transmission of these contents. It is my ethical posture in the course of teaching these contents that will make the difference. It is a posture made up of my commitment to thoroughness, my investment in excellence, and my competent preparation that reveals humility rather than arrogance. It is a posture of unconditional respect for the students, for the knowledge they have that comes directly from life and that, together with the students, I will work to go beyond. My coherence in the classroom is as important as my teaching of contents. A coherence of what I say, write, and do.

I am a teacher who stands up for what is right against what is indecent, who is in favor of freedom against authoritarianism, who is a supporter of authority against freedom with no limits, and who is a defender of democracy against the dictatorship of right or left. I am a teacher who favors the permanent struggle against every form of bigotry and against the economic domination of individuals and social classes. I am a teacher who rejects the present system of capitalism, responsible for the aberration of misery in the midst of plenty. I am a teacher full of the spirit of hope, in spite of all signs to the contrary. I am a teacher who refuses the disillusionment that consumes and immobilizes. I am a teacher proud of the beauty of my teaching practice, a fragile beauty that may disappear if I do not care for the struggle and knowledge that I ought to teach. If I do not struggle for the material conditions without which my body will suffer from neglect, thus running the risk of becoming frustrated and ineffective, then I will no longer be the witness that I ought to be, no longer the tenacious fighter who may tire but who never gives up. This is a beauty that needs to be marveled at but that can easily slip away from me through arrogance or disdain toward my students.

It's important that students perceive the teacher's struggle to be coherent. And it is necessary that this struggle be the subject of discussion in the classroom from time to time. There are situations in which the teacher's attitude or practice may appear contradictory to the students. This apparent contradiction usually occurs when the teacher simply exercises authority in coordinating the activities of the class in a way that seems to the students an excess of power. At times it may be the teacher who is uncertain whether she or he overstepped the limits of authority or not.

Freedom and Authority

In another part of this text, I referred to the fact that we have not yet resolved the problem of tension between authority and freedom. Because we were dedicated to overcoming the legacy of authoritarianism so prevalent among us, we fell into the opposite error of limitless freedom, accusing the legitimate exercise of authority of being an abuse of authority.

Recently, a young university professor with democratic principles was telling me about what seemed to him an abuse in his way of handling authority. He told me, with a certain air of affliction, that he reacted to the presence of a student from another class who was standing at the half-open door gesticulating to one of the students of his class. In fact, he had to interrupt his teaching because of the disturbance. In so doing, he managed to focus attention on what was central, namely, his teaching activity and the climate necessary for its proper execution, to say nothing of his right and that of his students not to be interrupted by a clearly unacceptable expression of freedom without limits. Even so, he thought his decision had been arbitrary. Not so, in my view. In fact, not to have intervened would have amounted to a demonstration of a lack of real authority, an act of omission in the face of a clearly unacceptable and prejudicial intrusion into his teaching space.

In one of the many debates in which I have participated on the question of freedom and authority and the limits inherent in both (limits without which freedom is perverted into license and authority into authoritarianism), I heard one of the participants say that my "singsong" reminded him of a reactionary teacher he had during the military regime. Freedom, according to my interlocutor, has no limits. It is above any and every limit. Obviously, I did not accept this position. Freedom without limit is as impossible as freedom that is suffocated or contracted. If it were without limit, it would take me outside of the sphere of human action, intervention, or struggle. Limitless freedom is a negation of the human condition of unfinishedness.

The great challenge for the democratic-minded educator is how to transmit a sense of limit that can be ethically integrated by freedom itself. The more consciously freedom assumes its necessary limits, the more authority it has, ethically speaking, to continue to struggle in its own name.

I would like to say once again how much I believe in freedom and how fundamental it is, in the exercise of freedom, to assume responsibility for our decisions. It was this kind of freedom that characterized my own experience as a son, a brother, a student, a teacher, a husband, and a citizen.

Freedom becomes mature in confrontation with other freedoms, defending its rights in relation to parental authority, the authority of teachers, and the authority of the state. It is clear, of course, that adolescents do not always makes the best decisions regarding their future. For that reason it is important for parents to take part in discussions about the future plans of their children. They cannot, ought not, deny that they must know and assume that the future of their children belongs to their children and not to the parents. In my view, it's preferable to emphasize the children's freedom to decide, even if they run the risk of making a mistake, than to simply follow the decision of the parents. It's in making decisions that we learn to decide. I can never learn to be who I am if I never decide anything because I always have the good sense and the wisdom of my mother and father to fall back on. The old arguments of "Imagine the risk you run and the time and opportunity wasted on this crazy idea," are simply invalid. What is pragmatic in our existence cannot be exalted above the ethical imperative that we must face. The child has, at the very least, the right to prove the craziness of his or her idea. However, it is essential to the learning experience of decision making that the consequences of any decision be assumed by the decision maker. There is no decision that is not followed by effects either expected, half expected, or not expected at all. Consequences are what make decision making a responsible process. One of the pedagogical tasks for parents is to make it clear to their children that parental participation in the decision-making process is not an intrusion but a duty, so long as the parents have no intention of deciding on behalf of their children. The participation of the parents is most opportune in helping the children analyze the possible consequences of the decision that is to be taken.

The position of the mother or father is that of someone who, without any risk to her or his authority, is able to accept, humbly, the extremely important role of adviser to a son or daughter. And as an adviser, will never impose a decision or become angry because the parental point of view was not accepted.

What is necessary, fundamentally, is that the son or daughter take on, responsibly and ethically, the weight of his or her own decision, which in fact amounts to a key moment in forging on the development of the individual's autonomy. No one is first autonomous and then makes a decision. Autonomy is the result of a process involving various and innumerable decisions. For example, why not challenge the child while still young to participate in a discussion and a decision about the best time to do schoolwork? Why is the best time for homework always the parent's time? Why waste the opportunity to emphasize the duty and the right that the children have, as people, to engage in the process of forging their own autonomy? No one is the subject of the autonomy of someone else. However, no one suddenly becomes mature at twenty-five years of age. Either we become mature with each day that passes or we do not. Autonomy is a process of becoming oneself, a process of maturing, of coming to be. It does not happen on a given date. In this sense, a pedagogy of autonomy should be centered on experiences that stimulate decision making and responsibility, in other words, on experiences that respect freedom.

One thing is very clear to me today. I have never been afraid of believing in freedom, in seriousness, in genuine love, in solidarity, or in the struggle in which I learned the value and importance of indignation. I have never been afraid of being criticized by my wife, by my children, or by the students with whom I have worked down the years because of my profound conviction of the value of freedom, hope, the word of another, and the desire of someone to try and try again as a result of having been more ingenuous than critical. What I have feared, at different times in my life, is that I might, through my words or gestures, be interpreted as an opportunist, a "realist," "a man with his feet on the ground," one of those experts at balancing things who sits forever on the fence waiting to see which way the wind blows to safely follow it.

Out of respect for freedom I have always deliberately refused its distortion. Freedom is not the absence of limits. What I have sought always is to live the tension, the contradiction, between authority and freedom so as to maintain respect for both. To separate them is to provoke the infraction of one or the other.

It's interesting to note how people who are fond of being authoritarian often think of the respect that is indispensable for freedom as a sort of incorrigible taste for the spontaneous. And those who imagine freedom to have no limits are forever discovering authoritarianism in every legitimate manifestation of authority. The undoubtedly correct position, though the most difficult, is the democratic one, coherent in its utopian pursuit of solidarity and equality. Here, it is not possible to have authority without freedom or vice versa.

Education Is Ideological

What is equally fundamental to the educational practice of the teacher is the question of ideology. Sometimes its presence is greater than we think. It is directly linked to that tendency within us to cloak over the truth of the facts, using language to cloud or turn opaque what we wish to hide. We become myopic. Blind. We become prisoners of artifice. Trapped.

The power of ideology makes me think of those dewy mornings when the mist distorts the outline of the cypress trees and they become shadows of something we know is there but cannot really define. The shortsightedness that afflicts us makes our perception difficult. More serious still is the way we can so easily accept that what we are seeing and hearing is, in fact, what really is and not a distorted version of what is. This tendency to cloud the truth, to become myopic, to deafen our ears, has made many of us accept without critical questioning the cynical fatalism of neoliberal thought, which proclaims that mass unemployment is an inevitable end-of-the-century calamity. Or that the dream is dead and that it is now the era of the pedagogical pragmatism of the technico-scientific training of the individual and not of his or her total education (which, obviously, includes the former). The capacity to tame, inherent in ideology, makes us at times docilely accept that the globalization of the economy is its own invention, a kind of inevitable destiny, an almost metaphysical entity rather than a moment of economic development, subject to a given political orientation dictated by the interests of those who hold power, as is the whole of capitalist economic production. What we hear is that the globalization of the economy is a necessity from which we cannot escape. A given aspect of the capitalist system, an instant of the productive forces of capitalism as experienced and played out in the centers of world economic power, is made universal, as if Brazil, Mexico, and Argentina ought to participate in the globalization of the economy in the same way as the United States, Germany, and Japan. It's a question of jumping on the train in the middle of the journey without discussing the conditions, the cultures, or the forms of production of the countries that are being swept along. And there is no talk about the distance that separates the "rights" of the strong and their power to enjoy them from the fragility of the weak in their attempts to exercise their rights. Meanwhile, responsibilities and duties are leveled—equal for all. If globalization means the abolition of the frontiers and the opening without restriction to free enterprise, those who cannot compete simply disappear.

For example, no one asks whether societies now at the forefront of globalization would, in a previous stage of capitalism, have been ready and willing to accept a radical opening of their frontiers—the type of opening that they now consider imperative for the rest of the world. They demand of the rest of the world now what they were unwilling to demand of themselves. One of the tricks of their fatalistic ideology is the capacity to convince submissive economies (which will be engulfed in this process) that the real world is this way, that there is nothing to be done about it except to follow the natural order of the facts. It passes off this ideology as natural or almost natural. It does not want us to see and understand the phenomenon as a product of historical development.

Globalization theory, which speaks of ethics, hides the fact that its ethics are those of the marketplace and not the universal ethics of the human person. It is for these matters that we ought to struggle courageously if we have, in truth, made a choice for a humanized world. A world of real people. Globalization theory cleverly hides, or seeks to cloud over, an intensified new edition of that fearful evil that is historical capitalism, even if the new edition is somewhat modified in relation to past versions. Its fundamental ideology seeks to mask that what is really up for discussion is the increasing wealth of the few and the rapid increase of poverty and misery for the vast majority of humanity.

The capitalist system reaches, in its globalizing neoliberal crusade, the maximum efficacy of its intrinsically evil nature.

It is my hope that the world will get over its fascination with the end of communism and with the fall of the Berlin wall. And thus remake itself so as to refuse the dictatorship of the marketplace, founded as it is on the perverse ethic of profit.

I don't believe that women and men of the world, independent of their political positions yet conscious of their dignity as men and women, will not want to reflect on the sense of foreboding that is now universal in this perverse era of neoliberal philosophy. A foreboding that one day will lead to a new rebellion where the critical word, the humanist philosophy, the commitment to solidarity, the prophetic denunciation of the negation of men and women, and the proclamation of a world worthy of human habitation will be the instruments of change and transformation.

A century and a half ago, Marx and Engels cried out in favor of the unity of the working classes of the world against their exploitation. Now, in our time, it is essential and urgent that people unite against the threat that looms over us. The threat, namely, to our own identity as human persons caught up in the ferocity of the ethics of the marketplace.

It is in this sense that I say that I have never abandoned my first preoccupation, one that has been with me since my early experiences in the field of education. Namely, my preoccupation with human nature. It is in this preoccupation that I continue to proclaim my loyalty. Even before I ever read Marx I had made his words my own. I had taken my own radical stance on the defense of the legitimate interests of the human person. There is no theory of socio-political transformation that moves me if it is not grounded in an understanding of the human person as a maker of history and as one made by history. If it does not respect men and women as beings of decision, rupture, option. As ethical beings who in their ethicality are capable of being unethical, of transgressing the ethical code indispensable for human living. Of this I have spoken insistently in this text. I have affirmed and reaffirmed the extent to which I rejoice in knowing that I am a "conditioned" being, capable of going beyond my own conditioning. The place upon which a new rebellion should be built is not the ethics of the marketplace with its crass insensitivity to the voice of genuine humanity but the ethics of universal human aspiration. The ethics of human solidarity.

I prefer to be criticized as an idealist and an inveterate dreamer because I continue to believe in the human person, continue to struggle for legislation that would protect people from the unjust and aggressive inroads of those who have no regard for an ethical code that is common to us all. The freedom of commerce cannot be ethically higher than the freedom to be human. The freedom of commerce without limits is no more than the license to put profit above everything else. It becomes a privilege of the few, who in certain favorable conditions increase their own power at the expense of the greater part of humanity, even to the point of survival itself. A textile factory that is forced to close because it cannot compete with the price of labor in Asia, for example, not only brings down the factory owner (who may or may not be a transgressor of that universal ethical code of which I have spoken) but signals the expulsion of hundreds of workers from the process of production. And what about their families? I refuse, with all the conviction I can muster, to accept that our presence in history can be reduced to a deterministic adaptation to our socio-historical condition. As I have said before, worldwide unemployment is not a fatalistic inevitability. It is the result of the economic globalization and the scientific and technological advances that lack a form of ethics that serves the interests of all human beings and not just the unfettered greed of the power minority who control the world today. The application of technological advances, which requires the sacrifice of thousands of people, is one more example of how we can be transgressors of a universal human ethic in the name of the market, of pure profit.

One of the transgressions of a universal human ethic that ought to be considered criminal is programmed mass unemployment, which leads so many to despair and to a kind of living death. Thus, the preoccupation with techno-professional education for the retraining of those who have become redundant would have to be greatly increased to begin to redress the balance.

I would like to make it clear that I know full well how difficult it is to put in practice a policy of development that would put men and women before profit. However, I believe that if we are going to overcome the crises that at present assail us, we must return to ethics. I do not see any other alternative. If it is impossible to have development without profit, then profit of its own accord cannot be the sole object of development in such a way that it justifies and sanctifies the immoral gain of the investor. It may be the utopia of a minority (which will also wither like the grass) to create a society robotized by highly intelligent machines that can substitute men and women in a whole range of activities, creating millions of Peters and Marys without anything to do. But such a utopia is worthless.

I also do not believe that a universal human ethic can be squeezed into the narrow confines of dictatorship, whether of the left or of the right. The authoritarian road is in itself a denial of our restless, questioning, searching nature, which, if lost, means the loss of liberty itself.

It's exactly for this reason that I, as a teacher, ought to be aware of the power of ideological discourse, beginning with discourse that proclaims the death of all ideologies. In truth, I can only put an end to all ideologies by proclaiming a new ideology, even if I am not aware of the ideological nature of my proclamation. It is a very subtle question because all ideological discourse has an immense persuasive power. It anesthetizes the mind, confuses curiosity, blurs perception.

The following statements reveal explicit and implicit ideological contents. They are often spoken uncritically. They deserve, however, a minimum of critical consciousness.

"Negroes are genetically inferior to whites. It's a pity, but it's a fact established by science."

"He killed his wife in legitimate defense of his honor."

"What can be expected of them anyway? Only a band of rabble-rousers would invade land."

"These people are always the same. Give them an inch and they will take a mile."

"We already know what the people need and want. Asking them is a waste of time."

"He is from the northeast of Brazil. But he is a good chap. Serious and helpful."

"Do you know to whom you are talking?"

"Imagine it! A man marrying a man. And a woman marrying a woman!"

"If a black man doesn't dirty the place coming in, he'll do it on the way out."

"The government ought to invest in those places where the taxpayers live!"

"There is no need for you to do the thinking. All you have to do is vote for this candidate and he will do the thinking for you."

"Even if you are unemployed, don't be ungrateful. There is a candidate who will help you. Vote for him."

"Brazil was discovered by Cabral."

In the course of the critical exercise of my resistance to the manipulative power of ideology, I bring to birth certain qualities that in turn become a store of wisdom, indispensable to my teaching practice. On the one hand, the necessity for this critical resistance creates in me an attitude of permanent openness toward others, toward the word; on the other hand, it generates in me a methodical mistrust that prevents me from becoming absolutely certain of being right. To safeguard myself against the pitfalls of ideology, I cannot and must not close myself off from others or shut myself into a blind alley where only my own truth is valid. On the contrary, the best way to keep awake and alert my capacity for right thinking, to sharpen my perception, and to hear with respect (and therefore in a disciplined manner) is to allow myself to be open to differences and to refuse the entrenched dogmatism that makes me incapable of learning anything new. In essence, the correct posture of one who does not consider him- or herself to be the sole possessor of the truth or the passive object of ideology or gossip is the attitude of permanent openness. Openness to approaching and being approached, to questioning and been questioned, to agreeing and disagreeing. It is an openness to life itself and to its vicissitudes. An openness to those who call on us and to the many and varied signs that catch our interests, from the song of the bird, to the falling rain or the rain that is about to drop from the darkening sky, to the gentle smile of innocence and the sullen face of disapproval, to the arms open to receive and the body stiff with refusal and fear. It is in my permanent openness to life that I give myself entirely, my critical thought, my feeling, my curiosity, my desire, all that I am. It is thus that I travel the road, knowing that I am learning to be who I am by relating to what is my opposite.

And the more I give myself to the experience of living with what is different without fear and without prejudice, the more I come to know the self I am shaping and that is being shaped as I travel the road of life.

THE ADULT LITERACY PROCESS AS CULTURAL ACTION FOR FREEDOM*

Every Educational Practice Implies a Concept of Man and the World

Experience teaches us not to assume that the obvious is clearly understood. So it is with the truism with which we begin: All educational practice implies a theoretical stance on the educator's part. This stance in turn implies—sometimes more, sometimes less explicitly—an interpretation of man and the world. It could not be otherwise. The process of men's orientation in the world involves not just the association of sense images, as for animals. It involves, above all, thought-language; that is, the possibility of the act of knowing through his praxis, by which man transforms reality. For man, this process of orientation in the world can be understood neither as a purely subjective event, nor as an objective or mechanistic one, but only as an event in which subjectivity and objectivity are united. Orientation in the world, so understood, places the question of the purposes of action at the level of critical perception of reality.

If, for animals, orientation in the world means adaptation to the world, for man it means humanizing the world by transforming it. For animals there is no historical sense, no options or values in their orientation in the world; for man there is both an historical and a value dimension. Men have the sense of "project," in contrast to the instinctive routines of animals.

The action of men without objectives, whether the objectives are right or wrong, mythical or demythologized, naive or critical, is not praxis, though it may be orientation in the world. And not being praxis, it is action ignorant both of its own process and of its aim. The interrelation of the awareness of aim and of process is the basis for planning action, which implies methods, objectives, and value options.

Paulo Freire, "The Adult Literacy Process as Cultural Action for Freedom," *Harvard Educational Review*, Volume 40, No. 2 (May 1970), pp. 205-225. Copyright © by the Center for the Study of Development and Social Change and Paulo Freire. Published and distributed by the Harvard Educational Review. All rights reserved. For more information, please visit www.harvardeducationalreview.org. Reprinted by permission.

*The author gratefully acknowledges the contributions of Loretta Slover, who translated this essay, and João da Veiga Coutinho and Robert Riordan, who assisted in the preparation of the manuscript.

Teaching adults to read and write must be seen, analyzed, and understood in this way. The critical analyst will discover in the methods and texts used by educators and students practical value options which betray a philosophy of man, well or poorly outlined, coherent or incoherent. Only someone with a mechanistic mentality, which Marx would call "grossly materialistic," could reduce adult literacy learning to a purely technical action. Such a naive approach would be incapable of perceiving that technique itself as an instrument of men in their orientation in the world is not neutral.

We shall try, however, to prove by analysis the self-evidence of our statement. Let us consider the case of primers used as the basic texts for teaching adults to read and write. Let us further propose two distinct types: a poorly done primer and a good one, according to the genre's own criteria. Let us even suppose that the author of the good primer based the selection of its generative words[1] on a prior knowledge of which words have the greatest resonance for the learner (a practice not commonly found, though it does exist).

Doubtlessly, such an author is already far beyond the colleague who composes his primer with words he himself chooses in his own library. Both authors, however, are identical in a fundamental way. In each case they themselves decompose the given generative words and from the syllables create new words. With these words, in turn, the authors form simple sentences and, little by little, small stories, the so-called reading lessons.

Let us say that the author of the second primer, going one step further, suggests that the teachers who use it initiate discussions about one or another word, sentence, or text with their students.

Considering either of these hypothetical cases we may legitimately conclude that there is an implicit concept of man in the primer's method and content, whether it is recognized by the authors or not. This concept can be reconstructed from various angles. We begin with the fact, inherent in the idea and use of the primer, that it is the teacher who chooses the words and proposes them to the learner. Insofar as the primer is the mediating object between the teacher and students, and the students are to be "filled" with words the teachers have chosen, one can easily detect a first important dimension of the image of man which here begins to emerge. It is the profile of a man whose consciousness is "spatialized," and must be "filled" or "fed" in order to know. This same conception led Sartre, criticizing the notion that "to know is to eat," to exclaim: *"O philoso-phie alimentaire!"*[2]

This "digestive" concept of knowledge, so common in current educational practice, is found very clearly in the primer.[3] Illiterates are considered "under-nourished," not in the literal sense in which many of them really are, but because they lack the "bread of the spirit." Consistent with the concept of knowledge as food, illiteracy is conceived of as a "poison herb," intoxicating and debilitating persons who cannot read or write. Thus, much is said about the "eradication" of illiteracy to cure the disease.[4] In this way, deprived of their character as linguistic signs constitutive of man's thought-language, words are transformed into mere "deposits of vocabulary"—the bread of the spirit which the illiterates are to "eat" and "digest."

This "nutritionist" view of knowledge perhaps also explains the humanitarian character of certain Latin American adult literacy campaigns. If millions of men are illiterate, "starving for letters," "thirsty for words," the word must be *brought* to them to save them from "hunger" and "thirst." The word, according to the naturalistic concept of consciousness implicit in the primer, must be "deposited," not born of the creative effort of the learners. As understood in this concept, man is a passive being, the object of the process of learning to read and write, and not its subject. As object his task is to "study" the so-called reading lessons, which in fact are almost completely alienating and alienated, having so little, if anything, to do with the student's socio-cultural reality.[5]

It would be a truly interesting study to analyze the reading texts being used in private or official adult literacy campaigns in rural and urban Latin America. It would not be unusual to find among such texts sentences and readings like the following random samples:[6]

> *A asa é da ave*—"The wing is of the bird."
> *Eva viu a uva*—"Eva saw the grape."
> *O galo canta*—"The cock crows."
> *O cachorro ladra*—"The dog barks."
> *Maria gosta dos animais*—"Mary likes animals."
> *João cuida das arvores*—"John takes care of the trees."

> *O pai de Carlinhos se chama Antonio. Carlinhos é um bom menino, bem comportado e estudioso*—"Charles's father's name is Antonio. Charles is a good, well-behaved, and studious boy."
> *Ada deu o dedo ao urubu? Duvido, Ada deu o dedo a arara. . . .*[7]

Se você trabalha com martelo e prego, tenha cuidado para nao furar o dedo.—"If you hammer a nail, be careful not to smash your finger."[8]

"Peter did not know how to read. Peter was ashamed. One day, Peter went to school and registered for a night course. Peter's teacher was very good. Peter knows how to read now. Look at Peter's face. [These lessons are generally illustrated.] Peter is smiling. He is a happy man. He already has a good job. Everyone ought to follow his example."

In saying that Peter is smiling because he knows how to read, that he is happy because he now has a good job, and that he is an example for all to follow, the authors establish a relationship between knowing how to read and getting good jobs which, in fact, cannot be borne out. This naiveté reveals, at least, a failure to perceive the structure not only of illiteracy, but of social phenomena in general. Such an approach may admit that these phenomena exist, but it cannot perceive their relationship to the structure of the society in which they are found. It is as if these phenomena were mythical, above and beyond concrete situations, or the results of the intrinsic inferiority of a certain class of men. Unable to grasp contemporary illiteracy as a typical manifestation of the "culture of silence," directly related to underdeveloped structures, this approach cannot offer an objective, critical response to the challenge of illiteracy. Merely teaching men to read and write does not work miracles; if there are not enough jobs for men able to work, teaching more men to read and write will not create them.

One of these readers presents among its lessons the following two texts on consecutive pages without relating them. The first is about May 1st, the Labor Day holiday, on which workers commemorate their struggles. It does not say how or where these are commemorated, or what the nature of the historical conflict was. The main theme of the second lesson is *holidays*. It says that "on these days people ought to go to the beach to swim and sunbathe . . ." Therefore, if May 1st is a holiday, and if on holidays people should go to the beach, the conclusion is that the workers should go swimming on Labor Day, instead of meeting with their unions in the public squares to discuss their problems.

Analysis of these texts reveals, then, a simplistic vision of men, of their world, of the relationship between the two, and of the literacy process which unfolds in that world.

A asa é da ave, Eva viu a uva, o galo canta, and *o cachorro late,* are linguistic contexts which, when mechanically memorized and repeated, are deprived of their authentic dimension as thought-language in dynamic interplay with reality. Thus impoverished, they are not authentic expressions of the world.

Their authors do not recognize in the poor classes the ability to know and even create the texts which would express their own thought-language at the level of their perception of the world. The authors repeat with the texts what they do with the words, i.e., they introduce them into the learners' consciousness as if it were empty space—once more, the "digestive" concept of knowledge.

Still more, the a-structural perception of illiteracy revealed in these texts exposes the other false view of illiterates as marginal men.[9] Those who consider them marginal must, nevertheless, recognize the existence of a reality to which they are marginal—not only physical space, but historical, social, cultural, and economic realities—i.e., the structural dimension of reality. In this way, illiterates have to be recognized as beings "outside of," "marginal to" something, since it is impossible to be marginal to nothing. But being "outside of" or "marginal to" necessarily implies a movement of the one said to be marginal from the center, where he was, to the periphery. This movement, which is an action, presupposes in turn not only an agent but also his reasons. Admitting the existence of men "outside of" or "marginal to" structural reality, it seems legitimate to ask: Who is the author of this movement from the center of the structure to its margin? Do so-called marginal men, among them the illiterates, make the decision to move out to the periphery of society? If so, marginality is an option with all that it involves: hunger, sickness, rickets, pain, mental deficiencies, living death, crime, promiscuity, despair, the impossibility of being. In fact, however, it is difficult to accept that 40% of Brazil's population, almost 90% of Haiti's, 60% of Bolivia's, about 40% of Peru's, more than 30% of Mexico's and Venezuela's, and about 70% of Guatemala's would have made the tragic *choice* of their own marginality as illiterates.[10] If, then, marginality is not by choice, marginal man has been expelled from and kept outside of the social system and is therefore the object of violence.

In fact, however, the social structure as a whole does not "expel," nor is marginal man a "being outside of." He is, on the contrary, a "being inside of," within the social structure, and in a dependent relationship to those whom we call falsely autonomous beings, inauthentic beings-for-themselves.

A less rigorous approach, one more simplistic, less critical, more technicist, would say that it was unnecessary to reflect about what it would consider unimportant questions such as illiteracy and teaching adults to read and write. Such an approach might even add that the discussion of the concept of marginality is an unnecessary academic exercise. In fact, however, it is not so. In accepting the illiterate as a person who exists on the fringe of society, we are led to envision him as a sort of "sick man," for whom literacy would be the "medicine" to cure him, enabling him to "return" to the "healthy" structure from which he has become separated. Educators would be benevolent counsellors, scouring the outskirts of the city for the stubborn illiterates, runaways from the good life, to restore them to the forsaken bosom of happiness by giving them the gift of the word.

In the light of such a concept—unfortunately, all too widespread—literacy programs can never be efforts toward freedom; they will never question the very reality which deprives men of the right to speak up—not only illiterates, but all those who are treated as objects in a dependent relationship. These men, illiterate or not, are, in fact, not marginal. What we said before bears repeating: They are not "beings outside of"; they are "beings for another." Therefore the solution to their problem is not to become "beings inside of," but men freeing themselves; for, in reality, they are not marginal to the structure, but oppressed men within it. Alienated men, they cannot overcome their dependency by "incorporation" into the very structure responsible for their dependency. There is no other road to humanization—theirs as well as everyone else's—but authentic transformation of the dehumanizing structure.

From this last point of view, the illiterate is no longer a person living on the fringe of society, a marginal man, but rather a representative of the dominated strata of society, in conscious or unconscious opposition to those who, in the same structure, treat him as a thing. Thus, also, teaching men to read and write is no longer an inconsequential matter of *ba, be, bi, bo, bu,* of memorizing an alienated word, but a difficult apprenticeship in naming the world.

In the first hypothesis, interpreting illiterates as men marginal to society, the literacy process reinforces the mythification of reality by keeping it opaque and by dulling the "empty consciousness" of the learner with innumerable alienating words and phrases. By contrast, in the second hypothesis—interpreting illiterates as men oppressed within the system—the literacy process, as a cultural action for freedom, is an act of knowing in which the learner assumes the role of knowing subject in a dialogue with the educator. For this very reason, it is a courageous endeavor to demythologize reality, a process through which men who had previously been submerged in reality begin to emerge in order to re-insert themselves into it with critical awareness.

The Adult Literacy Process as an Act of Knowing

To be an act of knowing the adult literacy process demands among teachers and students a relationship of authentic dialogue. True dialogue unites subjects together in the cognition of a knowable object which mediates between them.

If learning to read and write is to constitute an act of knowing, the learners must assume from the beginning the role of creative subjects. It is not a matter of memorizing and repeating given syllables, words, and phrases, but rather of reflecting critically on the process of reading and writing itself, and on the profound significance of language.

Insofar as language is impossible without thought, and language and thought are impossible without the world to which they refer, the human word is more than mere vocabulary—it is word-and-action. The cognitive dimensions of the literacy process must include the relationships of men with their world. These relationships are the source of the dialectic between the products men achieve in transforming the world and the conditioning which these products in turn exercise on men.

Learning to read and write ought to be an opportunity for men to know what *speaking the word* really means: a human act implying reflection and action. As such it is a primordial human right and not the privilege of a few.[11] Speaking the word is not a true act if it is not at the same time associated with the right of self-expression and world-expression, of creating and re-creating, of deciding and choosing and ultimately participating in society's historical process.

Notes

1. In languages like Portuguese or Spanish, words are composed syllabically. Thus, every non-monosyllabic word is, technically, *generative*, in the sense that other words can be constructed from its de-composed syllables. For a

word to be authentically generative, however, certain conditions must be present which will be discussed in a later section of this essay. [At the phonetic level the term *generative word* is properly applicable only with regard to a sound-syllabic reading methodology, while the thematic application is universal. See Sylvia Ashton-Warner's *Teacher* for a different treatment of the concept of generative words at the thematic level.—Editor]

2. Jean Paul Sartre, *Situations I* (Paris: Librairie Gallimard, 1947), p. 31.

3. The digestive concept of knowledge is suggested by "controlled readings," by classes which consist only in lectures; by the use of memorized dialogues in language learning; by bibliographical notes which indicate not only which chapter, but which lines and words are to be read; by the methods of evaluating the students' progress in learning.

4. See Paulo Freire, "La alfabetizacion de adultos, critica de su vision ingenua; compreension de su vision critica," in *Introducción a la Acción Cultural* (Santiago: ICIRA, 1969).

5. There are two noteworthy exceptions among these primers: (1) in Brazil, *Viver e Lutar,* developed by a team of specialists of the Basic Education Movement, sponsored by the National Conference of Bishops. (This reader became the object of controversy after it was banned as subversive by the then governor of Guanabara, Mr. Carlos Lacerda, in 1963.) (2) in Chile, the ESPIGA collection, despite some small defects. The collection was organized by Jefatura de Planes Extraordinarios de Educación de Adultos, of the Public Education Ministry.

6. Since at the time this essay was written the writer did not have access to the primers, and was, therefore, vulnerable to recording phrases imprecisely or to confusing the author of one or another primer, it was thought best not to identify the authors or the titles of the books.

7. The English here would be nonsensical, as is the Portuguese, the point being the emphasis on the consonant *d.*—Editor

8. The author may even have added here, ". . . If, however, this should happen, apply a little mercurochrome."

9. [The Portuguese word here translated as *marginal man* is *marginado.* This has a passive sense: he who has been made marginal, or sent outside society; as well as the sense of a state of existence on the fringe of society.—Translator.]

10. UNESCO: La situación educativa en América Latina, Cuadro no. 20, page 263 (Paris, 1960).

11. Paulo Freire, *op. cit.*

15

JACQUES RANCIERE

Jacques Ranciere, French philosopher, was born in 1940 and is today a professor emeritus at the University of Paris–VIII (St. Denis). During the 1960s in France, he was a student of the highly influential Marxist scholar Louis Althusser, with whom Ranciere and others co-authored the now classic book *Reading Capital*. But during the May 1968 uprising in Paris, when students and workers joined in a general strike against the conservative de Gaulle government, Ranciere broke his intellectual and political ties with Althusser. Ranciere felt that Althusser's notion of the role of the philosopher was elitist and that his interpretation of working-class culture was reductive and one-dimensional. As such, Ranciere began a series of archival investigations into the forgotten and distorted traditions of working-class men and women in France. Key to Ranciere's analysis was a rupture with traditional thinking (represented by Althusser), which assumed that only philosophers and intellectuals can think great thoughts while the masses labor. Through extensive research, culminating in the book *The Nights of Labor* (1981), Ranciere discovered that, in the 19th century, French workers not only were capable of thought but were publishing their own newspapers, writing poetry, dreaming of utopias, etc. In other words, workers had rich cultural traditions that disturbed the simplistic division of labor between thinkers and workers found in Althusser's writing.

Ranciere needed a new starting point for his political and educational philosophy. His new hypothesis became that everyone thinks and everyone speaks. This statement sounds simple, yet it has rarely been endorsed in the history of Western thought. For Ranciere, the philosopher tells us we are ignorant in order to maintain his or her power and prestige in society as the sole arbiter of truth. Here ignorance is an invention of an elite intellectual class; it is the result of power inequalities and a mechanism for maintaining power inequalities. The assumption that *some* think and *some* speak is, for Ranciere, a denial of the fundamental presupposition of democracy: we are all equal. In his book *The Philosopher and His Poor* (1983), Ranciere argued that even leftist educational sociologists, such as Pierre Bourdieu, simply reinforce the traditional division of labor. Sociology assumes that schools reproduce social inequality. As far as it goes, Ranciere agrees. But this thesis is problematic on two levels: (a) the strict divisions as described by Bourdieu miss those very real moments of mixing that introduce confusion into social stratification (as when excluded students suddenly reveal themselves capable of excelling in the very disciplines which schooling implicitly excludes them from) and (b) Bourdieu remains an elitist, for only the critical sociologist can read and correctly interpret how schools reproduce inequality. In other words, it is assumed that, without the sociologist, teachers and students would never be able to understand the ways in which the school system excludes or oppresses them. Thus, philosophy and sociology have consistently denied the ability of everyone to think and to speak.

Politics for Ranciere is the moment of disruption of the division of labor or the hierarchies in society by those who are commonly thought not to be able to speak or think. This disruption happens when the poor liberate the language of equality from those privileged few who have reserved it for themselves. For example, "All men are created equal" has been appropriated by African Americans and women who have traditionally been excluded from thinking and speaking by white, property-owning men. Thus, the division of labor that seemed "natural" is interrupted when the marginalized and the invisible appropriate the language of the oppressors in order to reveal that they, too, can think and speak.

Ranciere's educational philosophy is an attempt to found a new notion of pedagogy that does not assume that only some think and some speak. Once again turning to the French archives, Ranciere discovered a little-known educator by the name of Joseph Jocotot, who, in the 1830s, discovered that anyone can teach anything even if one is completely ignorant of the subject matter. The following excerpt is an analysis of Jocotot's controversial method. Jocotot makes us question what equality means in education, an important question to bear in mind, considering the ethical mandate of No Child Left Behind (NCLB). If we take Jocotot seriously, what is the presupposition behind NCLB? Is the presupposition democratic, or is there a latent belief that only some can think and some can speak? How can teachers act with students to create spaces in which traditional hierarchies and divisions are challenged?

REFERENCES

Cho, Daniel. "Teaching Abjection: A Response to the War on Terror." *Teaching Education* 16, no. 2 (2005): 103–15.

Hallward, Peter. "Jacques Ranciere and the Subversion of Mastery." *Paragraph* 28, no. 1 (2005): 26–45.

Ranciere, Jacques. *The Ignorant Schoolmaster: Five Lessons in Intellectual Emancipation.* Stanford, CA: Stanford University Press, 1991.

Ranciere, Jacques. *The Philosopher and His Poor.* Durham: Duke University Press, 2004.

Woodill, Gary. *"The Ignorant Schoolmaster* (Book Review)." *The Review of Education* 15, no. 1 (1993): 49–54.

THE IGNORANT SCHOOLMASTER

Five Lessons in Intellectual Emancipation

In 1818, Joseph Jacotot, a lecturer in French literature at the University of Louvain, had an intellectual adventure.

A long and eventful career should have made him immune to surprises: he had celebrated his nineteenth birthday in 1789. He was at that time teaching rhetoric at Dijon and preparing for a career in law. In 1792, he served as an artilleryman in the Republican armies. Then, under the Convention, he worked successively as instructor for the Bureau of Gunpowder, secretary to the Minister of War, and substitute for the director of the Ecole Polytechnique. When he returned to Dijon, he taught analysis, ideology, ancient languages, pure mathematics, transcendent mathematics, and law. In March 1815, the esteem of his countrymen made him a deputy in spite of himself. The return of the Bourbons forced him into exile, and by the generosity of the King of the Netherlands he obtained a position as a professor at half-pay. Joseph Jacotot was acquainted with the laws of hospitality and counted on spending some calm days in Louvain.

Chance decided differently. The unassuming lecturer's lessons were, in fact, highly appreciated by his students. Among those who wanted to avail themselves of him were a good number of students who did not speak French; but Joseph Jacotot knew no Flemish. There was thus no language in which he could teach them what they sought from him. Yet he wanted to respond to their wishes. To do so, the minimal link of a *thing in common* had to be established between himself and them. At that time, a bilingual edition of *Télémaque* was being published in Brussels. The thing in common had been found, and Telemachus made his way into the life of Joseph Jacotot. He had the book delivered to the students and asked them, through an interpreter, to learn the French text with the help of the translation. When they had made it through the first half of the book, he had them repeat what they had learned over and over, and then told them to read through the rest of the book until they could recite it. This was a fortunate solution, but it was also, on a small scale, a philosophical experiment in the style of the ones performed during the Age of Enlightenment. And Joseph Jacotot, in 1818, remained a man of the preceding century.

But the experiment exceeded his expectations. He asked the students who had prepared as instructed to write in French what they thought about what they had read:

> He expected horrendous barbarisms, or maybe a complete inability to perform. How could these young people, deprived of explanation, understand and resolve the difficulties of a language entirely new to them? No matter! He had to find out where the route opened by chance had taken them, what had been the results of that desperate empiricism. And how surprised he was to discover that the students, left to themselves, managed this difficult step as well as many French could have done! Was wanting all that was necessary for doing? Were all men virtually capable of understanding what others had done and understood?

Such was the revolution that this chance experiment unleashed in his mind. Until then, he had believed what all conscientious professors believe: that the important business of the master is to transmit his knowledge to his student so as to bring them, by degrees, to his own level of expertise. Like all conscientious professors, he knew that teaching was not in the slightest about cramming students with knowledge and having them repeat it like parrots, but he knew equally well that students had to avoid the chance detours where minds still incapable of distinguishing the essential from the accessory, the principle from the consequence, get lost. In short, the essential act of the master was to *explicate:* to disengage the simple elements of learning, and to reconcile their simplicity in principle with the factual simplicity that characterizes young and ignorant minds. To teach was to transmit learning and form minds simultaneously, by leading those minds, according to an ordered progression, from the most simple to the most complex.

The Old Master would say: such and such a thing must be learned, and then this other thing and after that, this other. Selection, progression, incompletion: these are his principle. We learn rules and elements, then apply them to some chosen reading passages, and then do some exercises based on the acquired rudiments. Then we graduate to a higher level: other rudiments, another book, other exercises, another professor. At each stage the abyss of ignorance is dug again; the professor fills it in before digging another. Fragments add up, detached pieces of an explicator's knowledge that put the student on a trail, following a master with whom he will never catch up. The book is never whole, the lesson is never finished. The master always keeps a piece of learning—that is to say, a piece of the student's ignorance—up his sleeve. I understood that, says the satisfied student. You think so, corrects the master. In fact, there's a difficulty here that I've been sparing you until now. We will explain it when we get to the corresponding lesson. What does this mean? asks the curious student. I could tell you, responds the master, but it would be premature: you wouldn't understand at all. It will be explained to you next year. The master is always a length ahead of the student, who always feels that in order to go farther he must have another master, supplementary explications. . . .

These are in fact the master's two fundamental acts. He *interrogates*, he demands speech, that is to say, the manifestation of an intelligence that wasn't aware of itself or that had given up. And he *verifies* that the work of the intelligence is done with attention, that the words don't say anything in order to escape from the constraint. Is a highly skilled, very learned master necessary to perform this? On the contrary, the learned master's science makes it very difficult for him not to *spoil* the method. He knows the response, and his questions lead the student to it naturally. This is the secret of good masters: through their questions, they discreetly guide the student's intelligence—discreetly enough to make it work, but not to the point of leaving it to itself. There is a Socrates sleeping in every explicator. And it must be very clear how the Jacotot method—that is to say, the student's method—differs radically from the method of the Socratic master. Through his interrogations, Socrates leads Meno's slave to recognize the mathematical truths that lie within himself. This may be the path to learning, but it is in no way a path to emancipation. On the contrary, Socrates must take the slave by his hand so that the latter can find what is inside himself. The demonstration of his knowledge is just as much the demonstration of his powerlessness: he will never walk by himself, unless it is to illustrate the master's lesson. In this case, Socrates interrogates a slave who is destined to remain one.

This is how all conscientious professors reason. This was how Joseph Jacotot, in his thirty years at the job, had reasoned and acted. But now, by chance, a grain of sand had gotten into the machine. . . .

The students had learned without a master explicator, but not, for all that, without a master. They did not know how before, and now they knew how. Therefore, Jacotot had taught them something. And yet he had communicated nothing to them of his science. So it wasn't the master's science that the student learned. His mastery lay in the command that had enclosed the students in a closed circle from which they alone could break out. By leaving his intelligence out of the picture, he had allowed their intelligence to grapple with that of the book. Thus, the two functions that link the practice of the master explicator, that of the savant and that of the master had been dissociated. The two faculties in play during the act of learning, namely intelligence and will, had therefore also been separated, liberated from each other. A pure relationship of will to will had been established between master and student; a relationship wherein the master's domination resulted in an entirely liberated relationship between the intelligence of the student and that of the book—the intelligence of the book that was also the thing in common, the egalitarian intellectual link between master and student. This device allowed the jumbled categories of the pedagogical act to be sorted out, and explicative stultification to be precisely defined. There is stultification whenever one intelligence is subordinated to another. A person—and a child in particular—may need a master when his own will is not strong enough to set him on track and keep him there. But that subjection is purely one of will over will. It becomes stultification when it links an intelligence to another intelligence. In the act of teaching and learning there are two wills and two intelligences. We will call their coincidence *stultification*. In the experimental situation Jacotot created, the student was linked to a will, Jacotot's, and to an intelligence, the book's—the two entirely distinct. We will call the known and maintained difference of the two relations—the act of an intelligence obeying only itself even while the will obeys another will—*emancipation*.

This pedagogical experiment created a rupture with the logic of all pedagogies.

One can teach what one doesn't know if the student is emancipated, that is to say, if he is obliged to use his own intelligence. . . . The ignorant person will learn by himself what the master doesn't know if the master believes he can and obliges him to realize his capacity: a circle of *power* homologous to the circle of powerlessness that ties the student to the explicator of the old method (to be called from now on, simply, the Old Master).

Granted, replies the critic. But that which makes the interrogator forceful also makes him incompetent as a verifier. How will he know if the child is losing his way? The father or mother can always ask the child: show me "Father" or "Heaven." But how can they verify if the child has pointed to the right word? The difficulty can only get worse as the child advances—if he advances—in his training. Won't the ignorant master and the ignorant student be playing out the fable of the blind man leading the blind?

Let's begin by reassuring the critics: we will not make of the ignorant one the fount of an innate science, and especially not of a science of the people as opposed to that of the scholar. One must be learned to judge the results of the work, to verify the student's science. The ignorant one himself will do *less* and *more* at the same time. He will not verify what the student has found; he will verify that the student has searched. He will judge whether or not he has paid attention. For one need only be human to judge the fact of work. Just like the philosopher who "recognizes" human footprints in the lines in the sand, the mother knows how to see "in his eyes, in the child's features, when he is doing work, when he is pointing to the words in a sentence, if he is attentive to what he is doing." The ignorant master must demand from his student that he prove to him that he has studied attentively.

This is the way that the ignorant master can instruct the learned one as well as the ignorant one: by verifying that he is always searching. Whoever looks always finds. He doesn't necessarily find what he was looking for, and even less what he was supposed to find. But he finds something new to relate to the *thing* that he already knows. What is essential is the continuous vigilance, the attention that never subsides without irrationality setting in—something that the learned one, like the ignorant one, excels at. The master is he who keeps the researcher on his own route, the one that he alone is following and keeps following.

We begin by asking the student to talk about what he is going to represent—let's say a drawing to copy. It would be dangerous to give the child explanations of the measures he must take before beginning his work. We know the reason for this: the risk that the child will sense in this, his inability. We will thus trust in the child's will to imitate. But we are going to *verify* that will. A few days before putting a pencil in his hand, we will give him the drawing to look at, and we will ask him to talk about it.

Perhaps he will only say a few things at first—for example, "The head is pretty." But we will repeat the exercise; we will show him the same head and ask him to look again and speak again, at the risk of repeating what he already said. Thus he will become more attentive, more aware of his ability and capable of imitating. We know the reason for this effect, something completely different from visual memorization and manual training. What the child has *verified* by this exercise is that painting is a language, that the drawing he has been asked to imitate *speaks* to him. Later on, we will put him in front of a painting and ask him to improvise on the *unity of feeling* present, for example, in that painting by Poussin of the burial of Phocion. The connoisseur will undoubtedly be shocked by this, won't he? How could you pretend to know that this is what Poussin wanted to put in his painting? And what does this hypothetical discourse have to do with Poussin's pictorial art and with the one the student is supposed to acquire?

We will answer that we don't pretend to know what Poussin wanted to do. We are simply trying to imagine what he might have wanted to do. We thus verify that all *wanting to do* is a *wanting to say* and that this wanting to say is addressed to any reasonable being. In short, we verify that the *ut poesis pictura* the artists of the Renaissance had claimed by reversing Horace's adage is not knowledge reserved solely for artists: painting, like sculpture, engraving, or any other art, is a language that can be understood and spoken by whoever knows the language. As far as art goes, "I can't" translates easily, we know, into "that says nothing to me." The verification of the "unity of feeling," that is to say, of the meaning of the painting, will thus be the means of emancipation for the person who "doesn't know how" to paint, the exact equivalent to the verification-by-book of the equality of intelligence.

Undoubtedly, there's a great distance from this to making masterpieces. The visitors who appreciated the literary compositions of Jacotot's students often made a wry face at their paintings and drawings. But it's not a matter of making great painters; it's a matter of making the emancipated: people capable of saying, "me too, I'm a painter," a statement that contains nothing in the way of pride, only the reasonable feeling of power that belongs to any reasonable being. "There is no pride in saying out loud: Me too, I'm a painter! Pride consists in saying softly to others: You neither, you aren't a painter."[21] "Me too, I'm a painter" means: me too, I have a soul, I have feelings to communicate to my fellow-men.

16

RICHARD RORTY

Richard Rorty (1931–2007) is emeritus professor of comparative literature and philosophy at Stanford University. His work combines American pragmatism with a philosophy of language inspired by Wittgenstein, and some influences from continental philosophy, particularly Martin Heidegger. Rorty's first and most influential book is *Philosophy and the Mirror of Nature* (1979). You will notice, reading the last chapter from this book, that Rorty refers to a variety of philosophers, including Hans-Georg Gadamer, Jurgen Habermas, Jean-Paul Sartre, and Immanuel Kant. He does not offer definitive accounts of these philosophies; rather, he mentions them in the process of reinterpreting the Western philosophical tradition's reliance on visual imagery to represent humanity's engagement with reality. In this respect, Rorty's methodology enacts the philosophical position he defends.

Rorty argues against philosophy's preoccupation with epistemology as a foundational science. He criticizes the underlying assumption that knowledge is a faithful, unbiased, accurate representation—or mirroring—of a mind-independent, objective reality. He refuses to accept that, in the final analysis, there can be only one true knowledge discourse. He understands what informs this view, for if different discourses are justified exclusively in relation to a unified and permanent reality, then only one of them will describe it correctly. If, for example, it is decided that science describes the true structure of reality, then aesthetics is reduced to the mere play of subjective appearances.

Rorty advocates abandoning epistemology as paradigmatic of both philosophy and humanity's relationship to reality. In his view, human worth is not a matter of justified true belief and cannot be reduced to the question of knowing reality. It is true that human life involves contemplation, yet it is not exclusively contemplative. According to Rorty, humans are poetic beings who constantly create new possibilities for thinking, living, and being. He argues that knowledge discourses—such as science, history, psychology, and astrology—should not presume to justify themselves according to a reality that transcends all appearance, for the justification of belief is simply what it appears to be: a social practice.

Rorty is not concerned that humans should want to understand themselves better, but he is concerned that they seek this self-understanding in transcendentalist and reductionist discourses. He thinks that a subtle and sophisticated cultural anthropology is needed. The purpose of inquiry is not to seek *the* Truth, as a mimetic representation of *the* real—Rorty refers to this as systematic philosophy—but to seek new, alternative truths distinct from previous iterations—which he calls hermeneutics, or edifying philosophy. The transformation of subjectivity plays an important role in edification. Systematic philosophy idealizes an absent subject. The subject's values, and inquiry into those values, is subordinated to knowledge of an "objective" world. In contrast, an edifying philosophy begins from subjective value. Individuals do not see the "facts" first and then evaluate them later; rather, evaluative, theoretical frameworks make certain features of experience salient as "facts." Rorty's philosophy raises questions about the role that subjective freedom plays in the determination of these evaluative frameworks. Can we choose them? According to what criteria? Or are they socially determined?

Rorty conceives of edification in conversational terms. The aim of edification is to maintain the conversation and one's own capacities as a conversational partner. Wisdom is defined as the ability to sustain conversation successfully. This raises many questions. Is conversation enough? What if the conversation is dysfunctional? Is it possible for conversation to be dysfunctional? As teachers, we should consider how edification would manifest in the classroom. How do Rorty's views inform curriculum and teaching? What pedagogical practices create participatory conversations in which students will participate?

Rorty does not see the history of human thought as a series of epistemic failures but as a vital tradition that re-envisions reality; it is a testament to the activity, creativity, and ingenuity of humanity. The establishment of conventions and the subsequent recognition of their limitations send us off in new directions to seek new descriptions that will inspire new conventions. Rorty views the history of human thought as an endless cycle of renewal and transformation.

REFERENCES

Arcilla, René Vincente. *The Love of Perfection: Richard Rorty and Liberal Education.* London and New York: Routledge, 1995.

Brandom, Robert B., ed. *Rorty and His Critics.* Oxford: Blackwell, 2000.

Rorty, Richard. *Philosophy and the Mirror of Nature.* Princeton: Princeton University Press, 1979.

Rorty, Richard. *Contingency, Irony and Solidarity.* Cambridge: Cambridge University Press, 1989.

PHILOSOPHY AND THE MIRROR OF NATURE

Philosophy Without Mirrors

1. Hermeneutics and Edification   Our present notions of what it is to be a philosopher are so tied up with the Kantian attempt to render all knowledge-claims commensurable that it is difficult to imagine what philosophy without epistemology could be. More generally, it is difficult to imagine that any activity would be entitled to bear the name "philosophy" if it had nothing to do with knowledge—if it were not in some sense a theory of knowledge, or a method for getting knowledge, or at least a hint as to where some supremely important kind of knowledge might be found. The difficulty stems from a notion shared by Platonists, Kantians, and positivists: that man has essence—namely, to discover essences. The notion that our chief task is to mirror accurately, in our own Glassy Essence, the universe around us is the complement of the notion, common to Democritus and Descartes, that the universe is made up of very simple, clearly and distinctly knowable things, knowledge of whose essences provides the master-vocabulary which permits commensuration of all discourses.

This classic picture of human beings must be set aside before epistemologically centered philosophy can be set aside. "Hermeneutics," as a polemical term in contemporary philosophy, is a name for the attempt to do so. The use of the term for this purpose is largely due to one book—Gadamer's *Truth and Method*. Gadamer there makes clear that hermeneutics is not a "method for attaining truth" which fits into the classic picture of man: "The hermeneutic phenomenon is basically not a problem of method at all."[1] Rather, Gadamer is asking, roughly, what conclusions might be drawn from the fact that we have to practice hermeneutics—from the "hermeneutic phenomenon" as a fact about people which the epistemological tradition has tried to shunt aside. "The hermeneutics developed here," he says, "is not . . . a methodology of the human sciences, but an attempt to understand what the human sciences truly are, beyond their methodological self-consciousness, and what connects them with the totality of our experience of the world."[2] His book is a redescription of man which tries to place the classic picture within a larger one, and thus to "distance" the standard philosophical problematic rather than offer a set of solutions to it.

For my present purposes, the importance of Gadamer's book is that he manages to separate off one of the three strands—the romantic notion of man as self-creative—in the philosophical notion of "spirit" from the other two strands with which it became entangled. Gadamer (like Heidegger, to whom some of his work is indebted) makes no concessions either to Cartesian dualism or to the notion of "transcendental constitution" (in any sense which could be given an idealistic interpretation).[3] He thus helps reconcile the "naturalistic" point I tried to make in the previous chapter—that the "irreducibility of the *Geisteswissenschaften*" is not a matter of a metaphysical dualism—with our "existentialist" intuition that redescribing ourselves is the most important thing we can do. He does this by substituting the notion of *Bildung* (education, self-formation) for that of "knowledge" as the goal of thinking. To say that we become different people, that we "remake" ourselves as we read more, talk more, and write more, is simply a dramatic way of saying that the sentences which become true of us by virtue of such activities are often more important to us than the sentences which become true of us when we drink more, earn more, and so on. The events which make us able to say new and interesting things about ourselves are, in this nonmetaphysical sense, more "essential" to us (at least to us relatively leisured intellectuals, inhabiting a stable and prosperous part of the world) than the events which change our shapes or our standards of living ("re-making" us in less "spiritual" ways). Gadamer develops his notion of *wirkungsgeschichtliches Bewusstsein* (the sort of consciousness of the past which changes us) to characterize an attitude interested not so much in what is out there in the world, or in what happened in history, as in what we can get out of nature and history for our own uses. In this attitude, getting the facts right (about atoms and the void, or about the history of Europe) is merely propaedeutic to finding a new and more interesting way of expressing ourselves, and thus of coping with the world. From the educational, as opposed to the epistemological or the technological, point of view, the way things are said is more important than the possession of truths.[4]

Since "education" sounds a bit too flat, and *Bildung* a bit too foreign, I shall use "edification" to stand for this project of finding new, better, more interesting, more fruitful ways of speaking. The attempt to edify (ourselves or others) may consist in the hermeneutic activity of making connections between our own culture and some exotic culture or historical period, or between our own discipline and another discipline which seems to pursue incommensurable aims in an incommensurable vocabulary. But it may instead consist in the "poetic" activity of thinking up such new aims, new words, or new disciplines, followed by, so to speak, the inverse of hermeneutios: the attempt to reinterpret our familiar surroundings in the unfamiliar terms of our new inventions. In either case, the activity is (despite the etymological relation between the two words) edifying without being constructive—at least if "constructive" means the sort of cooperation in the accomplishment of research programs which takes place in normal discourse. For edifying discourse is *supposed* to be abnormal, to take us out of our old selves by the power of strangeness, to aid us in becoming new beings.

The contrast between the desire for edification and the desire for truth is, for Gadamer, not an expression of a tension which needs to be resolved or compromised. If there is a conflict, it is between the Platonic-Aristotelian view that the *only* way to be edified is to know what is out there (to reflect the facts accurately—to realize our essence by knowing essences) and the view that the quest for truth is just one among many ways in which we might be edified. Gadamer rightly gives Heidegger the credit for working out a way of seeing the search for objective knowledge (first developed by the Greeks, using mathematics as a model) as one human project among others.[5] The point is, however, more vivid in Sartre, who sees the attempt to gain an objective knowledge of the world, and thus of oneself, as an attempt to avoid the responsibility for choosing one's project.[6] For Sartre, to say this is not to say that the desire for objective knowledge of nature, history, or anything else is bound to be unsuccessful, or even bound to be self-deceptive. It is merely to say that it presents a temptation to self-deception insofar as we think that, by knowing which descriptions within a given set of normal discourses apply to us, we thereby know ourselves. For Heidegger, Sartre, and Gadamer, objective inquiry is perfectly possible and frequently actual—the only thing to be said against it is that it provides only some, among many, ways of describing ourselves, and that some of these can hinder the process of edification.

To sum up this "existentialist" view of objectivity, then: objectivity should be seen as conformity to the norms of justification (for assertions and for actions) we find about us. Such conformity becomes dubious and self-deceptive only when seen as something more than this—

namely, as a way of obtaining access to something which "grounds" current practices of justification in something else. Such a "ground" is thought to need no justification, because it has become so clearly and distinctly perceived as to count as a "philosophical foundation." This is self-deceptive not simply because of the general absurdity of ultimate justification's reposing upon the unjustifiable, but because of the more concrete absurdity of thinking that the vocabulary used by present science, morality, or whatever has some privileged attachment to reality which makes it *more* than just a further set of descriptions. Agreeing with the naturalists that redescription is not "change of essence" needs to be followed up by abandoning the notion of "essence" altogether.[7] But the standard philosophical strategy of most naturalisms is to find some way of showing that our own culture has indeed got hold of the essence of man—thus making all new and incommensurable vocabularies merely "noncognitive" ornamentation.[8] The utility of the "existentialist" view is that, by proclaiming that we have no essence, it permits us to see the descriptions of ourselves we find in one of (or in the unity of) the *Naturwissenschaften* as on a par with the various alternative descriptions offered by poet's, novelists, depth psychologists, sculptors, anthropologists, and mystics. The former are not privileged representations in virtue of the fact that (at the moment) there is more consensus in the sciences than in the arts. They are simply among the repertoire of self-descriptions at our disposal.

This point can also be put as an extrapolation from the commonplace that one cannot be counted as educated—*gebildet*—if one knows *only* the results of the normal *Naturwissenschaften* of the day. Gadamer begins *Truth and Method* with a discussion of the role of the humanist tradition in giving sense to the notion of *Bildung* as something having "no goals outside itself,"[9] To give sense to such a notion we need a sense of the relativity of descriptive vocabularies to periods, tradition, and historical accidents. This is what the humanist tradition in education does, and what training in the results of the natural sciences cannot do. Given that sense of relativity, we cannot take the notion of "essence" seriously, nor the notion of man's task as the accurate representation of essences. The natural sciences, by themselves, leave us convinced that we know both what we are and what we can be—not just how to predict and control our behavior, but the limits of that behavior (and, in particular, the limits of our significant speech). Gadamer's attempt to fend off the demand (common to Mill and Carnap) for "objectivity" in the *Geisteswissenschaften* is the attempt to prevent education from being reduced to instruction in the results of normal inquiry. More broadly, it is the attempt to prevent abnormal inquiry from being viewed as suspicious solely because of its abnormality.

This "existentialist" attempt to place objectivity, rationality, and normal inquiry within the larger picture of our need to be educated and edified is often countered by the "positivist" attempt to distinguish learning facts from acquiring values. From the positivist point of view, Gadamer's exposition of *wirkungsgeschichtliche Bewusstsein* may seem little more than reiteration of the commonplace that even when we know all the objectively true descriptions of ourselves, we still may not know what to do with ourselves. From this point of view, *Truth and Method* (and chapters six and seven above) are just overblown dramatizations of the fact that entire compliance with all the demands for justification offered by normal inquiry would still leave us free to draw our own morals from the assertions so justified. But from the viewpoints of Gadamer, Heidegger, and Sartre, the trouble with the fact-value distinction is that it is contrived precisely to blur the fact that alternative descriptions are possible in addition to those offered by the results of normal inquiries.[10] It suggests that once "all the facts are in" nothing remains except "noncognitive" adoption of an attitude—a choice which is not rationally discussable. It disguises the fact that to use one set of true sentences to describe ourselves is already to choose an attitude toward ourselves, whereas to use another set of true sentences is to adopt a contrary attitude. Only if we assume that there is a value-free vocabulary which renders these sets of "factual" statements commensurable can the positivist distinction between facts and values, beliefs and attitudes, look plausible. But the philosophical fiction that such a vocabulary is on the tips of our tongues is, from an educational point of view, disastrous. It forces us to pretend that we can split ourselves up into knowers of true sentences on the one hand and choosers of lives or actions or works of art on the other. These artificial diremptions make it impossible to get the notion of edification into focus. Or, more exactly, they tempt us to think of edification as having nothing to do with the rational faculties which are employed in normal discourse.

So Gadamer's effort to get rid of the classic picture of man-as-essentially-knower-of-essences is, among other things, an effort to get rid of the distinction between fact and value, and thus to let us think of "discovering the facts" as one project of edification among others. This is why Gadamer devotes so much time to breaking down the distinctions which Kant made among cognition, morality, and aesthetic judgment.[11] There is no way, as far as I can see, in which to *argue* the issue of whether to keep the Kantian "grid" in place or set it aside. There is no "normal" philosophical discourse which provides common commensurating ground for those who see science and edification as, respectively, "rational" and "irrational," and those who see the quest for objectivity as one possibility among others to be taken account of in *wirkungsgeschichtliche Bewusstsein.* If there is no such common ground, all we can do is to show how the other side looks from our own point of view. That is, all we can do is be hermeneutic about the opposition—trying to show how the odd or paradoxical or offensive things they say hang together with the rest of what they want to say, and how what they say looks when put in our own alternative idiom. This sort of hermeneutics with polemical intent is common to Heidegger's and Derrida's attempts to deconstruct the tradition.

2. *Systematic Philosophy and Edifying Philosophy* The hermeneutic point of view, from which the acquisition of truth dwindles in importance, and is seen as a component of education, is possible only if we once stood at another point of view. Education has to start from acculturation. So the search for objectivity and the self-conscious awareness of the social practices in which objectivity consists are necessary first steps in becoming *gebildet.* We must first see ourselves as *en-soi*—as described by those statements which are objectively true in the judgment of our peers—before there is any point in seeing ourselves as *pour-soi.* Similarly, we cannot be educated without finding out a lot about the descriptions of the world offered by our culture (e.g., by learning the results of the natural sciences). Later perhaps, we may put less value on "being in touch with reality" but we can afford that only after having passed through stages of implicit, and then explicit and self-conscious, conformity to the norms of the discourses going on around us.

I raise this banal point that education—even the education of the revolutionary or the prophet—needs to begin with acculturation and conformity merely to provide a cautionary complement to the "existentialist" claim that normal participation in normal discourse is merely one project, one way of being in the world. The caution amounts to saying that abnormal and "existential" discourse is always parasitic upon normal discourse, that the possibility of hermeneutics is always parasitic upon the possibility (and perhaps upon the actuality) of epistemology, and that edification always employs materials provided by the culture of the day. To attempt abnormal discourse *de novo*, without being able to recognize our own abnormality, is madness in the most literal and terrible sense. To insist on being hermeneutic where epistemology would do—to make ourselves unable to view normal discourse in terms of its own motives, and able to view it only from within our own abnormal discourse—is not mad, but it does show a lack of education. To adopt the "existentialist" attitude toward objectivity and rationality common to Sartre, Heidegger, and Gadamer makes sense only if we do so in a conscious departure from a well-understood norm. "Existentialism" is an *intrinsically reactive* movement of thought, one which has point only in opposition to the tradition. I want now to generalize this contrast between philosophers whose work is essentially constructive and those whose work is essentially reactive. I shall thereby develop a contrast between philosophy which centers in epistemology and the sort of philosophy which takes its point of departure from suspicion about the pretensions of epistemology. This is the contrast between "systematic" and "edifying" philosophies.

In every sufficiently reflective culture, there are those who single out one area, one set of practices, and see it as the paradigm human activity. They then try to show how the rest of culture can profit from this example. In the mainstream of the Western philosophical tradition, this paradigm has been *knowing*—possessing justified true beliefs, or, better yet, beliefs so intrinsically persuasive as to make justification unnecessary. Successive philosophical revolutions within this mainstream have been produced by philosophers excited by new cognitive feats—e.g., the rediscovery of Aristotle, Galilean mechanics, the development of self-conscious historiography in the nineteenth century, Darwinian biology, mathematical logic. Thomas's use of Aristotle to conciliate the Fathers, Descartes's and Hobbes's criticisms of scholasticism, the Enlightenment's notion that reading Newton leads naturally to the downfall of tyrants, Spencer's evolutionism, Carnap's attempt to overcome metaphysics through logic, are so many attempts to refashion the rest of culture on the model of the latest cognitive achievements. A "mainstream" Western philosopher typically says: Now that such-and-such a line of inquiry has had such a stunning success, let us reshape all inquiry, and all of culture, on its model, thereby permitting objectivity and rationality to prevail in areas previously obscured by convention, superstition, and the lack of a proper epistemological understanding of man's ability accurately to represent nature.

On the periphery of the history of modern philosophy, one finds figures who, without forming a "tradition," resemble each other in their distrust of the notion that man's essence is to be a knower of essences. Goethe, Kierkegaard, Santayana, William James, Dewey, the later Wittgenstein, the later Heidegger, are figures of this sort. They are often accused of relativism or cynicism. They are often dubious about progress, and especially about the latest claim that such-and-such a discipline has at last made the nature of human knowledge so clear that reason will now spread throughout the rest of human activity. These writers have kept alive the suggestion that, even when we have justified true belief about everything we want to know, we may have no more than conformity to the norms of the day. They have kept alive the historicist sense that this century's "superstition" was the last century's triumph of reason, as well as the relativist sense that the latest vocabulary, borrowed from the latest scientific achievement, may not express privileged representations of essences, but be just another of the potential infinity of vocabularies in which the world can be described.

The mainstream philosophers are the philosophers I shall call "systematic," and the peripheral ones are those I shall call "edifying." These peripheral, pragmatic philosophers are skeptical primarily *about systematic philosophy*, about the whole project of universal commensuration.[12] In our time, Dewey, Wittgenstein, and Heidegger are the great edifying, peripheral, thinkers. All three make it as difficult as possible to take their thought as expressing views on traditional philosophical problems, or as making constructive proposals for philosophy as a cooperative and progressive discipline.[13] They make fun of the classic picture of man, the picture which contains systematic philosophy, the search for universal commensuration in a final vocabulary. They hammer away at the holistic point that words take their meanings from other words rather than by virtue of their representative character, and the corollary that vocabularies acquire their privileges from the men who use them rather than from their transparency to the real.[14]

The distinction between systematic and edifying philosophers is not the same as the distinction between normal philosophers and revolutionary philosophers. The latter distinction puts Husserl, Russell, the later Wittgenstein, and the later Heidegger all on the same ("revolutionary") side of a line. For my purposes, what matters is a distinction between two kinds of revolutionary philosophers. On the one hand, there are revolutionary philosophers—those who found new schools within which normal, professionalized philosophy can be practiced—who see the incommensurability of their new vocabulary with the old as a temporary inconvenience, to be blamed on the shortcomings of their predecessors and to be overcome by the institutionalization of their own vocabulary. On the other hand, there are great philosophers who dread the thought that their vocabulary should ever be institutionalized, or that their writing might be seen as commensurable with the tradition. Husserl and Russell (like Descartes and Kant) are of the former sort. The later Wittgenstein and the later Heidegger (like Kierkegaard and Nietzsche) are of the latter sort.[15] Great systematic philosophers are constructive and offer arguments. Great edifying philosophers are reactive and offer satires, parodies, aphorisms. They know their work loses its point when the period they were reacting against is over. They are *intentionally* peripheral. Great systematic philosophers, like great scientists, build for eternity. Great edifying philosophers destroy for the sake of their own generation. Systematic philosophers want to put their subject on the secure path of a science. Edifying philosophers want to keep space open for the sense of wonder which poets can sometimes cause—wonder that there is something new under the sun, something which is *not* an accurate representation of what was already there, something which (at least for the moment) cannot be explained and can barely be described.

The notion of an edifying philosopher is, however, a paradox. For Plato defined the philosopher by opposition to the poet. The philosopher could give reasons, argue for his views, justify himself. So argumentative systematic philosophers say of Nietzsche and Heidegger that, whatever else they may be, they are not *philosophers*. This "not really a philosopher" ploy is also used, of course, by normal philosophers against revolutionary philosophers. It was used by pragmatists against logical positivists, by positivists against "ordinary language philosophers," and will be used whenever cozy professionalism is in danger. But in that usage it is just a rhetorical gambit which tells one nothing more than that an incommensurable discourse is being proposed. When it is used against edifying philosophers, on the other hand, the accusation has a real bite. The problem for an edifying philosopher is that qua philosopher he is in the business of offering arguments, whereas he would like simply to offer another set of terms, *without* saying that these terms are the new-found accurate representations of essences (e.g., of the essence of "philosophy" itself). He is, so to speak, violating not just the rules of normal philosophy (the philosophy of the schools of his day) but a sort of meta-rule: the rule that one may suggest changing the rules only because one has noticed that the old ones do not fit the subject matter, that they are not adequate to reality, that they impede the solution of the eternal problems. Edifying philosophers, unlike revolutionary systematic philosophers, are those who are abnormal at this meta-level. They refuse to present themselves as having found out any objective truth (about, say, what philosophy is). They present themselves as doing something different from, and more important than, offering accurate representations of how things are. It is more important because, they say, the notion of "accurate representation" itself is not the proper way to think about what philosophy does. But, they then go on to say, this is not because "a search for accurate representations of . . . (e.g., 'the most general traits of reality' or 'the nature of man')" is an *in*accurate representation of philosophy.

Whereas less pretentious revolutionaries can afford to have views on lots of things which their predecessors had views on, edifying philosophers have to decry the very notion of having a view, while avoiding having a view about having views.[16] This is an awkward, but not impossible, position. Wittgenstein and Heidegger manage it fairly well. One reason they manage it as well as they do is that they do not think that when we say something we must necessarily be expressing a view about a subject. We might just be *saying something*—participating in a conversation rather than contributing to an inquiry. Perhaps saying things is not always saying how things are. Perhaps saying *that* is itself not a case of saying how things are. Both men suggest we see people as saying things, better or worse things, without seeing them as externalizing inner representations of reality. But this is only their entering wedge, for then we must cease to see ourselves as *seeing* this, without beginning to see ourselves as seeing something else. We must get the visual, and in particular the mirroring, metaphors out of our speech altogether.[17] To do that we have to understand speech not only as not the externalizing of inner representations, but as not a representation at all. We have to drop the notion of correspondence for sentences as well as for thoughts, and see sentences as connected with other sentences rather than with the world. We have to-see the term "corresponds to how things are" as an automatic compliment paid to successful normal discourse rather than as a relation to be studied and aspired to throughout the rest of discourse. To attempt to extend this compliment to feats of *ab*normal discourse is like complimenting a judge on his wise decision by leaving him a fat tip: it shows a lack of tact. To think of Wittgenstein and Heidegger as having views about how things are is not to be wrong about how things are, exactly; it is just poor taste. It puts them in a position which they do not want to be in, and in which they look ridiculous.

But perhaps they *should* look ridiculous. How, then, do we know when to adopt a tactful attitude and when to insist on someone's moral obligation to hold a view? This is like asking how we know when someone's refusal to adopt our norms (of, for example, social organization, sexual practices, or conversational manners) is morally outrageous and when it is something which we must (at least provisionally) respect. We do not know such things by reference to general principles. We do not, for instance, know in advance that if a given sentence is uttered, or a given act performed, we shall break off a conversation or a personal relationship, for everything depends on what leads up to it. To see edifying philosophers as conversational partners is an alternative to seeing them as holding views on subjects of common concern. One way of thinking of wisdom as something of which the love is not the same as that of argument, and of which the achievement does not consist in finding the correct vocabulary for representing essence, is to think of it as the practical wisdom necessary to participate in a conversation. One way to see edifying philosophy *as* the love of wisdom is to see it as the attempt to prevent conversation from degenerating into inquiry, into a research program. Edifying philosophers can never end philosophy, but they can help prevent it from attaining the secure path of a science.

3. Edification, Relativism, and Objective Truth   I want now to enlarge this suggestion that edifying philosophy aims at continuing a conversation rather than at discovering truth, by making out of it a reply to the familiar charge of "relativism" leveled at the subordination of truth to edification. I shall be claiming that the difference between conversation and inquiry parallels Sartre's distinction between thinking of oneself as *pour-soi* and as *en-soi,* and thus that the cultural role of the edifying philosopher is to help us avoid the self-deception which comes from believing that we know ourselves by knowing a set of objective facts. In the following section, I shall try to make the converse point. There I shall be saying that the wholehearted; behaviorism, naturalism, and physicalism I have been commending in earlier chapters help us avoid the self-deception of thinking that we possess a deep, hidden, metaphysically significant nature which makes us "irreducibly" different from inkwells or atoms.

Philosophers who have doubts about traditional epistemology are often thought to be questioning the notion that at most one of incompatible competing theories can be true. However, it is hard to find anyone who actually does question this. "When it is said, for example, that coherentist or pragmatic "theories of truth" allow for the possibility that many incompatible theories would satisfy the conditions set for "the truth," the coherentist or pragmatist usually replies that this merely shows that we should have no grounds for choice among these candidates for "the truth." The moral to draw, they say, is not that they have offered inadequate analyses of "true," but that there are some terms—for example, "the true theory," "the right thing to do"—which are, intuitively and grammatically, singular, but for which no set of necessary and sufficient conditions can be given which will pick out a unique referent. This fact, they say, should not be surprising. Nobody thinks that there are necessary and sufficient conditions which will pick out, for example, the unique referent of "the best thing for her to have done on finding herself in that rather embarrassing situation," though plausible conditions can be given which will shorten a list of competing incompatible candidates. Why should it be different for the referents of "what she should have done in that ghastly moral dilemma" or "the Good Life for man" or "what the world is really made of"?

To see relativism lurking in every attempt to formulate conditions for truth or reality or goodness which does not attempt to provide uniquely individuating conditions we must adopt the "Platonic" notion of the transcendental terms which I discussed above (chapter six, section 6). We must think of the true referents of these terms (the Truth, the Real, Goodness) as conceivably having no connection whatever with the practices of justification which obtain among us. The dilemma created by this Platonic hypostatization is that, on the one hand, the philosopher must attempt to find criteria for picking out these unique referents, whereas, on the other hand, the only hints he has about what these criteria could be are provided by current practice (by, e.g., the best moral and scientific thought of the day). Philosophers thus condemn themselves to a Sisyphean task, for no sooner has an account of a transcendental term been perfected than it is labeled a "naturalistic fallacy," a confusion between essence and accident.[18] I think we get a clue to the cause of this self-defeating obsession from the fact that even philosophers who take the intuitive impossibility of finding conditions for "the one right thing to do" as a reason for repudiating "objective values" are loath to take the impossibility of finding individuating conditions for the one true theory of the world as a reason for denying "objective physical reality," Yet they should, for formally the two notions are on a par. The reasons for and against adopting a "correspondence" approach to moral truth are the same as those regarding truth about the physical world. The giveaway comes, I think, when we find that the usual excuse for invidious treatment is that we are shoved around by physical reality but not by values.[19] Yet what does being shoved around have to do with objectivity, accurate representation, or correspondence? Nothing, I think, unless we confuse *contact* with reality (a causal, non-intentional, non-description-relative relation) with *dealing with* reality (describing, explaining, predicting, and modifying it—all of which are things we do under descriptions). The sense in which physical reality is Peircean "Secondness" —unmediated pressure—has nothing to do with the sense in which one among all our ways of describing, or of coping with, physical reality is "the one right" way. Lack of mediation is here being confused with accuracy of mediation. The absence of description is confused with a privilege attaching to a certain description. Only by such a confusion can the inability to offer individuating conditions for the one true description of material things be confused with insensitivity to the things' obduracy.

Sartre helps us explain why this confusion is so frequent and why its results are purveyed with so much moral earnestness. The notion of "one right way of describing and explaining reality" supposedly contained in our "intuition" about the meaning of "true" is, for Sartre, just the notion of having a way of describing and explaining *imposed* on us in that brute way in which stones impinge on our feet. Or, to shift to visual metaphors, it is the notion of having reality unveiled to us, not as in a glass darkly, but with some unimaginable sort of immediacy which would make discourse and description superfluous. If we could convert knowledge from something discursive, something attained by continual adjustments of ideas or words, into something as ineluctable as being shoved about, or being transfixed by a sight which leaves us speechless, then we should no longer have the responsibility for choice among competing ideas and words, theories and vocabularies. This attempt to slough off responsibility is what Sartre describes as the attempt to turn oneself into a thing—into an *être-en-soi*. In the visions of the epistemologist, this incoherent notion takes the form of seeing the attainment of truth as a matter of *necessity*, either the "logical" necessity of the transcendentalist or the "physical" necessity of the evolutionary "naturalizing" epistemologist. From Sartre's point of view, the urge to find such necessities is the urge to be rid of one's freedom to erect yet another alternative theory or vocabulary. Thus the edifying philosopher who points out the incoherence of the urge is treated as a "relativist," one who lacks moral seriousness, because he does not join in the common human hope that the burden of choice will pass away. Just as the moral philosopher who sees virtue as Aristotelian self-development is thought to lack concern for his fellow man, so the epistemologist who is merely behaviorist is treated as one who does not share the universal human aspiration toward objective truth.

Sartre adds to our understanding of the visual imagery which has set the problems of Western philosophy by helping us see why this imagery is always trying to transcend itself. The notion of an unclouded Mirror of Nature is the notion of a mirror which would be indistinguishable from what was mirrored, and thus would not be a mirror at all. The notion of a human being whose mind is such an unclouded mirror, and who *knows* this, is the image, as Sartre says, of God. Such a being does *not* confront something alien which makes it necessary for him to choose an attitude toward, or a description of, it. He would have no need and no ability to choose actions or descriptions. He can be called "God" if we think of the advantages of this situation, or a "mere machine" if we think of the disadvantages. From this point of view, to look for commensuration rather than simply continued conversation—to look for a way of making further redescription unnecessary by finding a way of reducing all *possible* descriptions to one—is to attempt escape from humanity. To abandon the notion that philosophy must show all possible discourse naturally converging to a consensus, just as normal inquiry does, would be to abandon the hope of being anything more than merely human. It would thus be to abandon the Platonic notions of Truth and Reality and Goodness as entities which may not be even dimly mirrored by present practices and beliefs, and to settle back into the "relativism" which assumes that our only useful notions of "true" and "real" and "good" are extrapolations from those practices and beliefs.

Here, finally, I come around to the suggestion with which I ended the last section—that the point of edifying philosophy is to keep the conversation going rather than to find objective truth. Such truth, in the view I am advocating, is the normal result of normal discourse. Edifying philosophy is not only abnormal but reactive, having sense only as a protest against attempts to close off conversation by proposals for universal commensuration through the hypostatization of some privileged set of descriptions. The danger which edifying discourse tries to avert is that some given vocabulary, some way in which people might come to think of themselves, will deceive them into thinking that from now on all discourse could be, or should be, normal discourse. The resulting freezing-over of culture would be, in the eyes of edifying philosophers, the dehumanization of human beings. The edifying philosophers are thus agreeing with Lessing's choice of the infinite *striving for* truth over "all of Truth."[20] For the edifying philosopher the very idea of being presented with "all of Truth" is absurd, because the Platonic notion of Truth itself is absurd. It is absurd either as the notion of truth about reality which is not about reality-under-a-certain-description, or as the notion of truth about reality under some privileged description which makes all other descriptions unnecessary because it is commensurable with each of them.

To see keeping a conversation going as a sufficient aim of philosophy, to see wisdom as consisting in the ability to sustain a conversation, is to see human beings as generators of new descriptions rather than beings one hopes to be able to describe accurately. To see the aim of philosophy as truth— namely, the truth about the terms which provide ultimate commensuration for all human inquiries and activities—is to see human beings as objects rather than subjects, as existing *en-soi* rather than as both *pour-soi* and *en-soi,* as both described objects and describing subjects. To think that philosophy will permit us to see the describing subject as itself one sort of described object is to think that all possible descriptions can be rendered commensurable with the aid of a single descriptive vocabulary—that of philosophy itself. For only if we had such a notion of a universal description could we identify human-beings-under-a-given-description with man's "essence." Only with such a notion would that of a man's *having* an essence make sense, whether or not that essence is conceived of as the knowing of essences. So not even by saying that man is subject as well as object, *pour-soi* as well as *en-soi,* are we grasping our essence. We do not escape from Platonism by saying that "our essence is to have no essence" if we then try to use this insight as the basis for a constructive and systematic attempt to find out further truths about human beings.

That is why "existentialism"—and, more generally, edifying philosophy—can be *only* reactive, why it falls into self-deception whenever it tries to do more than send the conversation off in new directions. Such new directions may, perhaps, engender new normal discourses, new sciences, new philosophical research programs, and thus new objective truths. But they are not the point of edifying philosophy, only accidental byproducts. The point is always the same— to perform the social function which Dewey called "breaking the crust of convention," preventing man from deluding himself with the notion that he knows himself, or anything else, except under optional descriptions.

4. *Edification and Naturalism*   I argued in chapter seven that it would be a good idea to get rid of the spirit-nature distinction, conceived as a division between human beings and other things, or between two parts of human beings, corresponding to the distinction between hermeneutics and epistemology. I want now to take up this topic again, in order to underline the point that the "existentialist" doctrines I have been discussing are compatible with the behaviorism and materialism I advocated in earlier chapters. Philosophers who would like to be simultaneously systematic and edifying have often seen them as incompatible, and have therefore suggested how our sense of ourselves as *pour-soi,* as capable of reflection, as choosers of alternative vocabularies, might itself be turned into a philosophical subject matter.

Much recent philosophy—under the aegis of "phenomenology" or of "hermeneutics," or both—has toyed with this unfortunate idea. For example, Habermas and Apel have suggested ways in which we might create a new sort of transcendental standpoint, enabling us to do something like what Kant tried to do, but without falling into either scientism or historicism. Again, most philosophers who see Marx, Freud, or both as figures who need to be drawn into "mainstream" philosophy have tried to develop quasi-epistemological systems which center around the phenomenon which both Marx and Freud throw into relief—the change in behavior which results from change in self-description. Such philosophers see traditional epistemology as committed to "objectivizing" human beings, and they hope for a successor subject to epistemology which will do for "reflection" what the tradition did for "objectivizing knowledge."

I have been insisting that we should not try to have a successor subject to epistemology, but rather try to free ourselves from the notion that philosophy must center around the discovery of a permanent framework for inquiry. In particular, we should free ourselves from the notion that philosophy can explain what science leaves unexplained. From my point of view, the attempt to develop a "universal pragmatics" or a "transcendental hermeneutics" is very suspicious. For it seems to promise just what Sartre tells us we are not going to have—a way of seeing freedom as nature (or, less cryptically, a way of seeing our creation of, and choice between, vocabularies in the same "normal" way as we see ourselves *within* one of those vocabularies). Such attempts start out by viewing the search for objective knowledge through normal discourse in the way I have suggested it should be viewed—as one element in edification. But they then often go on to more ambitious claims. The following passage from Habermas is an example:

> . . . the functions knowledge has in universal contexts of practical life can only be successfully analyzed in the framework of a reformulated transcendental philosophy. This, incidentally, does not entail an empiricist critique of the claim to absolute truth. As long as cognitive interests can be identified and analyzed through reflection upon the logic of inquiry in the natural and cultural sciences, they can legitimately claim a "transcendental" status. They assume an "empirical" status as soon as they are analyzed as the result of natural history—analyzed, as it were, in terms of cultural anthropology.[21]

I want to claim, on the contrary, that there is no point in trying to find a general synoptic way of "analyzing" the "functions knowledge has in universal contexts of practical life," and that cultural anthropology (in a large sense which includes intellectual history) is all we need.

Habermas and other authors who are impelled by the same motives see the suggestion that empirical inquiry suffices as incorporating an "objectivistic illusion." They tend to see Deweyan pragmatism, and the "scientific realism" of Sellars and Feyerabend, as the products of an inadequate epistemology. In my view, the great virtue of Dewey, Sellars, and Feyerabend is that they point the way toward, and partially exemplify, a nonepistemological sort of philosophy, and thus one which gives up any hope of the "transcendental." Habermas says that for a theory to "ground itself transcendentally" is for it to

> become familiar with the range of inevitable subjective conditions which both make the theory possible *and* place limits on it, for this kind of transcendental corroboration tends always to criticize an overly self-confident self-understanding of itself.[22]

Specifically, this overconfidence consists in thinking that

> there can be such a thing as truthfulness to reality in the sense postulated by philosophical realism. Correspondence-theories of truth tend to hypostatize facts as entities in the world. It is the intention and inner logic of an epistemology reflecting upon the conditions of possible experience as such to uncover the objectivistic illusions of such a view. Every form of transcendental philosophy claims to identify the conditions of the objectivity of experience by analyzing the categorical structure of objects of possible experience.[23]

But Dewey, Wittgenstein, Sellars, Kuhn, and the other heroes of this book all have their own ways of debunking "truthfulness to reality in the sense postulated by philosophical realism," and none of them think that this is to be done by "analyzing the categorical structure of objects of possible experience."

The notion that we can get around overconfident philosophical realism and positivistic reductions only by adopting something like Kant's transcendental standpoint seems to me the basic mistake in programs like that of Habermas (as well as in Husserl's notion of a "phenomenology of the life-world" which will describe people in some way "prior" to that offered by science). What is required to accomplish these laudable purposes is not Kant's "epistemological" distinction between the transcendental and the empirical standpoints, but rather his "existentialist" distinction between people as empirical selves and as moral agents.[24] Normal scientific discourse can always be seen in two different ways—as the successful search for objective truth, or as one discourse among others, one among many projects we engage in. The former point of view falls in with the normal practice of normal science. There questions of moral choice or of edification do not arise, since they have already been preempted by the tacit and "self-confident" commitment to the search for objective truth on the subject in question. The latter point of view is one from which we ask such questions as "What is the point?" "What moral is to be drawn from our knowledge of how we, and the rest of nature, work?" or "What are we to do with ourselves now that we know the laws of our own behavior?"

The primal error of systematic philosophy has always been the notion that such questions are to be answered by some new ("metaphysical" or "transcendental") descriptive or explanatory discourse (dealing with, e.g., "man," "spirit," or "language"). This attempt to answer questions of justification by discovering new objective truths, to answer the moral agent's request for justifications with descriptions of a privileged domain, is the philosopher's special form of bad faith—his special way of substituting pseudo-cognition for moral choice. Kant's greatness was to have seen through the "metaphysical" form of this attempt, and to have destroyed the traditional conception of reason to make room for moral faith. Kant gave us a way of seeing scientific truth as something which could never supply an answer to our demand for a point, a justification, a way of claiming that our moral decision about what to do is based on *knowledge* of the nature of the world. Unfortunately, Kant put his diagnosis of science in terms of the discovery of "inevitable subjective conditions," to be revealed by reflection upon scientific inquiry. Equally unfortunately, he thought that there really was a decision procedure for moral dilemmas (though not based on *knowledge*, since our grasp of the categorical imperative is not a *cognition*).[25] So he created new forms of philosophical bad faith—substituting "transcendental" attempts to find one's true self for "metaphysical" attempts to find a world elsewhere. By tacitly identifying the moral agent with the constituting transcendental self, he left the road open to ever more complicated post-Kantian attempts to reduce freedom to nature, choice to knowledge, the *pour-*

soi to the *en-soi*. This is the road I have been trying to block by recasting ahistorical and permanent distinctions between nature and spirit, "objectivizing science" and reflection, epistemology and hermeneutics, in terms of historical and temporary distinctions between the familiar and the unfamiliar, the normal and the abnormal. For this way of treating these distinctions lets us see them not as dividing two areas of inquiry but as the distinction between inquiry and something which is *not* inquiry, but is rather the inchoate questioning out of which inquiries—new normal discourses—may (or may not) emerge.

To put this claim in another way, which may help bring out its connections with naturalism, I am saying that the positivists were absolutely right in thinking it imperative to extirpate metaphysics, when "metaphysics" means the attempt to give knowledge of what science cannot know. For this is the attempt to find a discourse which combines the advantages of normality with those of abnormality—the intersubjective security of objective truth combined with the edifying character of an unjustifiable but unconditional moral claim. The urge to set philosophy on the secure path of a science is the urge to combine Plato's project of moral choice as ticking off the objective truths about a special sort of object (the Idea of the Good) with the sort of intersubjective and democratic agreement about objects found in normal science.[26] Philosophy which was utterly unedifying, utterly irrelevant to such moral choices as whether or not to believe in God would count not as *philosophy,* but only as some special sort of science. So as soon as a program to put philosophy on the secure path of science succeeds, it simply converts philosophy into a boring academic specialty. Systematic philosophy exists by perpetually straddling the gap between description and justification, cognition and choice, getting the facts right and telling us how to live.

Once this point is seen, we can see more clearly why epistemology emerged as the essence of systematic philosophy. For epistemology is the attempt to see the patterns of justification within normal discourse as *more* than just such patterns. It is the attempt to see them as hooked on to something which demands moral commitment—Reality, Truth, Objectivity, Reason. To be behaviorist in epistemology, on the contrary, is to look at the normal scientific discourse of our day bifocally, both as patterns adopted for various historical reasons and as the achievement of objective truth, where "objective truth" is no more and no less than the best idea we currently have about how to explain what is going on. From the point of view of epistemological behaviorism, the only truth in Habermas's claim that scientific inquiry is made possible, and limited, by "inevitable subjective conditions" is that such inquiry is made possible by the adoption of practices of justification, and that such practices have possible alternatives. But these "subjective conditions" are in no sense "inevitable" ones discoverable by "reflection upon the logic of inquiry." They are just the facts about what a given society, or profession, or other group, takes to be good ground for assertions of a certain sort. Such disciplinary matrices are studied by the usual empirical-cum-hermeneutic methods of "cultural anthropology." From the point of view of the group in question these subjective conditions are a combination of commonsensical practical imperatives (e.g., tribal taboos, Mill's Methods) with the standard current theory about the subject. From the point of view of the historian of ideas or the anthropologist they are the empirical facts about the beliefs, desires, and practices of a certain group of human beings. These are incompatible points of view, in the sense that we cannot be at both viewpoints simultaneously. But there is no reason and no need to subsume the two in a higher synthesis. The group in question may itself shift from the one point of view to the other (thus "objectivizing" their past selves through a process of "reflection" and making new sentences true of their present selves). But this is not a mysterious process which demands a new understanding of human knowledge. It is the commonplace fact that people may develop doubts about what they are doing, and thereupon begin to discourse in ways incommensurable with those they used previously.

This goes also for the most spectacular and disturbing new discourses. When such edifying philosophers as Marx, Freud, and Sartre offer new explanations of our usual patterns of justifying our actions and assertions, and when these explanations are taken up and integrated into our lives, we have striking examples of the phenomenon of reflection's changing vocabulary and behavior. But as I argued in chapter seven, this phenomenon does not require any new understanding of theory-construction or theory-confirmation. To say that we have changed ourselves by internalizing a new self-description (using terms like "bourgeois intellectual" or "self-destructive" or "self-deceiving") is true enough. But this is no more startling than the fact that men changed the data of botany by hybridization, which was in turn made possible by botanical theory, or that they changed their own lives by inventing bombs and vaccines. Meditation on the possibility of such changes, like reading science fiction, does help us overcome the self-confidence of "philosophical realism." But such meditation does not need to be supplemented by a transcendental account of the nature of reflection. All that is necessary is the edifying invocation of the fact or possibility of abnormal discourses, undermining our reliance upon the knowledge we have gained through normal discourses. The objectionable self-confidence in question is simply the tendency of normal discourse to block the flow of conversation by presenting itself as offering the canonical vocabulary for discussion of a given topic—and, more particularly, the tendency of normal epistemologically centered philosophy to block the road by putting itself forward as the final commensurating vocabulary for all *possible* rational discourse. Self-confidence of the former, limited sort is overthrown by edifying philosophers who put the very idea of universal commensuration, and of systematic philosophy, in doubt.

Risking intolerable repetitiveness, I want to insist again that the distinction between normal and abnormal discourse does not coincide with any distinction of subject matter (e.g., nature versus history, or facts versus values), method (e.g., objectivation versus reflection), faculty (e.g., reason versus imagination), or any of the other distinctions which systematic philosophy has used to make the sense of the world consist in the objective truth about some previously unnoticed portion or feature of the world. *Anything* can be discoursed of abnormally, just as anything can become edifying and anything can be systematized. I have been discussing the relation between natural science and other disciplines simply because, since the period of Descartes and Hobbes, the assumption that scientific discourse was normal discourse and that all other discourse needed to be modeled upon it has been the standard motive for philosophizing. Once we set this assumption aside, however, we can also set aside the various anti-naturalisms about which I have been complaining. More specifically, we can assert all of the following:

Every speech, thought, theory, poem, composition, and philosophy will turn out to be completely predictable in purely naturalistic terms. Some atoms-and-the-void account of micro-processes within individual human beings will permit the prediction of every sound or inscription which will ever be uttered. There are no ghosts.

Nobody will be able to predict his own actions, thoughts, theories, poems, etc., before deciding upon them or inventing them. (This is not an interesting remark about the odd nature of human beings, but rather a trivial consequence of what it means to "decide" or "invent.") So no hope (or danger) exists that cognition of oneself as *en-soi* will cause one to cease to exist *pour-soi*.

The complete set of laws which enable these predictions to be made, plus complete descriptions (in atoms-and-the-void (terms) of all human beings, would not yet be the whole "objective truth" about human beings, nor the whole set of true predictions about them. There would remain as many other distinct sets of such objective truths (some useful for prediction, some not) as there were incommensurable vocabularies within which normal inquiry about human beings could be conducted (e.g., all those vocabularies within which we attribute beliefs and desires, virtues and beauty).

Incommensurability entails irreducibility but not incompatibility, so the failure to "reduce" these various vocabularies to that of "bottom-level" atoms-and-the-void science casts no doubt upon their cognitive status or upon the metaphysical status of their objects. (This goes as much for the aesthetic worth of poems as for the beliefs of persons, as much for virtues as for volitions.)

The assemblage, *per impossibile*, of all these objective truths would still not necessarily be edifying. It might be the picture of a world without a sense, without a moral. Whether it seemed to point a moral to an individual would depend upon that individual. It would be true or false that it so seemed, or did not seem, to him. But it would not be objectively true or false that it "really did," or did not, have a sense or a moral. Whether his knowledge of the world leaves him with a sense of what to do with or in the world is itself predictable, but whether it *should* is not.

The fear of science, of "scientism," of "naturalism," of self-objectivation, of being turned by too much knowledge into a thing rather than a person, is the fear that all discourse will become normal discourse. That is, it is the fear that there will be objectively true or false answers to every question we ask, so that human worth will consist in knowing truths, and human virtue will be merely justified true belief.

This is frightening because it cuts off the possibility of something new under the sun, of human life as poetic rather than merely contemplative.

But the dangers to abnormal discourse do not come from science or naturalistic philosophy. They come from the scarcity of food and from the secret police. Given leisure and libraries, the conversation which Plato began will not end in self-objectivation—not because aspects of the world, or of human beings, escape being objects of scientific inquiry, but simply because free and leisured conversation generates abnormal discourse as the sparks fly upward.

5. Philosophy in the Conversation of Mankind I end this book with an allusion to Oakeshott's famous title,[27] because it catches the tone in which, I think, philosophy should be discussed. Much of what I have said about epistemology and its possible successors is an attempt to draw some corollaries from Sellars's doctrine that

> in characterizing an episode or a state as that of *knowing,* we are not giv-
> ing an empirical description of that episode or state; we are placing it in
> the logical space of reasons, of justifying and being able to justify what
> one says.[28]

If we see knowing not as having an essence, to be described by scientists or philosophers, but rather as a right, by current standards, to believe, then we are well on the way to seeing *conversation* as the ultimate context within which knowledge is to be understood. Our focus shifts from the relation between human beings and the objects of their inquiry to the relation between alternative standards of justification, and from there to the actual changes in those standards which make up intellectual history. This brings us to appreciate Sellars's own description of his mythical hero Jones, the man who invented the Mirror of Nature and thereby made modern philosophy possible:

> Does the reader not recognize Jones as Man himself in the middle of his
> journey from the grunts and groans of the cave to the subtle and polydi-
> mensional discourse of the drawing room, the laboratory, and the study,
> the language of Henry and William James, of Einstein and of the philoso-
> phers who, in their efforts to break out of discourse to an ἀρχή beyond dis-
> course, have provided the most curious, dimension of all? (p. 196)

In this book I have offered a sort of prolegomenon to a history of epistemology-centered philosophy as an episode in the history of European culture. Such philosophy goes back to the Greeks, and goes sideways into all sorts of non-philosophical disciplines which have, at one time or another, proposed themselves as substitutes for epistemology, and thus for philosophy. So the episode in question cannot simply be identified with "modern philosophy," in the sense of the standard textbook sequence of great philosophers from Descartes to Russell and Husserl. But that sequence is, nevertheless, where the search for foundations for knowledge is most explicit. So most of my attempts to deconstruct the image of the Mirror of Nature have concerned these philosophers. I have tried to show how their urge to break out into an ἀρχή beyond discourse is rooted in the urge to see social practices of justification as more than just such practices. I have, however, focused mainly on the expressions of this urge in the recent literature of analytical philosophy. The result is thus no more than a prolegomenon. A proper historical treatment would require both learning and skills which I do not possess. But I would hope that the prolegomenon has been sufficient to let one see contemporary issues in philosophy as events in a certain stage of a conversation—a conversation which once knew nothing of these issues and may know nothing of them again.

The fact that we can continue the conversation Plato began without discussing the topics Plato wanted discussed, illustrates the difference between treating philosophy as a voice in a conversation and treating it as a subject, a *Fach*, a field of professional inquiry. The conversation Plato began has been enlarged by more voices than Plato would have dreamed possible, and thus by topics he knew nothing of. A "subject"—astrology, physics, classical philosophy, furniture design—may undergo revolutions, but it gets its self-image from its present state, and its history is necessarily written "Whiggishly" as an account of its gradual maturation. This is the most frequent way of writing the history of philosophy, and I cannot claim to have avoided such Whiggery entirely in sketching the sort of history which needs to be written. But I hope that I have shown how we can see the issues with which philosophers are presently concerned, and with which they Whiggishly see philosophy as having always (perhaps unwittingly) been concerned, as results of historical accident, as turns the conversation has taken.[29] It has taken this turn for a long time, but it might turn in another direction without human beings thereby losing their reason, or losing touch with "the real problems."

The conversational interest of philosophy as a subject, or of some individual philosopher of genius, has varied and will continue to vary in unpredictable ways depending upon contingencies. These contingencies will range from what happens in physics to what happens in politics. The lines between disciplines will blur and shift, and new disciplines will arise, in the ways illustrated by Galileo's successful attempt to create "purely scientific questions" in the seventeenth century. The notions of "philosophical significance" and of "purely philosophical question," as they are currently used, gained sense only around the time of Kant. Our post-Kantian sense that epistemology or some successor subject is at the center of philosophy (and that moral philosophy, aesthetics, and social philosophy, for example, are somehow derivative) is a reflection of the fact that the professional philosopher's self-image depends upon his professional preoccupation with the image of the Mirror of Nature. Without the Kantian assumption that the philosopher can decide *quaestiones juris* concerning the claims of the rest of culture, this self-image collapses. That assumption depends on the notion that there is such a thing as understanding the essence of knowledge— doing what Sellars tells us we cannot do.

To drop the notion of the philosopher as knowing something about knowing which nobody else knows so well would be to drop the notion that his voice always has an overriding claim on the attention of the other participants in the conversation. It would also be to drop the notion that there is something called "philosophical method" or "philosophical technique" or "the philosophical point of view" which enables the professional philosopher, *ex officio,* to have interesting views about, say, the respectability of psychoanalysis, the legitimacy of certain dubious laws, the resolution of moral dilemmas, the "soundness" of schools of historiography or literary criticism, and the like. Philosophers often do have interesting views upon such questions, and their professional training as philosophers is often a necessary condition for their having the views they do. But this is not to say that philosophers have a special kind of knowledge about knowledge (or anything else) from which they draw relevant corollaries. The useful kibitzing they can provide on the various topics I just mentioned is made possible by their familiarity with the historical background of arguments on similar topics, and, most importantly, by the fact that arguments on such topics are punctuated by stale philosophical clichés which the other participants have stumbled across in their reading, but about which professional philosophers know the pros and cons by heart.

The neo-Kantian image of philosophy as a profession, then, is involved with the image of the "mind" or "language" as mirroring nature. So it might seem that epistemological behaviorism and the consequent rejection of mirror-imagery entail the claim that there can or should be no such profession. But this does not follow. Professions can survive the paradigms which gave them birth. In any case, the need for teachers who have read the great dead philosophers is quite enough to insure that there will be philosophy departments as long as there are universities. The actual result of a widespread loss of faith in mirror-imagery would be merely an "encapsulation" of the problems created by this imagery within a historical period. I do not know whether we are in fact at the end of an era. This will depend, I suspect, on whether Dewey, Wittgenstein, and Heidegger are taken to heart. It may be that mirror-imagery and "mainstream," systematic philosophy will be revitalized once again by some revolutionary of genius. Or it may be that the image of the philosopher which Kant offered is about to go the way of the medieval image of the priest. If that happens, even the philosophers themselves will no longer take seriously the notion of philosophy as providing "foundations" or "justifications" for the rest of culture, or as adjudicating *quaestiones juris* about the proper domains of other disciplines.

Whichever happens, however, there is no danger of philosophy's "coming to an end." Religion did not come to an end in the Enlightenment, nor painting in Impressionism. Even if the period from Plato to Nietzsche is encapsulated and "distanced" in the way Heidegger suggests, and even if twentieth-century philosophy comes to seem a stage of awkward transitional backing and filling (as sixteenth-century philosophy now seems to us), there will be something called "philosophy" on the other side of the transition. For even if problems about representation look as obsolete to our descendants as problems about hylomorphism look to us, people will still read Plato, Aristotle, Descartes, Kant, Hegel, Wittgenstein, and Heidegger. What roles these men will play in our descendants' conversation, no one knows. Whether the distinction between systematic and edifying philosophy will carry over, no one knows either. Perhaps philosophy will become purely edifying, so that one's self-identification as a philosopher will be purely in terms of the books one reads and discusses, rather than in terms of the problems one wishes to solve. Perhaps a new form of systematic philosophy will be found which has nothing whatever to do with epistemology but which nevertheless makes normal philosophical inquiry possible. These speculations are idle, and nothing I have been saying makes one more plausible than another. The only point on which I would insist is that philosophers' moral concern should be with continuing the conversation of the West, rather than with insisting upon a place for the traditional problems of modern philosophy within that conversation.

Notes

1. Hans-Georg Gadamer, *Truth and Method* (New York, 1975). p. xi. Indeed, it would be reasonable to call Gadamer's book a tract against the very idea of method, where this is conceived of as an attempt at commensuration. It is instructive to note the parallels between this book and Paul Feyerabend's *Against Method*. My treatment of Gadamer is indebted to Alasdair MacIntyre; see his "Contexts of Interpretation," *Boston University Journal* 24 (1976), 41–46.
2. Gadamer, *Truth and Method*, p. xiii.
3. Cf. ibid., p. 15. "But we may recognize that *Bildung* is an element of spirit without being tied to Hegel's philosophy of absolute spirit, just as the insight into the historicity of consciousness is not tied to his philosophy of world history."
4. The contrast here is the same as that involved in the traditional quarrel between "classical" education and "scientific" education, mentioned by Gadamer in his opening section on "The Significance of the Humanist Tradition." More generally, it can be seen as an aspect of the quarrel between poetry (which cannot be omitted from the former sort of education) and philosophy (which, when conceiving of itself as super-science, would like to become foundational to the latter sort of education). Yeats asked the spirits (whom, he believed, were dictating *A Vision* to him through his wife's mediumship) why they had come. The spirits replied, "To bring you metaphors for poetry." A philosopher might have expected some hard facts about what it was like on the other side, but Yeats was not disappointed.
5. See the section called "The Overcoming of the Epistemological Problem . . ." in *Truth and Method*, pp. 214ff., and compare Martin Heidegger, *Being and Time*, trans. John Macquarrie and Edward Robinson (New York, 1962), sec. 32.
6. See Jean-Paul Sartre, *Being and Nothingness*, trans. Hazel Barnes (New York, 1956), pt. two, chap. 3, sec. 5, and the "Conclusion" of the book.
7. It would have been fortunate if Sartre had followed up his remark that man is the being whose essence is to have no essence by saying that this

went for all other beings also. Unless this addition is made, Sartre will appear to be insisting on the good old metaphysical distinction between spirit and nature in other terms, rather than simply making the point that man is always free to choose new descriptions (for, among other things, himself).

8. Dewey, it seems to me, is the one author usually classified as a "naturalist" who did not have this reductive attitude, despite his incessant talk about "scientific method." Dewey's peculiar achievement was to have remained sufficiently Hegelian not to think of natural science as having an inside track on the essences of things, while becoming sufficiently naturalistic to think of human beings in Darwinian terms.

9. Gadamer, *Truth and Method,* p. 12.

10. See Heidegger's discussion of "values" in *Being and Time,* p. 133, and Sartre's in *Being and Nothingness,* pt. two, chap. 1, sec. 4. Compare Gadamer's remarks on Weber (*Truth and Method,* pp. 461ff.).

11. See Gadamer's polemic against "the subjectivization of the aesthetic" in Kant's Third Critique (*Truth and Method,* p. 87) and compare Heidegger's remarks in "Letter on Humanism" on Aristotle's distinctions among physics, logic, and ethics (Heidegger, *Basic Writings,* ed. Krell [New York, 1976], p. 232).

12. Consider the passage from Anatole France's "Garden of Epicurus" which Jacques Derrida cites at the beginning of his "La Mythologie Blanche" (in *Marges de la Philosophic* [Paris, 1972], p. 250):

. . . the metaphysicians, when they make up a new language, are like knife-grinders who grind coins and medals against their stone instead of knives and scissors. They rub out the relief, the inscriptions, the portraits, and when one can no longer see on the coins Victoria, or Wilhelm, or the French Republic, they explain: these coins now have nothing specifically English or German or French about them, for we have taken them out of time and space; they now are no longer worth, say, five francs, but rather have an inestimable value, and the area in which they are a medium of exchange has been infinitely extended.

13. See Karl-Otto Apel's comparison of Wittgenstein and Heidegger as having both "called into question Western metaphysics as a theoretical discipline" (*Transformation der Philosophie* [Frankfurt, 1973], vol. 1, p. 228). I have not offered interpretations of Dewey, Wittgenstein, and Heidegger in support of what I have been saying about them, but I have tried to do so in a piece on Wittgenstein called "Keeping Philosophy Pure" (*Yale Review* [Spring 1976], pp. 336–356), in "Overcoming the Tradition: Heidegger and Dewey" (*Review of Metaphysics* 30 [1976], 280–305), and in "Dewey's Metaphysics" in *New Studies in the Philosophy of John Dewey,* ed. Steven M. Cahn (Hanover, N. H., 1977).

14. This Heideggerean point about language is spelled out at length and didactically by Derrida in *La Voix et le Phénomène,* translated as *Speech and Phenomenon* by David Allison (Evanston, 1973). See Newton Garver's comparison of Derrida and Wittgenstein in his "Introduction" to this translation.

15. The permanent fascination of the man who dreamed up the whole idea of Western philosophy—Plato—is that we still do not know which sort of philosopher he was. Even if the *Seventh Letter* is set aside as spurious, the fact that after millenniums of commentary nobody knows which passages in the dialogues are jokes keeps the puzzle fresh.

16. Heidegger's *"Die Zeit des Weltbildes"* (translated as "The Age of the World-View" by Marjorie Grene in *Boundary II* [1976]) is the best discussion of this difficulty I have come across.

17. Derrida's recent writings are meditations on how to avoid these metaphors. Like Heidegger in "Aus einem Gespräch von der Sprache zwischen einem Japaner und einem Fragenden" (in *Unterwegs zur Sprache* [Pfullingen, 1959]), Derrida occasionally toys with the notion of the superiority of Oriental languages and of ideographic writing.

18. On this point, see William Frankena's classic "The Naturalistic Fallacy," *Mind* 68 (1939).

19. What seems to be a sense of being shoved around by values, they reductively say, is just physical reality in disguise (e.g., neural arrangements or glandular secretions programmed by parental conditioning).

20. Kierkegaard made this choice the prototype of his own choice of "subjectivity" over "system." Cf. *Concluding Unscientific Postscript*, trans. David Swenson and Walter Lowrie (Princeton, 1941), p. 97.

21. Jürgen Habermas, "Nachwort" to the second edition of *Erkenntnis und Interesse* (Frankfurt: Surkamp, 1973), p. 410; translated as "A Postscript to *Knowledge and Human Interests*," by Christian Lenhardt in *Philosophy of the Social Sciences* 3 (1973), 181. For a criticism of the line Habermas takes here—a criticism paralleling my own—see Michael Theunissen, *Gesellschaft und Geschichte: Zur Kritik der Kritischen Theorie* (Berlin, 1969), pp. 20ff. (I owe the reference to Theunissen to Raymond Geuss.)

22. Habermas, "Nachwort," p. 411; English translation, p. 182.

23. Ibid., pp. 408–409; English translation, p. 180.

24. Wilfrid Sellars uses this latter Kantian distinction to good effect in his insistence that personhood is a matter of "being one of us," of falling within the scope of practical imperatives of the form "Would that we all . . .," rather than a feature of certain organisms to be isolated by empirical means. I have invoked this claim several times in this book, particularly in chapter four, section 4. For Sellars's own use of it, see *Science and Metaphysics* (London and New York, 1968), chap. 7, and the essay "Science and Ethics" in his *Philosophical Perspectives* (Springfield, Ill., 1967).

25. See Kant's distinction between knowledge and necessary belief at *K.d.r.V.*, A824–B852ff., and especially his use of *Unternehmung* as a synonym for the latter. This section of the First Critique seems to me the one which gives most sense to the famous passage about denying reason to make room for faith at Bxxx. At many other points, however, Kant inconsistently speaks of practical reason as supplying an enlargement of our *knowledge*.

26. The positivists themselves quickly succumbed to this urge. Even while insisting that moral questions were noncognitive they thought to give

quasi-scientific status to their moralistic attacks on traditional philoso-phy—thus making themselves subject to self-referential criticisms concern-ing their "emotive" use of "noncognitive."

27. Cf. Michael Oakeshott, "The Voice of Poetry in the Conversation of Mankind," in his *Rationalism and Politics* (New York, 1975).

28. Wilfrid Sellars, *Science, Perception and Reality* (London and New York, 1963), p. 169.

29. Two recent writers—Michel Foucault and Harold Bloom—make this sense of the brute factuality of historical origins central to their work. Cf. Bloom, *A Map of Misreading* (New York, 1975), p. 33: "All continuities possess the paradox of being absolutely arbitrary in their origins and absolutely inescapable in their teleologies. We know this so vividly from what we all of us oxymoronically call our love lives that its literary counterparts need little demonstration." Foucault says that his way of looking at the history of ideas "permits the introduction, into the very roots of thought, of notions of *chance, discontinuity* and *materiality.*" ("The Discourse on Lan-guage," included in the *Archaeology of Knowledge* [New York, 1972], p. 231) It is hardest of all to see brute contingency in the history of *philosophy,* if only because since Hegel the historiography of philosophy has been "pro-gressive," or (as in Heidegger's inversion of Hegel's account of progress) "retrogressive," but never without a sense of inevitability. If we could once see the desire for a permanent, neutral, ahistorical, commensurating vocab-ulary as itself a historical phenomenon, then perhaps we could write the history of philosophy less dialectically and less sentimentally than has been possible hitherto.

17

MAXINE GREENE

Maxine Greene (born in 1917) is professor emeritus at Teachers College, Columbia University. Her academic career is distinguished by an indefatigable faith in humanity, the arts, and the possibility of a more just and inclusive future. Like no other philosopher of education, her texts proliferate with quotations drawn broadly from philosophers, novelists, poets, and dramatists. Her writing reaches a diverse audience of professors, artists, arts administrators, and musicians, as well as a legion of educators across the globe. Greene addresses her readers as human beings. She appeals to teachers' tacit understanding that they teach because they love learning.

Globalization has left individuals overwhelmed with choices for consumption, entertainment, fashion, design, health, diet, appearance, lifestyle, and even credit. Rarely are they encouraged to question and resist the conditioning forces that underlie these so-called choices. Frequently, individuals are called to teaching because they are concerned about the "birth of meaning" for children, and not because they want to raise test-scores, make good citizens, or provide a workforce. Teachers want children to ask questions in an effort to reveal the unrevealed and reach toward what is not yet. The cognizance of perspective brings about the proliferation of interpretation, the transformation of experience, and the realization of new possibilities. Newly imagined possibilities prompt individuals to recognize, articulate, and overcome the obstacles to their shared becoming.

Teachers enlist multiple perspectives from different vantage points because what is familiar and ordinary to one might be radically unfamiliar and strange to another. Passionate about ideas, Greene is adamant that they are not the exclusive purview of the armchair philosopher. Ideas are of great existential and political consequence because they animate the lives of individuals, communities, cultures, and societies. The arts reflect this. In her own work, Greene uses literature to document and elaborate philosophical understandings. In her view, literature not only instantiates different conceptual understandings of freedom but also promotes existential freedom by exposing readers to diverse perspectives.

For Greene, to be educated is to be free. To be free is to ask critical questions about the world we inhabit in order to create new initiatives. Unfortunately, our thinking about freedom has become infected by a certain lassitude: we accept it as given, assert it as right, or consider it negatively as the absence of interference from others. Greene argues that freedom is not a given: it is an ability to look at situations, individuals, actions, and ourselves, as if they could be otherwise. It is to take responsibility for oneself in the presence of others. It is to risk becoming different. Freedom is the imaginative consideration of alternative possibilities, and it only emerges when individuals come together to overcome obstacles by envisaging new possibilities. Greene cites Frederick Douglass as an exemplar of freedom because, throughout his life, he managed to find new meanings by questioning what he already knew.

A free act is a particularized act. Greene states that "it is undertaken from the standpoint of a particular, situated person trying to bring into existence something contingent on her/his hopes, expectation, and capacities." It follows that an individual's ability to envision new possibilities relies on the quality of our public spaces and the kinds of reflection available to identities circumscribed by race, gender, class, age, and ability within those public spaces. Greene argues in support of Michel Foucault and others, that the social constitution of identity is a manifestation of power. The possibility for envisaging new possibilities also relies on the accidents of history which bring changes to our situations. For these reasons, freedom must involve both the deconstruction of myths of education, family, femininity, and marginalization, for example, and the honest scrutiny of lived actualities. As an endless cycle of constructing and deconstructing our lived realities, the human condition is neither a case of absolute determinism nor choice.

For Greene, freedom necessarily implies pluralism. An education that aims at freedom strives "to discover how to open spaces for persons in their plurality, spaces where they become different, where they can grow." Drawing on Arendt, Green argues that these spaces must have features of "equality and distinction." Without equality of regard, there can be no public spaces and without distinctiveness there is no need for the words and actions that make us intelligible to others.

REFERENCES

Ayers, William, and Janet Miller, eds. *A Light in Dark Time: Maxine Greene and the Unfinished Conversation*. New York: Teachers College Press, 1998.

Greene, Maxine. *Teacher as Stranger: Educational Philosophy for a Modern Age*. Belmont, CA: Wadsworth, 1967.

Greene, Maxine. *The Dialectic of Freedom*. New York: Teachers College Press, 1988.

Greene, Maxine. *Variations on a Blue Guitar: The Lincoln Center Institute Lectures on Aesthetic Education*. New York: Maxine Greene and the Lincoln Center, 2001.

Pinar, F. William, ed. *The Passionate Mind of Maxine Greene "I Am . . . Not Yet."* Bristol, PA: Taylor and Francis, 1998.

TEACHER AS STRANGER

. . . And must not an animal be a lover of learning who determines what is or is not friendly to him by the test of knowledge and ignorance?

Most assuredly.

And is not the love of learning the love of wisdom, which is philosophy?

They are the same, he replied.

And may we not say confidently of man also, that he who is likely to be gentle to his friends and acquaintances, must by nature be a lover of wisdom and knowledge?

That we may safely affirm.

Then he who is to be a really good and noble guardian of the State will require to unite in himself philosophy and spirit and swiftness and strength?

Undoubtedly.

Then we have found the desired natures; and now that we have found them, how are they to be reared and educated?

—Plato
The Republic

The University! So he had passed beyond the challenge of the sentries who had stood as guardians of his boyhood and had sought to keep him among them that he might be subject to them and serve their ends. Pride after satisfaction uplifted him like long slow waves. The end he had been born to serve yet did not see had led him to escape by an unseen path: and now it beckoned to him once more and a new adventure was about to be opened to him.

—James Joyce
A Portrait of the Artist as a Young Man

To take a stranger's vantage point on everyday reality is to look inquiringly and wonderingly on the world in which one lives. It is like returning home from a long stay in some other place. The homecomer notices details and patterns in his environment he never saw before. He finds that he has to think about local rituals and customs to make sense of them once more. For a time he feels quite separate from the person who is wholly at home in his ingroup and takes the familiar world for granted.

From *Teacher as Stranger, Educational Philosophy for the Modern Age, 1st edition* by Maxine Greene. 1973. Reprinted with permission of Wadsworth, a division of Thomson Learning: www.thomsonrights.com. Fax 800 730-2215.

Such a person, writes Alfred Schutz, ordinarily "accepts the ready-made standardized scheme of the cultural pattern handed down to him by ancestors, teachers, and authorities as an unquestioned and unquestionable guide in all the situations which normally occur within the social world."[1] The homecomer may have been such a person. Now, looking through new eyes, he cannot take the cultural pattern for granted. It may seem arbitrary to him or incoherent or deficient in some way. To make it meaningful again, he must interpret and reorder what he sees in the light of his changed experience. He must consciously engage in inquiry.

When thinking-as-usual becomes untenable for anyone, the individual is bound to experience a crisis of consciousness. The formerly unquestioned has become questionable; the submerged has become visible. He may become like Meursault in Albert Camus's *The Stranger*, when he looks at his own murder trial and sees an ingroup ritual:

> Just then I noticed that almost all the people in the courtroom were greeting each other, exchanging remarks and forming groups—behaving, in fact, as in a club where the company of others of one's own taste and standing makes one feel at ease. That, no doubt, explained the odd impression I had of being *de trop* here, a sort of gate-crasher.[2]

Or he may come to resemble Hester Prynne, in Nathaniel Hawthorne's *The Scarlet Letter*. Ostracized for having committed adultery. Hester is forced to live at the edge of the wilderness, on the outskirts of the Puritan community. Because she has "a mind of native courage and activity," her "estranged point of view" enables her look critically at institutions once taken for granted, to criticize all "with hardly more reverence that the Indian would feel for the clerical band, the judicial robe, the pillory, the gallows, the fireside, or the church."[3] Both Mersault and Hester are strangers in the sense that they do not share the conventional vision. Camus describes an entirely honest man who will not pretend to share the cultural pieties; Hawthorne describes a woman who is "emancipated." Both see more than their less conscious fellow citizens could possibly see. Both are ready to wonder and question; and it is in wonder and questioning that learning begins.

We do not ask that the teacher perceive his existence as absurd; nor do we demand that he estrange himself from his community. We simply suggest that he struggle against unthinking submergence in the social reality that prevails. If he wishes to present himself as a person actively engaged in critical thinking and authentic choosing, he cannot accept any "ready-made standardized scheme" at face value. He cannot even take for granted the value of intelligence, rationality, or education. Why, after all, *should* a human being act intelligently or rationally? How *does* a teacher justify the educational policies he is assigned to carry out within his school? If the teacher does not pose such questions to himself, he cannot expect his students to pose the kinds of questions about experience which will involve them in self-aware inquiry.

Maurice Merleau-Ponty attributes the feeling of certainty that rules out questioning to the ancient notion that each human being carries within him a *homunculus,* or "little man," who can "see" what is real and true. This *homunculus* represents what is best in the human being; and, unlike the person involved with the natural world and other people, the phantom creature inside always knows the Ideal. Merleau-Ponty writes:

> The "little man within man" is only the phantom of our successful expressive operations; and the admirable man is not this phantom but the man who—installed in his fragile body, in a language which has already done so much speaking, and in a reeling history—gathers himself together and begins to see, to understand, and to signify. There is no longer anything decorous or decorative about today's humanism. It no longer loves man in opposition to his body, mind in opposition to its language, values in opposition to facts. It no longer speaks of man and mind except in a sober way, with modesty: mind and man never are; they show through the movement by which the body becomes gesture, language an oeuvre, and coexistence truth.[4]

The teacher is frequently addressed as if he had no life of his own, no body, and no inwardness. Lecturers seem to presuppose a "man within man" when they describe a good teacher as infinitely controlled and accommodating, technically efficient, impervious to moods. They are likely to define him by the role he is *expected* to play in a classroom, with all his loose ends gathered up and all his doubts resolved. The numerous realities in which he exists as a living person are overlooked. His personal biography is overlooked; so are the many ways in which he expresses his private self in language, the horizons he perceives, the perspectives through which he looks on the world.

Our concern throughout this book has been to make that person visible to himself. If the teacher agrees to submerge himself into the system, if he consents to being defined by others' views of what he is supposed to be, he gives up his freedom "to see, to understand, and to signify" for himself. If he is immersed and impermeable, he can hardly stir others to define themselves as individuals. If, on the other hand, he is willing to take the view of the homecomer and create a new perspective on what he has habitually considered real, his teaching may become the project of a person vitally open to his students and the world. Then he will be in a position to define himself as "admirable" in Merleau-Ponty's sense. He will be continuously engaged in interpreting a reality forever new; he will feel more alive than he ever has before.

Seeking the communicative gesture and the expressive word, such a teacher will try consciously to move among and reflect together with his students. Coexisting with them, opening up perspectival possibilities along with them, he and they may journey toward some important truths as the days go on. "Sometimes one starts to dream," Merleau-Ponty writes, "about what culture, literary life, and teaching could be if all those who participate, having for once rejected idols, would give themselves up to the happiness of reflecting together."[5] The teacher in the United States, facing the adversity of his historic moment, facing violence and inequities and irrationality, may believe the dream to be impossible. Yet, at some level of his consciousness, he may insist on just this kind of happiness. In Albert Camus's *The Plague*, the doctor says he thinks it is *right* to refuse to be balked of happiness. Later, when the plague has reached its peak and he is exhausted by the hopeless battle against it, he still can smile at a young journalist who wants to break the quarantine and escape from the town; in fact, he tells the journalist to hurry "because I, too, would like to do my bit for happiness." There are no good arguments against such a desire. The teacher who feels he too is fighting plague can still nurture the dream.

In this final chapter, we shall have the dream in mind as we talk of possibility and moral choosing and the arts. There will be no closure for us; there cannot be. The questions implicit in our initial chapter remain open: the questions having to do with defining *education*, determining educational purposes, achieving democracy. Customarily, books on educational philosophy conclude with talk of the democratic character, summon up visions of a "good society," or explain the relationships between world understanding and effective public schools. There is always a tendency to drive toward completion, to finish the design, to stand back and look at an articulated whole. Recognizing that each reader must strive toward such completion for himself, we choose to

conclude in the mood expressed by Nick Henry in Ernest Hemingway's
A Farewell to Arms:

> I was always embarrassed by the words sacred, glorious and sacrifice and
> the expression in vain. We had heard them, sometimes standing in the rain
> almost out of earshot, so that only the shouted words came through, and
> had read them, on proclamations that were slapped up by billposters over
> other proclamations, now for a long time, and I had seen nothing sacred,
> and the things that were glorious had no glory and the sacrifices were like
> the stockyards at Chicago if nothing was done with the meat except to
> bury it. There were many words that you could not stand to hear.[6]

Of course, the teacher's experience is not identical with that of a
soldier trapped in a retreat; but most teachers know the meaning of the
slogans and pieties they hear on loudspeaker systems and the procla-
mations they read on bulletin boards, reminders of the glorious purposes pursued by the institution. What teacher has seen anything
sacred in the corridors? Do the things called "glorious" have glory?
Charles Silberman quotes a high school principal, who says: " 'Maybe
the public may think the schools are democratic. They are democratic
as far as the rights of the individual, but as far as the operation, they
are not democratic. In order to get efficiency in a school system, there
has to be a clear pattern of operation, behavior, rules and regulation.
Then there's not time for a group of people to sit down and thrash out
a variety of ideas and to come up with a quick, clear-cut and efficient
policy.' "[7] Writing about a singing lesson in an American school, Jules
Henry describes how the student must substitute the teacher's criteria
for his own: "He must learn that the proper way to sing is tunelessly
and not the way *he* hears music; that the proper way to paint is the
way the teacher says, not the way he sees it; that the proper attitude is
not pleasure but competitive horror at the success of his classmates,
and so on."[8]

Names and concrete nouns are not the only words that ought to be
used in talk about education. But if the teacher can think what he is
doing in the concrete situations of his life, he must be aware of the conventions currently used to organize reality. He must be conscious that
the "fictions" used in sense making (in the schools as well as outside
the schools) are mental constructs, man-made schemata, deserving only
"conditional assent."[9] This point is particularly important in a time like
the present, an era distinctive for the walls of images and words con-

stantly being erected between us and actuality. We need only recall the bombardment of media images that replace the "reality" they purport to represent, that make "the 11 o'clock News" out of wartime atrocities, protest demonstrations, prison riots, political pronouncements, accidents, deformities, deaths. We need only recall the proliferating euphemisms, "waste the enemy," "protective reaction," "correctional facility," "national security," "behavioral engineering," "off the pig," "power to the people," and the rest. It has become all too easy to distance and distort what is experienced with language of that kind. It has become all too easy to cope with social relationships through the taking on and the assigning of roles.

The teacher is continually being asked (at least obliquely) to write a pious and authoritative role for himself and submissive or savage or special roles for the young people he teaches. He has to make a deliberate effort to realize that no role can fully encompass a personality, just as no slogan or abstraction or popular phrase can do justice to a human situation. Unless he is careful, the teacher may tend to oversimplify by means of language, to smooth over the rough places, to live by self-serving myths. For this reason, we are unwilling to end this book by spelling out overarching purposes or slapping still another proclamation on the schoolroom wall.

It makes little difference if the proclamation calls for the defense of the nation or personal liberation, citizenship or spontaneity. Once we spell out aims in general, we are in danger of "embarrassing" ourselves. Moreover, the teacher's feeling of responsibility may well be eroded by an implicit demand that he be the agent of an externally defined purpose, which he can only understand as a slogan or still another expression of prevailing piety. We would emphasize once more the need for self-consciousness and clarity on the part of the individual, the need to frame conditional orders. His aims, therefore, can only be specific ones, identified in concrete situations with respect to concrete tasks and subject matters, where structures and relevancies are not always clear. They must be pursued as lacks are perceived and actions undertaken. Because persons differ, achievements vary, horizons shift, perspectives alter, his aims can never be twice the same.

It must be clear by now that, no matter how carefully he deliberates, how artfully he develops alternative modes of instruction, the teacher is forever involved in constituting meanings. This act of forming applies to perspectives on the teaching act, on education viewed as intentional undertaking and as social enterprise. It applies to the perspectives through which persons are seen, knowledge structures apprehended, ethical problems resolved. Also it applies to questions touching on dissent, reform, and the transformation of cultural institutions; it applies to the methods chosen for responding to the inhumanities of the time. The teacher can not assert that the schools should or should not "dare to change the social order." He must choose the part he will play in such an effort. He must even choose how to conceive the "social order": as an oppressive, impersonal system, as a series of fluid human communities, as "the best of all possible worlds."

At a time of major tensions among groups and moral systems, no educator is in a position to impose designs for harmonizing clashing interests. In his school, for example, the teacher may *propose* resolutions when racial groups are fighting with each other; he may, in time of dire emergency, suppress conflict by force. But it appears to be immoral, at this time, to decide *for* any individual or group what is fair, decent, or humane. Expertise no longer possesses transfer value for other people's private, immediately apprehended experiences, for predicaments that must be phenomenologically understood. The educational task, in the moral domain as well as in others, is to find out how to enable individuals to choose intelligently and authentically for themselves. It involves learning how to equip them with the conceptual tools, the self-respect, and the opportunities to choose—in specific circumstances—how to do what they consider right.

This may be a troubling solution for the teacher who is committed to certain values, causes, or patterns of social change. As citizen or layman, he has the right (and perhaps the obligation) to work for the reforms in which he professes to believe. If he does not act on his beliefs, in fact, he may be said to be in "bad faith," expected to feel "shame." If he has no commitments, if he remains uninvolved, he may not be the engaged, wide-awake teacher young people appear to need. But this causes an inevitable conflict once he commits himself to arousing students to create their own values and seek their own resolutions. Impartial in some areas (when dealing with students as individuals or in their groups), he cannot be impartial or neutral on, say, the Vietnamese War, racial discrimination, drug addiction, or the many injustices that plague American life. Some philosophers, as we have seen, attach so much importance to cool rationality that they would advise the teacher to sublimate his political and social enthusiasms when he is working at school. The teacher has enough to do, they would say, to initiate young people into such activities as "science, poetry, and engineering and possibly a variety of games and pastimes. Most of these are intimately connected not only with occupations and professions but also with possible vocations and ideals of life."[10] Other philosophers would recommend the temperate use of intelligence in cooperative attempts to solve such problems. Still others would draw attention to crisis and adversity. They would insist that political and social commitments permeate an individual's life and that the teacher defines himself as much by the ends he pursues outside the school as by the values he creates within. Conceivably, the activist teacher can struggle for peace and justice for the same reasons he tries to liberate the young to choose for themselves. He knows, as well and as clearly as the analytic philosopher (although on different grounds), that it is morally indefensible to indoctrinate or to tell students categorically that only one mode of action is "right." He may feel, as Jean-Paul Sartre has said, that: "in choosing myself I choose man";[11] but his sense of the universality, even the absoluteness of his choice does not justify his willing against others' freedom. And this is precisely what he would be doing if he tried to use his position to impose his own beliefs.

To lecture against smoking marijuana is obviously questionable; and to proscribe, on moral grounds, use of heroin is futile. What of the student who refuses to attend school regularly because he thinks (as, indeed, his teacher might) that the compulsory school manipulates and imprisons, that he learns far more outside? What of the controversies over sex education? What of the books (such as Piri Thomas's *Down These Mean Streets* or George Jackson's *Soledad Brother*) some charge with being pornographic, subversive, or "inciting to violence"? What, more traditionally, of education for truth telling, decency, cooperativeness, playing fair?

We cannot presume that the teacher functions in an ordered world or a spacious society, where each person's duties in the various departments of his life are clearly set forth. Nor can we take for granted that fundamental agreements lie below the surfaces on a morality viewed as "an instrument of society as a whole for the guidance of individuals and smaller groups."[12] The assumption may be true in the few homogeneous small towns left in America; but it is not likely to be generally true. We have talked about the disintegrating norms throughout the culture, about the loss of trust, about the defiance of codes and the sometimes shocking acceptance of lawbreaking. Much has been written recently about so-called "new crimes": "trashing," pointless vandalism, shoplifting for sport. Gresham Sykes uses divorce as an example, because divorce was once considered shameful and now has little stigma attached to it. He goes on to say that "there are a number of areas of behavior labeled criminal by the law, for which this same sort of 'slipping out from morality' may be occurring for a number of people. The use of drugs, particularly in the case of marihuana, may often be of this order; similarly, certain kinds of sexual behavior, such as premarital sexual relations, seem to be losing a good deal of their moral resonance. The question of whether to engage in such behavior becomes very pragmatic; the question is whether one will be caught."[13]

Complicated problems confront any teacher who attempts "moral education." If he believes, as the positivist philosophers do, that only principles can be taught, along with the nature of good reasons, he still must determine which principles can be made meaningful to the contemporary young. He must determine what sorts of actions have "moral resonance," which do not and which should not. If he considers that guidelines are impossible to define any longer, if he is more concerned with the way people respond to appeals from "conscience" and the way they create themselves as norm-regarding beings, he will still find himself in tension as he watches individuals do violent and careless things. And indeed, no matter what his philosophical approach, the teacher cannot help recognize that human beings are always being demeaned and maltreated, that his students are capable of hatred and bigotries, that it is difficult for anyone *not* to falsify himself. Whether he tries consistently to remain "calm and cool" in the knowledge "that the way of life he prefers, all things considered, includes the moral way of life,"[14] whether he chooses to live "in unsatisfied indignation" because "too high a price is asked for harmony,"[15] he will find himself entangled in the problematic, haunted by open questions. In his capacity as teacher he is expected to know the answers, to have prescriptions at hand which tell the young how they ought to live. Unable to tolerate major personal uncertainties when he is engaged in teaching, he is likely to tell himself that he does indeed have it all worked out, that he *knows*. Camus once wrote: "There is not one human being who, above a certain elementary level of consciousness, does not exhaust himself in trying to find formulae or attitudes which will give his existence the unity it lacks. . . . It is therefore justifiable to say that man has an idea of a better world than this. But better does not mean different, it means unified."[16] This desire for unity or meaning may be the source of the impulse to reach out and to learn; but it can be extremely disquieting, especially for the self-conscious teacher. He can only engage in the movement we have spoken of, at the side of his students, making efforts to constitute meanings—caring intensely about the kind of thinking going on and the choices being made. As aware of his students' incompleteness as he must be of his own, the teacher can only strain to encounter his students without objectifying them; he can only act to help them, as autonomous beings, to choose.

Let us take, as an example, the predicament of a teacher confronted with a Peace Moratorium, a day on which students stay away from classes in symbolic protest against a war. Like many other such situations, this gesture may provide occasion for a considerable amount of moral education if the teacher makes no arbitrary decisions and if the students are free to decide what they think is right to do. Let us suppose the teacher has been much involved with peace campaigns, has belonged to various peace organizations, and has participated in marches and demonstrations. Let us also suppose the teacher is deeply convinced that atrocities are being committed in the current war and that they present a moral issue of consequence for every American. He may believe a widespread indifference partly accounts for the massacres that have taken place, the torture, the indiscriminate bombings, and the rest. He may be convinced the Moratorium will have positive results, so positive that they will erase the negative effects of violent protests carried on in the past. As he sees it, then, he has every reason for saying the Moratorium is worth supporting. He is eager, in fact, for his students to turn out in a body to demonstrate their support.

He has, however, other convictions too. The particular lessons he has been teaching are important to him. He does not believe learning sequences ought to be whimsically or foolishly interrupted; he thinks classroom activity, because it brings him in contact with his students, contributes measurably to their education. A lost day, as he sees it, might mean a setback for some of his pupils, missed learning opportunities for others; and, obviously, observing the Moratorium means his losing the day in that sense. He realizes, in addition, that observing it might suggest to the less motivated that there are more worthwhile things to do than studying; to others it might seem an excuse for time off to observe minor holidays, to celebrate World Series victories, and so on. Taking all this into account, he still believes it is more worthwhile to support the peace action than to do nothing at all.

Some would say that, in coming to this conclusion, the teacher should anticipate the consequences (moral and pedagogical) of each course. Others would stress that he must be clear about his own priority system. Still others would talk about the extremity of the war situation and the need, if only in the interests of decency, for each person to rebel. We have been describing a fairly deliberate and rational teacher, who is preoccupied with acting justly in and outside of school. He might well set up as a first principle the idea of justice: human beings ought to be treated with a proper concern for their interests; that they ought never to be discriminated against unless there are relevant grounds for treating them differently (as infant children, criminals, and mentally ill people are treated differently). Thinking of the war and the men, women, and children suffering because of it, the teacher can reasonably say that it is unjust for them to be deprived not only of the right to live in peace but of opportunities for education, economic security, and the kinds of fulfillment Americans take for granted. It makes good sense for him to present this idea to his students as well as to explain why commitment to such a principle makes relevant their idea that the war should be ended, that people should do whatever is in their power to see that this end is brought about.

The same principle of justice, however, may require that he provide each member in his class with the freedom to deliberate on what ought to be done in this instance: whether they should support the Moratorium. If he does not permit this kind of deliberation, he will be interfering with their freedom; and such interference would also be unjust. Personally involved with the Moratorium as he is, he can still recognize that as a teacher his primary obligation is to teach his students the principle of justice in the hope that they will be able to make future decisions, holding that principle clearly in mind. "Morality," writes R. M. Hare, "retains its vigour when ordinary people have learnt afresh to decide for themselves what principles to live by, and more especially what principles to teach their children."[17] The children, too, have to learn afresh as they make decisions of principle. Neither teacher nor parent can feel assured that the young will act as their elders would have done or even as their elders recommend. The point is that the young understand certain principles, make clear the reasons for their decisions, and revise their norms intelligently in response to the contingencies of the world. For the man of rational passion this ought to be enough. He wants the young to know, above all, what they are doing and why; he wants them to be able to explain in understandable language; he wants them to make sense.

When they do understand and make sense, the teacher we have been describing can say he has been successful as a moral educator in one specific situation. To demonstrate his success, he can ask people to listen to the talk proceeding in his classroom, to the way the students go about deliberating on the matter of the Moratorium. Perhaps they will decide not to support it; and they may make their decision cooperatively, slowly, rationally, paying attention to consequences and to the logic of what they are saying. The teacher can only feel gratified because they have achieved a type of mastery new to them. Of course, they could always have decided, with equivalent deliberateness, to support the Moratorium. Or, without much thought, they could have decided to march out of the classroom to join the action because it was so highly publicized, because their friends and their teacher were so much involved. In the latter case, the good teacher (activist or not) would have to feel he had failed.

A kind of heroism is demanded of the principled teacher eager to initiate his students into principled decision making and a rational way of life. *What* they decide is always in question. There are no guarantees that they will be "good" or humane people. The teacher must acknowledge that he can only deal justly with individuals he hopes will learn how to learn. When faced with issues more personally consequential than a Peace Moratorium or when dealing with elementary school children, he may focus on the formation of good habits or the cultivation of the dispositions required for reflective conduct. But here too there are no certainties, even if he resorts to traditional "habit training" or the use of punishments and rewards. We might consider the problem of drugs, for instance—clearly a far more complex question than whether existing laws should be obeyed. Peter Marin has written sympathetically about young people in search of a supportive community life, who "turn to drugs for all the things they cannot find without them." He describes the ways in which the drug cultures answer young people's needs for communities protected from adults, adult ambitions, and what the young see as adult hypocrisy. "They can walk the streets high or sit stoned in class and still be *inside it* (meaning, their own community)—among adults but momentarily free of them, a world *within* which one is at home."[18] Marin recommends a kind of loving detachment, dealing with these young people as if they composed a friendly neighborhood tribe. Whether he is right or wrong in a pragmatic sense, the detachment he recommends may enable the teacher at least to help them articulate the criteria governing their choices of life-style. Refusing to blame them, simply asking them to talk about how and why they live as they do, the teacher may be in a position to make them aware of their principles, which have often turned out to be much akin to "Christian" principles. Even though he may not convince them to give up marijuana, for example, the teacher may help them see the "moral resonance" of the decisions they are making day by day. Marin, of course, has marijuana in mind when he speaks so empathetically about the "stoned"; and he knows, as most teachers do, that far more serious issues are raised by the "hard" and dangerous drugs. When confronted with proselytizing addicts, the teacher can do little; nor can he be persuasive with youth who boast experiences of "expanding consciousness" they know he cannot share. Trying, sometimes in the face of chaos, to suggest alternative ways of getting through life, he can point to consequences and dangers, even as he gives reluctant credence to the delights that are claimed. The least productive road here, as in other moral domains, is the path of tyranny and suppression. Even here many teachers will opt for the values of justice, which (in Lawrence Kohlberg's words) "prohibit the imposition of beliefs of one group upon another."[19] But this does not mean the teacher will give license to the self-destructive; nor does it mean that he will do nothing to change their habits or their style. He might even call in legal authorities and still feel that he was, in Kohlberg's sense, "just." He is a teacher; and, in the case we have been discussing, a teacher with a prior commitment to rationality. His obligation, as he perceives it, is primarily to induce young people to decide in principled fashion what they *conceive* (not merely "feel" or "intuit") to be worthwhile.

How would a teacher with a more existential orientation handle the problems of moral education? There are many different problems, not all revolving around the matter of principles and guidelines. Obviously, he would put great stress on his and his students' freedom and on the need to make choices within frequently "extreme" situations. He would take seriously what the analytically inclined teacher is prone to ignore: the moods he and his student are bound to experience— anguish, boredom, guilt. For him these are anything but pathological states. They are appropriate responses to the contemporary universe with its injustice and impersonality, its underlying "absurdity." Furthermore, they create the affective and subjective context in which choices are made and values defined; doing so, they make unthinkable the predominantly cool, calculative approach to moral life. This does not mean that human beings are determined by their passions, because they can choose whether to give in to them. Nor does it mean that mere impulse or feeling governs moral choice. Sartre talks about "creating the man we want to be." Every act we perform creates an image of man as we *think* he ought to be. "To choose to be this or that is to affirm at the same time the value of what we choose, because we can never choose evil. We always choose the good, and nothing can be good for us without being good for all."[20] Our responsibility, then, is immense, especially when we consider that (for the existentialist) there are no predefined values, no moral principles which determine in advance what is good. Alone and condemned to freedom, the individual *must* choose. He experiences anxiety or anguish because he cannot even be sure that the person he chooses himself to be at one moment is the same as the one he will be at a later time. A student, for example, choosing to be a chemist, investing all his energies in what he has determined to be valuable, cannot know that the "essence" he has fashioned for himself will be the same the following year; yet, in the interim, he will have chosen *not* to do a great many things that might have been relevant to what he eventually decided to become. Anguish is the way freedom reveals itself. It is the expression of the nagging desire for completion— without any guarantee that the completion sought will be valuable when it is achieved. Boredom is the way the threat of nothingness and indifference reveal themselves to consciousness. Choices are made in the face of a "profound boredom" many times, "drifting" (as Martin Heidegger says) "hither and thither in the abysses of existence like a mute fog," drawing all things together in "a queer kind of indifference."[21] What, after all, does it matter? What is the point? These questions, too, are functions of the dreadful freedom in which the individual decides; and the existential teacher would have to take this notion seriously into account. Then there is the matter of guilt, so frequently suppressed or ignored. Guilt may be the expression of a feeling that the individual is not acting on his possibilities, not shaping his future; and yet here too the teacher can never be sure. The existential teacher would not try to assuage such feelings or to evade them. He would consciously stimulate the disquietude they entail; he would provoke to responsible action persons absolutely free to choose themselves.

Given the problem of a Peace Moratorium, such a teacher could not will against his students' freedom or enforce his commitments on them. He would, however, emphasize the evasions that lead to refusals to act. Simply to sit back and condemn a war one recognizes to be unjust and evil is to be guilty of bad faith, especially if there is the possibility of action. For this reason, the German who detested Nazism and still did nothing to demonstrate his opposition is called so ironically a "good German," someone who took no responsibility, who lived his life in bad faith. Therefore, more explicitly than the analytically inclined teacher, the existential educator would underline the inescapability of responsibility. Each person is "the author" of the situation in which he lives; *he* gives meaning to his world, but through action, through his project, not by well-meaning thought. If a student declared his opposition to a war but was not inclined to do anything about it or to be actively concerned about what was being done in his name, he could be charged with evasion and irresponsibility, even though no one would *tell* him what to do.

An article appearing in *The New Yorker* magazine soon after the My Lai massacre in Vietnam was exposed captures some of the feeling that stirs the existential thinker or teacher. The writer says that the war going on was not made by "Man" but by particular men.

> To lay the responsibility on Man or on War is to make nobody accountable, and is to move in the direction of regarding the massacre as part of a natural, acceptable course of events. . . . And we are as accountable for our self-deceptions as for our deceptions. With the report of the My Lai

massacre, we face a new situation. It is no longer possible for us to say that we did not know. When we look at the photographs published in *Life* and see bodies of women and children in piles, and look into the faces of an old woman and a young girl who (we are told) are about to be shot, we feel that a kind of violence is being done to our feelings, and that the massacre threatens to overpower us. To block it out, we may freeze. If we face the massacre for what it is, we are torn by almost unbearable grief, but if we turn away and let the rationalizations crowd into our minds to protect us, we are degraded.[22]

This statement is reminiscent of Camus's *The Plague* and Tarrou's conversation with Doctor Rieux on the night they go swimming:

> "Have you ever seen a man shot by a firing-squad? No, of course not; the spectators are hand-picked and it's like a private party, you need an invitation. The result is that you've gleaned your ideas about it from books and pictures. A post, a blind-folded man, some soldiers in the offing. But the real thing isn't a bit like that. Do you know that the firing-squad stands only a yard and a half from the condemned man? Do you know that if the victim took two steps forward his chest would touch the rifles? Do you know that, at this short range, the soldiers concentrate their fire on the region of the heart and their big bullets make a hole into which you could thrust your fist? No, you didn't know all that; those are things that are never spoken of. For the plague-stricken their peace of mind is more important than a human life. Decent folks must be allowed to sleep easy o' nights, mustn't they? Really it would be shockingly bad taste to linger on such details, that's common knowledge. But personally I've never been able to sleep well since then."[23]

The "plague" represents evasion and indifference. We are repeatedly reminded in the course of Camus's book that enormous vigilance is necessary to combat the plague, that acts of will are required if a person is to achieve health and integrity, if he is to be pure. Significantly enough, the inhabitants of the town of Oran in Camus's novel are called either townspeople or volunteers, once the plague strikes. The townspeople are victims; they suffer and lash out at each other and find that fighting back is useless. The volunteers, like Tarrou, Rieux, and their "sanitary squads," do fight back. But there is no "good reason" because no one knows how to heal the sickness or stop the epidemic. Doctor Rieux keeps struggling because it is his job, it is only "logical," and because "a fight must be put up, in this way or that, and there must be no bowing down." He and his comrades talk of decency, happiness, love; Tarrou is committed to becoming "a saint without God." And they remain whole persons (out of "common decency"); they show compassion and refuse to become merely passive victims, at the mercy of the inhuman plague. They do not act on predetermined principle; in no way could they rationally justify a fundamentally "absurd" heroism. Yet, if they remain vigilant and take responsibility for themselves at this last point, they can move beyond victimization and survive (for however long they have to live) as men.

The existential teacher recognizes that he cannot *tell* another person how to live; nor can he demand that his students exercise their will and become, in their own way, volunteers. But he can set up classroom situations that make it difficult to maintain "peace of mind." He may use literature and the arts; he may focus on crisis situations—such as a Peace Moratorium; he may engage students in concrete questioning and confrontation; he may urge them to take stands. The task will not be easy for such a teacher, anymore than it will for his students because they are forever condemned to the freedom that requires them to create themselves over and over without a sense of comforting constraint or a priori norm.

The same idea applies to drug experiences. Confronted by students who praise psychedelic cultures, the teacher can do no more than ask them to choose for themselves, to avoid following the "crowd." Often he will find some who present an alternative ethic of hedonism, sensualism, gentleness, oceanic love. He will find others who say they cannot help what they are doing: their peers made them sample drugs, they may tell him; they could not be accepted unless they followed their peers. In the first case, the teacher can do little more than say that these youth are only hedonists if they make pleasure their primary value. They are only sensualists if they pursue the delights of the various senses and live for such pursuits. The point is that a mere expression of value means nothing; the expression must be acted on and realized. Sartre says that "man is nothing other than his project, he exists only in so far as he realizes himself, thus he is nothing other than the whole of his actions, nothing more than his life."[24] The teacher can ask the drug enthusiast who says he has an ethic what kind of person he is choosing himself to be, whether he has freely acted to open his way to the future. The teacher can scarcely do more. As for the student who says he cannot help his actions: the teacher can only tell him that he is rejecting his freedom and that his choices are dishonest. He can be charged with bad faith; he can be called "a coward or a stinker," not because he takes drugs but because he has refused responsibility. He has not exercised his will.

Because of the absoluteness of the freedom assumed, because the existentialist appears to have no grounds for saying any moral choice is wrong, his approach to choosing is sometimes considered incompatible with morality. "Any choice is as good as another," writes Alvin Plantinga; "there is no possibility of making a moral mistake. And that is fatal to morality."[25] The recognition that many existentialists have been and are concerned with *engagement* in a world of fellow creatures, an intersubjective world, does not lessen such disapproval. Sartre has said that "the protected status of the intellectual is over, that there are no more sanctuaries." This notion comes partly from a recognition that the intellectual too often leads a life of ease, which prevents him from confronting "the injustices and inhumanities in our own bailiwicks, in the very places we live," and partly from the realization that moral responsibility entails responsibility for the effects of his actions on others. This still does not suggest criteria for determining which effects are desirable and which are not; but it does imply that a commitment to one's own and to others' freedom *means* a confrontation with injustice and inhumanity. Existentialists occasionally speak of a "conversion," which will enable an individual to respond to the calls of his conscience. Perhaps, after all, a converted conscience always makes an appeal for justice and humanity, as it seems to be doing in Sartre's case. Perhaps "anything" is *not* possible once a man wills himself to be free. None of this, however, discounts the extreme difficulty a teacher experiences in stirring others to action they know is authentic. Nothing is more difficult than to be—and to ask others to be—in good faith. Nevertheless, a rebellion against indifference and abstractness appears necessary at the present moment. Perhaps, in the last analysis, only the rebel can summon the courage to identify himself as a passionately rational man.

Every teacher is familiar with the vast looming structures of the corporate society, which set up so many obstacles before those who strive to be reflective and to live in good faith. Every teacher knows the dehumanizing pressure of bureaucracies; he understands something about the anonymity of crowds, the ease with which one can deny responsibility. Also he knows, from encounters with his high school or college students, how easily the aesthetic can overcome the moral, how people can simply "groove" on what is made available instead of acting to constitute their own worlds. Despair, boredom, a kind of indolence may be to blame. But many young people are averse to making serious choices, "not so much," as Kierkegaard says, "on account of the rigorous cogitation involved in weighing the alternatives, not on account of the multiplicity of thoughts which attach themselves to every link in the chain, but rather because there is danger afoot, danger that the next instant it may not be equally in my power to choose, that something already has been lived which must be lived over again."[26] Obscure powers in the personality, according to Kierkegaard, are always driving ahead to new choices. Personality cannot be kept a blank; personal life cannot be halted and started again. For this reason, when they do finally make their choices, people so often feel "that there is something which must be done over again, something which must be revoked. . . ." For some this feeling results in an unending, almost desperate search for freedom from what they have been in the past (in their families, in their schools). For others it results in a desire simply to live and experience without choosing or commitment. Kierkegaard calls this feeling a desire to remain at the first "stage"on life's way, the "aesthetic stage." The person who lives forever at this stage is like Don Juan, the perpetual romantic lover who exists in an erotic present, a discrete "now," which neither binds the past to the present nor anticipates any future time. "The aesthetic choice is entirely immediate, or it loses itself in the multifarious."[27] Actually, it is no choice at all, because it involves neither consideration nor commitment; and it ends, more often than not, in apathy or despair. The individual must move from the aesthetic to the ethical stage, where significant choices are made and the "personality" is consolidated. "I should like to say," Kierkegaard writes, "that in making a choice it is not so much a question of choosing the right as of the energy, the consciousness, the pathos with which one chooses."[28]

We may now be emerging from a period in which "image," "style," and other such aesthetic concepts have been more important than creeds and codes. Lionel Trilling, writing about the generation of the early 1960s, has said many were more concerned with their relation to the "sources of life" than with moral decision. He means their relation to what they believe will yield sensual excitement, self-transcendence, and various kinds of liberation, rather than meaning or value or truth. Charles Reich, speaking on behalf of such persons, bears out what Trilling said. Reich places much stress on the appearance of those blessed with "Consciousness III." Describing what he saw as a "conversion," he writes: "What happens is simply this: in a brief space of months, a student, seemingly conventional in every way, changes his haircut, his clothes, his habits, his interests, his political attitudes, his way of relating to other people, in short, his whole way of life."[29] Reich conveys the impression that the student, treating himself as a species of art object, first alters the way he *looks* and then changes his habits and attitudes as if they too were mere accouterments. The term *life style* becomes far more appropriate than the existential term *project* because (with few exceptions) so little passionate engagement, so little difficult choice, seems to be involved. Such a person is tempted to distance himself from life as if it were a drama, to treat politics as theater, to perceive history as a vast, formless "happening" or a kind of empty dance.

Persistence in this tendency provides another argument for the existential teacher's efforts to stimulate the energy, the consciousness, the pathos involved in serious choice. In fact, most moral philosophers are likely to see this as a significant phase of moral education. Henry David Aiken, for instance, says: "Morality . . . is a form of self-discipline for moral subjects who hold themselves responsible for their actions."[30] Few would disagree that the principles we have spoken of are "first-personal" that is, principles a moral agent believes he *ought* to acknowledge (or he chooses to acknowledge) and then become binding on him. "Moral freedom," Aiken also says, "is not the freedom to do as you please, but the freedom to decide what sort of person you ought to be." The teacher and his students may need to move beyond the aesthetic stage to make meaningful such freedom to decide. Varied experience, expansion of consciousness, sensual enjoyment, expressiveness are important for development. But it is not enough for an individual to spend his life as a dilettante or wanderer, for all the vividness of perspective these roles make possible. At some point he must perceive himself as a potential person; he must experience what may be a *moral* demand to become, to create himself. Only then does freedom descend as it does on Sartre's Orestes. This moral demand is understood as a freedom to choose resolutely and without assurances, "the freedom to decide what sort of person you ought to be."

Here, of course, philosophic disagreements begin; the teacher may reach a fork in the road. Many philosophers say free, authentic choice is not necessarily better than choice which is not so free. A decision that an action is right for the individual does not, they say, *make* that action right. Iris Murdoch writes: "The ordinary person, unless corrupted by philosophy, does not believe he creates values by his choices. He thinks that some things really are better than others and that he is capable of getting it wrong. We are not usually in doubt about the direction in which Good lies."[31] An even more serious charge against existential views on choosing is that a nonpurposeful act or a decision for which no reasons can be given is not a choice at all. Rather, it appears to be a type of instinctive, impulsive, or merely whimsical behavior. If the appeal from conscience is held in mind, however, if it is remembered that the self exists in the world, in the midst of community, and that each person is held—and holds himself—morally responsible for everything he does, the approach cannot be disposed of as merely emotive. Relativism, however, does result from such an approach. Many existentialists would answer as did Friedrich Nietzsche's Zarathustra when asked about "the way". " 'This is *my* way: where is yours?' " And then: "For *the* way—that does not exist." And this response is understandable, because each person is thought to be creating his project, his life-world. A class of high school students may be confronted with the same curriculum materials, the same moral principles and rules of behavior. But each student will order his experience in his own fashion; each will transcend himself and appropriate dimensions of the culture as these dimensions are presented to *his* consciousness. He is bound to his fellow student not because of similar patterns in their life-worlds but because of the intersubjectivity of language, cumulative meanings, history. However, his perspectives, reciprocal as they may be, are his own. If he perceives his freedom and is enabled to act on it, he has his own way.

There arises, then, the question of authority, or what William Frankena calls a "transpersonal standard" or a "moral direction" transcending the individual. Analytical philosophers insist that direction can be found in a properly impersonal consideration of such principles as justice and respect for persons. These (and a few others, including freedom, impartiality, and truth telling) strike R. S. Peters, for example, as fundamental. But they are "nonarbitrary in the sense that they are presuppositions of the form of discourse in which the question 'What are there reasons for doing' is asked seriously." These principles, says Peters, are "of a procedural sort in that they do not tell us precisely what rules there should be in a society but lay down general guidance about the ways in which we should go about deciding such matters. . . ."[32] Experimentalist philosophers, well aware of precariousness and open opportunity, believe that sufficient study of the relevant facts of any situation, of the surrounding circumstances and the living interests involved, leads to decisions as free of relativism as possible. A "transpersonal standard" is implicit in creative intelligence itself. Using a standard of this kind, moral and social agreements can be made, ideal possibilities projected, and "control of the future" achieved.[33] Others (like William K. Frankena) talk of instilling a sense of a "Way" or "Tao," which finds expression in a set of rules, principles, and ideals.[34] Internalizing these, developing a sense of obligation, young people will be able to choose—both freely and knowledgeably—in the situations that confront them. They will find themselves on the road to the good life.

What should govern? An understanding of protocols, of procedures? A range of fundamental principles? Authenticity—the sense of the person one ought to be? Again, the teacher will have to decide, to take a stand. However, whatever he decides, whatever orientation makes the most sense to him, he will not *impose* values or virtues on his students; he will *pose* questions, do what he can to move them toward increasing awareness, deepening conviction. Granting them dignity, freedom, and autonomy (unless they are little children), he becomes a catalyst in the process of their self-identification, their learning how to learn. He may address himself to the task, more or less assured about "the good life" and "desirable dispositions." But, no matter who he is, he will not deliberately guide his students toward a boring, empty, dissatisfying life; he will not deliberately encourage the development of dispositions he believes to be destructive or "bad." And just as he must be convinced about the worthwhileness of what he is teaching, so he is convinced about the value of his own tastes and commitments.

At this point the tension originates for the teacher who is truly concerned to stimulate *action* rather than merely mechanical behavior on the part of each student. If he finds his norm in community standards of "good," in public traditions, or in the requirements of the academic disciplines, the tension is likely to be least. If he is concerned with cognitive action, with the formation of belief systems having specifiable characteristics, with evidence, with reasons, he obviously has to exert himself to critical questioning and thinking; but committed to clarity and analysis as he must be, he will not suffer fundamental doubts. If he is primarily interested in a "democratic" classroom, where cooperative experience and full participation in decision making take priority, he may suffer the inevitable frustrations when "all" affected by policies have a share in making them; but the doubts he experiences are likely to be fruitful, leading to new definitions of problem, new possibilities of resolution. If his commitment is to self-disclosure and free choosing, the tension is likely to be greatest. Something like a dialectical struggle will be under way as the teacher attempts to reconcile his commitments with his desire for his students to choose themselves. He must guide, stimulate, and challenge intentional ignorance wherever he perceives it; but, at the same time, he must feel the most tender regard for each person's being—for each person's privacy, inner time. The existential teacher, "nondirective" as he may appear to be, cannot permit floundering, careless thinking, or flaccidity anymore than can the most "directive" classroom authorities. Curiosity, wonder, the sense of problem: these may be taken as starting points here as in any other teaching situation. There must be a similar awareness of the way rationality contributes to freedom, of the way freedom of mind and widening perspectives enrich the life-world and expand the scope of choice. The existential teacher is simply more attuned than others to the implicit threat of coercion in a classroom situation. He, far more than others, must confront his freedom along with the alien freedoms of his students; and because he is bound to attend to so much more than performance, speech, and observable instances of mastery, he can never be sure of what he or they achieve.

We have already talked of B. F. Skinner's alternative and the certainties associated with a determinist point of view. We have also said that, even if the past is fixed and in some sense "necessary" from the vantage point of the present, the future is not; and willing or choosing moves forward into that future. The teacher, like his students, is concerned with projecting and with possibilities. His prime preoccupation may be with the tasks his students will be able to perform, with the achievements at which they will arrive. It may be with the degrees by which they master the principles fundamental to the disciplines or with the ways in which they gain new perspectives on their life-worlds. Whatever the teacher's concern, it is directed at the future, at what is not yet; and in no way can the future be empirically tested. By each of his actions, each of his efforts to move his students toward inquiry, he asserts his freedom; and, implicitly, he affirms that choosing is significant for himself and for those trying to learn. If choosing were not significant, he could scarcely justify intervening in the endless chain of cause and effect except by saying that he intended to ensure that what was meant to happen did indeed occur. As every teacher knows, sometimes it is all too easy to accede to disadvantage, to retardation, to apparent incorrigibility; and other times it is mysteriously necessary to say "No!"

The troubling question of how much freedom to grant young people still remains open. For one thing, there is the matter of the age of the students involved. If, indeed, freedom means (as it does in the simplest sense) an absence of restraint, the teacher of preschool children must confront the issue differently than does the teacher of persons old enough to decide for themselves. Individuals who work with the very young have long prized the values of spontaneity and expressiveness. In many Head Start programs and nursery schools, where children are given diverse opportunities to play and express themselves, there is an appearance of almost total freedom. Yet we are aware that a great number of constraints exist and that these are not always explained to the children. Little children may not go home at will or run up and down the halls or interfere with each other's activity or injure others. All too frequently, they are not permitted to stand apart (in the closet, on the windowsill) and be alone. Their options, in actual fact, are limited, presumably because they are not old enough to understand why certain reasons are relevant and others are not. The result is what Peters calls the "paradox" of moral education: certain habits must be cultivated before children are old enough to know why; certain wants must be constrained; certain rules must be imposed.[35] Were it not for such a foundation, children could not move from their original egocentrism to a conception of pleasing others or doing what the community thinks is right.

Aristotle talked of the need for "good habits"; Dewey wrote of the need to develop "dispositions," attitudes "not to this and that thing nor even to the aggregate of known things, but to the considerations which govern conduct."[36] Schooling, traditionally, has focused on the cultivation of certain dispositions rather than others, depending on what the culture values at the moment and what attitudes are considered "necessary to the continuous and progressive life of [the] society."[37] As we have seen, the romantic critics of the present take issue with this approach. A. S. Neill, John Holt, Paul Goodman, and others like them believe that the deliberate cultivation of dispositions is manipulative. They talk of the "retroflected rage and shame" experienced by children compelled to go to school and "coerced" into accommodation with what is considered right. They think that intervention on the part of adults assigned to socialize prevents spontaneous learning that would take place if young pupils were left free. Neill, for example, objects to "hothousing" children. The implication is that habit training and the imposition of rules create an artificial environment. Natural growth becomes impossible. Moral education becomes a sham.

Bill Ayers, a young black radical who worked at a Michigan free school called Children's Community, expresses the romantic view in simple terms:

> What we try to do is allow these groups of kids to learn from each other, to exchange things, throw things away, pick things up, without any kind of value judgments. I think that more than anything it is dangerous to consciously create models for kids to emulate.[38]

Children, says Paul Goodman, should be exposed to diverse models in and out of school. They should be brought into contact with "unlicensed" adults in their home neighborhoods. They could then choose their models and ego ideals spontaneously: a skillful bricklayer; a "nice cop"; a hard-working druggist; a humane priest; an old man good at working with his hands. The school, ideally, should be a mini-school (like George Dennison's First Street School) or a storefront school open to the life on the street. Children should be permitted to participate on an equal basis in community activities and to learn through friendly association with their elders. Under such circumstances, there would be no need for deliberate teaching of norms and rules. Civility, like literacy, would develop naturally through and by means of everyday experience. The total environment would educate; there would be no need for compulsory schools.

Certain teachers, anticipating alternative modes of education for the young, respond warmly to this imaging of what might be. Others are troubled by the implication that most teachers have no worthy roles to play. The reality confronting both groups, however, is the complex reality of the present moment when schools are inadequately supported and continually accused of ineffectuality. It may be that decentralization, community control, and local participation in policy making will overcome feelings of powerlessness and effect significant change. It may be that increased localism will intensify separatism and hostility between ethnic groups. The teacher, as citizen, will want to take positions on local control, busing, integration, voucher systems, and the rest; he may even want to play a part in supporting what he conceives to be reforms. It is likely, as we have said, that he will be a more vital teacher if he becomes involved in the public world.

Nevertheless, his fundamental project is pursued in his classroom, where he must cope with the effects of injustice and inequity on children, with the terrible discrepancies between the lives of the poor and the well-to-do. If he teaches in the slums, where models may be drug addicts or gang members or desperate and jobless men, he must confront the question of moral teaching squarely. Ought he not to acquaint his students with existing cultural norms? Ought he not to teach them principles to counteract what they learn on the streets? Are they being given an equal chance if they are not taught the rules of the game? Their parents, more often than not, will demand the kind of formal, even rigorous teaching that presumably equips the young to play the game. The teacher, no matter how committed he is to self-determination and free choice, must hold himself accountable to his pupils, to their parents, *and* to the community. This means he must take personal responsibility for the choices he makes in his classroom, for the accommodations he makes, and for the refusals his values demand.

The same is true in a suburb, in a working-class neighborhood, in a homogeneous small town, in an ordinary middle-class community. There may be groups of people who object to the discussion of controversial issues, other groups who emphasize "character education," still others who consider all extrinsic discipline to be bad. The teacher may be instructed to devote most of his energies to the gifted or to preparing certain students for the better colleges. He may be asked to put his main reliance on teaching machines, to substitute multimedia teaching for literature teaching, to discourage interest in such "frivolities" as art. Not only will he have to make decisions of principles with regard to curricular emphases; he will also have to make continual choices with respect to the norms he teaches as well as the way the local parents think their children *ought* to live.

The problems are inescapable, wherever the teacher is assigned to teach, because he is asked to function as a self-conscious, autonomous, and authentic person in a public space where the pressures multiply. Unlike an artist or a scholar or a research scientist, he cannot withdraw to studio, study, or laboratory and still remain a practitioner. He is involved with students, colleagues, school board members, and parents whenever and wherever he pursues his fundamental project; he cannot work alone. Moreover, he cannot avoid the great social structures beyond his classroom doors. There is always a sense in which he must mediate between those structures and the young people he hopes to liberate for reflection and choice. He must initiate them in certain patterns of thinking and acting; he must enable them to recognize and choose among the options presented to them. He must sensitize them to inhumanity, vulgarity, and hypocrisy; he must help them seek equivalents for violence and for war. And, at some level, he must enable them to comprehend their society's professed ideals: freedom, equality, regard for the individual. These are all fundamental to the democratic credo; they distinguish and dignify the democratic way of life. But they are norms, conceptions of what *ought* to be; and they must be created anew with each generation, by each person choosing to live a principled or norm-regarding life, if they are to become viable ideals that summon human beings to moral action in the world they know.

The teacher's responsibilities become more and more complex; and he is required every day to reinterpret, to make his own sense of modern life. Because modern life has so many aspects and dimensions, because it cannot be fully apprehended by conventional means, we turn one last time to the arts and their relevance for the teacher who is willing to take a stranger's view. The relevance is dual. In the first place, works of art have the capacity to disclose things about which (according to Ludwig Wittgenstein) philosophy must be silent. Imaginative presentations can engage individuals with the changing meanings of human existence, reality, and time in a manner mere description cannot achieve. In the second place, experiences with the arts offer possibilities for self-confrontation and self-identification to those willing to try to understand. Such experiences may be of peculiar significance for the teacher wishing to be present as a full person, as the "single one" Kierkegaard describes.

Traditionally, the arts were thought to be imitative forms, representations of universal and recurrent patterns. To apprehend them was to look through the windows of a time-bound world into a domain that was larger, purer, glowing, and serene. Even today, people afflicted by the banalities and brutalities on the visible surfaces of things long to find some countervailing force in the arts. In Herman Melville's *Billy Budd*, Captain Vere (attempting to justify his execution of the young sailor) says: "With mankind, measured forms are everything; and that is the import couched in the story of Orpheus with his lyre spellbinding the wild denizens of the wood." He means, of course, that the ambiguity and "formlessness of the "primeval" have to be in some manner counteracted by human orders and human laws. There is still a desire, often frustrated in these times, for orders that will sustain. For many young people, however, nothing could be more alien than "measured forms." They perceive life as fluid, encompassing, an affair of discontinuous events to be felt, to be celebrated, to be sensed. Threatened by anonymity, conditioning, and quantification, they seek occasions for "grooving," for engagement, for acting out, for expansion of consciousness, for discovering what it is to *be*. The tension between their conception of art forms and traditional conceptions (which their teachers frequently maintain, no matter what) has heightened the problematic character of the arts. Not only is it necessary to decide among the multiple artistic offerings in every field; it becomes more and more important to decide the significance of the arts and aesthetic experiences in one's personal life. This experience ought to heighten perceptiveness and sensitivity, as it intensifies self-consciousness with respect to the arts. Authorities (scholars, critics, museum curators) are no longer in position to legislate standards for individual taste and appreciation. Connoisseurship has become questionable to many. "Art" can no longer be satisfactorily defined.

Nevertheless the nostalgia remains; and it is significant too. When a person thinks, for example, of *The Iliad*, with its heroic seekers after excellence, its speakers of words and doers of deeds, of the Greek tragedies with their imitation of the forms of human action, or of

Shakespeare's plays, the magnitude of these works makes them seem truer, more intrinsically artistic than, say, Samuel Beckett's *Waiting for Godot*, Bernard Malamud's *The Fixer*, John Barth's *End of the Road*, Sylvia Plath's *Ariel*, Francois Truffaut's *Jules and Jim*. The blues and golds, the burnished surfaces of one of Raphael's Madonnas, Michelangelo's giant young David, Rembrandt's obliquely lit Saul seem to reveal a veritable ultimate to certain modern viewers, especially when they compare Pablo Picasso's *Guernica*, Francis Bacon's screaming figures in their glass boxes, Alberto Giacometti's spare and desolated images frozen in the void. Even though they feel the peculiar nostalgia induced by the great and familiar classical works, many people still recognize that they can no longer speak of universals, of enduring, luminescent truths. Some agree that none of the traditional explanations or theories of art can account for all the phenomena classified as "art" since the beginning of time—that, in effect, "art" cannot be defined. It is impossible, we are told, to discover a single element or essence (an x-quality, perhaps, or "artness") common to works as disparate as *Hamlet, A Clockwork Orange, Vanity Fair, A Farewell to Arms, Hedda Gabler, Waiting for Godot, Mona Lisa,* and *Guernica*. How can anyone state categorically that Andy Warhol's rendering of the Campbell soup can should not be included along with Claude Monet's *Waterlilies* in the art world because it cannot be construed to be art? Morris Weitz says that, instead of asking "What is art? How is it to be defined?", we should ask "What sort of concept is 'art'?"—and go on to discover the conditions under which we can correctly apply the term.[39] Weitz takes from Ludwig Wittgenstein the notion of "strands of similarity" and says that the best we can do is identify similarities between the new forms and such paradigm cases as those created by Shakespeare, Raphael, Dickens, Ibsen. Weitz believes that "art" should be treated as a concept with an open texture, meaning that the conditions of its applications should be held open for correction or revision. If a new form appears—such as a work of "earth art" (a cliff draped in sheets or a pile of stones on sand) or a novel without narrative or transitions—decisions on whether to extend the use of the concept or to invent a new one will have to be made. When a self-aware individual makes such a decision, he will likely consider his expectations of an aesthetic experience, the principles that underlie his judgments when he says something *is* a work of art, his criteria for recognizing "great" works, the kinds of recommendations he can reasonably make. He has been moved to self-questioning and perhaps to deeper enjoyments. Also, he is not prevented from talking about the art forms he cherishes and knows best.

Few would disagree (despite the lack of definitions) that a work of art does differ from a natural object and requires a different stance on the part of the beholder. Encountering a work as art, the beholder is expected to set aside his everyday modes of apprehending. *Guernica* cannot be encountered as if it were a cartoon or a distorted rendering of an actual bombing. Nicolas Poussin's *The Death of Socrates* cannot be "read" as an illustration of an actual event. Neither work is transparent; neither is a glass through which the beholder is meant to look at some historic occasion. Both are opaque, complete unto themselves, made of colors, shapes, lines in relationship to one another. Painted on canvas, those colors, shapes, and lines compose an equivalent, a secondary world: They are paintings, not photographs or reflections. The creators of both works were impelled, perhaps, to transmute rage, grief, or philosophic pondering into image. They were deliberately wrought to embody feeling in complex form, to objectify it as an independent existence in the world, a possibility for others to choose.

Sartre once said, of *Guernica:* "Does anyone think that it won a single heart to the Spanish cause? And yet something is said that can never quite be heard and that would take an infinity of words to express. . . ."[40] The meaning, more than likely, is in some manner inexplicable in words. Like a poem, a painting cannot be paraphrased. Too few people give it sufficient time or hold in mind the potential it offers for those willing to experience it. Too few people remember that a painting—like the Picasso and the Poussin, like a Cezanne still life, a De Kooning woman—is not a representation of some outer "real." They do not remember often enough that a painter, working with inherited conventions, seeking his vision, his style, creates formal equivalents of the subject matter with which his desire to paint began. It may be the legendary drinking of the hemlock, the bombing of the small town. It may be a landscape the painter has encountered somewhere, which he sees with lights glancing and shadows going black. It may be a loss or feeling of horror he has experienced; it may be the rush of steam, the sense of speed, or the clash of colors in the light. Working with his medium, the artist must transmute the idea, vision, feeling, or memory into gradations of color, arrangements of planes, "cryptograms" the beholder can translate into a private message incommunicable in words. The more his perceptiveness, the more his willingness to attend and prehend, the more the beholder will find his repertoire of feelings expanding, his emotional palette becoming enriched. He may find that his vision of his life space is sharpened because of his experiences in looking at painting. He may become sensitized to forms and colors never previously noticed; he may become participant in another dimension of the quest for clarified vision and for modes of ordering reality. The teacher who is drawn in this direction may well find continuities between his teaching effort and his effort to *see* more. Perceptively engaged, he may find that he cannot take a self-righteous or proprietary stance toward painting. He may be gaining opportunities to enable those he teaches to see as well, truly to see, not through his eyes but through their own.

Somewhat the same things may be said about film, that art form of such peculiar significance for the contemporary young. We are told that experiences with film are primarily visual, that film is an art of moving images. The member of the audience often forgets the illusionism involved in film making; and, as in the case of the painting, he too frequently perceives films as photographed "reality" and recalls them as if they were dreams. To encounter a film as a potential work of art is to keep in mind the ways in which the editing process alters and shapes, imaginatively transforming "shots" of an existing world. To prehend a film as a created thing is to be somehow familiar with its grammar, the syntax of its images, the uses of montage, flashback, and visual metaphors. Knowing what to look for, how to "aspect" a film, a viewer has a greatly increased opportunity to engage with it as art—and, in engaging, to discover or rediscover aspects of the self. Many people consider such films as *Bonnie and Clyde, Easy Rider*, and *A Clockwork Orange* to be morally questionable because viewers are given opportunities to identify only with delinquent characters. These films may or may not be works of art, may or may not be equal in impact to Ingmar Bergman's *The Seventh Seal*, Michelangelo Antonioni's *L'Avventura*, Charles Chaplin's *Modern Times*, Jean Renoir's *Grand Illusion*, and other works now taken to be masterpieces. But they deserve to be heeded, felt, reflected on, and criticized. They deserve to be presented to the young, not as photographs of actuality, but as fictions, *films* that have been deliberately crafted by artists working with a new technology. Only then will film experiences enable individuals to move within themselves, tap the fund of life within them, and look with somewhat different eyes on other persons and the concreteness of the world. Only then can the morally questionable be confronted honestly by people free to reflect on what they have imaginatively made their own.

There are connections between film and literature, as there are between film and the other arts. Literature, of course, is made of language, the same stuff used for factual statements, for ordinary conversations about everyday things. The imaginative writer, however, structures and shapes the raw material of language to exploit possibilities of ambiguity and indirection, to permit the words to function figuratively as well as denotatively, to permit them to be visible, sometimes almost palpable. He creates, at length, a totality composed of many interrelated levels of potential meaning. Attending to the work—be it Shelley's *Ode to the West Wind*, Hemingway's "The Killers," Joyce's *A Portrait of the Artist as a Young Man*—as a formed expression of some speaker, engaging himself with the language in its permutations, the characters and their enactments, the movement of motifs, the development of theme, the reader is bound to shape his experience in the process. How else can he read—except in the light of his experience, except as he builds out of what has evoked in him an imaginary, fictive world—the illusioned world that is the book?

A book, after all, is a dead thing once it is written. It simply exists, as does Keats' Grecian urn"a still unravish'd bride of quietness"—until someone lends it his life. And a reader can only truly lend a work of literature his life if he moves, with the aid of his imagination, into his consciousness, his inwardly apprehended world. "Raskolnikov's waiting is *my* waiting which I lend him," writes Sartre. "Without this impatience of the reader he would remain only a collection of signs. His hatred of the police magistrate who questions him is my hatred which has been solicited and wheedled out of me by signs, and the police magistrate himself would not exist without the hatred I have for him via Raskolnikov." Only at that point does Dostoevsky's *Crime and Punishment* come alive; coming alive, the book becomes an event in the reader's consciousness. In the same discussion, Sartre goes into particulars about the specific activity involved. He points out that reading is a synthesis of perception and creation, that the "object" (the novel or the poem, with its distinctive structure) is just as important as the "subject" (the reader, who discloses the work of art, brings it into being):

> In a word, the reader is conscious of disclosing in creating, of creating by disclosing. . . . If he is inattentive, tired, stupid, or thoughtless, most of the relations will escape him. He will never manage to "catch on" to the object (in the sense in which we see that fire "catches" or "doesn't catch"). He will draw some phrases out of the shadow, but they will appear as random strokes. If he is at his best, he will project beyond the words a synthetic form, each phrase of which will be no more than a partial function: the "theme," the "subject," or the "meaning."[41]

Wide-awakeness is important; so is the ability to generate (out of the reader's accumulated experience) the structure of the literary work. Not only is the reader released into his subjectivity, his inner time; his imagination can—and usually will—move him beyond the artist's traces "to project beyond the words a new synthetic form," an order of meanings which is distinctively his.

This approach is neither permissive nor relativistic. Attention is continually drawn to the work and its multiple facets. Its structure and multivalent levels of meaning are slowly and carefully to be explored; "one must wait for it," Sartre says, "and observe it." But the work as such refers to the subjectivity of the reader, who journeys into his interior under the guidance of the literary artist—Robert Frost or Herman Melville, Samuel Beckett or William Shakespeare. For instance, there may have been woods and snow, horses and sleds in the experience of a person who comes to Frost's "Stopping by Woods on a Snowy Evening." He may have been reared in New England and known the winters; and somewhere in the background of his consciousness may be imprints of early perceptions of sleighbells, mysterious silences, sudden falls of darkness. Entering the poem, engaging with the images and sounds, he may well discover some of those perceptions rising to the surface, accompanied by feeling-tones and shreds of memory. The poem itself, however, is ready to impose its structure on amorphous materials; and, as he discloses that structure, the reader will find himself forming those materials as he has never done before. "The woods are lovely, dark and deep. . . ." He may feel, as never before, the dangerous seductiveness of darkness and all it represents: sleep, forgetfulness, even death. "But I have promises to keep. . . ." He may experience the tension of obligation, the risks involved in leaving village conventions behind"without a farmhouse near." Almost certainly, he will see what he has never seen before in his stream of consciousness. And yet, even as he recognizes the new-ness of the perspective, he will probably feel that that is how the moment truly was—except that he never realized it before. He will have become visible to himself in a new way—discovering materials within his life-world through the patterns he has imposed on them, seeing them with opened eyes.

To respond to Frost's poem it is not necessary to have lived in New England, of course. Everyone has experienced dark places and pulls to nothingness, in inner city or on open plains. Nor is it necessary to have sailed on whaling ships to understand *Moby Dick.* What human being has not felt the temptation to look "into coffin ware-houses" or to dash out into the middle of a busy street? What human being has not (feeling self-destructive and despairing) wanted to make a transition "from a schoolmaster to a sailor," to go off in search of whatever he imagines the "great whale" to be? The teacher who risks experience with such works must involve himself fully, aiming at pri-vate possession, at a discovery of his own inwardness. If he makes these works available to his students, he ought also to respect their privacy—certainly at the beginning and the end. Of course, there should be talk among them, interchange, mutual involvement. And the teacher may function like a good critic—affording "new perceptions and with them new values," as Arnold Isenberg has said.[42] The teacher will *know* that there is no final explanation of any particular experience with a work of art; he will also know that no one can bring about appreciation or enjoyment in another, that he can only help make oth-ers see. Nevertheless, he can try to make his students discern certain qualities they may have overlooked. He can articulate (without forc-ing) certain of his ideas about the work. The ideas may even take the form of directions for focusing in certain ways, for tracing the emer-gence of various patterns, for clarifying figures of speech, paradoxes, ironies. Knowing something of his inner voyages, however, the teacher will not try to persuade his students to adopt his evaluations or share his feelings. He will offer good reasons, try to elicit good reasons for the judgments his students make; but in the end, when they return to the work at hand, the students must embark on their own journeys—and no one can accompany them.

Confronting any art form, the teacher can only involve himself and bring his convictions to his class when he is done. He is not a missionary, not a museum guard; he is a human being trying to recapture some of his original perceptions, trying to identify himself, trying to see. He can only be present to his students *as a human being* engaged in searching and choosing, as someone who is willing to take the risk of new perspectives, as someone who cares.

The poet Rainer Maria Rilke, in "Torso of an Archaic Apollo," communicates the sense of what confrontation with works of art can do:

> Never will we know his fabulous head
> where the eyes' apples slowly ripened.
> Yet his torso glows: a candelabrum set before his
> gaze which is pushed back and hid,
>
> restrained and shining. Else the curving breast
> could not thus blind you, nor through the soft turn
> of the loins could this smile easily have passed
> into the bright groins where the genitals burned.
>
> Else stood this stone a fragment and defaced,
> with lucent body from the shoulders falling,
> too short, not gleaming like a lion's fell:
>
> nor would this star have shaken the shackles off,
> bursting with light, until there is no place
> that does not see you. You must change your life.[43]

Rilke is describing a torso sculptured by Auguste Rodin. It is a torso of Apollo, the god of light, knowledge, and art, who is "archaic" for so many modern men. Working with his own medium and out of his own experience, Rodin was able to transmute a form that would otherwise have been dead. Through his imagination he was able to restore to life a mere fragment of the past and create significance where there had been a void. That significance now calls out to the person willing to look through his own eyes. It makes a demand of the one who can encounter the vitality and radiance of the sculpture without a desire to run away and hide. "You must," the great work exhorts, "change your life."

The teacher can find an analogy here, since his very project involves making that demand. He is also engaged in transmuting and illuminating material to the end of helping others see afresh. If he is able to think what he is doing while he is vitally present as a person, he may arouse others to act on their own freedom. Learning to learn, some of those persons may move beyond the sheltered places until they stand by their own choice in the high wind of thought. They may experience the adventure Rilke speaks of in the poem entitled "Initiation":

> Whoever you are, go out into the evening,
> leaving your room of which you know each bit;
> your house is the last before the infinite,
> whoever you are.
> Then with your eyes that wearily
> scarce lift themselves from the worn-out door-stone
> slowly you raise a shadowy black tree
> and fix it on the sky: slender, alone.
> And you have made the world (and it shall grow
> and ripen as a word, unspoken, still).
> When you have grasped its meaning with your will,
> then tenderly your eyes will let it go. . . .[44]

The tree may represent the order, pattern, or perspective the individual creates when he learns. To grasp its meaning with one's will may signify the personal choice to integrate what has been disclosed, to put it to use in interpreting and ordering one's own life-world. The teacher, too, must raise his shadowy trees and let them ripen. Stranger and homecomer, questioner and goad to others, he can become visible to himself by doing philosophy. There are countless lives to be changed, worlds to be remade.

Notes and References

1. Alfred Schutz, "The Stranger," in *Studies in Social Theory, Collected Papers* II (The Hague: Martinus Nijhoff, 1964), p. 95.
2. Albert Camus, *The Stranger* (New York: Vintage Books, 1954), p. 104.
3. Nathaniel Hawthorne, *The Scarlet Letter,* in *The Portable Hawthorne*, ed. Malcolm Cowley (New York: Viking Press, 1955), p. 425.
4. Maurice Merleau-Ponty, "Man and Adversity," in *Signs*, tr. Richard C. McCleary (Evanston, Ill.: Northwestern University Press, 1965), p. 240.
5. Maurice Merleau-Ponty, "Man and Adversity," in *Signs*, p. 242.
6. Ernest Hemingway, *A Farewell to Arms* (London: Jonathan Cape, 1952), p. 186.
7. Charles E. Silberman, *Crisis in the Classroom* (New York: Random House, 1970), pp. 126–127.
8. Jules Henry, *Culture Against Man* (New York: Random House, 1963), p. 291.
9. Frank Kermode, *The Sense of an Ending* (New York: Oxford University Press, 1967), p. 39.
10. Richard S. Peters, "Concrete Principles and the Rational Passions," in *Moral Education: Five Lectures by James M. Gustafson, Richard S. Peters, Lawrence*

Kohlberg, Bruno Bettelheim and Kenneth Keniston (Cambridge, Mass.: Harvard University Press, 1970), p. 39.

11. Jean-Paul Sartre, *Existentialism*, tr. Bernard Frechtman (New York: Philosophical Library, 1947), p. 21.

12. William K. Frankena, *Ethics* (Englewood Cliffs, N.J.: Prentice-Hall, 1963), pp. 5–6.

13. Gresham M. Sykes, "New Crimes for Old," *The American Scholar,* autumn 1971, p. 598.

14. William K. Frankena, *Ethics*, p. 98.

15. Fyodor Dostoevsky, *The Brothers Karamazov*, tr. Constance Garnett (New York: The Modern Library, 1945), p. 291.

16. Albert Camus, *The Rebel*, tr. Anthony Bower (New York: Alfred A. Knopf, 1954), p. 231.

17. Richard M. Hare, *The Language of Morals* (New York: Oxford University Press, 1964), p. 73.

18. Peter Marin and Allan Y. Cohen, *Understanding Drug Use* (New York: Harper & Row, Publishers, 1971), p. 15.

19. Lawrence Kohlberg, "Education for Justice: A Modern Statement of the Platonic View," in *Moral Education: Five Lectures by James M. Gustafson, Richard S. Peters, Lawrence Kohlberg, Bruno Bettelheim and Kenneth Keniston*, p. 70.

20. Jean-Paul Sartre, *Existentialism*, p. 20.

21. Martin Heidegger, "What Is Metaphysics?", in *Existence and Being*, tr. R. F. C. Hull and Alan Crick (Chicago: Henry Regnery Company, 1965), p. 334.

22. "Notes and Comment," *The New Yorker*, December 20, 1969, p. 28.

23. Albert Camus, *The Plague* (New York: Alfred A. Knopf, 1948), pp. 226–227.

24. Jean-Paul Sartre, *Existentialism*, pp. 37–38.

25. Alvin Plantinga, "An Existentialist's Ethics," in *Ethics*, ed. Julius R. Weinberg and Keith E. Yandell (New York: Holt, Rinehart & Winston, 1971), p. 23.

26. Søren Kierkegaard, "Either/Or," in *A Kierkegaard Anthology*, ed. Robert Bretall (Princeton, N.J.: Princeton University Press, 1947), p. 103.

27. Søren Kierkegaard, "Either/Or," in *A Kierkegaard Anthology*, p. 105.

28. Søren Kierkegaard, "Either/Or," in *A Kierkegaard Anthology*, p. 106.

29. Charles A. Reich, *The Greening of America* (New York: Random House, 1970), pp. 223–224.

30. Henry David Aiken, "Morality and Ideology," in *Ethics and Society*, ed. Richard T. De George (Garden City, N.Y.: Doubleday & Company, 1966), p. 159.

31. Iris Murdoch, *The Sovereignty of Good* (New York: Schocken Books, 1971), p. 97.

32. Richard S. Peters, "Concrete Principles and the Rational Passions," in *Moral Education*, p. 36.

33. John Dewey, "The Present and Future," in *Human Nature and Conduct* (New York: The Modern Library, 1930), p. 266.

34. William K. Frankena, "Toward A Philosophy of Moral Education," in *Philosophy and Education,* 2nd ed., ed. Israel Scheffler, (Boston: Allyn and Bacon, 1966), pp. 237–238.

35. Richard S. Peters, "Reason and Habit: The Paradox of Moral Education," in *Theories of Value and Problems of Education,* ed. Philip G. Smith (Urbana: University of Illinois Press, 1970), pp. 164–166.

36. John Dewey, *Democracy and Education* (New York: The Macmillan Company, 1916), p. 379.

37. John Dewey, *Democracy and Education,* p. 26.

38. Bill Ayers, "Traveling with Children and Traveling On," in *This Book Is About Schools,* ed. Satu Repo (New York: Pantheon Books, 1970), p. 334.

39. Morris Weitz, "The Role of Theory in Aesthetics," in *Problems in Aesthetics,* ed. Morris Weitz (New York: The Macmillan Company, 1959), pp. 149–151.

40. Jean-Paul Sartre, *Literature and Existentialism,* tr. Bernard Frechtman (New York: The Citadel Press, 1965), p. 11.

41. Jean-Paul Sartre, *Literature and Existentialism,* p. 43.

42. Arnold Isenberg, "Critical Communication," in *Contemporary Studies in Aesthetics,* ed. Francis J. Coleman (New York: McGraw-Hill Book Company, 1968), p. 154.

43. Rainer Maria Rilke, "Torso of an Archaic Apollo," in *Rilke: Selected Poems,* tr. C. F. MacIntyre (Berkeley: University of California Press, 1958), p. 93.

44. Rainer Maria Rilke, "Initiation," in *Rilke: Selected Poems,* p. 21.

FURTHER READING

Sylvia Ashton-Warner, *Spearpoint: Teacher in America* (New York: Alfred A. Knopf, 1972).

Richard Barnet, *Roots of War* (New York: Atheneum, 1972).

William Barrett, *Time of Need: Forms of Imagination in the Twentieth Century* (New York: Harper & Row, Publishers, 1972).

Gregory Battcock, ed., *The New American Cinema: A Critical Anthology* (New York: E. P. Dutton & Company, 1967).

Gregory Battcock, ed., *The New Art: A Critical Anthology* (New York: E. P. Dutton & Company, 1966).

Ernest Becker, *Beyond Alienation* (New York: George Braziller, 1967).

Daniel Bell, *Work and Its Discontents* (New York: League for Industrial Democracy, 1970).

Kenneth D. Benne, *A Conception of Authority: An Introduction* (New York: Russell and Russell, 1961).

Bruno Bettelheim, *The Informed Heart* (New York: The Free Press, 1960).

Kenneth Boulding, *The Meaning of the Twentieth Century* (New York: Harper & Row, Publishers, 1964).

Theodore Brameld, *The Climactic Decades: Mandate to Education* (New York: Frederick A. Praeger, 1970).

Harry S. Broudy, *The Real World of the Public Schools* (New York: Harcourt Brace Jovanovich, 1962).

Gloria Channon, *Homework! Required Reading for Teachers and Parents* (New York: Outerbridge and Dienstfrey, 1970).

George Dennison, *The Lives of Children: The Story of the First Street School* (New York: Random House, 1969).

John Dewey, *Experience and Education* (New York: Collier Books, 1963).

Elizabeth Cleaners Street School People, *Starting Your Own High School* (New York: Vintage Books, 1972).

Estelle Fuchs, *Teachers Talk: Views from Inside City Schools* (Garden City, N.Y.: Doubleday & Company, 1969).

William H. Gass, *Fiction and the Figures of Life* (New York: Alfred A. Knopf, 1970).

Paul Goodman, *The New Reformation: Notes of a Neolithic Conservative* (New York: Random House, 1970).

Thomas F. Green, *Work, Leisure, and the American Schools* (New York: Random House, 1968).

Nat Hentoff, *Our Children Are Dying* (New York: Viking Press, 1966).

John Holt, *Freedom and Beyond* (New York: E. P. Dutton & Company, 1972).

Judson Jerome, *Culture Out of Anarchy* (New York: Herder & Herder, 1970).

Herbert R. Kohl, *The Open Classroom: A Practical Guide to a New Way of Teaching* (New York: Vintage Books, 1969).

Rollo May, *Love and Will* (New York: W. W. Norton & Company, 1969).

Maurice Natanson, *The Journeying Self: A Study in Philosophy and Social Role* (Reading, Mass.: Addison-Wesley Publishing Company, 1970).

A. Harry Passow, ed., *Urban Education in the 1970s* (New York: Bureau of Publications, Teachers College, Columbia University, 1971).

Paul Ricoeur, *Fallible Man: Philosophy of the Will,* tr. Charles Kelbley (Chicago: Henry Regnery & Company, 1965).

Ross V. Speck and others, *The New Families: Youth, Communes, and The Politics of Drugs* (New York: Basic Books, 1972).

Stephen Spender, *The Struggle of the Modern* (Berkeley: University of California Press, 1965).

Paul Tillich, *The Courage To Be* (New Haven: Yale University Press, 1963).

Miriam Wasserman, *The School Fix* (New York: Outerbridge and Dienstfrey, 1970).

René Wellek and Austin Warren, *Theory of Literature* (New York: Harcourt Brace Jovanovich, 1956).

John Wilson, Norman Williams, Barry Sugarman, *Introduction to Moral Education* (Baltimore: Penguin Books, 1967).

18

NEL NODDINGS

It would be fair to claim that, nowadays, any form of discussion on caring in education includes references to Nel Noddings (born 1929). A veteran scholar, Noddings has established her academic career in association with the ethics of caring in education. Her prime argument is that anything we learn needs to stem from the ethics of caring, including science and math, because the goal of education is first and foremost to cultivate caring and good human beings.

Noddings's academic career is very impressive, and to summarize it is a challenge. She started her academic adventure at Montclair State University, where she received her bachelor's degree in mathematics. She then went on to receive a master's degree in mathematics from Rutgers University. In 1973 she received her Ph.D. in philosophy of education from Stanford University. Prior to her academic career, she taught grades 6–9. She also taught K–12 teachers modern math and served as a high school assistant principal. Her vast experience as a teacher has always been the guiding voice in her writings. Altogether, she has been involved in many writing projects, has received many honorary awards, has been invited to teach and to lecture in many places (including Columbia University and Stanford) in many parts of the world, and her books have been translated into many languages.

Overall, her philosophy of education has two important influences. First, Carol Gilligan's book *In a Different Voice: Psychological Theory and*

Author: Tammy Shel

Women's Development (1984) emphasizes a feminist ethic of care. While this book has been criticized for overgeneralizing women's experiences and essentializing caring, Noddings found in it a new notion of ethics that was not reliant on masculine forms of thought. While traditional ethics is often concerned with death and the afterlife, Noddings and Gilligan argue that starting ethics from a feminist perspective would focus more on questions of birth and life. Noddings then combined Gilligan's groundbreaking work with the existential philosophy of Martin Buber. To help the reader understand caring, Noddings borrowed Buber's theory of the "I-Thou" relationship. Rather than see students as passive objects, a caring theory of educational ethics would see students as active subjects.

Caring, Noddings contends, has three major components: engrossment, motivational displacement, and reciprocity. The first, *engrossment*, is related to how the carer understands the needs of the cared-for. It is the notion of "feeling with . . . I receive the other into myself, and I see and feel with the other. I become a duality." The second, *motivational displacement*, occurs when we transcend our own interests to the cared-for experience, with empathy. That is, we feel the cared-for from his or her standpoint. The last one, *reciprocity*, is recognition of our acts by the cared-for that helps us to complete the caring relationship. Reciprocity does not oblige, in Noddings's view, though, equal exchange of acts but it does require acknowledgment of the receiver.

With respect to education, Noddings writes: "The fundamental aim of education is to help children grow in desirable ways. This is best accomplished by modeling, dialogue, practice, and confirmation." First, a teacher must be a role model of good behavior. Then a teacher needs to establish a genuine dialogue with his or her students through mutual exploration. In practice, teachers rationalize what they require from their students to practice instead of just giving them instructions. In confirmation, the teacher encourages the students and reinforces their confidence in the process of learning. In other words, the teacher gives constructive and positive feedback. Caring is more than emotions. Noddings's main contribution is to promote caring as an approach to life, to others, and it is an approach to teaching and learning. While traditional, male-oriented curricula focus on the training of reason and abstraction, Noddings focuses on the need to develop an overall ethical disposition that includes reason, practical action, and feelings.

What are Noddings's main contributions? There are many, and it is impossible to cover them all in this brief introduction. To begin with, Noddings synthesized many scholars' philosophies into a well-established theory. Likewise, she does not attempt to get the entire credit for herself and, by that, she demonstrates and promotes a more humble and genuine academic discourse. Her other contribution is equally important in changing the academic discourse vocabulary. Because of her, caring, which is traditionally associated with women and the private sphere, has become an acceptable word in any academic discourse, especially in education. Prior to her, philosophers of education did not use the term on a regular basis, and if care was mentioned, it was stigmatized as "unintellectual" women's work associated with the home. Nowadays, even male scholars focus on caring and elaborate on it as an important way of rethinking ethics, yet there are significant problems with Noddings's theory. For instance, she does not provide readers with ethnographic and empirical studies to support her arguments. Second, her theories do not address multicultural possibilities in understanding caring. Her theories need to be examined and developed by including multiple individual and cultural experiences and interpretations of care.

In conclusion, Noddings poses a series of questions to educators: Are there multicultural possibilities for understanding care differently? How would one imagine care for ideas, strangers, objects, and community? How can we redesign a school around centers of care?

REFERENCES

Buber, Martin. *I and Thou.* New York: Charles Scribner, 1970.

Clement, Grace. *Care, Autonomy, and Justice: Feminism and the Ethics of Care.* Boulder: Westview, 1996.

Gilligan, Carol. *In a Different Voice.* Cambridge, MA: Harvard University Press, 1982.

Noddings, Nel. *Caring: A Feminine Approach to Ethics and Moral Education.* Berkeley: University of California Press, 1984.

Noddings, Nel. *The Challenge to Care in Schools.* New York: Teachers College Press, 1992.

Noddings, Nel. *Starting at Home: Caring and Social Policy.* Berkeley: University of California Press, 2002.

Shel, Tammy. *The Ethics of Caring: Between Utopia and Pragmatism.* New York: Peter Lang, 2007.

White, Brian. Caring and the Teaching of English. *Research in the Teaching of English.* 37, no 3 (2003): 295–328.

CARING

The German philosopher Martin Heidegger (1962) described care as the very Being of human life. His use of the term is very broad, covering an attitude of solicitousness toward other living beings, a concern to do things meticulously, the deepest existential longings, fleeting moments of concern, and all the burdens and woes that belong to human life. From his perspective, we are immersed in care; it is the ultimate reality of life.

Heidegger's full range of meanings will be of interest as this exploration continues, but the meaning that will be primary here is relational. A *caring relation* is, in its most basic form, a connection or encounter between two human beings—a carer and a recipient of care, or cared-for. In order for the relation to be properly called caring, both parties must contribute to it in characteristic ways. A failure on the part of either carer or cared-for blocks completion of caring and, although there may still be a relation—that is, an encounter or connection in which each party feels something toward the other—it is not a *caring* relation. Even before I describe the contributions of carer and cared-for, one can see how useful this relational definition is. No matter how hard teachers try to care, if the caring is not received by students, the claim "they don't care" has some validity. It suggests strongly that something is very wrong.

In *Caring* (1984), I described the state of consciousness of the carer (or "one-caring") as characterized by engrossment and motivational displacement. By engrossment I mean an open, nonselective receptivity to the cared-for. Other writers have used the word "attention" to describe this characteristic. Iris Murdoch (1970), for example, discussed attention as essential in moral life, and she traced the concept to Simone Weil. Weil placed attention at the center of love for our neighbors. It is what characterizes our consciousness when we ask another (explicitly or implicitly), "What are you going through?" Weil wrote:

> This way of looking is first of all attentive. The soul empties itself of all its own contents in order to receive into itself the being it is looking at, just as he is, in all his truth. Only he who is capable of attention can do this. (1951, p. 115)

To say that the soul empties itself of all its own contents in order to receive the other describes well what I mean by engrossment. I do not mean infatuation, enchantment, or obsession but a full receptivity. When I care, I really hear, see, or feel what the other tries to convey. The engrossment or attention may last only a few moments and it may or may not be repeated in future encounters, but it is full and essential in any caring encounter. For example, if a stranger stops me to ask directions, the encounter may produce a caring relation, albeit a brief one. I listen attentively to his need, and I respond in a way that he receives and recognizes. The caring relation is completed when he receives my efforts at caring.

As carer in the brief encounter just described, I was attentive, but I also felt the desire to help the stranger in his need. My consciousness was characterized by motivational displacement. Where a moment earlier I had my own projects in mind, I was now concerned with his project—finding his way on campus. When we watch a small child trying to tie her shoes, we often feel our own fingers moving in sympathetic reaction. This is motivational displacement, the sense that our motive energy is flowing toward others and their projects. I receive what the other conveys, and I want to respond in a way that furthers the other's purpose or project.

Experiencing motivational displacement, one begins to think. Just as we consider, plan, and reflect on our own projects, we now think what we can do to help another. Engrossment and motivational displacement do not tell us what to do; they merely characterize our consciousness when we care. But the thinking that we do will now be as careful as it is in our own service. We are seized by the needs of another.

What characterizes the consciousness of one who is cared for? Reception, recognition, and response seem to be primary. The cared-for receives the caring and shows that it has been received. This recognition now becomes part of what the carer receives in his or her engrossment, and the caring is completed.

Some critics worry that my account puts a tremendous burden on the carer and very little on the recipient of care. But we must keep in mind that the basic caring relation is an encounter. My description of a caring relation does not entail that carer and cared-for are permanent labels for individuals. Mature relationships are characterized by mutuality. They are made up of strings of encounters in which the parties exchange places; both members are carers and cared-fors as opportunities arise.

Even in the basic situation, however, the contribution of the cared-for is not negligible. Consider the mother-infant relationship. In every caring encounter, the mother is necessarily carer and the infant cared-for. But the infant responds—he or she coos, wriggles, stares attentively, smiles, reaches out, and cuddles. These responses are heartwarming; they make caregiving a rewarding experience. To see just how vital the infant's response is to the caring relation, one should observe what happens when infants cannot respond normally to care. Mothers and other caregivers in such situations are worn down by the lack of completion—burned out by the constant outward flow of energy that is not replenished by the response of the cared-for. Teachers, too, suffer this dreadful loss of energy when their students do not respond. Thus, even when the second party in a relation cannot assume the status of carer, there is a genuine form of reciprocity that is essential to the relation.

The desire to be cared for is almost certainly a universal human characteristic. Not everyone wants to be cuddled or fussed over. But everyone wants to be received, to elicit a response that is congruent with an underlying need or desire. Cool and formal people want others to respond to them with respect and a touch of deference. Warm, informal people often appreciate smiles and hugs. Everyone appreciates a person who knows when to hug and when to stand apart. In schools, all kids want to be cared for in this sense. They do not want to be treated "like numbers," by recipe—no matter how sweet the recipe may be for some consumers. When we understand that everyone wants to be cared for and that there is no recipe for caring, we see how important engrossment (or attention) is. In order to respond as a genuine carer, one does have to empty the soul of its own contents. One cannot say, "Aha! This fellow needs care. Now, let's see—here are the seven steps I must follow." Caring is a way of being in relation, not a set of specific behaviors.

I have put great emphasis on caring as relation, because our temptation is to think of caring as a virtue, an individual attribute. We do talk this way at times. We say, "He is a caring person," or even, "She is really a caring person, but she has trouble showing it." Both of these comments capture something of our broad notion of care, but both are misleading because of their emphasis on caring as an individual virtue. As we explore caring in the context of caregiving—any long-term unequal relation in which one person is carer and the other cared-for—

we will ask about the virtues that support caring. But for now, it is important not to detach carers from caring relations. No matter how much a person professes to care, the result that concerns us is the caring relation. Lots of self-righteous, "caring" people induce the response, "she doesn't really care about me at all."

Even though I will often use the word *caring* to apply to relations, I will also need to apply it to capacities. The uses should be clear in context. I want to avoid a concentration on judgment or evaluation that accompanies an interpretation of caring as an individual virtue, but I also want to acknowledge that people have various capacities for caring—that is, for entering into caring relations as well as for attending to objects and ideas.

When we discuss teaching and teacher-learner relationships in depth, we will see that teachers not only have to create caring relations in which they are the carers, but that they also have a responsibility to help their students develop the capacity to care. What can this mean? For Heidegger care is inevitable; all aware human beings care. It is the mark of being human. But not everyone develops the capacity to care for others in the way described above. Perhaps very few learn to care for ideas, for nonhuman life, for objects. And often we confuse the forms of caring and suppose caring to be a unitary capacity that transfers easily from one domain to another.

Simone Weil is a good example of an outstanding thinker who seems to have believed that intellectual caring and interpersonal caring are closely related. In the essay from which the earlier passage was extracted, Weil observed that the study of geometry requires attention and that attention so learned could increase students' concentration in prayer. Thence, we may suppose, Weil concluded that closer connection in prayer would produce more sensitive interpersonal relations; that is, she believed that intellectual attention could be transferred to interpersonal attention. This is doubtful. Evidence abounds that people can attain high levels of intellectuality and remain insensitive to human beings and other living things. Consider the Nazi high command or the fictional Professor Moriarty (Sherlock Holmes's nemesis) who attended lovingly to his orchids but was evil incarnate in the human domain. So the varieties of care need analysis.

Unequal caring relations are interesting not only in the human domain but also in the realm of nonhuman animals. It is doubtful whether any animal can be a carer with respect to humans (although there are those who have argued the case for dogs), but many animals are responsive cared-fors, and taking care of animals can be a wonderful way to learn caring. In our interaction with animals, we also have an opportunity to study the forms of response that we value. Some animals respond with intelligence, and we usually value that. Some respond with affection; they like to be stroked, cuddled, held, or scratched. Still others respond vocally. All of these responses affect us and call forth a caring attitude. Further, certain physical characteristics that suggest the possibility of a valued response also affect us. Most of us feel sympathy for baby seals threatened by hunters, because they look as though they might respond in the ways mentioned. Creatures that are slimy, scaly, or spiny rarely evoke a sympathetic response in us. The nature of our responses will be seen as important when we consider the roots of ethical life.

In another sense of care, human beings can care about ideas or objects. An approach to education that begins with care is not, as I pointed out earlier, anti-intellectual. Part of what we receive from others is a sense of their interests, including intellectual passions. To enhance a student's understanding and skill in a given subject is an important task for teachers, but current educational practices are riddled with slogans and myths that are not very helpful.

Often we begin with the innocent-sounding slogan mentioned earlier, "All children can learn." The slogan was created by people who mean well. They want teachers to have high expectations for all their students and not to decide on the basis of race, ethnicity, sex, or economic status that some groups of children simply cannot learn the subject at hand. With that much I agree.

But I will argue that not all individual children can learn everything we might like to teach them. Further, the good intentions captured in the slogan can lead to highly manipulative and dictatorial methods that disregard the interests and purposes of students. Teachers these days are expected to induce a desire to learn in all students. But all students already want to learn; it is a question of *what* they want to learn. John Dewey (1963) argued years ago that teachers had to start with the experience and interests of students and patiently forge connections between that experience and whatever subject matter was prescribed. I would go further. There are few things that all students need to know, and it ought to be acceptable for students to reject some material in order to pursue other topics with enthusiasm. Caring teachers listen and respond differentially to their students. Much more will be said on this highly controversial issue in later chapters. For now it is enough to note that our schools are not intellectually stimulating places, even for many students who are intellectually oriented.

Few students learn to care for ideas in school. Perhaps even fewer learn to care for objects. I am not talking about mere acquisitiveness; this seems to be learned all too well. I am talking about what Harry Broudy (1972) called "enlightened cherishing" and what the novelist and essayist John Galsworthy (1948) called "quality." This kind of caring produces fine objects and takes care of them. In a society apparently devoted to planned obsolescence, our children have few opportunities to care lovingly for old furniture, dishes, carpets, or even new bicycles, radios, cassette players, and the like. It can be argued that the care of many tools and instruments is a waste of time because they are so easily replaced. But one wonders how long a throwaway society can live harmoniously with the natural environment and also how closely this form of carelessness is related to the gross desire for more and more acquisitions. Is there a role for schools to play in teaching care of buildings, books, computers, furniture, and laboratory equipment?

Caring for ideas and objects is different from caring for people and other living things. Strictly speaking, one cannot form a relation with mathematics or music or a food processor. The cared-for cannot feel anything for us; there is no affect in the second party. But, oddly, people do report a form of responsiveness from ideas and objects. The mathematician Gauss was "seized" by mathematics. The poet Robert Frost insisted that "a poem finds its own way" (see the accounts in Noddings & Shore, 1984). And we know that well-tended engines purr, polished instruments gleam, and fine glassware glistens. The care we exert induces something like a response from fields of ideas and from inanimate objects. Do our students hear enough—or anything at all—about these wondrous events?

Finally, we must consider Heidegger's deepest sense of care. As human beings, we care what happens to us. We wonder whether there is life after death, whether there is a deity who cares about us, whether we are loved by those we love, whether we belong anywhere; we wonder what we will become, who we are, how much control we have over our own fate. For adolescents these are among the most pressing questions: Who am I? What kind of person will I be? Who will love me? How do others see me? Yet schools spend more time on the quadratic formula than on any of these existential questions.

In reviewing the forms of care, it becomes clear that there is a challenge to care in schools. The structures of current schooling work against care, and at the same time, the need for care is perhaps greater than ever.

The Debate in Ethics

No discussion of caring today could be adequate without some attention to the ethic of care. In 1982 Carol Gilligan published her now famous *In a Different Voice*, describing an alternative approach to moral problems. This approach was identified in the voices of women, but Gilligan did not claim that the approach is exclusively female, nor did she claim that all women use it. Still, the avalanche of response from women who recognized themselves in Gilligan's description is an impressive phenomenon. "This is me," many women said. "Finally someone has articulated the way I come at moral problems."

Gilligan described a morality based on the recognition of needs, relation, and response. Women who speak in the different voice refuse to leave themselves, their loved ones, and connections out of their moral reasoning. They speak from and to a situation, and their reasoning is contextual. Those of us who write about an ethic of care have emphasized affective factors, but this is not to say that caring is irrational or even nonrational. It has its own rationality or reasonableness, and in appropriate situations carers draw freely on standard linear rationality as well. But its emphasis is on living together, on creating, maintaining, and enhancing positive relations—not on decision making in moments of high moral conflict, nor on justification.

An ethic of care—a needs- and response-based ethic—challenges many premises of traditional ethics and moral education. First, there is the difference of focus already mentioned. There is also a rejection of universalizability, the notion that anything that is morally justifiable is necessarily something that anyone else in a similar situation is obligated to do. Universalizability suggests that who we are, to whom we are related, and how we are situated should have nothing to do with our moral decision making. An ethic of caring rejects this. Next, although an ethic of care puts great emphasis on consequences in the sense that it always asks what happens to the relation, it is not a form of utilitarianism; it does not posit one greatest good to be optimized, nor does it separate means and ends. Finally, it is not properly labeled an ethic of virtue. Although it calls on people to be carers and to develop the virtues and capacities to care, it does not regard caring solely as an individual attribute. It recognizes the part played by the cared-for. It is an ethic of relation.

In moral education an ethic of care's great emphasis on motivation challenges the primacy of moral reasoning. We concentrate on developing the attitudes and skills required to sustain caring relations and the desire to do so, not nearly so much on the reasoning used to arrive at a decision. Lawrence Kohlberg (1981) and his associates, following Plato and Socrates, have focused on moral reasoning. The supposition here is that moral knowledge is sufficient for moral behavior. From this perspective, wrongdoing is always equated with ignorance. Gilligan explicitly challenged Kohlberg's scale or hierarchy of moral reasoning (suggesting a powerful alternative developmental model), but others of us have challenged the whole idea of a developmental model, arguing that moral responses in a given individual may vary contextually at almost any age. (The language used to discuss what one is doing and why may, of course, depend on intellectual development, but moral behavior and its intellectual articulation are not synonymous.)

Moral education from the perspective of an ethic of caring has four major components: modeling, dialogue, practice, and confirmation (Noddings, 1984). Modeling is important in most schemes of moral education, but in caring it is vital. In this framework we are not trying to teach students principles and ways of applying them to problems through chains of mathematical reasoning. Rather, we have to show how to care in our own relations with cared-fors. For example, professors of education and school administrators cannot be sarcastic and dictatorial with teachers in the hope that coercion will make them care for students. I have heard administrators use this excuse for "being tough" with teachers"because I care about the kids of this state"—but, of course, the likely outcome is that teachers will then turn attention protectively to themselves rather than lovingly to their students. So we do not tell our students to care; we show them how to care by creating caring relations with them.

There is a second reason why modeling is so vital. The capacity to care may be dependent on adequate experience in being cared for. Even while a child is too young to be a carer, he or she can learn how to be a responsive cared-for. Thus our role as carer is more important than our role as model, but we fill both simultaneously. We remind ourselves when we are tempted to take short cuts in moral education that we are, inevitably, models. But otherwise, in our daily activities we simply respond as carers when the need arises. The function of modeling gets special attention when we try to explain what we are doing and why in moral education. But the primary reason for responding as carers to our students' needs is that we are called to such response by our moral orientation.

Dialogue is the second essential component of moral education. My use of the term *dialogue* is similar to that of Paulo Freire (1970). It is not just talk or conversation—certainly not an oral presentation of argument in which the second party is merely allowed to ask an occasional question. Dialogue is open-ended; that is, in a genuine dialogue, neither party knows at the outset what the outcome or decision will be. As parents and teachers, we cannot enter into dialogue with children when we know that our decision is already made. It is maddening to young people (or any people) to engage in "dialogue" with a sweetly reasonable adult who cannot be persuaded and who, in the end, will say, "Here's how it's going to be. I tried to reason with you. . . ." We do have to talk this way at times, but we should not pretend that this is dialogue. Dialogue is a common search for understanding, empathy, or appreciation. It can be playful or serious, logical or imaginative, goal or process oriented, but it is always a genuine quest for something undetermined at the beginning.

Dialogue permits us to talk about what we try to show. It gives learners opportunities to question "why," and it helps both parties to arrive at well-informed decisions. Although I do not believe that all wrongdoing can be equated with ignorance, I do believe that many moral errors are ill-informed decisions, particularly in the very young. Thus dialogue serves not only to inform the decision under consideration; it also contributes to a habit of mind—that of seeking adequate information on which to make decisions.

Dialogue serves another purpose in moral education. It connects us to each other and helps to maintain caring relations. It also provides us with the knowledge of each other that forms a foundation for response in caring. Caring (acting as carer) requires knowledge and skill as well as characteristic attitudes. We respond most effectively as carers when we understand what the other needs and the history of this need. Dialogue is implied in the criterion of engrossment. To receive the other is to attend fully and openly. Continuing dialogue build up a substantial knowledge of one another that serves to guide our responses.

A third component of moral education is practice. Attitudes and "mentalities" are shaped, at least in part, by experience. Most of us speak regularly of a "military mind," a "police mentality," "business thinking," and the like. Although some of this talk is a product of stereotyping, it seems clear that it also captures some truth about human behavior. All disciplines and institutional organizations have training programs designed not only to teach specific skills but also to "shape minds," that is, to induce certain attitudes and ways of looking at the world. If we want people to approach moral life prepared to care, we need to provide opportunities for them to gain skills in caregiving and, more important, to develop the characteristic attitudes described earlier.

Some of the most fascinating work in contemporary feminist theory is devoted to the study of women's experience and its articulation. It seems likely that women's traditional experience is closely related to the moral approach described in ethics of care. Women, more often than men, have been charged with the direct care of young children, the ill, and the aged. They have been expected to maintain a pleasing environment, to look after the needs of others, and to mediate disputes in ordinary social situations. If we regard this experience as inseparable from oppression, then we might agree with Nietzsche that what I am describing is merely "slave mentality." But if we analyze the experience, we find considerable autonomy, love, choice, and consummate skill in the traditional female role. We may evaluate the experience as essential in developing fully human beings.

Women have learned to regard every human encounter as a potential caring occasion. In nursing theory, for example, Jean Watson (1985) defined the moment in which nurse and patient meet as a "caring occasion." It is not just that the nurse will provide care in the form of physical skills to the patient. Rather, it is a moment in which each must decide how to meet the other and what to do with the moment. This is obviously very different from defining a medical encounter as a problem-solving event. Problem solving is involved, of course, but it is preceded by a moment of receptivity—one in which the full humanity of both parties is recognized—and it is followed by a return to the human other in all his or her fullness.

If we decide that the capacity to care is as much a mark of personhood as reason or rationality, then we will want to find ways to increase this capacity. Just as we now think it is important for girls as well as boys to have mathematical experience, so we should want both boys and girls to have experience in caring. It does not just happen; we have to plan for it. As we will see, such planning is complex and loaded with potential pitfalls.

Some schools, recognizing the needs just discussed, have instituted requirements for a form of community service. This is a move in the right direction, but reflection produces some issues to worry about. The practice provided must be with people who can demonstrate caring. We do not want our children to learn the menial (or even sophisticated) skills of caregiving without the characteristic attitude of caring. The experience of caregiving should initiate or contribute to the desired attitude, but the conditions have to be right, and people are central to the setting. This is a major point, to which I will return.

Next, practice in caring should transform schools and, eventually, the society in which we live. If the practice is assimilated to the present structures of schooling, it may lose its transformative powers. *It* may be transformed—that is, distorted. If we were to give grades for caregiving, for example, students might well begin to compete for honors in caring. Clearly, then, their attention could be diverted from cared-fors to themselves. If, on the other hand, we neither grade nor give credit for such work, it may inevitably have second-class status in our schools. So long as our schools are organized hierarchically with emphasis on rewards and penalties, it will be very difficult to provide the kind of experience envisioned.

The fourth component of moral education from the perspective of caring is confirmation. Martin Buber (1965) described confirmation as an act of affirming and encouraging the best in others. When we confirm someone, we spot a better self and encourage its development. We can do this only if we know the other well enough to see what he or she is trying to become. Formulas and slogans have no place here. We do not set up a single ideal or set of expectations for everyone to meet, but we identify something admirable, or at least acceptable, struggling to emerge in each person we encounter. The person working toward a better self must see the attribute or goal as worthy, and we too must see it as at least morally acceptable. We do not confirm people in ways we judge to be wrong.

Confirmation requires attribution of the best possible motive consonant with reality. When someone commits an act we find reprehensible, we ask ourselves what might have motivated such an act. Often it is not hard to identify an array of possible motives ranging from the gross and grubby to some that are acceptable or even admirable. This array is not constructed in abstraction. We build it from a knowledge of this particular other and by listening carefully to what she or he tells us. The motive we attribute has to be a real, a genuine possibility. Then we can open our dialogue with something like, "I know you were trying to help your friend . . ." or "I know what you're trying to accomplish. . . ." It will be clear that we disapprove of this particular act, but it will also be clear to the other that we see a self that is better than this act. Often the other will respond with enormous relief. *Here is this significant and percipient other who sees through the smallness or meanness of my present behavior a self that is better and a real possibility.* Confirmation lifts us toward our vision of a better self.

It is worth repeating that confirmation cannot be done by formula. A relation of trust must ground it. Continuity is required, because the carer in acting to confirm must know the cared-for well enough to be able to identify motives consonant with reality. Confirmation cannot be described in terms of strategies; it is a loving act founded on a relation of some depth. When we turn to specific changes that should occur in schooling in order to meet the challenge to care, I will put great emphasis on continuity. Not all caring relations require continuity (some, as we have seen, are brief encounters), but teaching does require it.

Confirmation contrasts sharply with the standard mode of religious moral education. There we usually find a sequence of accusation, confession, penance, and forgiveness. The initial step, accusation, causes or sustains separation. We stand in moral judgment and separate the other from ourselves and the moral community. In contrast, confirmation calls us to remain in connection. Further, accusation tends to produce denial or rationalization, which we then feel compelled to overthrow. But the rationalization may in fact be an attempt on the part of the accused to find that possible motive and convey it to us, the accuser. Because we have to reject it in order to proceed with confession, penance, and forgiveness, offenders may never understand their own true motives. This sequence also depends heavily on authority, obedience, fear, and subordination. We can be harsh or magnanimous in our judgment and forgiveness. Our authority is emphasized, and the potential power of the offender's own moral struggle is overlooked.

I do not mean to suggest that there is never a place for accusation and confession in moral education. It is not always possible for us to find a motive that is morally acceptable; sometimes we have to begin by asking straight out, "Why did you do that?" or "How could you do such a thing?" But it is gratifying how often we really can see a better self if we look for one, and its identification is a first step in its realization.

This whole way of looking at ethics and moral education challenges not only parts of the religious tradition but also the ideas of Freud and like-minded theorists. Freud believed that our sense of morality develops out of fear. The superego, Freud said, is an internalization of authority—of the father's voice—and its establishment results from resolution of the oedipal conflict. Sons fear castration by the father if they disobey or compete with him. Resolution of this desire to rebel and compete involves acceptance of the father's power and authority, and the superego (Freud's guide to acceptable behavior) takes up residence within the son. This account of moral development led Freud to conclude that women must be morally inferior to men. Because girls need not fear castration (having been born in that dread condition), their moral voice never attains the strength and dependability of men's.

Recent criticisms of Freud suggest that more attention should be given to the preoedipal period. Nancy Chodorow (1978) has theorized that girls and boys develop different psychological deep structures because females are almost exclusively the primary caregivers for both. Girls can find their gender identity without separating from their mother and, hence, develop a relational personality structure and perhaps even a relational epistemology or way of knowing (Keller, 1985). Boys, however, must construct their gender identity in opposition to all that is female. Here we have the possible roots of the different moral voices described by Gilligan. We will consider other alternatives as well.

Eli Sagan (1988) has also suggested that moral development begins and is strongly affected by preoedipal life. Without rejecting the Freudian framework entirely, Sagan recommends a shift in emphasis. If we give due weight to early childhood, we see that conscience (a sense of right and wrong, not mere internalization of authority) develops as much out of love and attachment as out of fear. Further, the primary fear is not of harm and punishment but, rather, of disappointing a loved parent and, at worst, losing that parent's love. This is a major challenge to masculinist psychology and a suggestion compatible with an ethic of caring and the model of moral education outlined here. Love, caring, and relation play central roles in both ethics and moral education.

I want to suggest that caring is the very bedrock of all successful education and that contemporary schooling can be revitalized in its light. Before describing a broad plan to make caring central in education, I need to explain why the current ideal is inadequate. Liberal education has been the Western ideal for centuries. Even when it is poorly funded in comparison with technical and professional education, it is still the ideal that puts pressure on precollegiate education. It is the form of education—done well or poorly—that most of us experienced. What is wrong with it, and why should it be rejected as a model of universal education?

CARING FOR IDEAS

In our discussion so far, I have concentrated on ideas as they are connected to actual life, existential questions, and general education. Now I will consider how we should approach ideas for their own sake. How should we teach students who are passionately interested in a realm of disciplined thought? How should we teach those who have an instrumental interest in a subject? In short, how should we teach the disciplines as long as they remain in the curriculum?

I have already argued that the disciplines as we now know them should not be used as the heart—or organizing organ—of the curriculum. A first step toward weakening the hegemony of the disciplines is to cease teaching them for their own sake except to those who show a passionate interest in them. Everywhere today, educators in the particular disciplines want to teach their subject from the perspective of experts in the field. Students are supposed to learn to think like mathematicians, scientists, historians, literary critics, aestheticians, and ethicists. This attitude is pernicious and actually does violence to the disciplines thus presented. The average student need not think like a mathematician; lots of people other than mathematicians use mathematics effectively, and students should be encouraged to find their own uses for mathematics and choose their own attitude toward it. Pedagogy should begin with the purposes, interests, and capacities of students. But some students have a passionate interest in particular subjects. These students should have an opportunity to learn those subjects in considerable depth.

In this chapter I will look at two subjects from this perspective. The first, mathematics, I have had extensive experience in teaching. The second, art, I will look at as a philosopher and general educator. My major claim in both cases is that students who have passionate interest in a subject should be initiated into the discourse of the disciplinary community; others need not be. Further, beyond providing the best possible education for individual students, a pedagogy that posits different objectives for students with different capacities and interests stands the best chance of meeting our needs as a nation. If we need mathematicians, engineers, and scientists, then we should invite those students who have the appropriate interests and capacities into a rigorous and wondrous working partnership in the relevant disciplines. Otherwise the threat is not just mediocrity but outright intellectual rebellion.

Mathematics

There is now a tremendous push to get more students involved in mathematics. Many colleges and universities require three years of mathematics for entrance, and this requirement presses high schools to increase their enrollments in college preparatory mathematics. Preparation for college is highly standardized. Whether students plan to study art, religion, or engineering, three years of mathematics is supposed to be good for them.

What jobs really require algebra, geometry, and trigonometry? Think of all the things one could do in this society without using algebra. One needs to be literate in numbers, of course, and everyone should be able to compute percents, compare rates, and understand simple descriptive statistics. Beyond such basic skills, people should understand the mathematics involved in their own spheres of interest, but as I said earlier, this mathematics need not be taught by expert mathematics teachers. Indeed, it could be more convincingly taught by people using it in the fields where it is needed. Consider a problem suggested for students in an algebra class. A set of data is presented on soil acidity and plant growth (Goldin, 1990, p. 20). Students are asked to construct a scatter plot and look for trends. No explanation of pH is given, no mention is made of the type of plants, and no other variable is considered. This problem does not belong in a mathematics class! If it is to be treated at all, it should be done in a biology class where, preferably, students will actually grow plants. Students should consider the variables to be controlled (light, heat, water, nutrients) and the type of plants. They should be thoroughly familiar with the pH scale and the range preferred by most plants. They should also know how to change soil acidity. Selecting one kind of plant, they might experiment by varying the pH; then they should try another type of plant. In this context the statistical exercise becomes real. If scientists and science teachers do not use the mathematics described in this exercise, why should students be interested in looking for trends in a meaningless scatter plot?

Mathematics has served as a well-oiled piece of sorting machinery. Many students are discouraged from college preparation because they hate or fear mathematics, and if they drop it in high school and then decide at the community college level that they want a four-year education, they still have to take mathematics even if it's irrelevant to their projected field of study.

The schools are caught in a web of paradox. There is no question that mathematics, foreign language, and laboratory science were thought to be effective testing-sorting instruments for college entrance. Thus there has long been great pressure to make these courses rigorous and demanding. But now there is even greater pressure to give all children—especially minority children—a fair opportunity to get to college. That means enrolling many more children in college preparatory mathematics. One way to force students into algebra and geometry is to offer no alternative mathematics, and schools that make this choice must enroll everyone in college preparatory mathematics. In our eagerness to give everyone "a fair chance," we offer minimal courses—two years of mathematics taken over a three-year period with everything deep and interesting removed. It does

not occur to us to change the requirement—to insist that students prepare well for a line of study and to study mathematics only if it is relevant to that line. Such a requirement would mean that students taking
mathematics (or any other subject) would usually see the point of
their involvement.

At the level of national interest, we are shooting ourselves in the
foot with good intentions. Instead of coining slogans"All children can
learn!"—and forcing all children into algebra "for their own good," we
should be teaching college preparatory mathematics to fewer students
and doing a better job at it. The mathematics supposedly necessary to
understand other subjects should be taught there.

I do not mean to suggest that students should be kept out of mathematics classes by grade requirements, or unless they show proof of
aptitude. Classes should be totally open—even, as I said earlier, honors
classes. Teachers should talk with students about the receptivity
required in caring about mathematics. People can become engrossed in
mathematics, hear it "speak to them," be seized by its puzzles and challenges. It is tragic to deprive students of this possibility. "Honors"
classes should be classes for the passionately interested. Any student
who wants to tackle the work and has at least minimal prerequisite
experience should be allowed to do so. The key here is that we accept
students' legitimate aims and desires.

The complaint has been made against such a mode of operation
that some students will short-change themselves. Ignorant or uncon-
vinced of what a rigorous education can mean in their lives, they will
choose courses and topics based on how little work they require. But
this complaint rests on a misunderstanding. I am certainly not suggesting that some courses be challenging and others "mickey mouse."
Nor am I suggesting that students be left alone to choose what they
will do on the basis of mere whim. Rather, the idea is for teachers and
students to establish relations of care and trust so that valuable information can be effectively exchanged, advice given, and challenging
projects undertaken. I do not believe that many teenagers will down-
grade their own education. When they seem to be doing that, it is
because we have already told them that their interests are irrelevant
to schooling and (explicitly or implicitly) that engineers are better
than child care workers, physicians better than nurses, lawyers better
than police-persons, executives better than cooks, and so forth. In

such a system, choosing what one really wants to study can be—by definition—downgrading one's education. However, it need not be so, and it should not be so.

But, perverse as it is, let's face the reality of today's schools. Students who want to "make it" in life have to take academic mathematics. Can we do anything to improve life in mathematics classrooms without changing the whole system?

There is a movement in mathematics education that is growing in influence and popularity. It is called constructivism. (See Davis, Maher, and Noddings, 1990.) I want to say a little about it here because it offers some positive possibilities, but at the same time, it contains the seeds of its own destruction. Unless it is embedded in an encompassing moral position on education, it risks categorization as a *method*, as something that will produce enhanced or slightly modified traditional results.

Constructivism is a cognitive position holding that all mental acts, both perceptual and cognitive, are acts of construction. No mental act is a mere copy or externally imposed response. If you pass some information to me, I must actively listen to make out what you are saying, and then I have to fit what I have heard into what I already know and decide what to do with the new material. What I do with it depends on my purposes. I may respond with a sympathy-like interest because I care about you even though I do not care about the topic you are discussing. Or I may care deeply about the topic and realize that what you are saying suggests that I have been wrong about something. Or I may evaluate your remark and decide that *you* have made a mistake.

Constructivists believe that people are internally motivated and that they construct their own mental representations of situations, events, and conceptual structures. Constructivist teachers, then, usually spend time trying to find out what their students are trying to do and why. They are ready with suggestions and challenges that will help students to make strong and useful constructions.

What motivates constructivist mathematics educators? For the most part, they want to teach mathematics in ways that are compatible with their beliefs about how people learn. They also tend to believe that mathematical thinking is rich, complex, tolerant of ambiguity, filled with attempts that may or may not succeed, and broadly useful in many human activities. Believing all this, they want to promote their students' mathematical growth. This is fine to the degree that students are concerned for whatever reason with their own mathematical growth.

But constructivism as a pedagogical orientation has to be embedded in an ethical or political framework. The primary aim of every teacher must be to promote the growth of students as competent, caring, loving, and lovable people. Teachers with this aim will work flexibly in teaching mathematics—inspiring those who care about mathematics for itself to inquire ever more deeply, helping those who care instrumentally about mathematics to prepare for the line of work they desire, and supporting as best they can those students who wish they never had to encounter mathematics. To have uniformly high expectations for all students in mathematics is morally wrong and pedagogically disastrous. It is part of a sloganized attempt to make our schools look democratic and egalitarian, when in fact they are systems continually struggling for tighter control.

Now I want to describe in detail an actual program that embodies some of the ideas discussed here. First I will describe the program itself, and then I will present an analysis of what could go wrong if the primary aim is forgotten.

The mathematics department of an average suburban high school (about 1,500 pupils) was faced with an increasing number of students enrolled in third-year college preparatory mathematics"11th algebra/trig." The school was also pressed for space, and this fact made the plan proposed by the department administratively attractive. They proposed to work with two large classes (seventy-five to eighty students each) taught by a team of teachers in the school cafeteria. Each student could choose a minimum course, a standard course, or an accelerated course. This provision was designed to accommodate students who disliked math but needed the third year to qualify for university entrance, as well as students who loved math and wanted as much as they could get. The syllabi made clear that students could change their minds—slow down or speed up if they preferred. The minimum course covered six chapters of the course text and required students to pass one chapter test each marking period; completing this course would not qualify a student for twelfth-year mathematics. The standard course required completion of nine chapters, and the accelerated course demanded twelve or more chapters. Further, assignments varied. Students in the accelerated course might skip the easy exercises, but they had to do the difficult ones.

A serious attempt was made to reduce test anxiety. Grades were earned cumulatively. Everyone started the marking period with a grade of 50. When a test was passed, the grade became, say, 70; a second test passed meant perhaps an 85; a third test 95. This method reduces anxiety considerably because nothing can be lost by taking a test. The old (almost tribal) fear of entering the last test of a marking period with a 92 and leaving with a 72 is removed. All tests were graded "passing," "not passing," or "passing + 1." This last acknowledged a top-notch performance, and the extra point was added to the student's basic grade at the end of a marking period.

The course was designed as a continuous progress program. Students could not move on to chapter 3 until they had passed a test on chapter 2. One teacher, Ms. Jones let us say, would start the whole group off with an introduction to chapter 1, and then the students would work together at tables while the teachers circulated to give help. Fridays were test days, and on the very first Friday there were always some students ready to take the test on chapter 1. Students who passed the chapter 1 test would move on to work with the teacher who had major responsibility for chapter 2. This process continued until some students were ready for chapter 4, for which Ms. Jones again had responsibility. Usually there were still a few students working on chapter 1, so Ms. Jones divided her time between students in chapter 1 and those in chapter 4.

Every week, one day was designated for "enrichment," and one of the team teachers took a group of students to a separate classroom for discussion of some topic that did not appear in the text. Enrichment topics included Diophantine equations, cryptography, abstract algebra, logic puzzles, history of mathematics, and computer problems. Any students could elect to participate. If I were working with such a team today, I would want to introduce topics from each of the centers of care. Possibilities: our own psychology of learning math, effective tutoring, population and hunger studies, animal populations, matrices for agricultural studies, the special contributions of various ethnic groups, women mathematicians, religious interests of great mathematicians.

In the years that I was involved with this program, results—traditionally interpreted—were good. On year-end standardized tests, no student scored in the bottom decile and very few in the lowest fifth. Everyone learned something. The span of achievement in terms of material covered ranged from the minimum six chapters to more than sixteen! Motivation to do mathematics varies enormously.

For me, however, and certainly for our present discussion, traditional results are not the main concern. Our concern should center on what the students are learning about themselves, about helping each other, about contracts and meeting obligations, about the fascinating applicability of mathematics to human endeavors, and—for some students—about the nature and beauty of mathematics itself. Many things can go wrong if the primary purposes are not kept firmly in mind, and it is worthwhile to analyze the program from this perspective because in doing so we can learn much about why educational reforms fail.

One temptation is to overdo the individual, continuous progress aspect of such a program. Our students were encouraged to work together; they were not placed on individualized schedules. Teachers provided mini-lectures, special help, and advice on which other students to consult; they were not bogged down in checking work as often happens in individualized programs. The press to scientize teaching and learning could easily lead to an overemphasis on tests, to isolation in learning, and to standardized roles for teachers. Participants have to remember why they are engaged in a program of this sort and resist that pressure.

When team teaching is used, there may be a move (as mentioned above) to differentiate the functions of team members: a lead teacher to lecture, one to supervise individual tutoring, one to check work, and so forth. This is deadly and works against the primary purpose. Teachers and students must work together cooperatively as whole human beings, not as bits of pedagogical machinery. From the perspective of caring, team teaching can be a wonderful idea; differentiated staffing, however, is a terrible one.

As the year moves along, teachers may question the capacity of students for self-evaluation and self-governance. This actually happened in our program. Sometimes students would achieve their desired grade, say an 85, by the middle of a marking period and prepare to do something other than math for the next two or three weeks. Although I always tried to persuade such students to try for a top grade, I accepted their decision. After all, we had a contract. One team member, let's call her Ms. Smith, was aghast at this acceptance on my part. She believed that it was our duty to *make* students do their best, and she also believed that they should do nothing but math in math class. Ms. Smith's attitude was thoroughly conditioned by the control ideology that pervades our schools. Students must be controlled—for their own good, of course. To give way to Ms. Smith on this, I now understand even better than I did then, is to distort the whole program.

Another form of distortion is equally troubling. Over the years, a few teachers trying the approach in other courses (algebra 1, for example) interpreted the facilitative function of the teacher to mean that the teacher should only respond to student requests for help. These teachers never intervened and actually let students sit idle for days, even weeks. Nothing could be further from the spirit we are discussing here. Of course teachers should initiate! They should suggest, persuade, inspire, encourage, negotiate compromises, offer concrete help. Above all they should engage students in dialogue so that decisions are well informed. We do not respect students when we leave them alone to make decisions on whim.

Ms. Smith introduced another concern about control. She complained that too many students were electing to take tests on Fridays even though they were unprepared. Clearly many had not completed the assignments and were simply hoping to pass by luck. She insisted that their notebooks should be checked before they were allowed to take a test. Again, there was the need to control. Indeed Ms. Smith honestly felt it was her duty to control student work in this way. She staggered home every Thursday night under a tremendous load of notebooks. I compromised. On Thursday in class I would gather around me those students who wanted to take Friday's test. Then I would choose specific problems in their notebooks and ask how they had been done, why some had been skipped, whether the student had considered an alternative method that seemed important. These sessions were more conversations than quality checks, and other students would regularly chime in with suggestions. This way of operating is compatible with induction into a community of discourse. We ask different questions of students who are passionately interested in mathematics and expect a different level of response from them. From some students an answer that tells "how it works" is entirely adequate; from others we should expect a response that reflects deep structural understanding.

Finally, someone might challenge the whole notion of mixing minimum, standard, and accelerated classes in one program for which all students would get five credits. The question would be raised: Is this fair? My response is that a criterion of fairness is irrelevant here. Needs are being identified and met. That is what matters. One might want to argue that meeting needs *is* fair, but I have learned to identify that language as a danger signal. It means that the system wants tighter control.

With the ideology of control so firmly entrenched in our professional and personal lives, it is very difficult to move to an approach that emphasizes mutual respect, responsible freedom, self-evaluation, open cooperation, caring, and sharing. Even well-intentioned people can make or accede to decisions that will press promising programs back into the control mode. Constructivists risk having this happen when they insist on *understanding* as a legitimate goal for all students without analyzing the varieties of understanding. The goal should be for students to understand what they are doing and to what end. This need not require a deep structural understanding of mathematics.

Here I want to say a little more about Jaime Escalante, of whom I spoke appreciatively earlier. I cannot admire everything Escalante does. In particular I cannot approve throwing students out of class, browbeating them for not working as hard as the teacher wants, and using sarcasm as a pedagogical strategy. Many of Escalante's students see the caring that lies underneath the surface cruelty, but some probably do not. We have to ask whether getting students to pass an advanced-placement calculus test is an adequate reason for treating them impolitely. On the positive, polite side, Escalante says repeatedly to his students, "You are the best!" But that lovely compliment means, You can do A.P. calculus!" It also implies that other students (those not studying A.P. calculus) are less than best. My preference is to respect the full range of human capacities and to help students do high-quality work in whatever field they choose. A student should not have to succeed at A.P. calculus to gain a math teacher's respect.

There is another point to consider with respect to Escalante's methods. It is probably true that a majority teacher could not treat minority students so; complaints would be thunderous. Perhaps minority students and teachers need the freedom to work out methods that are mutually acceptable to them. But, as coprofessionals, we should continue to question as we support. Surely not all minority students respond favorably to coercion. Again, it is not a sign of respect to simply shrug and accede. At every stage and in all of our interactions, we must remind ourselves of what we are trying to achieve, and everything else must be examined in light of our major purpose.

Minorities and women, like majority students, may sometimes fall into the passionately interested category. But often their interests are instrumental. Such interests should be respected. Teachers need to experiment with a range of methods that may be especially effective for particular groups. They should be acquainted with works that treat the various ways of knowing (Belenky, et al., 1986; Culley & Portuges, 1985; Bunch & Pollack, 1983), and, where there are mathematical topics of special interest to these groups, they should be offered for study.

Mathematics teachers should also attend to capacities other than the mathematical. Those with linguistic capacities might learn a lot of mathematics through reading and writing. (We seldom spend time on the intelligent reading of math texts, for example.) Those with artistic talent might enjoy mathematical studies of aesthetics, the mathematics of design, or even the aesthetics of mathematics. Those with strong interpersonal skills might learn best through tutoring others. Our methods must vary.

Finally, although we should encourage students to study mathematics if their interests suggest such study, and we should help minorities and women to see themselves as potentially competent in mathematics, we should not create an environment in which mathematical competence defines a student's self-worth. Lots of successful, competent, morally upstanding people hate math and find their passionate interests elsewhere. Rather than press the question, Why aren't more women interested in math?, we should ask what they *are* interested in and why. We can use the answers to those questions both to encourage alternative interests and to design more appropriate math courses.

Art

I cannot examine every subject that appears in the school curriculum in detail. Among the arts, I have chosen fine arts rather than music or drama because its current direction illustrates the major mistakes I have been criticizing throughout this book.

Many art educators are now recommending a curricular approach called Discipline-Based Art Education (DBAE). This approach is highly cognitive and appeals to the same linguistic and mathematical/logical capacities that support the rest of the curriculum. It suggests that art education should comprise aesthetics, art criticism, art history, and art production. (See Getty Center for Education in the Arts, 1985; also *Journal of Aesthetic Education*, 1987). It should, in short, look more like other disciplines in the precollege curriculum and be subject to the same high-powered cognitive teaching and testing.

I think this movement is wrongheaded even though I have a high regard for many of its proponents. (For other criticisms see a collection of articles in *Educational Theory*, 1990; Gehlback, 1990.) I want to start the discussion with some recollections from my early days as a math teacher. Before I became convinced that the major job of every teacher is much like that of a parent—to foster growth and shape acceptable children—I was certainly a discipline-oriented math educator. There's a story to be told about my conversion from that position, but the point I want to make is different; it centers on the place of art as a very special elective in high schools. Year after year there were kids in my math classes who were terrible in math. When a marvelous art teacher joined the faculty, I found out that some of these people were outstanding young artists; art boomed in that school. They became part of what was known as the "art room crowd," and they held a proud position in our high school. I came to know them because there was a "math office bunch," too, and a few students belonged to both groups, one of my own daughters among them. Once I got to know the art room crowd and moved away from the rigidities of my early position on math (a lot of factors were involved here), I started to do a better job as a teacher. I came to appreciate a multitude of talents. My students no longer appeared to me as just good and bad math students.

In that high school, art played a significant role in the lives of a substantial number of young people. It was different from the other subjects, and the "crowd" was different from the other kids. They were serious about their work, had their own jokes, were trusted in the art rooms on their own and for as many hours as they could manage. I know they did art history and criticism—that they watched slides even during lunch—and that they were involved in evaluating and eventually arranging exhibits at the county museum. These young people were aiming at postsecondary schools my math kids rarely considered—Cooper Union, the Rhode Island School of Design, Pratt Institute; they were working hard at assembling portfolios. They had their service projects, too, and were often involved in designing sets for dramatic presentations, preparing posters for various events, and even producing political cartoons.

I don't know whether tests were given on the slides shown, whether student progress was systematically evaluated as we are so fond of claiming today. I doubt it. Students who took four years of art—sometimes the equivalent of six years by packing in extra hours—treasured their status as members of a community. They were learners but not ignorant learners; they were more like talented apprentices, and their talents were cultivated. The cognitive dimension of art grew out of their passionate involvement with art production. I suspect that their knowledge was active and well integrated with their central interests. It was not that flabby stuff Whitehead called "inert knowledge."

So far I have depended on experiential evidence, personal recollection, to initiate an argument. The major concern that emerges is that students who are really talented in art will be disenchanted by the standard cognitive approach. The people who will do well in these courses are just the people who do well generally in academic courses. In a recent dissertation, Liora Bresler (1987) showed that exactly this occurred in a cognitively oriented music class at a major university. Musically talented and experienced students dropped out or did poorly; the relatively ignorant and untalented did remarkably well. Art educators should launch a careful study of this phenomenon before converting art education to a more heavily cognitive base.

You can see what worries me in the move to DBAE. I am afraid that art will lose its unique place in schools. I understand the political reasons for advocating DBAE. To a large degree, art has lost its place entirely in many schools (what occurred in my old school is no longer so familiar) and so long as it sports an arty look, it will continue to be suspect in its very difference—to be relatively unimportant in college admission, to appeal to a limited number of students, to be at the mercy of the budget ax. DBAE advocates believe that one way to make art important is to make it just like English, math, and science: require it, make it heavily cognitive, sequence it, test the daylights out of it. But I wonder, if you do this, what will happen to all those young people who for years have found the art room the only place in school worth attending, whose interest in art has kept them in school long enough to qualify for a chance at life's standard goods. Of course it is clear by now that I reject the disciplinary approach to general education, but the example of art underscores the features that worry me most.

My concern so far has focused on the possible loss of uniqueness in art education and the effects of that loss on artistically talented students. Now I want to push the argument up a notch and consider the relation between DBAE and societal goals. "A fundamental premise," say Clark, Day, and Greer (1987), "is that general education, to be balanced and complete, must attend to all major domains of human experience, including the aesthetic domain" (p. 139). This sort of statement has a nice ring to it and has appeared perennially in arguments for the advancement of various curricula. The fact of the matter is, however, that education does not attend to all major domains of human experience, nor do many of its practitioners and theorists show signs of wanting it to do so. We have, instead, intellectualized human experience, and we have been so successful at doing this that we really suppose reading and writing about various domains is equivalent to "having experience" in those domains. Attending to all the major domains of human experience has come to mean—for schools, at least—extending the range of intellectual experience. If art educators are serious about introducing students to an experience they might otherwise not encounter in school, they might well emphasize art production, crafts, and decoration of various sorts.

DBAE does, of course, advocate balance, and art production will be given attention, but as I will argue later, balance does not have to mean equal time. Further, balance is not the point here; respect for a unique set of talents is more the point. In casting its program as it has, DBAE clearly places itself in the liberal arts tradition. "Classical approaches to selection of domains as bases for school programs rely on philosophical analysis," Clark, Day, and Greer state. Further, "These analyses identify domains of human experience that should be addressed in a well-rounded education" (p. 139). It is true that programs that use such language—that talk about the ideal of an educated person and a well-rounded education—are accompanied by or under-girded by philosophical analysis. But a philosophical analysis need not of necessity produce such a view of education. It might, as mine attempts to do, support a view of education as learning to care or, alternatively, as self-actualization, or growth, or mere training. Whether or not to speak of the ideal of an educated adult is itself a fundamental choice that must be supported by philosophical argument.

Because DBAE, like so many other curriculum movements, defends requiring art on the grounds that a democratic society wants all its people to be "truly educated," this is a good place to review our initial argument against liberal education. Two very different views of democracy have been prominent in American education: the more or less static Greek view advocated by Robert Maynard Hutchins and the more dynamic one described by John Dewey.

The first lays out a picture of a society already formed and in decent order and asks how it can be kept that way. Its concept of virtue is reminiscent of the Greeks; it depends heavily on a demonstration of excellence in ways of life (Alasdair MacIntyre [1981] calls them "practices") that demand reflection on ends as well as skilled performance. The masses learn virtue from virtuous masters, and indeed virtue itself is ultimately defined this way. It is the constitutive quality of the good (or virtuous) person. Thus the authority of moral experts plays a large role in such a society, and of course moral expertise is coextensive with intellectual expertise in this vision. The "best" in this society are, happily for them, the best in all ways.

Greek democracy clearly was not classless, and the education recommended by its philosophers reflected this fact. In Plato's *Republic*, children were to be educated according to their diagnosed abilities for one of three main functions in adult life. The "best" education was reserved for the "best" students—those who would become guardians of the Republic. This society was certainly a democracy of sorts. Those who were citizens were expected to participate appropriately in the affairs of the society, and gaining a position in the ruling class was supposedly a matter of merit.

The Greek notion of an elite education for guardians is retained in the contemporary ideal of an educated person. In the liberal arts tradition, an educated person is described in terms of the content with which he or she has become familiar, the shared language of this content, and the practices open to persons with such preparation. The education of such persons has long been considered the "best education." But notice that there is a good Greek circularity built into this

conception. What is the best education? It is the sort that our finest citizens must have had. Look at them to see what is good. How did they
get that way? Through the wonderful education provided for them
and through their talent and diligence. Thus the education already
experienced by the "best" becomes the best education.

The contemporary version of this doctrine was beautifully
described by Hutchins in the 1930s and still proficiently advocated, as
we saw earlier, by Mortimer Adler in his *Paideia Proposal* (1982).
Because our conception of democracy rejects a classed society, Hutchins
and Adler insist that, in Hutchins' words, "The best education for the
best is the best education for all." In other words, the education once
frankly designed for an elite should now be the education offered to
everyone.

The static assumptions in this recommendation are obvious. We
know what education is best because we have its best products as
examples. All we need to do is to replicate their education for each new
generation, being careful of course to give each child a genuine opportunity to succeed at it. Operation of the plan must be scrupulously fair.
Besides fairness to individuals, we are urged to consider the benefits
such a scheme promises for our democracy. From Adler's perspective a
democracy cannot long survive unless its citizens share a common
heritage—a common language, set of concepts, knowledge of their past,
understanding of the finest products of their culture. The society, for
Adler, is a given; at least its ideal is given, and this ideal is realized in a
nucleus of living experts who manifest the qualities needed in a good
society. What we need to do, he suggests, is to maintain and extend this
model.

The practicality of Adler's recommendations can safely be ignored
for the moment, and I have so far said nothing about the practicality
of DBAE either. It is the vision that I ask you to analyze and critique.
Are the persons who have governed, produced acknowledged works
of art, built fortunes, and conducted military campaigns really our
best persons? Did their education produce a goodness we really want
to replicate, or has its acquisition merely been the defining mark of
those who claimed themselves to be the best? If a different sort of
education had been offered, might our best have been a more compassionate, more generous, more open, less judgmental, less acquisitive,
and wiser set of persons? These are important questions, and no

scheme for general education should be seriously put forward without exploring them. There is enormous arrogance in the *Paideia Proposal*. It says, in effect, "Look at us! We are clearly the best, and our education should supply the pattern for all education. Let us be generous and give all children the opportunity to be just like us." The *Paideia* totally ignores the riches of pluralistic culture—especially those cultures, such as our Native American, that reject the very premises of liberal education as it has been traditionally defined.

In contrast to the static notion of democracy, there is Dewey's dynamic conception. A democracy is not given, nor is it even illustrated in the workings of a cadre of similarly educated elites all capable of discussing the Peloponnesian Wars, Picasso, and nuclear throw weights—thereby demonstrating their competence to govern. Democracy is not the outcome of a common set of words and customs. Rather, it is an achievement—one that depends on the desire to communicate and the goodwill to persist in collaborative inquiry. common language, customs, and values are the marks of achievement in the effort at building a democracy, not its prerequisites. To achieve a democracy we must try things out, evaluate them without personal prejudice, revise them if they are found wanting, and decide what to do next through a process of reasoned consensus or compromise in which the authority of expertise is consulted but not allowed to impose its views with no discussion of how, why, and on what grounds.

The same advice is applied to education. For Dewey education, too, is a constructive achievement. It is not a matter of absorbing something already laid out, tried and true. It is a matter of trying things out with the valued help of experts (teachers), of evaluating, revising, comparing, sharing, communicating, constructing, choosing. Strictly speaking, there is no end product—no ideally educated person—but a diverse host of persons showing signs of increasing growth. There will be commonalities, of course, but these will have been achieved in the process and not necessarily through exactly similar experiences. Even when common values are achieved by one group, they cannot be simply transmitted to another. The new group can be guided; we can share what we have learned. But as soon as we *impose* our values on a new generation we risk losing those values that are most needed in a dynamic society—those that encourage reflective criticism, revision, creation, and renewal.

Present debate over plans like the *Paideia Proposal* often concentrates on feasibility. Too seldom are we encouraged to think reflectively about the total pattern of education to which we are committed and how any plan under consideration relates to it. Adler himself has discouraged such reflection by glossing over the great differences between Hutchins and Dewey. One would think, to read the *Paideia,* that the two men were both advocates of the Hutchins-Adler program. He says, for example:

> There is no acceptable reason why trying to promote equality should have led to a lessening or loss of quality. Two decades after John Dewey, another great American educator, Robert Maynard Hutchins, as much committed to democracy as Dewey was before him, stated the fundamental principle we must follow in our effort to achieve a true equality of educational conditions. "The best education for the best," he said, "is the best education for all." (1982, p. 6)

From what has already been said, it is clear that this paragraph of Adler's is very misleading; it conveys a monumental distortion of Dewey's position, since Dewey's conception of democracy was very different from that of Hutchins. Further, Adler makes it sound as though the two men never actually discussed these issues, when in fact their published debates make lively reading. My point here is that we live and work in a time when the history and philosophy of education are not regularly drawn upon to enlighten our debates. That Adler would put Dewey and Hutchins into one compartment with respect to their views on democracy and be persuasive to so many people who should know better is a dangerous sign. It is a sign that the curriculum field is still not paying much attention to its own history. (This is not a reason for forcing all education students to study curriculum history. It is, rather, part of an argument for extended dialogue between professors and students.)

Now what has all this to do with DBAE? Several paragraphs of the monograph suggest that DBAE does hold an ideal of the educated person, that education in art is thought to be necessary for an educated or enlightened citizenry, and that education in the four art disciplines should provide the basis for advanced study in art. This is part of an old and time-honored position in education, but it is one we have good reasons to reject.

There is a tone in DBAE suggesting that persons unfamiliar with, for example, Botticelli's *Birth of Venus* fall somehow short of the ideal of an educated person. As I mentioned earlier, I have colleagues in math education who feel the same way about people who do not know the difference between a definite integral and an indefinite integral. At most meetings of such professional groups, lots of speeches include the words, "It is deplorable that . . ." Now, surely in a complex society such as ours, we cannot insist that every person attain even a minimum level of sophistication in every discipline for which there are living advocates. To insist on this is to have a faulty (static) vision of what it means to be educated. There just *are* well-educated people who have never heard of Botticelli, and there *are* well-educated people who know nothing whatever of integrals, definite or indefinite. There is nothing deplorable in this state of affairs. What would indeed be deplorable is a society in which no one cared enough to make these things available to those who might like to learn them. DBAE is a bit ambivalent on the issue of access versus compulsion. It seems right, for example, to take the position that "DBAE is based on the assumption that all members of society, not only the wealthy or elite, deserve access to the visual arts" (p. 42). I have no quarrel whatever with this. But if "access" means required study, I fear that the objective is to make competency in art a component of the static ideal so widely embraced by advocates of a host of disciplines—each seeking its own place in the educational sun. Neither the worth of persons nor their educational attainment should be measured by whether or not they can appreciate a joke involving Botticelli's Venus—or one, however improbable, involving definite and indefinite integrals.

DBAE draws in a balanced fashion from aesthetics, art criticism, art history, and art production. This tells us the domains from which content will be extracted, but it does not tell us how that content will be presented. Even if we look at the suggested three dimensions of each discipline—the community of scholars/artists, methods of inquiry, and conceptual structure—we find little help in deciding on methods of instruction. Talking about methods of inquiry, for example, is quite different from employing those methods of inquiry. Do people best learn methods of inquiry by actually inquiring and being pressed to evaluate both methods and results, or do they learn best by being given an explicit mode of inquiry and lots of practice in its use? Should the method of instruction vary, depending on the age of the learners and the method of inquiry under consideration? These are crucial questions for curriculum developers, because we know from experience that curriculum and instruction cannot be neatly separated.

I am sure that advocates of DBAE want to respect the autonomy of teachers; one of the contrasts listed between the 1960s discipline-centered reform and DBAE is that the former "attempted to make 'teacher-proof' curricula," whereas the latter "recognizes essential roles of teachers and administrators in curriculum implementation" (Clark, Day, & Greer, 1987, p. 132). But this contrast, though capturing a good intention, is not exactly accurate. Some curricula developed in the 1960s were in fact designed to be teacher-proof, but most were not. They embodied the more fundamental error of ignoring instruction entirely. The new math was notorious in this respect. In many versions it left an absolutely crucial pedagogy at an implicit level. Its makers took for granted that teachers who understood the new material would also see that the old methods were not adequate for this new material. To this day, math educators argue over whether more blame for the failure of new math should be charged to teachers' lack of understanding of the content or their failure to adopt an appropriate pedagogy. A deeper point that I have emphasized repeatedly is that student interests, capacities, and purposes were ignored.

Consider the matter of structure. An emphasis on structure was paramount in new math, and it seems to be in DBAE also, in spite of a contrast explicitly made—"Focused on structure of disciplines as content source" versus "Focused on dynamic view of art disciplines including concepts, methods of inquiry, and communities of scholars" (Clark, Day, & Greer, 1987, p. 132). There is an admirable breadth here—roughly comparable to that of Harvard Project Physics over the Physical Science Study Committee (PSSC)—but the emphasis on conceptual structure is still clear. Therefore, essential pedagogical questions arise: Should an understanding of the fundamental concepts and structure precede the manipulation of objects in the disciplinary domain? Or is this understanding a developmental outgrowth of long years of manipulative work in the field? Is knowledge of structure necessary for all students?

Another great error in the new math seems now to have been the assumption that we could teach children effectively something about the structure of mathematics before they had learned the usual algorithms. Indeed the claim was that children might then invent their own algorithms and would in any case not require hours of practice on routine computations, because they would know what to do as a result of their basic understanding. There may still be something true in this claim, but by failing to consider the sort of pedagogy that would replace didactic instruction in routine practice, we missed an opportunity to validate the claim in any form. Most of us now think that structural understanding is a product of growth through manipulating objects and applying skills rather than a prerequisite or substitute for either. Thus I think it is essential for art curriculum makers to study problems of instruction carefully. Curriculum implementation is part of curriculum making, not a totally separate enterprise.

The problem discussed here is related to the one with which I started out. It seems to me that many children and adolescents are drawn to art by a desire to *do* art; in earlier discussion, I worried over the possible loss of art's unique place in the high school curriculum. The reservation of electives emphasizing art production might relieve this worry, provided the electives do not have heavily cognitive prerequisites. But a basic issue for art curriculum makers remains. It may be that the only sound mode of curriculum-and-instruction requires placing art production at the center of the enterprise; instruction in aesthetics, art criticism, and history might then grow out of and serve this central function. Art education should serve the artistically interested or talented. Where else in school do they get the respect they deserve?

Advocates of DBAE discuss the necessity of informing students about the social, historical, intellectual, and psychological contexts in which art is produced and critiqued. (See Clark, Day, & Greer, 1987.) Issues that arise here should be considered by specialists in all disciplines, because every discipline has an aesthetic dimension, a history, and a mode of evaluation or criticism, amd all of these activities are conducted in and help to define a variety of contexts. Art educators should be applauded, then, for emphasizing these connections. These dimensions are central to caring for ideas.

When we decide to include such matters in our curricula, however, it becomes necessary to consider ideological biases and preferences. There is a temptation to teach a particular view of aesthetics, to teach history as a set of facts quite apart from the set of conflicting interpretations that characterize historical research, and to lay out criteria for criticism without engaging in real evaluation of those criteria. I see no reason to accuse advocates of DBAE of making these errors, but I want to ask how they will avoid them.

The program as it is now outlined assumes a continuous chain of instruction from kindergarten through grade 12. Quite apart from my earlier objections to *requiring* art, the likelihood of such universal continuity must now be considered. If all students were to study art in the fashion advocated for twelve or thirteen years, curriculum makers could plan for progressive involvement with controversial matters of interpretation and the politics of art. Without this continuity, instruction in these highly complex domains might do more harm than good. Even carried through the 12th grade, there should be legitimate concern about the scope and purposes of such instruction. Concentration on the aesthetic can induce an odd and frightening form of amorality, even immorality, as Kierkegaard (1959) so dramatically reminded us. The Nazis were, for example, possibly among the best educated generation—from an aesthetic perspective—the world has yet produced.

Proceeding by example might be useful here. In a powerful historical work, Bram Dijkstra (1986) demonstrates how intimate the connection between art and immorality—in this case misogynism—can be. His opening words are these: "This is a book filled with the dangerous fantasies of the Beautiful People of a century ago. It contains a few scenes of exemplary virtue and many more of lurid sin" (p. vii). He shows convincingly that works of art, art criticism, and versions of art history have all contributed vigorously to the oppression and exploitation of women. "This book," he asserts, "amply demonstrates that there is cause to assume that works of art are by no means beyond involvement in the dominant ideological movements of the time in which they were created" (p. ix). None of us, I am sure, would deny this, but there remains the tough educational question of when and how we introduce such material to students. If, for example, we simply talk about the depiction of historical events in art or, acknowledging the ideological aspect of art, we even discuss the antiwar sentiments of a famous painting, we have not come close to the sort of influence Dijkstra documents so well. Only if education is organized around centers of care are we likely to avoid the domination of groups in power.

Feminist scholars are among those deeply concerned with these issues. This is because the masculinist ideologies pervasive in the disciplines are only now being uncovered and studied. Merlin Stone (1976) has documented the bias in archeology and religious history in her fascinating study of the ancient Goddess religion. Nina Auerbach (1982) has shown how both the literature and art of the Victorian age revealed or held hidden awaiting interpretation a combination of awe, fear, and hatred for the ancient power of the feminine. Her study focuses on the latent power of the feminine. "The mermaids, serpent-women, and lamias who proliferate in the Victorian imagination suggest a triumph larger than themselves, whose roots lie in the antiquity so dear to nineteenth-century classicists" (pp. 8–9). Dijkstra, as already noted, focuses on the misogyny and evil in these and other images of the fin de siècle. His themes of therapeutic rape, extinguished eyes, clinging vines, the nymph with the broken back, maenads of decadence, and many others are persuasively and heartbreakingly documented with art. In many cases, the art—both visual and literary— used as documentation has been greatly admired even though both creators and critics were aware of its dreadful endorsement of misogyny. Octave Mirbeau, for example, is quoted by Dijkstra as saying the following in his commentary on Remy de Gourmont's *Lilith:*

> The symbolic genesis of woman, as interpreted by Remy de Gourmont, corresponds exactly with the conclusions of anthropological science. Woman does not have a brain; she is simply a sexual organ. And that is the beauty of it. She has but one role in the universe, but that is a grandiose one: to make love, that is to say, to perpetuate the species. According to the irrefutable laws of nature, of which we feel rather than perceive the implacable and dolorous harmony, woman is not fit for anything that does not involve love or maternity. Certain women, very rare exceptions, have been able to give, either in art or literature, an illusion of creative energy. But those are either abnormal creatures, in revolt against nature, or simply the reflections of males, of whom, through sexual dysfunction, they have been able to maintain certain characteristics. (Dijkstra, 1986, p. 182)

This is not an isolated or unusual case. The world of art and literature is filled with such material. Marina Warner (1976), in her study of the Virgin Mary and Mariology, comments on the horror and significance of paintings of Mary crushing the serpent's head beneath her foot. The serpent, after all, was once a symbol of immortality, knowledge, and feminine power. Mary Daly (1984) also comments on the importance of this self-destroying act depicted in religious painting. Many other examples of the association of women with dragons, serpents, evil, and death are described in J. A. Phillips' (1984), *Eve*. He, too, discusses the significance of Mary—as the second Eve—crushing the serpent.

As we consider in some depth the treatment of women in art, we uncover related ideologies in religion, psychology, anthropology, literature, philosophy, and even science. The present revival of interest in Jungian psychology, for example, is accompanied by new interpretations of old symbols, legends, and art. Here, too, we see interest in both the alleged power of the feminine and fear of its reputed dark and evil side.

Art educators are in a better position than I to know whether the profession is prepared to cope honestly with these matters. Are there texts that discuss the treatment of women in art openly? The issues that I have pointed to clearly go well beyond current concern about pornography. They appear everywhere in the history of art and literature. In general education, my preference would be to make these matters of central interest in themes of care and to draw on the disciplines in connection with them. But so long as art is a separate subject and discipline-based, these matters must be incorporated.

Just as not all students are interested in mathematics, not all are interested in art. My preference would be for "aesthetic education across the curriculum." All subjects have an aesthetic aspect that should be considered. But if art must be taught as a separate subject to those uninterested, it should be designed to capitalize on the capacities and affiliations of students. It should be possible for students to study engineering or mechanistic art, religious art and its themes, the art and crafts of various racial and ethnic groups, the aesthetics of motion, environmental art, political art, and the like. In response to this recommendation, many educators will say: But shouldn't all students have experience X? And, isn't X especially important for just those kids who would never choose it? By now, you (the reader) know my answer: probably not. It does no harm to suggest, to invite. But we need to entrust students with important choices concerning their own education. Indeed, helping them to choose intelligently *is* education, and we must reject the pernicious notion that some areas of study are intrinsically more valuable than others.

Conclusion

I have argued that caring for a set of ideas such as mathematics or art has much in common with caring for people. We can be engrossed—passionately interested—in ideas, and schools should make it possible for students to become so engrossed. However, this level of interest cannot be demanded, and students whose interests lie elsewhere should be respected and encouraged to choose what is useful for them in each subject.

We should expect a very different level of performance from the passionately interested. They should be introduced to the full rigor and beauty of the disciplines they study. Hard questions should be asked, and epistemologically excellent responses should be expected. For other students the level of performance and understanding might well be instrumentally defined. They should be able to do and to explain whatever is required by their own purposes. This level is not necessarily *lower*; it is just different.

Devising educational programs along the suggested lines requires careful analysis of levels of understanding. Understanding does not have to refer to *structural* understanding; it does not have to be tied to the basic nature of the discipline. Rather, it is properly defined with respect to legitimate purposes, capacities, and interests.

19

ANN MARGARET SHARP

Ann Margaret Sharp (born 1942) is an internationally acclaimed proponent of Philosophy for Children (P4C) and co-founder, with Professor Matthew Lipman, of the Institute for the Advancement of Philosophy for Children (IAPC) at Montclair State University (MSU). Her greatest philosophical influences are Fredrick Nietzsche (1844–1900) and John Dewey (1859–1952). In a recent interview, she stressed that "[from her perspective] Philosophy for Children is rooted in Dewey's conception of education, his commitment to open inquiry, fallibilism, faith in democracy as a social way of life, non-sexism, non-racism, egalitarianism, communal living, and the importance of aesthetic and ethical creativity." Sharp has been responsible for the international dissemination and coordination P4C and she has written P4C curriculum materials for early childhood. Imagine five-year-olds discussing friendship or justice in an effort to determine suitable criteria for loyalty or fairness!

Sharp's work in P4C is informed by her commitments first to the idea that children deserve to learn philosophy because it is a fundamental human right and second to the community of inquiry conceived as a transformative educational pedagogy. Sharp's first principle is grounded by her belief that contemporary society does not respect children as persons. She argues that, in order for children to be taken seriously, they must be given a voice and listened to as individuals striving to live meaningfully. Adults have an ethical obligation to respect children as persons, and this respect is the only way to create a more peaceful and equitable future. Actively resisting our "adultist" prejudicial attitudes toward children—rationalized by developmental psychology, popular culture and education—should, Sharp hopes, undermine future sexism, racism, and adultism.

According to Sharp, children's engagement in philosophical inquiry is one way to acknowledge their personhood and work toward a better future. Philosophy provides students with the opportunity to inquire cooperatively about concepts that are shared and important but profoundly contestable, such as faith, justice, friendship, and beauty. It is by this means that P4C students are encouraged to explore the aesthetic, ethical, political, and metaphysical dimensions of their experience. Philosophy provides them with the intellectual resources to articulate and evaluate alternative visions for the future and challenges them to supply reasons for otherwise unsupported opinions, make inferences based on the implications of what is said, identify assumptions, and correct fallacious reasoning.

Sharp's commitment to Philosophy for Children is foundational to her understanding of the P4C pedagogy, otherwise known as the "community of inquiry." Its procedural values are compassionate regard for others and respect for wondering and questioning (over knowing and answering). The P4C pedagogy assumes that meaningful inquiry is an enterprise that grows out of, and should be evaluated according to, an ability to improve our social interactions and daily life. Participants forge relationships of tolerance, care, and friendship that are not based on gender, race, religion, or ethnicity. They come to appreciate each member of the community in virtue of his or her difference—that is, in terms of the distinctiveness of what it is that he or she has to offer. Participants assist one another as they learn to think for themselves.

According to Sharp, learning to think for oneself requires more than just the rules of logic: "imagination and a strong feeling for natural affinities and differences, such as are expressed in similes, metaphors, and analogies" are essential. Sharp's later work in P4C is enriched by her holistic approach to thinking as an intellectual, emotional, and bodily activity. She argues that educating children to intervene reflectively in their bodily and emotional lives will protect them from many of the key psychological and social issues that children face today, including child abuse, anorexia, obesity, and homophobia.

In conclusion, Sharp has no tolerance for the minutiae of theoretical speculation and point scoring, the *techne* of professional philosophy. For Sharp, the point of engaging with a theory is to get to the essence of what it says and then to work out its implications for understanding and engaging in our ordinary lives. Philosophical theories provide multiple perspectives from which to interpret situations, but one should not remain at this level of abstraction, for it is their impact on the ordinary, the conversational, and the practical that matters.

REFERENCES

Sharp, Ann M. "Children's Intellectual Liberation." *Educational Theory* 31, no. 2 (1983): 197–214.

Sharp, Ann M. "And the Children Shall Lead Them." *International Journal of Applied Philosophy* 18, no. 2 (2004): 177–87.

Sharp, Ann M. Transcribed interview with the author, 2006.

Sharp, Ann M., with Laurance J. Splitter. *Teaching for Better Thinking: The Classroom Community of Inquiry.* Melbourne: ACER Press, 1995.

THE COMMUNITY OF INQUIRY

Education for Democracy

In this essay I would like to focus on the classroom community of inquiry as an educational means of furthering the sense of community that is a pre-condition for actively participating in a democratic society. Such a community cultivates skills of dialogue, questioning, reflective inquiry and good judgement. In the course of the paper, I will attempt to answer the following questions: When I enter a classroom, how do I know a community of inquiry is in formation? What behaviors are the students and teacher performing and what dispositions are manifest? What are some of the theoretical assumptions of these behaviors? And more importantly, what are some of the practical social, ethical and political consequences of such behavior?

I will assume that a community of inquiry is characterized by *dialogue* that is fashioned collaboratively out of the *reasoned* contribution of all participants. Over time, I assume that the classroom discussions will become more disciplined by *logical, epistemological, aesthetic, ethical, social* and *political* considerations that are applicable. In such a community, the teacher monitors the logical procedures but, in addition, philosophically becomes one of the community. Students learn to *object to weak reasoning, build on strong reasoning,* accept the responsibility of making their contributions within the context of others, accept their dependence upon others, follow the inquiry where it leads, respect the perspective of others, collaboratively engage in *self-correction* when necessary and take pride in the accomplishments of the group as well as oneself. Further, in the process, they practice the art of making *good judgements* within the context of dialogue and communal inquiry.[1]

There are cognitive behaviors that can be observed: giving and asking for good reasons, making good distinctions and connections, making valid inferences, hypothesizing, generalizing, giving counter-examples, discovering assumptions, using and recognizing criteria, asking good questions, inferring consequences, recognizing logical fallacies, calling for relevance, defining concepts, seeking clarification, voicing implications, perceiving relationships, judging well, standard-

"The Community of Inquiry: Education for Democracy" by Ann Margaret Sharp, from *Philosophy of Education, Revised 3e* edited by William Hare and John P. Portelli, 2001. Reprinted with permission from Detselig Enterprises Ltd.

izing, using good analogies, sensitivity to context, offering alternative points of view, building logically on contributions of others and voicing fine discriminations.

Participants come to regard the production of knowledge as contingent, bound up with human interests and activities and therefore always open to revision. Further, students become more tolerant of complexity and ambiguity and recognize that justification for belief is rooted in *human* action. The human condition often might require that we make a provisional commitment to one belief or one course of action because of the need to act, but this in no way means that the particular belief can be justified as absolute truth. It is this need to act that calls for *good practical judgement* that will only be as good as one has been educated dialogically in making fine discriminations and learning how to do full justice to particular situations. Ultimately this capacity to judge is based on *communal civic sense* that is necessary for making moral and political judgements.[2] Such judgements are intersubjective and appeal to, and require testing against, the opinions of other judging persons.

Since there is no criterion, independent of various practical concerns, that will tell us when we have arrived at truth, and since knowledge is inescapably linguistic and inseparable from human activity, knowledge is a product of practical reasoning. It is for this reason that the acquisition and retention of knowledge must always be an *active* process.[3]

There are *social behaviors* that can be observed: listening to one another, supporting one another by amplifying and corroborating their views, submitting the views of others to critical inquiry, giving reasons to support another's view even if one doesn't agree, taking one another's ideas seriously by responding and encouraging each other to voice their views. A certain *care* is manifest in the group, not only care for the logical procedures but for the growth of each member of the community. This care presupposes the disposition to be open, to be capable of changing one's view and priorities in order to care for the other. In a real sense to care presupposes a willingness to be transformed by the other—to be affected by the other. This care is essential for dialogue. But it is also essential for the *development of trust,* a basic orientation toward the world that accounts for the individuals coming to think they have a role to play in the world, that they can make a real difference. Further, the world is such a place that will receive not only their thoughts but their actions. Trust, in turn, is a pre-condition for the development of *autonomy* and *self-esteem* on the part of the individual participants. Care, then, makes possible a conception of the world as a play in which one can shape outcomes and create beauty where none has existed before.[4]

Participants appear to be capable of giving themselves to others, speaking when they think they have something relevant to say or when they think they have a responsibility for getting the dialogue back on track. Students appear to have repudiated the *prima donna* role and seem able to collaborate and co-operate in inquiry. They can hear and receive what others have to say in such a way that meaning and vitality is shared.[5] They are free of the need always to be right. They have the courage and ability to change their minds and to hold their views tentatively. They do not appear defensive but rather delighted to be in a community of inquiry. With respect to the ideas of others, it implies also an openness to emerging truth, a giving of oneself in the broadest sense, even though one realizes that the truth one gains in the end is only provisional. To do this, students must be capable of coming to understand that they do not know many things, if anything at all.

There are *psychological* or *socio-psychological* characteristics that can be observed. These involve the growth of the self in relation to others, putting of the ego in perspective, disciplining of self-centredness and eventually the transforming of oneself. Participants refrain from engaging in extended monologues that pre-empt dialogue or do not really call for a response. They know how to dialogue with each other. Dialogue implies a certain capacity for intellectual flexibility, self-correction and growth.[6] Have we not all had the experience of submitting a question to the group and then seeing emerge from the painful yet exciting dialogue an insight or understanding that is far more profound than that offered by any single contribution? Such an event should not only be evaluated in terms of the product but in terms of the process—the relationships experienced during the course of the inquiry.

Teachers and participants can mute themselves in order to encourage others to speak their own ideas. They have the ability to let go of their positions in order to listen openly, hear and follow the inquiry where it leads. The latter requires letting truth emerge even though one knows it will be provisional and might require that one reconstruct one's own cherished belief-system. In a working community of inquiry, participants will move from considering themselves and their accomplishments as all important to focusing on the group and its accomplishments. They are not only conscious of their own thinking but begin examining and correcting each other's methods and procedures. Once they internalize the self-correcting methodology, they have the possibility of becoming critical thinkers—individuals who are open to self-correction, are sensitive to context and use criteria consciously in the making of practical judgements.[7]

The relationship of the individual to the community is thus interdependent. The success of the community is compatible with, and is dependent on, unique expressions of individuality. Yet, each participant accepts the discipline of making his or her contribution in the context of the contributions of others. This means accepting interdependence and repudiating an attitude of "knowing-it-all." The community will not function unless the participants can conform to the procedures of that community—logical and social. If one of the procedural principles is brought into question, other procedures must be adopted so that the discussion can proceed. Conformity is also manifest in a growing commitment to the underlying principles and practices that govern the enterprise itself: tolerance, consistency, comprehensiveness, open-mindedness, self-correction, conscious use of criteria, sensitivity to context and respect for all participants as potential sources of insight. Zaniness is tolerated only if it produces progress for the group's inquiry. If not constructive, the group will self-correct and eliminate the behavior. Often this is done with silence—not responding to behavior that blocks dialogue or reflective inquiry.[8]

When one observes a functioning community of inquiry, one does not simply see a group nor simply individuals. What one observes is a community in which individual opinions are exchanged and serve as the source for further inquiry. Participants are capable of being fully *present* to each other in such a way that the entire meaning and vitality of the dialogue is shared.[9] Participants do not talk about themselves but rather offer meanings to which others may make a response. They can take the risk of communicating. If the trust and care of the community are in place, the individual is far more likely to take this risk. And at times it is a real risk. One is exposing ones beliefs, aware that one will probably be challenged and be forced to rethink one's position. This rethinking or restructuring takes time, which means that there will be a period during which the individual will feel confused and perhaps insecure and maybe even frightened. I have seen shy students finally muster the courage to express their belief verbally only to have it fall to the floor with a thud of silence. And yet, many were capable of accepting the silence and trying again and again to make some kind of contribution to the on-going inquiry. Participants tend to refrain from voicing their views dogmatically. If one observes closely one sees that individual convictions more often relate to basic character, always in formation, rather than to knowledge claims.

Individuals in a community of inquiry must be able to hear and respond to the *meaning* of the dialogue itself. Such meaning comes from two sources: (1) the participants willing to be involved in the inquiry and (2) the subject under discussion in light of the intellectual tradition of which we are all heirs. One must be willing to listen to the question behind the question, the fear behind the bravado, the insecurity behind the pretence, the courage behind the timidity, all of this being an essential component of the meaning of the dialogue itself. Further, one must be able to see—to read the faces of the speakers and the non-speakers and to interpret what they are saying and not-saying. Some might be silent because they have nothing to say. Others might be silent because they are afraid to voice their views. Others might be shy. Others might be afraid that their views will be challenged—this is a sign that something is wrong.

The breakdown of the community occurs when there is an obliteration of persons. This takes place when one person exploits another, that is, uses the relations that have been formed for any purpose other than its intended one: the pursuit of meaning and understanding and the furthering of the growth of each member of the community. To the extent that individuals engage in monologues, they block inquiry. To the extent that they make assumptions about what the other is going to say before the other has the opportunity to say it they block inquiry. To the extent that they engage in image making when another is speaking, they block inquiry. To the extent that they take it upon themselves to speak for others out of fear or insecurity, they destroy the trust essential for dialogical inquiry.

One purpose of the dialogue among participants is to bring *vitality* or life to the *form* of the community of inquiry. Without this vitality, the form is empty or meaningless. Asking questions means nothing if one is not actively involved in the quest for understanding. Tension among members of the group may produce conflict but it is not itself conflict.

For example, when violin strings have just the right tension, they can be used to produce beautiful music. Similarly, when a creative tension exists among participants, a tension between the vitality of the many relationships and the form of the community of inquiry, the group has the potential for open debate, growth, and each participant has the potential for self-transformation. Because tension is painful, we tend to want to get rid of it at any cost. Often we find ourselves choosing instead the mere form of a dialogue, the mere form of communal inquiry. The purpose, however, of a community of inquiry is to restore the tension between vitality and form, to bring participants into deeper and more significant relationships, to shake them free of their complacency, their false convictions and to make them available for more comprehensive understanding.[10] Therefore, it follows that dialogical thinking within the community requires a willingness to be disturbed and to be challenged by the ideas of the other, a process of active reconstruction using criteria of comprehensiveness, coherence and consistency, together with sensitivity to the particularity of each situation.

As mentioned before, individuals in a community of inquiry have learned to hold their beliefs tentatively. Given the nature of human knowledge and justification—that is, to justify any belief, we have to base our belief on another belief that is language-dependent—it is a matter of finding coherence among our beliefs and correspondence with the world. What I mean here is the world independent of language, perception and human understanding. But there is no such thing as knowledge of the world-as-it-really-is, since we can never be separated from the language and activities of particular groups or communities of human beings. Thus knowledge is always inescapably contingent, open to revision, and a matter of practical judgement. It is not a matter of aiming some mirror that is highly polished at the world as it really is and then passively noting the way things really are, independent of human practical concerns, social and personal. Rather, knowledge is an historical, linguistic and social *activity* and, as such, always open to self-correction as new data or evidence has to be taken into account. There is no ultimate foundation for our knowledge.[11] What we have is reason as a regulative ideal, and even the form of this reasoning process is open to revision within the context of questioning, dialogue and *praxis*.

Thus, one could say that the community of inquiry provides a process of communication for the students, a moving back and forth between a narrower and wider framework, which may allow meaning and understanding to emerge and which each participant may be able to actively judge at the end, the dialogue of the community itself. When one is actively involved in a community of inquiry, one assumes that subjective individual experience, as an unconsidered given, cannot reveal even provisional truth. It is the starting point of inquiry, not the end result. Further, the meanings that totally subjective experience do reveal are narrow and paltry compared to the meanings one can derive from communal inquiry.

Lastly, there are *moral* and *political* considerations that one must take into account when considering the nature of a community of inquiry. If we assume that the purpose of education is not only to transmit a body of knowledge but also to equip children with the skills and dispositions they need to create new knowledge and make better practical judgements, then the traditional classroom of "telling" is not appropriate. If we further assume that the purpose of education is the bringing into being of persons—persons of responsibility and integrity, persons of moral character who are capable of making wise judgements about what is right and wrong, beautiful and ugly, appropriate and inappropriate, then, if we are correct above, dialogue becomes an inescapable instrument or means of education and the community of inquiry becomes a means and an end satisfying and worthwhile in itself, while at the same time giving rise to the traits essential for a morally discriminating person.

The community of inquiry requires not only perseverance and courage but all of the Socratic virtues. It calls further for a commitment to stay with the group through its growth and change. It involves persons in a way of being-in-the-world aimed at struggling for understanding and self-knowledge by means of a process that is intersubjective. Further, the end products of such a community of inquiry are also intersubjective. However, in multiplying persons we do not simply multiply intelligences, experiences and perspectives. Rather we aim to produce practical knowledge in the *exchange* of perspectives, opinions, the sharing of experiences and the questioning of the assumptions of the beliefs that we do hold. Note that this is very unlike the working out of an argument. It is more akin to the playing of a quartet in which each instrument has an important role to perform in the production of the music. And, in all likelihood, there will be many quartets and many pieces of music played with integrity and beauty. The ideal of one universal community of inquiry embracing all of mankind is highly unlikely.[12] But this in no way invalidates the vision of many communities in which there is genuine inquiry, genuine participation of all human beings (rather than just white Western men) with *open communication* between the various groups.[13]

Thus, the community of inquiry constitutes a *praxis*—reflective communal action—a way of acting on the world. It is a means of personal and moral transformation that inevitably leads to a shift in meanings and values which affect the daily judgements and actions of all participants. One striking characteristic of a community of inquiry over time is that its members change. In time, they will be capable of saying to themselves such things as:

- I find I'm no longer bullied into accepting views that lead to consequences that I think are harmful.
- I think I've always thought that way, but now I can explain why I think that way.
- I am no longer in need of pretending what I feel or what I think.
- My taste in many things is changing.
- I'm beginning to realize what patterns of behavior make more sense in my daily life.
- I can change my mind about matters of importance.
- What other people say can make a difference in what I think.
- I'm beginning to understand how very little I really know.

One can explain such claims as a slow progressive release from subjectivism, intellectual and social isolation, finding the world an alien and confusing place into discovering what it is to participate in a community of inquiry that enables one to live actively, reasonably and responsibly in the world rather than merely accepting it, escaping it or ignoring it. It's as if the process itself of participating *in* such a community becomes a sense-finding enterprise. Participants discover the moral guidelines they want to live by and the moral virtues they want to exemplify in their daily lives. They gain practice in making discriminating, sensitive and appropriate moral judgements. In a real sense they, at one and the same time, discover and create themselves as they inquire together—they discover and create the persons they think they ought to be.

Lastly, the commitment to engage in a community of inquiry is a *political* commitment even at the elementary school level. In a real sense, it is a commitment to freedom, open debate, pluralism, self-government and democracy. Practical reason, reflective inquiry and practical judgement reflected in communal political, *praxis* presupposes that the people in the society have a sense of communal dialogue and inquiry and a facility with the skills of such inquiry. It is only to the extent that individuals have had the experience of dialoguing with others as equals, participating in shared, public inquiry, that they will be able to eventually take an active role in the shaping of a democratic society. Shared understandings and experiences, inter-subjective daily practices, a sense of affinity and solidarity, together with all the tacit affective ties that bind people together in a community are *pre-conditions* of communal reflection action in the political sphere.[14]

Thus, in answer to the question, "How can we further the type of community participation, dialogue, inquiry and mutual recognition and respect that is presupposed in political communities?" one can propose the conversion of educational classrooms into communities of inquiry beginning with kindergarten and extending such a conversion right through graduate school experience. It is only in this way that the next generation will be prepared socially and cognitively to engage in the necessary dialogue, judging and ongoing questioning that is vital to the existence of a democratic society and the maintenance of the planet earth and survival of the species. In these times when the threat of nuclear extinction and ecological disaster is so very real, it is all the more crucial to try to foster and nurture classroom communities of inquiry at the elementary school level and throughout the educational experience so that the next generation will be able to act in such a way that the human community will not only continue to exist, but to exist in a more reasonable and just manner. Such a conversion of the educational institutional structure moves us beyond arguments and beyond theories into the realm of concrete actions aimed at changing the world for the better.

Notes

1. See, Hannah Arendt, "Crisis in Culture: Its Social and Political Significance" in *Between Past and Future* (New York: Viking Press, 1961), 197–226. Arendt goes on to say "that the ability to judge is a specifically political ability in exactly the sense denoted by Kant, namely, the ability to see things not only from one's own point of view but in the perspective of all those who happen to be present: even judgement may be one of the fundamental abilities of man as political being insofar as it enables him to orient

himself in the public realm, in the common world." (221) See, also Richard Bernstein. "Judging the Actor and the Spectator," in Robert Boyers (ed.), *Proceedings of History, Ethics, Politics: A Conference based on the work of Hannah Arendt* (Saratoga Springs, NY: Empire State, 1982.) Also see Michael Dennery, "The Privilege of Ourselves: Hannah Arendt on Judgment," in R. Boyers, *Proceedings of History, Ethics, Politics,* 245–274; and Hannah Arendt, *The Life of the Mind* (New York: H.B. Jovanovich, 1978) Volume I and II.

2. This communal civic sense is what John Dewey calls taste. See *The Quest For Certainty* (New York: Minton, Balch, 1929.), 262. Also for a development of the same idea see John Dewey, *Art as Experience* (New York: Minton, Balch, 1934).

3. Richard Rorty, *Consequences of Pragmatism* (Minneapolis: University of Minnesota Press, 1982), xii–xxxix.

4. I am indebted to Monica Velasca from Guadalajara, Mexico for innumerable comments on the importance of care in the community of inquiry contained in her various papers submitted as a requirement for the degree of Masters of Arts in Teaching Philosophy for Children, Fall and Spring, 1988–89. For a philosophical analysis of the status of "Being-As-Care," see Martin Heidegger, *Being and Time* (New York: Harper and Row, 1962), 235–241. And for a psychological analysis of the importance of care in the cultivation of trust, autonomy and self esteem, see Erik Erikson, *Childhood and Society* (New York: Norton, 1950) and *Insight and Responsibility.*

5. See Martin Buber, *Between Man and Man.* (New York: Macmillan, 1947). In this volume one can find two essays, one on "Education," and the other on "The Education of Character." Both speak to the role of dialogue in education.

6. See, Martin Buber, *I and Thou* (New York: Scribners, 1970) Part I.

7. Here I am indebted to Matthew Lipman, "Critical Thinking: What Can It Be?" *Educational Leadership, 46,* 1, 1988, 38–43.

8. Here I am indebted to James Heinegg, "The Individual and the Community of Inquiry," ms. submitted as requirement for the degree of Master of Arts in Teaching Philosophy for Children at Montclair State College, Fall of 1988.

9. Buber says, "The present exists only insofar as presentness, encounter and relation exist. Only as the You becomes present does presence come into being." (*I and Thou,* 63).

10. I am indebted to Ronald Reed, who pointed out to me that John Dewey, in "My Pedagogic Creed" (Reprinted in Reginald D. Archambault [ed.], *John Dewey on Education: Selected Writings* [New York: Random House, 1964]), talks about vitality in relation to informal education. One could argue that a good classroom dialogue is modeled on what one finds in an informal environment, conversations that deal with real problems and real concerns of the participants. Usually such discussions focus on real questions that the participants have a stake in getting it right. However, in the informal environment no one looks askance if one excuses oneself because one is no

longer interested in talking. But the child in the classroom cannot do this. Once the child loses interest (if he or she ever had any) he or she tends to be condemned to play the spectator role. Dewey's point is that active participation and involvement in the discussion seems to go together with vitality and mere spectating seems to go together with dry sterility.

11. When I say that there is no ultimate philosophical foundation for our knowledge, I am relying here on Rorty, in particular. See Richard Rorty, *Philosophy and the Mirror of Nature* (Minneapolis: University of Minnesota Press, 1982). For the argument of reason as a regulative ideal, see Hilary Putnam, "Why Reason can't be Naturalized," *Synthese 52*, 1, 1982: 1–23. For an argument against complete relativism, see Alasdair MacIntyre, "Relativism, Power and Philosophy," the Presidential Address delivered before the 81st Annual Eastern Division Meeting of the American Philosophical Association in New York, December 29, 1984, in Proceedings and Addresses of the American Philosophical Association, (Newark, Delaware: APA, 1985), 5–22; and his postscript to the second edition of *After Virtue* (Notre Dame, IN: University of Notre Dame Press, 1984), 265–272. Also see MacIntyre, *Whose Justice? Which Rationality?* (Notre Dame, IN: University of Notre Dame Press, 1988, 1–11, 370–388, and 389–403). Also see: Richard Rorty, "The Contingency of Language," *London Review of Books* (April 17, 1986), 3; Bernard Williams, *Ethics and the Limits of Philosophy*, (Cambridge: Harvard University Press, 1985); and Richard Bernstein, *Beyond Objectivism and Relativism* (Philadelphia: University of Philadelphia Press, 1983).

In my previous article, "What is a Community of Inquiry?," *Journal of Moral Education, 16,* 1, 1987: 37–45, I argued that the community of inquiry is not condemned to relativism and endless self-correction, that some progress can be made and that the concepts of truth and justification cannot be reduced to the conceptual scheme of the tradition. Rorty thinks that all we have is the dialogue itself, the endless conversation spoken within the philosophical tradition. Further, he and others think the dialogue in connection with the establishment of local communities is sufficient to make the world more reasonable. Other philosophers, like Hilary Putnam, Jurgen Habermas and Alasdair MacIntyre, disagree. Putnam argues that the very fact that we can speak of our different conceptions as different conceptions of rationality posits truth. The very fact that we can agree that some thinkers in the past have been wrong-headed, presupposes that reason can serve as a regulative ideal. (See: *Reason, Truth and History* [Cambridge: Cambridge University Press, 1982], 163–216.)

In this essay, I argue that dialogical thinking and speaking takes courage, letting the truth emerge even if it forces one to reconstruct one's own cherished beliefs. (When I use the word "truth," I mean "warranted assertion"—Dewey's term.) No one captures this idea of the necessary courage more than Alasdaire MacIntyre in his APA presidential address (1984):

> *What can liberate rationality is precisely an acknowledgement only possible from within a certain kind of tradition, that rationality requires a readiness on our part to accept, and indeed to welcome, a possible future defeat of the forms of theory and practice in which it has up till now been taken to be embodied within our own tradition, at the hands of some alien and perhaps even as yet largely unintelligible tradition of thought and practice; and this is an acknowledgement of which the traditions that we inherit have too seldom been capable.*

It is just this disposition of "readiness" that the community of inquiry cultivates in the young child.

12. As Alasdair MacIntyre contends: "What matters at this stage is the construction of local forms of community within which civility and the intellectual and moral life can be sustained." *After Virtue,* 244.

13. Here see the works of Hans-Georg Gadamer and Habermas on communication and the need for community. In particular, Gadamer's autobiographical sketch, *Philosophische Lehrjahre* (Frankfurt am Main: Vittoria Klostermann, 1977); *Truth and Method* (New York: Seabury Press, 1975), 306–310, and 278–89; and for a treatment of practical judgement, "Problem of Historical Consciousness," in Paul Rabinow and William M. Sullivan (ed.), *Interpretive Social Science: A Reader* (Berkeley, CA: University of California Press, 1979), 120–30. And Habermas, "Dialectics of Rationalization: An Interview," *Telos, 49* 1981: 7; "A Reply to My Critics," in John B. Thompson and David Held, *Habermas: Critical Debates* (Cambridge, MA: M.I.T. Press, 1982), 263–269.

    I am also indebted to a paper, "Community of Inquiry," by Marcello Marer, from Sao Paulo, Brazil, submitted in requirement for the Masters of Arts in Philosophy for Children, Montclair State College, Spring 1989. In this paper, Marer tries to show the Peircean foundations of the concept, "Community of Inquiry," and the way in which the theory of Habermas plays an important role in the theoretical foundations of the concept, "community of inquiry," as it is used in Philosophy for Children.

14. See Richard Bernstein, *Beyond Objectivism and Relativism: Science, Hermeneutics and Praxis* (Philadelphia: University of Pennsylvania Press, 1983), 171–231. In this section, Bernstein discusses Praxis and practical discourse as seen in the works of Rorty, Gadamer, Habermas and Hannah Arendt.

20

CLEO CHERRYHOLMES

Cleo Cherryholmes is one of the contemporary intellectual leaders in pragmatism and education. His work has stimulated those in the field to rethink how a critical pragmatist's lens can inform discourse and practice. In his analysis of educational policies, curricula, and research methods he utilizes a variety of conceptual, theoretical, and methodological frameworks, including critical perspectives. As a political scientist, his early work in education served the development of social studies curricula.

He is professor emeritus of teacher education and political science at Michigan State University, were he taught for almost forty years. Cherryholmes grew up in the Midwest and attended Yale University, where he obtained his B.A. in 1960. He completed an M.S. in social science from Kansas State Teachers College in 1964. He studied at Northwestern University and finished his Ph.D. in political science in 1966. A prolific writer of journal articles, book chapters, and essays, he also wrote and edited books on education. Perhaps the two books he authored that had a significant impact in the field of education are *Power and Criticism: Post-structural Investigations in Education* (1988) and *Reading Pragmatism* (1999).

One of Cherryholmes's chief concerns has been the question of how educational ideas, explanations, theories, practices, methods, and inquiry are constituted. He has been interested in unpacking the notions of absolute truths in education that at one time or another have informed, for instance, policies, teaching, evaluation, school organization, concepts of learning, preparation programs, or classroom procedures. By engaging in the pursuit of these issues, he also contributed to a better understanding of the strengths, limitations, and temporalities (not eternal) of various theoretical lenses, such as critical theory, feminist theories, functionalism, structuralism, or behaviorism, which have attempted to explain educational phenomena practically in a totalizing manner.

His work has encouraged researchers, scholars, policy makers, administrators, and teachers to consider that the curriculum used in schools does not have to be the way it is. For instance, he has challenged the assumptions that subject matter and the established disciplines have to be the center of school learning experiences. Furthermore, he provokes debate by suggesting that what has been accepted as truth in developing higher-order thinking through a well-organized and planned curriculum, such as utilizing rationalistic models of curriculum development or structured and objective taxonomies, is a limited construction that resulted from a combination of contextual factors, including how research was done and how power arrangements operated. Thus, this implies that what has been taken for granted in terms of objectivity, truth, structures, generalizations, and rationalistic practices in education are illusions that cannot be foundational. However, as a pragmatist, he does not shelve away these constructs; he points to their limitations and the need to elaborate alternatives.

Cherryholmes's work has been influenced by a wide array of philosophical traditions. Well grounded in political philosophy and in phenomenology, he also studied and discussed the work of the French thinker Michel Foucault and utilized the poststructural contributions of Jack Derrida, both of whom have looked at text and textuality in the context of literary criticism. These perspectives have had implications for Cherryholmes's advancement of "deconstruction" as a tool for understanding educational research. For example: questioning how categories, interpretation, representation, and arguments about what counts as "data" or what is "valid" are mediated by discourses that are products of a context—that is, contingent to what has been accepted as truth and conditioned by time, place, ideologies, culture, language, politics, and other factors that limit the attempt to fully explain phenomena in objective and neutral terms. He also has investigated critical theory in the tradition of the Frankfurt school and the work of Habermas to better discuss power and educational discourses-practices. Certainly, traditional American pragmatism has had an impact on his work, but particularly contemporary pragmatists, such as Richard Rorty, have informed his discussions, theories, and proposals in education.

Cherryholmes offers a theory of action in education grounded in his critical pragmatism, which he distinguishes from vulgar pragmatism. In his view, critical pragmatism understands that power is at play in educational experiences and disciplinary relationships—including curricula and pedagogies—as well as in policy postulates and educational organizations. A vulgar pragmatist just would make choices and actions on the merits of the consequences without considering the a priori limitations of the choices or without considering how these consequences apply if different frameworks are utilized to judge their merits. Therefore, if actions and choices are pragmatic decisions that derive from the circumstances and contexts in which educators operate and give meaning to their experiences, and these meanings are mediated by our visions of what is good and better, then a critical stance will force us to investigate further not only these conditions and contexts but also the visions, which tend to be subjective in contrast to the discourses of structured objectivity that dominate education.

REFERENCES

Cherryholmes, C. *Power and Criticism: Poststructural Investigations in Education.* New York: Teachers College Press, 1988.
Cherryholmes, C. *Reading Pragmatism.* New York: Teachers College Press, 1999.

POSTSTRUCTURALISM, PRAGMATISM, AND CURRICULUM

> There is no power that is exercised without a series of aims and objectives. But this does not mean that it results from the choice or decision of an individual subject; let us not look for the headquarters that presides over its rationality. . . . It is often the case that no one is there to have invented them [the rationality of power and its tactics], and few who can be said to have formulated them: an implicit characteristic of the great anonymous, almost unspoken strategies which coordinate the loquacious tactics whose "inventors" or decisionmakers are often without hypocrisy. (Foucault, 1980c, p. 95)

> With the linguistic resourcefulness and mobility accruing from an extreme language-scepticism, deconstruction had the capacity to come in under existing or emerging critical systems at their weakest point, the linguistic bad faith on which they were built. (Felperin, 1985, p. 110)

Curriculum is not derivative, as are many subfields of education, from other academic or applied disciplines. For example, educational psychology has roots in psychology; social foundations of education, in history and sociology; philosophy of education, in philosophy; the study of educational policy, in political science and the policy sciences; and educational administration, in the applied fields of business and public administration. Curriculum deals with problems that are uniquely educational in much the same way that instruction has its own special tasks. But instruction is confronted with the concrete situation of classrooms, students, content, and teachers. The tasks facing curriculum are less immediately demanding.

Such independence is rare. It is enviable, however, if one desires to chart one's course by picking and choosing among problems and orientations. But there are also costs. There is a sense of security, if not certainty, when it is possible to rely on an academic discipline to orient one's research, to help identify "important" problems, and to outline accepted research techniques and methodologies. Given the disciplinary independence of curriculum, it is not surprising that its history is marked by repeated turmoil and conflict, because it is always possible to question its purposes, beliefs, values, assumptions, metaphors, and orientations that fix its purpose and meaning.

An array of metaphors related to death and illness have been used to describe the field: in 1969 Schwab used the word *moribund*, in 1975 Dwayne Huebner wrote about a *wake*, and in 1980 Philip Jackson questioned the *existence* of a field of curriculum. But there was plenty of counterevidence that curriculum was alive and, if not well, at least kicking. There were heated exchanges among so-called reconceptualists, conceptual-empiricists, and traditionalists (Jackson, 1980; Pinar, 1980; Tanner & Tanner, 1979). Additionally, remnants of old positivist debates (Eisner, 1983; Phillips, 1983) and discussions of phenomenology (Macdonald, 1982; van Manen, 1982), critical theory (Anyon, 1981; Cherryholmes, 1980, 1982; Giroux, 1983a,b), and neo-Marxist criticism (Apple, 1982; Popkewitz, 1982) were explored in terms of curriculum. Curriculum, it is safe to conclude, is not dead. It is fair to ask, however, whether its conflicts and disagreements signify illness, moribundity, or death. These metaphors, I will argue, misconceptualize curriculum and its dynamics. Furthermore, its internal conflicts and turmoil are not anomalous but characterize all fields of study (for one argument along these lines, see Kuhn, 1974). It just happens that the disciplinary and task independence of curriculum exacerbates this condition.

This chapter proposes one argument to answer two questions: (1) Why has the study of curriculum been turbulent and full of conflict? (2) What is its central project? First, a definition of curriculum and then the 1960s movement to teach the structure of the disciplines will be described and given a poststructural reading. Then some implications of this for curriculum and education will be outlined.

One caveat before proceeding: any profession operates simultaneously at many levels. Some practitioners implement research findings and engage in the practices of the field on a day-to-day basis. Some researchers try to clarify and extend the knowledge of the field. Some trainers teach the literature, norms, and practices of the field to new entrants. Some developers work, in the case of curriculum, on new classroom materials and new approaches to school and classroom organization. Such different activities have distinct yet reinforcing discourses. They are concerned with different immediate tasks, while sharing larger goals and purposes. The substantive focus of this chapter is with curriculum knowledge, purposes, and goals; how a particular movement proposed to organize the field; why it was persuasive at the time; and why it failed to live up to its promise. This analysis, I submit, clarifies the dynamics of the study of curriculum.

What Is Curriculum?

What is curriculum? Is it a program of studies? Course content? Planned learning experiences? Experiences "had" under the auspices of the school? A structured series of intended learning outcomes? A "written" plan for action? Or something more involved? This ground will not be covered in detail, since Mauritz Johnson (1967) and Robert Zais (1981), among others, have already analyzed and discarded many of these definitions.

Johnson defines curriculum as a structured series of intended learning outcomes. This is rejected for two reasons. First, Johnson's definition was selected in part because it distinguishes between curriculum and instruction, but this criterion is flawed because it presumes a categorical distinction between curriculum and instruction *before* curriculum is defined. Obviously, without a definition of curriculum it is not possible to know whether or not curriculum is distinct from instruction. Second, Johnson argues that curriculum cannot be defined *post hoc*; that is, it has to be defined before the act of instruction so that curriculum can guide instruction. Defining curriculum in this way has obvious instrumental and utilitarian appeal, but it places the study of curriculum, curriculum development, and so on at the service of immediate administrative and instructional demands. The functionalist nature of this definition is highlighted when one realizes that it would have administrative and instructional needs drive curriculum.

Zais, drawing on Hilda Taba's work, argues for a continuum between curriculum and instruction rather than a sharp distinction:

> The suggestion and central thrust of Taba's conception of curriculum, however, is that the broader (that is, more general) aspects of purposes, content, and method belong in the realm of curriculum, while the more proximate and specific aspects are properly allocated to teaching and instruction. (1981, p. 40)

Gail McCutcheon captures Zais's meaning with more fruitful results:

> By curriculum I mean *what students have an opportunity to learn* in school, through both the hidden and overt curriculum, and what they do not have

an opportunity to learn because certain matters were not included in the curriculum, referred to by Eisner (1979, p. 83) as the "null curriculum." (1982, p. 19; emphasis added)

What students have an opportunity to learn refers to legitimate and approved communications and actions. What students do not have an opportunity to learn are those things off-limits. This definition refers to the substance of what students have an opportunity to learn and to the rules and procedures by which those opportunities are provided.

One might be tempted to criticize this definition because it includes everything: everything present and not present (*p* and *not p* in symbolic notation). This criticism both grasps and misses the point of the definition. It captures the point that when we have an opportunity to learn, our attention is directed toward an object and away from other objects. When students learn about the American Civil War, they are not learning about the French Revolution. Does this definition include everything and exclude nothing? No! The missed point is that what students have an opportunity to learn focuses attention on selecting an object of study and how it is presented to the exclusion of other objects. Students learn from excluded opportunities as well as from those overtly provided. But different things are learned, depending upon whether an object is present or absent. This distinction makes a difference. One task for the study of curriculum, in this view, is to discover how and why some opportunities are provided and others are bypassed. Curriculum, in part, is a study of what is valued and given priority and what is disvalued and excluded.

Curriculum defined as what students have an opportunity to learn has several advantages:

1. It acknowledges curriculum as a guideline for planning and evaluation, including intended learning outcomes.
2. It includes what students learn from school structure and organization; school administration is not *just* administration but is also part of the instructional system.
3. It includes what students learn from their peers, including what the Supreme Court discussed in *Brown* v. *Board of Education*.
4. It includes the fact that students learn from that which is excluded, from that which is not part of the discourse.
5. It avoids the error of distinguishing curriculum from instruction before defining curriculum.

6. It avoids making curriculum dependent on organizational needs of school administrators and teachers.

Structural analysis identifies categories and binary distinctions of an argument, myth, novel, poem, or, in the present case, curriculum theory, textbook content, curriculum guideline, or assessment test. Examples of binary distinctions that structure curriculum are achievement/failure, theory/practice, concept/fact, learner-centered/subject-centered, accountability/lack of accountability, terminal objective/intermediate objective, literate/illiterate, cognitive/affective, organization/disorganization, synthesis/knowledge of specifics, and sociocentric/egocentric. Several approaches to curriculum value the first over the second term in many of the preceding pairs, and which term is valued depends upon which transcendental signified is queen or king for a day. Some versions of humanistic education might be: learner-centered/subject-centered, practice/theory, lack of accountability/accountability, and affective/cognitive. Approaches to curriculum are topsy-turvy because these and other distinctions could be reversed and reversed again, depending upon the reigning transcendental signified. This is less likely to happen in other fields, such as educational administration or educational psychology, because their meaning is fixed, in part, by academic disciplines outside professional education, even if this dependence is unattributed. Privileged meanings that organize other fields also shift and change but often give the appearance of stability, or at least of slow evolution—not many Kuhnian evolutions having been reported recently. One point of Kuhn's (1974) analysis of scientific revolutions, although it is rarely read this way, is that a dominant paradigm functions as a transcendental signified until it is overthrown and replaced. A structural analysis of curriculum theory and practice offers insight into how the field is (or has been) conceptually organized, what the central tasks of the field are (or have been), and how curricularists are to go about their work (or have gone about their work). But, as pointed out in Chapter 3, structural assumptions contain elements that eventually undermine structural interpretations.

Poststructural analysis, in part, addresses questions about transcendental signifieds: Where do they come from? How were they produced? Why did they originate? What do they assert? Meaning is not centered or fixed because it is caught in a play of references between words and definitions. This can be seen in written texts, which give the appearance of stability but have no center, no transcendental signified, no transcendental semantic meaning. In curriculum we have seen a succession of candidates, and many educators hope, no doubt, that one will come along to organize now and for all time the study of what students have an opportunity to learn. This seems to be what educators have in mind when yearnings are expressed for "a" curriculum theory that will tell us what to do. But what would such a theory look like? How could it endure?

A Poststructural Analysis of the Structure of the Disciplines

The succession of ideas put forward since World War II to serve as transcendental signifieds in curriculum attest to two things: (1) there has been a continuing search for a center to fix and ground thinking and arguments about curriculum, and (2) none has been found. In the early 1960s educators were urged to teach the structure of the academic disciplines. In many ways this was the highwater mark of structuralism and positivism in American curricular thought. The discursive practice of leading educators of the early 1960s is my concern here, not classroom discourse (which from this vantage point would certainly be hard to document). It is not clear to what degree national curriculum-development projects or teacher training institutes induced changes in classroom content or style. Textbooks published from the curriculum-development projects of that period eventually were used in classrooms across the nation, but classroom practices may have remained largely unchanged. The immense size, complexity, and decentralized nature of American education mitigates against quickly instituted, enduring changes. Foucault's approach to discursive practices provides a likely characterization of American education as an anonymous, powerful, slowly changing discourse that we inherit and over which we have little control.

It is always easy for politicians and laypeople to kick the educational system around, but at the end of the 1950s American education was particularly vulnerable due to national embarrassment over Sputnik I. On October 4, 1957, the Soviet Union launched the first artificial earth satellite. This was widely seen as a threat to the national security of the United States. It was important for the United States to compete technologically with and stay ahead of the Soviet Union. Therefore, for the sake of national security and in the name of patriotism, public education had to be upgraded.

How could schools be made better? One approach was "back to the educational basics." But making everyone proficient in reading, writing, and arithmetic was not going to save the nation. Another approach was to make schools more academic. What students henceforth had an opportunity to learn could be academically advanced, reflecting the structure of the disciplines. This was, perhaps, best expressed by Jerome Bruner.

In September 1959 a group of distinguished scientists, scholars, and educators met at Woods Hole on Cape Cod. The task was to consider how science education in primary and secondary schools might be improved. In 1960 Bruner reported their deliberations and recommendations in a small but very influential book, *The Process of Education*. A central theme was that students should be given "an understanding of the fundamental structure of whatever subjects we choose to teach" (p. 11). It was hypothesized that four outcomes would follow:

1. "Understanding fundamentals makes a subject more comprehensible" (p. 23).
2. "Learning general or fundamental principles ensure[s] that memory loss will not mean total loss, that what remains will permit us to reconstruct the details when needed" (p. 25).
3. "To understand something as a specific instance of a more general case—which is what understanding a more fundamental principle or structure means—is to have learned not only a specific thing but also a model for understanding other things like it that one may encounter" (p. 25).
4. "By constantly reexamining material taught in elementary and secondary schools for its fundamental character, one is able to narrow the gap between 'advanced' knowledge and 'elementary' knowledge" (p. 26).

This was a persuasive argument, advocated by distinguished scholars. The advantages were obvious to anyone seriously interested in educational achievement. Teaching the structure of a subject, tapping the center of disciplinary knowledge, was economic, in terms of the number of ideas to be learned, and long lasting in two ways, since there would be increased retention of what was learned and what was learned would become dated more slowly because of its fundamental character.

Two other discourses converged and contributed to the structure-of-the-disciplines movement. One was the explicit structural influence on education of Bloom et al.'s *Taxonomy of Educational Objectives* (1956). It was clearly stated by highly respected authorities that concepts were superior to facts; comprehension, to knowledge of specifics; application, to comprehension; analysis, to application; synthesis, to analysis; and evaluation, to synthesis. The valued and disvalued categories in discourse about educational objectives could not have been set forth more clearly. It was codified and certified. Not only was there a structure to the disciplines; there was also a structure to educational objectives. Conversely, the taxonomy assumed that subject matter had a structure conducive to such arrangement.

A third contributing discourse was Tyler's (1949) well-known rationale. Ten years before the Woods Hole Conference, Tyler applied principles of scientific management to education that showed educators how to think systematically: decide upon objectives, list learning experiences, organize learning experiences, and evaluate outcomes. Tyler's argument is a classic application of structuralism to education. Learning objectives by themselves mean little; but in a structure of organized learning experiences and evaluation, learning objectives contribute to systematic instruction. Likewise, by itself a measurement instrument used for evaluation has little significance; but in a structure of objectives and learning experiences, it can be given an interpretation straight off. By itself each stage of the Tyler rationale means little; the meaning of each stage depends upon differences from and relations to other parts of the process.

Structured interpretations were given to disciplinary knowledge, learning objectives, and curriculum. What had happened was remarkable: the disciplines had fundamental structures, which, if taught, had powerful and long-lasting benefits; learning objectives had been organized hierarchically; and systematic steps of scientific management had been applied to education. The interpretation of the Bloom et al. taxonomy and the Tyler rationale in support of teaching disciplinary structure was difficult to resist, to the degree resistance was considered. It all fit. Everything, from a curricular point of view, had seemingly fallen into place.

At this point a Foucauldian analyst might ask: How could it have turned out differently? Powerful discourses were operative. They reinforced each other: Bruner drew from positivist and logical-empiricist epistemology; Bloom et al., from educational psychology (also influenced by logical empiricism); and Tyler, from scientific (and efficient) management. Given the political imperatives of an internationally threatening situation, the discourse was set, limited, and legitimated. For a variety of reasons, each powerful and persuasive in its own way, teaching the structure of the disciplines had become for the time being the transcendental signified for the field of curriculum. It *centered* the system and it *fixed* meanings in education. Working from disciplinary structure, everything could be figured out, from objectives to evaluation. In retrospect, however, the idea of disciplinary structure was largely based on a positivist view of knowledge whose philosophical underpinnings had by then eroded.

The structure-of-the-disciplines argument seems to have presumed the following:

1. The structure of disciplinary knowledge was logically coherent and complete.
2. Disciplinary knowledge was logically valid and truth preserving, from first principles to testable hypotheses.
3. Disciplinary knowledge was factual and explanatory, not evaluative.
4. Scientific language was value neutral and passive in describing and explaining phenomena.

The first and second points assume a distinction between analytic and synthetic statements; the third, between facts and values; and the fourth, a view of language as passive and descriptive, not active or evaluative. An important consequence of the analytic/synthetic distinction is that a conclusion in a logically valid argument *necessarily* follows from the premises of the argument. Thus if a theory or explanation is stated in a valid deductive manner and its first principles are true, then its conclusion must also be true. It is easy to understand why this assumption is central to a structural approach to disciplinary knowledge. The latter two assumptions conceptualized knowledge and science somehow as separate from the world being described and explained.

Developments in modern logic by Quine (1953) and philosophy of language by Austin (1968) and Wittgenstein (1953) cut the ground from beneath these assumptions. Quine argued that it was not possible to account for truth-preserving natural-language arguments. (This depended on the notion of analyticity, which defied, then and now, clear characterization. See Quine, 1953, for the original argument.) Therefore it could not be shown that disciplinary knowledge was logically complete or truth-preserving. Austin and Wittgenstein, in different ways, showed that speech is action, not just description (which Austin called the descriptivist fallacy), and that value and institutional commitments infiltrate language and what is said. Disciplinary knowledge then, did not consist of passive, unambiguously truth-preserving factual arguments that excluded evaluation. A new account of disciplinary structure was in order. It was not forthcoming.

Not to be put off, many promoted curricula based on disciplinary structures that presumably were truth-preserving, objective, and cumulative, even though the precise nature of these structures, for good reason, was never spelled out. At Woods Hole there were six mathematicians, nine psychologists, four physicists, five biologists, and eight who represented history, classics, medicine, and cinematography. The issues discussed were philosophical to the core, but no philosophers participated. Elsewhere wars had been fought whose outcomes were important to a structural approach to the disciplines, but no one was there to report on battles, casualties, or outcomes.

These events illustrate Foucault's argument that power makes truth possible. The arguments of Quine, Wittgenstein, and Austin did not, nor would other contrary educational positions have been expected to, curb the structure-of-the-disciplines movement. The driving force was grounded in political exigencies internal as well as external to professional education, not in the substantive merits of the arguments.

Foucauldian analysis points to a continual movement from discourse (for example, Bruner's argument for a structural approach to curriculum) to history (for example, contemporary events within education and national and international political developments). That disciplinary structure became a transcendental signified for curriculum was an accident of history with no single author. Once it was in place, it determined who could speak and what could be said. Curricularists were not in control of their discourse; quite the reverse, dominant discursive practices dictated who was a curricularist. The discursive practice had shifted, and those who formerly had spoken with authority on curriculum were on the outside and those who had previously been on the outside of curriculum, for example, academic specialists, were now on the inside. And no one asked: Why not teach about racism, sexism, labor history, minority history, social inequality, or injustice. The configuration of power from several discourses, practices, and situations conferred upon the arguments of Bruner, Bloom et al., and Tyler the effects of truth. Power as well as truth had spoken, because power preceded and produced statements that were received as truth.

A deconstructive analysis in the manner of Derrida focuses less on the historical setting and more on the argument. One question is: What binary distinctions does a structure-of-the-disciplines approach advance and do they deconstruct? Disciplinary structure assumes the existence of a cumulative and hierarchical body of knowledge. It was assumed that academic scholars should set the educational agenda, and their assumptions about disciplinary structure led to a set of valued/disvalued categories. Some of these categorical distinctions were theory/practice, concept/fact, subject-centered learning/ learner-centered learning, and cognitive/affective, with the first terms valued over the second. These distinctions separate what is central from what is marginal.

Are these distinctions stable? Of the theory/practice opposition, Michael Ryan (1984) writes, "All theory is either a theory of a past practice which it describes, or of a future practice toward which it aims, in addition to being itself a practice. Pure practice . . . is always itself a certain theory of practice" (p. 14; see Chapter 5 in this volume for an argument deconstructing the theory/practice distinction).

As for the hypothesized superiority of concepts to facts, it is well known that scientific concepts are not empirical unless they point to the possibility of factual observations. Conversely, factual observations are only possible given a conceptual background. Concepts and facts point to things in the world and depend upon each other. If concepts and facts are mutually constitutive, one is led to ask why educators would value scientific concepts over facts. When disciplinary concepts are valued over facts, the world as conceptualized by academicians is privileged over alternative conceptualizations, such as artistic, humanistic, aesthetic, and political ones, and facts highlighted by such alternative orientations are slighted.

As for subject-centered learning and learner-centered learning, learners do not exist without subjects and a subject to learn does not exist without previous learners. When subjects are valued over learners, the interests of learners who constituted the subjects (experts) are valued over the interests of other learners (students). It is simply the case that the subject-centered/learner-centered distinction privileges learners who are subject-matter experts.

Finally, let us address the cognitive/affective distinction. Presumably a cognitive emphasis values "objective" knowledge and an affective emphasis deals with values, feelings, attitudes, and opinions. But a cognitive orientation cannot exist without prior value judgments that single out some cognitions as more important or worthwhile than others. What is cognitive can be neither produced nor taught without reference to prior evaluations. The cognitive/affective distinction operates to hide prior value judgments. Those hidden commitments turn out to be the ones held by authorities and experts.

By 1970 a number of developments illuminated the shortcomings of a structure-of-the-disciplines approach to curriculum. It deconstructed, although this term was not used, when it became widely recognized that the rhetorical claims of Bruner exceeded the logic of his argument. First, as noted earlier, logical positivism and its successor, logical empiricism, each of which had contributed to the epistemological foundation for teaching disciplinary structure, could no longer sustain claims made on their behalf. No alternative interpretation of disciplinary structure had surfaced; given Kuhn's influential 1962 book on *The Structure of Scientific Revolutions* (cited throughout this book in its 1974 edition), coming as it did two years after Bruner's, one was sorely needed. Second, academics who sought in the early 1960s to map the structure of their respective disciplines were less than successful in doing so (Bruner, 1971). Third, the international political situation vis-à-vis the Soviet Union had changed. Fourth, domestic politics in the United States was now dominated by the civil-rights movement, the War on Poverty, and rising controversy over United States military involvement in Vietnam. Disciplinary structure no longer drove curriculum efforts. By the 1970s there were voices, including Bruner's (1973), asking why we were not teaching about racism, sexism, and social inequality and injustice. By the 1980s these demands, in turn, had almost been silenced as the cry shifted to educational "excellence." Forces external to professional education were making different demands from those voiced ten years earlier. Power was speaking again and this time telling a different story. What is considered true and authoritative often shifts as power moves, settles, and is relocated. That is what happened in curriculum.

Critical Pragmatism and Curriculum

Teaching the structure of the disciplines is one proposal among many that have been promoted to center, organize, fix the meaning of, and bring coherence to curriculum. The history of curriculum theory and practice can be read as a series of repeated invasions of organizing ideas that command attention for a while before they are turned out by the next invasion. Each new invader was beyond the control of any individual educator, reflected political events external as well as internal to education, represented prominent contemporary ideologies, and could be deconstructed. Proposed transcendental signifieds, such as teaching disciplinary structure, recede for at least two reasons: (1) the material, external events that push for their adoption disappear or become less demanding and/or new developments disrupt the discourse and its related practices, a Foucauldian hypothesis; and (2) the organizing persuasiveness of the idea is subsequently shown to be suspect, due either to direct criticism or indirect analysis, a Derridean hypothesis. The argument from Foucault tends toward a synthetic, empirical claim, whereas the Derridean is more analytic.

The study and practice of curriculum determines where and on what grounds opportunities to learn are provided and at what point the deconstruction of those opportunities will stop. Construction and deconstruction circle around a central question: Why do we provide an opportunity to learn about something in the first place? Curricula can help students gain insight into their discourses, into how knowledge and power create and recreate each other, or it can focus on accepting existing discourses along with their unique opportunities, constraints, and oppressiveness. Curricular constructions and deconstructive criticisms allow judgments to be made about objectives, learning experiences, the organization of learning experiences, and their evaluation—all of which are necessary in some fashion some of the time but should not be mistaken as transcendental. If poststructural criticism teaches nothing else, it teaches us to be suspicious of argumentative, knowledge, and policy claims based on appeals to precision, certainty, clarity, and rigor.

This argument may seem a bit curious, unsettling, and unfamiliar because academic and professional arguments are expected to begin with a question and end with an answer. Academic and theoretical arguments push toward certainty and promise identity, by identifying—if nothing else—what it is we are studying, if not truth. For example, it would seem that curriculum theory should tell us what curriculum is and authoritatively tell us what to do when it comes to developing, implementing, and evaluating curriculum. The poststructural lesson is to be suspicious of such authority. Much of the unfamiliarity and strangeness of poststructuralism recedes when applied to everyday life. Work, relationships, beliefs, skills, and we ourselves are not identical from one day, or even one moment, to the next or from one place to another. There are always differences. Theories and organizing principles put forward as transcendental signifieds are products of human activity; therefore they are necessarily marked by the uncertainties and transience of human efforts.

Think of social practice and theory allegorically. Social practice, in this case curriculum and education, may be compared to humanity after the Fall. What we do in everyday life is negotiated, compromised, contingent, subject to miscalculation, and flawed. Theories and first principles promise redemption. There is hope, an expectation, that theory will tell us what is good and what is true, how to make correct calculations and avoid errors. Because theory is produced by humanity in its fallen state, it should not be surprising, then, that it is also characterized by incompleteness, ambiguity, error, and contradiction.

How to proceed? Both constructors and deconstructors are needed. Some people are better at constructing, others at deconstructing. Constructors must realize that what is built is temporal, fallible, limited, compromised, negotiated, and incomplete or contradictory. Each construction will eventually be replaced. And deconstructive arguments must be shaped so that construction will be encouraged and follow. The field of curriculum has unwittingly experienced cycles of construction and deconstruction. These have been interpreted as illness, moribundity, and a foreshadowing of the death of the field. The hope of finding a purpose or cause that grounds work in curriculum and education and fixes its meaning once and for all, however, is misplaced. It appears to be fictional. But the continuing search for meaning and purpose and the subsequent deconstruction of the candidates that turn up need not cause despair. The realization that this is the nature of history, politics, and texts brings with it important changes in thinking about curriculum and education. If the structure, pardon my usage, of curriculum and how it moves continues to be unrecognized, however, elation is likely to be followed by despondency by elation by . . . with no basis for sustained insight or dialogue.

If discourse in the field is accepted as fragmented, pushed and pulled, contradictory and incomplete, responding to professional and political forces beyond our control, subject to deconstruction; and we consciously choose to constitute a dialectic of construction-deconstruction; then the nature of curricular discourse will change. Instead of talking about taxonomies of objectives, structures of disciplines, learning objectives, and what "a" curriculum theory would be like, the conversation will turn to what kind of society and schools we want, knowing full well that they constitute each other. Our concerns will be pragmatic and focus, as Rorty puts it, "about what self-image our society should have of itself" (1985, p. 11). For example, do we want to provide opportunities to learn a structure of the disciplines at the expense of teaching about the causes and consequences of racism, sexism, and social inequality and injustice? If the argument Bruner made in 1960 is compared to that he came back with in 1971 and 1973—that social issues should be moved closer to center stage in curriculum—we see the ebb and flow. Each argument was persuasive when it was made, but *the discursive practices and social structures that made each argument persuasive were never addressed.* How to get behind the discourse? How to get at what structures what we say? Why do we choose the words and make the statements we do?

Even though poststructural criticism is relatively new to discussions of social practice, even though it promises no final, transcendent meaning, it is still possible to outline what curriculum and education might look like when criticism feeds into pragmatic choices. Curriculum is what students have an opportunity to learn. What students have an opportunity to learn depends upon what they do not have an opportunity to learn. Power distributes opportunities and nonopportunities. And curriculum is intimately linked to educational administration and instruction, because each set of activities produces opportunities and constrains what can be learned. Curriculum is not more isolated than any other field of education. They are all part of a larger society and are moved to and fro by the same rhythms that shape our politics, music, business, technology, and so forth. Complaints about the illness, death, or moribundity of curriculum resulted from a failure to grasp these connections in combination with monumental expectations made of the field. It was as though curricularists were expected to tell educators what to do. But the acceptability of what was uttered would have reflected the contemporary interests of those in power, and there is little reason to think the rhetoric of the answer would have matched its logic. The study of curriculum is the process of rolling over one answer onto the next when asked what students should have an opportunity to learn. To expect curricularists to give a definitive answer to what students should have an opportunity to learn is to display an ignorance of the question and the field. Given this, what curricular strategies seem promising?

Curricular work takes place in a wide variety of settings with different scope and generality: there are the United States Department of Education, publishing companies that market textbooks nationwide, state departments of education, teaching-methods classes, school district curriculum committees, and individual classrooms. What is constructed at each level is shaped by what is inherited from previous social, organizational, or professional generations. Saussure states this general point very clearly, and here structural and poststructural thought converge and then separate:

> The word, though to all appearances freely chosen with respect to the idea that it represents, is fixed, not free, with respect to the linguistic community that uses it. . . . No individual, even if he willed it, could modify in any way at all the choice that has been made; and what is more, the community itself cannot control so much as a single word; *it is bound to the existing language.* (1916/1966, p. 71; emphasis added)

Inherited discourses come into contact with each other, sometimes reinforcing, sometimes conflicting. A first step in a poststructural, critical, pragmatic strategy is to describe relationships between historical developments and political practices and curriculum theory and practice. For example, following up on the examples in Chapters 2 and 3, what were the historical and political conditions that made the Tyler rationale, the Bloom et al. *Taxonomy of Educational Objectives,* and Schwab's "Practical 4" persuasive? This should not be approached, however, in a simplistic and overdeterministic manner. Politics does not create curriculum out of whole cloth. Instead, power transforms discourses such that a category, like disciplinary structure, is given more salience and importance than others. International tensions did not create the notion of structure, but they did, however, assign an educational value it did not have before to disciplinary structure. Power creates opportunities for speech and discourse but does not create each category in the discourse. How does power shape curricular discourse and why are certain subjects privileged over others?

A second poststructural strategy follows from the point that power precedes curriculum discourse. Who, individually, or what group is rewarded and indulged and, conversely, who are those sanctioned and deprived? Who benefits under a curriculum organized in terms of disciplinary structure is easy to identify. Students from groups that did well in school would be expected to do well with an academic curriculum. Students from backgrounds that did not emphasize academic achievement would not be expected to do well. Academic specialists would be financially rewarded. Curricularists who argue humanistic or social-issue positions would be, for the time being, professionally marginalized.

A third poststructural move gives curricular discourse a close reading and analysis: Who listens? Who is excluded? What metaphors and arguments are deployed? Fourth, what are the dominant and valued categories? Since dominant categories cannot ground the logic of the system, it is only prudent to inquire into the values and ideologies that led to the choice of the organizing principles. Fifth, alternative interpretations of what students have an opportunity to learn should be generated, because it is a reasonable inference that subtexts tell stories different from those on the surface. Sixth, curriculum proposals, demands, and so forth should be examined in light of changes and developments in other disciplines, because their placement in a broader setting may provide insights into curricular discourses-practices, for example, that structural approaches to knowledge are not entirely defensible.

Structural approaches lend themselves to checklists; poststructural criticism defies the compilation of an enduring checklist. There are, to be sure, things to keep in mind in pursuing either Foucauldian or Derridean criticism, but it may be more productive to think of curriculum construction, the geneology of the construction, and its deconstruction more metaphorically. Poststructural criticism argues that linearity in text, organization, rationale, and argument is deceptive. Here are three metaphors offering contrasting yet dependent images useful in thinking about these things: normal and revolutionary science, normal and abnormal discourse, and canny and uncanny thinking. Although Kuhn in *The Structure of Scientific Revolutions* (1974) did not couch his account in poststructural terms, it roughly parallels the Derridean account. Scientific activity moves between normal science, which is governed by a paradigm that "stands for the entire constellation of beliefs, values, techniques, and so on shared by the members of a given community" or "denotes one sort of element in that constellation, the concrete puzzle-solutions . . . employed as models or examples" (1974, p. 175), and revolutionary science, which rejects and replaces paradigms. Normal science is, more or less, a hypothesis-testing activity wherein theories are elaborated and filled in. Occasionally the paradigm, the transcendental signified, breaks down. Scientific activity then takes on revolutionary overtones, and the search is on for a new set of governing principles and guiding puzzle-solutions, a new paradigm. Science, in this view, is movement between normal and rule-governed activity and a revolutionary search for new rules.

Normal and abnormal discourse is discussed by Rorty in *Philosophy and the Mirror of Nature* (1980). After recounting repeated failed attempts by twentieth-century philosophers to provide a foundation for knowledge, he notes that Wittgenstein, Dewey, and Heidegger came around to a common historicist message:

> Each of the three reminds us that investigations of the foundations of knowledge or morality or language or society may be simply apologetics, attempts to eternalize a certain contemporary language-game, social practice, or self image. (pp. 9–10)

This passes quite well as a general description of what was claimed for disciplinary structure in curriculum. In curriculum terms the search for "a" curriculum theory, "a" first principle, "an" organizing scheme, "an" evaluation procedure is an attempt to eternalize a particular social practice that is an accident of time and space. It represents an effort to deny our humanity by denying differences and movement.

Rorty devotes a fair amount of attention in his last chapter to education and edification, where *edification* stands for "finding new, better, more interesting, more fruitful ways of speaking" (p. 360). Edification begins with normal discourse dominated by "descriptions of the world offered by our culture (e.g., by learning the results of the natural sciences)" (p. 365). The move, then, is to abnormal discourse, which is always parasitic on normal discourse. On his final point he is worth quoting at length:

> The point of edifying philosophy is to keep the conversation going rather than to find objective truth. Such truth, in the view I am advocating, is the normal result of normal discourse. Edifying philosophy is not only abnormal but reactive. . . . The danger which edifying discourse tries to avert is that some given vocabulary, some way in which people might come to think of themselves, will deceive them into thinking that from now on all discourse could be, or should be, normal discourse. The resulting freezing-over of culture would be, in the eyes of edifying philosophers, the dehumanization of human beings. (p. 377)

Edifying discourse moves in and out from construction to deconstruction, from structure to its criticism, from normal to abnormal conversation and argumentation, always suspicious of certainty and precision.

Another way to think about structural and poststructural criticism is described by Culler in *On Deconstruction: Theory and Criticism After Structuralism* (1984). Building on work of J. Hillis Miller, he writes about canny and uncanny criticism about literature. The canny critic brings "literature out into the sunlight in a 'happy positivism'" (p. 23, quoting Miller). The uncanny critic pursues logical analysis into regions that are alogical and absurd, thus suggesting deeper meanings: "Uncanny post-structuralism arrives to waken canny structuralism from the dogmatic slumbers into which it was lulled by its 'unshakable faith' in thought and 'the promise of a rational ordering'" (p. 24). Being canny, shrewd, and clever about the world as it appears entraps, dehumanizes, and deludes us. Curriculum needs to be uncanny as well as canny.

It is time to bring the argument full circle and explain why historically the study of curriculum has appeared so turbulent. This has variously been interpreted as signifying illness, death, or moribundity, whereas other fields of education have seemingly displayed more stability. It is arguable that the disciplines from which educational psychology, social foundations of education, philosophy of education, educational policy analysis, and educational administration are, in part, derivative contribute to their apparent stability. Teacher education or instruction, as you will, attends to concrete situations. But curriculum is neither historically situated in the tradition of an academic discipline nor constrained by a concrete situation. The complexity of the demands thrust upon the study and practice of curriculum contribute to its looseness, its thrashing about, its contradictions, and its lack of a center, grounding, and foundation.

But the apparent stability of other fields in education and the lack of stability in curriculum are both illusory. Academic disciplines and the knowledge they produce are not stable, as Kuhn (1974) has persuasively demonstrated. But following a "scientific revolution," disciplines still have traditions and legacies. Questions shift and puzzle-solutions are discarded, but there is still some sense of what a field is about, whether it is philosophy or economics or political science. Transcendental signifieds for academic disciplines are in the long run fictional; but in the short run, say the length of an average professional career, they are stable. Life expectancy of foundational ideas may be longer in an academic discipline than in the field of curriculum for several reasons:

1. Academic disciplines are more loosely coupled to political events and exigencies, such as the surprise launching of an artificial earth satellite by the Soviet Union, than is the field of curriculum.

2. Research problems and tasks of disciplines are more closely framed and policed than the holistic tasks facing curriculum; for example, Kuhn argues that paradigms are often shared by communities of fewer than 100 members (1974, p. 178).

3. Disciplines do not have to respond to specific, immediate, and changing demands for excellence and performance as does professional education; for example, scholars can quietly admit within their community that they cannot solve a problem, as did political scientists who spent some 20 years trying to solve a problem known as Arrow's impossibility theorem. It turned out to be impossible to solve.

4. Whereas disciplines may reflect ideological orientations and problems of the larger society, such as a fixation on rational choice theories in microeconomics, psychology, and political

science, they are not continually confronted, as is curriculum, by the contradictions, frustrations, ambiguities, and, in some cases, helplessness of society.

The traditions, orientations, commitments, obligations, and, not least of all, focus of disciplinary and professional activity external to education give the appearance of stability to many fields in education. Curriculum does not have such a reserve.

Solid, immutable foundations do not exist for any of these endeavors. The absence of foundations is simply more noticeable in curriculum than in academic disciplines and other areas of professional education. The norm for curriculum, then, is not consensus, stability, and agreement but conflict, instability, and disagreement, because the process is one of construction followed by deconstruction by construction . . . of what students have an opportunity to learn. By explicitly adopting a poststructural attitude, educators will avoid the false hope of structural certainty and be in a stronger position to deal with, anticipate, and sometimes, perhaps, predict the fate of the latest proposal to guide curriculum. If the field of curriculum moves to a poststructural era along with its uncertainties, ambiguities, and criticisms, there is the promise of understanding more fully how we and others around us have become who we are. The possibility of such understanding brings with it the promise of increased freedom and power, increased freedom from existing social structures, and more power to create our societies and schools rather than the other way around.

21

NICHOLAS BURBULES

What are the underlying narratives that we tell ourselves about education? Most often these stories are full of utopian hope that education will transform society, realize our students' full potentials, create democratic citizens, etc., yet more often than not, when confronted with the daily trials and tribulations of teaching, educators find these aspirations frustrated by the ambiguities of teaching.

Nicholas Burbules (born 1954) has argued that we need a new way of understanding teaching that does not rely on narratives of utopian perfection or nihilistic pessimism. For him, education is inherently tragic—full of failures, uncertainties, and inconsistencies. According to Burbules, teachers should embrace education with a pragmatic modesty and humility concerning the hopes for success. In fact, doubt and uncertainty make for a better educational practice. In other words, a tragic sensibility accepts the intractable dilemmas of education without giving up or without providing naïve and overly simplistic solutions to complex problems. Thus, rather than repress the tragic, Burbules urges all educators to find productive possibilities within the tragic. This means that educational evaluation must rely less on positivistic forms of outcome measurements and more on the process of give and take inherent in dialoguing with students.

But if Burbules turns to dialogue as a way of exploring the tragic in education, this is not because dialogue is a "solution" to the problems of teaching. Much of Burbules's work concerns the question of communication, especially in contexts of multicultural difference. In his early work, we see a close relationship with Paulo Freire's pedagogy of the oppressed, as well as with the critical theorist Jurgen Habermas's notion of communicative action. More recently, Burbules has explored Wittgenstein's philosophy of language in order to better understand the tragic qualities of communication. Wittgenstein's use of dialogue as an investigation into his own doubts consciously ends with puzzlement rather than a definitive and universal answer abstracted from a particular social context.

Through his philosophical writings, Burbules argues that dialogue is not a one-size-fits-all solution but is itself a flawed educational method. It is through dialogue that teachers begin to learn that they do not have all the answers, that knowledge is incomplete, and that questioning rarely leads to final answers, yet this does not mean that we should abandon dialogue, for to abandon dialogue amounts to abandoning education itself. Thus, we must learn to live within the tragic and find it not so much as a source of frustration as a productive space of puzzlement.

Like others included in this volume, Burbules's scholarship is affected by real-world concerns. Thus, his inquiry into dialogue is in many ways a response to a multicultural and diverse world where communication is both necessary and fraught with misunderstandings. His most recent work has delved into two of the most important social and educational issues of the latter half of the 20th century: globalization and technology. For example, bringing his interest in Wittgenstein's philosophy to our experience of being lost on the World Wide Web, Burbules questions our pessimistic frustration in the face of "being lost." Rather than see this feeling of disorientation as an annoyance preventing us from reaching an intended destination, Burbules suggests we see the state of being lost as a productive opportunity to find surprising, new connections and interesting (if not challenging) alternatives to our preconceived plans and ideas. To be lost on the Internet thus becomes an analogy for learning in general, which, as indicated previously, is a maze of uncertainty and perplexity that lacks a clear road map to certainty.

In sum, a continuous theme of Burbules's work is the relation between teaching and uncertainty and the transformation of this uncertainty into an opportunity to ask new questions. Given the emphasis on the process of being lost, being uncertain, and asking good questions, how would Burbules view standardization in education? How would his educational theory look in a classroom mandated to fulfill strict performance outcomes? Besides standardization, we must also ask, how would Burbules critique Freire's theory of dialogue? In both cases, where is there room for a tragic sense of education?

REFERENCES

Burbules, Nicholas. "The Tragic Sense of Education." *Teachers College Record* 91, no. 4 (1990): 469–79.

Burbules, Nicholas. *Dialogue in Teaching: Theory and Practice.* New York: Teachers College Press, 1993.

Burbules, Nicholas. "Postmodern Doubt and Philosophy of Education." In Alven Neiman, ed. *Philosophy of Education Yearbook 1995* (pp. 39–48). Urbana, IL: Philosophy of Education Society, 1996.

Burbules, Nicholas. "Aporias, Webs, and Passages: Doubt as an Opportunity to Learn." *Curriculum Inquiry* 30, no. 2 (2000): 171–87.

Burbules, Nicholas, and Paul Smeyers. "Wittgenstein, the Practice of Ethics, and Moral Education." In *Philosophy of Education Yearbook* (pp. 248–57). Urbana-Champaign, IL: University of Illinois.

THE LIMITS OF DIALOGUE AS A CRITICAL PEDAGOGY

Introduction

It seems that hardly anyone has a bad word to say against dialogue. A broad range of political orientations hold out the aim of "fostering dialogue" as a potential resolution to social conflict and as a basis for rational public deliberation. A range of pedagogical approaches, from constructivist scaffolding to Socratic instruction to Freirean liberatory pedagogy, all proclaim the virtues of an interactive engagement of questions and answers in the shared pursuit of knowledge and understanding. Philosophical accounts of dialogue from Plato to the present employ the dialogical form as a literary genre that represents the external expression of an internal, dialectical thought process of back-and-forth ratiocination. Dialogue constitutes a point of opportunity at which these three interests—political, pedagogical, and philosophical—come together. It is widely assumed that the aim of teaching with and through dialogue serves democracy, promotes communication across difference, and enables the active coconstruction of new knowledge and understandings.[1]

Nevertheless, the ideal of dialogue has received withering criticism, particularly from poststructural feminist theorists in education and from those for whom "difference" is a lived experience of marginalization and not just a demographic category of identification. For these critics, "dialogue" has exerted a kind of hegemonic dominance that belies its emancipatory rhetoric, its apparent openness to difference, and its stress on equality and reciprocity within the dialogical relation. The way in which dialogue has become almost synonymous with critical pedagogy has tended to submerge the voices and concerns to groups who feel themselves closed out of dialogue or compelled to join it only at the cost of restricting their self-expression into acceptable channels of communication. Finally, an idealized, prescriptive conception of dialogue has abstracted the situated historicity of specific practices of communicative engagement from their consequences for people and groups who encounter the invitation to dialogue in difficult circumstances of conflict.

In light of such reactions, the claims made on behalf of dialogue as an inherently liberatory pedagogy need to be reassessed. The insistence that dialogue is somehow self-corrective, that if there are unresolved power differentials or unexamined silences and omissions within a dialogue, simply persisting with the same forms of dialogical exchange can bring them to light, seems not only counterproductive but itself a form of hegemony: if dialogue fails, the solution to the problem is more of the same.

Yet it also remains true that the ideal of "dialogue" expresses hope for the possibility of open, respectful, critical engagements from which we can learn about others, about the world, and about ourselves. Is there a space between the exaggerated claims made on behalf of dialogue entirely as an inherently liberatory pedagogy and the rejection of dialogue as an ideal?

Dialogue, Diversity, and Difference

As noted, one major point of criticism that has been raised against some accounts of dialogue is whether it is sufficiently sensitive to conditions of diversity, that is, the different forms of cultural communication, the different aims and values held by members of different groups, and the serious conflicts and histories of oppression and harm that have excluded marginalized groups from public and educational conversations in the past. Certainly, many accounts of dialogue have tried to respond positively to such criticisms.[15] Yet even these attempts to respond have pointed up serious limitations in the standard accounts of dialogue.

What seems to recommend dialogue as a pedagogy is its capacity for active participation by all parties; its room for the coconstruction of understanding of knowledge that can be negotiated between the perspectives of different members; its critical potential, which allows for not only questioning "within" the dialogue, but questioning its very terms and assumptions; and its open-endedness, its capacity for continuing and expanding the conversation to include multiple voices and perspectives—indeed, for many purposes, actively seeking them out. These are not trivial advantages, especially compared against many of the pedagogical practices currently in favor in education at all levels of schooling. Yet, as noted earlier, there is something self-confirming about this model: that its capacity to be self-corrective, in certain instances, is taken as proof that there is no legitimate "outside" to its procedures. One could call this "the hegemony of reasonableness": that precisely because dialogue seems to hold out the hand of inclusiveness and respect for all points of view, it makes those suspicious of its tacit rules of engagement, its "modes of address," as Ellsworth calls them, its scope of what is and is not up for discussion, appear as if *they* are at fault for remaining outside the conversation.

Dialogue runs up against difficulty in encounters with diversity. Not everyone speaks the same language. Whose language will be used? Are the ground rules for participation, however thinly procedural they might appear, actually substantive restrictions on what can be talked about, on how things can be talked about, and so upon who can or will be part of the conversation? What are the limits of reflexivity within dialogue? Is the invitation to participate already a kind of co-optation of *radical* critique and rejectionism? Are the dialogical aims of consensus, provisional agreement, and even understanding (across unresolved differences) based upon ideals of harmony and community that are always on *somebody's* terms, and so threaten the maintenance of separate, self-determined identities? Finally, are there some differences that are simply unbridgeable in dialogue, gaps of understanding or belief that cannot be bridged—but which, in the attempt to bridge them, put some people at risk more than others?

There are three broad ways that different models of dialogue have tried to address such issues of diversity. To an extent, these cut across the six traditions described above, although some are more amenable to certain approaches than others. None of them adequately addresses, in my view, the criticisms of radical diversity just discussed. The first, *pluralism*, or the "melting pot" ideal, regards social and cultural diversity as a positive resource for the exchange of beliefs, values, and experiences that can inform and invigorate dialogue, but with the specific aims of reconciling these differences in agreements or compromises that combine the best elements from each perspective or form new, common understandings with which all parties can identify. In many instances, however, pluralism in this sense simply comes to the end of assimilating diverse groups into predominantly mainstream beliefs and values (though, to a much lesser extent, dominant or mainstream views may be modified over time as well). This asymmetry of change threatens, in the long run, to erase significant cultural difference or to relegate it entirely to the private, not public, sphere.

The second approach to diversity, *multiculturalism*, perhaps the most widely held view in education today, emphasizes respecting (or celebrating) differences, not for the sake of assimilating them into dominant cultural forms but to preserve them, both out of respect for the integrity of diverse cultural traditions and out of an appreciation of cultural variety for its own sake. However, this inclusive or celebratory attitude can also have the effect of exoticizing differences, rendering them quaint or interesting as artifacts and not as critical points of reference against which to view one's self. The framework within which multiculturalism often takes shape, a broad (and sometimes patronizing) "tolerance" for difference, leaves dominant beliefs and values largely unquestioned—indeed even insulated from challenge and change—because they are shielded within the comforting self-conception of openness and inclusivity. But as Cameron McCarthy has noted, multiculturalism means little if it is only Other-regarding and does not become an occasion for questioning the dominant cultural orientation as itself one of many, unprivileged, and just as quaint or strange (needing to be "tolerated") when viewed from the outside. Where cultural dominance comes from, and how it settles into a taken-for-grantedness that makes its own specificity invisible, is a question rarely explored within the multicultural framework.[16]

A third view, *cosmopolitanism,* of growing interest recently, emphasizes the unreconciled coexistence of diverse cultures and diverse cultures and groups.[17] Informed to some extent by a global perspective that recognizes not only the radical diversity of cultural difference but also the attenuated circumstances that bring these cultures in contact with one another, this view of diversity (while often sharing many features with multiculturalism) acknowledges the limits of assimilation, agreement, or even understanding across certain cultural divides, and concludes that in many cases there must simply be an end to talk that seeks to bridge or minimize differences. Where such conversations exacerbate or heighten the awareness of disagreements or conflicting interests, continuing them may weaken rather than strengthen the prospects for a minimally harmonious condition in which each agrees to allow (and not necessarily respect or approve) the cultural domain and prerogatives of the other. The problem with this view, however, is that it abrogates—and sometimes prejudges and rejects out of hand—the value of engagement, excluding both the possibility of mutual accommodation and the possibility of a critical questioning of one view from a radically different other.

Because of the currency of debates over these three views, the question of the possibility and prospects for dialogue in contexts of diversity has become one of the central, if not *the* central, issues in contemporary educational theory and practice (to say nothing of larger social and political debates). The conventional view is that such dialogue is always a worthy effort and learning opportunity, even if in some cases it may unfortunately fall short of its ideals.

The problem here is that dialogue is variously viewed from these positions as a means of bridging differences, reconciling differences, coordinating action despite differences, or achieving understanding, respect, or tolerance in the face of differences. These objectives are clearly desirable under many circumstances, including educational circumstances; but these dynamics cannot be viewed symmetrically from all points of view. While some may view dialogue as a benefit, or a potential benefit, others may regard it as a threat, and others as an impossibility. The rejection of dialogue, or the refusal to submit one's views to questioning, compromise, or renegotiation, is not always a mark of irrationality. The very aim of dialogue to speak and understand across differences is not an unalloyed benefit to all potential parties to such dialogue. Moreover, "difference" here is constituted as a dimension of *diversity*—categorical differentiation according to demographic, cultural, or identity categories. Dialogue tends to construct differences as instances of diverse values and points of view along continuums where middle grounds may exist, where commonalties may be found, or where translations across gulfs of misunderstanding may be achieved. Sometimes these are realistic prospects. Sometimes they are not; and where they are not, the reasonable gestures of inclusion made within dialogue can actually constitute co-opting or even coercive moves that put upon those with strong differences the burden of justifying why they will not participate.

In some of my earlier work, I suggested that dialogue could yield a range of outcomes, ranging from *agreement*; to a *consensus* (or in Rawlsian terms an "overlapping consensus") that falls short of full agreement; to an *understanding* that falls short of agreement or consensus; to a respectful *tolerance* that falls short of full understanding. Each of these, I suggested, can have fruitful educational benefits. My main point was that dialogue does not have to achieve agreement, consensus, or even understanding to be educationally (or socially and politically) worthwhile. Theoretically, this represented my departure from Habermasian or Gadamerian views of dialogue. I now think that this view suffered from three serious limitations. One is that these outcomes cannot be placed easily along a single continuum, like railroad stations at which a train may stop; that they are actually quite discontinuous sorts of paths, often entailing very different sorts of dialogical interactions—and so one cannot simply say that dialogue moves along a single "track" and gets as far along it as possible, aiming toward agreement or consensus, perhaps, but being satisfied with something less than that if full "success" cannot be achieved. Instead, assumptions at the start concerning which of several ends is possible or desirable have a determinative effect upon the form and tone of the *type* of dialogue in which one is engaged (and into which one is inviting others).[18] *This* determination ("What type of dialogue are we having?") is one in which unilateral judgment and cultural dominance often play a central role.

The second failing was to underestimate the role of misunderstanding, and even incommensurability, as potentially necessary and even educationally beneficial ends under certain circumstances. I regarded them as failures of dialogue, or a sign that dialogue had not proceeded long enough. I stressed that one should never presume the outcome of incommensurability and suggested that one should always approach dialogue "as if" it need not end up that way. This was a mistake. There are instances in which the very encounter with a radically different, unreconciled, and unreconcilable point of view, value, voice, or belief can serve important educational purposes: to cause us to question the horizons of our own assumptions, to explore within ourselves (and not only within the other) the causes of why dialogue "fails," and to consider the possibility of a radically different way of approaching the world. Dialogue in the mode of resolving or dissolving differences provides no tools for coping with such encounters or deriving meaning from them; it regards them as failures or breakdowns, and not as limitations within the model of dialogue itself.

The third failing was to conceive difference solely in the sense of categorical diversity. As Homi Bhabha and others argue, cultural difference can be taken in a different way: as a less stable, noncategorical dimension that is a feature of lived experience and identity.[19] From this standpoint, differences are enacted. They change over time. They take shape differently in varied contexts. They surpass our attempts to classify or define them. Ellsworth puts it well, that the purpose of dialogue is not just speaking across given positions of difference, but a relation in which those very positions can be (need to be) questioned. Difference, then, is more than a matter of multicultural diversity, of speaking within and across stable identities; it is a challenge to these in three ways, which I have sketched in more recent work as *differences within*, *differences beyond*, and *differences against*.[20] Respectively, these three phrases refer to the ways in which: (1) difference stands not only as an external feature of the "other," but as an unexplored and unrecognized dimension of one's self (for example, in the ways by which heterosexuality is defined and defended implicitly as *not-homosexual*, thereby invoking its "opposite" as a part of its own self-conception); (2) difference exceeds categories of understanding, challenging these in ways that confound conventional vocabularies and assumptions (for example, when racial categories such as "black" and "white" become denaturalized and subject to all sorts of redefinitions, including those of skin color themselves [no one actually has black or white skin], the conflating of racial with national or ethnic differences, the emphasis on hybrid, creole, or border identities, and so on); and (3) difference is defined by its resistance, defined against dominant norms, and its persistent refusal to allow itself to be characterized from dominant, conventional points of view. In each of these three ways difference poses a fundamental challenge to views of dialogue oriented around achieving understanding or agreement—each, in its own way, is a repudiation of convergent models of discourse generally, and each, in its own way, resists the categorical characterization of diversity—no category can possibly contain these sorts of difference.

It is possible to put the point even more strongly: that the effect of traditional views of dialogue has been to "domesticate" difference: to make it safe and comprehensible by regarding all differences as elements of mere variation (diversity), and hence as starting points of potential reconciliation. This is not a neutral standpoint, even as it represents itself as such; it misses deeper, more radical conceptions of difference.

Dialogue as Decontextualized Pedagogy

The crucial shift in perspective outlined here is from a prescriptive model of dialogue as a neutral communicative process, a procedure in which all participants are treated equally, concerned only with the search for knowledge, understanding, and perhaps agreement, to dialogue as a situated practice, one implicated by the particulars of who, when, where, and how the dialogue takes place. The elevation of dialogue as a general pedagogical method abstracts its operations from those particulars and, as noted earlier, treats deviations from that ideal as either illegitimate violations of its rules or as unfortunate shortcomings that can be remedied through the application of more of the same—continuing with dialogue until these failures of understanding or agreement can be remedied. Radical difference, difference that *resists* accommodation or assimilation, is rendered inexplicable or perverse. But when one examines the who, when, where, and how of dialogue, such characterizations become much more difficult to defend.[21]

Who. The first issue begins with the growing diversity of classrooms (at all levels of education) and the increasing awareness of the margins or borders of common school culture as it interacts with the very different values and orientations that students bring to the classroom. The conditions of globalization and mobility have promoted both direct forms of migration across national/cultural categories and (especially with the rise of communication and information technologies) an increasing proximity and interaction of multiple lines of national/cultural influence. In this context, the central assumptions of common schooling—of a canon of texts, of a shared historical tradition, of a common language—are thrown into question, since even where such elements might be defended, their value and significance are going to be regarded differently from different positions as teachers and students. In some cases they will be directly challenged. The shift to a dialogical approach, in itself, does not remedy these conflicts; and when more radical conceptions of difference are at stake, the very notion of "remedying" such conflicts and disagreements becomes deeply problematic.

A dialogue is not an engagement of two (or more) abstract persons, but of people with characteristics, styles, values, and assumptions that shape the particular ways in which they engage in discourse. Any prescriptive conception of dialogue must confront the challenge of acknowledging persons who do not engage in communication through those forms and who might in fact be excluded or disadvantaged by them. Conversely, an account of dialogue that acknowledges the enormous multiplicity of forms in which people from different cultures do enact pedagogical communicative relations (let alone communicative relations generally) needs to address the question of why some versions are rewarded with the prescriptive label "dialogue" and others are not.

Aside from the multiplicity of communicative forms, there is also a multiplicity of communicative purposes in dialogue. In many contexts, for example, the formation and negotiation of identity may constitute the primary purpose in mind for some participants in a dialogical relation, supplanting more overt teaching-learning goals. Such dynamics may be only partly intended or conscious (and hence only partly susceptible to reflection or change). Participation in dialogue, even at the microlevel of apparent personal "choice," is not *simply* a matter of choice. The utterances that comprise an ongoing dialogue are already made (or not made) in the context of an awareness of the reactions— real, anticipated, or imagined—of other participants. The more that one pushes this sort of analysis, the more the achievement, or suppression, of dialogical possibilities comes to be seen as an expression of a group interdynamic, and not something resulting simply from the choices and actions of individuals.

WHEN. We do not just use language; language uses us. As Bakhtin argued, the nature of discourse is that the language we encounter already has a history; the words that we speak have been spoken by others before us (he calls this "the internal dialogism of the word").[22] As a result, what we speak always means more than we mean to say; the language that we use carries with it implications, connotations, and consequences that we can only partly intend. The words that others hear from us, how they understand them, and what they say in response are beyond our unilateral control. The multivalence of discourse situates specific speech acts or relations in a web of potential significations that is indeterminate, nonlinear, and highly susceptible to the effects of context and cultural difference.

WHERE. Recent years have seen a growth of interest in such problems as situated cognition, group learning, the relation of expert and novice understandings, real-world problem solving, distributed intelligence, and a whole range of similar notions that address in different ways the actual means by which the learning of individuals occurs in the contexts of existing social relations and practice.

These concerns apply directly to the matter of dialogue. The situatedness of dialogue, considered as a discursive practice, means that the dialogical relation depends not only upon what people are saying to each other, but the context in which they come together (the classroom or the cafeteria, for example), where they are positioned in relation to each other (standing, sitting, or communicating on-line), and what other gestures or activities work with or against the grain of the interaction.

How. Another aspect of this situatedness, or materiality, is that the texts and objects of representation that mediate classroom discourse can have distinctive effects on what can be said and how it can be understood. Where interaction takes place in an immediate, face-to-face circumstance, these "texts" include not only the words themselves, but facial expressions, gestures, and similar representational forms. Yet dialogue often also takes place in mediated forms: a dialogue between a book's reader and its author; a dialogue between correspondents writing to one another; a dialogue over a telephone; a dialogue through e-mail; and so on. The tendency of previous accounts of dialogue has been to ignore such factors or, if they are considered at all, to relegate them to trivial significance compared to what the words themselves express. Yet substantial research across a range of fields has high-lighted the ways in which the circumstances of form and medium are *not* trivial but can influence what is said and how it is understood and the ways in which these media are signifying elements themselves.[23]

In these four ways, then, the prescriptive account of dialogue has been impeded by the formal, idealized models through which it has been characterized: impeded because these models have often not taken account of the situated, relational, material circumstances in which such discursive practices actually take place. Attending to the social dynamics and contexts of classroom discourse heightens the awareness of the complexities and difficulties of changing specific elements within larger communities of practice. These communities may be the primary shapers of teaching and learning processes, but not always in ways that serve intended or ideal educational objectives; other purposes, such as identity-formation or negotiating relations of group solidarity, may predominate. The power of such social processes may restrict lines of inquiry, distort dialogical interactions, and silence perspectives in ways that conflict with the explicit purposes of education.

Rethinking dialogue along these lines holds promise for developing theoretical accounts of dialogue that are richer, more complex, and better attuned to the material circumstances of pedagogical practice. Dialogue, from this standpoint, cannot be viewed simply as a form of question and answer, but as a relation constituted in a web of relations among multiple forms of communication, human practices, and mediating objects or texts.

Engaging the Criticisms: From Prescriptivism to the Practice of Dialogue

I would like to think that I am open to criticism and try to learn from my mistakes. Still, I persist in thinking that some of these very criticisms reinforce the value of "dialogue" in some sense, if in a very different sense from its conventional uses. I believe that this alternative view of dialogue begins by questioning two elements in most conventional views of dialogue: *prescriptivism* and *proceduralism*.[29] Questioning prescriptivism entails reflecting on the ways in which "dialogue" has become a kind of unquestioned ideal, a norm, and a rhetorical device. To invite others into dialogue is seen as unassailable gesture of good will. Who could criticize or reject such a gesture, except the ill-willed, the alienated, the recalcitrant? Such a stance, however, ignores the many ways in which this invitation may *not* be open-ended or neutral, or not experienced as such by others, even when it is intended to be. To enter into a conversation is to accept a set of tacit communicative norms; it is to run the (often asymmetrical) risks of disclosure; it is to undertake to explain one's self, perhaps justify one's self, under questioning; it is to submit to a set of assumptions about what "the subject" of the dialogue is about and what it is not. The point here is not that these commitments are *never* fair expectations to have of participants to a dialogue; it is to acknowledge that for many parties, under specific circumstances, they represent a kind of entrapment, a kind co-optation, in which some persons have more to lose than do others. From this standpoint the humanistic ideal of "engaging in dialogue" comes to be seen as subtly coercive, even threatening. And for theorists, such as myself, who have tended to favor persistence and "keeping the dialogue going" as prescriptive norms, this criticism provides a much-needed rebuke.

Alison Jones provides a fascinating analysis of this problem in practice. Juxtaposing the ideal versions of dialogical pedagogy with the realities of conversation in a class where she brings together Maori (native, minority culture) and Pakeha (European, dominant-culture) students in New Zealand, she notes that "an ideal dialogical model for the classroom asserts that stories and meanings of less powerful as well as more powerful groups will intermingle and 'be heard' in mutual communication and progressive understanding. . . . [It] assumes that the opportunity for subordinate groups to express themselves in the critical classroom becomes an opportunity for 'empowerment.'" But Jones shows how in practice even this apparently benevolent, receptive stance by those in relative positions of power can in fact reinscribe their privileges and advantages: "Border-crossing and 'recognitions of difference' turns out to be *access for dominant groups to the thoughts, cultures, lives of others.*

The second, related issue is the proceduralism of most accounts of dialogue: the characterization of dialogue in terms of a particular set of communicative norms and the response, when conflict or friction arises, that the resolution of these can (and should) take place through a reinvigorated application *of those same norms.* Yet here we encounter a paradox (the first of several to follow), one that begins to turn the discussion of dialogue into a different, more productive theoretical vein. For if questioning the restrictive norms of dialogue is regarded as a good thing, is it not at least in part so that a fuller, fairer, more inclusive dialogue might be made *possible?* If persons choose to withdraw from a dialogue with those who do not or cannot understand them, is it not in part so that they are able to enter a dialogue with others who *can* understand them? If "analytic dialogue" seeks (rightly, I would say) to uncover the nonneutral, historically specific conditions under which its own interpretations proceed, is this not so that others might *come to share the same understanding, at least in part, about these conditions?* It seems strange indeed to imagine a dialogue in which *every* understanding emerges as entirely idiosyncratic and separate from every other or one that is so persistently pulling up the roots of its own genealogy that the participants never talk *about* the topic at hand.

These criticisms, in turn, confront some of their own difficulties. The first of these is that the elevation of difference, while an invaluable corrective to those views of "communicative dialogue" that emphasize the pursuit of agreement, consensus, or understanding as the only legitimate outcomes of dialogue, cannot stand as an absolute principle in its stead. Agreement, consensus, or understanding (which, as I have discussed, are very different sorts of outcomes) may sometimes be unobtainable in dialogue, and—even where attainable—they may be problematic, provisional, and properly subject to questions concerning *how* and *on whose terms* they have been obtained. Fair enough. But Ellsworth often writes as if these were inherently undesirable outcomes, never justifiable as voluntary and intersubjective. This cannot be true, both as a matter of experience and of history, where such outcomes—even in the face of deep difference and conflict—have been satisfactorily arrived at, and as a matter of social and political principle, where there are occasions in which the pursuit of such outcomes, with all their risks of difficulty and failure, is the sole alternative to violent adjudications of conflict. What the theory of dialogue needs is a modulated account of where and when such outcomes can be secured and how to be suspicious of them *while also* recognizing their value for different groups' purposes. If asymmetrical and unequal power were always conditions that abrogated the value of human engagement (including communicative engagement), then there would be no legitimate engagements at all, because power is never entirely asymmetrical and unequal. And, as I tried to show earlier, alternatives such as "analytic dialogue" believe in the value of understanding and agreement too.

Second, and building upon this point, the corrective elevation of radical difference sometimes segues into the presumption of incommensurability. I have addressed this issue in other writings. In the face of radical difference, misunderstanding or nonunderstanding are certainly possibilities. Sometimes dialogue reaches an impasse. But this account, taken on its own, is an oversimplification. For one thing, misunderstanding is not an all-or-nothing state; in real, situated contexts, degrees of misunderstanding are mixed with degrees of understanding, and the practical question at hand is where and for what purposes (and for whom) the degree of understanding is sufficient for the purposes—including the educational purposes—at hand. Too much rhetorical ink has been spilled, in my view, drawing the false alternatives of a realist, objectivist view of dialogue centered on a single "Truth," and a radically incommensurable alternative in which all knowledge is politically contested and culturally idiosyncratic. We need to get beyond these useless alternatives, especially if we are to speak in any constructive way about *educational* interactions. The paradoxical challenge here is to recognize the excess of meaning, the *differend,* as Lyotard calls it, that may be beyond translation or comprehension in many, even most, communicative encounters and to realize that sometimes this excess may be of crucial import in adjudicating, or failing to adjudicate, a serious difference of belief or value, while at the same time recognizing the practical need to pursue the degrees of understanding appropriate to particular purposes, including educational purposes. Sometimes, indeed, this endeavor fails—and, as noted earlier, this failure can have crucial educational import in alerting us to the horizons of our own assumptions, to our own culpability in why the dialogue "failed," and to the possibility of considering a radically different way of approaching the world. But if one believed truly that such encounters always fail, it is unclear what meaning "education" could ever have.

Notes

1. This point has been defended by the present author, among others: Nicholas C. Burbules, *Dialogue in Teaching: Theory and Practice* (New York: Teachers College Press, 1993); Nicholas C. Burbules and Suzanne Rice, "Dialogue across Differences: Continuing the Conversation," *Harvard Educational Review,* vol. 61, no. 4 (1991): 393–416.
15. See Burbules and Rice, "Dialogue across Differences."
16. Cameron McCarthy, "Multicultural Discourses and Curriculum Reform: A Critical Perspective," *Educational Theory,* vol. 44, no. 1 (1994): 81–98.
17. Cosmopolitanism covers a broad range of views. For example, see Martha Nussbaum, "Citizens of the World," in Martha C. Nussbaum, *Cultivating Humanity: A Classical Defense of Reform in Liberal Education* (Cambridge, MA: Harvard University Press, 1997), 50–84. For a very different vision of cosmopolitanism, see Iris Marion Young, *Justice and the Politics of Difference* (Princeton, NJ: Princeton University Press, 1990), especially Chap. 8. Young directly challenges the ideal of cosmopolitanism conceived as a form of "universal citizenship": see "Polity and Group Difference," in *Throwing Like a Girl and Other Essays in Feminist Philosophical and Social Theory* (Bloomington, IN: Indiana University Press, 1990), 114–137.
18. In *Dialogue in Teaching,* I argue that there are at least four discrete types of dialogue: conversation, inquiry, instruction, and debate. Each exhibits characteristic forms of communicative interaction, each pursues distinct sorts of outcomes, and each has a different quality of tone or feel in relation.
19. Homi K. Bhabha, "Cultural Diversity and Cultural Difference," in *The Post-Colonial Studies Reader,* Bill Ashcroft, Gareth Griffiths, and Helen Tiffin, eds. (New York: Routledge, 1995), 206.

20. Nicholas C. Burbules, "A Grammar of Difference: Some Ways of Rethinking Difference and Diversity as Educational Topics," *Australian Education Researcher,* vol. 24, no. 1 (1997): 97–116.

21. Some of this material is adapted from Burbules and Bruce, "Theory and Research on Teaching as Dialogue."

22. Bakhtin, M. M., *The Dialogic Imagination,* M. Holquist, ed. (Austin, TX: University of Texas Press, 1981).

23. Nicholas C. Burbules, "Technology and Changing Educational Communities." *Educational Foundations,* vol. 10, no. 4 (1996): 21–32.

29. Some of this material is adapted from Nicholas C. Burbules, "Dialogue," in *Power/Knowledge and the Politics of Educational Meaning,* David Gabbard, ed. (New York: Erlbaum, forthcoming).

22

BELL HOOKS

Professor bell hooks witnessed and experienced social and racial discrimination during the 1950s and 1960s in the United States. Born in 1952 in Kentucky, she was educated at Stanford University and the University of Wisconsin, and she obtained a Ph.D. from the University of California, Santa Cruz, in 1983. She decided to change her birth name, Gloria Watkins, to that of her grandmother in order to honor her mother's and grandmother's heritage and to reclaim her voice and identity. Her name, Gloria, did not represent who she was. Furthermore, she also decided to de-capitalize her name for two main reasons: (1) capitalization of names accepts a power structure imposed by privilege and (2) readers should focus on her writing and ideas, not her name. In spite of being a professor, she has argued that intellectual work is not produced only in academia, and furthermore academia sometimes disables intellectuals who want to advance transformation through their work.

bell hooks is one of the most influential thinkers of African-American feminism in cultural studies, education, and social issues. Her analysis of classrooms is grounded also in a theoretical framework that draws from anti-colonial, feminist, and Freirean perspectives. She is a well-regarded contemporary public intellectual because of her thoughtfulness and provocative discussions on the connections among class, gender, race, ethnicity, and language.

At a young age, she started the production of her first book, *Ain't I a Woman: Black Women and Feminism* (1981), which questioned feminism as a movement of white, upper-middle-class women that chose to ignore race and ethnicity in the formation of gender identity. She criticized feminism for not recognizing the suffering of discrimination and marginalization among African-American women. Her book *Talking Back: Thinking Feminist, Thinking Black* was published in 1989.

Influenced by the work of Freire in education, she calls for an "engaged" pedagogy. In *Teaching to Transgress* (1994), hooks calls for dialogical pedagogies in the classroom. Furthermore, she exhorts educators to analyze relationships created in their classrooms in order to point out oppression, advance opportunities that encourage action, and transform unjust social, cultural, political, human, environmental, and global situations.

She has also written about popular culture themes. In her writing, she illustrates how her critical perspectives and philosophy systematically questioning and analyzing how power works to the advantage of some while constructing others such as women, minorities, and poor people, as inferior. One engaging aspect of hooks's writing is her style in a personal, first-person approach. She includes her own stories in her social and educational analysis. In 2003, she wrote a well-received book: *Teaching Community: A Pedagogy of Hope*. The power of her style manifests through the texts by describing meaningful personal experiences that explain some difficult concepts in relevant and connecting ways, using her text as a dialogue with the reader and as an engaging pedagogy.

REFERENCES

hooks, b. *Ain't I a Woman? Black Women and Feminism*. Boston: South End Press, 1981.

hooks, b. *Feminist Theory: From Margin to Center*. Boston: South End Press, 1984.

hooks, b. *Teaching to Transgress: Education as the Practice of Freedom*. New York: Routledge, 1994.

hooks, b. *All About Love: New Visions*. New York: Morrow, 2000.

hooks, b. *Teaching Community: A Pedagogy of Hope*. New York: Routledge, 2003.

EMBRACING CHANGE

Teaching in a Multicultural World

Despite the contemporary focus on multiculturalism in our society, particularly in education, there is not nearly enough practical discussion of ways classroom settings can be transformed so that the learning experience is inclusive. If the effort to respect and honor the social reality and experiences of groups in this society who are nonwhite is to be reflected in a pedagogical process, then as teachers—on all levels, from elementary to university settings—we must acknowledge that our styles of teaching may need to change. Let's face it: most of us were taught in classrooms where styles of teachings reflected the notion of a single norm of thought and experience, which we were encouraged to believe was universal. This has been just as true for nonwhite teachers as for white teachers. Most of us learned to teach emulating this model. As a consequence, many teachers are disturbed by the political implications of a multicultural education because they fear losing control in a classroom where there is no one way to approach a subject—only multiple ways and multiple references.

Among educators there has to be an acknowledgment that any effort to transform institutions so that they reflect a multicultural standpoint must take into consideration the fears teachers have when asked to shift their paradigms. There must be training sites where teachers have the opportunity to express those concerns while also learning to create ways to approach the multicultural classroom and curriculum. When I first went to Oberlin College, I was disturbed by what I felt was a lack of understanding on the apart of many professors as to what the multicultural classroom might be like. Chandra Mohanty, my colleague in Women's Studies, shared these concerns. Though we were both untenured, our strong belief that the Oberlin campus was not fully facing the issue of changing curriculum and teaching practices in ways that were progressive and promoting of inclusion led us to consider how we might intervene in this process. We proceeded from the standpoint that the vast majority of Oberlin professors, who are overwhelmingly white, were basically well-meaning, concerned about the quality of education students receive on our campus, and therefore likely to be supportive of any effort at education for critical consciousness. Together, we decided to have a group of seminars focusing on transformative pedagogy that would be open to all professors. Initially, students were also welcome, but we found that their presence inhibited honest discussion. On the first night, for example, several white professors made comments that could be viewed as horribly racist and the students left the group to share what was said around the college. Since our intent was to educate for critical conscious-ness, we did not want the seminar setting to be a space where anyone would feel attacked or their reputation as a teacher sullied. We did, how-ever, want it to be a space for constructive confrontation and critical inter-rogation. To ensure that this could happen, we had to exclude students.

At the first meeting, Chandra (whose background is in education) and I talked about the factors that had influenced our pedagogical prac-tices. I emphasized the impact of Freire's work on my thinking. Since my formative education took place in racially segregated schools, I spoke about the experience of learning when one's experience is recog-nized as central and significant and then how that changed with deseg-regation, when black children were forced to attend schools where we were regarded as objects and not subjects. Many of the professors pres-ent at the first meeting were disturbed by our overt discussion of politi-cal standpoints. Again and again, it was necessary to remind everyone that no education is politically neutral. Emphasizing that a white male professor in an English department who teaches only work by "great white men" is making a political decision, we had to work consistently against and through the overwhelming will on the part of folks to deny the politics of racism, sexism, heterosexism, and so forth that inform how and what we teach. We found again and again that almost every-one, especially the old guard, were more disturbed by the overt recog-nition of the role our political perspectives play in shaping pedagogy than by their passive acceptance of ways of teaching and learning that reflect biases, particularly a white supremacist standpoint.

To share in our efforts at intervention we invited professors from universities around the country to come and talk—both formally and informally—about the kind of work they were doing aimed at trans-forming teaching and learning so that a multicultural education would be possible. We invited then-Princeton professor of religion and philos-ophy Cornel West to give a talk on "decentering Western civilization." It was our hope that his very traditional training and his progressive practice as a scholar would give everyone a sense of optimism about our ability to change. In the informal session, a few white male professors were courageously outspoken in their efforts to say that they could accept the need for change, but were uncertain about the implications of the changes. This reminded us that it is difficult for individuals to shift paradigms and that there must be a setting for folks to voice fears, to talk about what they are doing, how they are doing it, and why. One of our most useful meetings was one in which we asked professors from different disciplines (including math and science) to talk informally about how their teaching had been changed by a desire to be more inclusive. Hearing individuals describe concrete strategies was an approach that helped dispel fears. It was crucial that more traditional or conservative professors who had been willing to make changes talk about motivations and strategies.

When the meetings concluded, Chandra and I initially felt a tremendous sense of disappointment. We had not realized how much faculty would need to unlearn racism, to learn about colonization and decolonization, and to fully appreciate the necessity for creating a democratic liberal arts learning experience.

All too often we found a will to include those considered "marginal" without a willingness to accord their work the same respect and consideration given other work. In Women's Studies, for example, individuals will often focus on women of color at the very end of the semester or lump everything about race and difference together in one section. This kind of tokenism is not multicultural transformation, but it is familiar to us as the change individuals are most likely to make. Let me give another example. What does it mean when a white female English professor is eager to include a work by Toni Morrison on the syllabus of her course but then teaches that work without ever making reference to race or ethnicity? I have heard individual white women "boast" about how they have shown students that black writers are "as good" as the white male canon when they do not call attention to race. Clearly, such pedagogy is not an interrogation of the biases conventional canons (if not all canons) establish, but yet another form of tokenism.

The unwillingness to approach teaching from a standpoint that includes awareness of race, sex, and class is often rooted in the fear that classrooms will be uncontrollable, that emotions and passions will not be contained. To some extent, we all know that whenever we address in the classroom subjects that students are passionate about there is always a possibility of confrontation, forceful expression of ideas, or even conflict. In much of my writing about pedagogy, particularly in classroom settings with great diversity, I have talked about the need to examine critically the way we as teachers conceptualize what the space for learning should be like. Many professors have conveyed to me their feeling that the classroom should be a "safe" place; that usually translates to mean that the professor lectures to a group of quiet students who respond only when they are called on. The experience of professors who educate for critical consciousness indicates that many students, especially students of color, may not feel at all "safe" in what appears to be a neutral setting. It is the absence of a feeling of safety that often promotes prolonged silence or lack of student engagement.

Making the classroom a democratic setting where everyone feels a responsibility to contribute is a central goal of transformative pedagogy. Throughout my teaching career, white professors have often voiced concern to me about nonwhite students who do not talk. As the classroom becomes more diverse, teachers are faced with the way the politics of domination are often reproduced in the educational setting. For example, white male students continue to be the most vocal in our classes. Students of color and some white women express fear that they will be judged as intellectually inadequate by these peers. I have taught brilliant students of color, many of them seniors, who have skillfully managed never to speak in classroom settings. Some express the feeling that they are less likely to suffer any kind of assault if they simply do not assert their subjectivity. They have told me that many professors never showed any interest in hearing their voices. Accepting the decentering of the West globally, embracing multiculturalism, compels educators to focus attention on the issue of voice. Who speaks? Who listens? And why? Caring about whether all students fulfill their responsibility to contribute to learning in the classroom is not a common approach in what Freire has called the "banking system of education" where students are regarded merely as passive consumers. Since so many professors teach from that standpoint, it is difficult to create the kind of learning community that can fully embrace multiculturalism. Students are much more willing to surrender their dependency on the banking system of education than are their teachers. They are also much more willing to face the challenge of multiculturalism.

It has been as a teacher in the classroom setting that I have witnessed the power of a transformative pedagogy rooted in a respect for multiculturalism. Working with a critical pedagogy based on my understanding of Freire's teaching, I enter the classroom with the assumption that we must build "community" in order to create a climate of openness and intellectual rigor. Rather than focusing on issues of safety, I think that a feeling of community creates a sense that there is shared commitment and a common good that binds us. What we all ideally share is the desire to learn—to receive actively knowledge that enhances our intellectual development and our capacity to live more fully in the world. It has been my experience that one way to build community in the classroom is to recognize the value of each individual voice. In my classes, students keep journals and often write paragraphs during class which they read to one another. This happens at least once irrespective of class size. Most of the classes I teach are not small. They range anywhere from thirty to sixty students, and at times I have taught more than one hundred. To hear each other (the sound of different voices), to listen to one another, is an exercise in recognition. It also ensures that no student remains invisible in the classroom. Some students resent having to make a verbal contribution, and so I have had to make it clear from the outset that this is a requirement in my classes. Even if there is a student present whose voice cannot be heard in spoken words, by "signing" (even if we cannot read the signs) they make their presence felt.

When I first entered the multicultural, multiethnic classroom setting I was unprepared. I did not know how to cope effectively with so much "difference." Despite progressive politics, and my deep engagement with the feminist movement, I had never before been compelled to work within a truly diverse setting and I lacked the necessary skills. This is the case with most educators. It is difficult for many educators in the United States to conceptualize how the classroom will look when they are confronted with the demographics which indicate that "whiteness" may cease to be the norm ethnicity in classroom settings on all levels. Hence, educators are poorly prepared when we actually confront diversity. This is why so many of us stubbornly cling to old patterns. As I worked to create teaching strategies that would make a space for multicultural learning, I found it necessary to recognize what I have called in other writing on pedagogy different "cultural codes." To teach effectively a diverse student body, I have to learn these codes. And so do students. This act alone transforms the classroom. The sharing of ideas and information does not always progress as quickly as it may in more homogeneous settings. Often, professors and students have to learn to accept different ways of knowing, new epistemologies, in the multicultural setting.

Just as it may be difficult for professors to shift their paradigms, it is equally difficult for students. I have always believed that students should enjoy learning. Yet I found that there was much more tension in the diverse classroom setting where the philosophy of teaching is rooted in critical pedagogy and (in my case) in feminist critical pedagogy. The presence of tension—and at times even conflict—often meant that students did not enjoy my classes or love me, their professor, as I secretly wanted them to do. Teaching in a traditional discipline from the perspective of critical pedagogy means that I often encounter students who make complaints like, "I thought this was supposed to be an English class, why are we talking so much about feminism?" (Or, they might add, race or class.) In the transformed classroom there is often a much greater need to explain philosophy, strategy, intent than in the "norm" setting. I have found through the years that many of my students who bitch endlessly while they are taking my classes contact me at a later date to talk about how much that experience meant to them, how much they learned. In my professorial role I had to surrender my need for immediate affirmation of successful teaching (even though some reward is immediate) and accept that students may not appreciate the value of a certain standpoint or process straightaway. The exciting aspect of creating a classroom community where there is respect for individual voices is that there is infinitely more feedback because students do feel free to talk—and talk back. And, yes, often this feedback is critical. Moving away from the need for immediate affirmation was crucial to my growth as a teacher. I learned to respect that shifting paradigms or sharing knowledge in new ways challenges; it takes time for students to experience that challenge as positive.

Students taught me, too, that it is necessary to practice compassion in these new learning settings. I have not forgotten the day a student came to class and told me: "We take your class. We learn to look at the world from a critical standpoint, one that considers race, sex, and class. And we can't enjoy life anymore." Looking out over the class, across race, sexual preference, and ethnicity, I saw students nodding their heads. And I saw for the first time that there can be, and usually is, some degree of pain involved in giving up old ways of thinking and knowing and learning new approaches. I respect that pain. And I include recognition of it now when I teach, that is to say, I teach about shifting paradigms and talk about the discomfort it can cause. White students learning to think more critically about questions of race and racism may go home for the holidays and suddenly see their parents in a different light. They may recognize nonprogressive thinking, racism, and so on, and it may hurt them that new ways of knowing may create estrangement where there was none. Often when students return from breaks I ask them to share with us how ideas that they have learned or worked on in the classroom impacted on their experience outside. This gives them both the opportunity to know that difficult experiences may be common and practice at integrating theory and practice: ways of knowing with habits of being. We practice interrogating habits of being as well as ideas. Through this process we build community.

Despite the focus on diversity, our desires for inclusion, many professors still teach in classrooms that are predominantly white. Often a spirit of tokenism prevails in those settings. This is why it is so crucial that "whiteness" be studied, understood, discussed—so that everyone learns that affirmation of multiculturalism, and an unbiased inclusive perspective, can and should be present whether or not people of color are present. Transforming these classrooms is as great a challenge as learning how to teach well in the setting of diversity. Often, if there is one lone person of color in the classroom she or he is objectified by others and forced to assume the role of "native informant." For example, a novel is read by a Korean American author. White students turn to the one student from a Korean background to explain what they do not understand. This places an unfair responsibility onto that student. Professors can intervene in this process by making it clear from the outset that experience does not make one an expert, and perhaps even by explaining what it means to place someone in the role of "native informant." It must be stated that professors cannot intervene if they also see students as "native informants." Often, students have come to my office complaining about the lack of inclusion in another professor's class. For example, a course on social and political thought in the United States includes no work by women. When students complain to the teacher about this lack of inclusion, they are told to make suggestions of material that can be used. This often places an unfair burden on a student. It also makes it seem that it is only important to address a bias if there is someone complaining. Increasingly, students are making complaints because they want a democratic unbiased liberal arts education.

Multiculturalism compels educators to recognize the narrow boundaries that have shaped the way knowledge is shared in the classroom. It forces us all to recognize our complicity in accepting and perpetuating biases of any kind. Students are eager to break through barriers to knowing. They are willing to surrender to the wonder of re-learning and learning ways of knowing that go against the grain. When we, as educators, allow our pedagogy to be radically changed by our recognition of a multicultural world, we can give students the education they desire and deserve. We can teach in ways that transform consciousness, creating a climate of free expression that is the essence of a truly liberatory liberal arts education.

PAULO FREIRE

This is a playful dialogue with myself, Gloria Watkins, talking with bell hooks, my writing voice. I wanted to speak about Paulo and his work in this way for it afforded me an intimacy—a familiarity—I do not find it possible to achieve in the essay. And here I have found a way to share the sweetness, the solidarity I talk about.

Watkins:

> Reading your books *Ain't I a Woman: Black Women and Feminism,*
> *Feminist Theory: From Margin to Center,* and *Talking Back,* it is clear
> that your development as a critical thinker has been greatly influenced by the work of Paulo Freire. Can you speak about why his work has touched your life so deeply?

hooks:

> Years before I met Paulo Freire, I had learned so much from his work, learned new ways of thinking about social reality that were liberatory. Often when university students and professors read Freire, they approach his work from a voyeuristic stand-

point, where as they read they see two locations in the work, the subject position of Freire the educator (whom they are often more interested in than the ideas or subjects he speaks about) and the oppressed/marginalized groups he speaks about. In relation to these two subject positions, they position themselves as observers, as outsiders. When I came to Freire's work, just at that moment in my life when I was beginning to question deeply and profoundly the politics of domination, the impact of racism, sexism, class exploitation, and the kind of domestic colonization that takes place in the United States, I felt myself to be deeply identified with the marginalized peasants he speaks about, or with my black brothers and sisters, my comrades in Guinea-Bissau. You see, I was coming from a rural southern black experience, into the university, and I had lived through the struggle for racial desegregation and was in resistance without having a political language to articulate that process. Paulo was one of the thinkers whose work gave me a language. He made me think deeply about the construction of an identity in resistance. There was this one sentence of Freire's that became a revolutionary mantra for me: "We cannot enter the struggle as objects in order later to become subjects." Really, it is difficult to find words adequate to explain how this statement was like a locked door—and I struggled within myself to find the key—and that struggle engaged me in a process of critical thought that was transformative. This experience positioned Freire in my mind and heart as a challenging teacher whose work furthered my own struggle against the colonizing process—the colonizing mind-set.

GW: In your work, you indicate an ongoing concern with the process of decolonization, particularly as it affects African Americans living within the white supremacist culture of the United States. Do you see a link between the process of decolonization and Freire's focus on "conscientization"?

bh: Oh, absolutely. Because the colonizing forces are so powerful in this white supremacist capitalist patriarchy, it seems that black people are always having to renew a commitment to a decolonizing political process that should be fundamental to our lives and is not. And so Freire's work, in its global understanding of liberation struggles, always emphasizes that this is the important initial

stage of transformation—that historical moment when one begins
to think critically about the self and identity in relation to one's
political circumstance. Again, this is one of the concepts in Freire's
work—and in my own work—that is frequently misunderstood
by readers in the United States. Many times people will say to me
that I seem to be suggesting that it is enough for individuals to
change how they think. And you see, even their use of the *enough*
tells us something about the attitude they bring to this question. It
has a patronizing sound, one that does not convey any heartfelt
understanding of how a change in attitude (though not a completion of any transformative process) can be significant for colo-
nized/oppressed people. Again and again Freire has had to
remind readers that he never spoke of conscientization as an end
itself, but always as it is joined by meaningful praxis. In many different ways Freire articulates this. I like when he talks about the
necessity of verifying in praxis what we know in consciousness:

> That means, and let us emphasize it, that human beings do not
> get beyond the concrete situation, the condition in which they find
> themselves, only by their consciousness or their intentions—
> however good those intentions may be. The possibilities that I had
> for transcending the narrow limits of a five-by-two-foot cell in
> which I was locked after the April 1964 coup d'etat were not suffi-
> cient to change my condition as a prisoner. I was always in the cell,
> deprived of freedom, even if I could imagine the outside world. But
> on the other hand, the praxis is not blind action, deprived of inten-
> tion or of finality. It is action and reflection. Men and women are
> human beings because they are historically constituted as beings of
> praxis, and in the process they have become capable of transforming
> the world—of giving it meaning.

I think that so many progressive political movements fail to have
lasting impact, in the United States precisely because there is not
enough understanding of "praxis." This is what touches me about
Antonio Faundez asserting in *Learning to Question* that

> one of the things we learned in Chile in our early reflection on
> everyday life was that abstract political, religious or moral state-
> ments did not take concrete shape in acts by individuals. We were
> revolutionaries in the abstract, not in our daily lives. It seems to me
> essential that in our individual lives, we should day to day live out
> what we affirm.

It always astounds me when progressive people act as though it is somehow a naive moral position to believe that our lives must be a living example of our politics.

GW: There are many readers of Freire who feel that the sexist language in his work, which went unchanged even after the challenge of contemporary feminist movement and feminist critique, is a negative example. When you first read Freire what was your response to the sexism of his language?

bh: There has never been a moment when reading Freire that I have not remained aware of not only the sexism of the language but the way he (like other progressive Third World political leaders, intellectuals, critical thinkers such as Fanon, Memmi, etc.) constructs a phallocentric paradigm of liberation—wherein freedom and the experience of patriarchal manhood are always linked as though they are one and the same. For me this is always a source of anguish for it represents a blind spot in the vision of men who have profound insight. And yet, I never wish to see a critique of this blind spot overshadow anyone's (and feminists' in particular) capacity to learn from the insights. This is why it is difficult for me to speak about sexism in Freire's work; it is difficult to find a language that offers a way to frame critique and yet maintain the recognition of all that is valued and respected in the work. It seems to me that the binary opposition that is so much embedded in Western thought and language makes it nearly impossible to project a complex response. Freire's sexism is indicated by the language in his early works, notwithstanding that there is so much that remains liberatory. There is no need to apologize for the sexism. Freire's own model of critical pedagogy invites a critical interrogation of this flaw in the work. But critical interrogation is not the same as dismissal.

GW: So you see no contradiction in your valuing of Freire's work and your commitment to feminist scholarship?

bh: It is feminist thinking that empowers me to engage in a constructive critique of Freire's work (which I needed so that as a young reader of his work I did not passively absorb the worldview presented) and yet there are many other standpoints from which I approach his work that enable me to experience its value, that make it possible for that work to touch me at the very core of my being. In talking with academic feminists (usually white women) who feel they must either dismiss or devalue the work of Freire because of sexism, I see clearly how our different responses are shaped by the standpoint that we bring to the work. I came to Freire thirsty, dying of thirst (in that way that the colonized, marginalized subject who is still unsure of how to break the hold of the status quo, who longs for change, is needy, is thirsty), and I found in his work (and the work of Malcolm X, Fanon, etc.) a way to quench that thirst. To have work that promotes one's liberation is such a powerful gift that it does not matter so much if the gift is flawed. Think of the work as water that contains some dirt. Because you are thirsty you are not too proud to extract the dirt and be nourished by the water. For me this is an experience that corresponds very much to the way individuals of privilege respond to the use of water in the First World context. When you are privileged, living in one of the richest countries in the world, you can waste resources. And you can especially justify your disposal of something that you consider impure. Look at what most people do with water in this country. Many people purchase special water because they consider tap water unclean—and of course this purchasing is a luxury. Even our ability to see the water that come through the tap as unclean is itself informed by an imperialist consumer perspective. It is an expression of luxury and not just simply a response to the condition of water. If we approach the drinking of water that comes from the tap from a global perspective we would have to talk about it differently. We would have to consider what the vast majority of the people in the world who are thirsty must do to obtain water. Paulo's work has been living water for me.

GW: To what extent do you think your experience as an African American has made it possible for you to relate to Freire's work?

bh: As I already suggested, growing up in a rural area in the agrarian south, among black people who worked the land, I felt intimately linked to the discussion of peasant life in Freire's work and its relation to literacy. You know there are no history books that really tell the story of how difficult the politics of everyday life was for black people in the racially segregated south when so many folks did not read and were so often dependent on racist people to explain, to read, to write. And I was among a generation learning those skills, with an accessibility to education that was still new. The emphasis on education as necessary for liberation that black people made in slavery and then on into reconstruction informed our lives. And so Freire's emphasis on education as the practice of freedom made such immediate sense to me. Conscious of the need for literacy from girlhood, I took with me to the university memories of reading to folks, of writing for folks. I took with me memories of black teachers in the segregated school system who had been critical pedagogues providing us liberatory paradigms. It was this early experience of a liberatory education in Booker T. Washington and Crispus Attucks, the black schools of my formative years, that made me forever dissatisfied with the education I received in predominantly white settings. And it was educators like Freire who affirmed that the difficulties I had with the banking system of education, with an education that in no way addressed my social reality, were an important critique. Returning to the discussion of feminism and sexism, I want to say that I felt myself included in *Pedagogy of the Oppressed,* one of the first Freire books I read, in a way that I never felt myself—in my experience as a rural black person—included in the first feminist books I read, works like *The Feminine Mystique* and *Born Female.* In the United States we do not talk enough about the way in which class shapes our perspective on reality. Since so many of the early feminist books really reflected a certain type of white bourgeois sensibility, this work did not touch many black women deeply; not because we did not recognize the common experiences women shared, but because those commonalities were mediated by profound differences in our realities created by the politics of race and class.

GW: Can you speak about the relationship between Freire's work and the development of your work as feminist theorist and social critic?

bh: Unlike feminist thinkers who make a clear separation between the work of feminist pedagogy and Freire's work and thought, for me these two experiences converge. Deeply committed to feminist pedagogy, I find that, much like weaving a tapestry, I have taken threads of Paulo's work and woven it into that version of feminist pedagogy I believe my work as writer and teacher embodies. Again, I want to assert that it was the intersection of Paulo's thought and the lived pedagogy of the many black teachers of my girlhood (most of them women) who saw themselves as having a liberatory mission to educate us in a manner that would prepare us to effectively resist racism and white supremacy, that has had a profound impact on my thinking about the art and practice of teaching. And though these black women did not openly advocate feminism (if they even knew the word) the very fact that they insisted on academic excellence and open critical thought for young black females was an antisexist practice.

GW: Be more specific about the work you have done that has been influenced by Freire.

bh: Let me say that I wrote *Ain't I a Woman: Black Women and Feminism* when I was an undergraduate (though it was not published until years later). This book was the concrete manifestation of my struggle with the question of moving from object to subject—the very question Paulo had posed. And it is so easy, now that many, if not most, feminist scholars are willing to recognize the impact of race and class as factors that shape female identity, for everyone to forget that early on feminist movement was not a location that welcomed the radical struggle of black women to theorize our subjectivity. Freire's work (and that of many other teachers) affirmed my right as a subject in resistance to define my reality. His writing gave me a way to place the politics of racism in the United States in a global context wherein I could see my fate linked with that of colonized black people everywhere struggling to decolonize, to transform society. More than in the work of many white bourgeois feminist thinkers, there was always in Paulo's work recognition of the subject position of those most disenfranchised, those who suffer the gravest weight of oppressive forces (with the exception of his not acknowledging always the specific gendered realities of oppression and exploitation). This was a standpoint which affirmed my own desire to work from a lived understanding of the lives of poor black women. There has been only in recent years a body of scholarship in the United States that does not look at the lives of black people through a bourgeois lens, a fundamentally radical scholarship that suggests that indeed the experience of black people, black females, might tell us more about the experience of women in general than simply an analysis that looks first, foremost, and always at those women who reside in privileged locations. One of the reasons that Paulo's book, *Pedagogy in Process: The Letters to Guinea-Bissau,* has been important for my work is that it is a crucial example of how a privileged critical thinker approaches sharing knowledge and resources with those who are in need. Here is Paulo at one of those insightful moments. He writes:

> Authentic help means that all who are involved help each other mutually, growing together in the common effort to understand the reality which they seek to transform. Only through such praxis—in which those who help and those who are being helped help each other simultaneously—can the act of helping become free from the distortion in which the helper dominates the helped.

In American society where the intellectual—and specifically the black intellectual—has often assimilated and betrayed revolutionary concerns in the interest of maintaining class power, it is crucial and necessary for insurgent black intellectuals to have an ethics of struggle that informs our relationship to those black people who have not had access to ways of knowing shared in locations of privilege.

GW: Comment, if you will, on Freire's willingness to be critiqued, especially by feminist thinkers.

bh: In so much of Paulo's work there is a generous spirit, a quality of open-mindedness that I feel is often missing from intellectual and academic arenas in U.S. society, and feminist circles have not been an exception. Of course, Paulo seems to grow more open as he ages. I, too, feel myself more strongly committed to a practice of open-mindedness, a willingness to engage critique as I age, and I think the way we experience more profoundly the growing fascism in the world, even in so-called "liberal" circles, reminds us that our lives, our work, must be an example. In Freire's work in the last few years there are many responses to the critiques made of his writing. And there is that lovely critical exchange between him and Antonio Faundez in *Learning to Question* on the question of language, on Paulo's work in Guinea-Bissau. I learn from this example, from seeing his willingness to struggle non-defensively in print, naming short-comings of insight, changes in thought, new critical reflections.

GW: What was it like for you to interact personally with Paulo Freire?

bh: For me our meeting was incredible; it made me a devoted student and comrade of Paulo's for life. Let me tell you this story. Some years ago now, Paulo was invited to the University of Santa Cruz, where I was then a student and teacher. He came to do workshops with Third World students and faculty and to give a public lecture. I had not heard even a whisper that he was coming, though many folks knew how much his work meant to me. Then somehow I found out that he was coming only to be told that all the slots were filled for participants in the workshop. I protested. And in the ensuing dialogue, I was told that I had not been invited to the various meetings for fear that I would disrupt the discussion of more important issues by raising feminist critiques. Even though I was allowed to participate when someone dropped out at the last minute, my heart was heavy because already I felt that there had been this sexist attempt to control my voice, to control the encounter. So, of course, this created a war within myself because indeed I did want to interrogate Paulo Freire personally about the sexism in his work. And so with courtesy, I forged ahead at the meeting. Immediately individuals spoke against me raising these questions and devalued their importance, Paulo intervened to say that these questions were crucial and he addressed them. Truthfully, I loved him at this moment for exemplifying by his actions the principles of his work. So much would have changed for me had he tried to silence or belittle a feminist critique. And it was not enough for me that he owned his "sexism," I want to know why he had not seen that this aspect of earlier work be changed, be responded to in writing by him. And he spoke then about making more of a public effort to speak and write on these issues—this has been evident in his later work.

GW: Were you more affected by his presence than his work?

bh: Another great teacher of mine (even though we have not met) is the Vietnamese Buddhist monk Thich Nhat Hanh. And he says in *The Raft Is Not the Shore* that "great humans bring with them something like a hallowed atmosphere, and when we seek them out, then we feel peace, we feel love, we feel courage." His words appropriately define what it was like for me to be in the presence of Paulo. I spend hours alone with him, talking, listening to music, eating ice cream at my favorite cafe. Seriously, Thich Nhat Hanh teaches that a certain milieu is born at the same time as a great teacher. And he says:

> When you [the teacher] come and stay one hour with us, you bring that milieu. . . . It is as though you bring a candle into the room. The candle is there; there is a kind of light-zone you bring in. When a sage is there and you sit near him, you feel light, you feel peace.

The lesson I learned from witnessing Paulo embody the practice he describes in theory was profound. It entered me in a way that writing can never touch one and it gave me courage. It has not been easy for me to do the work I do and reside in the academy (lately I think it has become almost impossible) but one is inspired to persevere by the witness of others. Freire's presence inspired me. And it was not that I did not see sexist behavior on his part, only that these contradictions are embraced as part of the learning process, part of what one struggles to change—and that struggle is often protracted.

GW: Have you anything more to say about Freire's response to feminist critique?

bh: I think it important and significant that despite feminist critiques of his work, which are often harsh, Paulo recognizes that he must play a role in feminist movements. This he declares in *Learning to Question:*

> If the women are critical, they have to accept our contribution as men, as well as the workers have to accept our contribution as intellectuals, because it is a duty and right that I have to participate in the transformation of society. Then, if the women must have the main responsibility in their struggle they have to know that their struggle also belongs to us, that is, to those men who don't accept the machista position in the world. The same is true of racism. As an apparent white man, because I always say that I am not quite sure of my whiteness, the question is to know if I am really against racism in a radical way. If I am, then I have a duty and a right to fight with black people against racism.

GW: Does Freire continue to influence your work? There is not the constant mention of him in your latest work as was the case with the first books.

bh: Though I may not quote Freire as much, he still teaches me. When I read *Learning to Question,* just at a time when I had begun to engage in critical reflections on black people and exile, there was so much there about the experience of exile that helped me. And I was thrilled with the book. It had a quality of that dialogue that is a true gesture of love that Paulo speaks about in other work. So it was from reading this book that I decided that it would be useful to do a dialogical work with the philosopher Cornel West. We have what Paulo calls "a talking book," *Breaking Bread.* Of course my great wish is to do such a book with Paulo. And then for some time I have been working on essays on death and dying, particularly African American ways of dying. Then just quite serendipitously I was searching for an epigraph for this work, and came across these lovely passages from Paulo that echo so intimately my own worldview that it was as though, to use an old southern phrase, "My tongue was in my friend's mouth." He writes:

> I like to live, to live my life intensely. I am the type of person who loves his life passionately. Of course, someday, I will die, but I have the impression that when I die, I will die intensely as well. I will die experimenting with myself intensely. For this reason I am going to die with an immense longing for life, since this is the way I have been living.

GW: Yes! I can hear you saying those very words. Any last comments?

bh: Only that words seem to be not good enough to evoke all that I have learned from Paulo. Our meeting had that quality of sweetness that lingers, that lasts for a lifetime; even if you never speak to the person again, see their face, you can always return in your heart to that moment when you were together to be renewed—that is a profound solidarity.

23

DAVID KENNEDY

David Kennedy (born 1943) is a leading international theorist of childhood. He began his career as the curriculum director of the Berea (Kentucky) Children's Center, (1982–1988) and has held faculty positions at Northern Michigan University (1989–1993) and Western Carolina University (1993–1996). He is currently professor in the Educational Foundations Department at Montclair State University. Kennedy's research interests are distinguished by two concerns. First, he explores the relationship between childhood and philosophy, urging educators to understand and appreciate the standpoint of the child. Second, he seeks to identify educational settings and teaching practices that do justice to the standpoint of the child by acknowledging the inherent ambiguity of adult-child relations.

Kennedy's scholarly concerns are motivated by a desire to confront and overcome "ageism." Ageism, in Kennedy's view, operates like other forms of institutionalized discrimination, such as racism or sexism. For example, it is a reaction to difference that fulfills deep psychological, sociological, and political needs. Put simply, ageism generalizes and essentializes the identity of children—and, as a consequence, "adults"—framing all of society's interactions with children. Regardless of whether childhood is demonized or romanticized, ageism robs children of the right to negotiate their identity in their interpersonal relationships with others. In light of what we know about the dehumanizing effects of racism and sexism, Kennedy encourages us to think critically about how we conceptualize children today, and how we might reconceptualize them in the future.

To support his argument, Kennedy charts the changing conceptions of childhood in Western history. He employs a unique methodology that includes philosophical analysis, psychoanalytic interpretation, genealogy, and cultural studies. He uses representations of children in ancient mythology, religious iconography, poetry, and the visual arts to understand how the figure of the child has shifted over time. He connects shifts in "the child" with changes in our thinking about adulthood. As "childhood" and "adulthood" are terms that define each other, this implies that the study of childhood involves critical reflection on what it means to be an adult and to have adult responsibilities. Childhood studies move us to a consideration of the social relations between the young and the old within home, school, and community.

In the final chapter of *The Well of Being: Childhood, Subjectivity and Education*, Kennedy reconstructs the school to be a dynamic and open place that maximizes and encourages dialogue among administrators, academics, teachers, parents, children, and members of the larger community. He envisages a school that has permeable boundaries— between outside and inside, administration and education, education and recreation—and is populated with meeting rooms and passageways that facilitate emergent and differentiated activities, as well as fluid transitions between them. Kennedy views the school as an opportunity for intergenerational and intervocational dialogue: there is learning by children from other children; by adults from children; by adults from other adults; and by children from adults. The model for dialogue is based on a Socratic method of questioning combined with a pragmatic emphasis on reconstructive experience, as found in John Dewey's laboratory school. In the context of adult-child dialogue, the unique standpoint of the child is not repressed but considered an important resource for developing critical perspectives on the world and our future actions in it.

Kennedy advances his argument by claiming that dialogue is not only instrumental, but also *paradigmatic*, for identity. He cites rapid advances in new technologies—such as the Internet (chat rooms, e-mail, blogs, information sharing) and robotics—as instantiation and evidence for this revolution in human consciousness. Kennedy believes that we are now less likely to conceive of ourselves as discrete "subjects" engaged in oppositional encounters with one another and the world of "objects"—if we ever thought of ourselves in this way. He advocates a conception of the human as "intersubject." To be an intersubject is to participate in forms of relational subjectivity that involve constant exploration and interaction with others, in the absence of fixed and impermeable boundaries.

Overall, Kennedy's analysis urges us to reflect on how our conception of childhood affects classroom practices. As suggested in the introduction to this volume, understanding childhood is a key question that cannot be answered with reference to science alone but must also have a philosophical or speculative dimension. Thus, if we think of children as inherently good or inherently bad or perhaps blank slates ready to be filled up with adult knowledge, our classroom activities will change, as will our interaction with children. But to think through our assumptions concerning children is to ultimately reflect on ourselves as adult educators. As such, Kennedy's question is really a question concerning self-knowledge and its relationship to teaching and learning.

REFERENCES

Kennedy, David. "Communal Philosophical Dialogue and the Intersubject." *International Journal for Philosophical Practice* 18, no. 2 (2004):

Kennedy, David. *The Well of Being: Childhood, Subjectivity, and Education.* New York: SUNY Press, 2006.

Kennedy, David, and Pavel Lushun. "Power, Manipulation, and Control in a Community of Inquiry. *Analytic Teaching* 23, no. 2 (2003): 103–10.

THE ROOTS OF CHILD STUDY: PHILOSOPHY, HISTORY, AND RELIGION

Introduction: What Is the Philosophy of Childhood?

Child study as an academic activity is usually thought of as the natural domain of pediatrics, psychology, sociology, and education. But with the exception of education, none of those disciplines are more than a few hundred years old, and children have been around somewhat longer than that. Some philosophers of childhood go so far as to see the historical hegemony of psychology and sociology in child study that arose at the turn of the twentieth century as an impediment to genuine inquiry, because, like their hard science counterparts, they are so implicitly wedded to socially instrumental aims. Valerie Polokow, for example, speaks in The Erosion of Childhood (1982) of "the plethora of social psychological epistemologies" that "all attest in varying degrees to the impositional structures of consciousness that an adult world of 'experts' has unquestioningly brought to bear upon this life phase of childhood . . ." (p. 21). Gareth Matthews, in a recent book entitled The Philosophy of Childhood (1996), warns us about the epistemological status of scientific models of childhood. "We should be on the lookout," he says, "for what a given model may encourage us to overlook, or misunderstand, as well as for what the model may help us to understand better" (p. 26).

Neither Polokow nor Matthews is objecting to the scientific study of childhood per se, but to a form of human science that is not philosophically reflective—that does not examine its own assumptions, and thereby becomes a form of cultural imposition. One task of the philosophy of childhood is to reveal and clarify those assumptions. To do so promises to disentangle the study of childhood from its institutional matrix in the scientific establishment, at least to the extent to which the latter naively serves the prevailing social, economic, and political order. The outcomes of this project of disentanglement have potentially far-reaching practical implications for the future of child rearing, education, and the way adults think about children's rights.

The philosophy of childhood may be thought of as a subregion of the philosophy of persons. It emerges at a moment in the history of the field when the critique of Western metaphysics is paralleled by the critique of white adult male hegemony in the philosophical tradition and by an opening to "voices from the margins," including those of women and of non-Western forms of knowledge.

The philosophy of childhood tends to fall within two realms of discourse. First, it is an inquiry into what adults can know about children and the experience of childhood. This is represented by questions like: What is it to be a child? Just what kind of difference is the difference between children and adults? To what extent is childhood as we know it a historical and cultural construct? What are the hidden or unexamined assumptions underlying the explanatory constructs that adults apply to children? How does the construct "childhood" function in adult self-understanding, and in the history of culture and thought? What are the similarities and differences between the ways children and adults know the world?

The second realm of the philosophy of childhood is related to the first through this last question about knowledge. If children, for whatever reasons, do know the world differently—if children's knowledge is not just a weaker, or sketchier, or more rudimentary version of adults'—then what can they tell us? This is where the notion of child as a voice from the margins, hitherto excluded from adult discourse, and therefore from adult self-understanding, comes in.

The concepts "child" and "adult" are a mutually necessary contrastive pair. As there is no notion of "old" without a notion of "young," "child" is unthinkable apart from "adult." If everyone were born and remained "children," the term would no longer have any meaning; the same is true if we were all born and remained "adults." Thus, any philosophical inquiry into childhood is also necessarily an inquiry into adulthood. The concrete implications of this reflexive aspect of the inquiry into childhood are particularly significant, for they suggest that the adult who understands children and the conditions of childhood better understands him- or herself. Improved self-understanding leads to the possibility of a positive evolution of the adult-child relation in society; and it follows from the polar structure of the relation that adults who learn to identify and serve the needs of children with more sensitivity and precision learn to do so for each other as well.

The philosophy of childhood is both enriched and complicated by the discovery that childhood has meant and can mean different things to children and adults in different cultures and historical periods. The widespread documentation of variations in the cultural meanings of childhood began with the rise of cultural anthropology early in the twentieth century; the historical dimension has only begun to be investigated in the last 30 years, in the new field of study called history of childhood (Bellingham, 1988; Elder, et al, 1993; Hunt, 1970; Sommerville, 1982). To discover that "childhood" is at least to some degree a historically and culturally mediated social construct is to question, first of all, to just what degree it can be mediated. How much can childhood change over time, or differ from culture to culture, and still be what we call childhood? Are there clear and unambiguous universal criteria for calling someone a child? Is childhood a "hard" category, or could we imagine a culture or historical period in which either children thought, felt, and acted more like adults, or, conversely, adults thought, felt, and acted more like children? Just what do we mean by the current phrase, "disappearance of childhood" (Postman, 1982)?

The questions raised by our contemporary situation of ever-increasing cultural and historical intervisibility also touch on gender construction. Are children "male" and "female" in the same way that adults are? What are the limits of difference in the gendering of the two sexes, and what is the role of childhood in the gendering process? Then there is the question of just what drives and patterns historical change in the way adults construct and reconstruct childhood. Can we call the change we have noticed so far an "evolution"? (deMause, 1974). Can we make normative judgments about what constitutes positive change? Finally, if "child" and "adult" are indeed in polar conceptual relation, it follows that if childhood changes and varies, so necessarily does adulthood. If this is the case, what is the calculus of that mutual change? Is there some normative balance between the two that we recognize as inherently good, ethical, healthy, functional, etc.? Is there an inherent teleology of the adult-child relation? Is there a "model" adult? Is there a "model" child? If so, how are the two related?

The questions triggered by historical and cross-cultural inquiry into childhood move us beyond the philosophy of childhood in any narrow academic sense of the term "philosophy." They imply a further inquiry into the representation of children and childhood by adults in social and cultural history, in mythology and the history of spirituality, in the history of art and literature, in psychoanalytic theory, and in the history of science and of education. The images of children that we find in these fields are myriad and suggestive—for example the "divine child" archetype of ancient myth and Jungian psychology (Jung, 1963); the character of Pearl in Hawthorne's (1994/1850) Scarlet Letter; the representation of children in the photography of Ralph Meatyard (1970), or Sally Mann (1993); Freud's notion of the psychosexual stages of early childhood (Freud, 1957), or Emerson's (1965) characterization of infancy as the "perpetual Messiah." All of these images have an iconographic function: in each characterization, "child" functions symbolically as a carrier of deep assumptions about human nature and its potential variability and changeability, about the construction of human subjectivity, about the ultimate meaning of the human life cycle, and about human forms of knowledge.

The Child of the Philosophers

Looking back to the foundations of the Western philosophical tradition, the child does not fare particularly well in adult male construction (we do not hear from the females). Plato (1941) considered children—along with women, slaves, and the "inferior multitude"—to be liable to the "great mass of multifarious appetites and pleasures and pains" (p. 125) of the naturally immoderate. In his influential construal of the human soul as a dynamic combination—or "community"—of reason, will, and appetite, children are exemplars of the untamed appetite and the uncontrolled will. "They are full of passionate feelings from their very birth" (p. 138). The "boy, . . . just because he more than any other has a fount of intelligence in him which has not yet 'run clear,'. . . is the craftiest, most mischievous, and unruliest of brutes. So the creature must be held in check. . . ." (1961, p. 1379). For Plato, children's only virtue appears to be that they are "easily molded," that is, they are capable of being made into adults.

Aristotle (1962) develops Plato's argument by showing just how the community of self is skewed in children. The preponderance of the appetitive nature in childhood either leads to or is a result of the lack of the capacity of choice, or "moral agency," meaning the ability to deliberately engage in an action toward a final end, or "some kind of activity of the soul in conformity with virtue." For this reason the child cannot be called "happy"; and if we do call him happy, "we do so by reason of the hopes we have for his future" (1962, p. 23).

Aristotle seems to be engaging in something like what Erik Erikson (1965) called "subspeciation," or the attribution of ontological difference to racial, ethnic, or cultural variations, by the application of qualitative rather than quantitative distinctions. If the differences between adults and children are differences of kind rather than of degree, the child does not so much turn into an adult as be made into one. Aristotle's and Plato's analyses are first statements of a perennial symbolization of the child as both deficit and danger. Aristotle's might even be read as an implicit theory of monsters, in the sense that children are "like" humans—"human" understood as adult, male, free-born, and governed by reason—but are not. They combine the same elements in a different—and deficient—mixture. It is true that the child, if not born a slave or a female, has the chance of becoming an adult—that is, a being in which reason is in right relation to will and appetite—whereas the woman and the slave never will. But the presence of deficit and danger make that transition problematic. So Erasmus (1990/1529), 1800 years after Aristotle, tells parents:

> To be a true father, you must take absolute control of your son's entire being; and your primary concern must be for that part of his character which distinguishes him from the animals and comes closest to reflecting the divine. . . . Is there any form of exposure more cruel than to abandon to bestial impulses children whom nature intended to be raised according to upright principles and to live a good life? (p. 67)

We can be virtually certain that the tendency to place children on a lower rung of the great chain of being was challenged—if not in common sense or theory, then in practice—time and time again throughout history by sympathetic parents, educators, and other adult observers. But nothing remains, to my knowledge, in the Western philosophical, medical, and educational record to decisively challenge what we might call the "deficit theory" until the publication of Rousseau's (1979) Emile in 1763. Rousseau's challenge is fitful and ambivalent, but it opens a space for the reversal of the deficit theory. This reversal finds full expression in the Romantic reformulation of the image of the child in the early nineteenth century as a type of "genius," that is, a unified or integrated human being, not yet fallen into the psychological division that is characteristic of adulthood. The genius symbolization reoccurs continually in Romantic literature (Abrams, 1971) but is developed most forcefully by Wordsworth, Schiller, deQuincey, and Coleridge (Plotz, 1979). One of Novalis' (1989) aphorisms is representative:

> The first man is the first spiritual seer. To him, all appears as spirit. What are children, if not such primal ones? The fresh insight of children is more boundless than the presentiments of the most resolute prophets, (p. 50)

For the Romantic imagination, the child prophecies the highest goal of adult development. If the life cycle is understood as procession from a state of unity into division, and through division to a higher unity, then the child foreshadows and represents that higher unity. So Schiller (1966/1795), in Naive and Sentimental Poetry, says:

> They are what we were; they are what we should once again become. We were nature just as they, and our culture, by means of reason and freedom, should lead us back to nature. They are, therefore, not only the representation of our lost childhood, which eternally remains most dear to us, but fill us with a certain melancholy. But they are also representations of our highest fulfillment in the ideal, thus evoking in us a sublime tenderness (p. 85).

In fact the Romantic reformulation of childhood in the early nineteenth century was not new to the history of the image of the child. As any powerful symbolic image is ambivalent, the counter-image of the child that Romanticism seized and developed was also present as early as Plato, and before that in Taoism and Christianity. It is the other side of the deficit/danger symbolization: the child as somehow more in touch with spiritual reality than the adult. In ancient Athens, for example, a child selected by lot played an important role as intermediary in the Eleusinian Mysteries, where he or she went before the initiates, making the first contact with the gods (Golden, 1990). As Mark Golden says of this practice, "It is children's very marginality which makes their role appropriate. Not yet fully integrated into the social world of the polis, they are interested outsiders, a status they share with the gods with whom they intercede" (p. 44). Jesus' sayings in the New Testament regarding young children, in which they were held up as exemplars of open spirituality, brings this counter-image squarely into Christianity. As early as 600 B.C., The Tao de Ching (Lao Tzu, 1990) identified the infant with the spiritual master: "He who is in harmony with the Tao is like a newborn child. Its bones are soft, its muscles are weak, but its grip is powerful." And Pierre Erny (1973) summarizes African images of the child found in folktales: "Insensible, innocent, careless, unconscious, well-acquainted with the full condition of man, since he lives it, an ignorant being close to supreme wisdom, the child is thus a complete being, but closed, sealed, and impenetrable" (p. 88).

So there is a fundamental ambivalence—a double image—in the adult symbolization of childhood and children. Both sides of the image turn on the child as a liminal form of life, that is, a being at the threshold, still connected with "other worlds." whether it be the world of the animal or of the god. It must be noted that this is characteristic of the prejudgments that cultural insiders—in Western patriarchy anyway—bring, not just to children, but to other forms of human difference. There is also a long tradition in the West of seeing women, the insane, and "natives" as embodying both deficit/danger and a connection with other worlds, whether those worlds be represented as extreme sensuality, extreme spirituality, or some combination of the two.

The perennial power of this projective relation of cultural insiders to the culturally marginalized is demonstrated yet again in recent postmodern formulations of childhood. In Derrida (1976) for example, the child appears to assume the same position of limit condition of the human, except that in this case it is in the interests of the deconstruction of the modern subject:

> Man [sic] calls himself man only by drawing limits excluding his other from the play of supplementarity: the purity of nature, of animality, primitivism, childhood, madness, divinity. The approach to these limits is at once feared as a threat of death, and desired as access to a life without difference. (p. 245)

In his concern to deconstruct the notion of human subjectivity, Derrida makes a synthesis of the child of Aristotle and the child of the Romantics, while escaping the implications of both. For Aristotle, "man calls himself man" because he is ruled by reason. Aristotle's "man" occupies a particular station on the hierarchical chain of being, and to both fear and desire "nature, . . . animality," etc., would not be appropriate to the (true) nature of that station. For the Romantics on the other hand, "rational man" is merely a shrunken image of himself unless he is able to widen his subjectivity to the point where it incorporates "nature, . . . animality," etc., if in a sublimated form. Derrida, on the other hand, sees the human subject as constructed in contrast to what it is not—its "other," that is, "nature, . . . animality," etc. Therefore it is never itself, but only the production of a paradoxical relation. His "child" symbolizes both the ultimate possible unification of the human subject—an "access to a life without difference"—and its loss to itself through that very unification. Lyotard (1992) evokes the Romantic side of this paradox without mitigating its pathos in his formulation of "infancy" as

> . . . something that will never be defeated [by Western "emancipation" or "Enlightenment," or "reason"], at least as long as humans will be born infants, *infantes. Infantia* is the guarantee that there remains an enigma in us, a not easily communicable opacity—that something is left that remains, and that we must bear witness to it. (p. 416)

The image of the child as limit condition is re-evoked continually in modern and postmodern conceptions, and the tension between reason and nature or instinct, or Enlightenment and Romance, is never far from their surfaces. The most influential philosopher of childhood of the twentieth century, Freud, combines the two interpretations of childhood that I have been tracing by identifying early childhood as the site of a struggle between what he calls primary process and secondary process, or the pleasure principle and the reality principle. For Freud, infantile narcissism, although doomed to disappear in adulthood, represents a state of psychological unification—of self and world, the within and the without—which is thoroughly, if perversely, Romantic. Perversely because in adult terms this unification appears as psychosis, that is, "a life without difference." To become a functional adult, the child must be eradicated, if need be through psychoanalysis, which he describes as "a prolongation of education for the purposes of overcoming the residues of childhood" (1957, p. 48). On the other hand, Freud's symbolization inevitably evokes the counter-image of childhood as original wholeness, spelled out, for example, in N. O. Brown's (1959) classic interpretation of Freud's basic meaning: "Our indestructible unconscious desire for a return to childhood, our deep childhood-fixation, is a desire for a return to the pleasure-principle, for a recovery of the body from which culture alienates us, and for play instead of work." And he adds, "The possibilities adumbrated in infancy are to be taken as normative" (p. 66).

Freud's insights, ambivalent as they too were, did manage to synthesize the two perennial themes of child symbolization of deficit and wholeness. The power of his symbolization is suggested by the dramatic extent to which Freudian and post-Freudian theory and practice have contributed to contemporary Western understanding of actual children, as well as to our understanding the "residues of childhood" in adults. This, in turn, has influenced education—particularly early childhood education—and our appreciation of the significance of play for psychological, social, and cognitive development. Freud's philosophy of childhood has also changed adult self-conceptualization, in showing us the role of primary process in development throughout the life-course. Since Freud, we understand more consciously that, as Ashis Nandy (1987) has said of his influence, "Childhood and adulthood are not two fixed phases of the human life-cycle (where the latter has to inescapably supplant the former), but a continuum which, while diachronically laid out on the plane of life history, is always synchronically present in each personality" (p. 71).

Conclusion: Whither Childhood?

The implications of an archeology of Western childhood for those adults concerned with contemporary children are as varied as the disciplines this inquiry has traversed. The primary message of this material is that adults construct childhood, on the basis of deep-seated prevailing cultural images combined with the residues of their own childhoods. The parent or caregiver brings her construction into dialogue with real children, who, in turn, construct a world within the opportunities and limitations provided by the adults' construction (Wartofsky, 1983). Children bring to the dialogue what Dewey (1916) referred to as an extraordinary (relative to adults) "plasticity," or "the power to modify actions on the basis of the results of prior experiences, the power to develop dispositions" (p. 44). The child brings the power to grow—a power that adults, more often than not, have lost to one degree or another.

Perhaps the word "dialogue" is inappropriate, given the greater power of the adult's positioning in the interaction. But it is just in this disparity that the opportunity for growth among parents and caregivers lies. It seems to be the case that the more adults recognize that aspect of themselves that is still a "child," the more mature they become—i.e., the more both objective and empathic they are able to be in relation to children themselves (Misgeld, 1985). The more adults are able to recognize that the human life cycle involves a dialectical interplay between "adult" and "child," the less they see childhood as something to be outgrown or eradicated, and the more they are able to relate to children as persons, rather than as screens for projection.

A second, related implication of this inquiry is that there may be a historical movement—if not an "evolution" then a progression of some kind—in the history of the adult-child relation. This movement has radically affected the actual history of childhood per se—that is, the way adults construct the world for children, the attention they pay to them, the care they exercise for them, the extent to which they seek their good. If our new ideal of adult maturity includes childhood rather than excluding it, then our notions of optimal child rearing and education will change.

The most significant metaphor uncovered by thinking about childhood in this way seems to be a hermeneutical one. The adult is a "hermeneut" or interpreter of childhood. Through dialogue with the forms of life of childhood, the adult reappropriates, recreates, and reconstellates childhood as an element of the teleology of her own life-cycle. This makes not for more "childish" adults, but perhaps for more "childlike" adults—a new relationship to one's instinctual and affective life, and to one's sense of integration of the various elements of one's self. The adult's increased ability to overcome the ambivalence that the child's relative instinctual freedom produces leads to a reconstruction of the child construct, which allows the latter a greater voice in the adult-child dialogue, which leads to a further reconstruction, etc. Adults who are in dialogical relation to their own "child" have greater capacity to "grow," in Dewey's terms, and therefore to raise children who have that same capacity.

Are there more of these adult "hermeneuts" in the world today than there were in the past? It may be true that we cannot postulate a global evolution. There may be just as many murdering, abandoning, ambivalent, and intrusive adults raising children today as there are socializing and empathic ones. But if the psychohistorical processes that have led to the empathic mode have increased by even a small amount there is reason for hope, not only for childhood, but, necessarily, for human adulthood as well.

REFERENCES

Abrams, M. H. (1971). *Natural supernaturalism: Tradition and revolution in Romantic literature.* New York: Norton.

Aries, P. (1962). Centuries of childhood: A social history of family life, trans. R. Baldick. New York: Knopf.

Aristotle. (1962/350 B.C.). Nichomachean ethics, trans. M. Ostwald. New York: Bobbs-Merrill.

Bachelard, G. (1971). The poetics of reverie: Childhood, language, and the cosmos, trans. D. Russell. Boston: Beacon Press.

Bellingham, B. (1988). The history of childhood since the "invention of childhood": Some issues in the eighties. Journal of Family History, 13(2), 347–358.

Boswell, J. (1988). The kindness of strangers: The abandonment of children in western Europe from late antiquity to the Renaissance. New York: Pantheon.

Brown, N. O. (1959). Life against death: The psychoanalytic meaning of history. Middletown, CT: Wesleyan University Press.

Chartier, R. (1989). The practical impact of writing. In R. Chartier (Ed.), A. Goldhammer, (Trans.), A history of private life. Vol. 3: Passions of the Renaissance (pp. 111–160). Cambridge, MA: Harvard University Press.

Cocks, G., & Crosby, T. L. (Eds.). (1989). Psychohistory: Readings in the method of psychology, psychoanalysis, and history. New Haven: Yale University Press.

Derrida, J. (1976). Of grammatology, trans. G. C. Spivak. Baltimore: Johns Hopkins Press.

Dewey, J. (1916). Democracy and education. New York: Macmillan.

Elder, G. H. Jr., Modell, J., & Parke, R. D. (Eds.). (1993). Children in time and place: Developmental and historical insights. Cambridge, UK: Cambridge University Press.

Elias, N. (1978/1939). The civilizing process: The history of manners, trans. E. Jephcott. New York: Urizen Books.

Emerson, R. W. (1965). Nature. In R. E. Spiller (Ed.), Selected essays, lectures, and poems. New York: Washington Square Press.

Erasmus. (1990/1529). On education for children. In E. Rummel (Ed.), The Erasmus reader (pp. 65–102). Toronto: University of Toronto Press.

Erikson, E. H. (1963). Childhood and society (2nd ed.). New York: Norton.

Erny, P. (1973). Childhood and cosmos: The social psychology of the Black African child. Washington, DC: Black Orpheus Press.

Forsyth, I. H. (1976). Children in early medieval art: Ninth through twelfth centuries. Journal of Psychohistory 4(1), 31–70.

Foucault, M. (1979). Discipline and punish. New York: Vintage.

Franz, M. L. von (1979). Archetypal dimensions of the psyche. Los Angeles: Shambala.

Freud, A. (1946). The ego and the mechanisms of defense, trans. C. Baines. New York: International Universities Press.

Freud, S. (1957). Five lectures on psychoanalysis. In J. Strachey (Ed.), The standard edition of the complete psychological works of Sigmund Freud (Vol. 11). London: Hogarth Press.

Froebel, F. (1974/1826). The education of man. Clifton, NJ: Augustus M. Kelley.

Gadamer, H. G. (1975). Truth and method. New York: Crossroad.

Gelis, J. (1989). The child: From anonymity to individuality. In R. Chartier (Ed.), A. Goldhammer, (Trans.), A history of private life. Vol. 3: Passions of the Renaissance (pp. 309–325). Cambridge, MA: Harvard University Press.

Golden, M. (1990). Children and childhood in classical Athens. Baltimore: John Hopkins University Press.

Gottlieb, B. (1993). The family in the Western world from the black death to the industrial age. New York: Oxford University Press.

Hawthorne, N. (1994/1850). The scarlet letter. New York: Washington Square Press.

Huizinga, J. (1969). The waning of the Middle Ages: A study of the forms of life, thought, and art in France and the Netherlands in the 14th and 15th centuries. New York: Anchor.

Hunt, D. (1970). Parents and children in history: The psychology of family life in early modern France. New York: Basic Books.

Innes, H. (1951). The bias of communication. Toronto: University of Toronto Press.

Jacobi, J. (1959). Complex, archetype and symbol in the psychology of C. G. Jung. New York: Pantheon.

Jung, C. G. (1959). Archetypes of the collective unconscious. In V. S. de Laszlo (Ed.) The basic writings of C. G. Jung (pp. 286–325). New York: Modern Library.

Jung, C. G., & Kerenyi, K. (1963). Essays on a science of mythology: The myth of the divine child and the mysteries of Eleusis. Princeton, NJ: Bollingen Series XXII, Princeton University Press.

Kerenyi, K. (1977). Eleusis: Archetypal image of mother and daughter. New York: Schocken.

Koyre, A. (1957). From the closed world to the infinite universe. Baltimore: Johns Hopkins University Press.

Kuhn, R. (1982). Corruption in paradise: The child in Western literature. Hanover, NH: University Press of New England.

Kunstmann, J. (1970). The transformation of Eros, trans. M. von Herzfeld & R. Gaze. London: Oliver & Boyd.

Lao Tzu. (1990). Tao te ching, trans. V. H. Mair. New York: Bantam Books.

Lasareff, V. (1938). Studies in the iconography of the Virgin. Art Bulletin 20, 26–65.

Lifton, R. J. (1974). Explorations in psychohistory: The Wellfleet Papers. New York: Simon & Schuster.

Locke, J. (1968). Some thoughts concerning education. In J. L. Axtell (Ed.), The educational writings of John Locke. Cambridge, UK: Cambridge University Press.

Lorence, B. W. (1974). Parents and children in eighteenth century Europe. History of Childhood Quarterly 2 (1), 1–30.

Lyotard, J. F., & Larochelle, G. (1992). That which resists, after all. Philosophy Today 36 (4), 416.

Mann, S. (1993). Immediate family. New York: Phaidon Press.

Marcuse, H. (1966). Eros and civilization: A philosophical inquiry into Freud. Boston: Beacon Press.

Martin, L., Gutman, H., & Hutton, P. H. (Eds.). (1988). Technologies of the self: A seminar with Michel Foucault. Amherst: University of Massachusetts Press.

Matthews, G. (1996). The philosophy of childhood. Cambridge: Harvard University Press.

deMause, L. (1974). The evolution of childhood. In L. deMause (Ed.), The history of childhood. New York: Harper.

McLaughlin, M. M. (1974). Survivors and surrogates: Parents and children from the ninth to the thirteenth centuries. In L. deMause (Ed.), The history of childhood. New York: Harper & Row.

McLuhan, M. (1962). The Gutenberg galaxy. Toronto: University of Toronto Press.

Meatyard, R. E. (1970). Ralph Eugene Meatyard. New York: Gnomon Press.

Misgeld, D. (1985). Self-understanding and adult maturity: Adult and child in hermeneutical and critical reflection. Phenomenology + Pedagogy 3 (3), 191–200.

Nandy, N. (1987). Reconstructing childhood: A critique of the ideology of adulthood. In Traditions, tyranny, and Utopias: Essays in the politics of awareness (pp. 56–76). Delhi: Oxford University Press.

Neumann, E. (1969). The origins and history of consciousness. Princeton NJ: Princeton University Press.

Novalis. (1989). Pollen and fragments, trans. A. Versluis. Grand Rapids, MI: Phanes Press.

Ong, W. (1982). Orality and literacy: The technologizing of the word. New York: Methuen.

Pascal, B. (1962/1670). Pensees, ed. M. Turnell. New York: Harper & Row.

Petschauer, P. (1987). Intrusive to socializing modes: Transitions in eighteenth-century Germany and twentieth-century Italy. The Journal of Psychohistory 14(3), 257–270.

Petschauer, P. (1989). The childrearing modes in flux: An historian's reflections, The Journal of Psychohistory 17(1), 1–41.

Piaget, J. (1929). The child's conception of the world. London: Routledge & Kegan Paul.

Plato. (1941). The republic, trans. & ed. F. M. Cornford. New York: Oxford University Press.

Plato. (1961). Laws, trans. A. E. Taylor. In E. Hamilton & H. Cairns (Eds.), The collected dialogues of Plato (pp. 1225–1513). Princeton: Princeton University Press, Bollingen.

Plotz, J. (1979). The perpetual messiah: Romanticism, childhood, and the paradoxes of human development. In B. Finkelstein (Ed.), Regulated children/liberated children. New York: Psychohistory Press.

Pollock, L. A. (1983). Forgotten children: Parent-child relations from 1500 to 1900. Cambridge, UK: Cambridge University Press.

Polokow, V. (1982). The erosion of childhood. Chicago: University of Chicago Press.

Postman, N. (1982). The disappearance of childhood. New York: Delacorte.

Ricoeur, P. (1987). The hermeneutical function of distanciation. In Hermeneutics and the human sciences, trans. J. B. Thompson. Cambridge, UK: Cambridge University Press.

Rousseau, J. J. (1979/1763). Emile, or on education, trans. A. Bloom. New York: Basic Books.

Schiller, F. (1966). Naive and sentimental poetry and On the sublime: Two essays. New York: Norton.

Shahar, S. (1990). Childhood in the Middle Ages. London: Routledge.

Sommerville, C. J. (1982). The rise and fall of childhood. Beverly Hills, CA: Sage Publications.

Sommerville, J. (1992). The discovery of childhood in Puritan England. Athens: The University of Georgia Press.

Stearns, P. N. & Stearns, C. Z. (1987). Emotionology: Clarifying the history of emotions and emotional standards. In G. Cocks & T. L. Crosby (Eds.), Psychohistory: Readings in the method of psychology, psychoanalysis and history (pp. 284–309). New Haven, CT: Yale University Press.

Stone, L. (1979). The family, sex and marriage in England 1500–1800 (Abr. Ed.). New York: Harper.

Wartofsky, M. (1983). The child's construction of the world and the world's construction of the child: From historical epistemology to historical psychology. In F. Kessel & A. Siegel (Eds.), The child and other cultural inventions (pp. 188–215). New York: Praeger.

24

SANDRA HARDING

Sandra Harding (born 1935) is an internationally recognized and cele-brated philosopher of feminist standpoint theory, postcolonial theory, epistemology, research methodology, and philosophy of science. After receiving her Ph.D. from New York University, Harding taught at the University of Delaware for many years before moving to the UCLA School of Education, where she now teaches in the Social Sciences and Comparative Education division. She also directed the UCLA Center for the Study of Women (1995–2000) and co-edited the interdisciplinary journal *Signs: Journal of Women in Culture and Society* (2000–2005).

One of Harding's most important contributions to epistemology and to philosophy of science concerns her ongoing critique and reha-bilitation of the notion of objectivity. While traditional science meth-ods seek a neutral and impartial research process, Harding has demonstrated through her many books and articles that underlying these claims is a specific set of interests. In fact, Western science prac-tices and theories perpetuate the assumptions and values of white, heterosexual, Western patriarchy. Rather than deny the cultural, politi-cal, and economic location of all knowledge claims, Harding suggests a critical analysis of these underlying values and a recognition of objectivity's inherently political nature. Power and social interests are, in other words, not external to knowledge. We should not want to eliminate all values from philosophy or science but, rather, include those values that advance knowledge for social justice projects. Here power is not an obstacle to objectivity but helps produce what Harding refers to as "strong objectivity."

To make objectivity stronger, it thus follows that science should start from the experiences, activities, and knowledge claims of those traditionally marginalized in and by Western science (including women, minorities, and those in the global South). For instance, Harding strongly advocates that women have a unique standpoint on nature and social relations which has long been ignored and which would contribute to a better understanding of the world. Starting from the standpoint of women will expose male biases at work within science and will offer an opportunity to ask new questions and to gather new forms of data, in turn making science more democratic. Thus, oppression gives certain groups a unique, critical, and invaluable insight into how dominant society operates, which in turn can be the new starting point for the production of new kinds of knowing. In sum, Harding argues that we are entitled to be skeptical of knowledge claims produced by dominant groups. Authority here reduces "strong" objectivity which reveals the privileges of power and the exclusion of diversity. Second, strong objectivity recognizes the productivity of the relationship between science and politics (for example, AIDS research came from activism from within the gay community).

The importance of Harding's work in education is significant on two levels. First is the level of educational research. A standpoint methodology brings a strong notion of objectivity to both quantitative and qualitative methods. Second, for classroom practices, Harding asks teachers to teach science, and indeed all subjects, in a new way. "We need to make sure everyone gets a good science education," Harding has said. "As John Dewey pointed out, making democracy means ensuring that those who bear the consequences of decisions have a fair share in making them. But people who aren't scientifically literate can't share in making the decisions about science that will affect them, too." Educators should become more sensitive to how science practices in the classroom are gendered practices. Furthermore, to achieve a real democracy, both boys and girls need to become equally scientifically literate. Furthermore Harding's work poses a series of pedagogical problems: What would it look like to learn science by starting from the standpoints of the children being taught, especially those who come from marginalized cultures? What ways of knowing and seeing the world are unique to childhood and can be used as resources by teachers to ask new questions and investigate the world in a new way?

REFERENCES

Harding, Sandra. *Whose Science? Whose Knowledge?* Ithaca, NY: Cornell University Press, 1991.

Harding, Sandra. *Is Science Multicultural? Postcolonialisms, Feminisms, and Epistemologies.* Bloomington: Indiana University Press, 1998.

Harding, Sandra. *The Feminist Standpoint Theory Reader: Intellectual and Political Controversies.* London: Routledge, 2004.

HOW CAN WOMEN'S STANDPOINT ADVANCE THE GROWTH OF SCIENTIFIC KNOWLEDGE?

1. Does equal mean only "the same"? For more than a century feminists have argued that women should have equality with their brothers in sciences, mathematics and engineering. "We can do the same good science that they do," we have said. Women should be added to the sciences, mathematics and engineering professions.

Such claims have encountered strong resistance. It has been immensely difficult for women to achieve formal equality—that is equal access and treatment in scientific training, degrees, jobs, publication in scientific journals, and membership in scientific societies. And it has been even more difficult to achieve actual equality; often the climate and daily practices of knowledge production institutions fail to encourage and support girls and women as they do their brothers.[i] (Rossiter 1982, 1995, Schiebinger 1989) The recent report on the status of women faculty in the sciences at MIT revealed how the women who had earned their formal equality at that prestigious institution, and who denied that they had been discriminated against in any obvious ways, nevertheless testified to the greater difficulties they encountered in maintaining their careers compared to their male colleagues. And this was still the case for the youngest generation of women scientists, though the forms of informal discrimination varied at different stages in women's life cycles and careers. (Massachusetts Institute of Technology, 1999)

Yet I want to focus on a different set of issues here. Can "add women and stir" strategies actually achieve equality for women in the production of knowledge? To put the question another way, should the demand for equal treatment require only the same treatment? Under what conditions does real equality require different goals and strategies? Can women have a distinctive standpoint on nature and social relations? How does the growth of knowledge suffer when we understand equality as only sameness?

Such questions make women and their male defenders nervous—and for good reasons. For one thing, will asking for anything different

"How Can Women's Standpoint Advance the Growth of Scientific Knowledge?" by Sandra Harding. Reprinted with permission of the author.

from our brothers be regarded as claiming that women have "special interests"? Will we be perceived to be demanding the right to replace male or sexist biases with female and feminist biases, and thus not really advancing the objectivity of research? Won't the growth of knowledge suffer from such projects in ways similar to how it has suffered from sexist biases? A second concern focuses on why women always have to define our concerns in terms of our differences from the masculine norm; why should this be so? Furthermore, what effect do the answers to such questions have on how we think about recruiting and retaining women in the sciences? Finally, how might such issues influence the direction and design of research projects?

My intent here is to help us think about these difficult issues. But let me return first to remind us that a fair representation of women in scientific institutions brings benefits to society and to science itself, not only to women.

2. Who benefits from women's presence in the sciences?[ii] Of course fairness to women requires that they receive the same opportunities and resources as their brothers. The production of knowledge can be pleasurable and sometimes exciting work. It is frequently well-paid, so that women can support themselves and their dependents and achieve the upward mobility that often is characteristic of their brothers' careers in science, mathematics and engineering. Moreover, science, math and engineering are high status professions. Professional expertise is admired and respected. Modern science and engineering are models of enlightened progress. Thus, careers in such fields permit women, too, to contribute to widely-recognized human achievements, and to have the chance to improve the natural and social conditions under which we live in such ways.

Society benefits, too, from women's presence in science, math, and engineering institutions. For one thing, women's skills and talents at the production of knowledge are valuable social resources that enlarge the "human resources" pool on which the continued advance of science depends. Moreover, scientific forms of rationality, abstract, and critical thought have persistently been claimed as the significant marks of the fully human. Such traits are said (rightly or wrongly) to distinguish adults from children, and humans from members of other species. When women, too, are seen as rational, objective, careful observers and critical thinkers, membership doubles in the category of those who can get counted as fully human. Thus Marie Curie's achievements were immensely inspiring to women who had no intention of becoming chemists. If women can achieve in science, math and engineering, they can achieve in other fields that have been unfairly closed to them.

Finally, these days, after three decades of highly-visible feminist "revolution," the reputation, the perceived legitimacy, of scientific and technological institutions requires that women have equal status in scientific, mathematical, and engineering work. Science is supposed to be the paradigm of objective, rational, and critical thought. For many people it is still the ideal model of modernity, social progress, and even of enlightened civilization itself insofar as it confronts customary biases and superstitions. So its continued refusal to examine critically its own gender prejudices, where this occurs, damages that reputation these days. In the case of the social and life sciences these concerns are possibly even more critical. We are long past the day when it was regarded as appropriate for expertise about women's bodies, the health and welfare of children, and violence against women, for example, to be the possession only of men.

Important as these issues are, they are not the only important ones when the topic is women and science. Another one is the issue of women's differences from men that could be used to advance the growth of scientific knowledge. We have all learned to value biological diversity. But what about cognitive diversity? What is it, and how do sciences benefit from it? How can women's differences from men provide an undervalued source of cognitive diversity?

3. How can the sciences benefit from women's "difference"?[iii] According to modern sciences (as well as common sense), how we interact with the world around us both enables and limits what we can know about it. Different research designs offer the opportunity for different patterns of knowledge (and, we should remember, different patterns of ignorance). Moreover, not just how we study phenomena, but which ones we choose to study—or neglect to study—shapes both systematic patterns of knowledge and of ignorance. So we can ask: do women and men in any particular society tend to have characteristically different interactions with nature and social relations which might enable them to bring different concerns and sensitivities to research?

Mostly we do not. Men's and women's interactions with natural and social environments are more similar to each other than either are, say, to the interactions of horses or monkeys with their environments! Mostly men and women are found in the same places in nature—on deserts or mountains, islands or prairies, in the tropics or the Arctic. Moreover, in any particular environment men and women tend to have mostly the same or similar interests in the world around them; for example, they have similar interests in survival, shelter from hostile climates, sustainable food supplies, safety from dangerous plants and animals, and the pleasures of family, friends, and participation in their culture's distinctive activities. Men and women tend to share the same or similar cultural discourses: Christian or Islamic, Latino/a or Chinese religious narratives, models, and conceptual frameworks. And we mostly share the same or similar ways of organizing the production of knowledge: learning from sacred books or tribal elders, from daily agricultural and health care practices, from work in laboratories and field sites, classrooms, libraries and historical archives. So the life experiences and knowledge practices that men and women bring to their research are largely the same.

Moreover, whatever women may bring to their education as researchers, in scientific and scholarly disciplines they are trained to do the same things as men. We are all socialized into our disciplines. Moreover, the "strangers" to be welcomed, or at least tolerated, as a disciplinary group—whether these be women, racial, ethnic, religious or sexual minorities, or people of other classes—are those who already most fit the profile of the prevailing group. They are the most easily socialized, the most willing, docile, and unresistant to giving up their "difference" from the dominant group in order to share its activities.[iv] Women often are isolated as these strangers in our departments and labs, and punished in subtle and not so subtle ways for challenging on gender grounds the standard ways of conducting research.

However, paradoxically, this insistence on "becoming men" institutionalizes an important difference between women and men in educational and research institutions. Unlike our brothers, we must "leave our gender behind" when we open the lab or department door. The demand that women enter and engage in the production of knowledge only in the same ways as do men insures that in important respects women are thereby forbidden from achieving that goal. To do "the same science" as do men, women must restrict their subjectivity in way their brothers do not; we must limit our observations, reasoning strategies, intuitions, and critical thinking to ways that match such activities as they are performed by a socially distinctive group that is not us—namely, men.

This is significant because there are at least some respects in which women's interactions with nature and social relations differ from men's.[v] To the extent that women and men are assigned or choose different kinds of activities within a culture, they will tend to bring different resources to the production of knowledge. This is so even for the professional middle classes in which women's and men's life styles tend to be more similar than is the case in other classes. In both the North and the South these gender-differing patterns of scientific subjectivity have been noted. Thus there are distinctive resources women can bring to research that have the effect of expanding the comprehensiveness of patterns of knowledge and of correcting the errors that have infested research from which women's resources were excluded. Women's "cognitive difference" from men provides undervalued resources for the growth of scientific knowledge. We are all familiar with such cases. Here I briefly describe just a few.

4. Examples: Women's Health. It took the Women's Health Movement (and possibly the appointment of a woman to head the National Institute of Health: Bernadine Healy) to get federal funding for women's health issues up to the level assigned to men's issues. Of course both women and men have heart attacks and suffer other bodily failures. But studies such as the one on the effects of aspirin on the incidence of heart attacks had been conducted only on men, so no one knew if or how its effects might differ for women. Yet doctors were recommending aspirin as a way of preventing heart attacks to women, too. Here we have the Women's Health Movement raising additional research questions and calling for the study of additional phenomena, and insisting upon greater rigor in the procedures and reporting of drug trials.

Evolutionary theory. Have only men evolved? Ruth Hubbard (1979) pointed out two decades ago that standard interpretations of evolutionary theory treated females as making no contributions to human evolution. As Hubbard humorously put the point, mainstream theorists acted as if were it not for the lucky fact that girls inherit their fathers' genes as well as their mothers', contemporary men would have to be mating with apes! (Of course that is absurd, but that is the logic of then standard readings of evolutionary theory.) Hubbard and other biologists and anthropologists showed that women were hunters as well as gatherers, most likely providing more than half of such groups annual supplies of protein. Moreover, they developed tools for their hunting of small game, gathering and food preparation activities also. Here we have women asking questions about prevailing hypotheses, and about how the data was gathered and interpreted. Interpretations of evolutionary theory have persistently been used to argue for the legitimacy in today's world of the superior social status of one gender over another, and of one race over others. So it should not be surprising that members of the purportedly inferior gender (and races) should raise critical questions about such naturalizations of social hierarchy and the way data was collected to support them.

Moral development. Psychologist Carol Gilligan (1982) showed that Lawrence Kohlberg's influential stage theory of moral development gained its plausibility only through its failure to interrogate the androcentric assumptions guiding the research design. Women's responses to the study's set of moral dilemmas seemed to Kohlberg to support conventional views that women's morality was diffuse and less developed: a much higher proportion of women's than men's responses had to be set aside because they didn't fit the moral categories Kohlberg had prepared. Gilligan showed how women's moral reasoning was simply different, not inferior to men's, and that it was entirely appropriate for the kinds of decisions that women encountered in their assigned work of raising children and maintaining family relations. Women tended to develop and retain an "ethic of care" and responsibility. Men—at first comfortable with this ethic—gave it up for the "ethic of fairness" and of rights that are expected of moral decisions in the public realms of work and government. Did Gilligan's experience as a woman, a daughter, and a mother suggest insights to her that were less available to men? Whether or not this was the actual origin of her insights, her project started off from the standpoint of women's typical life activities in order to focus on widely accepted standards for what counts as moral development.

Human social relations. In the introduction to their early collection of feminist challenges to androcentric sociology, Millman and Kanter (1975) argued that this discipline's androcentric assumptions and practices prevented sociology from providing reliable accounts not only of women's lives, but also of men's lives and social relations in general.

For example, Sociology focused on "public, official, visible, and/or dramatic role players and definitions of the situation; yet unofficial, supportive, less dramatic, private, and invisible spheres of social life and organization may be equally important." Moreover, the discipline frequently assumed a single society inhabited by men and women in which generalizations can be made about all participants. Yet men and women in many respects inhabit different social worlds which must be taken into account when making generalizations. Social researchers concerned with racial and ethnic stratification have been making similar claims. For exampe, African American sociologist Patricia Hill Collins (1991/1999) has argued that sociology cannot understand white people's social worlds, let alone Black life, because of its assumptions about how white men are the unique exemplars of humanity. Collins and other social researchers have demonstrated the importance of thinking of social relations in terms of the "intersectionality" of gender with class, race and ethnicity rather than in the binary terms that feminist and other new social movements first favored. Learning to analyze how intersectional social relations affect the social structures and contents of the natural sciences too can only improve both.

In these cases, political struggles have become part of research processes, enabling researchers to "start off research" from the daily lives of people in oppressed groups in order to reveal more accurately their lives, the lives of the oppressing groups, and the institutional and discursive practices that tend to block such observation and understanding. In the language of standpoint theorists such as Dorothy Smith (1987, 1990a), we can take oppressed groups experiences of the everyday world as the starting point for understanding the "conceptual practices of power." It takes both empirical research—science—and political struggles to gain such understanding since, first, we are all forced to live in, and socialized to see as natural, social institutions that are in fact designed to serve members of the dominant groups and, second, the latter resist attempts to legitimate any public presentations of ways of understanding nature and social relations that are not their own.

Third World "Development." Yet one more example of how starting off thought from women's lives can reveal aspects of the "conceptual practices of power," in this case, the way Northern-directed international agencies think about Third World development, is available in the illuminating studies of women, the environment, and sustainable development. Researchers such as Braidotti et al (1994) have started off their research projects from the lives of the most politically and economically vulnerable of the world's women—the 60–80% of the world's poor women living "at the periphery of the Enlightenment." Thinking about development from such a standpoint, these researchers show how development policies in fact have increased the gap between the world's "haves" and "have-nots" through their reliance on economistic notions of what counts as development, narrow and counter-productive conceptions of what counts as "real science," androcentric and Eurocentric assumptions about sustainable environments, and persistent systematic blindness to the effects such concepts and policies have on the lives of women, their dependents, their communities, and the environments upon which their lives depend. Only policies designed from the standpoint of the daily interactions with nature and social relations of the most vulnerable citizens of the planet can stand a chance of actually providing access to development for them.

5. Conclusion: Gender and Cognitive Diversity. I have been arguing that women bring important resources to scientific research "as women," and as women of diverse classes, ethnicities, races, religions, sexualities, and cultures. Whether or not individual women in fact identify themselves as feminist, we can see that the last three decades of feminist research, scholarship, and politics have enabled all of us to see gender around us in ways that were invisible earlier. Feminisms have provided us with "gender lenses," by which I mean analytic frameworks and directions for identifying distorting gender assumptions that lurk in our sciences as in our social relations. Of course this means that men, too, could and should be looking at the world through "gender lenses"; these frameworks are analytic resources available for everyone who does the political and research work necessary to understand how they work. (Increasingly men have been using them, and in innovate ways. But this is a topic for another time and place.)

Let us summarize here some of the contributions to the growth of scientific knowledge that these "gender lenses" provide.

1. They identify important understudied social and natural phenomena, and what is problematic about them.
2. They propose new hypotheses and concepts that direct attention to unnoticed aspects of nature and social relations.

3. They create innovative research designs, enabling the collection of additional or different kinds of evidence, and insist on more rigorous deployment of existing research designs and their methods.

4. They interpret differently familiar data, enabling new patterns of nature and social relations to emerge into visibility.

5. They bring systematic critical scrutiny to bear on familiar conceptual frameworks, including the ones that have shaped their own training and research. Thus they insist that the observer's assumptions and practices be treated the same way as are the assumptions and practices of the observed. They develop a kind of "robust reflexivity" that counters the familiar insistence on treating observer and observed as different in kind.

6. They use ethical and political commitments to expand the growth of knowledge through all of the above processes. They understand that political struggle can expand our knowledge of nature and social relations. Thus while rejecting the possibility and desirability of the requirement to achieve value-neutral research, at the same time they develop stronger standards for maximizing objectivity."[vi]

Note that the arguments for the value of the standpoint of women or feminist standpoints focus on the importance of women's experiences and of feminist political movements as potential origins of scientific processes and as a check on their adequacy. While individual women have indeed used their experience to open up new lines of scientific research and illuminate familiar ones, pro-democratic political movements make possible the emergence of new kinds of group consciousnesses. Thus it is certainly true that some kinds of politics retard the growth of knowledge; but it is also clear that other kinds of politics have advanced it. (See Harding, forthcoming.)

I have been arguing that asking women to do research in only the same ways that men have done it in fact does not grant women equality in science, and additionally restricts the growth of knowledge. Instead, women will achieve equality, like their brothers, when they are permitted to do research that takes advantage of the distinctive interactions with nature and social relations characteristic of their gender—never forgetting how diverse gender relations are from class to class, race to race, and culture to culture. At the same time that women and men are mostly like each other within the same cultural context, it is also true that women tend to have distinctive locations in nature and social relations, distinctive interests in the world around them, distinctive discursive strategies—narratives, models, and metaphors—and distinctive ways of organizing the production of knowledge. Women's distinctive culturally-located subjectivities can provide rich resources for our sciences and our societies. Importantly, women can use our social disadvantage as an epistemological lever to pry open dominant theories and research practices so to observe the conceptual practices of power, and to strategize about how to create more democratic societies and more accomplished sciences.

Notes

  i. Note that thinking about such concerns only in terms of women's equality with their brothers avoids dealing with important issues of class, race, and ethnicity stratification in the sciences. Women—economically advantaged or disadvantaged, in the dominant or subordinate races and ethnicities—occupy distinctive class, race and ethnicity locations in the sciences, and their concerns differ in such different locations. For some analyses of racial inequality in the sciences and of forms of discrimination created by modern sciences' role within Western expansion see Harding 1993, 1998.
 ii. An earlier discussion of these issues appeared in Harding 1998.
iii. There is by now a large literature on this topic. Central arguments in it may be found in Cockburn 1985; Collins 1991/1999; Gender Working Group 1995; Haraway 1989, 1991; Harding 1986, 1987, 1991; Harding and McGregor 1996; Hartsock 1983; Keller 1984; Mayberry, Subramaniam, and Weasel 2001; Rooney 1994; Rose 1984; Rosser 1993; Rouse 1996; Schiebinger 1989, 1993; Shiva 1989; Smith 1987, 1990a, 1990b; Wajcman 1991; Wyer et al 2000.
 iv. I say this as one of the first in the 1970's wave of women to enter philosophy and its institutions—graduate schools, departments, journals, publishers' lists. In spite of considerable progress, these remain largely masculine preserves. The more prestigious the university, department, journal or publisher, the fewer women philosophers one can expect to find represented (with the occasional exceptions).
  v. See Harding 1998, Chapters 4 and 6: "Cultures as Toolboxes for Sciences and Technologies," and "Are There Gendered Standpoints on Nature?"
 vi. A number of philosophers have developed such strengthened standards for maximizing objectivity. Mine, under the label "strong objectivity," can be seen in Harding 1991, 1998. See also the related discussion of "robust reflexivity" in my 1998.

BIBLIOGRAPHY

Braidotti, Rosi et al. 1994. *Women, the Environment, and Sustainable Development.* Atlantic Highlands, N.J.: Zed.

Cockburn, Cynthia. 1985. *Machinery of Dominance: Women, Men, and Technical Know-How.* London: Pluto Press.

Collins, Patricia Hill. 1991/1999. *Black Feminist Thought: Knowledge, Consciousness, and the Politics of Empowerment.* New York: Routledge.

Gender Working Group, U.N. Commission on Science and Technology for Development. 1995. *Missing Links: Gender Equity in Science and Technology for Development.* Ottawa: International Development Research Centre.

Gilligan, Carol. 1982. *In a Different Voice: Psychological Theory and Women's Development.* Cambridge, Mass.: Harvard University Press.

Haraway, Donna. 1989. *Primate Visions: Gender, Race, and Nature in the World of Modern Science.* New York: Routledge.

————. 1991. "Situated Knowledges: The Science Question in Feminism and the Privilege of Partial Perspectives." In *Simians, Cyborgs, and Women.* New York: Routledge.

Harding, Sandra, 1986. *The Science Question in Feminism.* Ithaca: Cornell University Press.

———— ed. 1987. *Feminism and Methodology: Social Science Issues.* Bloomington: Indiana University Press.

————. 1991. *Whose Science? Whose Knowledge? Thinking From Women's Lives.* Bloomington: Indiana University Press.

————, ed.. 1993. *The 'Racial' Economy of Science: Toward a Democratic Future.* Bloomington, Ind.: Indiana University Press.

————1998. *Is Science Multicultural? Postcolonialisms, Feminisms, and Epistemologies.* Bloomington: Indiana University Press.

————. 1998. "Women, Science, and Society," *Science* Vol 281, 11 September 1998, p. 1599–1600.

————, ed. Forthcoming. *The Standpoint Reader.*

————and Elizabeth McGregor. 1996. "The Gender Dimension of Science and Technology." In UNESCO *World Science Report,* ed. Howard J. Moore. Paris: UNESCO.

Hartsock, Nancy. 1983. "The Feminist Standpoint: Developing the Ground for a Specifically Feminist Historical Materialism." In *Discovering Reality: Feminist Perspectives on Epistemology, Metaphyics, Methodology, and Philosophy of Science,* ed. Sandra Harding and Merrill Hintikka. Dordrecht: Reidel/Kluwer.

Heymann, S. Jody. 1995. "Patients in Research: Not Just Subjects, but Partners," *Science* 269, 797–98.

Hubbard, Ruth. 1979. "Have Only Men Evolved?" in *Biological Woman: The Convenient Myth,* ed. R. Hubbard, M. Henifin, and B. Fried. Cambridge, Mass.: Schenkman.

Keller, Evelyn Fox. 1984. *Reflections on Gender and Science.* New Haven: Yale University Press.

Massachuetts Institute of Technology. 1999. *A Study on the Status of Women Faculty in Science at MIT.* Available online at *http://web.mit.edu/fnl/women/women.html.*

Mayberry, Maralee, Banu Subramaniam, and Lisa Weasel, eds. 2001. *A New Generation of Feminist Science Studies.* New York: Routledge.

Meinert, Curtis. 1995. "The Inclusion of Women in Clinical Trials." *Science* 269, 795–96.

Millman, Marcia, and Rosabeth Moss Kanter, eds. 1975. *Another Voice: Feminist Perspectives on Social Life and Social Science.* New York: Anchor Books.

Rooney, Phyllis. 1994. "Recent Work in Feminist Discussions of Reason." *American Philosophical Quarterly.* 31:1. 1–21.

Rose, Hilary. 1984. *Love, Power, and Knowledge.* Bloomington: Indiana University Press.

Rossiter, Margaret. 1982 *Women Scientists in America: Struggles and Strategies to 1940.* Baltimore: Johns Hopkins University Press.

———. 1995. *Women Scientists in America: Before Affirmative Action.* Baltimore: Johns Hopkins University Press.

Rouse, Joseph. 1996. "Feminism and the Social Construction of Scientific Knowledge." In *Feminism, Science, and the Philosophy of Science,* ed. Lynn Hankinson Nelson and Jack Nelson. Dordrecht: Kluwer.

Schiebinger, Londa. 1989. *The Mind Has No Sex? Women in the Origins of Modern Science.* Cambridge: Harvard.

———. 1993. *Nature's Body: Gender in the Making of Modern Science.* Boston: Beacon.

———. 1999. *Has Feminism Changed Science?* Cambridge, MA: Harvard University Press.

Sherman, Ann, Robert Temple, and Ruth B. Merkatz. 1995. "Women in Cinical Trials: An FDA Perspective," *Science* 269, 793–94.

Shiva, Vandana. 1989. *Staying Alive: Women, Ecology, and Development.* London: Zed.

Smith, Dorothy E. 1987. *The Everyday World as Problematic: A Sociology for Women.* Boston: Northeastern University Press.

———. 1990a. *The Conceptual Practices of Power: A Feminist Sociology of Knowledge.* Boston: Northeastern University Press.

———. 1990b. *Texts, Facts, and Femininity: Exploring the Relations of Ruling.* New York: Routledge.

Wajcman, Judy. 1991. *Feminism Confronts Technology.* University Park: Pennsylvania State University.

Wyer, Mary, et al. 2000. *Women, Science, and Technology: A Feminist Reader.* New York: Routledge.

25

DOUGLAS KELLNER

Born in 1943, Douglas Kellner is one of the most important "third gener-ation" critical theorists in the tradition of the Frankfurt Institute for Social Research. During the 1960s, Kellner was a philosophy student at Columbia University in New York and partook in student protests against the Vietnam War. Then through his research into German critical theory at the University of Tubingen in Germany, Kellner examined the relationship between history and ideas, as well as the political nature of philosophy. While studying abroad in Germany, Kellner read the works of Theodor Adorno, Karl Korsch, Herbert Marcuse, and Ernst Bloch, all of whom were instrumental in theorizing a new form of Marxist criticism concerned primarily with questions of culture and subjectivity rather than with pure economic analysis.

As Kellner's autobiographical essay "Philosophical Adventures" on his website indicates (http://www.gseis.ucla.edu/faculty/kellner/essays/philosophicadventures.pdf), he went from Germany to France, where he attended lectures and read the books of Foucault, Deleuze, Baudrillard, Lyotard, and others who would be associated with post-modern theory. Hence, Kellner's philosophical explorations did not end with the Frankfurt School. With his co-author, Steven Best, Kellner has written a series of books critically interrogating what has come to be known as "postmodern" theory. Although adopting many insights from postmodernists, such as Michel Foucault, as well as many feminist and critical race theorists, Kellner retains the centrality of critical theory as a macrotheoretical lens capable of building conceptual bridges between various political movements and capable of critically evaluating and mediating competing philosophical perspectives.

Throughout his philosophical adventures, Kellner has consistently drawn from the Frankfurt School a concern for the industrialization and commercialization of culture under capitalist relations of production. This situation has become most acute in the United States, with its highly commercial media culture. Combining insights and methodological tools from the Frankfurt School and from British cultural studies, Kellner has written extensively on media culture as a complex political, philosophical, and economic phenomenon. For Kellner, media emerges as a "contested terrain" in which political struggles are played out in narrative and visual forms. Thus, films, television, the Internet, and so on articulate dominant, conservative, reactionary social values but also offer progressive resistance against these values. As an example of Kellner's method of media analysis, he has, most famously, read the image of the pop sensation Madonna as a complex representation of women that challenges gender, sexual, and fashion stereotypes while reasserting those very codes by offering a "new" notion of the self that is reliant upon hyper-consumerism. Kellner's work in the area of media culture has been highly influential for educators concerned with fostering "critical media literacy" capable of decoding the complexities of the visual culture that surrounds us.

Another, equally important line of inquiry defining Kellner's work is his interest in "techno-capitalism," or capitalism defined by ever-sophisticated advances in technology. Thus, Kellner has been at the forefront of theorizing new technologies and their social, political, and economic impacts. His interest in technologies began in the mid-1970s while a professor at the University of Austin. Here Kellner studied the political economy of television and launched his own, very successful alternative culture public access television show entitled *Alternative Views*. As with his theories of media images, Kellner offers a dialectical approach to new technologies, highlighting their progressive and democratic potentials while critiquing the undeniable reality of corporate interests that drive the technologies market. Again this work has become increasingly important for educators concerned with the role of technology in the classroom. Indeed, Kellner has focused studies in education on explicating media literacy and the multiple literacies needed to critically engage culture in the contemporary era. On this basis, he has called for a democratic reconstruction of education for the new digitized, mediated, global, and multicultural era.

Here his work poses the question how can technology be used to further democratic ends in the classroom and fight against global forms of oppression and exploitation? What forms of literacy are needed to read media critically and produce media that challenge dominant value systems? How can teachers bring new media into the classroom to teach critically?

REFERENCES

Kellner, Douglas. *Critical Theory, Marxism, and Modernity.* Baltimore: Johns Hopkins University Press, 1992.

Kellner, Douglas. *Media Culture: Cultural Studies, Identity and Politics Between the Modern and the Postmodern.* London: Routledge, 1995.

Kellner, Douglas. "Multiple Literacies and Critical Pedagogy in a Multicultural Society." *Educational Theory* 48, no. 1 (1998): 103–22.

Kellner, Douglas. "Technological Transformation, Multiple Literacies, and the Re-visioning of Education." *E-Learning* 1, no. 1 (2004): 9–37.

Ryan, Michael, and Douglas Kellner. *Camera Politica: The Politics and Ideology of Contemporary Hollywood Film.* Bloomington: University of Indiana Press, 1990.

MULTIPLE LITERACIES IN EDUCATION: AN INTRODUCTION

The dramatic proliferation of computer, information, communication, and multimedia technologies during the last century has drastically altered everything from the ways people work, to the ways they communicate with each other and spend their leisure time. Furthermore the rise of an "information society" poses tremendous challenges to educators to rethink their basic tenets, to deploy the new technologies in creative and productive ways, and to restructure schooling to respond constructively and progressively to the technological and other changes currently underway. In this study, I argue that educators need to cultivate multiple literacies for contemporary technological and multicultural societies, that teachers need to develop a range of literacies of diverse sorts to meet the challenge of restructuring education for a hi-tech, multicultural society, and global economy and culture.

To dramatize the issues at stake, we should consider the claim that we are now undergoing one of the most significant technological revolutions for education since the progression from oral to print and book based teaching (Castells 1996, 1997, 1998, and Best and Kellner 2001). Just as the transition to print literacy and book culture involved a dramatic transformation of education (Ong 1988), so too does the ongoing technological transformation demand a major restructuring of education today with novel curricula, pedagogy, literacies, practices, and goals. Furthermore, the technological developments of the present era makes possible the radical re-visioning and reconstruction of education and society argued for in the progressive era by Dewey and in the 1960s and 1970s by Ivan Illich, Paolo Freire, and others who sought radical educational and social reform. However, intense pressures for change now come directly from technology and the economy and not ideology or educational reformist ideas, with an expanding global economy and novel technologies demanding innovative skills, competencies, literacies, and practices. It is therefore a burning question as to what sort of restructuring of education and society will take place, in whose interests, and for what ends. More than ever, we need philosophical reflection on the ends and purposes of education, on what we are doing and trying to achieve in our educational practices and institutions.

With the proper resources, policies, pedagogies, and practices, educators can work to reduce the (unfortunately growing) gap between the technological haves and have nots (also known as the digital divide) by promoting broad training in information and computer literacy, that embraces a wide range of projects from providing technical skills to engaging students in the production of media projects. Although technology alone will not suffice to democratize and adequately reconstruct education, in a technological society providing proper access and training can improve education if it is taken as a supplement. That is, technology itself does not necessarily improve teaching and learning, and will certainly not of itself overcome acute socio-economic divisions.

In the following reflections, I propose multiple literacies in two respects. First, I call for media and visual literacies to be central to educational practices, thus taking seriously the media saturated lives of students. Second, I call for a new form of computer literacy that moves beyond questions of access and simple skill acquisition. Underlying both forms of literacy is the conviction that we should, as educators, provide *critical* lenses and perspectives for students to evaluate the positive and negative messages and effects of new media and information and communication technologies (ICTs) on their lives. Thus the critical perspective I encourage resists either technophilic enthusiasm (an uncritical embrace of all new technologies as inherently progressive and thus inherently good) or technophobic rejection (a ludic paranoia concerning the inherently negative effects of all new technologies). Both of these extremes lack a truly *critical* dimension, which is never either/or (either technology is good or it is bad), but rather embraces a vision of technology that recognizes its ambiguities (both its positive and negative sides). Critical literacies of new technologies insist on overcoming the digital divide not by simply rejecting technology but rather by refashioning and restructuring technologies in light of democracy as a guiding, normative ideal, thus enabling individuals to democratically and creatively participate in a new economy, society, and culture (see Feenberg 1991; 1999).

In sum, the question is not whether computers and multimedia technologies are good or bad in the classroom or more broadly for education. Rather, it is a question of what multimedia and computers can do and cannot do towards helping to produce a more democratic and equalitarian society and what their limitations are for producing more active and creative human beings and a more just society. Crucially, we must ask: What sort of skills do students and teachers need to effectively deploy computers and information technology, what sort of effects might ICTs have on learning, subjectivities, and social relations, and what new literacies, forms of education, and social relations do we need to democratize and improve education today?

In the new multimedia environment, *media literacy* is arguably more important than ever. Cultural studies and critical pedagogy have begun to teach us to recognize the ubiquity of media culture in contemporary society, the growing trends toward multicultural education, and the need for media literacy that addresses the issue of multicultural and social difference. There is expanding recognition that media representations help construct our images and understanding of the world and that education must meet the dual challenges of teaching media literacy in a multicultural society and sensitizing students and publics to the inequities and injustices of a society based on gender, race, and class inequalities and discrimination. Media education and the production of alternative media can help create a healthy multiculturalism of diversity and more robust democracy.

Yet despite the ubiquity of media culture in contemporary society and everyday life, and the recognition that the media themselves are a form of pedagogy, and despite criticisms of the distorted values, ideals, and representations of the world in popular culture, media education in K-12 schooling has never really been established and developed. It is highly irresponsible in the face of saturation by Internet and media culture to ignore these types of socialization and education; consequently a critical reconstruction of education should produce pedagogies that provide media literacy and enable students, teachers, and citizens to discern the nature and effects of media culture.

Media culture is a form of pedagogy that teaches proper and improper behavior, gender roles, values, and knowledge of the world (Kellner, 1995). Individuals are often not aware that they are being educated and constructed by media culture, as its pedagogy is frequently invisible and subliminal. This situation calls for critical approaches that make us aware of how media construct meanings, influence and educate audiences, and impose their messages and values. A media literate person is skillful in analyzing media codes and conventions, able to criticize stereotypes, values, and ideologies, and competent to interpret the multiple meanings and messages generated by media texts. Media literacy helps people to use media intelligently, to discriminate and evaluate media content, to critically dissect media forms, and to investigate media effects and uses (see Kellner 1995).

Indeed, teaching critical media literacy could be a participatory, collaborative project. Watching television shows or films together could promote productive discussions between teachers and students (or parents and children), with emphasis on eliciting student views, producing a variety of interpretations of media texts and teaching basic principles of hermeneutics and criticism. Students and youth are often more media savvy, knowledgeable, and immersed in media culture than their teachers, and can contribute to the educational process through sharing their ideas, perceptions, and insights. On the other hand, critical discussion, debate, and analysis ought to be encouraged with teachers bringing to bear their critical perspectives on student readings of media material. Since media culture is often part and parcel of students' identity and most powerful cultural experience, teachers must be sensitive in criticizing artifacts and perceptions that students hold dear, yet an atmosphere of critical respect for difference *and* inquiry into the nature and effects of media culture should be promoted.

One of the most effective ways of teaching critical media literacy is involving students themselves in the production of media texts (see Hammer in McLaren et al. 1995). Learning to produce different kinds of media texts teaches codes, formal features, and the role of technology in constructing media artifacts. In becoming literate in semiological and ideological codes of media culture, students not only can read and critique dominant modes of cultural hegemony, but they can produce oppositional forms of culture, subverting the dominant codes and ideologies and providing alternatives.

Teaching critical media literacy involves occupation of a site above the dichotomy of fandom (technophilic) and censor (technophobic). One can teach how media culture provides significant statements or insights about the social world, empowering visions of gender, race, and class, or complex aesthetic structures and practices, thereby putting a positive spin on how it can provide significant contributions to education. Yet critical educators should indicate also how media culture can advance sexism, racism, ethnocentrism, homophobia, and other types of prejudice, as well as misinformation, problematic ideologies, and questionable values, accordingly promoting a dialectical approach to the media that aims at critical and discriminating readers.

To fully participate in the hi-tech and global society, teachers and students should cultivate new kinds of computer literacy in ways that go beyond standard technical notions. Critical computer literacy involves learning how to use computer technologies to do research and gather information, as well as to perceive computer culture as a terrain containing texts, spectacles, games, and interactive multimedia which call for cultivating new literacies. As technologies like computers, telephones, televisions, and new multimedia devices converge, computer-mediated culture will increasingly provide an encompassing environment in which people work, play, relate, learn, and interact. Becoming computer-literate in this broad sense thus requires expanding notions of literacy and learning how to communicate, interact, and create in novel cybercultures.

The emergent cybercultures can be seen as a discursive and political location in which students, teachers, and citizens can all intervene, engaging in discussion groups and collaborative research projects, creating Web-sites, producing innovative multimedia for cultural dissemination, and engaging in novel modes of social interaction and learning. Computer culture enables individuals to actively participate in the production of culture, ranging from dialogue concerning public issues to creation of their own cultural forms. However, to take part in this culture requires not only accelerated skills of print literacy, which are often restricted to the growing elite of students who are privileged to attend adequate and superior public and private schools, but also demands multiple literacies.

To respond intelligently to the dramatic technological revolution of our time, we need to begin teaching computer literacy from an early age. Computer literacy, however, itself needs to be theorized. Often the term is synonymous with technical ability to use computers, to become proficient in the use of existing programs, and maybe undertake some programming. I suggest expanding the conception of computer literacy from using computer programs and hardware to a broader concept of information and multimedia literacy. This necessitates promoting more sophisticated abilities in traditional reading and writing, as well as the capability to dissect and read cultural forms taught as part of critical media literacy and multimedia pedagogy.

Information literacy thus requires learning how to distinguish between good and bad information, identifying what Burbules and Callister (2000) identify as misinformation, malinformation, messed-up information, and mostly useless information. Such literacy necessitates heightened capacities for critically accessing, analyzing, interpreting, processing, and storing both print-based and multimedia material. In a novel information/entertainment society, immersed in transformative multimedia technology, knowledge and information come not merely in the form of print and words, but through images, sounds, and multimedia material as well. As such, visual and auditory literacies take on increased importance. On the whole, computer screens are more graphic, multi-sensory, dynamic, and interactive than conventional print fields that disconcerted many of us when first confronted with the new environments. Icons, windows, mouses, and the various clicking, linking, and interaction involved in computer-mediated hypertext dictate new competencies and a dramatic expansion of literacy. Visuality is obviously crucial, compelling users to perceptively scrutinize visual fields, perceive and interact with icons and graphics, and use technical devices like a mouse to access the desired material and field.

Moreover, with ever-expanding Internet subcultures and online communities, more and more people have the possibilities of participating in cultural production and expression. Innovative web sites, such as blogs and wikis, have emerged as important new developments of the Net's hypertextual architecture and provide opportunities for new voices, alternative online communities, and political activism (Kahn and Kellner 2003). Participation in this new cultural and political environment accordingly requires the cultivation of multiple literacies.

In short, "multiple literacies" points to the many different kinds of literacies needed to access, interpret, criticize, and participate in the emergent multimedia culture and society. The key root here is the "multiple," emphasizing the proliferation of media which demands a multiplicity of competencies and skills and abilities to access, interact, and help construct a new semiotic terrain. Multiple literacies involve reading across varied and hybrid semiotic fields and being able to critically and hermeneutically process print, graphics, moving images, and sounds. Perpetually multiplying media provide the challenge for multiplying uses, always recreating and reconstructing media forms and practices. While traditional literacies concern practices in contexts that are governed by rules and conventions, the conventions and rules of multiple literacies are currently evolving so that their pedagogies comprise a fresh although bustling and competitive field. Critical educators need to theorize the literacies necessary to interact in these emergent multimedia environments and to gain the skills that will enable individuals to learn, work, and create in emergent cultural spaces and domains.

Cultivating multiple literacies and reconstructing education for democratization will also involve constructing traditional pedagogies and social relations. Emergent multimedia technologies enable group projects for students and more of a problem-solving pedagogy in the spirit of Dewey and Freire than traditional transmission top-down teaching models. To enable students to access information, engage in cultural communication and production, and to gain the skills necessary to succeed in the global economy and culture, they need to acquire enhanced literacies, abilities to work cooperatively with others, and to navigate emergent cultural and social terrains. Such group activity may generate more egalitarian relations between teachers and students and more democratic and cooperative social relations. Of course, it also demands reconsideration of grading and testing procedures, rethinking the roles of teacher and student, and constructing projects and pedagogies appropriate to the new cultural and social environments.

Finally, adequately meeting the challenges of ever-multiplying technologies raise the question of design and reconstruction of technology itself. As Andrew Feenberg has long argued (1991; 1999), democratizing technology often requires its reconstruction and re-visioning by individuals. Within the technology world, "hackers" have redesigned technological systems and much of the Internet itself is the result of individuals contributing collective knowledge and making improvements that aid various educational, political, and cultural projects. Of course, there are corporate and technical constraints in that dominant programs impose their rules and constraints on users and the open source movement has challenged users to participate in alternative computer programs and sites, freely providing novel innovations, programs, and content of various modes. There has been an on-going struggle within computer world between corporations and users with governments usually intervening on the side of major corporations. Critical educators, however, should help teach students and themselves to become producers as well as consumers, thus helping to redesign and reconstruct the very forms and programs of computers.

In sum, the critical dimension is needed more than ever as we attempt to develop improved teaching strategies and pedagogy, and design more emancipatory and democratizing technologies and curricula. In this process, we should avoid extreme positions, realizing the potentials of technologies and also their limitations in light of democratic ends. Guiding this critical, philosophical perspective are key questions such as: Whose interests are emergent technologies and pedagogies serving? Are they helping all social groups and individuals? Who is being excluded and why? We also need to raise the question both of the extent to which multiplying technologies and literacies are preparing students and citizens for the present and future and producing conditions for a more vibrant democratic society, or simply reproducing existing inequalities and inequity. It appears that technology will certainly drive the reconstruction of education, but we should make sure that it works to enhance democracy and empower individuals and not just corporations and a privileged techno-elite.

REFERENCES

Best, Steven, and Kellner, Douglas (2001) *The Postmodern Adventure.* New York: Guilford Press.

Burbules, Nicholas C. and Callister, Thomas (2000) *Watch IT. The Risks and Promises of Information Technology.* Boulder, Col.: Westview Press.

Castells, Manuel (1996) *The Rise of the Network Society.* Oxford: Blackwell.

_____ (1997) *The Power of Identity.* Oxford: Blackwell.

_____ (1998) *End of Millenium.* Oxford: Blackwell.

Feenberg, Andrew (1991) Critical Theory of Technology. New York: Oxford University Press.

_____ (1999) *Questioning Technology.* New York and London, Routledge.

Kahn, R. and Kellner, D. (2003) "Internet Subcultures and Oppositional Politics", in D. Muggleton (ed), *The Post-subcultures Reader,* London: Berg.

Kellner, Douglas (1995) *Media Culture.* London and New York: Routledge.

McLaren, Peter, Rhonda Hammer, David Sholle and Susan Reilly, (1995) *Rethinking Media Literacy. A Critical Pedagogy of Representation.* New York: Peter Lang.

Ong, Walter (1988) *Orality and Literacy: The Technologizing of the Word.* London and New York: Routledge.

26

PHILIP WEXLER

Professor Philip Wexler, born in 1943 in the United States, is a world-recognized scholar whose work on the sociology of education and spirituality—as well as on pedagogy, social psychology, and curriculum theory—is recognized as groundbreaking. He completed his Ph.D. at Princeton in 1972. He was appointed professor of sociology and of education in 1979 and dean of the Warner School of Education at the University of Rochester in 1989. In 1983 his book *Critical Social Psychology* was published, and in 1987 *Social Analysis of Education: After the New Sociology* became a required reading for scholars in the field. His work has been informed by critical theory, which he questioned, as well as by the work of other intellectual giants of the 20th century, such as Martin Buber and Basil Bernstein. Much of his contemporary writing on education discusses the intersections among education, society, and religion. In 1996 *Holy Sparks* and in 2000 *Mystical Society* were published. In 2002 he accepted a professorship at The Hebrew University of Jerusalem.

His work has provided the field of educational thought with a strong foundation of social theory and a better understanding of education as social practice. Wexler is one of the most thoughtful thinkers of education at the beginning of the 21st century. His work interrogates critical work, which usually focuses on how power operates, from a supportive but challenging perspective, pointing to the limitations of a reduced focus on power. He was one of the few and first to recognize that dogmatic critical perspectives fail to explain the complex aspects of human agency. He also questioned methodological and conceptual approaches in the social analysis, social psychology, and education, which tend to provide prescriptive explanations of phenomena by offering generalizations and rigid constructions of social categories without complexity. Furthermore, he also has interrogated and challenged postmodern explanations of educational and social experience. In his present work, he explores the role of spirituality and religion as a way of knowing which informs, as well as is informed by, social analysis. His emphasis on the spiritual aspects of education engages the reader not only within the mystical experience of becoming educated or the "new wave" ideas in a holistic sense but also with how these ideas connect with relevant traditions of philosophical and social analysis.

In *Mystical Society* he argues for a new approach to social and educational analysis by also utilizing what he labels "ethnography of the self." His arguments connect with a number of traditions that include phenomenology, aspects of critical social theory, some variation of psychoanalysis, and the work of Webber, Durkheim, and Buber—particularly *I-Thou* and "Man-to-Man." In addition, he also connects in his writing with several Talmudic and other Jewish sources. What is particularly appealing in this work is that he takes spirituality not at face value but as a form of social analysis, which develops into new theoretical frameworks. Furthermore, his "ethnography of the self" builds beyond phenomenological or even psychoanalytic or lacanean traditions of autobiography where the self is the subject matter of study and it is not in isolation from that socio-spiritual context.

In spite of an intricate writing style, which reflects the complex sophistication of his analysis and propositions, his arguments are visionary and invite readers to question predictability grounded on rigid interpretations, especially in the context of education. The following short selections illustrate some of Wexler's propositions.

REFERENCES

Wexler, P. *Sociology of Education: Beyond Equality*. Indianapolis: Bobbs-Merrill, 1976.

Wexler, P. *Critical Social Psychology*. Boston, MA: Routledge, 1983.

Wexler, P. *Social Analysis of Education: After the New Sociology*. New York: Routledge, 1987.

Wexler, P. *Holy Sparks: Social Theory, Education, and Religion*. New York: St. Martin's, 1996.

Wexler, P. *Mystical Society: An Emerging Social Vision*. Boulder, CO: Westview, 2000.

THE MYSTICAL SOCIETY

Prophetic Education

These are the topics that constitute an ethnography of being. A radically changing historical, social, educational context and new research in fields adjacent to education show how an ethnography of being can be actualized in studying education. Societal change has led to new research in adjacent fields by raising questions that are considered "educational."

This is a move away from the textualist aspect of postmodernism to the *existential situation* that the new social formation produces in everyday life; it is represented in new topics, resources, and practical and academic problematics and strategies. The topical move is to the reinterpretation of education as a process of being and meaning, for which "healing" may be the ideal, paradigmatic type. Its topics are consciousness, embodiment, emotions, and transcendence as altered states, the senses, energy, and complex transformations across lived worlds of timeless time that reframe consciousness and experienced embodiment.

In terms of the interest and emphasis in research, everyday problem solving, and socially shared individual practices, this entails a shift from discourse to an interactional study of beings and worlds. These are not simply constructions; they are imaginary recreations in which the "secondary interest," to use Toulmin's term, is not identity stabilization in an ambiguous world, but creation and sensorial transformation (Stein 1999). In this regard, its practice is not reproductive, critical, or disruptive, but revitalizing. The aim is vivification and enlivenment, the filling of a self emptied in an earlier time. The medium of this practice is not deconstructive mass media, but an analytical privileging of the charismatic and mystical religious movements and revitalizing practices of mind/body healing.

Under these historical conditions, the socially induced alteration in the meaning of education is taken actively; in Buber's terminology, it is a practice that "goes beyond mere liberation." At its apex, it moves from renewal of life sense to realization and enlightenment. This is not a new teleology, but an enlightenment of the present and a sociology of presence (Wexler 1996) in which there is a "practicing of

From "Education: From Postmodernism to Ethnography of Being" in *Mystical Society* by Philip Wexler, 2000. Reprinted by permission of Westview Press, a member of Perseus Books Group.

eternity" (Stein 1998) in this world. Its cosmology abandons both the linear narrative of progress and the fetishism of spatialized temporal incoherence; this is abandoned in favor of an intentional fusion of worlds that is also present instead of being dualized as this- and often-worldly. The reframing of experience requires not a simple demolition of contemporary authority, but a reauthorization of traditions that can mythologize and reenchant without losing the capacity for intentional, rational critique: a cosmic social criticism.

Here I am not going to enter into the more fine-grained discussion of detailed research practice, of the "techniques" that will be the "proof of the pudding." I hint at a turning in technique as well: away from deconstruction to "the truth of the way things are," or "dharma" as J. Goldstein (1993) puts it. Empirically, I think there will be a move in research practice to liken its techniques increasingly to the sorts of disciplines of *present awareness* that are currently more characteristic of meditation than of "research," as it has traditionally been conceived.

These practices of awareness move outward as well as inward, in a new regime of mystical informationalism. With cultural reintegration, research is again about "objectivity," but a new objectivity of awareness that works through the social limitations of consciousness instead of denying it. Goldstein puts it aphoristically in the language of the Buddha:

> The mind is radiant, shining, glowing forth; but it is stained by the defilements that visit it. The mind is radiant, shining, glowing forth, and from uprooting of defilements that visit it, it is freed. (1993, p. 8)

However, in educational practice cognitivism continues the seventeenth-century cultural regime of decontextualizing knowledge and separating epistemology from ontology and cosmology. This remains the regnant educational theology, despite the more socially historicized (but no more living or deeply reintegrated) contextualism of the educational, political so-called radicals.

Rather, the counterpractice is the return to heaven and earth, to being and cosmos, in the practices of revitalization. But as an opposition, even the revitalizing process from within mystical informationalism is prey to rigidification in a dualistic polarity of rationalism and mysticism. This is the problem that I attributed to Durkheim, in whose practical, educational analogue we find in the combined desiccation of standardized school performance and identity-desperation that compensates by violent self-assertions.

Ecstatic mysticism, then, is an effect of the mystical informational dynamics that we have considered. But in education, as in society more generally, the danger associated with it is a proliferation of violently destructive cults, reminiscent of Lasch's condemnation of gnostic Hellenism and its New Age parallels. The alternative is a nondualist interweaving of epistemology and ontology or, more precisely, of intellectual vision within existentially mystical states.

This is the "contemplative seeing" that Elliot Wolfson (1994) documents in his history of medieval Jewish mysticism. Contrary to the usual expectations about Jewish textualism, Wolfson shows the "ocularcentrism" of mystical practice; a visionary, symbolic intellectualism that goes well beyond the text, the word, or even the letters for its "enthronement," in what scholars of Sufism have called the "imaginal body." Vision, body, and emotion are combined in a practice of "the heart": "In the Islamic-Jewish Neoplatonic tradition, the vision of the heart is an intellectual intuition of that which is incorporeal and thus invisible in a physical sense" (1994, p. 171). Since "imagination is critical in shaping the vision of the luminous forms in terms of corporeal substance, then the whole inside/outside dichotomy is overcome" (1994, p. 112).

The mystical process here is not a simple desocialized ego surrender to the collective ecstasy. Instead, there are complex interchanges, which might be referred to as alchemies, of intellectual and theoretical assumptions, imagination, visual images, sounds, phantasms, and the physical body. This sort of mysticism is more than simple merging in the cosmos to find "timeless time." It is an active capacity of mind and heart, strength and receptivity of body, openness to nature (water, for example, is a "medium through which the glory can be seen," 1994, p. 242), and conscious cultivation of practices for reintegration with the eternal, energic Presence. This is a reintegration that in Kabbalah is "intensely eroticized." It is dialogical: "The movement of the imagination is from the human body to God and from God back to the human body again" (Wolfson 1994, p. 397).

Abraham Heschel (1962) wants to differentiate intellectual, symbolic visionary mysticism of the heart from undifferentiated ecstatic mysticism. He argues for a type of rational mysticism, despite the substantial debate about the role of ecstasy in emotional and intellectual vision, or prophecy. Heschel uses biblical examples and language to express this in his analysis of prophecy, describing Moses' mysticism as rational in this way: "Moses received his revelation while retaining his full power of consciousness. . . . [He] sees the vision of the Almighty, falling down, yet with opened eyes" (1962, p. 119).

This difference between prophecy and ecstasy in and of itself, even prophetic ecstasy, also signals the non-consummatory aspect of prophecy. It is a call, and the prophetic act is always incomplete. Perhaps that is because "the prophets' field of concern is not the mysteries of heaven, but the affairs of the marketplace; not the spiritual realities of the Beyond, but the life of the people. . . . What the prophet's ear perceives is the word of God, but what the word contains is God's concern for the world" (1962, p. 144).

It is this "falling down with opened eyes" that is a necessary condition for the work that lies ahead. This work is *to create a social vision from the mediating revitalization practices by a shared rediscovery of redemptive traditions, both in a study of the traditional texts and in an active renewal of the ancient techniques of self-realization.* A prophetic mysticism, even in deformed expressions of closed-eyed irrationalism, already hovers about the cognitive schoolhouse.

Pedagogy of Revitalization

The "respiration" of society is blocked in education. Although popular innerworldly mysticism represents what I have called a decentered curriculum, engaging a vast apparatus of New Age adult educational activities, in-school education remains unilinearly aimed toward the accumulation of cognitive capital. Although there are counterinstances of New Age education and the existence of revitalization practices in marginal, alternative school movements, school education is caught in the paroxysm of a duality of everyday school repression in the name of "academic achievement" and sporadic episodes of violent outbursts against schooling and society.

Elsewhere (1996, 1998) I have tried to describe an interactive mutuality of teacher and student, or even a "redemptive" teaching, but there is still no school-based curriculum to match the informal educational movement for the revitalization of everyday life. Although Pinar (1999) and his colleagues have worked to articulate such a curriculum for more than twenty years, it remains idiosyncratic and detached from an embeddedness in a wider movement of society.

As we saw in the discussion of revitalization, this is an education: of the imagination (for an exception, see Maxine Greene 1995); the capacity for cognitive reframing rather than cumulative information processing; ecological self-integration (Laura 1998); and a reselfing reunion through connection to some transcendental Jamesian "More," Kabbalistic "Ein Sof," or unboundedness and an embodied, continual process of recreation within society.

The articulation of the "small signs" (Pinar 1999; Greene 1995; Laura 1998) of such a curriculum into an active pedagogy of revitalization means less an encounter with the state apparatus (though public schools remain static on these dimensions, despite more than a decade of school "reform") and more a challenge to the economic logic of fast-track mobility via educational credentialism. Yet it is precisely in this arena, submerged in the informational and not the mystical aspect of the new society, that we look for the next round of educational transformation.

Such a pedagogy will require first a change in the pedagogues and their theories and practices. As Marx put it, "the educators must be educated." Our educators and educational theorists remain deeply committed to the logics of modernity and, more critically, to models of postmodern education. Yet, as with changing social practice, we already see the emergence of questions on the overlapping domains of religion, education, and society. The intersection of Buddhism and critical pedagogy, curricula of spirituality in the workplace, ecofeminism as a sacred pedagogy, and the dynamics of faith and reason, are examples of issues posed by a new generation of educators raised in the mystical society (Wexler 2000). Along with a redefinition of social concepts, there is a beginning also toward a new pedagogy—of revitalization.

"Forgotten Things"

A mystical society and a pedagogy of revitalization do not occur outside of history. Informationalism's slogan of an "end of history" is a new form of alienation, a deracination of collective being not from place, but from time. Even flowing time can have a memory. Without an intentional memory or a practice of remembering, "forgotten things" do return, but in misshapen forms, encrypted in the deformations of denial and repression. Mystery is emplaced in traditions of meaning, I think (concurring here with Gimello and Katz against "pure consciousness events," if that means outside any social history).

Without memory of those traditions, mystical experience dissolves into momentary pleasure and is easily caught up in the commodity machine of consumption as a new product for sale: mystical experience. If we need a "wild" hunger to quench our ontological thirst, a dialogue with place that creates wholeness that we feel as ecstasy, then we also need a "wild" history to satisfy our being in time. This is an active, living, remembered history and not a facticized accumulation of a dead, inert otherness.

The antidote to the alienation-antidote of mystical experience becoming a new social poison is the intellectual and emotional work of connecting such experience not simply with the momentary unification (Merkur 1999) of psychological gratification and understanding, but also with the long, historical way of collective memory of shared life. This entails both a scholarly and an experiential effort. Alongside the conceptual work of creating a mystical sociology and the educational work of creating and articulating a pedagogy of revitalization, there is also the historical-experiential work of remembering and the scholarly work that feeds memory. This involves an uncovering and a renewal of the mystical traditions that have, until very recently, been erased by the claims of the modern world. The element of the traditions that are now returned to us are only invitations, only beginnings.

As Murray wrote, these forgotten things can "help still in the forward groping of humanity" (1925, p. 238). In these tasks of reimagining, teaching anew, and creating vivid, presently active memories from traditions, we too participate in a historic revitalization of culture, theory, and education. This is the creative work of being truly alive everyday; this is the passion enlightened by mysticism.

HOLY SPARKS

Teaching as Being

Buber's dialogical interaction—and particularly dialogical teaching—works from the starting point of "presence." Here, Buber does not ordinarily mean the in-dwelling spiritual presence that we have described kabbalistically as Shekhinah. Education, for Buber, is openness toward what he calls "the creative Spirit." Presence is existential, concrete,

From "Resacralizing Education" in *Holy Sparks: Social Theory, Education and Religion* by Philip Wexler, 1996, pp. 144-152. Reproduced with permission of Palgrave Macmillan.

mutual and inclusive of the other in a way that goes beyond psychological empathy. "Inclusion is the extension of ones own concreteness, the fulfillment of the actual situation of life, the complete presence of the reality in which one participates" (1965:97). This presence entails an ingathering of the other's presence, by "that subterranean dialogic, that steady potential presence. . . . Then there is reality *between* them, there is mutuality" (1965:98).

Through this presence, the teacher—or "educator" in Buber's term—represents both the opening and the emanation of vital cultural traditions, for which concrete presence, or being, enables the child or student to "receive," in kabbalistic (or, for Buber, Hasidic) imagery. He writes:

> Yet the master remains the model for the teacher. For if the educator of our day has to act consciously he must nevertheless do it "as though he did not." That raising of the finger, that questioning glance, are his genuine doing. . . . the selection of the effective world must be *concentrated* in him; and doing out of concentration has the appearance of rest . . . but a hidden influence proceeding from his integrity has an integrating force. (1965:90)

Integration and unity, concentration and fullness rather than separation, diffusion and emptiness are the goals of such a conscious/unconscious educational interaction. In this version of "character education," there is an "education for community," but not the collective internalization of shared values that typifies contemporary discussions. Instead, Buber observed:

> The mass of contradictions can be met and conquered only by the rebirth of personal unity, *unity of being,* unity of life, unity of action—unity of being, life and action together. . . . It is the longing for personal unity from which must be born a unity of mankind, which the educator should lay hold of and strengthen in his pupils. (1965:116)

For us, this longing is, of course, at first a compensatory desire, a residual effect of the reorganization of self that takes place in the culture of the postindustrial workplace (Casey, 1995). The desire for presence and unified being, for mutuality and dialogical relation grows only with the evident failures of corporate recodings and revivals of a shattered self, an emptiness encased by rigidified shells that are nourished by consumption of the "ten thousand things." Creativity, which Buber calls the "instinct of origination," is an antidote to the false solution of "having," because it "never becomes greed, because it is not directed to 'having', but only to doing" (1965:87).

This doing is the as-though-not-conscious naturalness of being, the same doing/being that Fromm opposed to the alienated market consumerism of "having" (Fromm, 1976).

One implication for an educational movement that is not merely oppositional or marginally corrective, but creatively different, is to cultivate that being of presence which is the existential, at first apparently individual and subjective, alternative to a devitalized (do we really believe that "chronic fatigue syndrome" is an entirely intrapersonal, physiological phenomenon?), performance-structured, commodity-oriented, decaying, postmodern self. The new age cultural wave makes possible (just as it may also limit) not only an initially narcissistic resubjectification, but also a deeper cultural shift of basic premises, as Pitirim Sorokin (1957) argued. In turn, a new vocabulary and consciousness that can reverberate in social theory and education offers a new cultural foundation for both social theory and education.

For teaching, as for the revitalization of everyday social life, there is no protocol or formula for being. But our emphasis here on the sociocultural conditions or context for changes in social theory and education—the refusal of a postmodern antihistory—does not deny intentionality, which is the directed action of Hasidic sanctification of everyday life that Buber so much praised as different from the rabbinic, legal rationalist Judaism of the European mainstream. The emphasis on presence or being in education, and in teaching especially, is not spontaneism, but a sort of Taoist conscious naturalness that Buber idealized in the teacher as master. While not routine, this ideal does imply disciplined practice or, in Western terms, "virtue."

Fromm's posthumously published (1994) book, *The Art of Being*, represents a condensed effort to catalog such disciplined practices that could realize an alternative to the alienated, consumer-driven culture and self against which he struggled in all of his work. Fromm offers a short road map to what he had earlier (Fromm, 1976) called a "city of being." His insights into practicing being are drawn not only from a socialist critique of what we now call postmodern society, or a psychoanalytic background and commitment to rational demystification, or even a radical reading of the Old Testament as a blueprint for an historical, collective path toward a nonidolatrous, dealienated social existence. Drawing upon so-called Eastern religions and what are unmistakably instances of new age "bodywork," Fromm offers an outline of

practices that could well constitute a different path of teacher formation, based on a different sociocultural premise.

What I am suggesting is not only that this reconceptualized practice of
virtue—these "arts of being"—is of general interest for the transformation
of social interaction and individual identity, but also that as a schematic
catalog it offers an alternative model for "educating the educator." These
"arts of being" suggest the possibility of a curriculum of teacher education
that is different than the traditional, industrial-bureaucratic teacher education, with its interest in transmission of the rules and regulation of pedagogy and disciplinary subjects. The *presence* of the educator also suggests a
different path than the current postindustrial education curriculum
emphasis on managed forms of collaboration that blur institutional
boundaries, and thereby further corporatist social forms of regulation and
governance. This new alternative curriculum also stands in contrast to a
so-called radical, slogan-like authoritarianism that parades under the banner of "critical pedagogy" in both modern and postmodern forms.

This entirely different training of educators is a training for being,
for presence, for the concentrated intelligence of awareness that enables
inclusion of the other side—the student—as an organic, living being and
not as an object of mechanical or electronic desire for control and manipulation in the name of performance standards, new skills, and personal
and national success in global competition. Are these latter terms not the
watchwords of contemporary educational change around the postindustrial, postmodern world? For subjective and culturally creative revitalization the teacher has, first of all, to be alive, not dead. I have argued
that a generative source for this resubjectification is in a broader cultural
revitalization, one that flows from a transcendental mediation of intersubjectivity, and that rationalizes and elaborates world views deriving
from renewals of ancient symbolic traditions of the sacred.

Although Fromm secularizes his catalog of the arts of being, these
arts develop historically as cultural integrals and are most fully
expressed in religious or sacred aspects of those historic, core civiliza-
tional cultures. Like the soul traveler of Dante's Inferno, Fromm's
seeker of "attaining optimal being," must pass through the "suggestion
apparatus of society," which produces the "inner chains" that block
both inner and outer liberation (1994:4–10). Socially produced obstacles
to liberation are the "great shams" of promises of power and fame,
excessive cerebral orientation, and the illusions, including the illusion
of what we are calling new age cultural practices (1994:11). Fromm

already foresaw commodification of forces for the "transformation from within." He warned of what he referred to as the "commercialization of the salvation business": "Has the spirit of big business and its selling methods already made such inroads that one must also accept them in the field of individual spiritual development?" (1994:17).

Fromm poses an alternative, drawing on Eastern traditions for disciplined practices designed to shed illusions, in much the same way as Csikszentmihalyi (1993) offers a cognitive psychological evolutionary theory of attention. Here too, the key is the cultivation of awareness. Fromm writes:

> The conclusion from all these considerations is that the most important step in the art of being is everything that leads to and enhances our capacity for heightened awareness and, as far as the mind is concerned, for critical, questioning thinking. (1994:43)

He also uses the language of energy in discussing awareness, concentration and the goal of revitalization: "Mobilization of energy, which has a psychic as well as a physiological aspect, has the effect of making one feel alive" (1994:45).

Buber and Fromm coalesce in the emphasis on concentration and attending to the presence of the other as a formative, necessary element of any intersubjectivity: "the Buddhist concept of *mindfulness* [emphasis added] means precisely a way of being in which one is fully concentrated on everything one is doing at any given moment" (1994:49). This ideal of integration of attention is quite different from the superficial, postmodern celebration of noisy, carnivalesque polyvocality.

Concentrated, mindful presence is a protection against the attachment of energies to a mode of dependent submission to powerful others, which is now identified as idolatry (alienation). For even in a psychoanalytically oriented secularization of sacred disciplines of being, Fromm intersperses the more culturally foundational vocabularies drawn from traditions of collectively organized, subjective sacred experience. Fromm aims to cultivate cognitive, rational, intersubjective presence in his recollected arts of being. He wants to resuscitate the feeling, "affect," that has been severed from intellection. This severance of feeling blocks the vitalizing experience of joy, and the capacity for what Jessica Benjamin (1988) and Buber both call "mutuality," but which Fromm refers to simply as the "capacity for giving," and, as we have seen, "for loving." "In summary," he writes: "modern man *has* many things and uses many things, but he *is* very little. His feelings and thinking processes are atrophied like unused muscles (1994:96). Here the echo of Marx's theory of alienation (see Bertell Ollman, 1971) is very loud.

Postmodern idolatry is consumption, having, trying to fill the emptiness with food, devouring sex, and other manifestations of "hostile possessiveness." In the end, culturally and religiously derived, individuated practices of being can change identity: "To sum up once more: Awareness, will, practice, tolerance of fear and new experience, they are all necessary if transformation of the individual is to succeed" (Fromm, 1994:120).

Teaching in Sociocultural Movement

Fromm's educative interest in culling and communicating eclectic practices to transform identity and society certainly can provide a basis for creating an alternative curriculum for teacher education. Transformative teaching requires that the teacher herself or himself be fully whole, and sufficiently aware to respond concretely to the student, opening a dialogic path for individual growth and development. In a time when mechanical petrification pervades teacher-student interaction, the existential emphasis on awareness is a mild corrective.

Indeed, Fromm's catalog is easily assimilable to new age cultural trends, commercialized and otherwise. In part, this is because the arts of being are consistently separated from any of their generative sources. Putting it severely, they are desocialized and decultured, appearing as interactional devices, interpersonal knacks that can obstruct a much larger apparatus working to inhibit the development of full human being. Despite the intention, the effect is to separate and extricate the individual from society, culture, history, and dynamic closeness to such energizing approaches to the sacred that we have touched upon. While I do think that an orientation to a dialogic teaching of presence is a salutary corrective to the educational trends that we have described and that the arts of being can be fruitfully brought to teacher education, still, as decultured devices, they are ironically alienated from the broader sociocultural movements within which educational change is contained.

Resacralizing teaching, as a revitalizing alternative to postmodern educational forms in both corporatism and its critiques, can avoid the very commercialization that Fromm feared only by itself being integral to a larger, dynamic whole. Practically, the expression of resacralized social forms is much more evident in socioeducational activities less institutionalized than teaching (in its current professionalized organization). Such oppositional resacralization would require a deprofessionalization and debureaucratization of teaching to the extent that teaching could become a personal "calling" to actualize the transformation of identity.

While Weber (1946) railed against ersatz prophecy in the university lecture hall, simultaneously he described prophetic styles as dynamic elements in historic transformation. Indeed, one of the responsibilities that intellectuals had forsaken was the work of rationalizing and sublimating religious salvation ethics. Weber's (1958) typology of prophecy does show an example of how resacralized teaching can become a socially dynamic force.

Without intersubjectivity, teaching from within cultural movements becomes the sort of collectivist "box of scorpions" that Buber shunned in his anticentralist utopian socialism. Yet, without contextualization in sociocultural movement, any arts-of-being, new age, or resacralized teaching becomes, despite its advance on the present, an individualized interaction device to produce student-workers as arrays of surface or flexible skill performers.

I suggest then, a combination of teaching with styles of prophecy, as a heuristic way of underlining the sociocultural embeddedness of any durable effective teaching. This no more means that all teachers should become prophets (sacralized "transformative intellectuals") than does my attempt to resacralize social theory and education as explanation indicate a predilection for religious schools, as currently constituted. Rather, it is a simultaneous recognition of the historic sociocultural preeminence of religion and an effort to revitalize decadent cultural, theoretical and educational ways of thinking and being. It is a method of breaking out of current ways of thinking about teaching.

This interest in prophecy is found in Weber's juxtaposition of prophet and priest, and the educational analogues for deinstitutionalizing routine or "priestly" teaching, in favor of an enlivening, engaging "prophetic" teaching. Weber indicates the difference:

> For our purposes here, the personal call is the decisive element distinguishing the prophet from the priest. The latter lays claim to authority by virtue

of his service in a sacred tradition, while the prophet's claim is based on personal revelation and charisma. (1964:46)

Weber differentiates the prophet from founders of schools of philosophy, teachers of ethics, and even those traditionally classed as prophets whom he categorizes as theorists of social reform. What does link teachers and prophets is the strength of the bond between a teacher of religious or philosophical wisdom and his disciple. But, what finally differentiates prophets from other teachers is not the reverence of the "disciple-master relationship", but teachers' "lack of that vital emotional preaching which is distinctive of prophecy" (Weber, 1964:52,53). It is then hyperbolic to suggest that teachers can, or should, become more like prophets as sociocultural and educational sacralization increases. But, the exaggeration does underline both the necessity of emotional bonding and the integration of teaching within a living cultural tradition that feeds organic social, individuated identities. These are elements that are barely present in the contemporary model of education, which posits flexible standards and performance-accountability.

To state the analytical interest even more baldly, if Bernstein's sociology is a recontextualization of Durkheim's sociology of religion, at a cultural time of resacralization movements, should we not ask what other sociologies of religion, such as Weber's, imply for a social understanding of education? Further, without advocating religious schools, should we not ask more, following our larger analytic pattern of reading sociology back into culture and culture into religion, about the implications of religious theory and practice for creating new models of educational theory and practice?

So, for example, Weber's types of ethical and exemplary prophecy offer clues to understanding different types of teaching—first, as modes of interaction, but then more generally, as analyses of individual being, teaching practice and cultural movement. These are very different sorts of linked analyses: an ethical prophecy of obligatory correction of action according to abstract norms; and an exemplary prophecy that does not preach ethical obligation, but "rather directs itself to the self-interest of those who crave salvation, recommending to them the same path as he himself traversed" (Weber, 1964:55).

According to this resacralized approach, teaching would be seen more as a cultural practice aligned with other institutional practices. The social effect of postindustrialism in production and postmodernism in consumption has been a blurring of practices and meanings across sectors of society. This reversal, if not of the division of labor in fact, then of its representations, is heightened also by current resacralization movements which, commercialized, authoritarian or not, aim to reduce boundaries between the sacred and profane. Just as changing production and communication technologies and organizational devices migrate to the educational sector, so too does a changed cultural premise and practice inevitably press for expression in various forms of resacralized education.

The resacralization of culture means, theoretically, a rethinking of education in terms of religion, to the extent that the sociocultural foundations of education are resacralized. Theoretically, it implies the borrowing and adaptation of categories such as ethical and exemplary prophecy in order to understand changes in teaching and to be able to contextualize those changes in wider sociocultural movements. Practically, it means a new complement to the postindustrial press for educational restructuring. The interesting analytical issue is precisely the interaction of these apparently contradictory tendencies: postindustrialism and resacralization. Perhaps the most apparent manifestation of the effects of this interaction is the comfort of religious, politically rightist groups with corporatist school reform. On a subtler side of the social realignment process, religious groups interested in education join the liberal and libertarian communalists, who may demur from economic education reform as excessive instrumentalism in the name of remoralization and character education.

These contradictions are not going to be resolved theoretically, but in political, social, cultural educational practice and movement. What is possible is that these sociocultural movements can at least be attended to by social theorists of education, since they may provide an opportunity to move paradigmatically into more open space. From this place we look away from an ever more strident critical sociology of education and an appropriately superficial and fragmented collaging of postmodern icons and aesthetics to social analyses of education.

Instead, there is now an opening toward the religious foundations of culture, which reappear, subject both to a fundamentalist appropriation and to a contemporary revisionist reading. This revisionism is fused with a socially transformative interest in a revolutionary renewal of theory and practice in society and education.

POSTSCRIPT

Playing with Ideas: Some Notes About Learning Communities and Connected Teaching Elements

Learning communities, communities of learners, communities of inquiry, socially constructed learning, and learning in community have been discussed, analyzed, defined, and criticized too many times. However, in contemporary educational environments an overwhelming number of classrooms at different levels and in different school contexts have been using some version of group work, group discussion, group project, group inquiry, or group cooperation with or without modern technologies in varied ways, at least a few times in the course of an academic year. In the following notes, I will play with some of these ideas.

Although in these notes there are implicit themes related to the larger purposes of education, the reasons for schooling, what constitutes a classroom, the nature of a school's institutional organization, and what must be taught (the overt curriculum) and what does not (the null curriculum), these issues will not be addressed directly. That is the reason for the title of this postscript; these are only some notes, not a comprehensive essay. I will first discuss three prevalent dimensions of learning communities. Then, I will proceed to play and explain some teaching elements within the framework of classrooms that foster a learning community.

LEARNING COMMUNITIES

In general terms, "learning communities" refers to at least three dimensions of group or class centered practices, which include the individual student within the classroom context by emphasizing some levels of cooperation, exchange, support, dependency, and collective exploration. These dimensions complement each other and often develop simultaneously, but they do not function as taxonomy. In addition, fostering learning communities as a teaching approach does not mean that eventually there is no room for good lectures, direct instruction, or traditional memorization. The teacher is not divorced from the learning community; rather, he or she is a member and participates actively. However, the teacher is the authority and cannot and should not relinquish such responsibility, for the teacher has experience and expertise in addition to the trust that is inherent in the role. The authority is not only that of the role but also that which emerges from the relationships and environment created to support the learning community; thus, it includes that of expertise and inquiry knowledge. The issue for the teacher is to ask how that authority is used, for what purposes, and under which circumstances.

The first common dimension is that of learning together as a community. Such a dimension assumes that it is possible to learn not only from each other but also under the right classroom environment and with the right direction from a teacher; this is desirable. The argument is that enough research, such as that within the framework of constructivism, and practical experience, such as that done by programs such as Philosophy for Children, support the assumption and that such learning experience enhances understanding while facilitating the development of critical thinking skills. For this to happen, the tasks, projects, discussions, or inquiries have to be relevant, connected, engaging, and intellectually stimulating in a way that are challenging enough to demand effort but are developmentally tailored to avoid frustration.

The focus of the second dimension of learning communities is on learning the communities. While much of it can be related to learning the local environments, the cultural milieu, the organization of social life, the social institutions within a civil and a political society, rules, regulations, or legal rights, all of which tend to resemble much of what is taught in social studies disciplines, it is not limited to that. It is also a process of learning about each other member of the learning community, including cultural traditions, languages, literature, music, art, dance, sports, and media, by looking at similarities and differences, commonalities, and legitimization of diversity but in a unifying experience. This dimension also includes a very important aspect: systematic inquiry. Such communities not only are geographic, cultural, or institutional, they are also disciplinary. Systematic inquiry, exploring, discussing, validating, rejecting, accepting, organizing, and building relationships within a discipline have similarities and differences. Learning the ways by which different scholarly communities engage in such systematic activities that ultimately deal with the "nature of knowledge," or epistemologies and some of their politics, is a process, a developing habit of learning to think and understand these ways of disciplinary knowing. This is not to reject the learning of skills and the acquisition of information, but the assumption is that this aspect of learning the community (or a community) is indeed a way of inducting youngsters into the discourses of the discipline, engaging them in tasks that would create, for example, communities of "young geographers," "young artists," or "young biologists."

The third dimension involves learning to live in a community. For the inquiry to happen, for the learning environment that builds on the assumptions that lead into the other dimension of learning communities, this third dimension has to be an ongoing development. Learning to live in a community, to be a member of a community, it is not an easy task and requires much effort, not only from the participants but also fundamentally from the teachers. There is a need to create an inclusive climate of comfort and trust, respect and engagement, tolerance and acceptance, caring and listening, with the ambitious expectation that students will gain ownership over their own experiences, individually and collectively. Procedures for discussion, the right expressions, the language and tone, and the body language and silences have to be moderated in such a way that students feel at ease with others while maintaining their own individuality without imposing on each other. This is not easy to accomplish, it takes time, and it is somehow idyllic.

Conflict emerges from time to time. Teachers who foster this framework of community learning do deal with conflict and often utilize conflict resolution as a learning experience in order to further inquiry into how to live in community, as well as a way of validating multiple and diverse voices. For instance, in a process of inquiry where there has to be argumentation, demonstration, and defense of a proposition or a speculation within a project, an investigation, or problem posing and problem solving, how do students challenge each other, how do they accept or reject each other's alternative perspectives, how do they contemplate the merits of these arguments—and not only within the norms of the subject matter but also in terms of personal styles and emotions? At times, as in Talmudic disputes, members of the community have to learn to accept "teikko," meaning that both or all points of view are equally valid and valued; there is no resolution in favor of one, at least for the time being. Thus, learning to live in community involves the development of a classroom culture that leads beyond the learning of the content into learning about oneself and about others. This educational concept resembles one of the established concepts of the Talmud, which argues that if one is not for oneself, it is not good; but if one is *only* for oneself, it is not good either.

These dimensions are particularly difficult, considering that in most schools, and in most classrooms, students have little choice over who will be their teachers or their classmates—and teachers often have little or no choice over who their students will be. Therefore, the building of these learning communities is a necessary imposition on the members. Individual differences in terms of needs and personalities, cultural backgrounds, and motivations present both a challenge and a resource to teachers and students. There can be a "hidden curriculum" in learning communities that forces its members to participate—to be exposed to the rest of the group through discussions, silence, observation, or documentation—which results in the unintended consequences of "surveillance" or even control of students and teachers.

It would be naïve not to realize that, even in the best situation, group dynamics involve power dynamics and, under some circumstances, can become oppressive to some members. Yet they can provide a stimulating intellectual journey—the same power dynamics can become a source of support and mutual dependency for a more sophisticated, vibrant, and exhilarating learning experience. Certainly, this is also challenging for the teacher who did not experience learning communities as a student, in a nonformal environment, as a student of teaching, or with colleagues in his or her own disciplinary communities. Teacher education programs, as well as professional development opportunities, must provide experiences in learning communities in order to support teachers who foster or want to foster a framework of learning communities in their own classrooms.

TEACHING ELEMENTS

Inquiry-Based Practice

In order to sustain, develop, and enhance a learning community, teachers need to share their experiences with others, which is counter-culture in most school environments, where teachers tend to be isolated from their colleagues. By engaging in systematic inquiry into their own practices, teachers can involve themselves and their colleagues as researchers; they can also engage their students as researchers vis-à-vis the learning experience in their own particular learning community.

In a sense, the assumption is that, when a teacher makes instructional decisions, he or she is grounded in a body of knowledge. However, that knowledge not always has been tested in the particular conditions of a classroom with a particular and distinctive group of students. Thus, in spite of generic understanding of the so-called knowledge base, the application translates into who the teacher and students are and what the situations are. For these decisions to be better informed, teaching should be practiced as a form of research that takes into consideration the complexity of the factors or variables at play, the testing of assumptions, the analysis of information gathered, and the implications for further action. Furthermore, the accumulation of varied evidence, at times in contradiction, serves as a source for learning. In addition, these bodies of accumulated information have to be presented, shared, discussed, dissected, challenged, and reinterpreted in light of new evidence and within a learning community of educators who have similar commitments.

The habit of inquiry, as previously mentioned, is present also within learning communities where students research various subjects, pose and find problems that need to be investigated, and converse with the field of study in a way that they do not reinvent the wheel but make the road by walking, as much as the road might have been traveled before. What this means is that the engagement is not only with a problem posed by a teacher or by the field but with questions that emerge as the students immerse themselves in the study of the subject matter. At times, this might be challenging and complex but engaging, because the questions and the inquiry process might require multiple disciplinary lenses, multiple processes, and multiple perspectives, including the propensity to analyze, make connections, see relationships and patterns, and provide alternative explanations of what constitutes experience, truth, fiction, and fact. These learning communities will not only experiment and practice "hands-on" activities but also practice "minds-on" and at times even "emotions-on" activities.

Listening to and Seeing the Whole Student

Students, and teachers, bring with them baggage of experiences into these communities. They are more than a good or bad math student, student-athlete, or writer. Even though, for purposes of understanding youngsters, aspects of growth and development are isolated, they do function as a unity. A student might have high cognitive development, an appropriate-to-age psychomotor ability, a limited social experience or ability, and/or a "balanced" emotional level; however, the student is not one or the other but all of these combined.

Listening is not just hearing the student. It means to actively engage in a dialogical mode, looking at the student's point of view, attending to his or her need, and focusing on the meaning and messages conveyed. This does not mean that all is legitimate and valid, or that there has to be agreement. It means that the student realizes that the teachers, and classmates, understand what they are articulating and engage with them. Seeing the student also adds the element of visibility, seeing the person not just as a presence but also as an individual and as a member of the group. Seeing the whole child includes seeing the strengths and limitations—the needs and potentials—and providing opportunities for growth, not only within a subject area but also as persons.

Teaching as a Form of Building Relationships

While it is clear that relationships are created between teachers and students and among students, the primary function of these relationships is to enable growth, development, and learning. Needless to say, in any relationship there are ups, downs, tensions, and expectations. These are also ethical, and incorporate mutual caring, with feelings and emotions not detached from cognitive processes. Yet the relationship between individuals—the I–Thou—includes a context (such as the classroom), and a content (such as the subject matter). This content tends to mediate the relationship in terms of interactions, but not always in terms of quality, as all the other elements of trust, respect, safety, and high expectations of learning are also present.

Creating the classroom climate—the environment for developing, nurturing, and growing the relationships—without the social, academic, spiritual, or emotional content renders a vacuum of learning. There is learning about relating to each other and about how to treat each other, even learning about the self, which is very important, but this is not enough for a classroom. The inquiry, the project, the problem finding, the problem posing, and the problem solving are sine qua non for a learning community.

While experiencing and growing within a learning community, members develop a sense of self, identities. For instance, students learn to be mathematicians and artists; they build a sense of themselves as such. But this is not the only aspect of their building identities, since in these relationships they also interact with each other and build other aspects of themselves, including many psychological and emotional, at times even spiritual, dimensions of who they are. These multiple opportunities to participate can be empowering or repressing—often both simultaneously. Teachers who see and listen to the whole student are attuned to the issues of relationships with and among students, individually and collectively.

Aesthetic relationships are also included in seeing and listening to the whole child. Aesthetics are a central component of a whole education and a whole person. Furthermore, the incorporation of music, plastic arts, drama, dance, and other forms of human expression and communication—including, in my judgment, sports—enhances the learning experience both as forms of disciplinary knowledge and as a form of involvement of the body, the feelings, and the sense of beauty. Such experiences open up the whole experience to more complex and sophisticated means of relating, understanding, and critical thinking.

Problematization

This crucial element is an intellectual tool that enables ways of looking at situations, experiences, information, and arguments by unveiling and challenging underlying assumptions, revising ideas, and thinking of different ways of analyzing, explaining, and interpreting. For example, a way of starting to think about subject matter connections and building relationships is through incorporated explorations and inquiry. However, problematization is more than this. It does involve critical thinking and problem solving, but problems have to be identified, created, developed, and framed. Problematization involves interrogating what has been taken for granted, asking questions that were or were not asked before, and eliciting imagination and scrutiny. There has to be a dimension of discomfort, confusion, and uncertainty about what is known and what is unknown, a daring to ask and to search for more than common sense to further problematization—something that scientists in the social sciences or natural sciences do, not just because of curiosity but because of understanding the limitations of their own knowledge.

Using facts and information by themselves, without individual and collective problematization, presents the danger of manipulating the facts to fit the needs of a few at the expense of the rest, a way of maintaining hegemonic dominance. What is important to consider, then, are questions such as how facts and information are used and how facts are judged. Whose facts and whose information are presented? What facts or information is not presented and why? Who can and who cannot benefit from these facts and information? Moreover, for problematizing further, what facts and information need to be investigated?

This not only engages the mind (thinking) but also engages the body (feelings, behaviors, aesthetics dimensions), and even the "spirit." It requires a process of gaining awareness, begun by questioning the given conditions of our own experience and existence—what we are told are the facts. To problematize implies that we ought to consider multiple possible alternatives; it invites us to play with what counts as facts, true or false, and to consider possible multiple coexisting realities. In consequence, what starts with questions, with finding the problems, leads into critical habits that also analyze power arrangements as well as connections with larger contextual issues, such as gender, social class, and race.

Importance of Contexts

As previously discussed, aspects of knowledge are located and shaped by the particularities of place and time. Spaces—physical and metaphysical, virtual and material—are elements that contextualize relationships, cooperation, and even identities. A learning community constitutes such space, but it is not the only space. The classroom is part of a larger institution, which in turn is part of multiple systems that include families, networks, neighborhoods, and listserves (in a micro sense) and those with cultural and political dimensions (in a macro sense).

While a subject matter—say, biology—would be relatively stable regardless of where is it studied, a number of contextual elements would influence and shape the learning community vis-à-vis the subject. One obvious element is resources. What a second-grade or a high school biology class has in terms of equipment, materials, rooms, teacher expertise, or natural environments to extend the class beyond the school walls depends at least on the geography, economy, and politics of the place. If a school has technological resources and another does not, that influences what students have access to. Although a learning community can be resourceful within itself, external factors can limit or enable it. Besides some clear conditions that the context provides, there are students and teachers who might be influenced by culture or other factors. For instance, looking at the same cell through a microscope, different students in the same learning community might ask very different questions, or they might be interested in different issues regarding the cell. Furthermore, in different places, given the geography, the culture, the environmental experiences, and/or the weather, students might ask very different questions. Variation can be two-fold: within a group and that between groups. Yet in both cases a learning community would center some practices utilizing local resources and the community at large as a place to learn. This also implies that the context can provide opportunities for learning.

Teacher as Intellectual and Artist (and Citizen)

Much has been written and discussed about the elements of teaching in a learning community. Teachers invest a tremendous amount of energy in developing, supporting, sustaining, and enhancing learning communities. They invest intellectual energy, since their work is intellectual by definition. They also display an authentic intellectual respect for students and foster such respect as part of the everyday life in learning communities. However, they also invest emotional, physical, and even spiritual energies. Students, too, invest these energies in a learning community.

The artistry of teaching involves the nuances, the unpredictability, the uncertainty, and the beauty of building meaningful relationships. Often intellectual and artistic are presented as dichotomies; this is a false dichotomy. There is an intellectual aspect to the artistic in teaching and there is an artistic aspect to the intellectual. In this discussion, I prefer to include two dimensions that capture this element in somehow a different way. In the following lines, I will discuss "Passion and Coraje to teach."

These are not only intellectual dispositions but also are feelings and emotions. Passion is often associated with an intense emotion, and it occurs with devotion and dedication, with love, and with physical energy. It also includes a level of risk-taking because it can produce suffering. Oftentimes teachers have been instructed to control their passions and not to be too directive of the students' innate interests, to avoid being intrusive. However, passion is an important element, particularly in communities and with students who learn to value and understand passion and who themselves are open about being passionate.

"Coraje" can be translated in a number of ways. Often it means courage—the courage to take on unpopular positions, the courage to confront authority, the courage to risk one's own privilege, the courage to accept one's own limitations, the courage to confront injustice, the courage to teach everybody's children, or the courage to learn from one's students. Coraje is also anger, even rage—at least indignation. The condition of schooling in some places—including historical structural inequities, the expectation that some students will drop out, and the perpetuation of discriminating against "others"—provoke coraje. Coraje is also daring; it is in many ways a form of cheerful disrespect toward institutions and toward people who exploit their positions to their own advantage. Coraje is "chutzpah," a way of both daring and cheerfully disrespecting authority, norms, and power arrangements.

Passion and coraje are elements of the "teacher as citizen" because they develop the qualities of acting, of doing, of being involved—beyond the classroom and beyond the school. Eventually, this teacher works to alter difficult conditions, acts to defend the spaces that enable meaningful learning, and negotiates for and with students to control the environment of their learning. Teachers and students fuel each others' coraje and passion through responsibility and mission. These teachers, and on occasion their students, learn to make things happen rather than letting things happen to them.

Last Notes: Bridging False Dichotomies?

An important challenge for learning communities is the bridging of false dichotomies. Throughout these notes, I have addressed that problematization is an important aspect of inquiry and that inquiry is at the center of learning communities' experiences. I have implied that some elements complement each other and that at times we explain dimensions as separate entities, but they are connected and related and as a total are more than the addition. Learning communities provide opportunities to challenge and to bridge these dichotomies. Some of them are mind and body, emotion and cognition, practice and theory, school and home, and virtual and physical communities. They are part of the same. While one might help define the other, maintaining the dichotomy is problematic because it can privilege one over the other or might create the sense that they are separate. This is an open note to play with more ideas.

The potential and limitations of virtual and mediated learning communities were not discussed in these notes. However, technology has presented a tremendous potential for reaching out and broadening the ways in which learning communities can operate. Physical proximity or human warmth is not sine qua non anymore. Although I prefer to see energy generated in a direct and constrained physical environment, I recognize that this can also be limiting, and at times oppressive. Virtual learning communities, given time and multiple confluent conversations, have the potential to add new dimensions of reflectiveness, problematization, alternative points of view, multiple resources, and access to variety and quality. Virtual learning communities also necessitate many of the elements previously discussed, such as trust, safety, respect, and intellectual curiosity, to name a few. In addition, a virtual learning community is as much or even more surveillant than the traditional classroom, because it requires more exposure; what is written, especially with e-mail, is permanently recorded and may be accessed by anyone, including non-members of the community. Ultimately, much depends on the type of relationships constructed. Playing with ideas is the challenge that these "Notes" attempt to instigate in you, the reader.